firefly

A CELEBRATION

FIREFLY:
A CELEBRATION

ISBN: 9781781161685

Published by
Titan Books
A division of Titan Publishing Group Ltd.
144 Southwark St.
London
SE1 0UP

First edition: September 2012
10 9

The contents of the book were originally published as
Firefly: The Official Companion Volume One and *Volume Two*, and *Firefly: Still Flying*.

Based on the series created by Joss Whedon

Book designed by Marcus Scudamore and Martin Stiff.
Production by Bob Kelly.

Acknowledgements
Volume One and Two:
The publishers would like to thank the cast, crew and writers of *Firefly* for all their enthusiasm and cooperation, particularly Joss Whedon. Thank you to the 'shiny' crew who conducted the interviews, wrote material and helped out with the book: Abbie Bernstein (Joss Whedon, Jewel Staite, Michael Fairman, Christina Hendricks, Shawna Trpcic, Carey Meyer, Greg Edmonson, Ben Edlund, Jeff Ricketts, Melinda Clarke, David Boyd, Jose Molina, Lisa Lassek), Bryan Cairns (Adam Baldwin, Morena Baccarin, Gina Torres), Karl Derrick (Chris Calquhoun, Mike Gibbons, Jonathan A. Logan, Brennan Byers, Regina Pancake, Randy Eriksen, Chris Gilman, Skip Crank), Tara DiLullo (Nathan Fillion, Ron Glass, Summer Glau, Alan Tudyk, Tim Minear, Loni Peristere, Brett Matthews, Cheryl Cain). Many thanks to star photographers Angie Thomas and Elena Kanaouris. Thank you to the Ariel Ambulance Rescue Group www.arielambulance.org. Thank you to Julie Thompson at still-flying.net, Barbara Johnson, Harry Harris and BrilliantButCancelled.com. Many thanks also to Shawna Trpcic for allowing us to photograph her costume designs. Finally thank you to Debbie Olshan and Jamie Waugh at Fox for their help.

Props and costumes courtesy of Karl Derrick.

For Still Flying acknowledgments, see page 541.

Did you enjoy this book? We love to hear from our readers.
Please e-mail us at: **readerfeedback@titanemail.com** or write to Reader Feedback at the above address.
You can also visit us at **www.titanbooks.com**

A CIP catalogue record for this title is available from the British Library.

Printed and bound in China by C&C Offset Printing Co., Ltd.

A CELEBRATION

TITAN BOOKS

CONTENTS

Transport Class

载 : FF : 这种

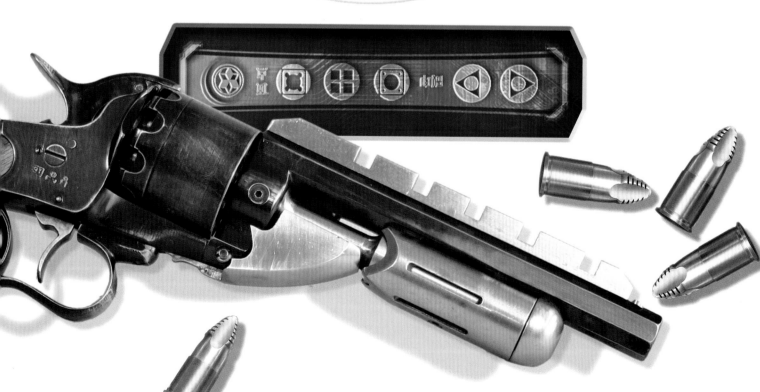

C O N T E N T S

VISIT HISTORIC

SERENITY VALLEY

NATIONAL PARK

宁静
ALRICH

BIRTHPLACE OF UNITY

CONTENTS

A MESSAGE FROM YOUR CAPTAIN

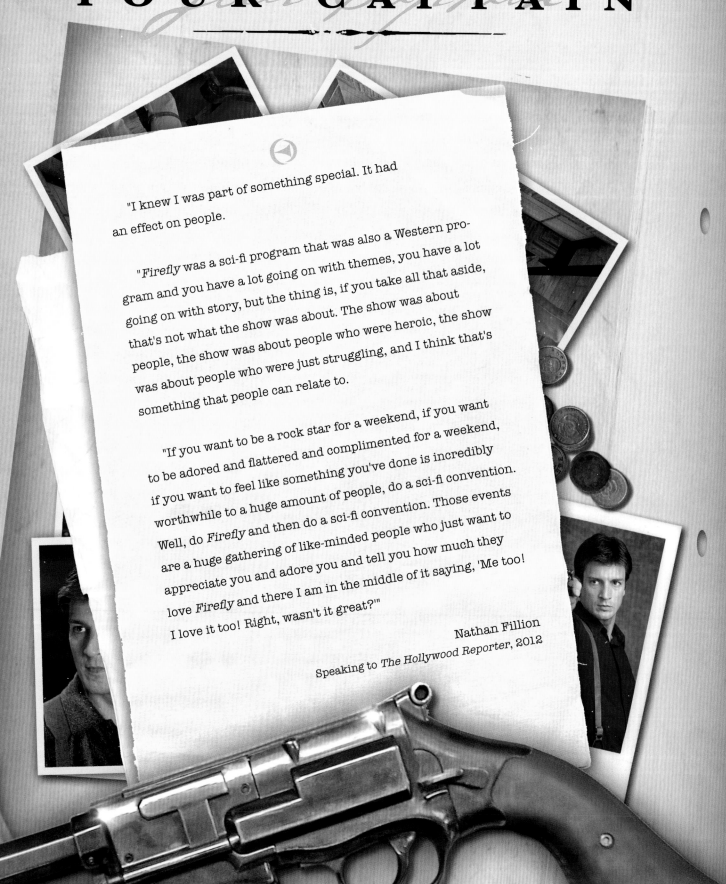

"I knew I was part of something special. It had an effect on people.

"*Firefly* was a sci-fi program that was also a Western program and you have a lot going on with themes, you have a lot going on with story, but the thing is, if you take all that aside, that's not what the show was about. The show was about people, the show was about people who were heroic, the show was about people who were just struggling, and I think that's something that people can relate to.

"If you want to be a rock star for a weekend, if you want to be adored and flattered and complimented for a weekend, if you want to feel like something you've done is incredibly worthwhile to a huge amount of people, do a sci-fi convention. Well, do *Firefly* and then do a sci-fi convention. Those events are a huge gathering of like-minded people who just want to appreciate you and adore you and tell you how much they love *Firefly* and there I am in the middle of it saying, 'Me too! I love it too! Right, wasn't it great?'"

Nathan Fillion

Speaking to *The Hollywood Reporter*, 2012

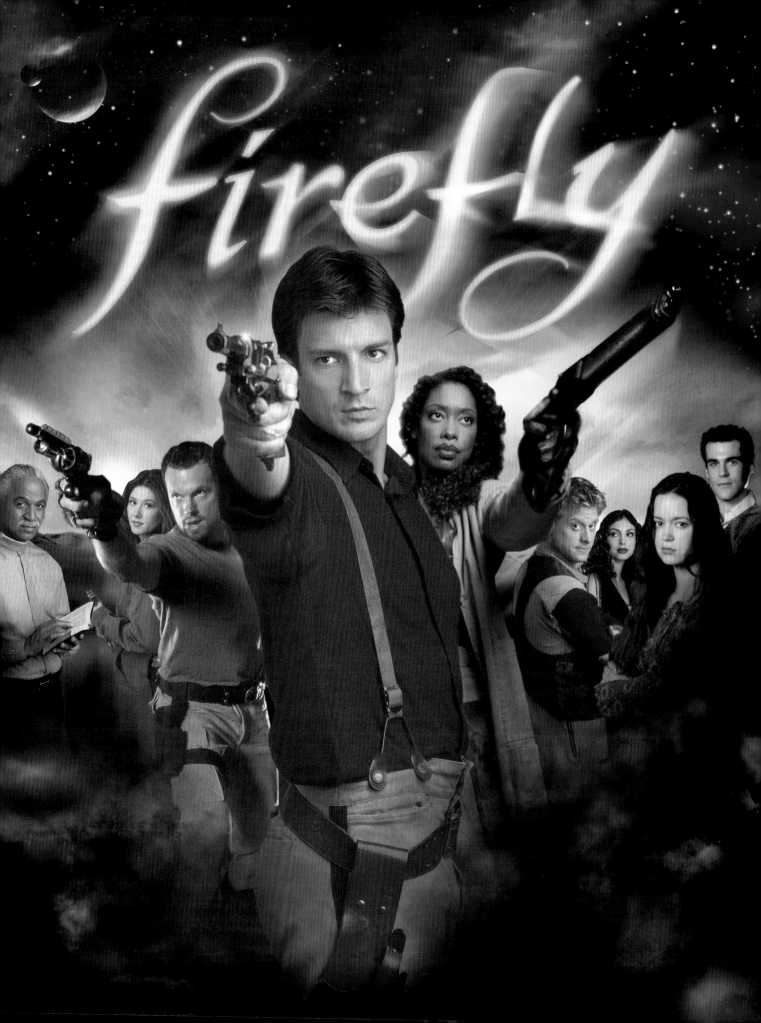

THE OFFICIAL
COMPANION

VOLUME ONE

Features and Interviews by Abbie Bernstein, Bryan Cairns,
Karl Derrick & Tara DiLullo

INTO THE
BLACK

An interview with Joss Whedon

Did _Firefly_ wind up being about what it started out being about?

JOSS WHEDON: Ultimately, mostly yes. Because what it set out to be was a mixture of genres, a _Stagecoach_ kind of drama with a lot of people trying to figure out their lives in a bleak and pioneer environment. There was one major sea change during the process and it came from [the network] Fox, which was obviously that they wanted it to be more an action-oriented drama. I wanted it to be the kind of show where guns would not be drawn often, so that when they were, it was that much more dire a thing. They wanted gunplay a-plenty and it was both a rhythmic and something of a moral adjustment to go, 'Okay, we're going to go a little more _Wild Bunch_ than _Stagecoach_' [laughs]. I still got to have the things that I was looking for, the moments between people. Those are the things that people remember and love, and I explained early on, that the most important scene in the pilot ['Serenity'] is the scene of Kaylee eating that strawberry. That to me was the essence of the entire show. But when Mal came in and shot the agent [Dobson] in the head, it was really because he had no other choice. Reavers were coming; this was the most efficient thing to do. He did it very cold-bloodedly and that was on purpose, but not gratuitously. By the time we made the first episode ['The Train Job'], he kicked a guy into the ship's engine for a laugh. That's a bit of a change. I think if we had been able to do something without _any_ adjustment, and that's very rare, it would have been somewhat quieter. But as it was, the integrity of the characters and the show and the rhythm and the feeling they had about each other was very much the show that I had originally intended; and the episodes that I had thought to do, that I now never will, were still very much in place. It was just a question of easing the audience into it with something a little more exciting than contemplative.

❖ Opposite: Meet the crew of Serenity.

❖ Below: _Firefly_ creator Joss Whedon

You have previously said that most of your stories are about discovering strength or discovering what to do with strength. Which is _Firefly_?

It's interesting. I wouldn't have classified it as either, but it's definitely both and more. Because ultimately, _Firefly_ is also about perhaps discovering strength through weakness, simply because the idea that these people could get through the day at all, make a living, avoid the Alliance and not get eaten is kind of a triumph. But it's a triumph because they have no power, which is of course different than strength. But because I had so many different people on so many different journeys, I would say that this sort of fits every mode. We have River, who is obviously the classic adolescent with power who is going to learn that she has it and how to control it, something we paid off in the movie; and Mal, who at this point in his life has rejected the idea of the power he had, even though he was a captain, because the power he used to have, a lot of it came from idealism and faith and momentum, and when that was kicked out of him, he's sort of empty. I would say, power is not what I was thinking about when I made the show. This is part of the difference between the show and the movie, because the show was really about what is it like to be the little guy, and the movie was, what is it like to be the little guy — in an awesome epic! Where you win! Because it's a movie! [laughs] And the paradigm adjustment for the movie is much greater than any that I had from the network.

When you were putting _Firefly_ together, out of all of the people that you were working with at that time, how did you select Tim Minear as the other show-runner?

Through deceit and evil. I wish I were kidding. I had not intended to use Tim. I was desperate to use Tim. I had three people that I absolutely knew could run a show, and they were David [Greenwalt on _Angel_] and Marti [Noxon on _Buffy the Vampire Slayer_] and Tim [on _Angel_], and David and Marti already were show-runners. And I promised David Greenwalt, to his face, I would not take Tim away from him when I did _Firefly_. But I could not find anybody even remotely of the caliber of Tim, and somebody — a very smart person and a good friend — took me aside and

❖ Top: Cast and crew in the galley.

❖ Above: Joss Whedon and Morena Baccarin during filming.

❖ Right: Executive producer Tim Minear.

of a sudden, I had an even better reason to spend a lot of time on *Buffy* and *Angel* — I had no show-runners. So it really was difficult, because I just had so much work, but once I made the decision, once I knew I had to do it [laughs], it was so easy. And Tim had been dying to do it. And then all of a sudden, I had a second half. I mean, as much as anybody I've ever worked with, Tim had the same voice and came in at the very beginning, the way David did with *Buffy*, and informed the voice of *Firefly* so much and did so much of the great stuff. He was the guy I wanted, and I realized eventually that he was the guy I *needed*; and my god, from the first moment, he understood the show as well as any human being, and just brought so much to it that I think of it as though he were always a part of it. There was never a time when I hadn't hired him.

Was there a defined division of responsibilities, or did you both just jump in and handle whatever came up?

It really was just, 'Tag, you're it.' I obviously ended up with final say on all things, because that's how it worked, but I could leave anything in Tim's hands and know that it would come back to me the way it should. It was my show, in the sense of it was something I had been nurturing for years, and he didn't have to go through a lot of the incredibly painful casting process and stuff like that, but had I had to shuffle off this mortal coil or move to Gdansk and change my name, I would have had perfect confidence the show would be just about everything it could with only Tim on working it.

How did you select the writing and production staff?

Basically, the production staff as much as possible was made up of people that I knew and loved: ADs [assistant directors] and producers and people like that, I had used before. The big find was David Boyd, the DP [director of photography], whose style fit the show so perfectly, who is full of joy and energy and lit faster than anybody I'd ever worked with. Which was great, because we had a smaller budget than either *Buffy* or *Angel*, and we had to move as down and dirty as possible, and so it was a piece of luck. When a guy like that walks in a room, you feed off his energy, you know you've got a problem-solver. DPs come in two kinds — problem-solvers and the other kind. David lit environmentally, so you could turn around and shoot the other way. Very often, DPs can kill you. [Boyd's] stuff looked cinematic, just beautiful, but he always achieved it with as little work as possible. He thought the lenses were too clean and he knew I was going for that 1970s Western look, so he found some beautiful old lenses that caught flares off of everything and really helped the look of the thing. I brought a camera operator over from *Buffy* and sound people — anybody that I could spare, where

said, 'Be realistic. If you don't move Tim to *Firefly*, you will never see *Buffy* or *Angel* again. If you don't have a second-in-command who can control the set when you walk away from it, you never will. And the only way to make things even out is to put him on that show.' And it was true. And I didn't want to admit it, because I had made a promise and then I had to go back on it. And needless to say, David Greenwalt did not take that lightly, nor should he have. Not just because of that, there were many factors involved, but David left *Angel* [he went to ABC to produce *Miracles*] and then Marti had her baby right away, and all another show was dialed in enough that the show wouldn't suffer if the person moved. I brought them over, so that I would have that comfort factor.

As far as the writing staff, we did it the way you normally do it. We read scripts and we met with people. Jose [Molina] we had known for a while, as Howard Gordon's assistant and then as a writer. Tim is very active in following writers and nurturing writers. Obviously when we found Ben [Edlund], we grabbed him pretty quick, because he has a sensibility that's so left of center. Cheryl [Cain] had written a beautiful spec; and Brett [Matthews], who was my assistant, knew the show from being with me and from being a young writer himself, so he wrote one of the scripts. And we pilfered staff: we used Drew Greenberg and Jane Espenson from *Buffy*. The first year of a staff is always difficult. But we actually started out very strong and that's rare.

The two-hour episode 'Serenity' was originally conceived as the première, but it wound up airing last; Fox required you to make a new first episode, 'The Train Job'. Do you think *Firefly* would have been the same if the network had not made you reiterate the premise several times in different episodes?

You know, the only time it was egregiously difficult was obviously 'The Train Job'. And I still think that's a sweet episode. The fact of the matter is, I am a firm believer in reiterating the premise of any show anyway. Because you don't catch the first one every time. And I believe that for the first thirteen, you should always make it as easy as possible for people to come in and be told what's going on. If you have to tell them too much, maybe you're doing something wrong. But there are some things you can take for granted. If you see the Shepherd with his collar, you don't have to say, 'Look! He's a Shepherd, he's a man of God!' He's got the collar. You see Jayne — do you *have* to explain he's a mercenary? Not so much. There are certain things that we'd throw out there every time, but certain things do take care of themselves. I do believe that you should always explain the show kind of up-front, let people know what they're in for. 'The Train Job' was a bit more extreme, because we really had to assume people hadn't seen anything ever — and as it turned out, we would be right. It's the same thing I had to do for [the feature film] *Serenity*, except I only had a weekend to do 'The Train Job'. But I had Tim.

In the two-hour 'Serenity' episode, there are some shots that are almost like thought voiceovers — shots of the character's reaction outside the scene…

I wanted to be a little stylistically funky and people pretty much wanted me to turn that down, because it is a little odd, it throws some people. Every now and then, I wanted to be a little stylistically bizarre. I found [Steven Soderbergh's] *The Limey* an extremely influential film for me stylistically, and I've never really gotten away from it. I wanted the thing to feel like little found bits of footage that got stuck together, and I think it's a nice way to get into somebody's head, to hear them saying one thing and to

❖ Bottom: Serenity flying through space.

❖ Below: Bridge control panel detail.

see another. It's something I would have liked to have done more of, but again, the mission statement became, 'Tell the story, get people through it and earn your indulgence.'

Did you ever consider actually killing off a member of the crew in the opening episode?

No. No. No. Because you just can't do it — you want to do it [laughs] and I think about it every show I ever create — the fact of the matter is, it never doesn't get out. So it's too difficult. I wanted to create a world with all these people, and then I wanted to live with them. So that was my only mandate. I did intend to kill at least one of them at some point, suddenly and unexpectedly, because it is my nature to do so. And it's very much the nature of the show that things are pulled out from under you suddenly; that you can depend on nothing; that you are floating in the midst of nothing. But I wasn't planning to do that for a while.

Can you talk about the design of Serenity the ship?

The design of the ship is something that I worked on very hard and then [production designer] Carey Meyer worked on very hard. To me, the design of the ship was very crucial just in terms of the idea of a known space; the idea of, 'We live on this space, and here's where the rooms are, and here's why, and here's where the cargo bay is, and here's why,' and there are not fourteen hundred decks and a holodeck and an all-you-can-eat buffet in the back. It's very utilitarian. If you actually watch *Stagecoach*, they spend a long time introducing the stagecoach, because that space is very important. We did a lot of collaboration. I knew everything I was looking for and which space related to which character. We spent a lot of time talking about paint. Because you're going into this knowing you're going to spend most of your time on the ship, and every room represented either a feeling or a character. The engine room was rusty brown because that's very earthy and likable and real, and that's Kaylee's space — that was very deliberate. The hall next to it is very cool and blue, because that space doesn't really serve a purpose [laughs], except for action or suspense. Everything was done exactly like that. Obviously, the blue of the infirmary is like Simon.

Did you ever write scenes for certain parts of the ship that had to be moved to a different part because the mood of the scene didn't match the specific environment?

Not particularly. It wasn't like I ever made a huge mistake like I did on *Buffy* of putting a bedroom scene on a front lawn [in the episode 'Innocence'; the scene was reshot to take place inside a bedroom]. Ultimately, every space had that Serenity feel. It was beat-up but lived-in

❖ Opposite top: The
engine room.

❖ Opposite below:
Exterior ramp set.

❖ This page clockwise
from the top: Kaylee's
room, a futuristic
advert, living quarters,
the infirmary door.

and ultimately, it was home. Having said that, there certainly were specific things you could go for from one
space to another, but we pretty much knew as we broke
the story, that we said, 'We want to be here with this
character, we want to be here with this one.'

The design used different influences, like the sliding
doors and — you couldn't see them, we didn't build one,
we only had little doors for them — but those tiny cubicles — I should say 'tubicles', you could only lie down in
them — that are found in little Japanese hotels. Those
sliding doors were influenced by that idea, the idea that
there were a couple of cubicles even smaller than the
ones that Simon and River and Book had.

When we designed the ship, the only thing I learned
really was that you don't put the opening of a cargo ship in
the front, because it really goes in the back, aerodynamic-
ally speaking [laughs], and that was a bit of awkward
design that was my fault. But basically, once we created the
environment for them to live in, Carey not only built it
beautifully, he built the entire thing with ceilings, so that
we could always look every which way *and* the entire thing
was adaptable — you could pull it away or move
something huge, so that you could get in and around
everything. That meant the environment worked for us
and there weren't a lot of adjustments that needed to be
made. It was more like discovering, 'Oh! I can shoot here!
I can shoot there! I can get behind these stairs!' It was a
dream set, because there was always something interesting to look at, and it wasn't difficult to get there.

The crew's bunks being down ladders was a very
important thing to me. I'm a huge believer in vertical
space, and one of the reasons I loved doing the show,
something that had dropped out of televised science fiction to an extent, was the idea of vertical space, because

it's just easier to do things horizontally; everything's out on a soundstage and you can roll the cameras around. But we knew we were going to be carrying the cameras hand-held most of the time anyway. In fact, our Steadicam operator lamented at one point, 'I used to have a Steadicam for a job...' because we made him do so much hand-held. This was Bill Brummond. He was so damn steady holding the thing that a lot of his hand-held looked like Steadicam. I used to yell at him, 'What do I have to do — get behind you and tickle you? C'mon, make it dirty.'

Anyway, the idea of the ship was that you lived in it. And that's the same idea behind the camerawork: don't be arch, don't be sweeping — be found, be rough and tumble and docu and you-are-there.

We knew we were going to have to be on the ship a lot — like 'Objects in Space' — as an attempt to save some dough [laughs], because we didn't have any. In the case of the world, we always had to sort of build a little something or find a little something. In that sense, we were flying a little blinder, because we didn't know what we were going to be able to pull off or come up with. Something like 'Heart of Gold', which is very rustic, or 'Shindig', which is very old-fashioned but also modern and opulent — to create either of those is going to mean a lot of cheating, a lot of building and a lot of using what's already there. Carey Meyer, (who had worked with me on *Buffy* forever) again, like David Boyd, was endlessly inventive. Except I did have to tell him at one point, 'You have to stop using wine crates on every set,' because I was starting to notice [laughs] — but my god, they saved us a ton of money. The mall in 'The Message', where they go and get the dead body, was basically a piece of every set that we'd ever built that we still had, but it had a look of its own. He did an extraordinary job creating those worlds. But with exceptions, they were difficult to visualize, because you know, how much can we get away with? It's part of why I gave every planet Earth atmosphere and Earth tones, because quite frankly, I knew that I couldn't afford to make alien worlds. I didn't want to go to Yucca Flats every other episode and transform it into Bizarro World by making the sky orange.

A number of episodes conclude with a shot of Serenity flying away from us as a few guitar notes are played. Was this conceived as a signature shot for *Firefly*?

I didn't think of it as that, but it's not the 'Let's fly at camera in the *Back to the Future* shot' and it's not the warp speed end of *Star Trek* shot, 'It's a small ship, we've had some fun, but we're still all alone out here.' The guitar is very small. The idea of the instrumentation was to highlight the sparseness of their environment and the teeniness of them. So, yeah. It wasn't 'Let's have that — this will sum it all up,' but it does.

Four of your actors who had guest roles in *Firefly* — Andy Umberger as the Captain of the Dortmunder and Carlos Jacott as Dobson in 'Serenity', Jeff Ricketts as a Blue-Gloved Man in 'The Train Job' and 'Ariel' and Jonathan M. Woodward as Tracey in 'The Message' — were 'hat-trick' actors who all also appeared in both *Buffy* and *Angel*. Would you have had more hat-trick actors if *Firefly* had gone on longer?

I don't do it in order to do it, I do it because I have somebody I love and they fit a space. Carlos had actually read for Wash and when Alan [Tudyk] got Wash, it occurred to me that Carlos was that guy who can appear very menacing, but he's also the most disarming fellow in the world, so he worked perfectly for Dobson. I don't go into these things saying, 'We absolutely must,' but when you have a guy who's right, it saves you some time. Jonathan [Woodward] had worked on *Buffy* but not *Angel* yet when he did 'The Message'.

Were Niska and Saffron designed to be recurring characters?

Only if they worked. I mean, you want everybody to be so good that you want them to be ongoing. And that worked out. I didn't even close the door on Early, or for that matter, even Dobson. I planned to bring him back — when I couldn't, I brought him back in the comic. He got shot in the eye. In the show, he was going to have a whole run about how Mal had shot him in the eye and not killed him and how pathetic Mal was. It was going to be really funny.

What about the Blue-Gloved Men?

This was another change: they [the network executives] were very interested in the over-reaching arc. I wanted the show to play more episodically, because *Buffy* and *Angel* had gotten so caught up in their own mythos that I couldn't tell what was going on; and so I was like, 'Let's be very standalone,' and also because it reflected the sort of day to day pointlessness of these [*Firefly*] people's lives, not in a harsh way, just 'We got through today, now we have to get through tomorrow, so let's not be part of a grander scheme right away.' Eventually, we were going to build to it, because I think you have to, but [the network] wanted to bring that out sooner, so I created the Blue-Handed fellas for that purpose, so there was sort of the ticking clock of the thing following [the main characters]. I had not actually intended to use the same two actors. I wanted to indicate that there were a bunch of them, but nobody knew that [laughs], so when we had the Blue-Hand Men again, they had the same guys [Jeff Ricketts and Dennis Cockrum]. So I was like, 'Okay, apparently there's only two of them.' Because I was running three shows and so I missed that one, that fell between the cracks. That's not a diss on the actors, they did a great job,

but yeah, the original idea was that there would be these guys everywhere. Blue Sun [Corporation, the employer of the Blue-Gloved Men] was going to be a big thing, part of the whole Miranda thing, but the movie just didn't have room for that.

Interviews with the cast often give the impression that their characters really had a continued life beyond just 'action — cut.' Did you get that feeling from your cast on this?

I did. Here were very, very dedicated craftsmen, who were working on making it work and getting it right, but they lived their characters to such an extent that, yeah, sometimes the issue would become confused. I thought for a long time that Sean [Maher] was looking at all of us going, 'How did I get on board with these idiots?' Because he's very quiet and reserved. He's actually the sweetest guy in the world and was having a lot of fun, but I didn't know it for a while [laughs]. I thought he was just looking at us like, 'I'm smarter than them,' because he's got such incredible self-containment. But then, like Simon, he's just all mushy heart. Jewel's mom actually talked to me about what it was like when Jewel was playing Kaylee, that it was exciting for her to be playing somebody so optimistic and so full of love and life, because she had been cast in a different kind of role before that and it was like playing Kaylee opened her up, to an extent. Yeah, [the entire cast] embodied their characters to the point where I can't remember a time when those characters existed without those faces.

Did they ever discuss with you what allowed them to jump into it so wholeheartedly?

I don't know. Part of it was a feeling — there was a history to the thing, that if they had a question, there was an answer, or we would work out an answer, we would find it together. But I don't know how I got so many grossly talented people all in one place who really enjoyed what they were doing and really liked each other. I've worked with great ensembles every time out and I've been very lucky, but there was something going on here that was really different than anything I've seen on any set. Nobody ever went to their trailer — they all just wanted to watch each other. It's not something to be taken lightly. Or canceled.

(End of part 1. Continued in Volume 2.)

SERENITY

Written & Directed by Joss Whedon

The most difficult shot we did is in the pilot. It's Mal coming out of his quarters on the ladder. The camera is in his quarters and then goes up the ladder above him and into the hall. That required building a piece of the hall above his room and [director of photography] David and his guys designing a rig that they attached the camera to, that basically ran on tracks which they attached to the ceiling, so they could stick the camera all the way down in the room. Then I actually asked them to adjust it and the next day, they had completely reworked it so you went up the track and then they'd literally pull it with a rope, while someone was operating the head of the camera so that it could look down. It could go up and then go out again when he came up the hall, so that

it really felt like it was just hanging with him. And that kind of last-minute, low-rent but elaborate inventiveness to get that feeling of being there was something that I adored, that I got from everybody I worked with, and that I thrived on, because we were making something that felt very epic, but at the same time, it felt so little regional theatre, intimate, no-budge [no-budget], we are a little band of brothers, little artists having our moment. And that kind of energy is very rare in television. Usually somebody is stepping on it, and very often, it's the actors [laughs]. But again, in this case, they all were very much in the same spirit of 'How much can I bring to the party?' and not 'What's in it for me?'

TEASER

EXT. SERENITY VALLEY – NIGHT

Battle rages. Dead bodies, explosions — we see rapidfire images of bloody conflict. The IN-DEPENDENTS hold a narrow gulch that overlooks a desert valley, which the ALLIANCE troops swarm through, trying to take the position. From above, a small Alliance SKIFF flies by, strafing the ground and several men.

ANGLE: behind an outcropping:

are six soldiers, all in conference, sweaty, haggard, shouting over the din. Amongst them are SGT. MALCOLM REYNOLDS, clearly in charge, ZOE, his unflappable corporal, BENDIS, a terrified young soldier, and GRAYDON, an exhausted but tough radio operator. Around them, other soldiers are laid out, firing, keeping back the onslaught of Alliance troops.

GRAYDON
Sergeant! Command says air support is holding til they can assess our status!

MAL
Our status is that we need some gorramn air support! Get back on line and —

ZOE
That skiff is shredding us, sir —

GRAYDON
They won't move without a lieutenant's authorization code, sir —

Mal breaks past them, moves to a corpse of at least two days in officer's gear. He rips a rank symbol off the corpse's arm.

Hands it to Graydon, flipping it over so we can

SERENITY VALLEY

Production designer Carey Meyer: "Serenity Valley was in several places. In flashbacks, we had this interior that looked like an old decrepit church — it had parts of columns and an old Buddha. The exterior was in the deep San Fernando Valley, in Lake Los Angeles — where there is no lake. It's not easy to light, but you can get equipment in and it's a nice place to shoot because you can light it up and see a pretty large environment. Often, if you get to an exterior and your geography is not controlled or you have a very close horizon, you just can't afford to light it. So you try to find a space that has a high horizon that is close to you, where you can control the lighting. Even though it's still a big space, the valley is essentially like a large bowl, where you can see the ground in front of you, light it and actually shoot it at night. It also was somewhere we could set off those large fireballs and have a lot of gunfire late at night and not disturb the community."

see a series of numbers and letters on the other side.

MAL
That's your code. You're lieutenant Baker, congratulations on your promotion, now get me air support!

Turns to the two other soldiers.

MAL (cont'd)
(to one)
Pull back just far enough to wedge 'em in here.
(to the other)
Get your squad to the high ground, you pick 'em off.

THE BROWNCOATS

Costume designer Shawna Trpcic: "We actually designed the Serenity battle before we designed Mal's individual look. That was a lot of [original *Firefly* designer] Jill Ohanesson's input. We went everywhere from chain mail to these red vests with the Asian closures and Civil War pants and torn-up rags for keeping warm. We had images from around the world, from wars in Genghis Khan's time to Civil War time, and captured a little bit of everybody's armor and everybody's layers to try to convey the homespun look of the Serenity battle."

❖ Above right: Costume designs for Mal and Zoe as Independent soldiers.

❖ Right: The Independents' rank symbols, including the lieutenant's patch Mal rips from the arm of a dead soldier.

❖ Above: The anti-aircraft gun Mal fires up.

ZOE
High ground's death with that skiff in the air.

MAL
That's our problem and thank you for volunteering.
(to the scared guy)
Bendis, you give us cover, we're going duck hunting.

A soldier falls back between them, dead.

MAL (cont'd)
(to all)
Just focus. Alliance said they were gonna waltz through Serenity Valley and we've choked 'em with those words. We've done the impossible and that makes us mighty. Just a little while longer, our angels'll be soaring overhead, raining fire on those arrogent cods, so you hold. You HOLD! Go.

Two of them scamper off, Bendis moving into position, back to the rock, ready to give cover fire but still scared shitless.

Mal and Zoe move over to a small cache of arms and he picks up a rifle.

ZOE
Really think we can bring her down, sir?

MAL
Do you even need to ask?

Unseen by her, he pulls a small cross from a

chain on his neck, silently kisses it, puts it back.

MAL (cont'd)
Ready?

ZOE
Always.
(shouts)
Bendis! BENDIS!

But he is too scared. Can't move.

ZOE (cont'd)
Rut it.

She pops up herself, firing a machine gun, strafing the area. A moment, and Mal goes, also firing, Zoe behind.

As they run to an anti-aircraft gun, three Alliance troops come into view.

They each shoot one but one gets in close to Mal and they tangle, Mal adroitly outfighting him, knocking him on his ass and moving on as Zoe follows, firing a burst into the gut without even stopping.

She reaches a little cover, throws herself down. He goes higher, for a clear view of the sky.

ANGLE: THE SKIFF

streaks through the night sky, firing short, deadly bursts. A single-person fighter, it looks like nothing so much as a boomerang.

Mal shoots the soldiers by the anti-aircraft gun, then jumps in and grabs it. There is much with buttons and dials and whirring and clicking. He sights up...

MAL
Give me a lock...

ANGLE: THROUGH THE SCOPE:

More of the skiff, but with calibrations and infravision and whatnot.

A moment, and Mal fires.

ANGLE: THE SKIFF

is hit direct, explodes, fragments of it coming straight for camera —

Mal bolts, slamming into Zoe and diving with her out of the way as a huge flaming chunk of skiff spins over them and into his position, exploding.

They hit the ground and roll, fire raining down around them.

ANGLE: behind the outcrop —

They return, Bendis still unmoving.

ZOE
Nice cover fire.

MAL
What's the status on —

But they see that Graydon is dead.

MAL (cont'd)
Zoe.

She starts pulling the radio off his corpse. Mal moves to Bendis, gets in his face.

MAL (cont'd)
Listen to me. Look at me! Listen. We're holding this valley. No matter what.

BENDIS
We're gonna die...

MAL
We're not gonna die! We can't die, Bendis, and do you know why? Because we are so very pretty. We are just too pretty for God to let us die, look at that chiseled jaw, come on...

BENDIS
I'm sorry...

Mal hears something — a growing roar. He smiles.

MAL
You won't listen to me, listen to that.

That's our angels, come to blow the Alliance right to the hot place.

Bendis hears it too. It changes him, hope suffusing his expression.

MAL (cont'd)
Zoe, tell the eighty second to —

ZOE
They're not coming.

Mal stops. Zoe lowers the radio.

ZOE (cont'd)
Command says it's too hot. They're pulling out. We're to lay down arms.

Mal is uncomprehending at first.

MAL
But... what...

The noise grows louder. IN SLO MO, Mal rises, the first light of day hitting his face as he scans the valley.

ANGLE: THE VALLEY

As out of the sunrise come dozens of Alliance ships, filling the sky.

ANGLE: MAL

as he sees everything lost — everything he believes, everything he fought for... In the background of the shot, we see Bendis, also looking in horror, be strafed with bullets and fall out of frame.

Mal just stares.

INT. BLOWN-OUT SHIP - NIGHT

We are in a some kind of burnt out wreck - all we see is twisted black metal, a few stars visible through breaches in the hull. It's 'night' because it's space, so it's always night. But the wreck is not empty.

From top of frame, Mal floats upside-down into a closeup. He is in a spacesuit, the light from inside his helmet glinting off the sweat on his face. He is visibly changed, older and less sickly, so the title reading

SIX YEARS LATER

should not be any surprise.

MAL
I'm gonna boil it. Give me the sticky.

WIDEN to see Zoe, also six years older, also suited up. She and Mal are in zero grav, floating by a big iron door that has buckled but not burst during whatever tore this ship apart.

Floating nearby is JAYNE: a hulking, wary mercenary who keeps watch as the other two work. His face says "thug". His face don't lie.

Zoe hands Mal a sort of glue gun looking thing. He squeezes and a clear gel comes out. In the center of the gel is a thin thread, like a wire.

Mal squeezes a circle about a foot around on the middle of the door. Zoe reaches in and snips the wire with pliers.

Since there is no sound in space, all we hear is the labored breathing of three very tense people.

Mal pulls out a small device, looks almost like electric nosehair clippers, and clamps it onto the end of the wire.

He hits a switch on the device and a charge runs through the wire, causing a reaction in the gel that turns it incredibly acidic — it starts melting through the metal in a circle.

Mal moves away from the door, holds onto something near Zoe.

ANGLE: THE GEL

as it eats through the door, further and further...

INT. BRIDGE - CONTINUING

This (as we will learn in detail later) is the bridge of SERENITY, a small transport ship. The bridge itself is small and cluttered, more like someone's car than a pristine futuristic space vessel. In the pilot's seat sits WASH, a slightly shlumpy, unassuming fellow. He's concentrating intensely.

WASH
Everything looks good from here...
(beat)
Yes. Yes, this is a fertile land, and we will thrive.

It is at this point that we realize he's playing with little plastic dinosaurs. He holds a Stegosaurus and a T-rex (or whatever the hell they call 'em these days). The dinosaurs look out over his dash/console, toward the window.

WASH (cont'd)
(as Steg)
We will rule over all this land, and we will call it... This Land.
(as T-rex)
I think we should call it... your grave!
(Steg)
Curse your sudden but inevitable betrayal!
(T-rex)
Ha HA! Mine is an evil laugh! Now die!

He makes them fight. As he does, a light near him flashes red.

He stops fighting, looks, then looks at a sort of radar screen.

ANGLE: THE RADAR SCREEN

has got three other dinosaurs on it. He sweeps them off as a blip appears in the upper right quadrant, closing fast.

WASH (cont'd)
Oh, motherless son of a b —

FWOOSH! The circle of door shoots out toward us, as we're back in:

INT. BLOWN-OUT SHIP - CONTINUING

The piece of door flies across the room, bouncing off the wall right by Jayne — he catches it as it's ricochetting. What looks like steam pours out through the hole for a few moments.

ZOE
Full pressure. The goods should be intact.

MAL
Assuming they're still there.

He's floating to the door — sticks his hand in the hole and shoves, the door slides aside and Jayne shines a flashlight in there.

ANGLE: INSIDE THE CHAMBER

WASH'S DINOSAURS

Prop master Randy Eriksen: "I bought Wash's dinosaurs in the downtown LA toy district. I repainted them. They were made in China and were pretty cheap."

Three crates, roughly the size of haybales, sit in the dark.

MAL (cont'd)
Okay. Looking good.

A voice sounds simultaneously in all three headsets: Wash.

WASH (O.S.)
We have incoming! Alliance Cruiser, bearing right down on us!

MAL
<Ta ma de.> [Dammit.]
(continuing)
Have they spotted us?

WASH
I can't tell if —

MAL
Have they hailed us?

JAYNE
If they're here for the salvage, we're humped.

ZOE
This ship's been derelict for months. Why would they —

MAL
<Bizui.> [Shut up.]
(continuing)
Shut it down, Wash. Everything but the air.

INT. BRIDGE - CONTINUING

WASH
Shutting down.

He is flipping switches, we hear engines running down, lights go off — he hits the com:

WASH (cont'd)
Kaylee! KAYLEE!

INT. ENGINE ROOM - CONTINUING

KAYLEE rolls into frame from underneath a huge engine part, ups and runs to the com. She is young, zaftig — as cheery as she is sexy. She and her jumpsuit are, as usual, speckled with grease.

WASH
Kaylee! Go to black out! We're being buzzed!

She hits the com —

KAYLEE
<Shi> [Affirmative],
(continuing)
going dark —

and keeps moving, hitting switches — climbing atop the engine to pull the last lever. Everything goes pretty damn black.

KAYLEE (cont'd)
Okay. Now I can't get down.

INT. BLOWN-OUT SHIP - CONTINUING

Jayne, Zoe and Mal all hold their positions, tense.

MAL
(softly)
Wash. Where's the Crybaby?

INTERCUT WITH:

INT. BRIDGE - CONTINUING

WASH
Right where we left her. You want her to cry?

MAL
Not yet. They slowing down?

WASH
That's a neg. Don't think they're interested in us. We should be eating wake in a minute or two.

MAL
All right. They do a heat probe, you holler.

WASH
<Shi.> [Affirmative.]

Mal looks at the other two. They wait.

EXT. SPACE - CONTINUING

And we see it, in all its glory: An Alliance Cruiser. Sleek, huge, antiseptic. The AngloSino flag painted above the name, I.A.V. DORTMUNDER.

CAPTAIN (O.S.)
What am I looking at?

INT. DORTMUNDER BRIDGE - CONTINUING

Hey, it's big. And clean, and everything a spaceship is supposed to be. The CAPTAIN speaks with an ENSIGN. They are rigid, formal, their clothes somewhat Trekkian, with a more militaristic edge to it. They're Cops, Army, Ambassadors — they're the Man.

ENSIGN
It's a carrier, blew out a few months back. No survivors, but it was only run by a skeleton crew anyway.

Now we see their view: a huge window, in which the twisted wreck of a ship is a tiny speck, and a computerized window within in which it's magnified, a rotating 3D image.

CAPTAIN
Damn shame. No point in checking for survivors...?

ENSIGN
Locals swept it right after.

A moment, and the Captain takes off his hat. The Ensign follows suit as the Captain hits the com, his voice booming out around the ship:

CAPTAIN
Crew, a moment of respect, if you please. Passing a graveyard.

The other men in the ship respond by pulling off their hats and slightly bowing their heads, a couple looking out at the approaching ghostship.

INT. BLOWN-OUT SHIP - CONTINUING

Mal waits as through a piece of ripped out wall behind him, the ship, impossibly huge and dangerously close, passes by.

ANGLE: MAL'S FACE

is set with grim dislike, as the reflection of the passing ship plays across his faceplate.

He is silent. So are the others.

EXT. BLOWN-OUT SHIP - CONTINUING

As the Cruiser passes by, leaving the ship behind, all clear...

INT. DORTMUNDER BRIDGE - CONTINUING

A MAN seated at a screen suddenly brow-furrows.

MAN
Sir, there is a reading on that thing. Some residual heat...

CAPTAIN
Do a sweep.

INT. BRIDGE - CONTINUING

An alarm sound, lights blink.

WASH
<Aiya! Huaile.> [Something's wrong.]
(continuing)
Captain! We're humped!

INT. BLOWN-OUT SHIP - CONTINUING

MAL
Fire it up! Now!
(to the others)
We move these in, double-time!

They float to the crates, start dragging them (not hard in zero g).

INT. ENGINE ROOM - CONTINUING

It's still pitch black in here.

WASH (O.S.)
Fire it up! Kaylee!

KAYLEE
I'm all over it! I just gotta find the damn...

She hits the switch that gives her light. But in the action, topples off the engine she was perched on and out of frame.

KAYLEE (cont'd)
Wahh!

EXT. BLOWN-OUT SHIP

Mal, Jayne and Zoe move straight up through twisted metal, pushing their crates. Jayne is first, reaching the top and then proceeding forward, pushing off with crate in hand before him.

INT. BLOWN-OUT SHIP/AIRLOCK OF SERENITY - CONTINUING

Mal, Zoe and Jayne all float their crates past the twisted wreckage and into the airlock. Mal hits the button and the airlock door shuts. Hits another and gravity hits, the three of them landing on their feet, crates dropping, as air rushes in.

Mal hits the com.

MAL
Wash! We're on! Go!

EXT. BLOWN-OUT SHIP - CONTINUING

The Cruiser is a good ways away as part of the black, twisted shadow begins to disengage itself, and we see for the first time that Serenity was anchored to the wreck, hidden almost in her bowels.

Serenity is a small, buglike ship, patched together, rusted in parts — everything the Dortmunder is not. And teeny in comparison. It somewhat unfolds itself as it gets free.

INT. DORTMUNDER BRIDGE - CONTINUING

The Captain is watching on his screen.

CAPTAIN
What the hell?

INT. BRIDGE - CONTINUING

Wash is seated, all business now.

WASH
Hang on, travelers...

INT. AIRLOCK - CONTINUING

Everyone grabs something, as Jayne pulls off his helmet.

JAYNE
Let's moon 'em.

EXT. SERENITY - CONTINUING

As the ship turns away from us, the back lights up — the entire bulbous back end glowing beneath a metal grid.

The ship fires away from us.

INT. AIRLOCK - CONTINUING

Mal hits the com:

MAL
Cry, baby, cry.

WASH (O.S.)
Make your mother sigh. Engaging the Crybaby.

EXT. SPACE - CONTINUING

Behind some little moon, we see a tiny jet-propelled satellite-looking thing, beeping out its distress signal. It's roughly the size of a thermos, and has written on a piece of tape: "Crybaby #6".

INT. DORTMUNDER BRIDGE - CONTINUING

The Captain and Ensign are near the screen. The Captain's face goes cold with disgust.

MAN
It's a transport ship. Firefly class.

ENSIGN
They still make those?

CAPTAIN
Illegal salvage. Lowlife vultures picking the flesh off the dead.

ENSIGN
Should we deploy gunships, bring her in?

CAPTAIN
Do it.

MAN
Captain, I am picking up a distress signal thirteen clicks ahead... From a... it sounds like a personnel carrier...

EXT. DORTMUNDER - CONTINUING

We move from a front shot of the bridge below

the Dortmunder, to see gunships preparing to launch.

EXT. SPACE - CONTINUING

The Crybaby beeps.

INT. DORTMUNDER BRIDGE - CONTINUING

MAN
Definitely a big ship, sir, and she is without power.

CAPTAIN
(considering)
Gunships'd never get back to us in time... all right. Let's go help those people.
(to the Ensign)
Put a bulletin out on the Cortex, and flag Interpol: a Firefly with possible stolen goods aboard.
(almost to himself)
Maybe someone'll step on those roaches...

INT. CARGO HOLD - CONTINUING

The airlock feeds right into the cargo hold. It's a cavernous space with a great deal of junk cluttering it. The airlock door opens and Mal and the other two step out, clearly a bit tense. They all pull off their helmets.

WASH (O.S.)
We look shiny, Captain. They are not repeat not coming about.

ZOE
Close one.

JAYNE
Any one you walk away from, right? Long as those crates aren't empty, I call this a win.

MAL
Right.

He looks away, darkness in his gaze.

MAL (cont'd)
We win.

END OF TEASER

ACT ONE

INT. CARGO HOLD - LATER

A crate is jimmied open. It is Jayne with the crowbar, Mal who pulls the top off, looking in. Zoe, Wash and Kaylee are also about. Zoe, Jayne and Mal are already dressed in their regular clothes. [Add shot from inside hidden compartment.]

MAL
Well. There we are.

ANGLE: IN THE CRATE are bars that look a lot like gold.

KAYLEE
(excited)
They're awfully pretty...

WASH
I'd say worth a little risk.

JAYNE
Yeah, that was some pretty risky sitting you did there.

WASH
That's right, of course, 'cause they wouldn't arrest *me* if we got boarded, I'm just the pilot. I can always say I was flying the ship by accident.

MAL
(harshly)
<Bizui.> [Shut up.]

He has a bar in his hand, is looking at it up close.

ZOE
Problem, sir?

Clearly, there is. But Mal tries to cover — just a bit of tension creeping into his voice.

MAL
(after a moment)
Couldn't say.
(tosses the bar back)
But we'd best be rid of these 'fore we run into another Alliance patrol.

JAYNE
What the hell they doing this far out, anyhow?

KAYLEE
Shining the light of civilization.

JAYNE
Doesn't do us any good...

KAYLEE
Well, we're uncivilized.

As they talk, Mal approaches Wash, talking over them.

MAL
How long til we reach Persephone?

WASH
Three or four hours.

MAL
Can we shave that?

WASH
(shakes his head)
We're down to the wire on fuel cells. We run hot, we might not even make it.

MAL
Play it as close as you can. This catch is burning a hole in my hull.

ZOE
You think that Cruiser could've I.D.'d us?

MAL
Gotta hope not. Contact Badger, tell him the job's done. Don't go to mentioning the Cruiser, though. Keep it simple.

ZOE
Sir, we're sure there's nothing wrong with the carg —

MAL
It's fine. I just wanna get paid.

They head up the ladder as Mal turns his attention to:

MAL (cont'd)
Jayne, Kaylee, let's get these crates stowed. I don't want any tourists stumbling over them.

KAYLEE
We're taking on passengers at Persephone?

ANGLE - POV FROM HIDDEN COMPARTMENT

MAL
That's the notion. We could use a little respectability on the way to Boros. Not to mention the money.

JAYNE
I hate tourists...

INT. UPPER CORRIDOR/BRIDGE - CONTINUING

As Wash and Zoe crest the ladder and head to their positions, talking.

ZOE
I know something's not right.

WASH
Sweetie, we're crooks. If everything was right we'd be in jail.

ZOE
It's just, the Captain's so tense...

WASH
Man needs a break. In fact...

He pulls her towards him.

WASH (cont'd)
We could all use a couple days leave.

ZOE
We still gotta drop the goods —

WASH
And when we do, we'll fly off to Boros rich and prosperous. Well, less poor. But with enough to find some sweet little getaway...

ZOE
(loosening up)
Wouldn't mind a real bath...

WASH
And a meal that included some form of food... Just a couple of days, lying around... you with the bathing, me with the watching you bathe...

They're so close...

ZOE
If the Captain says it's all right...

Wrong. Wash shuts his eyes a moment, rests his head on hers, quietly pissed. He breaks apart.

WASH
What if we just told Mal we needed a few days, 'stead of asking him?

ZOE
He's the Captain, Wash.

WASH
Right. I'm just the husband.

He lands in his seat. She still stands.

ZOE
Look, I'll ask him.

WASH
Don't forget to call him "sir". He likes that.

MAL
Who likes what?

Instinctively, Zoe's demeanor changes as Mal enters, her bearing more erect, military.

ZOE
It's nothing, sir.

Wash looks at her excitedly, mouths, "good!" and gives the thumbs up. She looks away.

MAL
Has the Ambassador checked in?

WASH
Nah, I think she had a pretty full docket.

MAL
Well, after you talk to Badger, let her know we may be leaving Persephone in a hurry.

ZOE
Inara knows our timetable, she should be checking in.

WASH
I can tell her to cut it short, meet us at the docks.

MAL
No, no. Don't wanna get in her way if we don't have to.
(leaving)
Someone on this boat has to make an honest living.

INT. INARA'S CHAMBER - NIGHT

We are close on INARA's face. She is being made love to by an eager, inexperienced but quite pleasingly shaped YOUNG MAN. She is beneath him, drawing him to his climax with languorous intensity. His face buried in her neck.

INARA
Oh... Oh... Oh my god...

He tightens, relaxes, becomes still. She runs her hand through his hair and he pulls from her neck, looks at her with sweaty insecurity.

PERSEPHONE

She smiles, a worldly, almost motherly sweetness in her expression. He rests his head on her breast, still breathing hard.

INARA (cont'd)
(softly)
Oh my boy...

INT. SAME - LATER

They are seated on cushions, close to each other with their legs entwined, sipping tea from small cups. She has a robe on.

INARA
Sihnon isn't that different from this planet. More crowded, obviously, and I guess more complicated. The great city itself is... pictures can't capture it. It's like an ocean of light.

THE YOUNG MAN
Is that where you studied? To be a Companion?

INARA
(nodding)
I was born there.

THE YOUNG MAN
I can't imagine ever leaving.

There is but half truth in her reply, and a hint of weariness.

INARA
Well, I wanted to see the universe.

THE YOUNG MAN
My cousin hopes to become a Companion. But I don't think the Academy will take her unless her scores come up.

INARA
It was the languages I struggled with. And music, at first.

THE YOUNG MAN
You play beautifully.

INARA
Thank you.

He looks down at his cup a moment.

THE YOUNG MAN
Do you really have to leave? I mean... I, my father is very influential, we could... I could arrange for you to be with...

She smiles that knowing smile again, just a tinge of sadness in it. He doesn't continue.

INT. SAME - LATER

He is dressed and exiting, his manner slightly more diffident.

THE YOUNG MAN
A very — it was very good. Thank you.

INARA
The time went too quickly.

THE YOUNG MAN
Your clock's probably rigged to speed up and cheat us out of our fun.

The smile vanishes from her face. He looks guilty, then ducks out of the chamber, shutting the door behind him.

She takes a moment, then hits a button by the door, locking it and sealing it. She moves across the room and pulls aside a tapestry that conceals the cockpit of what we now see to be a small shuttle. Gets in the pilot's seat and hits a switch (and continues hitting them as she talks).

INARA
Serenity, this is Shuttle One, what's your ETA?

WASH (O.S.)
Inara, hey. We're touching down at the Eavesdown docks in about ten minutes.

INARA
I'll join you there, thanks.

WASH (O.S.)
Looking forward. We missed you out here.

INARA
(softly)
Yeah. Me too.

She punches a few buttons, rides the joystick, and the cockpit begins to shake slightly as we CUT TO:

EXT. CITY - DAY

The outside of the shuttle, which rises slowly into the air. As it does we see it is perched atop a sky-scraper in a fairly big and ritzy city. It flies off.

INT. COCKPIT - DAY

Wash deftly pilots Serenity, light shifting across his face as the ship descends into atmo.

EXT. DOCKS - DAY

We see Serenity as she touches down at the Eavesdown docks. It's a bustling bazaar, ships lined up next to each other, each one advertising passage or selling goods. The place is filled with people of all races, modes and languages. It's chaos; trade, theft and outright violence all happening amidst the jumble of humanity.

This district is clearly poorer than the gleaming city in the distance, and every ship parked looks a tad haphazard — though Serenity does seem particularly small and ratty next to the ships it docks between.

The airlock opens, the ramp coming down and our gang piling out.

MAL
(to Kaylee)
This shouldn't take long. Put us down for depar-ture in about three hours.
(to Wash)
Fuel her up, and grab any supplies we're low on.

Kaylee moves to a computerized placard in front of their 'parking space', starts entering data. We arm up to see it reads: DESTINATION: and that BOROS appears below that. The rest is filled in thus:

CAPACITY: TWELVE

DEPARTURE TIME: 1500

KAYLEE
I'd sure love to find a brand new compression coil for the steamer.

MAL
And I'd like to be king of all Londinum and wear a shiny hat. Just get us some passengers. Them as can pay, all right?

KAYLEE
Compression coil busts, we're drifting...

MAL
Best not bust, then.

Zoe, Jayne and Mal start off.

WASH
Zoe.
(then)
<Zhu yi.> [Watch your back.]

ZOE
We will.

He watches her move through the crowd.

EXT. EAVESDOWN DOCKS - DAY

We're in the middle of the hubbub. We see a sign that advertises: Good DOGS! Arm down to see a pen of scrawny, listless dogs of various breeds. Arm further down to see a griddle, with some sus-picious looking cuts of meat sizzling on it. A man works the griddle.

We see, passing through frame, Shepherd BOOK. He's about sixty, weathered and worldly, with a quiet kindness in his eyes. Farmer stock, not a trace of bullshit and a workingman's hands. He drags a few boxes and suitcases on a sort of wheeled papoose, carries another suitcase in his hand. His clothes are plain and instantly identify him as some kind of protestant minister. As he moves on, looking about him, he is approached by a MAN, who's in his face a bit.

MAN
You going on a trip, grandpa? Need safe passage? We're cheap, we're cheap and clean, The BRUTUS is the best ship in the 'verse. What's your des, grandpa, we're hitting the outer rings —

BOOK
I never married.

MAN #2
What?

BOOK
I'm not a grandpa.

The guy just looks at him like he's crazy, lets him move on past the next barker, MAN #2. This guy is fancy, with people gathered around — his ship is clearly high class.

MAN #2
— three berths left, junior suites, we are not inter-ested in Asian or Catholic passengers, thank you, we will be bidding for the last three berths —

Book moves on. Comes to the third dock in the row. It's Serenity's. Kaylee sits outside it in a lawn chair. He looks at it, never stopping, til Kaylee says, smiling:

KAYLEE
You're gonna come with us.

BOOK
Excuse me?

KAYLEE
You like ships. Don't seem to be looking at the destinations. What you care about is the ships and mine is the nicest.

She's completely innocuous. It's hard not to be

charmed by her. He does stop, gives the ship a look-over.

ANGLE: THE BRIDGE sticking out above them, SERENITY painted on the side.

BOOK
She don't look like much.

KAYLEE
She'll fool ya'. Ever sailed in a Firefly?

BOOK
Long before you were crawling. Not an aught three, though. Didn't have the extenders, tended to shake.

KAYLEE
You wanna shake, sail the PARAGON there. Guarantee you'll barf before you break atmo.

Book looks over at the fancy ship he just passed, clearly agreeing.

BOOK
They can dress her up pretty, but a Gurtlser engine's always gonna get twitchy on ya.
(re: Serenity)
The aught three still use the trace compression block?

KAYLEE
Til they make something better.

Now she pretty much thinks he's the cool fool too. There is a moment between them.

KAYLEE (cont'd)
So how come you don't care where you're going?

BOOK
'Cause how you get there is the worthier part.

KAYLEE
You a missionary?

BOOK
I guess... I'm a Shepherd, from the Southdown Abbey. Book, I'm called Book. Been out of the world for a spell. Like to walk it a while, maybe bring the word to them as need it told.

KAYLEE
I'm Kaylee. This is Serenity, and she's the smoothest ride from here to Boros for anyone can pay.
(beat, worried)
Can you pay?

BOOK
Not what they're charging on the Paragon. But I expect we could come to terms. I've got a little cash, and, uh...

He approaches her, with a small wooden box. Shows her the contents. She goes a little bit wide eyed, eyeing the contents lustfully.

KAYLEE
Oh, Grampa...

BOOK
I never married.

KAYLEE'S COSTUMES

Costume designer Shawna Trpcic: "At first, I thought that she was going to be Asian, so I got a bunch of books on Chinese and Japanese youths and girls — one book in particular was called *Fruit*. I was also inspired by the World War Two figure Rosie the Riveter and Chinese Communist posters, with Chairman Mao and everybody smiling. We blended all these ideas together.

"I loved it when Kaylee wore her little flirty dress [in 'The Message'] — I loved it when I got to break out of the army green or metric yellow jumpsuit. I also found some fabric downtown in a remnant store, and we just made a bunch of t-shirts from it, because that was kind of her uniform. The frilly little dress I made out of actual antique Japanese kimono fabric, from the pattern of a 1970s flower girl dress."

INT. - HALLWAY - DAY

Mal, Zoe, and Jayne walk down a hallway, past a row of gunmen.

INT. UNDERGROUND 'OFFICE' - DAY

This is BADGER's place. It's not too large, and kind of dingy. The ceiling has what looks like subway grates over it — we can hear the traffic above, and every now and then the bright white of a flying vehicle pours through the grate. On one side are stairs leading up to ground level and a door beside, at the other end an oversized, beat up desk and a way into the back through a curtain.

Badger is a petty thug with pretensions to Kingpinery. He has bad facial hair, bad teeth, a crushed derby and he wears a woolly three piece and tie, though he has only a wifebeater beneath.

We find him in the room with three thugs in the corners. A fourth, an old man, is holding the arm of a clearly frightened but slightly hopeful young woman. Badger inspects her.

BADGER
Let me see your teeth.

She gives him a big smile. He pulls her lip up, the other one down.

BADGER (cont'd)
Yes.

She looks apprehensively pleased as she is shuttled behind the curtain. As she is, yet another thug leads Mal, Zoe and Jayne down the stairs. Badger doesn't look at them, heading for his desk.

BADGER (cont'd)
You're late.

MAL
You're lying.

Everybody tenses as Badger turns.

BADGER
What did you just say to me?

MAL
You're well aware we landed two hours 'fore we planned to, with all the goods you sent us after intact and ready to roll. So your decision to get tetchy and say we're late means you're looking to put us on the defensive right up front. Which means something's gone wrong and it didn't go wrong at our end so why don't we start again with you telling us what's up?

A beat. A mean little smile from Badger.

BADGER
You're later than I'd like.

MAL
Well I am sorry to hear that.

Badger sits. Briefly holds up what appears to be digital paper: a clear, pliable piece of plastic with words and images running across it, constantly changing.

BADGER
If you'd gotten here sooner, you might've beaten the bulletin that came up saying a rogue vessel, classification "Firefly", was spotted pulling illegal salvage on a derelict transport.

MAL
They didn't ID us. Doesn't lead to you.

As he speaks he sticks an apple on a rusty old peeler, slowly turns it.

BADGER
No, it doesn't. But the government stamp on every molecule of the cargo just maybe might.

Zoe looks at Mal — that's what he didn't say when he examined the bars.

BADGER'S APPLE PEELER

Prop master Randy Eriksen: "Another great prop was the hand-cranked apple peeler in Badger's place. I think it was Joss Whedon's. It looked really cool."

BADGER (cont'd)
Oh, you noticed that. You were gonna hand over imprinted goods and just let me twist, is that the case?

MAL
We didn't pick the cargo.

BADGER
And I didn't flash my ass at the gorramn law. There's no deal.

ZOE
That ain't fair.

BADGER
Crime and politics, little girl: the situation is always fluid.

JAYNE
Only fluid I see here is the puddle of piss refusing to pay us our wage.

Guns are raised, cocked.

Mal shoots Jayne a look that shuts him right up.

Mal steps forward and Badger rises — but Mal is reasonable of tone.

MAL
Doesn't have to go this way. You know you can still unload those goods. So I can't help thinking there's something else at work here.

As he talks, two more girls are hustled in. They are nudged, and both smile at Badger.

BADGER
(re: one)
Yes.
(re: other)
No.
(to Mal)
I don't like you.

He makes a face, reconsidering —

BADGER (cont'd)
(to his thug, re: other)
Dyeahh... yes.

The girl is pushed through the curtain after the first one. Badger calls after them:

BADGER (cont'd)
But keep her in the back, yeah?

MAL
I'm not asking you to like me —

BADGER
(overlapping)
What were you in the war? That big war you failed to win — you were a sergeant? Yeah, Sergeant Malcolm Reynolds, Balls and Bayonets Brigade, big tough veteran, now you got yourself a ship and you're a captain! Only I think you're still a sergeant, see. Still a soldier, man of honor in a den of thieves.
(in his face)
Well it's my gorramn den and I don't like the way you look down on me. I'm above you. Better than. I'm a businessman, yeah? Roots in the community. You're just a scavenger.

MAL
Maybe I'm not a fancy gentleman like you with your... very fine hat... but I do business. We're here for business.

BADGER
Try one of the border planets — they're a lot more desperate there. Of course they might kill you, but you stay here and I just know the Alliance'll track you down. I have that feeling.

M A L

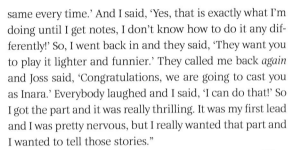

"We've done the impossible, and that makes us mighty."

For anyone confused about what *Firefly* is really about, all one needs to do is look past the spaceships and Western attire. Ignore the rag-tag heists and wacky, ethnically fused colloquialisms. Bypass the terrifying Reavers and omnipotent Alliance to get to the actual heart of the series, which is the story of a dark, world-weary man with an unshakeable love and loyalty for his adopted family. That man is Captain Malcolm Reynolds and it's on his shoulders that *Firefly* firmly rests. Suffice to say, only the right actor could bring Mal's particular mix of pathos, humor and strength to life in perfect harmony and Joss Whedon found his casting zen with actor Nathan Fillion. Equal parts handsome, rugged, goofy and tragic, Fillion inhabited the character from the moment he stepped on set and made Malcolm his own.

The actor still remembers landing the part with enthusiasm. "I walked into [casting director] Amy Britt's office to have a meeting with Joss," Fillion says. "It was dimly lit and warm and cozy in there. I knew of Joss Whedon but had never met him, nor did I know what he looked like. There was this scroungy-looking fella in the corner. He had a purple sweater on with a hole in it on the left side on his chest and I thought, 'Who's this guy and when do I meet Joss?' Halfway through the meeting, it dawned on me who *he* was," the actor laughs. "Joss told me a great deal about the show. I had so many questions and Joss had the answers. For whatever I asked, he had an entire universe planned. I was enthralled. We talked about the show, personal experiences, work ethics, how to keep things smooth on sets and it became apparent that we had similar sensibilities. He said, 'Why don't you come back and audition for Malcolm Reynolds?' I said, 'Great', and did just that. I remember I auditioned and they had me come back and do it again. I left and they had me come back and do it *again*. Joss then came out and said, 'They think you are doing it the

same every time.' And I said, 'Yes, that is exactly what I'm doing until I get notes, I don't know how to do it any differently!' So, I went back in and they said, 'They want you to play it lighter and funnier.' They called me back *again* and Joss said, 'Congratulations, we are going to cast you as Inara.' Everybody laughed and I said, 'I can do that!' So I got the part and it was really thrilling. It was my first lead and I was pretty nervous, but I really wanted that part and I wanted to tell those stories."

The key to Mal's motivations became clear once Fillion figured out what his Serenity family truly represented. "I always imagined that since he's had so much taken away from him that he had such a fear of losing anything else, especially something that might make him happy, and that's sad. Somebody asked me why he so zealously guards over the safety of his crew and I look at it that Mal gathers to him that which he no longer has within himself. In Wash, he has a lust for life and a sense of humor he's lost. In Jayne, he has selfishness. In Book, he has spirituality. In Kaylee, he has innocence. Everybody represents a facet of himself that he has lost and that's why he keeps them close and safe, and yet at arm's length."

The cast in reality brought just as much to Fillion too. "It was very much a family. They all knew exactly what they were doing and I credit Joss with that. He found not only talented actors, not only people who understood the kind of lilt to the language or the personas for their characters, but everybody brought so much to the table that it made my job so incredibly easy. People are looking at me like I'm the Captain, like I might be dangerous, like I'm their friend — everybody did my work for me. I also credit Joss with having created a family. I don't know how you do that but he did it and I am a richer man for it. The quality of my life has improved because of *Firefly*, not just because of the employment and things it did for me, but because of the people. It sounds corny and hokey, but I loved being Mal Reynolds. I really, really did. I loved having all the adventures, riding horses, flying spaceships, shooting guns. I had a great time being cool, being funny, the awesome coat and the wicked gun, but I walked away from that with close friends. I'm a lucky man."

Long beat. Mal is inches from starting a firefight — Jayne is less than inches. Zoe merely waits to back Mal's play.

But Mal turns to go. As he's leaving, he says:

MAL
Wheel never stops turning, Badger.

BADGER
That only matters to the people on the rim.

EXT. EAVESDOWN DOCKS - LATER

OPEN ON: The clash of wooden swords as two kabuki actors fight on a raised dais for the crowd. Whip pan off this action to track quickly in front of Mal, Zoe and Jayne as they head back to the ship.

JAYNE
I don't understand why we didn't leave that sumbitch in a pool of his own blood.

MAL
We'd be dead. Can't get paid if you're dead.

JAYNE
Can't get paid if you crawl away like a bitty little bug, neither. I got a share in this job, and ten percent of nothing, uh — hold on. Let me do the math here... nothing into nothing... carry the nothing...

ZOE
(overlapping him)
We'll just find a buyer on Boros. There's gotta be —

MAL
Boros is too big. It's crawling with Alliance, they could just be waiting for us.

ZOE
You really think Badger'd sell us out to the feds?

Mal looks over at:

ANGLE: TWO COPS looking around them, as though searching for something.

MAL
If he hasn't already.

ZOE
Alliance catches us with government goods, we'll lose the ship.

MAL
That's never gonna happen.

She stops, turns to him.

ZOE
We could just dump the cargo, sir.

JAYNE
No rutting way! We ain't had a job in weeks! I didn't sign up with this crew to take in the sights, all right? We need coin!

MAL
Jayne, your mouth is talking. You might wanna look to that.

JAYNE
(belligerent)
I'm ready to stop talking whenev —

MAL
You're right, though.

This stops Jayne — didn't expect to hear that.

MAL (cont'd)
Last two jobs we had were weak tea. We got nothing saved, and taking on passengers won't help near enough. We don't get paid for this cargo, we won't have enough money to fuel the ship, let alone keep her in repair. She'll be dead in the water.

ZOE
So we do like Badger said? The border planets?

MAL
(nodding)
I'm thinking we can hit Whitefall, maybe talk to Patience.

Zoe is clearly unhappy with this notion.

ZOE
Sir, we don't wanna deal with Patience again.

MAL
Why not?

ZOE
She shot you!

MAL
Well, yeah, she did a bit. Still...

He starts walking again, the others falling into step.

ZOE
So we find someone else. Horowitz.

MAL
He can't afford it.

ZOE
The Holden boys.

MAL
They wouldn't touch it. You want me to run down the list? The Capshaws are brainblown, Gruviek's dead...

ZOE
He's dead?

MAL
Town got hit by Reavers. Burned it right down.

JAYNE
Hey, I'm not going anywhere near Reaver territory. Those people ain't human.

MAL
Whitefall is the closest and the safest. Been a long

while since Patience shot me, and that was due to a perfectly legitimate conflict of interest. I got no grudge. She owns half that damn moon now, she can afford what we got and she might just need it.

ZOE
I still say the old lady's not —

MAL
(turns to her)
There's only one thing that matters.

She looks at him, then up past him, as he turns as well to look at:

ANGLE: SERENITY. They have reached her.

MAL (cont'd)
I'm not saying it won't be tricky. But we got no kind of choice.

MAL'S POV: still looking at Serenity, he sees Kaylee welcoming another passenger, introducing himself as:

DOBSON
Dobson... Thank you...

He stumbles, nearly dropping his luggage — he's just a bit bumbly and sweet. Over this we hear:

MAL
We just gotta keep our heads down and do the job. Pray there ain't no more surprises.

He is standing by the airlock ramp as he says it, looking at:

ANGLE: A BOX. Being loaded on by Wash on a dolly/truck is, among a few other things, a clearly special, futuristic-looking dark blue box with many dials and readouts.

The box clears frame to reveal SIMON, a young, clearly affluent man. He wears a dark suit and round glasses. He seems to be looking directly at Mal, then glances over to the box.

SIMON
(to Wash)
Please be careful with that.

KAYLEE
Mal, this is Simon. This is our Captain.

Both men size each other up, neither particularly anxious to make conversation.

SIMON
Captain Reynolds.

MAL
Welcome aboard.
(to Kaylee)
This all we got?

INT. CARGO BAY

Wash and Jayne are unloading stuff. We see Book and Simon unpacking — pan over to find Zoe moving to Mal, who is near the hidden compartment.

ZOE
So now we got a boatload of citizens right on top of our stolen cargo. That's a fun mix.

MAL
There's no way in the 'verse they could find that compartment, even if they were looking.

ZOE
Why not?

MAL
...'Cause.

ZOE
Yeah, this is gonna go great...

MAL
If anybody gets nosy, you just, you know... shoot 'em.

ZOE
Shoot them.

MAL
Politely.

INT. BRIDGE - DAY

Wash is prepping her for take off, sees a signal, flips a switch.

WASH
Inara. You're just in time.

INARA (O.S.)
Let me guess. We're in a hurry.

WASH
Looks like. Port hatch green for docking.

INARA (O.S.)
Locked in five. Four.

EXT. SERENITY - CONTINUING

As Inara's flying shuttle locks onto a side of the still-parked ship.

INT. INARA'S SHUTTLE - CONTINUING

As she feels the lurch of lock. She doesn't leave the pilot's seat.

INT. BRIDGE - CONTINUING

Wash turns, calls back:

WASH
The Ambassador has returned.

He is talking to Zoe, who moves to the

INT. CARGO BAY/AIRLOCK - CONTINUING

and calls down to Mal, who is stowing cargo with Jayne:

ZOE
We got a full house, Captain.

He turns to the airlock:

MAL
Kaylee. Lock it up!

EXT. AIRLOCK - CONTINUING

Kaylee looks around once...

KAYLEE
(softly)
All aboard...

ANGLE: SIMON

as he passes his box, looking at it, looking coldly at Mal.

EXT. PERSEPHONE - DAY

As Serenity shoots away from the atmosphere and into the black of space.

END OF ACT ONE

ACT TWO

EXT. SPACE - LATER

Serenity moves silently through. It is a tiny light in the black of space.

INT. PASSENGER DORM - LATER

MAL (O.S.)
Meals are taken up here in the dining area, the kitchen is pretty much self explanatory, you're welcome to eat what there is any time...

NATHAN FILLION

I put on my costume in my trailer and took one last look in the mirror. They called me to the set and I remember coming right from my trailer to inside the door of the set. When you walked into the studio, the ship was just to your left with the big open cargo bay door looking at ya. I remember walking up the cargo bay door for the first time in costume. I believe it was David Boyd, our director of photography, who turned and saw me walking up and turned back around to the crew and said, 'Captain on deck.' Some people clapped and it was kind of neat. It was a reception I will remember always.

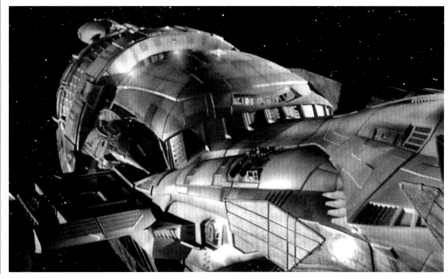

We see Dobson hurriedly coming out of the bathroom and up the stairs from the passenger section to the upstairs

INT. DINING ROOM - CONTINUING

as Mal has already begun addressing the other two passengers. Zoe and Kaylee are there as well.

MAL
...What there is is pretty standard fare, I guess, protein in all the colors of the rainbow. We do have sit-down meals, the next being at about 1800 —

KAYLEE
(excited)
I think Shepherd Book has offered to help me prepare something.

MAL
(to Book, less excited)
You're a Shepherd.

BOOK
Thought the outfit gave it away. Is it a problem?

KAYLEE
Of course not!
(to Mal)
It's not a problem, 'cause it's not.

MAL
No.
(to the bunch)
As I said, you're welcome to visit the dining area any time. Apart from that, I have to ask you to stay in the passenger dorm while we're in the air. The bridge, the engine room and the cargo bay are off limits without an escort.

SIMON
Some of my personal effects are in the cargo bay.

MAL
I figure you all got luggage you'll need to get into. Soon as we're done here we'll be happy to fetch 'em with you. Now I have to tell you all one other thing and I apologize in advance for the inconvenience — Unfortunately, we've been ordered by the Alliance to drop some medical supplies on Whitefall. It's the fourth moon on Athens, a bit out of our way, but we should have you on Boros no more than a day off schedule. Is that gonna be all right for everyone?

BOOK
Jake by me...

SIMON
What medical supplies?

MAL
I honestly didn't ask.

ZOE
Probably plasma, insulin, whatever they ain't got enough of on the border moons.

MAL
Alliance says jump...

SIMON
All right.

These two clearly already don't trust each other. Book watches the both of them, sensing the dynamic.

DOBSON
I'm supposed to be meeting my wife's sister. I've only a few days to see her...

ZOE
I wish there was another way...

DOBSON
Oh, no, no. That woman is like a dragon. I mean, I believe she has a tail. If there's any other moons we need to visit, or if we could just fly very slowly...

The tension is broken — people smile at Dobson's disarming relief.

WASH
One last thing, sorry — Your Firefly is a solid boat, but she's older... We've been having a bit of interference with our aeronautics, the new frequencies... we need to ask you all to stay off the Cortex, at least til we get to Whitefall. We should be able to correct the problem there.

MAL
Zoe, why don't you take 'em down to the cargo bay?

ZOE
Yes sir.

As the others start leaving, Mal moves close to Wash:

MAL
You send word to Patience?

WASH
Ain't heard back. Didn't she shoot you one time?

MAL
Everyone's making a fuss...

INT. CARGO BAY - LATER

People are getting the luggage they need. Dobson is spilling clothes out of his case — he's a perpetual bumbler.

Simon is also placing things into an elegant little valise — all the while eyeing his special blue box.

Book places something wrapped in tissue into a wooden box, hands it to Kaylee, who beams at him.

ANGLE: THE SECOND SHUTTLE HATCH

opens, showing Inara's shuttle. She steps out of it, in a simple but elegant dress. The hatch opens onto a catwalk that runs above the space in an 'X', the opposite side being the entrance to the first shuttle. She descends stairs as the group notices her.

MAL
The Ambassador graces us with her presence.

Book looks up — and Inara does indeed look the part of a lady of state.

INARA
Hello, Mal. I see we have some new faces.

KAYLEE
Hey you.

INARA
Hey you.

There is sweetness between those two. Not so much with Mal, whom Inara approaches.

MAL
Ambassador, this is Shepherd Book.

INARA
I'd have to say this is the first time we've had a preacher on board.

BOOK
Well, I wasn't expecting to see a state official, either.
(takes her hand, bows slightly)
Ambassador.

Mal laughs. Inara glowers at him.

BOOK (cont'd)
I'm missing something funny.

KAYLEE
(glaring at Mal)
Not so funny.

INARA
"Ambassador" is Mal's way of —

MAL
She's a whore, Shepherd.

Book's clearly a little thrown. And disapproving.

KAYLEE
The term is "Companion".

MAL
Yeah, but the job is whore.
(to Inara)
How's business?

INARA
None of yours.

MAL
(to Book)
She is pretty much our Ambassador. There's plenty of planets won't even let you dock without a decent Companion on board. This isn't a problem for you, is it?

BOOK
Well, I... no, I certainly...

INARA
(turns to go)
It's all right. I mostly keep to myself.

(passing Mal)
When I'm not whoring.

MAL
Don't you wanna meet the rest of the bunch?

INARA
Why don't you make sure they want to meet me first.

Inara and Kaylee start out together.

KAYLEE
So how many fell madly in love with you and wanted to take you away from all this?

INARA
Just the one. I think I'm slipping.

INT. DINING ROOM - CONTINUING

Kaylee has made her way up with the box, lays it on the counter. Quietly excited, she opens it, looks in. A beat, then she pulls out a strawberry.

It's just as red and luscious as it could be. She smells it, slowly puts it in her mouth, eyes closing. Watching her savor it is not an entirely unsensual experience.

She swallows it. Smiles, broad and bright.

INT. DINING ROOM - LATER

We see a sparse but none-the-less inviting spread — Book and Kaylee have made a salad of tomatoes, and grilled up some root vegetables along with the pasta and protein/starch mush that is the usual diet of space travelers. To us, not much. To this crowd, a banquet.

People are gathering, sitting, helping themselves to things — everybody's moving and talking over each other and everyone's there save Wash and Inara.

ZOE
Oh, this is incredible.

BOOK
It's not much — I had a garden at the Abbey, thought I should bring what I could.

SIMON
It's very kind of you to share with all of us.

ZOE
I'm gonna make a plate for Wash...

BOOK
(to Simon)
Well, it won't last, and they're never the same when they're frozen.

The important thing is the spices. A man can live on packaged food from here til Judgement Day if he's got enough Marjoram.

DOBSON
(over this, to Jayne)
Can you pass me the tomatoes?

He does, after taking several slices. People settle.

BOOK
Captain, would you mind if I say grace?

MAL
Only if you say it out loud.

A beat — Mal has broken the mood. He starts eating, others follow. Book lowers his head a moment, as do Kaylee, Dobson and Jayne, then they eat as well.

SIMON
So, does it happen a lot? Government commandeering your ship, telling you where to go?

MAL
That's what governments are for. Get in a man's way.

DOBSON
But it's good, if the supplies are needed...

JAYNE
Yeah, we're just happy to be doing good works.

DOBSON
I hear a lot of the border moons are in bad shape. Plagues, and famine...

ZOE
Well, some of that's exaggerated, and some of it ain't. All those moons — just like the central planets, they're as close to Earth-That-Was as we could make 'em: atmosphere, gravity and such, but...

MAL
Once they're terraformed, they'll dump settlers on there with nothing but blankets and hatchets and maybe a herd. Some of them make it, some of them...

SIMON
Then I guess it's good we're helping.

KAYLEE
(to Simon)
You're a doctor, right?

SIMON
Oh. Uh, yes. Yes, I was a trauma surgeon on Osiris, in Capital City.

MAL
Long way from here.

KAYLEE
(to Simon)
You seem so young. To be a doctor.

SIMON
(changing the subject)
You're pretty young to be a ship's mechanic.

KAYLEE
Know how. Machines just got workings, and they talk to me.

BOOK
That's a rare gift.

KAYLEE
Not like being a doctor, helping fix people, that's important. It's kind of comforting to have a doctor on board.

JAYNE
Little Kaylee just wishes you was a gynecologist.

Kaylee, visibly humiliated, looks down.

MAL
Jayne. You'll keep a civil tongue in that mouth or I will sew it shut, is there an understanding between us?

JAYNE
(pushing)
You don't pay me to talk pretty.

MAL
Walk away from this table. Right now.

FOOD

Prop master Randy Eriksen: "I had to do all the weird food. We used Heirloom tomatoes, you know, the purple ones. We had orange ones and we used risotto and Israeli couscous. Adam ate like crazy. The crew was all sitting down eating and they make Jayne get up and leave because he was rude. He was shoveling this food into his mouth and I had to keep resetting his plate over and over. He must have eaten like five plates of this couscous. Adam is a big guy."

A beat, and Jayne goes, grabbing a bunch of food as he does. Everyone is silent a moment.

SIMON
What do you pay him for?

MAL
What?

SIMON
I was just wondering what his job is. On the ship.

Mal stares a moment.

MAL
Public relations.

INT. INARA'S CHAMBER - LATER

Inara is kneeling, robe pooled at her waist. She is sponging off — the only kind of bathing you'll find on this ship. A knock on the hatch...

INARA
<Qing jin.> [Come in.]

Book enters. She is facing mostly away from him, but she sees it's him. She continues to bathe herself, running the sponge over her breasts, more in defiance than seduction.

MORENA BACCARIN

On bathing semi-nude: "I prepared by just getting really nervous! It is basically one of those things you have to do and luckily, I had a great director who was very respectful. I can't imagine doing anything like that with somebody who doesn't give a crap. It was a great crew, everybody was quiet and silent and looking down the whole time unless they happened to be looking through a camera. Of course, they reshot it three times because Joss kept saying something about a filter — to this day, I don't believe him! However, that wasn't my most embarrassing scene, because I had my back to everyone. What was more embarrassing was when I had to orgasm. That was much worse. Hopefully, you just make noises and Joss goes 'Okay, that's enough!'"

BOOK
If I'm intruding...

INARA
Not at all. I expected you.

BOOK
Couldn't really say the same.

INARA
So. Would you like to lecture me on the wickedness of my ways?

BOOK
I brought you some supper. But if you'd prefer a lecture, I've a few very catchy ones prepped. Sin and hellfire. One has lepers.

INARA
I think I'll pass. But thank you for these.

BOOK
The Captain said you might like them. I was surprised at his concern.

INARA
For a lowly whore?

BOOK
It was unjust of him to say that.

INARA
Believe me, I've called him worse. Anyway, I suspect he has more interest in making you uncomfortable than me.

BOOK
He's not wildly interested in ingratiating himself with anyone. Yet he seems very protective of his crew. It's odd.

INARA
Why are you so fascinated by him?

BOOK
Because he's something of a mystery. Why are you?

A beat, as she decides to play cards up.

INARA
Because so few men are.

She sounds almost weary when she says it. Her feelings for him are clearly complex.

INT. MAL'S ROOM - CONTINUING

It's a tiny cell, just a bunk and a tiny fold-down desk. A ladder runs up to the hatch (the crew rooms are under the foredeck hall). The room is cluttered with junk, pictures, general mess.

Mal is in the heroic act of doing up his trousers as we find him. There is a kind of metal drawer that hinges open to knee level. It's the toilet, and Mal kicks it shut, causing a flushing sound not unlike an airplane toilet. Above it is another metal drawer. He pulls it open and it's a small sink. He runs a little water on his hands, splashes his face, when the com sounds.

WASH (O.S.)
Mal, you might wanna get up here...

Mal's up the ladder in a flash.

INT. FOREDECK HALL - CONTINUING

The hatch, set at the side of the hall at a forty-five degree angle between floor and wall, slides open and Mal climbs up. He moves through the hall to:

INT. BRIDGE - CONTINUING

Where Wash is studying a screen.

MAL
What is it?

WASH
Signal. Somebody went on the Cortex, hailed the nearest Alliance Cruiser.

❖ Above: Dobson's Astra 400 stunt pistol.

MAL
Tell me you scrambled it.

WASH
All to hell, but I don't know how much got through. Alliance got a pin in us for sure.

MAL
<Ni ta ma de. Tianxia suoyoude ren. Dou gaisi.> [Everyone under the heavens ought to die.]

WASH
We got a mole on board.

Mal's face hardens as he works it out...

INT. CARGO BAY - MOMENTS LATER

Simon is checking on his box, looking at lights and gages. The lights are low now and he is furtive and very quiet, crouching on the larger crate on which his luggage sits. He finishes and steps down.

He turns and Mal is standing before him.

MAL
Forget your toothpaste?

Mal SLUGS him, sends him sprawling. Simon feels his head, furious, as Mal shakes his hurt hand.

SIMON
Are you out of your mind?

MAL
Just about. What'd you tell them?

SIMON
(standing)
Tell who?

Mal draws his gun, puts in in Simon's face.

MAL
I have exactly no time for games. What do they know.

SIMON
You are a lunatic.

MAL
And you're a gorramn fed.

BOOK
Hate to say it, Captain, but you've got the wrong man.

Both men turn to him, Mal stunned to think the Shepherd is actually a fed. A beat, and both Mal and Simon realize Book is looking behind them. Slowly, they turn the other way, and understand Book's meaning.

Dobson holds a gun on Mal.

MAL
(defeated)
Son of a bitch.

DOBSON
Drop that firearm, Captain Reynolds.

A beat, and Mal does.

MAL
This is not my best day ever.

Dobson moves the gun to point it at Simon.

DOBSON
Simon Tam, you are bound by law to stand down.

Mal takes a moment to realize the man is after Simon. Switches gears instantly:

MAL
You — what — the Doctor? Oh!
(indignant at Simon)
Hey!
(hopeful, to Dobson)
Is there a reward?

END OF ACT TWO

ACT THREE

INT. CARGO BAY - CONTINUING

Right where we left off. Dobson is ignoring Mal, focusing on Simon. This bumbling businessman is now a very intense, tightly wound cop.

DOBSON
(to Simon)
Get on the ground. Get on the ground!

SIMON
Lawman, you're making a mistake.

MAL
I think you oughta get on the ground, son. Man seems a mite twitchy.

BOOK
I think everybody could stand to calm down a bit.

He is moving slowly towards Dobson, hoping to defuse.

DOBSON
This isn't your business, Shepherd.

BOOK
The boy's not going anywhere, Lawman. As I understand it, it's pretty cold outside.

Mal moves casually for his gun — he's of the righteous now.

MAL
Not to worry. We can hold Lord Fauntleroy in a passenger cell — won't make a peep til you hand him over to —

DOBSON
(pointing the gun at Mal again)
Get the hell away from that weapon! You think I'm a complete backbirth? You're carrying a fugitive across interplanetary borders and do you think I actually believe you're bringing medical supplies to Whitefall? As far as I care, everyone on this ship is culpable.

MAL
(icy calm)
Well now. That has an effect on the landscape.

BOOK
Please, we're very close to true stupidity here —

DOBSON
I got a Cruiser en route for intercept, so talk all you want. You got about twenty minutes.

MAL
Might have less than that.

DOBSON
Yeah, threaten me...

BOOK
(still moving)
For God's sake —

DOBSON
You think I wouldn't shoot a Shepherd? Back off!

Mal grabs Simon — and everybody's shouting —

MAL
Just take the kid!

SIMON
Get your hands off —

DOBSON
Stand the hell down —

KAYLEE
Hey, what's —

Dobson spins and FIRES.

Kaylee steps backwards, puzzled, as Jayne steps in behind her —

KAYLEE (cont'd)
Wait, why are you...

She puts her hand to her belly. Blood runs over it.

A lot of things happen. Kaylee slumps to the ground as Simon rushes to her, Mal dives for his weapon, Jayne draws his, Dobson swings to fire at Mal —

— and Book is in Dobson's face, a brutal jab in

the throat as he grabs his gun-hand whip-quick, twists and pulls the gun out, cracking Dobson across the face with it in the same motion and Dobson is down. In seconds.

INARA
Kaylee!

She is on the upper level, having come out of her shuttle at the sound of the shot. She races to Kaylee, as does Mal, seeing that Dobson is no longer a threat.

Jayne comes toward Dobson with a purpose, gun in hand, and Book turns to face him.

JAYNE
Get out of the way.

BOOK
You're not killing this man.

JAYNE
Not right away...

BOOK
He's not a threat.

JAYNE
Move.

BOOK
Not gonna happen.

JAYNE
(raising his gun)
I'm not joking with you, Preacher —

ZOE
Jayne!

She's got her gun out, pointed at Jayne.

ZOE (cont'd)
Just tie him up. Do it!

A moment, and Jayne holsters his piece, moves to get some duct tape.

ZOE (cont'd)
(to Book)
The gun, Shepherd. Please.

Book hands her Dobson's gun. A bit of blood drips off it.

ANGLE: KAYLEE AND THE OTHERS

(NOTE: much of this action will be happening simultaneously with the other.)

Simon lays Kaylee prone, keeping her head up

til the others join him.

SIMON
Lie back. How do you feel?

KAYLEE
A little odd. Why'd he... oh...

Inara and Mal join them.

SIMON
(to Inara)
Put something under her head.

Inara pulls off her robe (she is dressed beneath) and bunches it under Kaylee's head, as Simon rips open Kaylee's jumpsuit, examines the wound. It's not pretty.

MAL
(to Kaylee)
Well, that ain't hardly a mosquito bite.

He and Inara exchange a glance that means something very different.

KAYLEE
Big... mosquito...

SIMON
Can you move your feet? Kaylee. Stay with me. Can you move your feet?

KAYLEE
Are you... asking me to dance...?

Her eyes start to roll back —

SIMON
She's going into shock.

INARA
Kaylee, <xiao meimei> [little sister], you gotta focus.

Simon pushes Kaylee's stomach and she screams.

SIMON
(to Mal)
The infirmary working?

MAL
We got it stocked.

They move to pick her up —

WASH (O.S.)
(on the com)
Captain, we've been hailed by a Cruiser. Ordered to stay on course and dock for prisoner transfer.

Mal and Simon look at each other.

Simon rises, steps away from Kaylee. He is tense, but surprisingly calm.

SIMON
Change course. Run.

MAL
Hell with you. You brought this down on us, I'm dumping you with the law.

INARA
Mal...

SIMON
She's dying.

MAL
You're not gonna let her.

SIMON
Yes I am.

MAL
You can't.

Simon looks at Kaylee, helpless and sweet.

ZOE
No way the feds'll let us walk.

MAL
Then we dump him in the shuttle and leave him for them.

KAYLEE
(delirious)
Everybody's so mad...

INARA
It's okay, baby...

SIMON
You know what a stomach wound does to a person?

MAL
I surely do.

SIMON
Then you know how crucial the next few minutes are.

ZOE
(to Simon)
You let her die you'll never make it to the feds.

SIMON
She'll still be dead.

MAL
You rich kids, you think your lives are the only thing that matters. What'd you do? Kill your folks for the family fortune?

SIMON
I don't kill people.

MAL
Then do your job!

SIMON
Turn the ship around!

INARA
Enough! Mal, do it.

MAL
Don't ever tell me —

Kaylee screams again.

Mal and Simon stare at each other.

MAL (cont'd)
(eyes on Simon)
Zoe. Change course.

SIMON
Help me get her up.

Mal and Inara hoist with Simon.

INARA
It's back behind you.

ZOE
(hits the com)
Wash, change course and go for hard burn. We're running.

EXT. SPACE - CONTINUING

As the ship turns and the back lights up wicked bright — and she shoots off.

INT. INFIRMARY - MOMENTS LATER

The three of them burst in, lay Kaylee on the table. It's small and not wildly sterile here, but it is clearly functional.

SIMON
You have an extractor?

MAL
Laser saw. We can go in —

SIMON
Not good enough. In my room, the red bag.

Inara goes. Simon raids the cupboards, finds a hypo-gun and vials.

MAL
This is over, you and me are gonna have a personal chat.

SIMON
Won't that be fun.
(tosses Mal the hypo)
Dope her.

INT. INFIRMARY - CONTINUING

We see, over time, VARIOUS ANGLES of Simon operating. What's clear here is that this guy is supremely confident and good at his job. Mal and Inara assist — mostly Mal, who has the most field experience. Among the images are:

— Simon using the extractor to find and pull out the bullet shards.

— Mal holding the wound open while Simon works a laser/scope inside her. Both men with bloody hands.

— Inara holding a breathing mask over Kaylee's face, looking at instruments indicating her vitals.

— a vid image of a laser sewing up a hole in her liver.

— Inara handing over bandages as Simon sews the wound shut.

INT. INFIRMARY - LATER

Simon washes off his hands. He turns to Mal.

SIMON
I can't do any more until she stabilizes.

MAL
Will she?

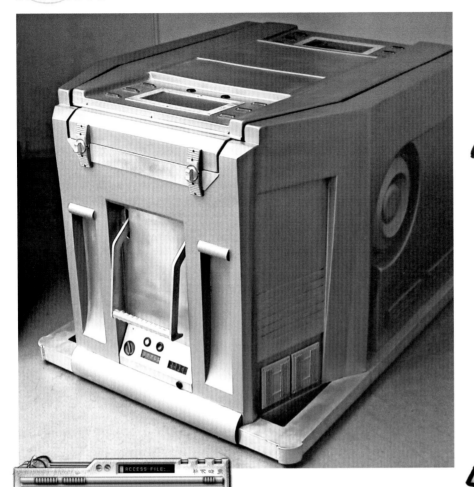

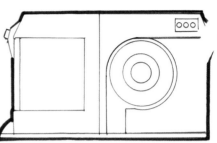

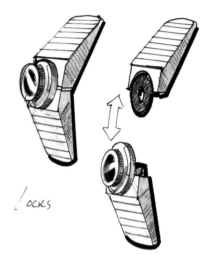

Locks

RIVER'S BLUE BOX

Prop master Randy Eriksen: "River's blue cryo box was the biggest prop we made for sure. We designed it and Neotech made it for us. I went to pick it up and it was gray. I told them it had to be this icy blue color, not gunmetal gray. We'd had to pick from color chips the size of your fingernail and maybe I was off by one color, or they were. When we repainted it, it looked great. The lid was rigged to fly off and I'd made this big aluminum handle. The first thing Nathan did when he came to rehearse is pull the handle as hard as he could! He totally wrenched it and bent the handle. It was a bad moment and he was really sorry. We sort of bent it back and nobody knew. It ended up working fine and they shot around it.

"It's one piece I wish still existed. Very cool. It was lined with this quilted material which was formed to fit around Summer's body as she lay inside. I remember I said to her, 'This is going to sound really weird, but I want you to lay down in a fetal position on this big piece of paper.' I drew around her and we used it as a pattern to cut the foam which lined the box. It fit her pretty well."

❖ Above: The finished article: River's cryo box.

❖ Left: Designs for River's cryo box.

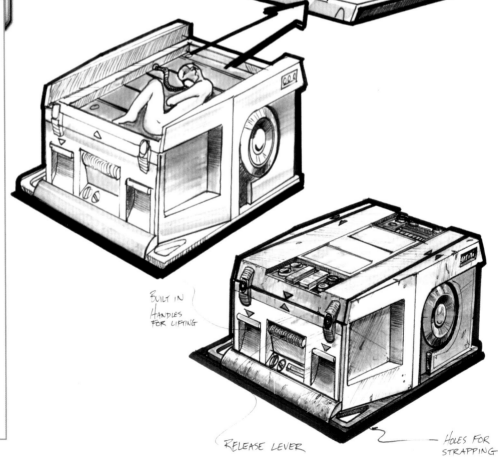

BUILT IN HANDLES FOR LIFTING

RELEASE LEVER

HOLES FOR STRAPPING DOWN

SIMON
Can't say yet.

INARA
I wanna know what's going on here.

MAL
Well then why don't we find out?

He moves quickly from the room.

SIMON
What are you... no!

Simon follows, as do we, back into

INT. CARGO BAY - CONTINUING

Mal overturns some crates and cases to reveal Simon's big blue box, sitting atop another box.

SIMON
Stay away from that!

He moves toward Mal — but is grabbed and easily held by Jayne.

MAL
(calmly, to Jayne)
Where's the fed?

JAYNE
Secured. Shepherd's with him. Seems to think he's not safe alone with me.

Mal hops atop the first crate and pushes the blue box.

It topples off the crate and lands hard on the metal floor as Wash and Zoe enter.

Mal hops down, turns some dials on the box and pulls a release lever.

There is much flashing of lights and four latches twist automatically at the corners.

The top comes slightly up with a hydraulic whoosh, dry ice pouring out the sides.

Zoe and Mal pull at the top. Inara enters, watches as well.

MAL
Let's see what a man like you would kill for.

The top won't go.

Mal rears back and slams his heel into it.

It flies off, clattering to the floor as the smoke clears from over what's inside.

Mal steps forward, looks.

ANGLE: ABOVE THE BOX

Curled inside is a naked, unconscious seventeen-year-old girl.

The box is clearly a cryo-chamber of some

sort, perfectly conformed to her body, a sleek metallic womb.

Mal looks at the girl. At Simon. At the girl.

MAL (cont'd)
Huh.

END OF ACT THREE

ACT FOUR

INT. CARGO BAY - CONTINUING

Simon tries to wrest himself free of Jayne, who's just holding his arm now.

SIMON
I need to check her vitals.

MAL
Is that what they call it?

SIMON
She's not supposed to wake up for another week! The shock could —

MAL
The shock of what? Waking up? Finding out she's been sold to some borderworld baron? Or, I'm sorry — was this one for you? Is it true love? 'Cause you do seem —

She SCREAMS as she lurches out of the box behind Mal. He actually gives a little yelp himself as he turns, startled.

She keeps screaming, and for a moment no one does anything.

She spills out of the box, crawling backwards, breathing hard and looking around her, wild-eyed.

Simon finally pulls himself free of Jayne — who's now more interested in Naked Girl than Struggling Man — and comes to her.

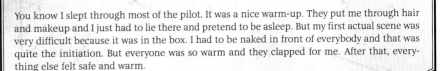

SUMMER GLAU

You know I slept through most of the pilot. It was a nice warm-up. They put me through hair and makeup and I just had to lie there and pretend to be asleep. But my first actual scene was very difficult because it was in the box. I had to be naked in front of everybody and that was quite the initiation. But everyone was so warm and they clapped for me. After that, everything else felt safe and warm.

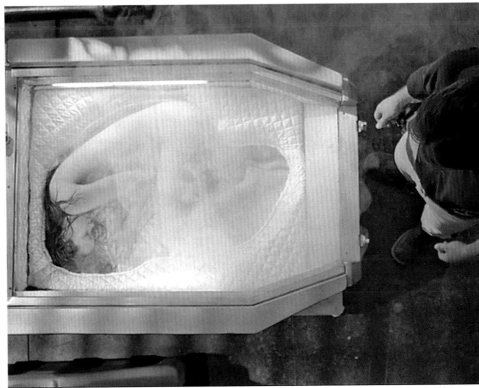

SIMON
River —

She screams at his touch — Inara instinctively moves forward — but he holds onto her, tries to get her to look in his eyes.

SIMON (cont'd)
River. It's okay. It's okay. I'm here.

Finally she looks at him, trying to focus, still breathing hard. Tears are welling in his eyes, but he just stays focused on her.

She looks about, at everyone, then back at him.

SIMON (cont'd)
River...

RIVER
Simon...?

And she realizes, begins to cry, as does he.

RIVER (cont'd)
Simon... They talk to me, they want me to... to talk...

SIMON
They're gone... they're gone and we're safe now, we're safe and I'm here.

Everyone in the room can tell this is not what Mal thought. There is a kind of respect in their silence. Well, til:

MAL
What the hell is this?

Simon pulls the weeping River to him, looks at Mal defiantly, unashamed of the tears in his eyes.

SIMON
This is my sister.

INT. DINING ROOM - LATER

Everyone is gathered, save Kaylee and River herself, to hear Simon speak. As he does, we will periodically INTERCUT to him taking care of River in the infirmary.

For a moment, they all just wait.

INT. INFIRMARY - EARLIER

River is brought — wrapped in the robe Inara used for Kaylee's pillow — into the infirmary. She sees the unconscious Kaylee, the operating room, and she freaks. Starts screaming again, struggling to get out of Simon's grip.

SIMON (O.S.)
I'm very smart.

INT. DINING ROOM - CONTINUING

SIMON
Went to the best Medacad on Osiris, top three percent of my class, finished my internship in eight months. Gifted. Is the term. So when I tell you that my little sister makes me look like an idiot child, I want you to understand my full meaning.

INT. INFIRMARY - EARLIER

Simon has calmed her down, she's sitting on the table now, looking at him with fresh tears. He prepares a hypo with a sedative. Her look of distrust at the hypo is comically grumpy — a little child's. Her eyes wander as he injects her, she mutters something to no one — this girl is gone.

INT. DINING ROOM - CONTINUING

SIMON
River was more than gifted. She was... a gift. Everything she did, music, maths, theoretical physics — even dance — there was nothing that didn't come as naturally to her as breathing does to us.
(smiles, remembering)
She could be a real brat about it, too. She used to tell me —
(losing the train)
I mean, she's a kid. You know? Like everyone else, except she *understands*. So much.

INT. INFIRMARY - EARLIER

River drifts off to sleep. We pan across to see Simon holding her hand.

INT. DINING ROOM - CONTINUING

Simon pauses a moment.

SIMON
There was a school... a, uh, government-sponsored academy, we'd never even heard of it but it had the most exciting program, the most challenging... We could have sent her anywhere, we had the money... but she wanted to go. She wanted to learn. She was fourteen.

A moment of bitter emotion, then he pulls it together.

SIMON (cont'd)
I got a few letters at first, then I didn't hear for months. Finally I got a letter that made no sense. She talked about things that never happened, jokes we never... it was code. I couldn't even figure... I talked to professors, spent a week trying to work it. It just said... "They're hurting us. Get me out."

He can't go on for a moment.

INT. INFIRMARY - EARLIER

She sleeps.

INT. DINING ROOM - CONTINUING

ZOE
How did you do it?

SIMON
Money. And luck — for two years I couldn't get near her, but I was contacted by some men, some underground movement. They said she was in danger, that the government was playing with her brain. If I funded them they could sneak her out in cryo. Get her to Boros and from there, I could take her... wherever.

MAL
How did you know it wasn't a scam?

SIMON
I didn't. Until you opened that box.

INARA
Will she be all right?

SIMON
She was supposed to reacclimate before I brought her out, she's in physical shock, but not serious. I don't know if she'll be all right. I don't know what they did to her, or why. I just have to keep her safe.
(to Mal)
You asked me what a man like me would kill for. And she's it.

There is a moment.

BOOK
That's quite a story, son.

MAL
Yeah, it's a tale of woe, very stirring but in the meantime you've heaped a world of trouble on me and mine.

SIMON
I never thought that —

MAL
No, I don't imagine you thought. In consequence of which we got a kidnapped federal officer on board, we got the Alliance hard on our trail and Kaylee...

He doesn't say it.

ZOE
(to Wash)
How much does the Alliance know?

WASH
Can't say. I killed the message pretty quick, so they might just have had our position.

MAL
Or they might have personal profiles on each and every one of us. Til that fed wakes up, we won't know.

JAYNE
What do we do?

A moment, as he thinks, looking at his crew.

At Inara.

MAL
The job. We finish the job. I got word from Patience, she's waiting for us.

Zoe looks unhappy at the prospect.

MAL (cont'd)
We circle round to Whitefall, make the deal, get out. Keep flying.

SIMON
What about us?

Mal looks at him a moment.

MAL
Kaylee comes through, you and your sister'll get off in Whitefall.

SIMON
If she doesn't come through?

MAL
Then you're getting off a mite sooner.

BOOK
That'd be murder.

MAL
Boy made a decision.

INARA
He didn't shoot her.

JAYNE
But somebody on this boat did and I'm scratching my head as to why we ain't dealt with him.

And now the room gets louder, people start talking over each other...

ZOE
Kill a fed? Can you think of a stupider thing to do?

JAYNE
He can I.D. us all.

SIMON
You wanna throw me out the airlock, fine, but River's not a part of this.

WASH
Can we maybe vote on the whole murdering people issue?

MAL
We don't vote on my ship because my ship is not the rutting town hall!

INARA
This is insanity. Mal...

WASH
I happen to think we're a ways beyond that now, sir.
(to Zoe)
Come on, we're gonna talk this through, yeah?

Zoe doesn't answer. Wash is truly pissed.

BOOK
I'll not sit by while there's killing here.

JAYNE
(smiling)
Shepherd's got a mean streak. We'd best walk soft.

Book looks down, ashamed.

MAL
<Ta ma de! Nimen de bizui!> [Everybody shut the hell up!]
(they do)
Way it is is the way it is. We got to deal with what's in front of us.

INARA
Mal, you know those two wouldn't survive a day in Whitefall anyway.

She comes close to him.

INARA (cont'd)
You throw them out, I'm leaving too.

Mal looks at her, furious at being confronted publicly, truly upset by the thought of her leaving, taking a moment to push both below the surface.

MAL
Might be best you do. You ain't a part of this business.

They stare at each other a moment. He exits towards the back.

INT. AFT HALL - CONTINUING

Simon follows him.

SIMON
What business is that, exactly?

Mal turns and gives him a murderous look, but Simon doesn't back down.

SIMON (cont'd)
I'm a dead man, I can't know? Gold? Drugs? Pirate treasure? What is it that makes you so afraid of the Alliance?

MAL
You don't wanna go down this road with me, boy.

SIMON
You're not afraid of them? I already know you'd sell me out to them for a pat on the head — Hell, you should probably be working for 'em, you certainly fit the profile —

Mal decks him. He goes tumbling. Mal looks down at him, looks back to see:

ANGLE: THE DINING ROOM

The rest are looking at him, Book and Jayne in foreground.

JAYNE
Saw that coming...

INT. INFIRMARY - LATER

The girls are asleep. Simon finishes injecting something into Kaylee, goes to return a bottle to a cabinet.

ZOE

"Big damn heroes, sir."

Whether it is as a pirate captain (Nebula in *Hercules: The Legendary Journeys*), an immortal-life-gobbling goddess (Jasmine in *Angel*), or an animal-enhanced superhero (Vixen in *Justice League*), Gina Torres has certainly made her mark on the science-fiction universe in various TV shows and films over the last twelve years. Nonetheless, it was her role as the warrior Zoe Washburne on *Firefly* which has earned the actress her most passionate fans to date. Initially, after all her genre work, it was not a role she immediately gravitated towards; however, she was won over by the quality of the source material. "I would say that even though there were several elements that were familiar, Joss had managed to create an incredibly unique world in the way that he combined and juxtaposed those elements," says Torres. "So you had these challenged characters inhabiting a challenging world and that makes for great storytelling. AND NO ALIENS!"

A former soldier in the Unification War where she served under Sergeant Malcolm Reynolds, Zoe became his loyal second-in-command on the spaceship Serenity. Despite Zoe's tough outer shell, Torres somehow managed to infuse a sense of vulnerability into her married character. Still, when it came to further fleshing out or discussing Zoe, Torres recalls, "Joss and I spoke very little actually. He said two things about her that were of great value to me: she's career military and she loves her husband. After that, it was up to me to add the flesh and bone and heart and psyche. And it was lovely to be trusted to do that."

In many ways, the characters that made up the *Firefly* crew were based on some well-known archetypes. Mal's swashbuckling heroics have been described as Han Solo-esque, while Jayne was clearly influenced by old Westerns. Similarly, Zoe's roots can be traced back. "Several different women and a couple of men went into Zoe," explains Torres. "It was important that Zoe be somewhat of a mystery, that during each episode another layer of her person be revealed, so there would be an element of surprise and maybe even shock."

On the one hand Zoe never shied away from a fight, she was never afraid to butt heads or lock and load her heavy-duty weapons. However, she was also frequently found stepping in as peacemaker on Serenity. "Her job was to get along with everybody and make sure things ran smoothly," offers Torres. "It's what Mal wasn't particularly good at. Was she perfect? Hell no!"

Besides her statuesque height and stunning looks, Zoe's costume immediately made a striking impression. In keeping with her warrior status, she opted for a rugged look with a war-torn leather vest, tight pants, and boots. "As far as the Zoe uniform goes, I thought it was pretty hot," says Torres. "I liked that it was practical and comfortable and quite appropriate. As for the necklace, I like to think it was one of the laces off the boots she wore to war."

The episode 'The Train Job' replaced the original intended pilot 'Serenity' yet still served to set up the *Firefly* world in the minds of the audience. "Having done the pilot where we got to learn so much about who these people are, setting them in motion in 'The Train Job', as an example of their everyday life, was a lot of fun," says Torres. "We were able to launch the viewers into our 'verse at about two hundred and fifty miles per hour."

The feature film *Serenity* may have blown open the secrets concerning those cannibalistic nightmares, the Reavers, but the crew came across their handiwork in the memorable episode 'Bushwhacked'. "There was a lot going on in that episode," recalls Torres. "It went from being one of our scariest to, at times, one of our most amusing. Mostly I remember Doug Savant [who played Commander Harken] not quite sure what to make of us on our set, and I mean that in the best way. We laughed a lot."

Zoe's no-nonsense attitude and combat experience made her a formidable adversary, yet Torres believes she struck a chord with viewers for another reason. "I think it was because she can be trusted," she explains. "Zoe is a great friend, in good times and bad."

Even years after *Firefly* was canceled, the actors still carry a burning torch for the series and Torres is no exception. "Ultimately, being part of something that lives on in people's memories with such affection is reward enough," she concludes. "I am still honored that Joss saw something in me that day and trusted me to bring Zoe to life." ◖

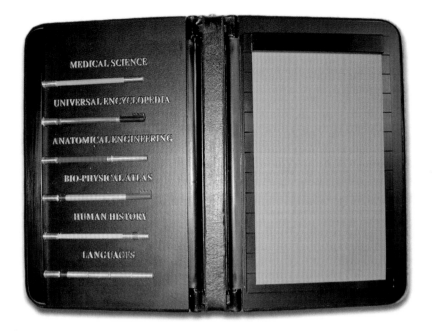

MEDICAL SCIENCE

UNIVERSAL ENCYCLOPEDIA

ANATOMICAL ENGINEERING

BIO-PHYSICAL ATLAS

HUMAN HISTORY

LANGUAGES

ACCESS·FILE:

THE UNIVERSAL ENCYCLOPEDIA

Chris Colquhoun of Applied Effects explains why this prop seems strangely familiar: "It's a Franklin personal organizer. Randy [Eriksen] asked me to modify it. I laid it all out in Illustrator and had a design for the left side. My chemical etcher etched the brass plate away from the lettering. It was sprayed semi-flat black, as production wanted a slightly matt finish, and then I cleaned the paint off the tops of the letters, leaving the brass showing. I sealed it all with Crystal-Clear."

The organizer shell was completely gutted and the new brass face-plate installed in the left side. On the right side, a piece of Plastruct with a grid pattern was fitted. The piece of translucent material was intended as a futuristic Etcha-Sketch, a page which could be written on and erased. For shots where a data screen or animated graphic was required, it was created in postproduction.

"The data-sticks were made to fit into the pen-recess on the top. I made them from some rod, some PDA styluses and some heat shrink and I also turned some of the pieces on the lathe. They had to read on camera so we made them all different colors."

BOOK
How is she?

Startled, Simon shuts the door. Turns to the Shepherd.

SIMON
Touch and go.

BOOK
I might pray over her a bit, if you don't mind.

SIMON
Of course.

BOOK
She's a special girl. We kinda got to be friendly right away.

SIMON
That's a talent I seem to lack.

BOOK
If I can ask, what made you pick this ship?

SIMON
It looked disreputable.

Book smiles. Simon does too, though his is a bleak one.

BOOK
Well, you're not without critical judgement. Didn't happen to look at the name, I suppose?

SIMON
Um, what — "Serenity", right? That's a joke.

BOOK
I believe it's not.

SIMON
<Duibuqi?> [I'm sorry?]

BOOK
You want to get the lay of the land here, it might be what you lack isn't psychological insight. Might be it's history.

Simon looks at him.

INT. SIMON'S ROOM - LATER

Simon opens a small notebook. It's got a sheet of digital paper inside on the right, and a series of what look like little plastic pointers inserted on the left. He picks one, slides it in the spine of the notebook, and the paper lights up, reading: Universal Encyclopedia. He touches a section that says: VOICE, and says:

SIMON
Serenity.

Up comes the dictionary definition, and below that, SERENITY, BATTLE OF. He touches it and a paragraph forms with photos next to it.

SIMON (cont'd)
Read.

As the book reads, in a soft female voice, the images fill the page. Planets, banners, then images of battle and carnage, the aftermath of which we saw in the flashback.

ENCYCLOPEDIA
In the war to unite the planets, The Battle Of Serenity was among the most devastating and decisive. Located on Hera, the valley was considered a key position by both sides, and was bitterly fought over. The Independent Faction, with sixteen brigades and twenty air-tank squads, held the valley against Alliance forces for almost two months, until superior numbers and a brilliant deep-flank strategy by General Richard Wil —

ZOE
What does it say under "bloodbath"?

Simon turns off the book, seeing Zoe in his doorway.

SIMON
I was just trying to —

ZOE
We're not in there. The book, I mean. We're not generals or diplomats, we didn't turn the tide of glorious history or whatever that thing is supposed to spew.

SIMON
You know what they say: history is programmed by the winners.

ZOE
Nearly half a million people lay dead on that field at day's end, about a third of them "winners". Can you imagine that smell? Can you imagine piling up the bodies of soldiers — of friends — to build a wall 'cause you got no cover? Blood just kept pouring out of them, you'd slip in it half the time, find

out bloodbath is not just a figure of speech.

SIMON
Mal was there with you.

She enters, sits across from him.

ZOE
He was my Sergeant. In command of thirty-odd grunts — five days in, there were so many officers dead he commanded two thousand. Kept us together, kept us fighting, kept us sane. By the time the fighting was over he had maybe four hundred still intact.

SIMON
Well that's a hell of a —

ZOE
I said the fighting was over. But you see they left us there. Wounded, and sick, and near to mad as can still walk and talk. Both sides left us there while they "negotiated the peace". For a *week*. And we just kept dying. When they finally sent in Medships, he had about a hundred and fifty left, and of our original platoon, just me.

She stands.

ZOE (cont'd)
Mercy, forgiveness, trust... Those are things he left back there.

What he has now is the ship, the ship and us on it. You get Kaylee through this and I think he'll do right by you. He won't kill unless he's got no other option.

SIMON
What if he tells you to kill me?

ZOE
I kill you.

SIMON
(grim smile)
Just getting the lay of the land.

She starts to go.

SIMON (cont'd)
If that battle was so horrible, why'd he name the ship after it?

She considers the question.

ZOE
Once you've been in Serenity, you never leave. You just learn to live there.

INT. BRIDGE - CONTINUING

Mal arrives on the bridge, moving fast.

Wash is watching a screen, very apprehensive.

MAL
How the hell did they find us? I thought you said we could get around 'em.

WASH
It's not Alliance.

MAL
You're sure?

WASH
It's a smaller vessel.

MAL
Commercial?

WASH
Um, yeah, I read it as an older model, Trans-U.

MAL
I didn't think Trans-U still operated.

WASH
They don't.

MAL
Get me a visual.

WASH
They're still too far out to —

MAL
Get me something!

WASH
I'm picking up a lot of radiation... they're burning without core containment. Well, that's <kwong-juh duh> [nuts], that's suicide...

He looks at Mal, getting it.

MAL
Reavers.

Mal looks out toward a tiny speck that approaches them.

EXT. SPACE - CONTINUING

Where we see, for the first time, the ship. Once it was a commercial spaceliner, now it's a war machine. Tricked out, ornamented and painted, with giant torpedo-looking tubes jerry-rigged near the front. Everything about this vessel says "savage".

INT. BRIDGE - CONTINUING

Where Mal continues to stare ahead, and Wash repeats softly:

WASH
Oh god... oh god... oh god...

END OF ACT FOUR

ACT FIVE

INT. INFIRMARY - CONTINUING

We see the two girls laid out, unconscious. Book is quietly standing at the foot of Kaylee's bed, bible folded in his hands. Mal's voice comes over the com:

MAL (O.S.)
This is the Captain.

INT. PASSENGER DORM HALL - CONTINUING

Zoe has started out of Simon's room, has stopped to listen. He steps out of his room, listening as well.

MAL (O.S.)
We're passing another ship. Looks to be Reavers. From the size, probably a raiding party.

INT. INARA'S CHAMBER - CONTINUING

She listens, too. Gravely.

MAL (O.S.)
Could be they're headed somewhere particular, could be they've already hit someone and they're full up. So everybody stay calm.

INT. JAYNE'S ROOM - CONTINUING

Jayne pulls down a decorative blanket to reveal an arsenal on his wall. He is silent and serious.

MAL (O.S.)
We're holding course. They should pass us in a minute, we'll see what they do.

INT. BRIDGE - CONTINUING

MAL
Zoe, you come on up to the bridge.

INT. PASSENGER DORM HALL - CONTINUING

Zoe is going as Simon stops her with:

SIMON
I don't understand.

ZOE
You've never heard of Reavers?

SIMON
Campfire stories... Men gone savage at the edge of space, killing, and...

ZOE
They're not stories.

SIMON
What happens if they board us?

ZOE
If they take the ship, they'll rape us to death, eat our flesh and sew our skins into their clothing and if we're very very lucky, they'll do it in that order.

She exits. Simon moves quickly to:

INT. INFIRMARY - CONTINUING

Where he moves near River. He and Book look at each other.

EXT. SPACE - CONTINUING

We see the ships nearing each other. Slowly and silently.

INT. INARA'S CHAMBER - CONTINUING

Inara digs out a small, hidden box. She opens it. Inside is a modern syringe gun, smaller than the one Simon used on River, and a vial of black liquid. Unmarked.

She stares into the box.

INT. JAYNE'S ROOM - CONTINUING

Jayne is loading bullets the size of D batteries into a big-ass rifle. His hands are shaking slightly.

INT. DOBSON'S ROOM - CONTINUING

Bound and gagged, Dobson waits in terror.

EXT. SPACE - CONTINUING

The ships are almost upon one another. The Reaver ship is nearly twice the size of the Firefly.

INT. BRIDGE - CONTINUING

Zoe enters, says nothing. She stands behind Wash, slips her hand onto his shoulder. He covers it with his own.

Wash looks out the window at the ship, sees the

attachments on the front. Also speaks softly.

WASH
Magnetic grappler. They get ahold of us with that...

MAL
Just tell me if they alter course.

They wait.

Everybody waits.

EXT. SPACE - CONTINUING

The ships pass silently. The Reaver ship comes close enough to cast a shadow on the smaller ship.

But it passes.

EXT. BRIDGE - CONTINUING

After a few long seconds...

WASH
They're holding course.

Mal lets out a looong breath. Looks at the other two.

WASH (cont'd)
I guess they weren't hungry. Sure didn't expect to see them here...

ZOE
They're pushing out further every year, too.

MAL
Getting awful crowded in my sky.

He hits the com:

MAL (cont'd)
Jayne.

INT. DOBSON'S ROOM - LATER

Jayne and Mal are in the room with the tied and gagged cop.

MAL
I'm in a situation, I think you're aware. Got me a boatload of terribly strange folk making my life a little more interesting then I generally like. Chief among them, an Alliance mole that likes to shoot at girls when he's nervous. Now, I got to know how close the Alliance is, exactly how much you told them 'fore Wash scrambled your call. So I've given Jayne here the job of finding out.

Jayne pulls out a big-ass knife.

JAYNE
He was nonspecific as to how.

Mal says to Jayne, very quietly:

MAL
You only gotta scare him.

JAYNE
(grinning at Dobson)
Pain is scary...

MAL
Do it right.

Mal exits, shutting Jayne in with Dobson. Jayne pulls the gag out and the cop drags in ragged breaths.

DOBSON
Do you have any idea how much trouble you're in?

JAYNE
Gee, I never been in trouble with the law before...

DOBSON
Not like this you haven't. You think this is just a smuggling rap? The package that boy is carrying —

JAYNE
It's a girl. Cute, too, but I don't think she's all there.
(ugly grin)
'Course, not all of her has to be...

DOBSON
That girl is a precious commodity. They'll come after her. Long after you bury me they'll be coming.

JAYNE
I ain't gonna kill you, Dobson — what's your first name?

DOBSON
Laurence.

JAYNE
Laurence, I'm just gonna cut on ya' til you tell me how much they know.

DOBSON
They know everything. Every name, every record — they know how many nosehairs you've got.

JAYNE
(genuinely disappointed)
Oh, see — they don't know a damn thing. It's all over your face and I ain't even...
(petulant)
I was gonna get me an ear. Aren't you an officer of the law, don't they teach you how to... you know, withstand interrogation? Can't even tell a damn lie.

DOBSON
Okay. I can see you're not an idiot.

JAYNE
Wish I could say the same, Laurence, but this is disappointing as hell.

DOBSON
Let me speak a language you will understand. Money. This girl is worth a lot of money. I mean a lot. You kill me, there's nothing. But you help me out, you'll have enough to buy your own ship. A better one than this piece of crap.

JAYNE
Does helping you out mean turning on the Captain?

DOBSON
Yes it does.

Jayne thinks a moment.

JAYNE
Let's talk money, Larry.

INT. INFIRMARY - LATER

Mal is looking at River, silent.

KAYLEE
Captain...?

He turns. She has woken, is woozy and quiet.

MAL
Hey... Hey little Kaylee, what's the news?

KAYLEE
I'm shiny, Captain. A-okay. Can't feel much below my belly, though. And I'm... it's gettin' cold.

Mal moves to get her another blanket, lays it on her — all the while hiding his feelings at hearing that.

MAL
You just gotta rest. Something on this boat's gonna break down real soon, and who else I got to fix it?

KAYLEE
Don't worry none... Doc fixed me up pretty. He's nice.

MAL
Don't go working too hard on that crush, <xiao meimei> [little sister]. Doc won't be with us for long.

KAYLEE
You're nice, too.

MAL
No, I'm not. I'm a mean old man.

KAYLEE
He wasn't gonna let me die. He was just trying to... It's nobody's fault. Promise you'll remember that?

MAL
(takes her hand)
I'll keep it in mind.

KAYLEE
You are a nice man, Captain. You always look after us. But you got to... you got to have faith in people.

He says nothing, just holds her hand.

Her eyes drift to River, still sleeping.

KAYLEE (cont'd)
She is a beauty, isn't she?

She smiles... and her eyes gently close.

Her hand slips from Mal's.

INT. INARA'S CHAMBER - LATER

Simon is there, as Inara hands him a couple of packets.

SIMON
Thank you.

INARA
This is just a standard Companion immunization package. I'm not sure it'll help in this —

SIMON
It won't hurt. The supplies down there are pretty rudimentary.

INARA
Is there anything else I can do?

SIMON
I don't think so. But I appreciate it.

INARA
Kaylee's very dear. To all of us.

SIMON
I'm sorry. For my part in what happened. I've never... I don't know how to —

INARA
You're lost in the woods. We all are. Even the Captain. The only difference is, he likes it that way.

MAL
(entering)
No the difference is, the woods are the only place I can see a clear path.
(to Simon)
What's your business here? .

INARA
It's my business, the usual. I gave the boy a free thrust, since he's not long for this world. What are you doing in my shuttle?

MAL
It's my shuttle. You rent it.

INARA
Then when I'm behind on the rent, you can enter unasked.

Simon elbows his way out. Mal and Inara look at each other a moment.

MAL
Thought you were leaving, anyhow.

INARA
Well I guess that depends on you.

Mal turns and goes.

INT. CARGO BAY - CONTINUOUS

Simon is walking away, but Mal stops him:

MAL
You'll ruin her, too, you know.

Simon turns.

MAL (cont'd)
This is the thing I see you're uncomprehending on. Everyone on this ship, even a "legitimate businesswoman" like her, their lives can be snatched away because of that fed. You got a solution for that? Got a way round?

SIMON
I don't.

MAL
Comes time, somebody's gonna have to deal with him. That should be you, but I don't think you have the guts. And I know you don't have the time.

SIMON
What do you mean?

MAL
Kaylee's dead.

He is steely, contained. Simon is quietly devastated.

Mal turns and walks toward the bridge. A moment, and Simon starts in a daze for the infirmary, running, unable to accept it as he enters:

INT. INFIRMARY - CONTINUING

To find Kaylee sitting up a bit, talking weakly but happily with Book. Simon turns and looks out

where Mal left, true shock in his eyes...

SIMON
The man's psychotic.

INT. BRIDGE - MOMENTS LATER

Mal, Wash, Jayne and Zoe are all laughing.

WASH
Okay, you are psychotic.

MAL
No, but you should have seen his face... ahhh... I'm a bad man.

ZOE
And Kaylee's really okay?

MAL
I'll tell you the truth, I didn't expect her to heal this quick. The Doctor knows his trade, I'll give him —

There is a noise from a console. Wash checks it out.

WASH
We're being hailed.

MAL
That'd be Patience. We're close enough for a vid, put her up.

We briefly see an image on a screen, a weathered, pioneer-looking woman of about fifty.

PATIENCE
Malcolm Reynolds.

MAL
Hello, Patience.

PATIENCE
I have to say, I didn't look to be hearing from you anytime soon.

MAL
Well, we may not have parted on the best of terms — I realize certain words were exchanged, also certain... bullets, but that's air through the engine, that's past. We're business people. 'Sides, your days of fighting over salvage rights are long behind you, what I hear. What are you, mayor, now?

PATIENCE
Just about. You telling the truth about that cargo? 'Cause your asking price is a bit too reasonable for that much treasure.

MAL
It's imprinted. Alliance. Hence the discount.

N A T H A N   F I L L I O N

The first scene that we shot on the pilot was Sean Maher and myself up on the catwalk talking about how Kaylee died from her gunshot wound, which was obviously a lie. It was the very first thing we did. I won't forget that.

PATIENCE
Government goods, huh?

MAL
If it doesn't work for you, no harm. Just thought you could use —

PATIENCE
Alliance don't scare me. Just collating data, as they say. I like you being up-front about it. We can deal. I'll upload coordinates for a rendezvous point outside of town.

MAL
See you in the world.

The screen goes black — no more Patience. There is a pause. Everyone knows:

MAL (cont'd)
I believe that woman's planning to shoot me again.

JAYNE
She meant to pay you, she'd a haggled you down some.

WASH
Just a little effort to hide it would've been considerate —

Mal angrily sweeps away a pile of stuff, including a tin cup and plate, off a console and into the wall. Everybody takes a moment to let the outburst pass.

ZOE
Sir, we don't have to deal with her.

MAL
Yes we do.

JAYNE
Well, here's a little concept I been working on: why don't we shoot her first?

WASH
It IS her turn...

MAL
That doesn't get us what we need either.

ZOE
There's moons on this belt we ain't seen. We could try our luck on one of —

MAL
Our LUCK? Have you noticed anything particular about our luck, last few days? Any kind of pattern? You depend on luck you end up on the drift, no fuel, no prospects, begging for Alliance make-work or being towed out to the scrapbelt. That ain't us. Not ever. Patience has the money to pay and she's going to. One way or another.

JAYNE
Still say there's gonna be gunplay.

MAL
Most like. And we'll be ready for that. There's obstacles in our path, we're gonna deal with them. One by one.

INT. DOBSON'S ROOM - CONTINUING

We see Dobson sawing away at his bonds with a tiny, jagged piece of metal.

MAL (O.S.)
We'll get through this. We will.

END OF ACT FIVE

ACT SIX

EXT. WHITEFALL - DAY

We see the desert planet below, as Serenity rockets down toward it.

EXT. WHITEFALL - LATER

We're on the surface now — rocks and sagebrush jutting out of low hills. Serenity touches down, the airlock door beginning to open.

EXT. DESERT - DAY

We see a small valley, dotted with brush, hills all about. Pan slowly across it to find our three looking at it.

ZOE
Nice place for an ambush.

MAL
That it is.

Jayne arrives, at a decent clip. He hands one bar from the crate to Mal.

JAYNE
I buried 'em good. Equipment's back on the boat.

He sticks an earwig in his ear.

JAYNE (cont'd)
Testing, test — Captain, can you hear me?

MAL
I'm standing right here.

JAYNE
You're coming through good and loud.

MAL
'Cause I'm standing right here.

JAYNE
Well, but the transmitter's...

He gives up. Mal steps forward, looking about him, the wheels in his head turning. After a time.

MAL
Patience is gonna figure we buried the cargo.

Which means putting us to our ease 'fore there's any action. She'll come at us from the east, talk the location of the cargo out of us. She'll have the coin to show us first. We get it, give the location, snipers hit us from...
(points)
There. And there.

JAYNE
Figure they're in place yet?

MAL
Should be. Feel like taking a walk around the park?

JAYNE
(grinning)
Sure you don't just wanna piss yourself and back down like you did with Badger?

Mal stares at him til he stops smiling.

MAL
Walk soft. I want Patience thinking they're in place. And don't kill them if you don't have to. We're here to make a deal.

Jayne takes off. Zoe and Mal look over the meeting place some more.

ZOE
I don't think it's a good spot, sir. She still has the advantage over us.

MAL
Everyone always does.
(turns back to her, smiling bleakly)
That's what makes us special.

INT. PASSENGER DORM HALL/DOBSON'S ROOM - CONTINUING

Book is there, wrestling with his conscience. He looks toward the infirmary, looks toward Dobson's room. After a moment, he heads toward the latter, stops at the door. Knocks.

BOOK
Lawman, it's Shepherd Book.

He opens the door —

BOOK (cont'd)
I believe you're in more danger than —

Dobson SLAMS his chair into the Shepherd, sending him flying back into the hall. Is on him in a second with a makeshift truncheon, hits him in the head. Book slumps, unconscious. Dobson looks out to make sure no one heard. Then, his face contorted with pent-up rage, he whips the truncheon down twice more, pure fucking spite. Starts dragging Book into his room.

EXT. DESERT - DAY

We are high and wide above Mal and Zoe, watching them walk across the valley. Them small, landscape big.

Closer in, we track with them, moving slow. They keep their eyes peeled all ways, hands near their

holsters.

A ways more, and they are nearing a rise — Over which appear:

ANGLE: PATIENCE and her crew of six — as they crest the hill on horseback — all but one, who drives a vehicle not unlike the one on Serenity. They're maybe twenty yards from our two.

Patience is in a weatherbeaten duster, grey hair flyblown about her face. Her men are a hodge-podge of old and modern clothes — not quite Road Warrior gear, but more eclectic and raggedy than even our gang is used to. One wears a shiny black top hat.

MAL
(quietly)
Jayne better come through...

PATIENCE
Mal! How you doing, boy?

MAL
Walking and talking.

PATIENCE
That Zoe? You still sailing with this old bum?

ZOE
That's an awful lot of men to haul three crates.

PATIENCE
Well, I couldn't be sure my Mal here wasn't

looking for some kind of payback. You understand.

MAL
We're just on the job, Patience. Not interested in surprises.

EXT. RIDGE OVERLOOKING THE MEETING PLACE - CONTINUING

A sniper is set to take a bead on Mal. Jayne drops on him like a stone, knocks him unconscious. Grabs his rifle and takes his position. He finds a mark, smiles.

ANGLE: IN HIS SIGHTS:

is Mal.

Jayne smiles, wicked-like.

INT. ANOTHER DORM ROOM - CONTINUING

As Dobson busts in, moves to his suitcase. He opens it, digs in and grabs his tiny computer, turns it on. The screen has icons on it, including CONNECT TO CENTRAL CORTEX. He hits it, waits. It comes up: INTERFERENCE. UNABLE TO CONNECT. Furious, he hurls the computer against the wall, smashing it. Reaches into the bottom of his suitcase.

He pulls out another gun. And another.

EXT. DESERT - CONTINUING

The exchange continues.

PATIENCE
I don't see my cargo anywhere...

MAL
And you're not gonna, til I'm holding two hundred in platinum.

PATIENCE
Oh, come on, Reynolds. I'm supposed to take it on faith you've got the goods?

Mal pulls out the bar from the crate. He tosses it to Patience.

MAL
It's pure, Patience.

She rips the foil off to reveal what looks like one of those awful energy bars, which, by the by, is what it is. She sniffs it.

MAL (cont'd)
Genuine A-grade foodstuffs. Protein, vitamins, immunization supplements... One of those'll feed a family for a month. Longer, if they don't like their kids too well.

She slices off a piece, chews the very end.

PATIENCE
Yeah, that's the stuff.

She pulls a small bag from her hip pocket, tosses it to Mal. He reaches in and pulls out a silvery coin.

PATIENCE (cont'd)
So where's the rest?

INT. INFIRMARY - CONTINUING

River pulls her hand from Kaylee's, sitting up. True fear is on her face.

RIVER
Simon...

KAYLEE
What's wrong, sweetie?

River doesn't answer — she moves to the door — where Dobson GRABS her, sticks a gun to her head.

DOBSON
Look at you, all woke up.

Kaylee starts to move — he pulls out the other gun, points it at her.

DOBSON (cont'd)
I'm sorry about what happened before. But make so much as a sound and the next one goes through your throat.

She looks at him with genuine terror. He pulls River back toward the dorm.

EXT. DESERT - CONTINUING

MAL
Then half a mile east, foot of the first hill. You'll

see where it's been dug.

PATIENCE
Reckon I will.

MAL
Well then.

PATIENCE
Yep.

Nobody moves.

MAL
I'd appreciate it if you all would turn around and ride out first.

PATIENCE
Yeah, well... see there's kind of a hitch.

MAL
We both made out on this deal. Don't complicate things.

PATIENCE
I have a rule. I never let go of money I don't have to. Which is maybe why I'm running this little world and you're still in that dinky old boat sniffing for scraps.

ANGLE: JAYNE'S POV, through the sights of the gun. Still on Mal, they now swing over to Patience and her gang as Mal tosses the money to her.

MAL
You got the money back. There's no need for killin'.

ZOE
We're just gonna walk away, sir?

MAL
Guess that's up to Patience here.
(to Patience)
Could be messy...

PATIENCE
Not terribly. Ah, Mal... you just ain't very bright, are you?

Mal looks at her men, notices one (with a shiny top hat) is carrying a fine looking rifle.

MAL
That's quite a rifle there. Boy must be your best shot, carry that.

PATIENCE
He's called Two-Fry. Always makes it quick and clean.

Two-Fry smiles.

MAL
Two-Fry. Nice hat.

Two-Fry is BLOWN off his horse by a shot from the unseen Jayne.

And then a lot of things happen at once.

Mal draws and nails a second man, Zoe a third (the one on the vehicle) — as the gang opens up, a fourth man blasts his shotgun, nailing Zoe right in the chest. She goes flying back — as Mal hits shotgun man, moving, diving behind some brush cover as Patience and the remaining two fire at him, their horses rearing in panic, one of them drops off his, comes up firing, Mal and he can't really find each other through the dust at this point —

INT. BRIDGE - CONTINUING

Simon and Wash are there, talking.

WASH
Should think about asking the Captain to drop you somewhere else. Whitefall ain't exactly civilization in the strictest sense...

SIMON
You don't have to worry about me.

WASH
Zoe's out on a deal, I always worry. So it's not out of my way —

Kaylee's voice comes over the com, weak and whispered...

KAYLEE
He took her...

Simon bolts out of the room. Wash is about to as well, but there is a beeping — a proximity warning.

He stops, looks at his screen.

WASH
Oh, don't... don't you dare...

INT. CARGO BAY - CONTINUING

Simon runs out, sees Dobson with River below, his grip on her loose right now as he looks around him, heading for the closed airlock —

Simon JUMPS right down on top of him — two men go tumbling, two guns go flying — and both men lie there in extreme pain, unable to get up and get the guns.

River backs into a corner, wild with terror.

EXT. DESERT - CONTINUING

ANGLE: JAYNE fires, but everything is moving too much — he misses, cursing.

JAYNE
<Hun dan!> [Damn!]

Patience dismounts, shooting from behind her horse, as Mal and the other man on the ground continue firing at each other —

The last man on his horse starts to ride away in panic —

ANGLE: ZOE

still flat on her back, Raises her gun and shoots him in the back. He falls off the still moving horse.

Now it's just Patience and the one other. He fires and clips Mal in the arm — Mal returns in kind, blasting his hip. The other guy goes down, screaming in pain.

Patience pulls out her shotgun, still with the cover of the horse.

Mal stands, no longer moving or hiding.

MAL
Zoe?

ZOE
Ahhhh... armor's dented.

MAL
Well, you were right about this being a bad idea...

ZOE
Thanks for saying, sir.

She pulls at her shirt — there is a beat up kind of superthin Kevlar underneath.

PATIENCE
Mal, don't take another step —

She doesn't really have a bead on him or she woulda shot him, but she's close, gun leveled on the back of the horse.

Mal walks toward her, shoots the horse and it collapses half onto her. He comes up to her and sticks his gun in her face.

MAL
I did a job. I got nothing but trouble since I did it, not to mention more than a few unkind words as regards to my character so let me make this abundantly clear. I do the job.

He takes the money back.

MAL (cont'd)
And then I get paid.

He moves his gun from her face.

MAL (cont'd)
Go run your little world.

Jayne runs up to him, holding out a walkie-phone.

JAYNE
Mal! It's Wash! We got a ship coming in. They followed us. The Gorramn Reavers followed us!

Everyone still alive looks scared.

EXT. SPACE - CONTINUING

As the Reaver ship whips past camera, heading towards Whitefall.

END OF ACT SIX

ACT SEVEN

INT. CARGO BAY - MOMENTS LATER

Dobson lunges for his gun — and Simon throws himself on top of him. They can both barely stand from their crash before. They struggle in an ugly fashion, until Dobson gets an elbow free and jerks it into Simon's face.

He gets free enough to crawl for the weapon, but Simon rolls around and grabs the other one, points it:

SIMON
Don't move!

WASH (O.S.)
(on the com)
REAVERS! Reavers incoming and headed straight for us. We are in the air in one minute!

INT. BRIDGE - CONTINUING

WASH
(to himself)
Guess they got hungry again.

He starts warming the ship up.

INT. CARGO BAY - CONTINUING
Inara comes out of her chamber, sees the action below.

Simon holds the gun on Dobson. His hand shakes.

❖ Above: Simon's Vektor stunt pistol.

DOBSON
You gonna do that? You gonna kill a lawman in cold blood. I know what you did for your sister and I understand. It doesn't make you a killer.

A barely conscious Book also comes to the entrance, holding onto it to stay up.

DOBSON (cont'd)
I don't wanna hurt anybody. I have a job to do. To uphold the law. That's what we're talking about here. There's nowhere you can take her that the law won't find. Nobody's gonna hurt her... unless you hurt me.

SIMON
I said don't move!

DOBSON
It's your call.

Simon doesn't know what to do. He looks over at River.

EXT. SPACE - CONTINUING

The Reaver ship breaks into atmo, headed down to the planet.

INT. BRIDGE - CONTINUING

Wash is getting more and more freaked —

WASH
Come on, come on...
(into walkie)
Where the hell are you guys!?!

EXT. DESERT - CONTINUING

As we see Mal, Zoe and Jayne RIDE into frame on horseback, moving just as fast as they can.

INT. CARGO BAY/AIRLOCK - CONTINUING

The airlock starts to open, the noise and motion distracting Simon long enough for Dobson to grab his gun and fire —

INARA
Simon!

— missing but sending Simon diving for cover as Dobson grabs River and puts himself behind her, gun to her head. Simon steps out, between him and the airlock.

DOBSON
I'm not playing anymore.

EXT. SERENITY - CONTINUING

The three pull up on their horses, jump off, Mal striding in as the others shoo the horses off.

INT. CARGO BAY/AIRLOCK - CONTINUING

Mal walks in behind Simon —

DOBSON
Anybody makes so much as a —

— and shoots Dobson in the face. He flies back, letting go of River and dead before he lands. Tilt up from him to see Book, unable to move.

MAL
Wash! We're on!

He pulls the Lawman's body up and dumps it out the closing airlock as Jayne and Zoe enter. Simon moves to River, just shocked and silent.

EXT. SERENITY - CONTINUING

The hatch is still closing as the ship takes off.

INT. BRIDGE - MOMENTS LATER

Mal and Zoe come up to Wash, Inara hanging back behind.

MAL
How close are they?

WASH
About twenty seconds from spitting distance.

JAYNE
Well lose 'em!

MAL
(to Zoe)
Give me rear vid.
She punches it up. ON THE SCREEN, we see the ship approaching from behind.

ZOE
<Ai ya. Women wanle.> [We're in big trouble.]

MAL
(to Wash)
How close do they need to be to fire the grapples?

JAYNE
Wash, you dumbass, dodge 'em!

WASH
If everybody could just be quiet a moment...

He's incredibly calm. He veers hard left, snakes through —

EXT. DESERT - CONTINUING

— the hills, where we see the ship moving fast — but the Reavers are right on them.

INT. BRIDGE/FOREDECK HALL - CONTINUING

Wash continues to pilot with serene expertise.

WASH
I need Kaylee in the engine room please.

ZOE
Can she even —

MAL
(to Jayne)
Get her in there. Now.

Jayne goes. Mal moves to Inara.

ZOE
(to Wash)
Can we lose them?

He doesn't answer. He's flying.

ANGLE: MAL and INARA.

MAL
I want you to get in your shuttle. Get the civilians and be ready to go.

INARA
We can't just leave you here.

MAL
Thought that was the plan.

INARA
Mal, don't —

MAL
We get boarded, you take off, head for town. We might be able to stop them from following.

INARA
They'll kill you.

MAL
Inara.

Just saying her name says more than he probably ever meant to. He puts his hand on the Companion's shoulder.

And pushes her gently away.

THE REAVER CHASE

Visual effects supervisor Loni Peristere: "My favorite sequence was definitely the Reaver chase. I liked it because it took spaceships that you are used to seeing in space and put them in atmospheric peril. I think for the first time on TV, and even film, you had two giant spaceships in atmosphere. Our Reaver ship was not only designed to look like a wild boar, it was painted with war paint and it was belching dirty smoke, which made it a monster coming to get you. I loved that we had a big monster trying to swallow our cute little bird, if you will. To 'shoot' the scene, we had a virtual 'chase plane', a mounted camera with a zoom lens that was not in focus all the time, smoke in the lens and lens flares blocking the view. It was all created in CGI and synthetically, but it really felt organic."

MAL (cont'd)
Go.

He turns back to the bridge. She is going as well, throws a look back, a little blown away by his caring, then continues on.

MAL (cont'd)
(to Wash)
How are we doing?

WASH
I don't want to alarm anybody... but I think... we're being followed...

EXT. DESERT - CONTINUING

The Reaver ship is hard on Serenity's heels.

INT. INFIRMARY - CONTINUING

Jayne is carrying Kaylee out as Inara enters. She speaks to Simon, River and Book:

INARA
You three. Come with me.

BOOK
I think I can help Kaylee out.
(to Simon, re: River)
Take her. Keep her safe.

Book and Inara share a glance before they go their separate ways.

INT. BRIDGE - MOMENTS LATER

Wash flies.

MAL
Can't keep this up, they get a bead, they're gonna lock us down.

WASH
(into com)
Kaylee, how're we doing?

INT. ENGINE ROOM - CONTINUING

Kaylee is propped in a corner, Jayne and Book at the ready.

KAYLEE
You want me go for full burn?

WASH (O.S.)
Not just yet, but set it up.

KAYLEE
(to Book)

You know where the press regulator is?

He looks about, heads to a part of the engine, opens a panel. Kaylee smiles.

KAYLEE (cont'd)
Head of the class.

She coughs, wincing at the pain.

INT. BRIDGE - CONTINUING

ZOE
Full burn in atmo? That won't cause a blowback? Burn us out?

MAL
Even if it doesn't, they can push just as hard, keep right on us. Wash, you gotta give me an Ivan.

WASH
See what I can do...
(into com)
Kaylee, how would you feel about pulling a Crazy Ivan?

INT. ENGINE ROOM - CONTINUING

KAYLEE
Always wanted to try one. Jayne. Open the port jet control. Cut the hydraulics.

JAYNE
Where the hell —

KAYLEE
Look. Look where I'm pointing.

He does, opens a panel near the floor.

KAYLEE (cont'd)
Okay. Now it's real simple.

ANGLE: JAYNE'S POV: A tangle mess of cables. Real simple.

EXT. DESERT - CONTINUING

The Reaver ship has Serenity locked in. The magnetic grapple warms up, latches flying off...

INT. BRIDGE - CONTINUING

MAL
They're on us...

INT. INARA'S SHUTTLE - CONTINUING

Inara moves into the pilot's seat as Simon sits River down.

INT. BRIDGE - CONTINUING

WASH
(into com)
Kaylee...?

No answer. Then:

KAYLEE (OS)
Okay!

WASH
Everybody hold on to something.
(softly, to the Reavers)
Here's something you can't do...

He SLAMS down a lever and

EXT. DESERT - CONTINUING

Serenity's port jet flips the other way and the ship LURCHES into a perfect one-eighty, spinning on a dime, the jet flips back and it's headed straight for the Reaver ship, which dodges at the last second —

INT. BRIDGE - CONTINUING

WASH
(into com)
NOW!

INT. ENGINE ROOM - CONTINUING

Book hits a big button with the heel of his hand and the room gets lighter —

EXT. DESERT - CONTINUING

As the ass-end of Serenity lights up, sending ripples of fire bursting into the atmosphere as the ship blasts out of there so fast, gradually arcing up toward space...

INT. BRIDGE - CONTINUING

Wash is pulling up at the controls with all his might. Finally he eases off, quietly pleased.

Mal and Zoe are kind of amazed.

ZOE
Ain't no way they can come around in time to follow us now.

Mal hits the com:

MAL
We're good, people.

INT. INARA'S SHUTTLE - CONTINUING

Extreme, solemn relief.

MAL (O.S.)
We're out of the woods.

INT. ENGINE ROOM - CONTINUING

Jayne whoops with delight. Even Book smiles.

Kaylee runs her hand along the hull.

KAYLEE
That's my girl... That's my good girl.

She looks at the boys and beams.

INT. BRIDGE - CONTINUING

WASH
(to Mal)
We should have just enough left in us to hit a fuel station. We'll need to do some patching up. Hope we got paid today.

MAL
We did.

Zoe exchanges a look with Wash.

ZOE
Sir? I'd like you to take the helm, please.
(re: Wash)
I need this man to tear all my clothes off.

Mal says nothing, just smiles and indicates the way out. Wash climbs out of the chair and exits with Zoe...

WASH
Work, work, work...

And Mal throws himself down into the pilot's seat. Lets out a breath he's been holding for, oh, about two days. And starts flying.

EXT. SPACE - LATER

As Serenity breaks out of atmosphere into the deep silence of space.

INT. INARA'S CHAMBER - LATER

Book sits as Inara takes a cloth from a bowl and dabs his head. He is sitting, she stands before him.

INARA
You should really have the young Doctor look at this.

BOOK
It's not so bad.

INARA
Well, I'm sure you'll be fine...

BOOK
I didn't say that.

He looks up at her and she sees how upset he is, how lost.

BOOK (cont'd)
Is this what life is, out here?

INARA
Sometimes.

BOOK
I've been out of the abbey two days, I've beaten a lawman senseless, I've fallen in with criminals... I watched the Captain shoot the man I swore to protect.
(the hard part...)
And I'm not even sure if I think he was wrong.

INARA
Shepherd...

He is shaking a bit, tearing up.

BOOK
I believe I just...
(a pained smile)
I think I'm on the wrong ship.

INARA
Maybe. Or maybe you're exactly where you ought to be.

He lowers his head. She puts her hand on it, a kind of benediction. We hold on them a moment.

INT. SIMON'S ROOM - LATER

He is tucking River into bed.

SIMON
The shot I gave you will help you sleep.

RIVER
I slept for so long...

SIMON
Just a little while. Then we'll find a place... we'll find a safe place.

He's not convinced, but he smiles at her anyway. She looks suddenly terribly sad.

RIVER
I didn't think you'd come for me.

SIMON
(welling up)
Well, you're a dummy.

He takes her in his arms, holds her tight.

JAYNE (O.S.)
The girl's a problem.

INT. BRIDGE - LATER

Mal is still at the helm as Jayne speaks to him.

JAYNE
The Lawman said they'd keep looking for her. Something about her brain being all special. Important to the Alliance brass. Sooner we dump those two, the better.

MAL
I suppose so.

Jayne gets up to leave.

MAL (cont'd)
Funny how the Lawman got out of his room. You having tied him up so well and all.

JAYNE
I didn't have nothing to do with that. Anyway it all turned out just fine. Buzzards're the only ones gonna find him...

MAL
But he did try to make a deal with you, right?

He looks at Jayne, who says nothing.

MAL (cont'd)
How come you didn't turn on me, Jayne?

JAYNE
Money wasn't good enough.

MAL
What happens when it is?

JAYNE
(smiling)
Well that'll be an interesting day.

MAL
I imagine it will.

Jayne leaves, passing Simon, who comes up next to Mal. He sees Mal's arm is a bit bloody.

SIMON
You need me to look at that?

MAL
Just a graze.

SIMON
(a beat, then:)
So where do you plan on dumping us?

MAL
There's places you might be safe. You want the truth, though, you're probably safer on the move.
(turns to him)
And we never stop moving.

SIMON
I'm confused. No wait — I think maybe you're confused.

MAL
It may have become apparent to you, the ship could use a medic. You ain't weak. I don't know how bright you are, but top three percent, but you ain't weak and that's not nothing. You live by my rule, keep your sister from doing anything crazy, you could maybe find a place here. Til you find a better.

SIMON
I'm trying to put this as delicately as I can... How do I know you won't kill me in my sleep?

MAL
You don't know me, son. So let me explain this to you once: if I ever kill you, you'll be awake, you'll be facing me, and you'll be armed.

SIMON
(smiles)
Are you always this sentimental?

MAL
I had a good day.

SIMON
You had the law on you, criminals and savages... half the people on the ship have been shot or wounded including yourself, and you're harboring known fugitives.

Mal looks out at the black sky.

MAL
We're still flying.

SIMON
That's not much.

Mal answers, almost to himself...

MAL
It's enough.

A beat, then Simon goes. Mal just keeps looking ahead.

END OF SHOW.

THE TRAIN JOB

Written by Joss Whedon & Tim Minear
Directed by Joss Whedon

JOSS WHEDON

Joss Whedon says that Mal was not originally intended to have a moral crisis as early as 'The Train Job'. "Besides the action," Whedon explains, "the other adjustment the network was very firm about was Mal being more likable. And, of course, Tim and I used to joke, 'But we thought you said, "More like a bull!" Ah, this is very embarrassing...' For me, part of the show was going to be unfolding Mal to the audience and to himself. But they said, 'We want to like him up front, but he can be a little caustic if you want.' And so, yeah, him giving back the medicine in 'The Train Job' wouldn't have happened [otherwise]. This is something we did for the network. Now, it's not something that goes against the ethos of the show. This is the thing you have to remember. We scrambled to get the show on the air because we believed in it, but I've also always believed that if the show changes beyond what it should be, you walk away. The idea that Mal would return the medicine did not offend me, did not make me go, 'I've compromised and now he's kissing puppies.' Because it's something that somebody like him would do. In a harsher version, he wouldn't, because his crew was starving and he needed to get them through. Shooting the guy in *Serenity* the movie was an example of that, it was an example of, 'I'm going to make the harshest possible decision, because of the safety of my peeps.' But in this instance, assuming they're not all starving, it is something that Mal as a person is capable of doing. It's just a side of him I wasn't planning to show so much of right away."

TEASER

INT. BAR - DAY

It's a small, disreputable place, doing a brisk but low-key business. Most of the people here are probably up to something they don't want other people to know about. The dark wood and clutter suggest a Western space, but it is definitely multicultural: a belly dancer makes her way about the room, and everyone's mode of dress is diverse — though none is too fancy.

We follow a BELLY DANCER's undulating belly through the space, coming to a table with three people sitting at it. ZOE and JAYNE are more or less facing us, MAL has his back mostly turned. The three are concentrating on a game we can't see.

Those who look carefully will spot the belly dancer's hand as it slips Mal a piece of paper, which he slips in turn into his pocket.

JAYNE
(to Mal)
Your move.

Camera ARMS UP to see the game on the table is Chinese Checkers. Mal moves.

ZOE
That's a bold move.

MAL
I live on the edge.

Zoe makes a much better move.

JAYNE
(to Mal)
Nice work, dumbass.

MAL
I've given some thought to moving off the edge, it's not an ideal location... might get a place in the middle...

VOICEOVER (O.S.)
A toast!

The VOICE is surly, loud. Trouble waiting to happen. As it speaks, Mal turns back towards camera and we see him in closeup. Calm, assessing the danger.

ANGLE: The guy who spoke, LUND. A drunken dick, holding court at the bar.

LUND
A toast. Shut up! Quiet, I'm, I got words. I'm say, this is an asspishus day. We all know what day it is...

ANGLE: The gang. Mal is stone-faced, Zoe the same. They clearly know where this is going. Jayne has no clue.

JAYNE
Suspicious? What day is it?

LUND
A glorious day for all the proud members of the Allied planets. Unification Day! The end of the Independent scumbags and the dawn of a new galaxy! Yeah-huh!

He downs a shot.

Mal is grabbing his empty glass, rising.

ZOE
Captain...

MAL
Just feeling the need for a drink.

JAYNE
(not paying attention)
What month is it?

Mal moves to the bar, far from Lund.

MAL
<Ching zie lie ee bay Ng-Ka-Pei?> [Can I have one more glass of Ng-Ka-Pei, please?]

Lund, naturally, sidles up to him.

LUND
You gonna drink to the Alliance with me?

Mal looks at him, looks away.

LUND (cont'd)
Six years today... The Alliance sent the browncoats running, pissing their pants.

Mal is not biting. He gets his drink, tosses a weird looking bill on the bar.

LUND (cont'd)
Your coat's kind of a brownish color...

MAL
It was on sale.

He drinks.

LUND
You didn't toast! You know, I'm thinking you're one of them. Independents.

MAL
And I'm thinking you weren't burdened with an overabundance of schooling. So why don't we just ignore each other til we go away?

He turns back to the bar. Lund pursues.

LUND
The Independents were a bunch of inbred, cowardly pisspots shoulda been killed off a every world spinnin'.

Mal turns, ready for the fight.

MAL
Say that to my face.

LUND
I said, you're a coward and a pisspot. Now what're you gonna do about it?

Mal smiles casually.

MAL
Nothing. I just wanted you to face me so she could get behind you.

Lund spins and Zoe SWAPS him with the butt of her sawed-off. He goes down.

Mal and Zoe smile grimly at each other as she

holsters the weapon.

MAL (cont'd)
Drunks are so cute.

Suddenly, seven GUYS stand up, seeing what happened to Lund. They are not wearing colors like Mal and Zoe's.

MAL (cont'd)
<Oh, juh jen sh guh kwai luh duh jean jan...> [Oh, this is a happy development...]

Zoe turns, sees the coming fight.

ZOE
Jayne...

ANGLE: Jayne: Sits, unconcerned.

JAYNE
Hey, I didn't fight in no war. Best of luck, though...

MAL
Fine. Let's do this.

EXT - BAR - CONTINUING (AFTERNOON)

Mal goes flying through the front window — only it's not glass, rather an ionized field that CRACKLES and REFORMS after he passes through.

He rolls in the dirt, stops. Looking up, he hears the sound of fighting within — we might notice at this point that the sky contains THREE MOONS, one so close it looks like another planet on the horizon.

Mal shakes off the punch, pulls out a transmitter.

MAL
(into transmitter)
Wash, we got some local color happening... a grand entrance would not go amiss...

Zoe comes flying out the door, takes two others

with her, giving them hell.

Mal rises, helps her put them down.

MAL (cont'd)
Is Jayne even —

Three guys come backwards out of the bar, driven by the table Jayne is wielding. Another comes behind and he elbows him into dreamland without even looking back. Jayne is an incredible fighter.

Our gang ends up side by side, facing an angry bunch of at least ten guys.

We might notice our three backed up at the EDGE OF A CLIFF.

MAL (cont'd)
Well, there's just an acre of you fellows...
(to Zoe)
This is why we lost, you know: superior numbers.

ZOE
Thanks for the reenactment, sir.

Lund forces his way through the crowd and pulls his gun. This changes things. Our gang look at each other.

JAYNE
Them ain't kosherized rules...

Others pull guns (even though they feel odd about it). Our gang don't yet.

LUND
I'm thinking someone should put you down, dog.
What do you think?

MAL
I'm thinking we'll rise again.

It is at this moment that SERENITY rises from
behind the cliff, dwarfing our combatants.

Wind rips through everyone, the assailants starting back in fear (and grit in their eyes). An amplified voice (WASH's) comes over a loudspeaker:

WASH (O.S.)
Every man there go back inside or we will blow a
new crater in this little moon.

Lund and the others back off, grumbling but
cowed.

ANGLE: Behind our heroes.

The airlock door opens and our gang step onto it
from the cliff face.

INT. AIRLOCK/CARGO BAY - CONTINUING

The doors shut behind them. Mal and Zoe head
upstairs as Jayne wanders off, saying:

JAYNE
Damn yokels can't even tell a transport ship ain't
got no guns on it.
(chuckling)
"Blow a new crater in this moon..."

**INT. FOREDECK HALL/BRIDGE - MOMENTS
LATER**

Mal and Zoe are entering the bridge as KAYLEE is

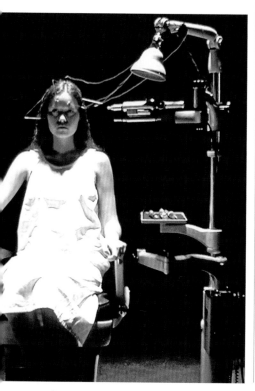

coming up the hall behind them, grease on her
face and some unidentifiable ship part in her
hand. She's thrilled by the drama.

MAL
(to Wash)
Nice save.

WASH
Pleasure.

MAL
How are our passengers?

KAYLEE
They're fine. What happened? Was there a terrible
brawl?

ZOE
(eyeing Mal)
Oddly enough, there was.

WASH
You getting my wife into trouble?

MAL
What? I didn't start it. Just wanted a quiet drink.

ZOE
Funny, sir, how you always find yourself in some
Alliance-friendly bar come U-Day, looking for a
"quiet drink".

MAL
See, this is a sign of your tragic space dementia.
All paranoid and crotchety, it breaks the heart.

WASH
Well, did we at least make a contact?

Mal smiles, produces the piece of paper handed
to him by the belly dancer.

MAL
Ladies and menfolk, we got ourselves a job.

He hands the paper to Zoe.

MAL (cont'd)
Take us out of the world, Wash.
(looking ahead)
Got us some crime to be done.

EXT. SERENITY - CONTINUING

As it blasts past camera, heading out of the
atmosphere.

END OF TEASER

ACT ONE

INT. LABORATORY

Flashes of bright lights, of people in masks
approaching camera with weird-looking instruments — classic operation nightmare.

ANGLE: RIVER

strapped to a chair, with electrodes on her,
needles attached to wires stuck into her head,
ears, nose, blood trickling from each wound,
terror in her eyes as a man's voice speaks
slowly:

VOICEOVER
I'm not going to speak. I'm not going to SAY a
word...

She opens her mouth to scream and —

INT. INFIRMARY

— wakes up on the operating table, freaking,
scrambling off as SIMON approaches her
tenderly.

SIMON
River. River. It's okay. It's me.

She says nothing.

SIMON (cont'd)
You know who I am...

RIVER
(duh)
Simon.

SIMON
Were you dreaming? Did you dream about the Academy?

RIVER
(scattered, muttering)
It's not relevant.

SIMON
If you can talk about what happened there... I know it's hard but the more I know, the faster you'll get better. I promise.

She gets up, looks around.

RIVER
This isn't home.

SIMON
No. No, we can't go home. If we go home they'll just send you back to the Academy. This is safer now.
(cheerfully)
We're on a ship.

RIVER
Midbulk transport, standard radion-accelerator core, classcode 03-K64, "Firefly".

Mal enters at that moment, saying:

MAL
Well, that's something. I can't even remember all that.

SIMON
I'm always amazed at what she knows. River, this is Captain Reynolds.

MAL
(to River)
Mal.

She curtsies with exaggerated elegance. A beat, as Mal doesn't know what to do. Then he curtsies back, somewhat awkwardly.

SIMON
(slightly amused)
You bow.

MAL
What?

SIMON
From the waist.
(he demonstrates)
The lady curtsies, the gentleman bows.

MAL
Well, I'm not overly gentle.

He makes his way to the sink, starts rinsing

his bloody knuckles.

SIMON
Need a weave on that?

MAL
It's nothing.

SIMON
I expect there's someone's face feels differently.

MAL
(smiles in reverie)
They tell you never hit a man with a closed fist, but it is on occasion hilarious.

SIMON
I suppose so. The fight didn't draw any... any attention?

MAL
No feds. Just an honest brawl between folk. Ain't none of us want the Alliance on us, Doctor. That's why you're here.

SIMON
I thought I was here because you needed a medic.

MAL
Well, not today.

He exits, River watching him. After he goes:

RIVER
Mal.
(turns to Simon)
Bad.
(looks after Mal)
In the Latin.

INT. PASSENGER DORM - CONTINUING

Mal is about to head upstairs when BOOK comes down the hall.

MAL
Shepherd Book.

BOOK
Captain. How's the girl?

They look back at the pair in the infirmary.

MAL
Still kinda whimsical in the brainpan. Seems calm enough, though.

River hurls a metal container on the ground with a great crash, starts crying as Simon tries to soothe her.

BOOK
That young man's very brave.

MAL
(whatever)
Yeah, he's my hero...

BOOK
Give up everything to free his sister from that... place... go from being a doctor on the

central planets to hiding on the fringes of the system... There's not many would do that.

MAL
Suppose not.

Mal starts up the stairs, but:

BOOK
There's not many would take him in, either.

He's going somewhere with this. Mal turns back.

BOOK (cont'd)
Why did you?

MAL
Same reason I took you on board, Shepherd. I need the fare.

He starts upstairs, the Shepherd following him.

BOOK
There's neither of us can pay a tenth of what your crew makes on one of your "jobs".

INT. UPPER AFT-HALL/ENGINE ROOM - CONTINUING

MAL
Are you referring to our perfectly legitimate business enterprises?

BOOK
I'm wondering why a man who's so anxious to fly under Alliance radar would house known fugitives. The Alliance had her in that institution for a purpose, whatever it was, and they will want her back. You're not overly fond of the boy, so why risk it?

Mal turns, with all mock seriousness.

MAL
Because it's the right thing to do.

He looks in at the engine room — which is an unholy mess of wires and patchwork and tools lying about.

MAL (cont'd)
Will you look at this? Kaylee...

BOOK
I begin to wonder if you yourself know why you're doing it.

MAL
What about you? How come you're flying about with us brigands? Shouldn't you be off bringing religiosity to the Fuzzie-Wuzzies or some such?

BOOK
Oh, I got heathens aplenty right here.

MAL
(smiling)
If I'm your mission, Shepherd, best give it up. You're welcome on my boat. God ain't.

He turns to go, grumbling to himself:

MAL (cont'd)
Where the hell is that girl...

INT. INARA'S SHUTTLE - CONTINUING

We see Kaylee in closeup, eyes closed, a dreamy smile on her (still grease-stained) face. Soft, classical music is playing.

Widen to see that she is sitting on the floor of Inara's sumptuous chamber, and that INARA herself is on the couch behind her, brushing Kaylee's hair.

INARA
Do you want me to put it up?

KAYLEE
Mmmmmm... that's okay...

INARA
You have lovely hair.
(knowingly)
I'm sure the Doctor would agree.

KAYLEE
Simon? No, he's much too... I'm just... Do you think it looks better up?

INARA
We can experiment... We might even get wild later and wash your face.

Kaylee smiles, shutting her eyes again.

KAYLEE
Do you ever do this for your clients?

INARA
Very occasionally. Not all of my clients have enough hair to get a brush through.

KAYLEE
I shouldn't much like a bald lover... some bald men have awfully furry backs.

INARA
Yes, hair often doesn't disappear so much as migrate south.

KAYLEE
Have you ever had to service a really hideous client? With boils and the like?

INARA
A Companion chooses her own clients; that's guild law. But physical appearance doesn't matter so terribly. You look for a compatibility of spirit... there's an energy about a person that's difficult to hide, you try to feel that...

MAL
(entering)
Then you try to feel the energy of their credit account. It has a sort of aura...

INARA
What did I say to you about barging into my shuttle?

MAL
That it was manly and impulsive?

INARA
Yes, precisely, only the exact phrase I used was "don't".

MAL
Well you're holding my mechanic in thrall and Kaylee what the hell is going on in the engine room? Were there monkeys, some terrifying space monkeys that maybe got loose?

KAYLEE
No monkeys, mister funny — I had to rewire the grav-thrust because somebody won't replace that crappy compression coil.

MAL
Well get the place squared away. It's dangerous in there and I ain't paying you to get your hair played at.

Kaylee rises, grumbly, and exits.

KAYLEE
<Kuh-ooh duh lao bao jurn...> [Horrible old tyrant...]

MAL
We work before we play.
(to Inara)
You're servicing crew now?

INARA
In your lonely, pathetic dreams.

MAL
How would you know what I dream about?

INARA
It never occurred to me that you did. What do you want?

MAL
We got a job.

INARA
Congratulations. This job wouldn't be on a decently civilized planet where I could screen some respectable clients, perhaps?

MAL
Respectable clients? Seems a contradiction —

INARA
Don't start.

MAL
I'm Captain Reynolds. My First Mate, Zoe, and this is Jayne.

NISKA
Very nice. I'm Adelai Niska, you've seen Crow, he loves to stand at the door to say "Boo!", but he is, you say it... my Good Right Hand.

MAL
We got word you might have a job for us.

NISKA
Yes, yes, an exciting job — a train! Has something I need. You've worked a train before?

MAL
We've hit a few.

NISKA
Are you going to ask me what it is I need?

MAL
As a rule, no.

NISKA
Yes, good, you have a reputation. You do the job, no complications, that's what. Malcolm Reynolds gets it done, is the talk.

MAL
Well I'm glad to hear that.

NISKA
Do you know what a reputation is? It's people talking, gossip, it's not... to hold, touch it, you can't. Not from gossip. Now I also have reputation, not so pleasant, I think you know. Crow.

Crow opens a door to another room.

ANGLE: in the room is a man hung from the ceiling, clearly dead from being hideously tortured. Crow steps in, brandishing a curved blade that is his trademark weapon.

MAL
We don't have the location yet. We're docking on a skyplex in a bit, it's run by a fellow called Niska.

INARA
Never heard of him.

MAL
Well I have, and while we're there you'll stay confined to the ship.

INARA
Is the petty criminal perchance ashamed to be riding with a Companion?

MAL
Niska has a very unlovely rep. If he's got work for me, fine, but I don't — I'm not sure you'd be safe.

INARA
Mal, if you're being a gentleman, I may die of shock.

Mal bows, slightly, and leaves. Pops his head back in:

MAL
Have you got time to do my hair?

INARA
Out.

He goes.

EXT. SPACE - LATER

We see Serenity docking on a large space station, Niska's SKYPLEX. It has docks for at least eight ships, and though somewhat dingy, it is bustling.

INT. BRIDGE - CONTINUING

As Wash settles her down.

INT. HALL/NISKA'S OFFICE - LATER

Mal, Zoe and Jayne are walked through the hall by two armed goons. The three are quiet and watchful. One of the goons knocks on a door and it is opened.

Standing behind it is CROW. He is as mean and large a tattooed motherfucker as ever stood behind a door. He stares grimly at the crew a moment, then:

NISKA (O.S.)
It's fine, Crow, they can come in.

The accent is heavily European, and the man (NISKA), when revealed by Crow stepping aside, is a slight, old, bespectacled fellow — looks more like Gepetto than the Godfather. He comes from around a desk, looks our gang up and down as they enter.

NISKA
Malcolm Reynolds is which?

W A S H

"Oh, gawd! What could it beee? We're doomed! Who's flyin' this thing?! Oh. Right. That'd be me. Back to work."

It's a long way from Plano, Texas to outer space, but in both his life and career, native Texan Alan Tudyk has always relished taking on roles that transport him from the ordinary to the extraordinary. He's built his career around his chameleon-like ability to play anyone convincingly, from a gay German drug addict (*28 Days*), a delusional pirate (*Dodgeball*), Lancelot à la Monty Python (*Spamalot*), to a machine with an awakening heart (*I, Robot*). Yet despite his varied résumé, Tudyk is arguably best known to his dedicated fan base as the goofy, wise-crackin', dinosaur-lovin' pilot — Hoban 'Wash' Washburne of *Firefly*. Interestingly enough, it's a role that the actor admits initially barely registered on his radar way back in the early months of 2002. "I was aware of the project and that Joss Whedon was involved," Tudyk remembers about his first audition for the pilot. He was rehearsing for a play in New York City at the time, Tudyk recalls, "I went on tape in a casting office in New York with the one scene from the original pilot, which has me playing with the dinosaurs. It was like, 'There's no script, here's a couple of lines, let's see what you can do with it.' They sketched a little paragraph that said it would be set in the future and in space, but not alien space, so there aren't prosthetics or bumpy foreheads and all that stuff. Basically, it was the outline of what we became."

After the audition, Tudyk details, "A month or so went by. I did a play and then flew out to LA to test for two other pilots. Originally, it was just one. I tested and it didn't go, so I was going back to New York and they said, 'Wait, they want you to test for this other thing.' I didn't get that one either and I was really done with LA and excited to go back home to New York. Then they said, 'Wait, they want to test you for *Firefly*.' I'm like, 'I don't even know what the hell that is. I auditioned for this, evidently?'" the actor deadpans. "They reminded me it was the Joss Whedon pilot and I said, 'Oh, wait! Cool! No, I liked that!' They got me the script and I went and auditioned.

"My first meeting with Joss was at that test. I just thought he was some guy. I remember he had a beard and I didn't think it was Joss Whedon," he laughs. "He came out to tell us all good luck and to have fun with it. So I went in and auditioned against two other guys; and they then said, 'Now, we are down to just two of you. You need to come back and we will pair you with our possible Zoes.' It was me and this guy, Carlos [Jacott] — who is Dobson in the original pilot. We were both up for Wash. We were there waiting to be paired up with the Zoes, but they didn't like any of the Zoes they had that day. They sent us both home and when I got back, I got a call saying I'd got it. I said, 'Okay, fine, great! I'm not going to argue!' And then it became the show."

Cast as Wash, the everyman, smart-ass of the crew, Tudyk says he immediately embraced the character because of their shared qualities. Full of humor with a true passion for flying and his wife Zoe, Wash became the voice of reason the audience could identify with amongst the crew. Wash was a character Tudyk says he understood and one that fit a familiar Whedon model. "*Buffy* was still on the air when we were doing the show — so I'm the space Xander," he jokes. And even if the actor is a little less Zen in reality about navigating the potholes in life, he smiles, "It's my instinct more to be... when everything is high-octane around you and moving fast, I can get caught up in it really easily. Wash reminds me that I can just relax and be calm."

Our gang sees this, takes it in.

None of them pleased, but all of them silent.

Crow starts cutting down the body as Niska shuts the door, shaking his head sadly before he turns to the group.

NISKA (cont'd)
Now, for you, my reputation is not from gossip. You see this man, he does not do the job. I show you what I do with him and now, my reputation for you is fact, is... solid. You do the train job for me, then you are solid. No more gossip. That is strong relationship.

MAL
Right...

NISKA
You do not like I kill this man.

MAL
Well, I'm sure he was a... very bad person...

NISKA
My wife's nephew. At dinner I am getting an earful, there is no way out of that. So. The train job.

He moves to his desk, hits a piece of clear paper, the train schematic appears.

NISKA (cont'd)
Here in fifth car, two boxes, Alliance goods. You don't mind taking from the Alliance, I think. From your reputation.

He smiles at Mal, who doesn't really have it in him to smile back.

NISKA (cont'd)
You get on the train at Hancock, heading to Paradiso. I give you cover story in case of questions, but you are not bothered, I think. You get the boxes off before you reach Paradiso and you deliver to Crow... here.

He touches the paper again and a map appears, with a point marked a few miles from the train line (where the city, PARADISO, is also clearly marked).

NISKA (cont'd)
Half the money now, Crow gives you the other half at rendezvous point. Anything goes wrong... then your reputation is only gossip, and things between us are not so solid. Yes?

Off Mal's look...

EXT. DESERT - DAY

We see the quiet countryside — and then the train WHIPS through frame. It has an old, wrought-iron and brass feel to it, but it HOVERS above a lit track, a series of slim metal dorsal fins arching out from the undercarriage, just above the ground.

INT. TRAIN - CONTINUING

Mal and Zoe, dressed in civvies that look not terribly unlike their usual clothes, sit in the crowded car.

MAL
How long til we hit Paradiso?

ZOE
Another twenty minutes. We should be at the foothills in five.

MAL
Best get to work.

They rise, start toward the back.

ZOE
He's a psycho, you know. Niska.

MAL
He's not the first psycho to hire us, nor the last. Do you think that's a commentary on us?

ZOE
I've just got an image in my head of a guy hanging from the ceiling.

MAL
And I got an image of it not being me. Let's do the thing.

They reach the end of the car, are moving into the next one:

MAL (cont'd)
It's a simple job. And we're simple folk, so it shouldn't be a problem.

He is finishing that sentence as they enter the next car.

ANGLE: THE CAR

is entirely filled with a regiment of Alliance soldier/cops (called FEDS), all facing this way. All armed.

ANGLE: MAL AND ZOE

stop and stare.

MAL (cont'd)
Hi.

END OF ACT ONE

ACT TWO

INT. DINING ROOM - DAY

Inara enters to find Book sitting at the dining room table, reading his bible distractedly. He rises, nods to her.

INARA
Shepherd.

BOOK
Good day.

He sits again. She fusses about getting food. A beat.

BOOK (cont'd)
So, how do you think it's going?

INARA
(slightly amused)
The "caper"?
(less amused)
Mal knows what he's doing.

BOOK
How long have you known him?

INARA
I've been on the ship eight months now. I'm not certain that I'll ever actually know the Captain.

BOOK
(laughs a bit)
I'm surprised a respectable Companion would sail with this crew.

INARA
It's not always this sort of work. They take the jobs they can get. Even legitimate ones. But the further you get from the central planets, the harder things are. So this is part of it.

BOOK
I wish I could help. I mean, I don't want to help, not help help, not with the thieving, but... I do feel awfully useless.

INARA
You could always pray they make it back safely.

BOOK
I don't think the Captain would much like me praying for him.

INARA
Don't tell him.

She turns a bit, says, mostly to herself:

INARA (cont'd)
I never do.

INT. TRAINCAR - CONTINUING

Mal and Zoe are still standing in front of the feds.

There is a beat, and then the door at the other end opens, an immigrant-looking family coming through towards Mal and Zoe. They take the opportunity to move as well, heading back and passing the family. A couple of feds eyeball them, but there is no comment made.

INT. THE NEXT TRAINCAR - CONTINUING

This one is filled with poor, immigrant families. Mal and Zoe take a moment, make sure they're out of earshot.

ZOE
Sir, is there some information we might maybe be lacking? As to why there's an entire fed squad sitting on this train?

MAL
It doesn't concern us.

ZOE
It kind of concerns me...

MAL
I mean they're not protecting the goods. If they were, they wouldn't be letting people past 'em.

ZOE
You don't think it changes the situation a bit?

MAL
I surely do. Makes it more fun.

ZOE
Sir, I think you have a problem with your brain being missing.

MAL
Come on. We stick to the plan, we get the goods and we're back on Serenity before the train even reaches Paradiso. Only now we do it under the noses of twenty trained Alliance feds and that makes them look all manner of stupid. Hell, this job I would pull for free.

He starts off, she follows.

ZOE
Then can I have your share?

MAL
No.

ZOE
If you die can I have your share?

MAL
Yes.

EXT. DESERT - DAY

We are moving with the train — and we suddenly move laterally, over low hills, to find Serenity flying low at the same pace, some 300 yards away.

INT. BRIDGE - CONTINUING

Wash is piloting. Jayne is with him.

WASH
We start flying with the hatch open, keeping her steady is gonna be a job of work, so you strap in.

JAYNE
You get me killed, I'm a come back as a ghost and punch your liver out.

WASH
Well, there goes Plan A...

JAYNE
I'm not messing around. You'd best run straight or you'll get a boxing.

WASH
You sound like my father. Which is weird because you look more like my mother.

JAYNE
One of these days —

A beeping. Wash looks at his monitors.

WASH
We're close. Get down there.

JAYNE
(as he goes)
Hell, I ever call you out, you'd probably just hide behind the Mrs.

WASH
(working the panels)
Go.
(a beat. To himself:)
My liver?

INT. CARGO BAY - CONTINUING

Kaylee opens the bay doors. She drags over some cable and winches, starts attaching them to the walls.

Simon appears, tentative.

SIMON
Hey.

KAYLEE
Oh hey Doctor.

SIMON
You really should just call me Simon.

KAYLEE
I'll do that then.

He a little bit causes the shyness in her.

SIMON
So what are we doing?

KAYLEE
Oh! Crime.

SIMON
Crime, good. Okay. Crime.

KAYLEE
It's a train heist. We fly over the traincar, The Captain and Zoe sneak in, we lower Jayne onto the car, they bundle up the booty and we haul 'em all back up. Easy as lyin'.

SIMON
You've done this before?

KAYLEE
(laughing)
Oh hell no!
(serious)
But I think it's gonna work. The captain is <jen duh sh tyen tsai> [an absolute genius] when it comes to plans.

SIMON
Is there anything I can... something I should be doing?

JAYNE
(entering)
Staying the hell out of everyone's way.

We can see he's added some layers, including a hat tied around his chin and a scarf to pull over his face. Gonna be windy.

KAYLEE
No call to be snappy, Jayne.

JAYNE
(to Kaylee)
Are you about to jump onto a moving train?

She backs off. He turns back to Simon.

JAYNE (cont'd)
Captain's not around, I'm in charge.

KAYLEE
Since when?

JAYNE
(ignoring her)
Just 'cause Mal says you're a medic don't make you part of the crew. You just play at figuring what's wrong with that moon-brained sister of yours til we call for you, <dong ma> [understand]?

ANGLE: UP ON THE CATWALK

is River herself, sitting and watching the exchange. It's impossible to tell if she even understands what she's hearing. Simon stares at Jayne a beat, weighing the advantages of arguing.

SIMON
Right.

He turns and goes. Kaylee starts strapping Jayne in.

KAYLEE
You shouldn't be so rude to him.

JAYNE
Why, 'cause he's all rich and fancible?

KAYLEE
He's not rich. Alliance crashed his accounts when he snuck out his sister.

JAYNE
Yeah, well, we could all be rich, we handed her back.

KAYLEE
You're not even thinking that!

JAYNE
Mal is.

KAYLEE
That's not funny.

JAYNE
He ain't stupid. Why would he take on trouble like those two if there weren't no profit in it? Captain's got a move he ain't made yet. You'll see.

He tests his straps and such. They're good.

JAYNE (cont'd)
Time for some thrilling heroics.

INT. TRAINCAR - CONTINUING

Mal and Zoe are at the door marked: STORAGE. NO PASSENGERS. Mal pulls out a keycard.

MAL
Niska's sources better be good...

A beat, and he inserts the card.

INT. TRAINCAR WITH FEDS - CONTINUING

One of the feds gets up, stretching, and heads back to where Mal and Zoe are.

INT. TRAINCAR - CONTINUING

The panel lights on the corners of the door turn from orange to purple. We hear locks withdrawing and the door swings open.

ZOE
Shiny.

She pulls a gas canister out of Mal's bag, prepares to hurl it as Mal readies himself and whips the door open.

ANGLE: INSIDE THE CAR

there are no guards. Just a room full of various crates and baggage. They enter, pulling the door shut behind them — but leaving it slightly ajar, as Zoe fiddles with the canister and some wire at the bottom of the doorway.

Mal moves to the center of the car, pulling what looks like a wicked powerful screw gun from his bag.

MAL
Find the cargo.

He steps up on some boxes. The ceiling is separated into three corrugated iron panels, all about eight feet by four. Mal puts the gun to one of the rivets in the center panel, triggers it, and we hear a ripping/sucking sound. He pulls the gun down, rivet stuck in it. Removes it and starts on the next.

ANGLE: ZOE

is going through boxes. Rips a tarp off some and sees two big metal crates with the AngloSino flag printed on top. They are the burnished purple of the soldiers' uniforms.

ZOE
All hail the great Alliance.

EXT. DESERT - CONTINUING

We are with the train as Serenity appears right above it, keeping pace with it.

INT. AIRLOCK/CARGO BAY - CONTINUING

The doors are closing behind Jayne and Kaylee as the bomb bay door is opening, letting in daylight and a shitload of wind. When the hatch is open all the way, Jayne gets down and crawls to the edge of it, looks over. He has a cable attached to him.

ANGLE: OVER JAYNE

We see the train some twenty feet below. Everything is moving very fast.

INT. BRIDGE - CONTINUING

Wash pilots, hands tight on the wheel, ship bucking slightly.

INT. AIRLOCK - CONTINUING

Jayne gives the thumbs up to Kaylee. She hits a lever on a winch and it starts letting out cable as Jayne jumps —

EXT. DESERT - CONTINUING

— from the ramp to the car twenty feet below, cables trailing out above him. He hits hard but holds on, keeping his head down. Waits.

INT. TRAINCAR - CONTINUING

Mal pops the last rivet and he and Zoe lower the panel down as gently as they can. It makes a bit of clatter as they lower it to one side —

INT. TRAIN - CONTINUING

The fed who moved back hears the noise, starts in that direction, curious...

PARADISO

Production designer Carey Meyer: "The town we used for 'Paradiso' is very Western. It's a little gold mining area with some mineshafts and other useful locations. We stumbled on it while location scouting for 'Serenity' and almost used it; we'd always liked it and Joss remembered it and so he went back to it when we came to do 'The Train Job'. I came up with a way to connect the train to the area — have the train tracks come up along the ridge. We built one traincar, for the actors to enter and exit, out on a ramp in this built up space; the train was all CG on the other side. Once we had connected the train to the location, everything else fell into place and we could use it and dress it the way we wanted to."

❖ Above: Building the set for the interior of the train.

INT. TRAINCAR - CONTINUING

Jayne flips in through the big hole in the roof as Zoe and Mal drag the crates in a net to right under the hole. They start pulling cable off Jayne and securing it onto the corners of the net. Jayne hops on top (still with his own line on) and calls into a walkie:

JAYNE
Fifteen seconds!

ANGLE: KAYLEE

ready to reverse the winch.

ANGLE: WASH

piloting. Tense as hell.

ANGLE: THE FED

sees the door ajar, pulls his rifle off his shoulder, approaches the door. Zoe hops on the crate with Jayne, about to buckle onto his line, as Mal is finishing his end of the net —

The soldier stands by the door, rifle ready, and rips it open —

ANGLE: THE GAS CANISTER

is popped when the wire is pulled.

It shoots gas up into the Fed's face before he can see anything. He shoots blind (the sound is a series of muffled pops), Mal moving towards him as Zoe dives off the crate for cover as boxes splinter by her head from stray bullets. One hits Jayne's leg, he sags but holds on.

ZOE
(to Jayne)
Go!

JAYNE
(into walkie)
Go! Go now!

Kaylee hits the winch —

And Jayne goes up with the netted crates, out of the traincar as Mal gets to the blinded soldier, fights him in the smoke. Mal is precise and brutal, and though it's messy, the guy is unconscious in moments.

MAL
(to Zoe)
Come on!

They head out of the traincar, towards the front —

EXT. DESERT - CONTINUING

As Serenity moves away from the train, Jayne and the crates still being pulled up.

INT. TRAIN - CONTINUING

THE ALLIANCE

Costume designer Shawna Trpcic: "The classic image was Nazi Germany, and to try to avoid it just being totally German, we again went to different wars. The first sketches that we did were way too Nazi," she laughs. "You don't need to be so obvious when you're conveying a bad guy, and Joss was like, 'Okay, pull it up a little...' but we took the hat shapes and things from that World War Two time period."

❖ Above: Trpcic's costume designs for the Alliance soldiers.

❖ Right: An Alliance soldier's armor.

Mal and Zoe reach the car — full with poorer passengers — between them and the car full of soldiers. They roll out a couple of gas canisters. Gas billows up just as feds are entering from the other side. Mal and Zoe blend in with the other civilians, choking and keeping low, as the soldiers pass them.

INT. CARGO BAY - CONTINUING

Jayne climbs up, the crates pulled up by the winch. As soon as the door is shut, Kaylee unhooks herself and moves to him, finally able to speak without the rushing wind:

KAYLEE
Where are the others?

JAYNE
Shot my gorramn leg!

KAYLEE
Jayne? Are they on the train? Are they gonna be okay?

EXT. PARADISO TRAIN STATION - DAY

The train has stopped. Many passengers have climbed off, still red eyed and coughing from smoke. Mal and Zoe are among them. Behind them, though paying them no particular mind, is Sheriff BOURNE, talking to a fed.

FED
Our man didn't get a look.

BOURNE
Well, Jesus, can someone at least find out what they took?
(calls out to a deputy)
Pendy, keep these people together! And quiet 'em down!

Mal is listening, but his attention is also drawn to:

ANGLE: A group of families, mostly women and children. Clearly very sick, clearly waiting for something on that train. Someone comes to talk to them and several of the women start crying, clutching their children to them.

A deputy comes up to the sheriff, and Zoe and Mal hear very clearly.

DEPUTY
It was the medicine, sir. All the supplies.

BOURNE
They stole the gorramn medicine? We been waiting — all of it?

DEPUTY
Every ounce.

BOURNE
God help us.

Zoe looks at Mal. Mal looks stone-faced.

ANGLE ON: the crying women. The sickly children.

MAL
Son of a bitch...

END OF ACT TWO

ACT THREE

EXT. SPACE - ALLIANCE CRUISER

A giant Alliance Cruiser moves slowly through space.

INT. ALLIANCE CRUISER - CONTINUING

Big. Clean. Corporate. No bantery chit-chat to be had. The crew is dressed in the same formal Alliance attire we saw the soldiers wearing in the traincar.

An OFFICER looks over an ENSIGN's shoulder to a viewing screen.

OFFICER
What's the fuss?

ENSIGN
All network alert. Cargo theft. Medical shipment lifted off a train in the Georgia System, en route to Paradiso.

OFFICER
(eyeing screen)

Two crates of Pasceline D. Right. Get you a tidy fortune on the black market.

ENSIGN
Paradiso's a mining community, sir. Most there are afflicted with Bowden's Disease. The miners pass it on to their children.

OFFICER
(almost to himself)
And yet they insist on breeding...
(then)
Tag it received and bounce it back. Locals can deal with it.

ENSIGN
Sir, there is a regiment holding in Paradiso. They were on the train, headed to the installation.

OFFICER
Then get 'em back on that train and get it moving. Who's holding them there?

ENSIGN
Sir, the Sheriff requested we deploy a few to help him inves —

OFFICER
Those are Federal Marshals, not local narcotic hounds. They have better things to do. And so do we.

The Ensign nods as the Officer moves off.

EXT. DESERT - NIGHT - SERENITY

is parked in a canyon, away from prying eyes and spying probes.

INT. SERENITY - INFIRMARY - CONTINUING

Simon is patching up the wounded Jayne who's on an operating table. Kaylee is nearby, trying to keep him steady while Simon works. We may or may not notice River quietly sitting in the b.g. On Wash's entrance, Jayne pulls away from Simon, starts to rise.

SIMON
(re: wound)
I'm not finished.

JAYNE
(ignoring Simon, rises)
Why you got us parked here? This ain't the <go tsao de> [dog humping] rendezvous spot.

WASH
It is now.

JAYNE
Niska's people're waitin'. They're not partial to waitin'.

WASH
Let 'em read a magazine. We don't make the sale until Mal and Zoe are back on the boat.

JAYNE
These are stone killers, little man. They ain't cuddly like me.

WASH
I'm not flying anywhere without my wife.

KAYLEE
She'll be okay. She's with the Captain.

JAYNE
See there? Everybody wins. Gahh!
(to Simon)
Dammit, Doc, I need a pop to quiet this pain some.

Simon goes for the medicine, loads it onto the hypo as he talks.

SIMON
What about the authorities? We're sitting here with stolen Alliance goods.
(no one denies it)
Won't they be looking for us?

WASH
They buzz this canyon, we'll hear 'em before they ever see us. I figure we're good for a...

RIVER
Won't stop. They'll never stop.

That was unnerving. Everyone just looks at her.

RIVER (cont'd)
They'll just keep coming until they get back what you took.

She laughs softly to herself, her eyes betraying fear.

RIVER (cont'd)
Two by two, hands of blue... two by two, hands of blue...

JAYNE
(to River)
How's about you keep your crazy mouth shut? Is that a fun game?
(to the others)
Now I'm in rutting charge here and I'm telling you how it works.

Simon injects him with painkiller as he continues.

JAYNE (cont'd)
Niska doesn't get the goods on time he will make meatpies of the lot of us. I ain't walking into that.

BOOK
This Adelai Niska you're talking about?

JAYNE
Now how would a Shepherd know a name like that?

BOOK
As I've heard it, he made a deal with the Captain. If the Captain's not there to finish it — If Niska finds out he's being held and may speak as to who hired him... I think we're better off being a little late.

A beat, as Jayne takes this in.

JAYNE
Fine. We wait. For a spell. Then we make our appointment.

That's good enough for Wash, for now.

INT. POLICE STATION - NIGHT

Mal and Zoe sit stiffly next to each other.

MAL
This is a nightmare.

❖ Top: Fed badges.

❖ Above: The Sheriff's badge.

INARA

"Mal, if you're being a gentleman, I may die of shock."

As a highly respected Companion, Inara Serra is a woman noted for her calm, graceful style, but as a late and integral addition to the cast, Julliard graduate Morena Baccarin felt far from calm on her first day. "I came on set and was *petrified*," she recalls. "I had auditioned probably two days before. It all happened very quickly. I had just come to Los Angeles; it was my first time here, and my first television show, so it was a first for a lot of things. I'm glad it happened so quickly because I didn't have a chance to freak out. I was so scared, but they were so warm and so sweet. They all seemed happy to meet me and see who the new Inara was going to be. [Baccarin replaced the originally cast Rebecca Gayheart shortly after filming began.] Joss brought me down from the testing room like a proud dad, holding my hand and introducing me."

Inara defied the conventions of her profession and despite being labeled a whore several times by Mal, she never warranted that description. Rather, she defined elegance and decorum — more closely resembling a Japanese Geisha than a traditional prostitute. "It was really important to Joss that she was regal, a woman of class, high standing, and moral grounds," says Baccarin. "She's against the stereotype and the way he described her is exactly what attracted me to the character and the project. We had a lot of conversations about how she would be an ambassador and bring all these people together on the ship. And she's got pride — which is why she can't express herself with Mal.

"I also liked the fact that she was a whore, even though it was kind of scary for me. I originally got just a few pages of the script. Even before I read those, there was just a treatment that

kind of explained what she did and I thought, 'This could be bad. This could really be *not* fun to do.' Then I met Joss, and he persuaded me that it would be a really good thing.

"I don't think I was conscious of what I was doing. It just came out of the text, what I was saying, and how I was dressed. It was a combination of a lot of elements coming together. I didn't really make a decision about what I was going to sound like. I did do some research on Geisha because I thought it was important that she had a sense of tradition and ceremony; but it is really difficult to do research for a show set in a world that doesn't exist. However, it was very clear in Joss's mind, so it was easy to translate for us."

Inara's beautiful Eastern-inspired wardrobe helped to define her character. "I loved those outfits!" smiles Baccarin. "Every day coming to work, I used to wonder, 'What am I going to be wearing today?' Shawna [Trpcic] did such a great job designing the costumes that I felt like a princess all the time. All the girls were like, 'You are so lucky. We're in grease and overalls all day long.' Although it could get kind of old after twelve hours of being in some of those corsets. You can't breathe. They were designed not to be too tight, but you wear anything like that for over ten hours and it's going to be uncomfortable. There was always something sticking into me. I was always the one standing while everyone was sitting. Some of that stuff I just wanted to rip off, so I could put on sweat pants! It's funny — Inara might be 'the stylish one', but any time we do conventions, I'm the one in the jeans and sneakers."

Baccarin really valued being directed by Joss Whedon: "It was a dream. He's great to work with because he's very specific and knows what he wants, but he'll let you put in your two cents. If you are wrong, he'll tell you; but for the most part, he will let you try stuff. It feels like a collaboration, which makes all the difference sometimes."

Although *Firefly* was a casualty in the ratings war, it inspired a legion of loyal fans. "It is one of those things people identify with," she offers. "It's a fantasy world, but so tangible. A part of you is in almost every one of the characters. People are really drawn to that, to stories that are like myths but teach you life lessons." ◀

ZOE
Nothing points to us yet, sir.

MAL
That ain't what I'm talking about.

WIDER - we see they're currently sitting alone. About them the place is a hive of activity. Hill-Street-Blues-meets-Rio-Bravo-by-way-of-Blade-Runner. The understaffed constabulary is working its way through questioning the train passengers.

And more of the sick women and children are near Mal and Zoe, a constant reminder of their crime.

The SHERIFF, no-nonsense, tired, finishes questioning A COUPLE that we might recognize from the train. He thanks them perfunctorily. They take their luggage, exit.

MAL (cont'd)
Whatever happens, remember I love you.

ZOE
(shocked)
Sir?

MAL
(you idiot)
Because you're my wife.

ZOE
Right. Sir. Honey.

The Sheriff confers with a deputy, who checks a list, points to Mal and Zoe. Sheriff crosses to them. Has the train manifest.

BOURNE
Car three, row twelve. Mister and Missus... Raymond.

Mal is suddenly the protective young husband.

MAL
Can you tell us what's going on? We've been here for so long. Did someone on the train get killed?

BOURNE
No, no. Nothing like that. I see here your fares were purchased by a third party...

MAL
My uncle. A wedding gift.

BOURNE
(it's unheard of)
Wedding gift... You spending your honeymoon in Paradiso?

ZOE
Actually we're here looking for work.

BOURNE
That right?

MAL
My uncle said he knew a Joey Bloggs out here. Said he might have an opening. Thought we'd try our luck.

BOURNE
You a miner by trade, either of you?

MAL
Not really.

BOURNE
Haven't seen many folk choose this life weren't born to it.

ZOE
Well, work's real scarce for a couple just starting out.

MAL
How come there's so many sick here?

BOURNE
Bowden's Malady. You know what that is?

ZOE
Affliction of the bone and muscle. Degenerative.

BOURNE
Very. Every planet that's been terraformed for human life has its own little quirks. Turns out the air down underground, mixed up with the ore processors, it's a perfect recipe for Bowden's. Everybody gets it: minors, dumpers — hell, I got it and I ain't ever set foot in a mine. It's worst on the kids, of course.

ZOE
But it's treatable.

BOURNE
There's medicine, Pasceline — works on the symptoms. Person could live like a person, they get it regular. But our shipment got stole right off that train you was ridin' in. Which is why you won't be seeing a parade in town today.

MAL
(feigned shock)
Stolen? Didn't we see an entire regiment of fine young Alliance Federals on the train?

BOURNE
You did. The same regiment that let the medicine get swiped from under their noses and then took off for their camp without so much as a whoopsie daisy.

MAL
That sounds like the Alliance. Unite the planets under one rule so everyone can be interfered with or ignored equally.

BOURNE
Alliance ain't much use to us on the border planets. But they ain't the ones stole that medicine. I find those people, they'll never see the inside of a jail. I'll just toss 'em in the mine, let 'em breathe deep for the rest of their lives.

MAL
Can't argue with that.

BOURNE
Mind telling me when it was you last spoke to Joey Bloggs?

Mal tenses, senses the trap.

MAL
Never did myself.

BOURNE
Right. Your uncle. And it was indicated to you that Joey had an opening?

MAL
Any job would do...

BOURNE
Funny your uncle never went to mentioning the Bowden's problem. Or that Joey Bloggs ate his own gun 'bout eight months back.

MAL
Did he.

BOURNE
Yep. Blew the back of his head right off.

MAL
(a long beat)
So... would his job be open?

The Sheriff gives a wan smile. The game's afoot and they both know it, neither one about to be so rude as to say so openly.

BOURNE
Say, I don't suppose you folks would mind if we took a retinal scan? We're doin' it with all the folks we don't know by sight. Just to make sure

ADAM BALDWIN

On improvising a drugged up and delusional Jayne during 'The Train Job': "I came up with that part about reaching out for the pixie dust, the little fairies, the shining lights... There were a few things Joss didn't write that would get added in. I would always try to busy it up because Jayne wasn't speechifying all over the place so I had to try and find things to do. I would work closely with the prop master and find doings with straps, belts, buckles, guns, gloves and wristbands. So Joss allowed me to play around. We did a few takes and I did a couple of takes just reaching for it. Then for whatever reason — Summer blew her line or something. You know, she was the set scapegoat. Anytime any of us would screw up a line or the camera would get out of focus, we'd all be 'Summer! Goddamit! Get your lines right!' The most innocent of us all! Anyway, Joss came up to me and said 'Why didn't you reach for the little fairies? Where were they?' I was like 'Oh, you like that huh?' And he's like 'Yeah, keep that. Okay good.'"

they are who they say.

INT. SERENITY - BRIDGE - NIGHT

Jayne comes barging into the bridge. Wash is there, with Kaylee. Wash stands up, knowing this will be unpleasant. Simon follows Jayne.

JAYNE
That's it. We waited long enough. Get this bird in the air.

WASH
No rutting way.

SIMON
(to Jayne)
You really should sit down...

KAYLEE
We can't just leave the Captain and Zoe here.

JAYNE
They ain't coming! We can't walk in there and get 'em so they're done.

Jayne shoves Wash back toward the controls.

JAYNE (cont'd)
Now fire it up.

Wash flares. He'll get trounced, but he's ready to fight. Inara and Book appear in the doorway.

INARA
What's going on?

JAYNE
(without looking at her)
Strap in. We're takin' off.

WASH
We're not.

JAYNE
Captain'd do the same if it were one of us —

KAYLEE
Not in a million years —

JAYNE
Shut it!

His intensity shuts them down. Wash is quiet but firm:

WASH
Listen to me —

JAYNE
Do you know what the chain of command is? It's the chain I go get and beat you with til you understand who's in rutting command here!

Wash is truly scared, but not backing down.

JAYNE (cont'd)
Now we're finishing this deal and then maybe — MAYBE we'll come back for those... morons... got themselves caught and you can't change that just by gettin' all bendy...

WASH
All what?

JAYNE
(drifting)
You got the light, from the console to keep you, to lift you up... they shine like little angels.

He topples forward, hits the floor hard, chin leading. Out like a two ton light. Everyone just blinks. Except for Simon.

WASH
Did he just go crazy and fall asleep?

SIMON
I told him to sit down...

KAYLEE
You doped him!

SIMON
It was supposed to kick in a good deal sooner. I just didn't feel comfortable with him in charge. I hope that's all right.

The look on everyone's faces tells him it is.

BOOK
So how do we get the others?

WASH
Jayne was right about them not making contact. Chances are they got pinched getting off that train.

KAYLEE
And we can't just waltz in and pull 'em out...

BOOK
Someone respectable enough might be able to.

WASH
A Shepherd can't just demand they hand over —

BOOK
I know. I wasn't talking about me.

INT. POLICE STATION - NIGHT

Mal and Zoe still cooling their heels. The Sheriff in the near distance conferring. Eyeballing them.

ZOE
You figure Serenity's still waitin' for us?

MAL
If they are, everyone's fired.

ZOE
And if they're not?

MAL
Everyone's fired.

ZOE
So how you wanna play this?

There is a buzz of activity. A deputy moves to the Sheriff with some news. He reacts with surprise.

Mal and Zoe watch, curious. Commotion as someone pushes through the deputies —

INARA - appears, the bearing of a monarch. Mal reacts to the sight. So does Zoe. Inara strides magnificently over to Mal. He opens his mouth to speak —

MAL
What the h—

SMACK -

she slaps him hard across the face.

INARA
Don't you dare speak to me.

A deputy has given the Sheriff Inara's official papers. He peruses them as he crosses to her.

INARA (cont'd)
Sheriff, I want this man bound by law at once. That's assuming he hasn't been already...

BOURNE
No one's been bound. Not yet.

INARA
Well thank god you stopped them.
(to Mal)
Did you honestly think you could access my accounts and I wouldn't find you?
(sadly, to Zoe)
And Zoe... what would your husband say if he knew you were here?

ZOE
I was weak.

BOURNE
(not surprised)
So I take it they ain't newlyweds?

INARA
Hardly. Malcolm's my indentured man. With three years left on his debt. I imagine we'll have to add another six months after this little adventure.

The deputies stare in awe and whisper amongst themselves, as they have been since her entrance. Inara glances to them. Gathers herself with tremendous dignity.

BOURNE
You'll have to pardon them. Don't think a one of em's ever seen a Registered Companion before. Fancy lady such as yourself don't pass through here everyday.

INARA
I apologize for my manner.

BOURNE
Not a bit.

INARA
(to Mal and Zoe)
Though I've half a mind to leave you both here. If your debt weren't so large, I would.
(then)
Should I contact my ship? Will you need to hold them very much longer?

BOURNE
Looks to me like we're done. We're having some

unrelated trouble. And his story had kind of an odor to it...

INARA
Yes. It's not the only thing about him that does.

Mal refuses to show that it burns him how much fun she's having.

INARA (cont'd)
Thank you very much, Sheriff.
(to Mal and Zoe)
Come along.

Mal and Zoe rise, follow her out.

The Sheriff watches them go. Something not sitting just right with him.

BOURNE
(to the deputy)
That's a hell of a lady. Her files were all in order?

DEPUTY
Ran 'em twice.

BOURNE
(lets out a breath)
Let's get started with the rest, then.

INT. CARGO BAY - LATER

Mal, Zoe and Inara all step off the shuttle. Kaylee and Wash are there to greet them. Zoe and Wash hug, make with smoochies.

KAYLEE
How'd it go?

MAL
She hit me.

He starts downstairs, they all follow.

They all react now to see Jayne sprawled out/propped against the stairs/catwalk. He's sort of in and out of consciousness. A floppy puppy. They have to step over him. Mal does a take.

KAYLEE
(approaching)
We tried to get him to the infirmary. He's just heavy.

Mal doesn't even ask.

WASH
Kept the engine running. We're good to go.

MAL
We're not going.

WASH
Not what? Not why?

MAL
We're bringing the cargo back.

Astounded looks from all save Zoe. Jayne moans in his full-body-novocaine stupor.

JAYNE
(slurred)
What? Whaddya mean back? I waited for you!

ZOE
Let's get this on the Mule.

WASH
What're you talking about? What about Niska? Won't that put him more or less in a killing mood?

Mal hits a button and the cargo bay ramp starts to lower.

MAL
There's others need this more.

INARA
My shuttle is faster —

MAL
You risked enough flying in there once. And I don't wanna get slapped around no more.
(to Wash)
Far as Niska goes, we'll just have to explain the job went south on us when we return the money.

Jayne groans.

WASH
You wanna explain, now's your chance...

He's seeing something that Mal doesn't. Mal turns, following Wash's gaze to see —

ANGLE - CARGO BAY RAMP

At the bottom of the ramp, just outside the ship are CROW and THREE MEN. Every man large, every man pissed.

END OF ACT THREE

ACT FOUR

INT. CARGO BAY/AIRLOCK - CONTINUOUS

Mal looks down on Crow and his men. They start to walk up the ramp. Mal takes a step forward.

CROW
You didn't make the rendezvous.

MAL
Ran into a few complications.

❖ Above and Below: Inara's official Companion papers and book.

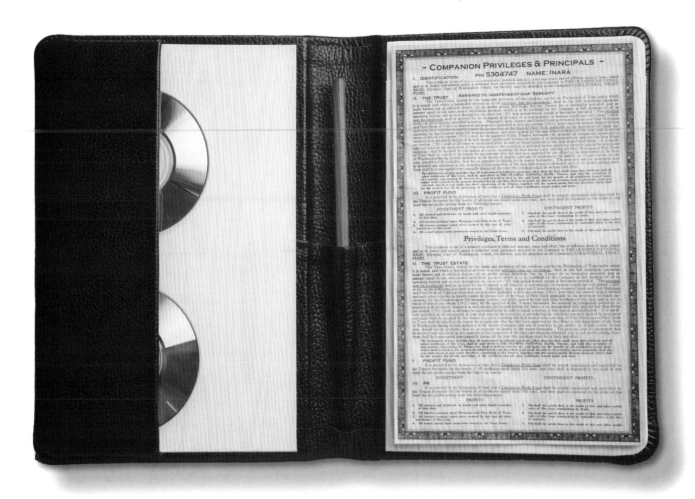

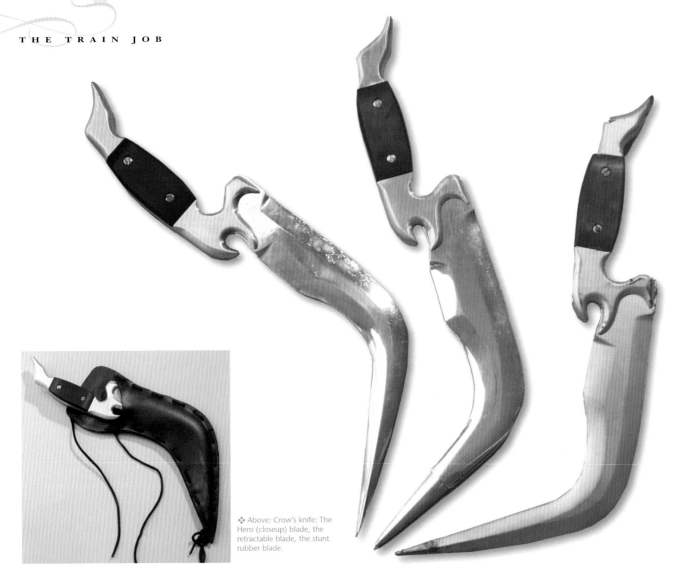

❖ Above: Crow's knife: The Hero (closeup) blade, the retractable blade, the stunt rubber blade.

CROW
You were thinking of taking Mister Niska's money and his property, maybe?

MAL
Interestingly — neither.

Crow furrows his brow.

CROW
I don't understand...

MAL
Yeah. Look. Here's what it is: deal's off.

Still with the brow furrowing from Crow.

MAL (cont'd)
We changed our minds.

CROW
You entered into an arrangement with Mister Niska. There is no mind-changing.

MAL
'Fraid that's where you're wrong. We just, we can't take this job. So you just relax, and we'll get you the money Niska paid us up front, you return it to him and call it even.

CROW
And there is no "even".

MAL
Is that right?

During all this...

MAL'S HAND

has been drifting toward his gun, as —

CROW

whip quick, releases his curved knife — buries it in Mal's right shoulder. Mal rears back, big pain.

And all hell, as they say, breaks loose —

Zoe is pulling her weapon, as...

Crow's men storm the cargo bay, guns out and firing...

MAL

Suddenly Crow is there, pulling out the knife, then slamming his fist into the wound. Mal fights back.

ZOE

Zoe has her gun out, takes out one of the guys right off, then lunges at Kaylee, pulling her down behind some cover as she avoids getting hit by the return fire. She looks over to make sure Wash is okay.

He is, nods to her from behind some crates, as...

CROW AND MAL

Crow just fucking wails on Mal, driving him staggering back up the ramp with each bone jarring blow.

Mal's pretty much only good with his left at this

point, and manages to get in a few good hits, but Crow's punishment is taking its toll on him.

Crow is distracted suddenly, as —

A ROAR

The MULE comes bouncing up over the top of the ramp, sending the other thugs scattering. Wash is driving it.

Mal presses his advantage. Gets in a few good licks. But Crow comes back strong. Sweeps up his fallen knife, is about to bury it in Mal's skull, when

A SHOT RINGS OUT

Crow goes down, screaming pain, a big hole in the back of his leg. Mal looks up, astonished to see —

JAYNE

still propped in the same spot, but with his gun out, sort of lazily aimed in that general direction. He still looks like a stroke victim, desperately trying to keep his eyes open.

MAL
Nice shot.

JAYNE
(slurred)
I was aimin' for his head.

EXT. JUST OUTSIDE TOWN - NIGHT

Mal and Zoe are on the Mule, Zoe driving, Mal on top of the crates, with a better view. The town becomes visible in the distance and he taps her shoulder. She cuts the engines and they get off, start untying the crates.

MAL
We're gonna have to drag 'em from here. We can leave 'em just off the street, notify the Sheriff once we're in deep deep space.

BOURNE
Why don't you tell him in person?

They draw — but SIX MEN with rifles appear from the brush. Mal and Zoe slowly holster their guns.

BOURNE (cont'd)
We got word of a ship not far out, came looking. Didn't expect to find you coming back.

MAL
Didn't expect to be coming.

The deputy from Act Two comes over as they speak, opens the crates.

DEPUTY
Nothin' missing.

Mal and the Sheriff stare at each other. Clearly an understanding, as he addresses the pair of them:

BOURNE
You were truthful back in town. These are tough times. Hard to find yourself work. A man can get a job, he might not look too close at what that job is.
(to Mal)
But a man learns all the details of a situation like ours, well then he has a choice.

MAL
I don't believe he does.

There is a moment then. The Sheriff slightly smiles.

BOURNE
(to his men)
Let's get these crates back to town. Make ourselves useful.

Two men each take a crate and haul them off. The Sheriff walks off with the rest of them, not saying anther word.

After a beat, Zoe climbs back onto the Mule and starts to turn it around.

EXT. SERENITY - NIGHT

Crow goes down in a heap onto his knees. He is on the ramp, the huge jet engine behind him just starting to whir to life, wind kicking up as the ship prepares to take off.

Mal stands before him, holding a wad of bills.

MAL
Now this is all the money Niska gave us in advance. You give it back to him, tell him the job didn't work out. We're not thieves — well, we are thieves, but — the point is, we're not taking what's his. We'll stay out of his way as best we can from here on in. You'll explain that's best for everyone, okay?

Crow rises. He towers over Mal, hatred on his face.

CROW
Keep the money. Use it to buy a funeral. It doesn't matter where you go, how far you fly — I will hunt you down and the last thing you see will be my blade.

MAL (sighs)
Darn.

He kicks Crow back — and the huge fellow is

❖ Above: The transparency of River produced by the Blue-Gloved Men.

instantly SUCKED into the engine of the ship. It's very sudden, but the resultant crunching noise goes on for a bit. A beat, and Zoe shoves one of Crow's henchmen in front of Mal.

MAL (cont'd)
Now. This is all the money Niska —

HENCHMAN
Oh I get it. I'm good. Best for everyone, I'm right there with you.

Mal smiles, puts the money in the man's breast pocket and pats it.

EXT. SPACE - NIGHT

As the ship leaves the planet behind.

INT. INFIRMARY/PASSENGER DORM/RIVER'S ROOM - NIGHT

Mal is being stitched up by Simon.

SIMON
You should have let me do this sooner.

MAL
I've had plenty worse. This is just a OWWW!

SIMON
Sorry.

MAL
Just be careful.
(a beat)

That was pretty fast thinking, dopin' up Jayne. Can't say you've made a lifetime friend...

SIMON
I'll deal with him.

MAL
I'm not too worried about you. How's your sister?

We begin drifting away from them as they speak, heading toward River's room as Simon's voice becomes a voiceover...

SIMON
The same. One moment she seems perfectly cogent, the next... she speaks nonsense. Like a child. It's so difficult to diagnose; I still don't know what the government was trying to do with her. So I have no idea if they succeeded.

and we land on River, sitting up in her bed and worrying the sheet with her hands, repeating to herself:

RIVER
Two by two, hands of blue, two by two, hands of blue...

over and over and

INT. ALLIANCE CRUISER - CONTINUING

The officer we saw before steps into a starkly lit room.

OFFICER
I'm sorry to keep you waiting. There's always one crisis or —

MAN
We're not interested.

OTHER MAN
We're here about a theft.

OFFICER
The medicine? On that planet... Word came up that was returned.

MAN
We didn't fly eighty-six million miles to track down a box of band-aids, Colonel.

The officer is increasingly uneasy. We finally

REVERSE ANGLE to see TWO MEN sitting at the table. They reek of government. Whatever the CIA is in the future, it's these guys. They are blank as slate.

OTHER MAN
We're looking for a girl. This girl.

As he says it the first man slides a folder forward, with a picture atop it. The picture is of River. The hand sliding it forward has, incongruously, a skin-tight latex glove on it. Blue.

Tilt back up to the men to see they are both wearing blue gloves.

They stare, impassively.

BLACKOUT.

END OF SHOW

RANDY ERIKSEN

I did a lot of the graphics on the show's props myself. I remember the money. I think I got a bunch of different foreign currency, including some Thai money, and Photoshopped and manipulated the colors and stuff and printed it. I got some parchment and some hand-made paper from the art store and printed and cut it in my office. The Hero money was printed on some translucent paper, like tracing paper but with sparkly bits in it. That way I only needed to print the bills one side and the design would show through to the other. Of course the sound guy hated the crackly paper I used!

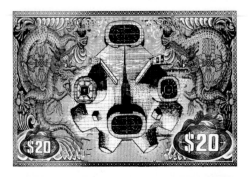

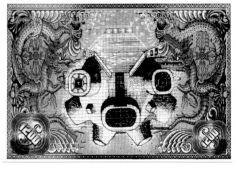

"I'M THINKING YOU'RE ONE OF THEM INDEPENDENTS"

Mal's Pistol & Browncoat

Once in a while, a prop comes along which is perfect for its purpose.

Television and film both need for us to suspend our disbelief if they're to tell the story, but never more so than in science fiction. The carefully contrived framework of a fictional universe is a fragile one. In the *Firefly* universe, everyone is armed as a matter of course. The Black is a dangerous place. Altercations with the Alliance, Reavers and disgruntled traders are all too common.

The pistol Mal carries is rather special. Its design captures both the antique romance of the Old West and the extravagant flair of golden-age science fiction. It has a timeless quality and would seem as at home strapped to the hip of H.G. Wells' time traveler, as it would on the Outlaw Josey Wales. Its robust but elegant lines evoke *Wild Wild West* retro-tech. It conjures brass robots, Disney's *Nautilus* and the fancifully spindly, almost organic look of black powder weapons like the Colt 1860 Army and 1851 Navy and, like the Navy, it has an octagonal barrel.

The sweeping, gracefully flared steel grip frame and wood grips announce it as the weapon of a gunfighter, born to be worn on the thigh. Its heavy, bullish barrel is offset by two intriguing thumbscrews which counter the blocky weight of the business end, adding a touch of delicacy and technical refinement. There's an almost whimsical scrolled fin on the base of the ammunition clip, which is mirrored by that of the lanyard attachment, at the grip's base. Though artful and interesting, it means business. Its owner may not start the fight, but he is certainly equipped to finish it.

Applied Effects, an LA prop shop, were tasked with creating this key prop for *Firefly*. Regina Pancake, Applied's co-founder, remembers it well. "Randy Eriksen showed up at the shop. And it was a big rush job. All of a sudden we had to deal with this gun. It was Mal's Hero [closeup] gun and you can imagine how much of a priority it was. I think Randy had a week and a half or something to get it done. It was a panic. But, even with all the hypertension of getting the pistols done in time, he was way mellow. He's a very mellow guy, he's like Bing Crosby. He even wears a hat like Bing Crosby, with a little feather in it."

The production called Applied and told them that they had the base guns for the prop. It was decided to build the prop on an existing, live-firing revolver. In sequences where Nathan Fillion had to actually fire the weapon, the blanks used would produce a realistic muzzle flash and the report would be a cue for the sound designer. (Actual gunfire is far too loud to be accurately recorded live. When gunfire is heard in a film it's invariably a sound effect, added in postproduction.) The two base guns were supplied by Gibbons Ltd, the show's armorer, and delivered to Applied's workshop. Randy Eriksen also provided a foamcore conceptual mock-up of the pistol, made by *Firefly*'s art department.

The foamcore model was laid on a desk next to one of the base guns, a five-shot .38 caliber Taurus model 85

❖ Above and opposite: Profiles of the Hero prop, photographed before it was fully weathered.

Courtesy of Applied Effects.

revolver, and they got to work. The main objective was to hide the shape and size of the Taurus. After much discussion it was decided that a set of investment-cast bronze dressing shrouds would do the job. They'd be hollow metal shells which still allowed operation of the revolver's mechanism, but which changed the lines of the gun radically, leaving only the Taurus' trigger, trigger guard and the bottom of the frame visible. Mal's pistol comprises the Taurus revolver with the original grip frame chopped off, a new custom-made steel grip frame, two wooden grips, a hollow octagonal barrel shroud, a front sight, two front shrouds, two middle shrouds and two rear shrouds, plus a slim top-strap which is the base of the rear sight. There is also a removable ammunition clip which slips into a recess just forward of the Taurus' trigger guard. The ammo clip is a dummy; the firing blanks are contained in the Taurus' original cylinder.

The first stage in the production process was to design and produce the bronze castings. Eric Haraldsted, Applied's co-founder and resident gun expert, designed the cast pieces using a CAD (computer aided design) program. Various versions were drawn up in different sizes. One problem was that they had no idea what the shrinkage ratio would be when the pieces were finally cast. To be certain they could produce the pistol within the time frame, it was decided to cast pieces in different sizes and test fit

them on the Taurus. Wax models were produced on a 3D wax printer and bronze castings were made by a jeweler. Finally they had a set just the right size, and another was made for the second pistol.

The Taurus' original grip was very small as the revolver is designed as a concealment sidearm. It wasn't at all in keeping with the large and robust captain's pistol. The original grip frame was chopped and discarded. A new frame was designed in CAD and produced from steel stock which was cut to shape with a high-pressure water jet. The witness marks from the cutting jet are visible on the side of the frame. To allow the revolver to operate, the Taurus' mainspring was reseated in the new frame. The grip panels themselves are carved from American Walnut wood and stained to a rich, reddish brown color. The final finish on the polished bronze shrouds is Plum Brown Barrel Finish, a chemical surface treatment. This was applied and left to weather naturally with use and handling, giving the prop the look of a weapon which isn't new and has probably spent a lot of time in its holster.

To load Mal's pistol, simply undo the thumb-screw on the pistol's left side, as held. As the screw retracts, the middle shroud will be released. The Taurus revolver is then visible inside the casing. The cylinder release catch is still present and functional on the revolver, but the bulky thumb-tab has been replaced by a low-profile brass piece. Push the cylinder release forward and the cylinder will swing out on its crane, through the gap where the side shroud was. Empty and reload as normal. Swing the cylinder back in and replace the shroud plate, tighten the thumbscrew and you're ready to defend some honor.

In the hand, the pistol initially feels a bit nose-heavy. The Colt single-action revolvers feel this way too, to start with. Like the Colt revolvers, the pistol does have that rare quality in a handgun — pointability. It seems to point naturally at the target. It isn't a light prop, the steel revolver and brass casings all add up to a hefty 1.48 kg (3.26 lbs), but it doesn't feel clumsy or awkward in any way. Holding it makes you want to do something just and reckless. Something brave but misguided. Like a Big Damn Hero.

RANDY ERIKSEN

Prop master Randy Eriksen: "Of course Mal's pistol was manufactured. We went through the design process, several drawings to get a look. We did a lot of research on the Civil War revolvers and kind of manipulating them and stretching them a little bit. To have it look like brass or bronze. Applied Effects did great work for me on that gun."

MAL'S HOLSTER

It's a great Western tradition to wear a sidearm proudly on display on the gunfighter's leg. Not only is this an essential show of force to ward off the more casual would-be aggressor, but it's also a purely practical arrangement. The hand hangs naturally at mid-thigh, the ideal location for the gun. The holster must be secure so the weapon doesn't fall out, it must allow an easy and fast draw (as the owner's life may depend on it) and it must be well made to stand up to the rigors of the trail.

Brennan Byers, of GBB Custom Gunleather in Los Angeles, has been handcrafting leather since he was ten. When Mal needed a gun rig, he was the logical choice to make it. "I went to the studio and met with Nathan to measure him, and I remember it seemed like he'd just got the call. He was beaming and very excited about the part. The first thing I said was 'Congratulations'. To be honest, sometimes when you hear an actor has landed a plum job, you think uncharitable things because maybe that actor is so unpleasant. With Nathan, I just felt really happy for him. He was on cloud nine and you were right there with him — what a nice guy."

The holster itself was constructed using traditional methods. Oak-tanned, five to six ounce (weight per square foot) carving leather, with no bug-bites or scars, was used for the exterior, and a soft 'Kip' leather for the lining. "I knew the show was set in space, but with Western influences too. I decided to hide any modern-looking hardware by lining the holster." Recalls Byers. "I only had Nathan for one initial fitting, so I made the holster adjustable for three hanging positions. The adjustment snaps were set in the leather first and then the back of the fittings covered by the lining. The lining also protects the gun from being scratched when drawn or being carried in the holster."

The pistol is retained in the holster by means of a 'thumb-break'. This is a strap which fits over the hammer of the pistol when in the holster. When the pistol is drawn, the natural action of gripping the weapon causes the thumb to pop the snap open on the strap, freeing the piece. The snap is positioned between the holster and the body so it is hidden from view when the holster is secure.

"I called the studio to tell them when the holster was done and they asked me if I thought it needed anything else. I said a leg-tie would be a good idea." A leg-tie is a simple leather thong, attached to the barrel end of the holster. It's tied around the wearer's leg and its job is to keep the holster down when the gun is drawn.

"I think they made a few changes after it was delivered. They put a strap and buckle around the middle, and it looks like they armed someone with some sandpaper! I appreciate the need for this; the holster has to look like it's been around."

❖ Below: Nathan Fillion wears the 'Number 1' Browncoat, one of three made for the series.

❖ Right top: The drawn on 'bullethole' on the Number 1 Browncoat.

❖ Right middle: The 'Hero' coat has a more detailed cut and sewn bullethole.

❖ Right bottom: Buckle detail.

The symbol of 'Browncoats' the world over, Mal's coat came about as the result of a collaboration between costume designer Shawna Trpcic and leather artist Jonathan A. Logan. Shawna and Jonathan are old friends and they've worked together on many TV shows. Shawna contacted Jonathan about making some garments for *Firefly* and took her conceptual sketches to show him.

When expensive material like deerskin is used for a garment, an initial conceptual proof is made in the shape of a cloth mock-up. The design is tweaked until it is approved. Leather samples are carefully selected and the right material for the job is chosen; in this case, domestic-farmed deerskin, dyed a deep mahogany. The closures were custom made in antique-finished brass. The oval clasps have a concealed spring-clip underneath to keep them securely closed. The sleeves of the coat appear to be leather trimmed but are, in fact, the very long sleeves themselves folded back to show the inside of the deerskin – a feature of Oriental robes where the sleeves are often lined with silk of a different color.

The coat embodies the very spirit of the production design of *Firefly*: East meets West. Although steeped in the traditions of Western, Victorian and Civil War garments, it still manages to evoke its oriental influences with flair. In all, three coats were made for Mal. They were sent to the studio in pristine condition and then dirtied-down by Shawna herself, to give them a lived-in look. Unlined, it's not the coat of a rich man or core-planet dandy.

Jonathan describes it: "I do love that coat, a warrior's coat, kind of like a kimono. Three-quarter length is great for heroes' coats, I think. It looks rugged and tough and it could give a very masculine presence to the person who wears it. It automatically looks like you're standing in the wind."

❖ Top: Front and back views of the Hero Browncoat.

❖ Above left: The Number 1 Browncoat.

❖ Above right: Shawna Trpcic's original design.

BUSHWHACKED

Written & Directed by Tim Minear

TIM MINEAR

"I felt really confident after 'Bushwhacked'," says Tim Minear. Detailing how the episode was developed, he adds, "Early on, I don't know that there really was a writers' room per se. Joss and I were still pretty much doing it ourselves, while we were looking for writers and hiring people. I do remember that 'Bushwhacked', being as close to 'The Train Job' as it was, was still servicing certain things because we didn't have the pilot aired and also because we were still trying to get the network on board. The network really, *really* hated the Western element, so my feeling on this episode was to try to keep it all in spaceships so it wouldn't have the onus of sage and tumbleweed. I think with 'Bushwhacked', at least the things I was attempting to do made sense for a second or third episode. If you look at it, every scene is a little piece of exposition. You want to reiterate the concept for the first few episodes, particularly when it's such a complicated concept; you kind of have to do it.

"So we wanted to make something scary because we had just done something funny ['The Train Job']. Plus, I was still trying to set up two things: the universe and the characters. I set up the universe by exploring the two extremes — the Reavers and the Alliance. The first half of the episode is about the Reavers and the second half is about the Alliance. In the first half they come upon this ship, and it's about homesteaders and regular people trying to get by. It's about the savagery of being too far away from civilization. The second half was about civilization being *so* civilized that it becomes this collectivist, bureaucratic behemoth that can't get anything done, and it's trying to control you too much. Really the story is about how our people inhabit a space in between those two extremes. The other thing I was trying

to do was, once again, establish who everyone was. The centerpiece of that episode is the interrogation. I needed some device in order to have these people talk explicitly about who they were. The whole interrogation scene, all the way to the reveal of Simon and River outside of the ship, it's like a movement of music. The inter-cutting of everyone being interrogated, building to, 'If those kids are on that ship, we will find them', and then pulling out from the dining room and then all the way out to Serenity, that's my favorite thing in the episode.

"I was trying to explain the world, the concept, the universe, and the characters. It's almost like a pencil sketch of what the show is. I don't think the episode gets under the skin of anything emotionally and it's not intended to do that. We hadn't earned anyone's allegiance to any of these characters in order to persuade them to identify with anybody emotionally. When you step back from it, like a painting, really what you see are the extremes of savagery and bureaucracy. It looks like they have no rules and it's just chaos, which is the metaphor of the whole Calvinball game at the beginning, they really do know what the rules are, even though to Simon it looks like there are none.

"It was the first one I directed and it was so much fun. There were three spaceships and it was just great, huge, giant fun. We found this great spaceship for the derelict on a stage in the San Fernando Valley. I think it was the set they used on *Power Rangers* or some kids show. It was a really cheesy spaceship set, but it worked perfectly. We took a piece of the airlock with us to the Valley so it looks like they are actually walking off of a giant hangar in Serenity into the airlock that is directly on this other ship."

TEASER

INT. SERENITY - CARGO BAY

BANG! MAL lands hard against a wall. Ouch. He's sweaty, out of breath. We're in the middle of some violence. Now a winded ZOE appears, coming to his aid.

MAL
We're dead.

ZOE
I believe we still have a shot, sir.

MAL
Haven't really learned a terrible lot about losing — have you, Zoe?

ZOE
Only since I've been under your command, sir.

MAL
Fair.

She pulls him back into the fray of a BASKETBALL GAME. Or some raucous, post-modern version of

one, anyway. BOOK joins them as they head back into it —

BOOK
I think we've got 'em on the run now!

MAL
Our cunning strategy of getting our asses plainly whooped must be starting to confound 'em.

The teams are: MAL, ZOE, BOOK versus JAYNE, KAYLEE, WASH. It's a messy free-for-all, with everyone pretty much all over the place. Kaylee has the ball, gets past Mal, passes over to Wash. Wash shoots to a sideways hoop which hangs high, connected to the hoist chain. Scores!

Mal goes after the ball, but Jayne barrels through, steals it, drives past Book, past Zoe, passes the ball back to Wash. Wash dribbles, looks for an opening.

WASH
Somebody cover my wife.

JAYNE
(has appeared at his side)

Everytime you ain't lookin'.

Jayne moves off. Wash to Kaylee:

WASH
He's dampening my team spirit.

Kaylee has noticed —

— SIMON appears on the uppermost catwalk level with RIVER. Here to watch. Kaylee sees him, grins. Simon smiles.

KAYLEE
Gimme the ball.

He does. She drives forward, Mal tries to intercept, but she sidesteps him.

He goes sprawling. Kaylee, intensely aware of the handsome Doctor watching, shoots — scores!

MAL
(aside to Zoe)
Don't s'pose I could threaten to put her off the boat, she does that again?

ZOE
You could, sir. But she's the only one who knows how anything works.

MAL
There's a point.

The bash and crash of the game resumes. Jayne gets the ball, passes it, but Zoe intercepts. It's keep-away time.

INARA emerges from her shuttle. Smiles at the camaraderie.

Wash scoops up the ball. Zoe is hot on him. Kaylee clatters to an upper level. Wash passes over Zoe's head, Kaylee catches the ball. Mal tears off after her, coming up the steps, gonna get her from behind.

KAYLEE
Ah! Jayne!

Jayne runs up, gets under Kaylee and she climbs up on his shoulders. She just escapes Mal. As she rides Jayne toward the hoop, she sees —

— Inara is moving along the catwalk, over to:

SIMON
Hello.

Kaylee shoots. Misses. Badly. The rest of the players dive in. The chaos is on again, as above...

Inara stands next to Simon. They both watch

the game.

INARA
Who's winning?

SIMON
I can't really tell... they don't seem to be playing by any civilized rules that I know.

INARA
Well, we're pretty far from civilization.

She glances over at River who seems delighted with the game unfolding below her, but we can just see that her mouth is moving, muttering to herself...

INARA (cont'd)
How is she?

SIMON
She's... good. Better. She has her days.

INARA
Don't we all.

SIMON
There're even moments when she seems like the little sister I used to know... but then it passes. She still won't talk about what it was they did to her at the Academy.

INARA
Perhaps she's not sure herself.

SIMON
She dreams about it. I know that much. Nightmares. I can't begin to imagine what the government...
(then)
You know I supported Unification?

INARA
So did I.

SIMON
I believed everything they told us. How the Alliance would solve our problems. Right the wrongs. I wanted to be a part of that.

INARA
Things are better for a great many.

SIMON
It would have been unthinkable, three years ago, that I'd be on a ship like this, with people like that.

INARA
They're good people.

SIMON
Yes. And I'm grateful. Very grateful that Captain Reynolds has allowed us to remain on board. I just... I don't know if I'll be able to help her here. And I need to help her.

INARA
Simon. You are. I think your sister understands what you risked to rescue her from that place... leaving your whole world behind. That was incredibly selfless.

SIMON
I "selflessly" turned us both into wanted fugitives.

INARA
(a wistful smile)
Well. We're all running from something, I suppose.

He looks at her, curious. She doesn't expound. But her wise smile hints at something. The moment is interrupted by an ELECTRONIC BEEP-ING, an alert.

The game is halted as everyone reacts to the BEEPING.

ZOE
Proximity alert. Must be comin' up on some-thin'...

WASH
Oh, gawd! What could it beee? We're dooomed! Who's flyin' this thing?
(then, deadpan)
Oh. Right. That'd be me. Back to work.

He tosses the ball to the others, heads off.

KAYLEE
Hey, guess that leaves us a man short, don't it?

JAYNE
Little Kaylee's always a "man short".

Kaylee slugs Jayne in the arm as she calls up to:

KAYLEE
Say, Doc? Why don't you come on down, play for our side. Inara won't mind.

INT. SERENITY - BRIDGE

Wash arrives on the bridge, the proximity alert still beeping. Through the cockpit window —

A DERELICT SHIP

A vessel about the size of Serenity, eerily

rolling in space.

Wash slides into the pilot's seat, absently switches off the alert, leans forward peering through the window to get a better look at the... DEAD BODY that lolls into view, directly in front of him. Eyes just black staring sockets in a pruned-up purple face, mouth stretched back in a grimace. Wash recoils with a start, instinctively grabs the controls and banks the ship hard.

INT. SERENITY - CARGO BAY

Simon is coming down the metal steps as the ship lurches. Simon grabs hold of the rail, manages not to take a tumble. Everyone reacts to the sudden shift —

INT. SERENITY - BRIDGE

The entire gang, Mal leading, appears.

MAL
Wash, you have a stroke or something?

WASH
Near enough.

ZOE
What happened...?

She trails off as they all now see the derelict ship.

JAYNE
<Wuh de ma.> [Mother of god.]

MAL
Anyone home?

WASH
Been hailing her. But if whoever's there's as healthy as the guy we just ran over, can't imagine they'll be pickin' up.

MAL
Bring us in a little closer.

WASH
Get you close enough to ring the doorbell.

SIMON
What is it?

Everyone craning to get a good look now at the dead ship just rolling, rolling... We move past this discussion to find...

...River who has pressed herself tight against the wall in the foredeck hall, just outside the cockpit. From where she is she can't see the ship, and still she says to herself:

RIVER
Ghosts.

Off that —

BLACK OUT.

END OF TEASER

ACT ONE

INT. SERENITY - BRIDGE

Where we left off. Everyone eyeing the derelict ship silently spinning in the distance.

MAL
So what do we figure? Transport ship?

WASH
(nods)
Converted cargo hauler or short range scow, maybe.

KAYLEE
You can see she don't wanna be parked like that. Port thrust's gone, which is makin' her spin like she is.

SIMON
A short range vessel? This far out into space?

WASH
Retrofitted to carry passengers.

ZOE
Travelers pick 'em up cheap at government auction. A few modifications and they serve well enough for a one-way push to the outer planets.

BOOK
(realizing)
Settlers.

WASH
Probably squeeze fifteen, maybe twenty families on a boat that size, you pack 'em tight enough.

INARA
Families...

JAYNE
Tell you what I think. I figure that fella we ran into did everyone on board, killed 'em all, then decided to go for a swim, see how fast his blood'd boil out his ears.

WASH
You're a very "up" person.

BOOK
Shouldn't we report this?

MAL
To who? Alliance? Right, 'cause they're gonna run right out here lickety-split, make sure these taxpayers are okay.

BOOK
Then we'll have to.

JAYNE
Rudderless boat this far out, probably canned fish by now.

KAYLEE
You can't know that for sure.

JAYNE
If there's folks in need of help, why ain't they beaming no distress call?

ZOE
(to Mal)
It's true. There's no beacon.

MAL
(taking her meaning)
Which means it's likely nobody's looking to find 'er.

BOOK
All the more reason for us to do the right thing.

JAYNE
How 'bout you just say a prayer while we slide on by? That oughta do it.

BOOK
Shall I remind you of the story of the Good Samaritan?

MAL
Rather you didn't.
(then)
But we will check it out.

JAYNE
So we a search and rescue tug now?

MAL
No. But the Shepherd's not wrong. Could be survivors. And if not, well — then no one's gonna mind if we take a look around, see if there's not something of value they might've left behind.

JAYNE
(hadn't thought of that)
Right. Yeah... No. Someone could be hurt.

MAL
(as he goes)
Wash, hook us up.

EXT. SPACE

Serenity is piloted in close, locks into the spin-cycle of the derelict ship. Ka-chunk — Serenity's airlock latches onto the other ship's standard matching bulkhead.

As it does, WE SEE a web of insect like electronic tentacles attach themselves at the seam. RED LIGHTS within this weird network start blinking...

INT. SERENITY - CARGO BAY

Simon appears, entering. He's carrying his portable med-kit. He slows and stops as he sees —

SIMON'S POV

over near the airlock, Mal and Zoe suiting up (there are several spacesuits hanging there), going through the checklist as they prepare to board the derelict.

JAYNE (O.S.)
Where you think you're headed?

Jayne is there, stepping up behind Simon. We see he's loading Zoe's shotgun, prepping weapons.

SIMON
I thought I'd offer my services, in case anyone on board required medical attention.

JAYNE
Yeah, well, Cap and Zoe are going in first. We'll holler if we need ya.

Simon's not looking at Jayne, a bit spellbound, watching as Mal and Zoe pull on their helmets. Jayne reads Simon's discomfort at the suits, smiles.

JAYNE (cont'd)
Somethin' wrong?

SIMON
Hmmm? Oh. No. I... I suppose it's just the thought of a little mylar and glass being the only thing separating a person from... nothing.

JAYNE
Impressive what "nothing" can do to a man. Like that feller we bumped into. Yeah. He's likely stuck up under our belly about now. That's what space trash does, ya know. Kinda latches onto the first big somethin' stops long enough. Hey — now that'd be a bit like you and your sister, wouldn't it?

Jayne works the pump action on the shotgun. Cha-chunk. He crosses off, toward Mal and Zoe. Off Simon —

INT. SERENITY - CARGO BAY/AIRLOCK

Mal's gloved hand hits the airlock control button. WHOOSH. The door opens. Mal and Zoe, fully suited and armed, step into the airlock. The door closes behind them.

INT. SERENITY - AIRLOCK

Mal speaks to Wash through the com-link in his suit.

MAL
Okay, Wash. Ask Serenity to knock for us.

WASH (O.S.)
Just as nice as you please...

A light on the derelict's airlock door goes from RED to GREEN. WHOOSH. It opens. A beat. Mal and Zoe fire up their flashlights, enter into —

INT. DERELICT

They take a few steps and — THUNK. The airlock door shuts automatically behind them. The ship is running on emergency power only. Footlights marking the way. Mal and Zoe move with caution, their weapons at the ready. As they go:

MAL
Emergency power's up. Dashboard light.

We move with them as they step carefully down the dark passageways. They pass an abandoned child's TRICYCLE. Share a look, keep moving, to

INT. DERELICT - MESS HALL

Mal and Zoe enter. They both stop, look to —

— cafeteria style. Several tables set up. A high chair here and there. Slop counter with sneeze guard. And here's what's weird — plates of food in various states of being consumed. Big ladles still buried in (gnarly old looking) grub in the tins behind the slop counter. Evidence that folks were in line with trays.

MAL
Whatever happened here happened quick.

Zoe nods. Mal starts moving again. Zoe follows, to —

INT. DERELICT - BRIDGE - CONTINUOUS

They enter the bridge — more of the same,

basically: a book is open, coffee cup, some board game in mid-play, etc. More personal detail which suggests habitation. But no people. Zoe looks at the controls, computers, etc.

ZOE
Everything was left on... Ship powered down on its own.
(continues looking)
No sign of struggle. Just —

MAL
— gone.

As Zoe moves to the control panels:

ZOE
(seeing something)
Sir.

He moves to her.

ZOE (cont'd)
Personal log. Someone was in the middle of an entry —

Her look says "shall I?" Mal nods. Zoe hits the log button — and the screen BURSTS with EAR PIERCING STATIC.

INT. SERENITY - RIVER'S QUARTERS

River sits up INTO FRAME, sweaty and freaked — GASPS.

Simon pushes into her room, never far from her. He moves to her bed, kneels down.

SIMON
Shhh. It's okay. I'm here. Bad dreams again?

RIVER
(shakes her head "no")
No. Can't sleep. Too much screaming.

He looks at her, his sadness for her state right there on his face. Gently:

SIMON
River. There is no screaming.

She looks at him, utterly lucid, and says, darkly:

RIVER
There was.

He holds her look for a beat. He starts a bit at —

JAYNE
Grab your med-kit and let's hoof it. Mal wants us both over there on the double.

Jayne is at the door, loading (yet another) weapon.

SIMON
They've found survivors?

JAYNE
(shrugs)
Didn't say.

SIMON
Right.
(torn)
I'll ask Inara to look in on River.

JAYNE
Yeah, whatever. I ain't waiting.
(as he goes)
Meet you over there. But don't take forever. Still gotta get suited up.

And he exits. Off Simon —

INT. DERELICT

The airlock door opens revealing... SIMON. All packed into one of the suits. He loathes this. He looks into the dark, creepy derelict. Hesitates. Finally he steps across the threshold.

WHOMP. The door shuts behind him. His breathing becomes more rapid.

As he moves, we play a lot of this from his point of view... through the faceplate of the helmet... that thin, transparent sliver of life. The building rhythm of his BREATHING practically scoring this sequence.

INT. DERELICT - MESS HALL

As Simon continues his tense passage.

INT. DERELICT - BRIDGE - CONTINUOUS

Simon comes around a corner, sees —

Mal, Zoe, Jayne and Kaylee. All of them spacesuit-and-helmet-less, having a conversation he can't hear. Simon reacts. So do the others. Bemused, Simon clutches at his helmet. It's not coming off. Kaylee runs to him, helps him with it. He's gasping for breath. Before Simon can ask anything —

MAL
What are you doing here?
(also)
And what's with the suit?

Simon glances over to Jayne who's trying to stifle his gales of laughter. Simon's furious, humiliated.

SIMON
(glaring at Jayne)
Oh, you're hilarious. Sadist.

MAL
(forces back his own smile)
All right. That's enough. We ain't got time for games.
(to Simon)
Long as you're here, you might as well lend a hand. You can run with Kaylee.

He tosses Simon a canvas loot bag. (Mal and the others also have their portable salvage kits with them now.)

MAL (cont'd)
Let's do this quick, people. Coupla loads each. No need to be greedy.

SIMON
Where are all the people?

MAL
Ship says the lifeboat launched more'n a week ago. We're gonna assume everyone got off okay. Anyway, we're just here to pick the bones. You two start in the engine room. Jayne, take the galley.

They head off. As they go:

KAYLEE
(re: helmet)
You had this on wrong.

That's kind of a horrible thought. Simon blanches. Makes Jayne laugh all the harder. Once Mal and Zoe are alone:

ZOE
Sir... I count sixteen families signed on. Lifeboat wouldn't hold a third of that.

MAL
I know.
(into transmitter)
Wash? Any luck?

INTERCUT WITH:

INT. SERENITY - BRIDGE - CONTINUOUS

Up on the screen, ship schematics. Wash scrolls through.

WASH
Think I found something pretty well matches that class. Layout looks about right. Seems to me any valuables, if there are any, likely be stored somewhere in C-deck, aft.

MAL (O.S.)
Good work. Keep the motor running. Won't be long.

Wash signs off, leans back/swivels in his chair. Sees Book standing in the doorway behind him.

BOOK
Can't say I much care for this business.

WASH
It's abandoned, Shepherd.

BOOK
And if that's the result of some violence? What if that ship's a crime scene?

WASH
Well — if it wasn't before, it certainly is now.

Book smiles unhappily at the attitude.

INT. SERENITY - PASSAGEWAYS

Inara approaches River's quarters with a tray of food. Knocks. No answer.

INARA
River? It's Inara. Are you hungry, sweetie?

She pushes the door open...

INARA (cont'd)
I brought you a little...

Inara reacts. The room is empty.

INARA (cont'd)
River?

Off the empty room —

INT. DERELICT - AIRLOCK

The door opens with a WHOOSH, revealing River. The gust from the door gently blowing her hair. She seems to be in an almost trance-like state. Barefoot, she pads onto the derelict ship.

INT. DERELICT - PASSAGEWAYS

Mal and Zoe arrive at a storage door.

MAL
This'd be it.

ZOE
(tries it)
Locked.

MAL
Well — now I'd say that's like to be a very good sign.

He brings up a mini-blowtorch. Sparks it.

INT. DERELICT - ENGINE ROOM

Kaylee and Simon going through the engine room. Kaylee examines the machinery.

SIMON
Aren't you the least bit curious?

KAYLEE
'Bout what?

SIMON
Well — what happened here. Why would anyone abandon their ship in the middle of nowhere like this?

KAYLEE
Oh, all sorts of reasons...
(as she realizes)
Just... not mechanical...

SIMON
What?

KAYLEE
(a little surprised)
Well.. there ain't nothing wrong with this. Not that I can see, anyhow. Some of this's like new.

SIMON
Well, that makes it even more...

KAYLEE
(brightening)
Oooh, here's a good'n!
(as she pries away)

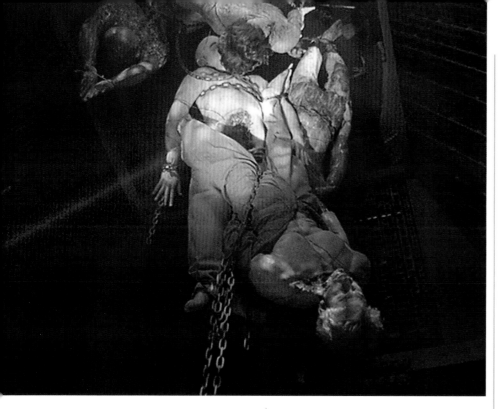

Hold the bag open.

She starts tossing pieces in, as —

INT. DERELICT - MESS HALL

Jayne tears the place apart, loading up, and snacking. He pauses, thinks he senses something. Takes out his gun... moves to the door. Nothing. He resumes his work, as —

INT. DERELICT - PASSAGEWAYS

River haunts this place like a ghost herself, drifting along, drawn by something —

INT. DERELICT - STORAGE ROOM

THUNK. The blowtorched door falls forward. Mal and Zoe enter. Very dim light in here. They use their flashlights.

Zoe whips a tarp off some crates, cracks one open. Within, family photo albums, heirlooms, like that. She runs her light along the front of the other crates — various FAMILY NAMES emblazoned there. All personal stuff.

MAL
Here —

Zoe joins him. Their FLASHLIGHT BEAMS illuminate stacks of government issue terraforming supplement materials. They are emblazoned with the AngloSino insignia of the Alliance.

MAL (cont'd)
Gen-seed, protein, crop supplements. Everything a growing family needs for a fresh start on a new world.

ZOE
Hard subsidies for fourteen plus families... that's...

MAL
...about a fortune.
(rising)
We forget the rest and just take this stuff. We'll need a hand hauling it out of here.

ZOE
Sir... even on a lifeboat. You'd think those who escaped would have found room for some of this.

MAL
(looking past her)
No one escaped...

ZOE
Sir?

MAL
I'm feelin' like nobody left this boat. Nobody...

She turns to see what he's looking at... Standing in the storage room doorway is...

RIVER. She seems to not even notice the two of them, her attention is directed above them. Mal turns, aims his flashlight upward, way up, into an overhead shaft. Zoe reacts with disgust...

THE BODIES

are strung up from the ceiling. Three clumps of twisted flesh. The skin pale, almost luminescent (the bits of it we do see).

ZOE
There's no blood. Not a drop anywhere...

MAL
<Jen dao mei!> [Just our luck!]
(pulls transmitter)
I know what did this.

River starts to wander in.

MAL (cont'd)
(re: River)
Keep her out of here.

Zoe moves to do that, as —

MAL (cont'd)
(into transmitter)
Jayne —

INT. DERELICT - MESS HALL

Jayne gorges and gathers — Mal's voice from his transmitter.

MAL (O.S.)
Jayne — drop what you're doing and get to the engine room. I want you to take Kaylee and the Doctor off this boat.

Jayne reaches for it, his mouth is full. He swallows, puts the transmitter to his mouth — but that's when the attack comes. The THING that ATTACKS him from behind is a BLUR. It comes so fast, so violently, he never had a chance to respond at all. Off his fallen transmitter and Mal's voice:

MAL (cont'd; O.S.)
Jayne? Jayne, do you read? Jayne?!

BLACK OUT.

END OF ACT ONE

ACT TWO

EXT. SPACE

Serenity still attached to the rotating derelict, as —

INT. SERENITY - BRIDGE

Wash sits up straight in his chair as he hears MUFFLED GUNFIRE over the two-way. He pounds on the mic —

WASH
Captain? Captain?
(then)
Zoe?

More GUNFIRE.

INT. DERELICT - PASSAGEWAYS

Mal and Zoe, who is steering River by the shoulders, emerge. Mal has his gun out. So does Zoe.

ZOE
Came from above, sir.

MAL
Galley —

They start to move but nearly collide with —

SIMON AND KAYLEE

coming around the corner, reacting to the

gunfire. Kaylee gasps, realizes it's Mal.

KAYLEE
We heard shootin' —

SIMON
River...? What are you...

RIVER
I followed the voices.

SIMON
(moves to her)
Don't ever leave the ship. Not ever.

MAL
(on the alert, to Simon, re: River)
Handle her, will you, son?

WASH (O.S.)
What the <tyen shiao duh> [name of all that's sacred] is going on in there?!

ZOE
(into transmitter, quickly and professionally)
Not now, dear.

She clicks him off. Nods to Mal that she's ready to roll. Together they move off, guns leading the way...

INT. DERELICT - MESS HALL

Tense beat as Mal enters the mess hall, his gun leading. Evidence of violence, upturned table, gross food on the floor. A noise — Mal whips around with his gun... and finds himself drawing down on...

JAYNE

who has his gun pointed right back at Mal. They both relax. Jayne is a bit mussed, but not really hurt.

MAL
What'd you see?

JAYNE
Didn't. Came at me from behind. Big, though. Strong. Think I mighta hit him.

Simon has entered with Kaylee and River.

SIMON
You did...

Simon points to tell-tale blood droplets. Mal moves to him, notes that the blood droplets lead to a grate in the wall. Mal eases Simon out of the way. Indicates to Zoe to hand him her shotgun. He pushes the grate up with the nose of it.

WALL GRATE

Mal's face appears. He squints at —

A YOUNG MAN

cowering in the shadows. He's feral, fearful, drawing himself as small as he can.

SURVIVOR
(muttering)
Mercy... mercy... no. Mercy.

MAL
Easy, now. Nobody's gonna hurt you.
(noticing gunshot wound in arm)
Anymore than we already did...

SURVIVOR
No mercy...

MAL
Oh, we got mercy. We got lots and lots of —

WHAM!, suddenly Mal comes up and gives the poor bastard the butt of the shotgun right in the kisser.

MESS HALL

As Mal pulls the unconscious guy out through the hole and lets him drop to the floor, a heap. Not big at all, just average. Practically a kid.

SIMON
(to Jayne)
Oh, yes. He's a real beast. It's a wonder you're still alive.

JAYNE
(confounded)
Looked bigger when I couldn't see him.

MAL
(grim)
Let's get him out of here.

INT. SERENITY - OUTSIDE INFIRMARY

In the common area are Inara, Kaylee, Jayne, Zoe, Wash. Book is there, too, sitting, clutching his bible. Kaylee and Inara are watching as inside the infirmary Simon can be seen tending to the Survivor, Mal over his shoulder.

INARA
I wonder how long he'd been living like that?

KAYLEE
Dunno. Must be real brave, though. Surviving like that when no one else did.

JAYNE
Yeah, a real hero. Killin' all them people.

KAYLEE
What? No. We don't believe that.
(turns toward Zoe)
We don't, do we?

ZOE
Captain wouldn't have brought him on board were that the case.

But she doesn't sound as convinced as she might.

INT. SERENITY - INFIRMARY

Simon has patched up the arm wound. The patient mutters in his delirium.

SIMON
Pulse is rapid, blood pressure's high side of normal. To be expected.

SURVIVOR
Weak. They were all weak.

SIMON
Other than the bullet wound, there doesn't appear to be any exterior trauma. Though that crack to the head you gave him probably didn't do him any good.

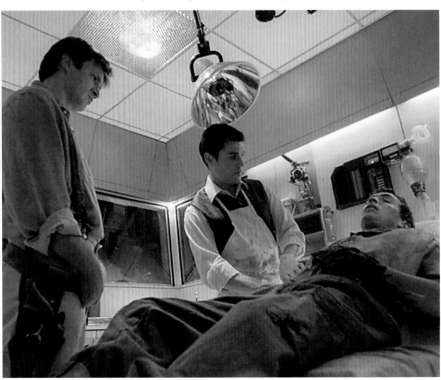

The patient rises up a bit, tries to focus on the faces outside the glass. This isn't lost on Mal.

SURVIVOR
Cattle. Cattle for the slaughter.

MAL
Dope him.

SIMON MAL
I don't think that's — Just do it.

Simon moves to load a syringe. Mal eyes the muttery patient.

SURVIVOR
No mercy... No resistance...

Simon leans over him. The man's hand grabs Simon's wrist.

SURVIVOR (cont'd)
Open up. See what's inside.

Simon gives him a shot. Pulls away from the man's weak grip.

MAL
Let's chat.

Mal moves to the door. Simon glances at his patient, who is slipping into semi-consciousness. He follows to —

INT. SERENITY - OUTSIDE INFIRMARY DOOR

As Simon appears here, he looks to Inara.

SIMON
River?

INARA
Resting in my shuttle. Not to disparage the other accommodations on this ship, but I think she'll find it more comfortable. And the door locks.

SIMON
Thank you.

KAYLEE
So? How's our patient?

SIMON
Aside from borderline malnutrition, he's in remarkably good health.

BOOK
(some relief)
So he'll live, then?

SIMON
Yes.

MAL
Which, to my mind, is unfortunate.

The others react, surprised.

BOOK
Not a very charitable attitude, Captain.

MAL
Charity'd be putting a bullet in his brainpan.

INARA
Mal!

MAL
Only save him the suffering.

Mal shuts the infirmary door, bolts it from the outside.

MAL (cont'd)
Nobody goes in there. Nothing more we can do for him now. Not after what he's seen.

SIMON
What do you mean?

MAL
That ship was hit by Reavers.

Mal turns, heads off. The others don't follow right away as the horror hits them.

JAYNE
(fear)
Reavers...

Wash looks to Zoe who doesn't deny it — she knows it, too.

WASH
<Tzao gao.> [Crap.]

Inara glances back into the infirmary, where the man is writhing in his delirium. She knows what this means.

INT. SERENITY - DINING ROOM - CONTINUOUS

Mal's pouring himself some coffee as the others follow him in.

INARA
Mal, how can you know?

JAYNE
He don't, that's how. No way.

Mal sips his coffee. Whatever you say.

JAYNE (cont'd)
It was that other fella. The one we run into. It's like I said before — he went stir crazy, killed the rest, took a walk into space.

KAYLEE
A second ago you were saying —

JAYNE
Don't matter what I said.

MAL
One of 'em was just lucky enough to get out, that's all.

WASH
He was the lucky one?

MAL
Luckier'n the rest.

JAYNE
Couldn't be Reavers. Wasn't Reavers. Reavers don't leave no survivors.

MAL
Strictly speaking — wouldn't say they did.

BOOK
What are you suggesting?

MAL
Don't matter we took him off that boat, Shepherd. It's the place he's gonna live from now on.

BOOK
I don't accept that. Whatever horror he witnessed, whatever acts of barbarism, it was done by men. Nothing more.

JAYNE
Reavers ain't men.

BOOK
Of course they are. Too long removed from civilization, perhaps — but men. And I believe there's a power greater than men. A power that heals.

MAL
Reavers might take issue with that philosophy. If they had a philosophy. And if they weren't too busy gnawing on your insides.
(then)
Jayne's right. Reavers ain't men. Or they forgot how to be. Now they're just... nothing. They got out to the edge of the galaxy, to that place of nothing. And that's what they became.

JAYNE
Why we still sittin' here? If it was Reavers, shouldn't we be gone?

WASH
Have to say I was kinda wondering that myself.

MAL
Work ain't done. Substantial money value still sitting over there.

JAYNE
Pffft. I ain't going back in there with them bodies. No rutting way. Not if Reavers messed with 'em.

ZOE
(stop your blubbering)
Jayne. You'll scare the women.

SIMON
I'll go.

They all look at him.

SIMON (cont'd)
I've dealt with bodies. They don't worry me.

BOOK
I'd like to go with him. Maybe see what I can do about putting those folks to rest.

MAL
They're already "resting" pretty good, Shepherd. Reavers saw to that.

BOOK
How we treat our dead is part of what makes us different than those did the slaughtering.

MAL
(considers)
All right. You go say your words.
(then)
Jayne, you'll help the Doctor and Shepherd Book cut down those people. Then you'll load up the cargo.

JAYNE
I don't believe this. Now we're gonna sit put for a funeral?

MAL
Yes, Jayne. That's exactly what we're going to do. I won't have these people lookin' over my shoulder once we're gone. Now I ain't sayin' there is any peace to be had. But on the off chance there is — then those folks deserve a little of it.

JAYNE
<Fong luh.> [Loopy in the head.] All of you.

He storms off. Simon follows. Book takes a beat,

might say something, decides against it then goes. Kaylee's beaming at her Captain. Inara now moves to Mal.

INARA
And just when I think I've got you figured out.

She holds the look. Might kiss him. Doesn't. Instead she moves off. He watches her go.

KAYLEE
That was real pretty, Captain. What you said.

WASH
Didn't think you were one for rituals and such.

MAL
I'm not. But I figure it'll keep the others busy for awhile. No reason to concern them with what's to be done.

ZOE
Sir?

CUT TO:

INT. SERENITY - BRIDGE

Mal pulls a visual up on a screen. The tendril like booby trap connected where the two airlocks joined.

MAL
It's a real burden being right so often.

Wash, Zoe and Kaylee at his side, looking at the screen.

WASH
What is it?

MAL
Booby trap. Reavers sometimes leave 'em behind for the rescue ships. We triggered it when we latched on.

WASH
And when we detach —

MAL
— it blows.

WASH
Okay — so we don't detach. We just, I don't know, sit tight until...

ZOE
What? Reavers come back?

Kaylee's been studying the image on the vid screen.

KAYLEE
Looks like they've jerry-rigged it with a pressure catch. Only thing that'd work with all these spare parts. Could pro'lly bypass that easy, we get to the DC line.

MAL
You tell me now, little Kaylee — you really think you can do this?

KAYLEE
Sure. Yeah. Think so. 'Sides, if I mess up, it's not like you'll be able to yell at me.

EXT. SPACE

Serenity and the derelict, locked together in a death grip. And under the soundlessness of space, MUSIC, carrying us through...

INT. DERELICT - STORAGE

Simon, Jayne and Book all have paper dust masks on as they lower down the bodies. This is done in an elliptical way, more a suggestion of the carnage than a strict depiction.

INT. SERENITY - CARGO BAY

The bomb bay doors are pulled open by Mal. Kaylee climbs in first, then Wash. Mal and Zoe stand topside, nervous.

INT. SERENITY - INFIRMARY

The tortured delirium of the survivor in his fever sleep. Somehow his distress seems to be affecting...

INT. SERENITY - INARA'S SHUTTLE

River, who is sleeping in Inara's bed. Her sleep becomes more and more fitful. Nearby, Inara reads a book, not yet noticing River's sleep become more and more agitated, as...

INT. SERENITY - INNARDS

Kaylee has to squeeze in tight to the confined space. She's looking at the seam where the two airlocks meet. The tendrils of the booby trap are visible, flashing RED.

WASH is in the pit, a bit above her, with a box full of tools. He hands her some wrench-like gadget. She blows a strand of hair out of her eyes, goes to work on the device.

INT. DERELICT - STORAGE

Jayne dragging crates, slamming them onto a dolly, looking over with some disdain, to —

Book reads from his bible, saying a few words for the dead. Simon shows respect, bowing his head.

INT. SERENITY - INARA'S SHUTTLE

Inara reacts now as she sees River's state, growing ever more agitated, as

INT. SERENITY - INFIRMARY

the patient's eyes SNAP OPEN.

INT. SERENITY - CARGO BAY

Kaylee working on the booby trap.

— Wash handing her down more tools.

— Mal and Zoe waiting helplessly, nervously, topside.

— Kaylee takes a stab at the booby trap. We see her recoil, nervous. Still here. She really concentrates, goes back at it. Cuts into some of the tubing and a dark OOZE drips out.

INT. SERENITY - INARA'S SHUTTLE

River's really thrashing now. Inara goes to her, gathers her in her arms, holds her close, tries to soothe her. River starts to calm, but GASPS with a START as...

INT. SERENITY - INFIRMARY

a drawer of SURGICAL TOOLS hits the floor, and with it returns the SYNCH SOUND. A HAND reaches in, picks up one of the more evocative- and lethal-looking surgical tools.

INT. SERENITY - CARGO BAY

WHOOSH — the airlock door opens and Jayne rolls in the dolly with the cargo. He reacts as he sees —

— CLANG. As the bomb bay doors are dropped shut. Mal, Kaylee, Wash and Zoe look over at him.

JAYNE
What's going on?

MAL
Not a thing.
(looks to Kaylee)
Right?

She nods her little greased smudged face.

KAYLEE
Not a gorramn thing.

Mal looks to Wash. Nods. Wash nods back, heads off.

JAYNE
Looks like a thing to me.

Book and Simon enter from the airlock. Mal hits the controls, closing it behind them:

MAL
Thought we might have had a situation, but it looks to be taken care of. Let's get that stuff stored.

Jayne, still not convinced, moves to the smuggling compartments, pops a panel.

MAL (cont'd)
(into transmitter)
Everybody's home, Wash. Let's go.

We HEAR the start of the detaching process.

EXT. SERENITY

As the two ships come apart, harmless remnants of the booby trap tearing away.

INT. SERENITY - CARGO BAY

Mal looks to Zoe and Kaylee. Now they can really breathe. In the b.g., Simon and Book move to Jayne.

Suddenly — that familiar PROXIMITY WARNING BEEPING. Everyone who was on pins and needles before is right back there — and Jayne freaks:

JEWEL STAITE

Jewel Staite on crawling in the vent: "It was built up on a platform, and it was a tiny, tiny little tunnel; there really wasn't much to crawl through. All the wires were filled with either water or this really weird oily substance. Tim Minear said, 'Just start fiddling around and then make a decision to cut one,' and I said, 'Which one should I cut?' and he said, 'Oh, whichever one you feel like cutting.' So the first take, I cut one and it was water, and that was fine. Then they reset the shot and I cut this other one and this weird oil came spurting out. It got me in the face, and it was gross and stank. I don't think they used that one, because I was sort of pissed off. I was like, 'Why didn't you tell me which one to cut?'" she laughs.

JAYNE

"Time for some thrilling heroics."

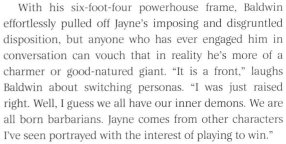

Every crew has one: that trigger-happy loose cannon who could explode at any given moment; the mercenary-for-hire whose top priorities are making a quick buck and bedding the ladies; the muscle who, even with his numerous faults, is invaluable in a scrap. On *Firefly*, that tough scruff is the man called Jayne Cobb, a character actor Adam Baldwin immediately latched on to. "Well, *Firefly* is a Western and I grew up watching Westerns like *The Magnificent Seven*, *The Wild Bunch*, *Once Upon A Time in the West*, *The Good, The Bad, and the Ugly*, movies like that," he explains. "I felt very comfortable slipping into such a role. I figured [adapting Jayne's drawl] 'Hell, I'll just try talking like this and see how far Joss lets me go.' I connected right away with the character and it fit at a time in my life where I was comfortable enough to stand there and just go broad. It can be a risky endeavor to go as broad as I did in some instances with Jayne, but Joss Whedon let me to a certain degree. That was sort of my deal with Joss: 'I'm gonna go as broad as I can in rehearsals and the first couple of takes and it is up to you to dial me back.' Once we had that communication established, you can find some things. You are not fearful of looking bad."

Despite carrying an extensive arsenal of guns including Jayne's beloved Vera, his other weapon of choice was a sharp wit and wounding sense of humor. "I forget the exact wording Joss used to describe Jayne but he was basically the guy who said what was on everybody's minds," says Baldwin. "It's like 'Cut to the chase guys! Quit your pussyfooting around and all your existential musings about the goodness of this existence. Let's go kill them!' I always thought of Jayne as this practical guy, a hands on problem solver — but selfish."

In fact with dialogue such as "Do you know what the chain of command is? It's the chain I go get and beat you with until you understand who's in rutting command here!" Jayne spouted some of the best lines of the series. "It's just the way I deliver them," chuckles Baldwin. "Everyone else had good lines too. I just said them better," he laughs. "I can say that now that I'm not on the show!"

With his six-foot-four powerhouse frame, Baldwin effortlessly pulled off Jayne's imposing and disgruntled disposition, but anyone who has ever engaged him in conversation can vouch that in reality he's more of a charmer or good-natured giant. "It is a front," laughs Baldwin about switching personas. "I was just raised right. Well, I guess we all have our inner demons. We are all born barbarians. Jayne comes from other characters I've seen portrayed with the interest of playing to win."

In 'The Message', viewers were treated to a glimpse of Jayne's family life when he received a letter and a knitted pompom hat from his dear old mom. "We kind of fantasized that Jayne was a middle-class cretin, not unlike the children of the late sixties, seventies, and eighties whose parents were a little bit too busy for them," offers Baldwin. "They got to the point where it was 'Screw this! I'm heading off to the Black! I want some adventure!' I think he had a good connection with his mom, and his dad not so much — but all this isn't Joss. He hadn't fleshed all that out because we only got to do half a season."

Captain Malcolm Reynolds recruited Jayne under strained circumstances and at times, the two experienced a volcanic relationship, although there was also respect and a warped loyalty there. "Jayne considers himself as a co-equal subservient," states Baldwin. "He considers himself a hired hand to Mal. His loyalty is as far as the money goes, although Mal's honor among thieves attitude had been growing on him. I think he was learning to respect that more. So they were sort of like brothers-in-arms."

However, their relationship was really put to the test when Jayne delivered Simon and River into the hands of the Alliance. "In 'Ariel', Mal knocks Jayne on the head with a wrench, throws him out the airlock and was going to space him," explains Baldwin. "Then Mal honors Jayne's last request to not tell the rest of the crew why he was dead. That was a turning point."

Joss is famous for killing off his characters but even at death's door, Baldwin wasn't worried about Jayne. "No, by then I was the favorite character on the show," he laughs. "Had that been the first episode, I'd have been worried. By then, I think my position was pretty secure."

JAYNE
No, no. Do not say that — it's the Reavers! Gorramn Reavers come back!

MAL
(already on the move)
Get that stuff stored.

JAYNE
Like it's gonna matter.

MAL
Just do it!

He's running, now. Zoe right behind him.

INT. SERENITY - BRIDGE

Wash just sits staring straight ahead, hasn't switched off the alert.

Mal and Zoe come running up the foredeck hall.

MAL
Reavers?

Wash absently shakes his head "no". A GREEN GLOW starts to overtake the cockpit. They all react as they see —

THROUGH THE COCKPIT WINDOW — outer space pretty well blotted out by the green glow of an enormous ALLIANCE CRUISER... Over the radio:

MALE VOICE (V.O.)
Firefly Class Transport, you are ordered to release control of your helm. Prepare to dock and be boarded.

MAL
Looks like civilization's finally caught up with us...

EXT. SPACE

Serenity dwarfed by the looming Alliance Cruiser.

And coming off the Alliance ship: several smaller GUNSHIPS, swarming around Serenity —

BLACK OUT.

END OF ACT TWO

ACT THREE

INT. ALLIANCE CRUISER

COMMANDER HARKEN watches from the bridge as Serenity moves toward us. An ENSIGN approaches. Harken points to Serenity.

HARKEN
No mandatory registration markings on the bow. Make sure we cite them for that. What is it, Ensign?

ENSIGN
Sir, we've identified the transport ship they were attached to. It was licensed to a group of families out of Bernadette. They were due to touch down in Newhall three weeks ago. Never made it. We've

DESIGNING THE 'VERSE

Prop master Randy Eriksen: "It was mixed technology from the brain of Joss Whedon. Starting with the whole look of the ship and the characters, it was very much influenced by the American Civil War. Especially the hand guns and the rifle. It really wasn't very 'spacey', we made a choice between Buck Rogers and the Old West, and this is like the Old West with some kind of technological twist in there. The Alliance was always glass and chrome and crisp and clean and bright, and everything else was all dingy and dirty and rusty and crappy. The Alliance look is what you classically think of as science fiction."

been hailing the vessel, get no response. It appears to be derelict.

HARKEN
Continue hailing. Once we secure these vultures, we'll send a team over. Check it out.

A RADIO OPERATOR sits at a communications station speaks:

RADIO OPERATOR
Didn't we have a flag a while back on a Firefly?

HARKEN
Check.

RADIO OPERATOR
Here it is. Alert issued for unidentified Firefly Class, believed to be carrying two fugitives. A brother and sister.

HARKEN
What are they wanted for?

RADIO OPERATOR
Not available. It's classified.

HARKEN
Forty thousand of these old wrecks in the air and that's all they give us? Well, I won't have any

surprises on a routine stop. We run into these two, we shoot first. Brass can sort it out later.

INT. SERENITY - CARGO BAY

Simon helps Jayne and Book finish loading the cargo into the smuggling hold. Mal appears, walking fast, entering the cargo bay. The three look over —

JAYNE
What was it? Was it Reavers?

MAL
Open the stash, pull out the goods.

JAYNE
What? Just got done putting it all in —

MAL
Yeah, and now I'm telling you to take it all out again.

JAYNE
Why for?

MAL
I got no notion to argue this. In about two minutes time this boat's gonna be crawling with Alliance.

SIMON
No...

Zoe, Wash and Kaylee appear. Kaylee hangs back, Zoe and Wash head further in, toward the others. Zoe and Wash help Book and Jayne with the goods. Simon's in a bit of shock.

SIMON (cont'd)
We've gotta run...

MAL
Can't run. They're pulling us in.

SIMON
If they find us they'll send River back to that place. To be tortured. I'd never see her again.

MAL
(to Jayne et al)
Stack everything right here in plain sight. Wouldn't want it to seem as if we're hiding anything. Might give them Alliance boys the wrong impression.

WASH
Or the right one.

MAL
That, too.

JOSS WHEDON

Obviously, 'Bushwhacked' had the basketball scene and a set with rotting food on it. Why they bothered to show rotting food, I don't know, but, man, that set was hard to be on. I think it is also an underrated episode. It was really an attempt to show just how creepy it could get out there, just how bad it was. And to show exactly where they were in the universe — caught between the most terrifying savages and the most antiseptic and annoying bureaucracy, and not really caring for either.

(turns to Simon)
Now run fetch your sister.

A beat. Simon suddenly becomes suspicious.

SIMON
What? Why? Are you going to put her in "plain sight", too?

MAL
Don't get tetchy. Just do as I say.

SIMON
Is that why you let us stay? So you could use us as bargaining chips?

JAYNE
I knew there was a reason!

SIMON
They're not taking her... and you're not giving her to them.

BOOK
(steps forward)
Don't be a fool, son. Do as the man says.

EXT. SPACE

As Serenity attaches to the bottom of the Alliance Cruiser, just a little bump now on the big ship.

INT. SERENITY - CARGO BAY

WHOOSH — the airlock doors open and a compliment of ALLIANCE SOLDIERS streams onto Serenity, their boots clicking on the hard cargo bay floor. Harken appears, looks at —

— Mal, Zoe, Jayne, Wash, Kaylee, Inara, Book, lined up. No sign of Simon or River. (We may or may not notice the smuggling compartments have been closed up again.)

Harken gives the signal to his lead man. Soldiers move in, start relieving our gang of any weapons.

MAL
Well now, ain't this a whole lotta fuss. I didn't know better, might think we were dangerous.

HARKEN
Is this your vessel?

MAL
It is. Bought and paid for. I'm Captain Malcolm Reynolds.

HARKEN
And is this everyone, Captain?

MAL
By way of crew, it is. Though you're gonna find in our infirmary a fella we rescued from that derelict. Saved him, guess you could say.

Harken nods to a couple of his guys, they head off.

MAL (cont'd)
(calling back)
Straight back, next to the common area.

HARKEN
(re: the goods)
And these items — I take it you "rescued" them as well?

INT. SERENITY - INFIRMARY

The two Alliance Soldiers force open the infirmary door. The operating table is empty. The place is a wreck. They look over, see something that WE DON'T. One of them turns away, loses his lunch right there. The other one reacts with similar, though less colorful, disgust. Off that —

INT. SERENITY - CARGO BAY

Harken eyes the "line up".

HARKEN
Looks to me like an illegal salvage operation.

MAL
Does it? That's discouraging.

HARKEN
Alliance property, too. You could lose your ship, Captain. But that's a wrist slap compared to the penalty for harboring fugitives. A brother and sister. When I search this vessel, I won't find them, will I?

MAL
No children on this boat.

HARKEN
I didn't say "children". Siblings. Adult siblings.

MAL
I misunderstood.

HARKEN
No chance they could have stowed-away? No one would blame you for that, Captain. I know how these older Firefly models often have those troublesome little nooks.

MAL
Do they?

HARKEN
Smugglers and the like tend to favor them for just that reason.

Now the two Alliance Soldiers return. The not-nauseated one approaches Harken. Whispers something to him. Harken eyes Mal, Mal looks back, wondering what's happened.

HARKEN (cont'd)
We'll continue this conversation in a more official capacity.

Harken motions to one of his men. Instantly some of the Alliance Men start to hustle our guys toward the door. Harken continues with the order-giving:

HARKEN (cont'd)
Every inch of this junker gets tossed.

KAYLEE
(as they go)
Junker?!

MAL
Settle down, Kaylee.

KAYLEE
But, Cap'n! You hear what that purple belly called Serenity?

MAL
Shut up.

INT. SERENITY - PASSAGEWAYS/VARIOUS

A MED TEAM wheels a gurney out with the survivor on it. We don't really get a good look at his current state, under an oxygen mask and sheet and the Med Team members mostly concealing him from us. They're moving fast, we follow them, passing SEARCHING SOLDIERS, and they take us to...

INT. SERENITY - CARGO BAY

...MUCH ACTIVITY. DOZENS of SOLDIERS searching Serenity — tossing it. We PICK UP a particular SOLDIER who moves into...

INT. SERENITY - INARA'S SHUTTLE

...Inara's shuttle. Reacting to the lavish difference.

HARKEN (O.S.)
You're a Companion.

INARA (O.S.)
Yes.

INT. ALLIANCE CRUISER - INTERROGATION ROOM

Inara sits in the sterile surroundings. Harken will be doing the grilling. (We'll be INTERCUTTING between INTERROGATIONS and THE SEARCH quite liberally throughout the following.)

HARKEN
You were based for several years on Sihnon. It's only been in the last year that you've been shipping out with the crew of The Serenity.

INARA
It's just "Serenity", and that's correct. In a few weeks it will be a year. Why is this important?

HARKEN
Just trying to put the pieces together. It's a curiosity. A woman of stature such as yourself falling in with these... types.

INARA
Not in the least. It's a mutually beneficial business arrangement. I rent the shuttle from Captain Reynolds, which allows me to expand my client base, and the Captain finds that having a Companion on board opens certain doors that might otherwise be closed to him.

HARKEN
And do you love him?

TIME CUT TO:

INT. ALLIANCE CRUISER - INTERROGATION ROOM

Zoe sitting rigidly in the interrogation room.

ZOE
I don't see how that's relevant.

HARKEN
Well, he is your husband.

ZOE
Yes.

INT. SERENITY - ZOE AND WASH'S ROOM

SOLDIERS moving in here, examining the evidence of Wash and Zoe's private life together...

HARKEN (V.O.)
You two met through Captain Reynolds?

ZOE (V.O.)
Captain was looking for a pilot, I found a husband. Seemed to work out.

INT. ALLIANCE CRUISER - INTERROGATION ROOM

HARKEN
You fought with Captain Reynolds in the war.

ZOE
Fought with a lot of people in the war.

HARKEN
And your husband?

ZOE
Fight with him sometimes, too.

HARKEN
Is there any particular reason you don't wish to discuss your marriage?

ZOE
Don't see that it's any of your business, is all. We're very private people.

TIME CUT TO:

INT. ALLIANCE CRUISER - INTERROGATION ROOM

Wash looking much more relaxed in the interrogation.

WASH
The legs. Oh, yeah. Definitely have to say it was her legs. You can put that down.

INT. SERENITY - VARIOUS

The search continues, moving into the engine room...

INT. ALLIANCE CRUISER - INTERROGATION ROOM

Still indignant.

KAYLEE
...six Gurstlers crammed right under every cooling drive so that you strain your primary artery function and end up having to recycle secondary exhaust through a bypass system just so's you don't end up pumping it into the main atmo feed and asphyxiating your crew. What [genius] thought up that lame design? Now that's "junk".

TIME CUT TO:

INT. ALLIANCE CRUISER - INTERROGATION ROOM

JAYNE just sits there, closed mouthed. Arms crossed. We play the silence for a moment, then —

INT. SERENITY - JAYNE'S ROOM

Knives. Guns. Girly magazine (with Chinese markings). Another knife.

INT. ALLIANCE CRUISER - INTERROGATION ROOM

Jayne sits silently. Not a word. More shifting. More silence.

INT. ALLIANCE CRUISER - INTERROGATION ROOM

KAYLEE
She ain't "junk".

INT. SERENITY - BOOK'S ROOM

As the Soldiers toss Book's room: bible, a cross, etc.

HARKEN (V.O.)
Pirates with their own Chaplain. There's an oddity.

INT. ALLIANCE CRUISER - INTERROGATION ROOM

BOOK
Not the only oddity this end of space, Commander. Way of things not always so plain as on the central planets. Rules can be a mite fuzzier.

HARKEN
Not for me. Our rules are written down. In books.

BOOK
I take my rules from a book, too. But just the one.

HARKEN
(smiles)
Southdown Abbey. Home to a fairly pious order. How long were you in residence there, Shepherd?

BOOK
Don't right recall. Didn't tend to keep track of the days there. Seemed like long enough, though.

HARKEN
You met up with Captain Reynolds and his crew on Persephone.

BOOK
That's true.

HARKEN
These fugitives we're looking for, the brother and sister... they were last seen on Persephone.

INT. SERENITY - VARIOUS

The swarm of the search team continues. One of the Soldiers looks at the panels of the stash. Moves to it...

BOOK (V.O.)
That a fact?

HARKEN (V.O.)
They also left port aboard a Firefly class transport. Just about the time you shipped out with Serenity.

He presses — a panel opens. He calls some others over. They rip the panels up — empty.

INT. ALLIANCE CRUISER - INTERROGATION

ROOM

BOOK
Well, Persephone's a big place.

HARKEN
Yes. But that Firefly isn't. And if there is anyone hiding anywhere on it — we will find them.

INT. SERENITY - DINING ROOM

The Soldiers are starting to pack up, file out. As the swarm begins to disperse... CAMERA pulls back and up, out past the overhead windows, moving to —

EXT. SERENITY

— the outside of the ship. Where WE FIND SIMON and RIVER both in spacesuits, clinging to the side of the ship.

Simon is just freaking out, his gloved hands the only thing keeping his sweaty palms from losing purchase on the side of the ship. He touches the seam of his helmet, making sure it's connected properly. He looks to River, worried. But he reacts —

River stares off into the limitless void of space, seemingly taking a kind of deep comfort from the vastness of it. She's doing something that we haven't really seen her do... she's smiling. Off Simon, continually amazed by his sister...

INT. ALLIANCE CRUISER - INTERROGATION ROOM

Mal sits alone in the room. Presently, the door opens. Harken enters, carrying a thick folder. Harken moves to the chair opposite Mal. Harken studies his documents. Won't look at Mal. A calculated move to put Mal on edge. Mal breaks the silence:

MAL
I figure by now you been over to that derelict. Seen for yourself.

HARKEN
Yes. Terrible thing.

MAL
You want my advice, you won't tow it back. Just fire the whole gorramn thing from space. Be done with it.

HARKEN
That ship is evidence. I'm not in the habit of destroying evidence.

MAL
'Course not. Be against the rules. I'm gonna make a leap and figure this is your first tour out here on the border.

Harken finally looks at Mal.

HARKEN
That's a very loyal crew you have there. But then I see by your record you tend to inspire that quality in people — Sergeant.

ACCESS·FILE

SERENITY CREW SPACESUITS

Chris Gilman's company, Global Effects, has produced high-end spacesuits and armor for countless movies and TV shows from *Bram Stoker's Dracula* to *Armageddon*. Chris recalls the origins of the suits used in *Firefly*. "They were originally created for Kurt Russell's movie *Soldier*. The movie's costume designer asked us to come up with some sort of 'soldier spacesuits'. I thought it was a perfect job for us as it combined two areas I'm really interested in: armor and spacesuits. The suits are a variant of the S10 high altitude flight suit."

Originally the *Firefly* production team rented the *Soldier* suits unmodified, but Shawna Trpcic asked Chris if they could create a new look for our crew when outside the ship in space. "We came up with a custom designed helmet for use on the *Soldier* suits. We wanted to give the impression that the helmet could retract back over your head, so we incorporated pleats of the suit material up on the back of the helmet so it would look collapsible. The helmet is basically in two parts, there's the front shell and faceplate, and the pleated back section which is on a plastic cap. The texture of the shell surface is in the molding and the finish is a drab olive, golden green color to match the suits. There's a drybrush effect over the top to make the helmets look used and armored. A fan system in the backpack forces air up the helmet hose and over the inside of the faceplate. All of our helmets have fans as they would fog up without this and create a big problem. They saw some pieces we did for *Armageddon* and liked the vents on them, so we sculpted some smaller ones for the helmets. The light tubes on the side were rigged by our guy on set, at the request of the production. They're a couple of flashlights and some tubing we usually use for air hose."

Jayne's yellow spacesuit is somewhat different. There were only two of the *Soldier* suits available for rent, so Jayne's suit is an exact replica of an SR-71/10-30 suit, originally made for Dolph Lundgren, who's a similar size to Adam Baldwin. The helmet is the same launch/entry model as those worn by current shuttle crews and is a basic grey color with a black stipple effect. The neck seal ring is a replica of that on an Apollo suit. "Replica spacesuits are surprisingly complicated to make. The *Firefly* suit has about 300 to 400 components. Our replica Shuttle EMU suits have over 1,200, but the real EMU has over 19,000."

Costume designer Shawna Trpcic: "We couldn't afford to make our own spacesuits. Joss said, 'Well, they're scavengers anyway, so just scavenge them from a couple of different shows.' I designed my own helmets to go with the suits, so that at least they would look a little different from the original. We tried to make them look like they'd been through a lot."

❖ Below right: The spacesuits as they originally appeared in the movie *Soldier*.

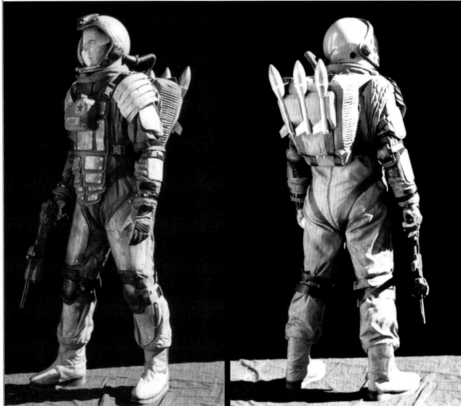

MAL
It's not "Sergeant". Not no more. War's over.

HARKEN
For some the war'll never be over. I notice your ship's called "Serenity". You were stationed on Hera at the end of the war. Battle of Serenity Valley took place there, if I recall.

MAL
(now let me think)
You know, I believe you may be right.

HARKEN
Independents suffered a pretty crushing defeat there. Some say after Serenity, the Browncoats were through. That the war really ended in that valley.

MAL
Hmmm.

HARKEN
Seems odd you'd name your ship after a battle you were on the wrong side of.

MAL
May have been the losing side. Still not convinced it was the wrong one.

HARKEN
Is that why you attacked that transport?

MAL
What — ?

HARKEN
You're still fighting the same battle, Sergeant. Only these weren't soldiers you murdered. They were civilians. Families. Citizens loyal to the Alliance, trying to make a new life for themselves. And you just can't stand that, can you?

MAL
So we attacked that ship then brought the only living witness back to our infirmary? That what we did?

HARKEN
I'd ask him... but I imagine he'll have some trouble speaking with his tongue split down the middle.

MAL
(realizing)
<Wuh de tyen, ah.> [Dear God in heaven.]

HARKEN
I haven't seen that kind of torture since... well, since the war.

Mal's stunned into silence for a beat, going internal as the full weight of his realization hits him.

MAL
(to himself)
Shoulda known... shoulda seen this comin'...

HARKEN
You and your crew will be bound by law. Formal charges will be transmitted to central authority —

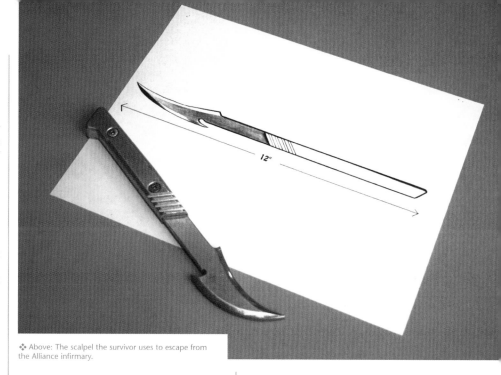

❖ Above: The scalpel the survivor uses to escape from the Alliance infirmary.

MAL
Commander, I am not what you need to be concerning yourself with right now. Things go the way they are — there's gonna be blood.

Off that —

INT. ALLIANCE SHIP - INFIRMARY

Again, we're only seeing bits and pieces of what's become of the survivor. Think Hannibal Lecter being worked on in the ambulance. His body lurches and convulses. Team of Alliance medics working to save him.

So involved in their good work are they, that they don't see his hand slip off the side of the operating table, dangling there, clutching the sharp, shining surgical tool that comes up now — slashing.

BLACK OUT.

END OF ACT THREE

ACT FOUR

INT. ALLIANCE CRUISER - INTERROGATION ROOM

Harken stares at Mal. Harken's unimpressed as he says:

HARKEN
Reavers?

MAL
That's what I said.

HARKEN
Can't imagine how many times men in my position hear that excuse. "Reavers did it."

MAL
It's the truth.

HARKEN
You saw them, did you?

MAL
Wouldn't be sitting here talking to you if I had.

HARKEN
No. Of course not.

MAL
But I'll tell you who did — that poor bastard you took off my ship. He looked right into the face of it. Was made to stare.

HARKEN
"It?"

MAL
The darkness. Kinda darkness you can't even imagine. Blacker than the space it moves in.

HARKEN
Very poetic.

MAL
They made him watch. He probably tried to turn away — they wouldn't let him. You call him a "survivor"? He's not. A man comes up against that kind of will, only way to deal with it, I suspect... is to become it. He's following the only course that's left to him. First he'll try to make himself look like one... cut on himself, desecrate his own flesh... then he'll start acting like one.

Harken seems to be considering that for a moment, hits a button on the table. The door opens and a SOLDIER appears.

HARKEN
Let's have two M.P.s up here to escort Sergeant Reynolds to the brig.

MAL
Lock me up. I'll thank you for it. But me and my crew're gonna be the only ones on this ship that's safe you don't move to act.

HARKEN
And let's not put him in with his compatriots. In fact, let's see to it they're all separated.

Off Mal's frustration...

INT. SERENITY - FOREDECK HALL

A HATCH OPENS and SIMON, still in his spacesuit, climbs down a ladder. He rips off his helmet as River descends down the ladder. He helps her off with her helmet.

RIVER
Let's go again.

SIMON
Later. Maybe. Captain said once the coast was clear we should lay low in the shuttle.

RIVER
(sensing something)
He's coming back.

SIMON
Yes. Yes, of course he is. They all are. Captain Reynolds is used to these sorts of situations. We just have to be patient. Come on.

They move off. Simon never saw the BLOODY FOOTPRINT nearby. They're not alone.

INT. ALLIANCE CRUISER - INTERROGATION ROOM

The interrogation is over. Harken is off to the side with an M.P. Two more M.P.s are pulling Mal out of his chair, cuffing his hands behind his back.

HARKEN
Your ship and its contents will be auctioned. The proceeds of the sale will be applied to the cost of your defense.

The Ensign now enters, looking a little pale. He moves close to Harken, whispers his report. Harken reacts. We can guess what's being reported to Harken. So can Mal.

HARKEN (cont'd)
(re: Mal)
Get him out of here.
(to Ensign)
Go to full lock down. I want guards on the nursery —

As Mal's hustled toward the door:

MAL
It won't matter. You won't find him.

Harken meets Mal's gaze, a little lost.

MAL (cont'd)
But I know where he'll go.

CUT TO:

INT. SERENITY - PASSAGEWAYS - CONTINUOUS

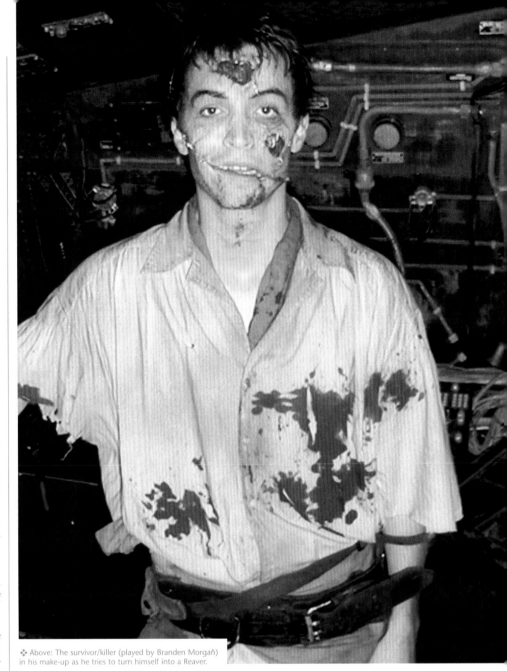
❖ Above: The survivor/killer (played by Branden Morgan) in his make-up as he tries to turn himself into a Reaver.

Simon tries to steer River into the dining room/kitchen area. She whimpers. Will go no further.

SIMON
River. It's okay. They've gone. Come on.

But she won't.

SIMON (cont'd)
We don't know how long it's going to be. Once we're settled, I don't think we should move around much. I'll just grab some some food and...

He tries to disengage from her, she's holding him back. He lists away, toward the dining room... CAMERA PULLS back...

...past scattered KITCHEN CUTLERY...

...finally REVEALING the FIGURE just two feet from the oblivious Simon who's trying to back yet closer, as...

INT. ALLIANCE SHIP - AIRLOCK/DOOR TO SERENITY

A DEAD GUARD marks the way of the killer. Mal is there with Harken and armed M.P.s.

HARKEN
Why would he come back here?

MAL
Looking for familiar ground. He's on the hunt.

HARKEN
All right.

Harken nods to his men. They ready themselves to enter. Before they can:

HARKEN (cont'd)
(to an M.P.)
Get him to the brig.

MAL
You should let me go with you.

HARKEN
Out of the question.

MAL
How many more men you feel like losing today, Commander? Nobody knows Serenity like I do. I can help you.

Harken considers that for a beat, then —

HARKEN
We'll let him go first.

MAL
(oh, good)
Great.

Harken is getting set again, Mal makes him pause with:

MAL (cont'd)
Uh — ?

Mal indicates his hands still cuffed behind his back. Harken takes the key from one of his men, undoes the cuffs himself — but just as quick pulls Mal's hands around front, recuffs him with his hands now in front of him.

MAL (cont'd)
Thanks. Now I'll really have the advantage.

HARKEN
(to his men)
Open it.

As his men move to do that —

INT. SERENITY - PASSAGEWAYS - CONTINUOUS

SIMON AND RIVER

She tries to hold him back as he backs close to the unseen (to him) Killer. He absently reaches behind himself, sets his helmet on the dining room table, as —

Simon stops suddenly at the SOUND of the AIRLOCK OPENING in the distance.

SIMON
Someone's coming...

The Killer also hears the approach of footsteps... feints out of frame...

INT. SERENITY - CARGO BAY - CONTINUOUS

Mal leads Harken and his men into the cargo bay.

HARKEN
(hushed)
We'll split up —

MAL
Best if we stick together. Unless you're in the

mood to get picked off.
Harken considers, nods. Sighs. Fine.

HARKEN
(to his men)
Keene, Escobar, you two stay here. Watch the door. Don't need this thing back on my ship.

Harken indicates for Mal to lead on. He does.

INT. SERENITY - OUTSIDE INFIRMARY

MOVING WITH MAL

Schmuck bait as he leads the team past the wrecked infirmary. Through the common area, coming up to the steep stairs which lead to the upper levels.

INT. SERENITY - ENGINE ROOM

Mal leads Harken and his men through the engine room, down into the dining area. Mal notes a spacesuit helmet sitting on the table. Knows what that means. He steels himself. Mushes on.

Mal sees the spilled cutlery. He and Harken share a look. They continue on...

Mal steps up into the foredeck hall. Tries not to react as he comes nearly face-to-face with —

SIMON AND RIVER

pressed tight up against a wall just around the corner, hidden by the lip of the passageway.

Harken's right on Mal's ass now, a step down in the dining room. Mal turns to him as —

THE KILLER

leaps from out of frame, attacking one of the men just behind Harken. Harken turns. THE KILLER slashes Harken's man. There is blood, splashing across Harken's surprised face.

Harken fumbles for his gun, the Killer knocks it away, lunges at Harken, as —

Mal leaps at the guy's back, brings his cuffed hands over his head and around his throat —

HARKEN'S POV

Of the HIDEOUS MUTILATED FACE, flesh peeled back, mouth pinned into a grimace by bits of metal. It SNARLS and SNAPS at Harken, trying to get at him. Right the fuck up in his face. Being held at bay only by Mal's strength. It is terrifying. Mal pulls hard. There is a crack.

Mal lets the body drop at their feet.

ANGLE: THE SURVIVOR

Mal uses the tip of his boot to turn the dead man's head slightly... Mutilated flesh. The skin of his mouth remains pulled back and pinned into that hideous grimace. Scarcely human.

MAL AND HARKEN

as they share a look. Harken's face sullied with blood. A baptism of sorts. There are no words. Off this —

EXT. SPACE

Serenity detaches from the Alliance Cruiser, floats down.

INT. SERENITY - BRIDGE

Mal, Wash, Zoe and Jayne. They watch as the big ship gets smaller.

JAYNE
You save his gorramn life. And he still takes the cargo. <Hwoon dahn.> [Jerk.]

MAL
Had to. Couldn't let us profit.

Mal doesn't stick around. He turns for the door.

MAL (cont'd)
Wouldn't be civilized.

Through the cockpit window, WE SEE the Alliance Ship send out what look like torpedoes. They connect with the spinning derelict, sending a series of SOUNDLESS EXPLOSIONS through its hull. As the derelict caves in on itself, glows to embers...

BLACK OUT.

END OF SHOW

"HAVE YOU EVER BEEN WITH A WARRIOR WOMAN?"

Zoe's Pistol & Vest

❖ Above: Profile views of Zoe's 'Mare's Leg' pistol.

Zoe's pistol is a fine example of a 'Mare's Leg'; a cut down Winchester rifle. Mike Gibbons, *Firefly*'s armorer, explains its origins: "The Mare's Leg pistols were originally made for a show called *The Adventures of Brisco County Jr.* I had them here in the shop, they saw them, liked them and used them in *Firefly*. The 'Zoe pistol' was inspired by Josh Randall's Mare's Leg in 1958's *Wanted, Dead or Alive*, a TV spin-off from *Trackdown*. Bounty hunter Josh Randall was played by Steve McQueen. He had this pistol which was cut down from a Winchester. The base gun for Zoe's pistol is a 44-40 caliber Rossi 92, a Winchester copy, which was cut down in the shop to remove the stock and some of the barrel length. We copied pictures of the Josh Randall prop — except that one was, I believe, a Winchester model 73. I did them on a 92 because they work better, they're shorter and lighter. They're more modern, have a shorter action and tend to be more reliable. Besides, at the time, there wasn't a ton of 73s lying around. *Firefly* had a small budget so we provided a lot of stuff for the show right off the shop wall."

Gina Torres would carry a rubber stunt pistol in the holster whenever the Hero (closeup) weapon wasn't required. The rubber guns weigh very little, but the Mare's Leg Hero pistol weighs in at 1.91 kg (4.21 lbs) unloaded.

As on Josh Randall's, the pistol's cocking lever is extended into a loop shape, but not for use as a hand-guard as might be expected. Armorer Mike Gibbons explains, "The loop is so you can 'swing' the gun to reload it. Swinging is the dangerous practice of cycling the gun's action by slinging the entire weapon in an arc around your firing hand. You see John Wayne do it in *True Grit*. It's a great way to shoot yourself or end up with the front sight embedded in your forehead!"

Costume designer Shawna Trpcic designed Zoe's trademark vest, which was made in collaboration with leather artist Jonathan A. Logan. The design evokes the Old West with its natural look and utilitarian economy. The rows of side-buckles were an inspiration of Shawna's.

Logan recalls, "That was a nice piece of work. We had the pleasure of actually fitting the garment to Gina Torres in the studio. We kind of made a vest which molded itself to her body. I have a lot of mock-up garments in fabrics, rather than the final leather material. So, when you have a concept like the vest, we try on a bunch of different bodies, then take whatever is the best for the purpose and apply that shape."

ZOE'S HOLSTER

The holster Zoe wears was also inspired by Josh Randall's. It's a slab of leather with a padded steel spring-clip at the barrel end and a bracket at the top upon which the pistol hangs by its saddle-ring. There's a leg strap, and a leather thong is used to keep the pistol snugly in its clip at the barrel end.

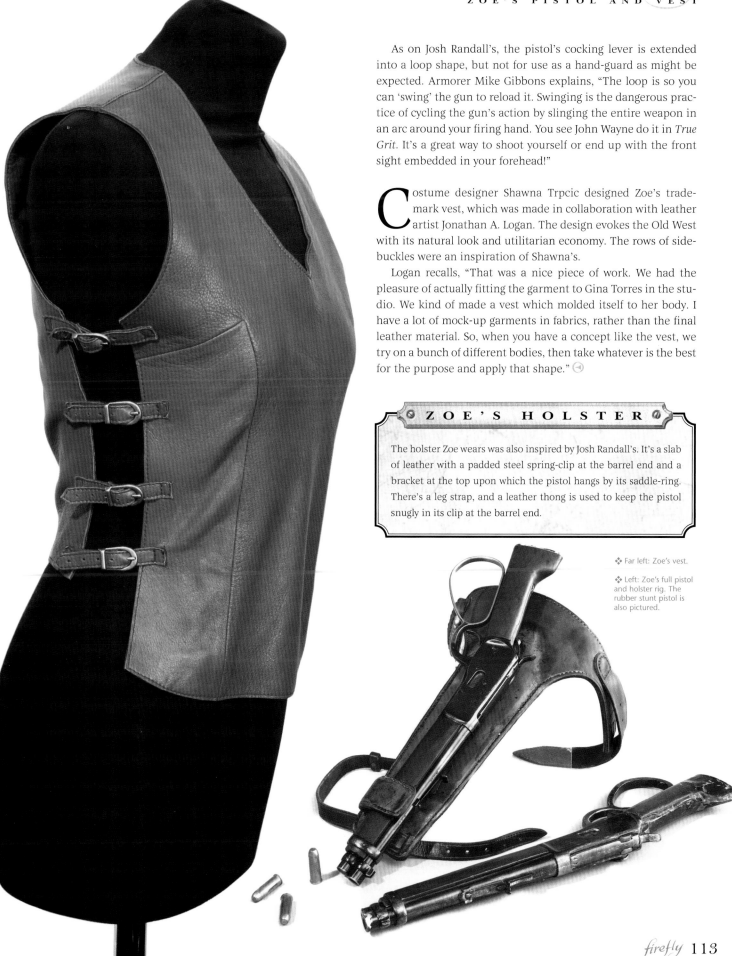

❖ Far left: Zoe's vest.

❖ Left: Zoe's full pistol and holster rig. The rubber stunt pistol is also pictured.

SHINDIG

Written by Jane Espenson
Directed by Vern Gillum

JANE ESPENSON

The idea of Mal having an adventure in Inara's world was one of several ideas that were already underway when I was brought into the process. Mal and Inara's attraction was one of the building blocks of the series. So all the romantic stuff was in place from the beginning of discussions about the story. But I had the immeasurable fun of finding the words. Unspoken attraction is a delight to put into dialogue because it's so unspoken. You get to dance with the words.

I know I came up with the title on my own. I loved the new-Old Western dialect and the chance to dust off an old word like 'shindig' again. Like the Badger-Jayne-Mal scene had a couple of interesting things going on. One of them was Adam Baldwin, as Jayne, constantly filling his cup with sugar. The other was a discussion about how to pronounce 'palaver'. It was another old word I dusted off. You've got to be careful with those old ones sometimes, because no one knows them anymore, except to read them.

I loved inventing sci-fi touches. This episode contains two of my favorites: the floating chandelier and the futuristic hotel key. I wrote the floating chandelier with very little thought. I imagined we'd see it briefly in one shot and then refer to it off-screen for the rest of the scene. But it turned into a major deal. The entire ballroom scene is filled with moving shimmering reflected light that is supposedly coming from the floating chandelier.

The hotel key I had imagined as a small metal knob with a shaft that became the doorknob when it was inserted into the right door-hole. The clever people in charge of such things found the coolest low-tech way of doing this. When Inara screws the knob into the door, the whole back half of the bulb lights up, because it's a light bulb — painted silver in front. Coolest thing ever! I also got to invent the poker descendant, tall card, in this episode.

Once the basic beats of the story were in place, there weren't a lot of adjustments made to them. One thing that I remember is that the first act break changed at least once. The problem was in deciding what exactly Inara was going to see and react to. Kaylee? Mal? Which one should enter first? Should Mal approach Inara in the moment? What we ended up with worked really well.

There is one other small rearrangement that happened after the shooting was done, in the editing process. The scene in which Mal comes to the engine room and tells Kaylee he's got a job for her is now used to break up two chunks of the party. In the shooting draft that scene falls before any of the party material. It's a great change. And the scene in which River is suddenly coherent and speaks to Badger in his own accent came from Joss knowing that Summer could do really good accents. He suggested we use this. I love doing stuff like that, building off the actors — the way they look or move, or stuff they can do.

The Wash-Zoe relationship was my favorite thing on *Firefly* and I was sad that they only had that one scene [the bed scene] alone together. I came up with the joke about Jayne taking over and the idea of Wash jokingly composing poetry for the funeral. Now, given the events of *Serenity*, it just all seems so sad and poignant and foreshadowy. In my version, I didn't have Wash actually quote any of the poem. But Joss liked the idea and he added the line that now ends the scene.

The episode turned out really well, and is one of the very few episodes in my entire career in which I was on the set for almost every take of every scene. I'm terribly proud of it.

TEASER

INT. POOL HALL - NIGHT (NIGHT 1)

It's dark, smoky. Four tables are in play. There are about fifteen people in here, mostly men. A BARTENDER serves beer in heavy wooden bowls. Small tables line the edges of the room.

MAL and JAYNE play two other men, WRIGHT and HOLDER. INARA, in a beautiful outfit, watches and holds a small glass of pink liqueur. She is the only color, only elegance.

WRIGHT is lining up a shot and talking at the same time. His cue has a ring of light right before the tip.

WRIGHT
Didn't hardly have to convert the ship, even.
(re: shot)
Six in the corner. Stronger locks, thicker doors, keep everybody where they're s'posed to be. Don't even need more rations.

As he sights along his cue, all the balls on the table flicker, disappearing for a moment, then reappearing. A general DISGUSTED GROAN comes from every player in the room.

WRIGHT (cont'd)
<Way!> [Hey!]

He looks toward the Bartender, as do other patrons. The Bartender points, bored, to a crude sign: "MANAGEMENT NOT RESPONSIBLE FOR BALL FAILURE" (It also says it in Chinese.)

Wright attempts his shot. Doesn't sink the ball.

WRIGHT (cont'd)
Flicker threw me off.

Mal's turn. He walks around, examines the table.

JAYNE
(to Wright)
You made money?

WRIGHT
Hand over fist, my friend. Border planets need labor. Terraforming crews got a prodigious death rate.

MAL
Side pocket.

Mal makes his shot, lines up another.

MAL (cont'd)
Labor. You mean slaves.

WRIGHT
They wasn't volunteers, for damn sure.

MAL
That why you didn't hafta lay in more rations?

WRIGHT
I didn't hear no complaints.

Wright and Holder laugh.

JAYNE
How much money? Lots?

Mal misses a shot and steps back by Inara. She's brushing cigarette ashes off a chair, making a place to sit.

MAL
There's a chance you may wanna head back to the ship.

INARA
Oh, I'm all right. This is entertaining, actually.

MAL
(amused, disbelieving)
Yeah? What's entertaining?

INARA
I like watching the game. As with other situations, the key seems to be giving Jayne a heavy stick and standing back.

ANGLE ON: Jayne, sinking one of the few remaining balls.

Mal smiles at Inara, but:

MAL
Still think you might oughtta clear out 'fore too much longer. Seems there's a thief about.

INARA
A thief?

Mal leans in close, slips Inara a handful of paper money.

MAL
He took this right off 'em. They earned that with the sweat of their slave-tradin' brows.

INARA
Mal!

MAL
Terrible shame. 'Course, they won't notice it til they go to pay for their next drink—

WRIGHT (O.S.)
<Way!> [Hey!]

MAL
(to Inara)
Good drinker, that one.

Wright's hand falls heavily on Mal's shoulder. Mal spins and LANDS A MIGHTY PUNCH.

Behind them, Holder jumps to help Wright. Jayne TACKLES HIM.

Inara jumps back against a wall, as Wright KICKS MAL'S LEGS from under him. Mal falls.

Holder is up again, swinging a pool cue at Jayne.

Mal, on the floor, grabs the base of a small table and rams it UP at Wright. Wright flies back.

It's a melee. Other patrons jump to join.

Inara jumps when a GLASS SHATTERS near her head. She heads toward the door, fast. She passes the Bartender as she goes.

INARA
(dryly)
Lovely place. I'll tell my friends.

END OF TEASER

ACT ONE

EXT. SERENITY/PERSEPHONE - EFFECT

Descending out of orbit over Persephone.

INT. SERENITY - BRIDGE - DAY (DAY 2)/ EFFECT

WASH pilots Serenity closer to the surface. ZOE stands behind his chair, hand on Wash's shoulder, looking out.

As they approach, Persephone comes between them and this system's sun; the planet's shadow moves over their faces. Zoe bends down close to Wash, a couple enjoying a sunset.

WASH
It seem to you we cleared outta Santo in a hurry?

ZOE
Seems to me we do that a lot. Heard tell though, we're gonna stay a while on Persephone, upwards of a week maybe.

Wash whistles through his teeth.

WASH
Shiny.

ZOE
Yeah? Thought you'd get land-crazy, that long in port.

WASH
Prob'ly. But I been sane a long while now, and change is good.

Mal joins them. Looks out past them at the planet.

MAL
Well, ain't that a joyful sight.

WASH
Gotta love a sunset.

ZOE
Startin' to get familiar, too. Like a second home.

MAL
(firmly)
Persephone is not home. Too many people we need to avoid. Resupply, look for work, move along. We sniff the air, we don't kiss the dirt.

JOSS WHEDON

Ultimately, it's time for a little romantic comedy with Mal and Inara and to see a little bit of her world, and Mal being the fish-out-of-water guy, because that's never not fun. And also, to have Kaylee have a dress, because not since I wanted Willow to have an Eskimo suit [on *Buffy*] have I been so excited about somebody's outfit.

ZOE
Wasn't planning on the dirt-kissing, sir.

WASH
I wouldn't stand for it anyways, Captain. Jealous man like me.
(re: piloting)
Closin' in.

ZOE
Planet's coming up a might fast.

WASH
Just means I'm going down too quick. Likely crash and kill us all.

As Mal exits:

MAL
That happens, let me know.

INT. INARA'S SHUTTLE - DAY

Inara sits facing a Cortex screen that hangs on the wall like a mirror. There is local data across the top of the screen: "Persephone", the local time (ten a.m.), ship's status (docked). The main part of the screen is labeled "Responses". The screen features twelve small pictures — ten men, two women. Text under each picture gives a name. Inara touches three pictures and they disappear.

Inara looks at the ones that remain. She touches one of the pictures and it expands to fill the screen. It's a taped request from a pale YOUNG HOPEFUL (man).

YOUNG HOPEFUL
(on tape, nervous)
I understand your time on our planet is limited. And if you've selected my proposal to hear, then the honor that you do me flatters my...
(searches for words)
My honor... and I hope—

Inara taps the screen. The field of nine photos is back. Before she can select another, a CHIME sounds and the screen fills with the live (not recorded) image of ATHERTON WING.

Atherton is handsome, thirties, with just enough charm to offset his aura of entitlement. Inara smiles at the sight of him.

ATHERTON
(over the link)
Now there's the smile made of sunlight.

INARA
Atherton! How wonderful to see you.

ATHERTON
Did you get my message? I was extra appealing.

INARA
Yesterday. I listened to yours first. What a flattering invitation. I had no idea I was arriving in time for the Social Event of the Season.

ATHERTON
We only have four or five of those a year, you know. So you'll accompany me, I ask, heart in my

throat? There is a certain offer I'm still waiting to hear about.

SFX: KNOCK AT THE DOOR

INARA
Yes, I imagine there is. I'm delighted to say I'll be there. Now, I'm sorry, Atherton, I have to run.

ATHERTON
I understand, I'll see you soon,
<bao bay.> [sweetheart.]

She severs the connection. His image freezes on the screen.

INARA
Come in.

Mal enters. Inara sets the screen on a table.

INARA (cont'd)
Good afternoon, Captain.

MAL
Morning. We're downing, and in case Wash don't kill us all, local time's gonna be in the a.m., ten or so.

INARA
(why are you really here?)
Yes, I saw that.

Mal gestures toward the screen, trying to seem casual.

MAL
Making plans?

Inara tenses. He doesn't wait for an answer from her. He looks closely at the screen.

MAL (cont'd)
"Atherton Wing". He's a regular, ain't he?

Inara blanks the screen.

INARA
I've seen him before.

MAL
Well, I never did. Not what I pictured. Young. Must be rich too, to afford your rates.

INARA
I suppose. He has engaged me for several days.

MAL
Days. The boy must have stamina.

INARA
He does.

Mal tries not to look stung.

MAL
Well... fine. Is he lettin' you out at all?

INARA
Actually, we're attending a ball tomorrow night.

MAL
Tell me, all the men there have to pay for their dates, or just the young rich ones with stamina?

INARA
Most of the women there will not be Companions, if that's what you're asking. Perhaps the other men couldn't attract one.

MAL
Huh. Sounds like the finest party I can imagine getting paid to go to.

INARA
I don't suppose you'd find it up to the standards of your outings. More conversation and somewhat less petty theft and getting hit with pool cues.

Inara moves to the door, a clear invitation to leave.

INARA (cont'd)
I understand, if you need to go prepare for that "it's ten in the morning" issue.

MAL
Yeah. Better do that. Cuz I think this is more of an evening look.

He exits.

EXT. STREET - DAY (DAY 2)

Outside a line of shops on Persephone. KAYLEE, Zoe, Jayne, Wash and Mal are carrying some supplies back to the Mule.

The women and Wash walk ahead, then Jayne, then Mal. Mal carries a heavy burlap sack.

They pass a high-class dress shop. There are three live MODELS behind the window, walking and posing, showing off their gowns. Kaylee stops short, and Zoe almost runs into her.

KAYLEE
Ooh. Look at the pretties.

Zoe looks, and Wash joins her.

WASH
What am I looking at? The girls or the clothes?

Jayne stops short:

JAYNE
(immediately)
There's girls?

ZOE
(answering Wash, overlapping)
The clothes, please.

Jayne looks too. Mal is forced to stop, wait.

KAYLEE
(pointing)
Say. Look at the fluffy one.

ZOE
Too much foofaraw. If I'm gonna wear a dress, I want something with slink.

WASH
(quickly)
You want a slinky dress? I can buy you a slinky dress. Captain, can I have money for a slinky dress?

JAYNE
I'll chip in.

ZOE
(casually, to Jayne)
I can hurt you.

KAYLEE
Only place I ever seen something so nice is some of the things Inara has.

MAL
We'd best be movin'—

ZOE
Guess she needs all that stuff, life she leads.

KAYLEE
Well, sure. And sometimes the customers buy her things. She knows some real rich men—

MAL
Come on. T'ain't feathers I'm toting here, you know.

KAYLEE
I like the ruffles. Inara gets to wear whatever she—

MAL
What would you do in that rig? Flounce around the engine room? Be like a sheep walkin' on its hind legs.

Jayne snorts a laugh at that. Kaylee's face shows she's hurt. Zoe shoots Mal a hard look. She takes Mal's burden effortlessly. She, Kaylee and Wash head o.s. toward the Mule.

ZOE
(coldly)
See you on the ship, Captain.

Mal instantly regrets what he said.

MAL
<Tee wuh duh pee-goo.> [Kick me in the bottom.]

JAYNE
Is she mad or something?

There's a series of meaningful CLICKS behind him.

Mal and Jayne turn to find themselves facing BADGER, a cockney criminal, a slice of local color with a fine hat.

Three of his LADS are with him, covering Jayne — the clicks were the cocking of their guns.

Mal nods politely, as if this is a normal way to run into an old acquaintance.

MAL
Badger.

BADGER
Captain Reynolds. Heard you was in town. Thought we might have a bit of a sit-down.

MAL
I'd prefer a bit of a "piss off".

BADGER
I'm very sorry. Did I give you the impression I was asking?

INT. BADGER'S LAIR - DAY

Badger, Mal and Jayne sit uncomfortably around a cable-spool table. Badger pours some English tea. Jayne eats from a plate of cucumber sandwiches.

MAL
Seems to me, last time there was a chance for a little palaver, we were all manner of unwelcome...

JAYNE
(re: tea)
That's not bad.

BADGER
(to Jayne, confidentially)
There's a trick to it. Wood alcohol.

Mal continues as if he hadn't been interrupted.

MAL
Now, we're favored guests, treated to the finest in beverages that make you blind. So what is it you need?

Jayne pours himself more tea, reaching across Mal.

JAYNE
'Scuse me.

BADGER
There's this local, name of Warrick Harrow. He's got some property he wants to sell off-planet, to fetch a higher price.

MAL
But the local powers won't let him sell off-world.

BADGER
It's a conundrum. What my man Harrow needs hisself, is a smuggler. 'M willing to cut you in on it.

MAL
Why me? You've got access to ships. You could do it yourself.

BADGER
(reluctant)
He won't deal with me direct. Taken an irrational dislike.

JAYNE
(mouth full)
What happened? He see your face?

BADGER
(ignoring Jayne)
He's a quality gent. Nose in the air like he never <wun gwo pee> [smelled a fart]. Don't find me respectable. You, I figure, you got a chance.

MAL
You backed out of a deal, last time. Left us hanging.

JAYNE
Hurt our feelings.

MAL
You recall why that took place?

BADGER
I had a problem with your attitude, is why. Felt you was, what's the word?

JAYNE
Pretentious?

Mal shoots Jayne a look.

BADGER
Exactly. You think you're better'n other people.

MAL
Just the ones I'm better than.
(then)
Now, I thinkin' that very quality is the one you're placing value on today.

BADGER
I place value on the fact that the stick up your <pee-goo> [bottom] is 'bout as large as the one Harrow's got.

Jayne barks a laugh at that. Mal shoots him

another look.

MAL
How would you even set up a meet, man won't deal with you?

BADGER
I know a place he'll be. Safe place, using some new-tech gun scans. High class, too. They wouldn't let me in there, but you might slip by. 'Course you couldn't buy an invite with a diamond size of a testicle. But I got my hands on a couple.

Mal raises his eyebrows for a pregnant beat.

BADGER (cont'd)
(clarifying)
..of invites. You want the meeting or not?

Mal considers.

BADGER (cont'd)
You want to do business in Persephone, you do it through me. But if you're so well off you don't need it...

INT. SERENITY - ENGINE ROOM - DAY (DAY 2)

Kaylee is working on the engine. Mal enters.

MAL
Kaylee.

She avoids his eyes, busies herself with her work. No answer.

MAL (cont'd)
Kaylee.

KAYLEE
I'm not speaking to you, Captain.

MAL
Got no need to speak... C'mon...

He turns to go, matching her coldness.

MAL (cont'd)
Got a job for you.

INT. PARTY - FOYER - NIGHT (NIGHT 2)

Atherton Wing ushers Inara into the richly decorated foyer of a large public building. They are dressy and elegant.

MARK A. SHEPPARD

London-born Mark A. Sheppard was a successful rock band drummer before he was cast in the docudrama *In the Name of the Father*. Since then, he's worked a lot, but says, "The fondest experience I have had is with *Firefly*. It was a lovely set full of people who actually cared about what they were doing, which is also rare. It's not rare that people care about what they're doing — it's rare that *everybody* cares about what they're doing."

Sheppard loved Badger's costume. "Shawna Trpcic gave me a flamingo pin, which was a great idea with the suit. No socks, an undershirt, a tie but no collar. Everything was slightly broken. We talked about 'very fine hats'. The Western bowler was the coolest-looking hat I'd ever seen. Everything had a reason. They explained to me that Badger having fresh fruit meant he had some power and influence; he also wasn't that interested in opulence, he was interested in enjoying the fruits of his labors."

Adam Baldwin, who had worked with Sheppard before on the films *Lover's Knot* and *Farewell, My Love*, broke the news to Sheppard that Joss Whedon had originally written the role of Badger for himself. "We got through [Badger's scene in 'Serenity'] and Joss said, 'I've got something to tell you,' and I said, 'Yeah, I know!'"

Part of the fun of playing Badger for Sheppard was leading Badger's gang. "The group of extras were extraordinary. I thought the nicest thing that Joss did was, when we went to do 'Shindig', I said, 'Please, get me the same guys.' They went out of their way to get the same guys. There was a wonderful guy, he looks like my accountant — he's sitting with the old adding machine, he's the first guy to draw down. I don't have a gang of big, tough guys — I've got a gang of interesting-looking human beings."

More was shot of the Badger/Mal/Jayne scene than we see in the episode. "Adam and I both have a tape from the editors of the whole scene with all of the pieces that we had put in," Sheppard explains. "Adam's eating my cucumber sandwiches, which is hysterical. It's a big deal to Badger and he's showing off what he has, and there's Jayne, stuffing his face with sandwiches, taking my wood alcohol tea and putting as much sugar into it as he possibly can. We went through the entire case of brown sugar cubes doing takes. They brought us real tea and real sandwiches, so Adam ate basically for about three hours and drank sugary tea. Jayne is staring Badger down, but as he's reaching for more food. It's one of my favorite scenes."

Sheppard helped Summer Glau with her English accent for their scene together. "She and I went to a café, we sat with a tape recorder and just worked on the accent. She said, 'Well, how would you say it?' I said it a few times and she was very self-deprecating, but she got what she needed to learn, she arrived on the set, boom. She won a round of applause after her first take, quite rightly so. She is so open when she does what she does; she's absolutely fearless."

Sheppard recalls his first scene on the Serenity interior. "That moment was about, wow, Badger gets that, Badger doesn't have this [a ship]. Badger thinks he owns it, because for some reason, he likes to think he can control Mal to a point — financially, certainly. I think Badger just wants to be liked — that's his fatal flaw — and I don't know that Malcolm Reynolds likes him that much," Sheppard laughs.

If *Firefly* is ever resurrected, Sheppard says, "It would be wonderful — I'd jump in a minute."

KAYLEE'S DRESS

Costume designer Shawna Trpcic: "Kaylee's dress was made completely from scratch. Because it was a ball and it was in the script that she was wearing this obnoxious hoopskirt, I instantly thought *Gone With the Wind*, and I found this delicate, beautiful little pencil drawing of this girl from about 1861 — I have no idea who did it or where it's from — in one of my history books. In the script, it said, 'layer cake', and she had layers and layers of ruffles. I found these fabrics that would do the ombre look, going from dark to light, echoing the layer cake. I used Indian saris for the fabrics, the pinks and the golds and the beads — that's all actually an antique Indian sari that we chopped to bits to make her ball gown. The first person to wear it was the model in the shop window, and the woman sweat acid. Even with dry cleaning, she turned the armpits dark yellow. It's an antique sari, so I didn't have more fabric lying around, so I couldn't replace the sleeves. The poor woman was sweating to death up in that window, but *oy*! Then I had to put that on my actress, but Jewel is always a good team player, so she worked with us.

"The ball was influenced by the Asian look and we just had fun with that. Banning Miller [Kim Onasch] had to be layer cake-ish to echo Kaylee, to show what Banning thought was a good way to do layer cake and a bad way to do layer cake. So she and her group were a little more hoopskirt-sy. But in the general crowd there weren't a lot of hoopskirts — including Inara, who just wears a full skirt. It wasn't particularly *Gone With the Wind*; I just used that for a touch of the way I tied the ties. But then we had sashes to show different ranks, so it was all over the map.

"Mal's suit was specially made for him. Again, I took it from *Gone With the Wind*, the quarter-length coat, tight style; making it a little bit Old West, with the little silk tie; and the tight pants were just the result of last-minute alterations. It was a standing joke for the rest of the season."

ATHERTON
After you...

The ballroom is beyond, through an ornate arch — there is no visible machinery associated with the arch. Two couples are in front of them, waiting to go through. A DECORATED OFFICIAL stands to the side of the arch.

ANGLE ON THE ARCHWAY

One couple passes through. A PORTER, his back visible through the arch, can be heard, slightly muffled, as he announces them to the room beyond.

PORTER
William and Lady Cortland.

The next couple, equally elegant, heads for the arch. The woman steps through, but the WELL-DRESSED MAN is held in place by something unseen.

A PLEASANT CHIME SOUNDS.

The Well-Dressed Man is not harmed, not struggling, but he can't move forward. He steps back, smiles at the Official. He removes a small pistol from a suit jacket pocket, hands it to the Official. He passes through the arch to join his date.

PORTER (cont'd)
Colonel Cyrus Momsen and escort.

Atherton and Inara step through.

INT. PARTY - BALLROOM - CONTINUOUS

Atherton and Inara enter.

PORTER
Atherton Wing and Inara Serra.

We see the room now, filled with elegant party-goers, circulating waiters, live musicians, a buffet table...

Fresh food means money, so many of the decorations feature huge bowls of fruit. There is also a hovering chandelier.

Atherton and Inara move into the room. Inara waves at someone, exchanges air kisses with another woman.

INARA
Roberta, it's been too long.

She greets an elderly man sitting in a chair:

INARA (cont'd)
<Lao pung yo, nee can chi lai hun yo jing shen.> [You're looking wonderful, old friend.]

They move on. Atherton talks softly into her ear.

ATHERTON
Half the men in this room wish you were on their arm tonight.

INARA
Only half? I must be losing my undefinable allure.

ATHERTON
Not that undefinable. All of them wish you were in their bed.

Inara finds that in bad taste. She looks away, changes the topic.

INARA
I'm looking for the boy with the shimmerwine.

ATHERTON
Oh, she blushes.
(considering)
Not many in your line of work do that. You, you are a singular woman and I find,
(stammering, sincere)

I find I admire you more and more.

Inara stops and looks at him, touched.

ATHERTON (cont'd)
I'm trying to give you something, you know. A life. If you want it.

INARA
Atherton...

ATHERTON
You can live here, on Persephone. As my personal Companion.

INARA
You are a generous man.

ATHERTON
That's not a "yes".

INARA
(after a beat)
It's not a "no" either.

Inara greets another acquaintance.

INARA (cont'd)
(to a woman)
You look gorgeous, dear.

Atherton spots a glass of champagne — a waiter is passing with a tray. Atherton lifts the glass and offers it to Inara in one smooth move. She smiles, delighted.

ATHERTON
You belong here, Inara, not on that flying piece of <gos se> [crap]. You see that, don't you?

INARA
Atherton, language.

ATHERTON
What, "piece of <gos se> [crap]"? But it is a piece of <gos se> [crap].

PORTER (O.S.)
Miss Kaywinnit Lee Frye and escort.

Inara turns her head sharply and a little rudely away from Atherton, startled into looking at the door.

INARA
Kaylee?

ON KAYLEE

She enters, eyes wide, soaking it all in. She wears the ruffled dress from the window and looks beautiful. She carries a glittery evening bag. She's Cinderella at the ball.

Mal steps forward to join her. He is in his Sunday best, something dark and Rhett Butler-y, maybe a cut-away coat.

ACROSS THE ROOM

Inara stares, locking in on Mal.

INARA
Oh <gos se>[crap].

END OF ACT ONE

ACT TWO

INT. PARTY FOYER - CONTINUING

Mal and Kaylee make their way into the party. Her eyes are bright and wide as she takes it all in at once. Mal is trying to look cool and cosmopolitan, but is actually almost as impressed as Kaylee. He tugs at his suit.

MAL
Does this seem kind of... tight?

KAYLEE
Shows off your backside. Didja see the chandelier?

MUSIC

Composer Greg Edmonson: "We used classical music for the ballroom stuff — Beethoven, Haydn. For filming they bought a performance, probably by a European orchestra, and then used the playback on set. Otherwise, they would have had nothing to dance to. Right about the time I got hired, they were already substantially into filming. They said, 'Here's the playback that we used. If you want to write something and replace this, feel free.' The problem was, number one, there was no time, and number two, I didn't have a symphony orchestra to do it with. So I said, 'I will find the scores to this music and go in and add instrumentation, so that it doesn't just sound like something you could just go into a Tower Classical store and pick up today.' I overlaid ethnic instruments, I would double a flute line with a shakuhachi or something, so that it sounded like classical music, except with a little bit of an ethnic twist. A shakuhachi is like a Japanese flute, but it's not polished like an orchestral flute, it's more of an organic, rough-sounding instrument."

It's hovering!

Mal looks up at the chandelier.

MAL
What's the point of that, I wonder?

KAYLEE
Ooh, pineapples.

Mal is still eyeing the chandelier.

MAL
I mean, I get how they did it. I just ain't seeing the why.

KAYLEE
These girls have the most beautiful dresses. And so do I, how 'bout that!

MAL
Well, careful with it. We cheated Badger outta good money to buy that frippery. You're s'posed to make me look respectable.

KAYLEE
Yes sir, Captain Tightpants.

Mal starts looking around, seeking someone out.

MAL
I'm looking for our guy, Harrow.

KAYLEE
And Inara. We should look for her, right? Just to halloo at her.

MAL
(too casual)
If we see her. Think she's wearing gold.

Kaylee is distracted by a passing group of attractive young men in fancy clothes.

KAYLEE
(to Mal, too loudly)
Say, lookit the boys!

Nearby party-goers glance over. Mal winces. Kaylee doesn't notice.

KAYLEE (cont'd)
Some of them's pretty as the Doctor.

She stares, struck speechless, as a waiter passes, carrying a huge BOWL OF ENORMOUS STRAWBERRIES to the buffet table.

MAL
Help me find our man. S'posed to be older, kinda stocky, wearing a red sash crossways.

Kaylee never takes her eyes off the strawberries.

KAYLEE
Why's he doing that?

MAL
Maybe he won the Miss Persephone pageant. Help me look.

KAYLEE
That him?

Mal looks where she's pointing, at the buffet table.

MAL
That's the buffet table.

KAYLEE
How can we be sure? You know, unless we question it?

MAL
Fine. Don't make yourself sick.

Kaylee flashes him a big smile.

KAYLEE
<Sheh-sheh> [Thank you], Cap'n!

And she's off to the buffet. Mal heads off on his own.

INT. SERENITY COMMON AREA/KITCHEN - NIGHT

SIMON, BOOK and Jayne play Chore Poker (it's actually a variant of poker which we'll call tall card). It's played with small metal playing cards. And instead of chips, they're playing for pieces of

METAL CARDS

Prop master Randy Eriksen: "The metal cards were great. I found them down in Chinatown and they were bright, shiny gold things. I ended up spray-painting them black and steel-wooling it off, to age them. The sound guy hated them since they were metal and clanked a lot. Anything that looks that good has got to be bad for sound."

paper. Each man has a collection of paper pieces in front of him — Simon has the least and Book the most. Simon starts to deal.

SIMON
Ante up, gentlemen.
(antes piece of paper)
Dishes.

BOOK
(anteing)
Dishes. Could do with less of them.

JAYNE
(anteing)
Garbage.

Simon completes the deal, five cards to each. The three men study their cards.

Simon lays A SINGLE ROUND CARD FACE-UP on the table.

SIMON
(re: round card)
Tall card... plum. Plums are tall.

BOOK
I'll take two.

SIMON
(giving cards)
Two. No tall card claim.

JAYNE
(re: his hand)
Speakin' of garbage.
(then)
Gimme three.

SIMON
(giving cards)
Three. And...
(taking the round card)
Dealer forced to claim the tall. I'd've cleared flower-side wasn't for this.

BOOK
What do you s'pose the Captain and Kaylee are doing now?
(betting)
Septic vac.

JAYNE
Eatin' steaks off plates made a' solid money, like as anything. I fold.

SIMON
Me too. Tall card's 'round my neck like a weight.

KAYLEE

"Yes sir, Captain Tightpants."

Embarking on an interview about her portrayal of Kaylee, Jewel Staite laughs. "I guess I've established that *Firefly* was the love of my life. I tend to gush like crazy, but it's totally genuine. I don't think anything will ever compare."

Staite began her screen acting career aged nine in the telefilm *Posing* and has since been a series regular on *Higher Ground* and *Da Vinci's Inquest* — she was also tapped for a recurring role on *Wonderfalls* by Tim Minear when *Firefly* ended.

"Initially, I was sent a very brief synopsis of the show and a very brief synopsis of the character," Staite recalls of her introduction to *Firefly* and Kaylee. She videotaped an audition in Vancouver, where she lives, then was asked to meet Joss Whedon in LA. After this she was offered the role, which meant relocating. "It all happened very fast. I had just gotten engaged and my fiancé, who's now my husband, decided to come with me. We just packed up all our things and left and that was that. And it was great. I love LA."

When she was first cast, Staite says she didn't know what the sets for the spaceship, Serenity, would be like. "I didn't know how much was going to be CGI and I didn't know how many soundstages we had access to or anything like that, so when I showed up and saw that each level of the ship was actually one long piece of set, it blew my mind. It was awesome."

As for Kaylee's look, "I remember when we had the hair and makeup test near the beginning and the character read as a bit of a tomboy. She loves boys and she loves dressing up — though she doesn't often get a chance to. I really saw her as this feminine person who loved love and was such a romantic — and she flirts with everybody shamelessly. I really wanted her to have that femininity in her, so I made sure that the hair was a little bit glamorous and she had a little bit of lip gloss — as much as Joss would allow. I really wanted her to be kind of cute and girly, and I really liked that Shawna [Trpcic] was really into that and got a bunch

of flowered shirts and cute, frilly kinds of stuff."

Just how flirty is Kaylee? "Very flirty," Staite laughs. "I think that's how Kaylee gets what she wants — whether she knows it or not, she's a huge flirt. She flirts with everybody on the whole ship. And I think that's part of her charm, whether she's aware of that or not."

One arguable exception is found in Kaylee's relationship with Jayne. "But at the same time, she's soft with Jayne," Staite points out. "I've always said that Kaylee is the one character that everybody trusts on that ship, and I think even Jayne trusts her, and he cares about her. It's obvious when she gets shot in the pilot episode and he's watching her in the infirmary that he really does care about her and really does like her. I think she and Jayne are kind of like brother and sister. I love that they have these scenes where they're just talking about everything that's going on around them and venting at each other. I think Kaylee's loyalty lies with the Captain, and since the Captain's not too hot on Jayne, she's not as nice to him as she could be, but I think she really does care about him."

The relationship between mechanic Kaylee and her beloved ship is key to *Firefly*. "I think Kaylee has always viewed Serenity as the tenth crewmember," Staite says. "It's very dear to her, it's her home, it's probably the only steady home she's ever really had, and I think she's just so proud of it. Right from the very beginning, Joss said that he wanted Kaylee's affection for the ship to be really obvious, so there was a lot of patting of the walls and admiration for the engine. She's just so amazed by how it all works and the fact that she gets to work on it."

As for Kaylee's self-imposed role as peacemaker, Staite says, "I've always thought that the reason why Kaylee steps in and defends people is that she wants everybody to get along. I think one of her biggest goals on that ship is to have everybody finally get along and nobody hate each other; she's always so upset and wringing her hands and doesn't know what to do when people are fighting. She doesn't want any negativity on that boat. She's kind of the only one who really gets the point that all they really have is each other, so it's important to her that everybody gets along."

JAYNE
Take it, Shepherd.

BOOK
Thank you, gents. That's a nice pile of things I don't have to do.

The CAMERA FINDS RIVER, sitting in the kitchen, next to a box of supplies. She takes the label off a can of peaches.

RIVER
There it is, there it is. It's always there if you look for it. Everybody sees and nobody sees it...

BACK AT THE GAME:

Jayne shuffles.

SIMON
The party is probably a buffet. And there'll be dancing. And beautiful women. Dozens of them.

JAYNE
And you can dance with any of 'em?

SIMON
Well, there are social conventions, ways of asking, ways of declining...

BOOK
It sounds very complicated. I'll never understand why it's considered a sacrifice to live a simple life.

JAYNE
Yeah. I wouldn't trade this for nothing, playing cards for a night off from septic vac duty.

IN THE KITCHEN

River has three cans unlabeled, and she's crushing a box of crackers. It has a visible, not emphasized, "Blue Sun" on it. She gets more violent and loud as she continues.

RIVER
These are the ones that take you! Little ones in the corner that you almost don't see. But they're the ones that reach in and do it. They're the ones with teeth and you have to smash them!

AT THE GAME

River's ranting is audible now. Simon drops his cards and goes to her. Book follows.

SIMON
River?

BOOK
Is she hurt?

JAYNE
Better see to her.
(called after)
Bad habit for a fugitive. She's gonna do that in public some day, get herself hauled off.

Jayne moves a few exemptions from Book's pile to his own.

IN THE KITCHEN

Simon has an arm around River, calming her down. Book looks at the supplies. River rants the whole time.

SIMON
(as River rants)
River, it's me. Calm down.

BOOK
(as River rants)
She didn't harm much.
(re: cans)
We'll have a few mystery meals.

SIMON
(as River rants)
River, it's okay. It's okay.

RIVER
A million things, and the little ends of the roots go everywhere and when you brush your teeth or all the little blue things are there but no one says it because, because sometimes they're afraid. And then they come...

She winds down, stops talking. Book and Simon relax.

JAYNE
So, we gonna play cards, or we gonna screw around?

INT. ZOE AND WASH'S QUARTERS - SAME TIME

Wash and Zoe in a post-coital tangle, limbs and sheets, exhausted and happy.

ZOE
Thought you wanted to spend time off-ship this visit.

WASH
Seems like out there it's all fancy parties. I like our party better. The dress code's easier and I know all the steps.

Zoe's eyes are closing.

ZOE
I'd say you do, at that.

WASH
Don't fall asleep now. Sleepiness is weakness of character, ask anyone.

Zoe starts to laugh, her eyes still closed.

ZOE
It is not!

WASH
You're acting Captain. You know what happens, you fall asleep?

ZOE
Jayne slits my throat and takes over?

WASH
That's right!

ZOE
And we can't stop it?

WASH
I wash my hands of it. Hopeless case. I'll read a nice poem at the funeral. Something with imagery.

ZOE
You could lock the door. Keep the power-hungry maniac at bay.

WASH
Don't know. I'm starting to like this poetry thing. "Here lies my beloved Zoe, my autumn flower, somewhat less attractive now that she's all corpse-ified and gross..."

Zoe hits him with a pillow.

INT. PARTY

Back at the party, Kaylee approaches an attractive BOY (early twenties) who is watching the dancers.

KAYLEE
(re: dancers)
Aren't they something? Like butterflies or little pieces of wrapping paper, blowing around...

The boy turns toward her and bows politely and moves away. But there's too much going on for Kaylee to be disappointed.

She joins a group of four GIRLS her age and younger, standing and gossiping. She waits until

JEWEL STAITE

On the hoopskirt: "It wasn't so bad getting in and out of it. It was just sitting in it — I couldn't sit in a normal chair, so I had to sit on an apple box and I couldn't support my back. Every time I had to go to the bathroom, somebody had to come and take my hoop off in front of the whole crew. They had to hike up my skirt and untie the thing and it was sort of embarrassing, but I got over it pretty fast. At one point, I kind of peed on my dress. I totally didn't mean to. But the hoopskirt was so huge and the stall was so small... For the rest of the episode, I had to go around knowing there was pee on the hem of my dress. I just learned to stop drinking so much water and not pee as much!"

a group-laugh subsides.

KAYLEE (cont'd)
Hello!

One of the girls, BANNING, seems to be the queen bee. She looks at Kaylee in surprise.

BANNING
I don't... have we been introduced?

Kaylee grabs Banning's hand, shakes it with enthusiasm.

KAYLEE
I'm Kaylee.

BANNING
Banning. And this is Destra, Cabott, and Zelle.

KAYLEE
Don't you love this party? Everything's so fancy and there's some kind of hot cheese over there.

CABOTT
It's not as good as last year.

KAYLEE
Really? What'd they have last year?

CABOTT
Standards.

Destra and Zelle giggle, but Banning looks sympathetic.

BANNING
You're not from Persephone, are you?

KAYLEE
I'm from Serenity. Neat little Firefly class. I keep the engines. She's a sweet runner.

BANNING
Uh-huh. Who made your dress, Kaylee?

KAYLEE
Oh, do you like it? When I saw the ruffles, I just couldn't — <Shuh muh?> [What?]

BANNING
You ought to see to your girl.

KAYLEE
<Shuh muh?> [What?]

BANNING
(confidential)

Your girl. She's not very good. She made you a dress looks like you bought it in a store.

The other girls giggle again, but Banning plays it off with a straight face.

KAYLEE
Oh. I... I didn't know...

BANNING
I'm only trying to help. No one wants you to look foolish...

A nearby guest, MURPHY, a kind-looking man in his fifties, interrupts.

MURPHY
(off-hand, for Kaylee's benefit)
Why Banning Miller, what a vision you are in that fine dress. Must have taken a dozen slaves a dozen days just to get you into that get-up. 'Course your daddy tells me it takes the space of a schoolboy's wink to get you out of it again.

Banning leaves, mortified. Her friends are suppressing giggles.

MURPHY (cont'd)
(to Kaylee)
Forgive my rudeness. I can not abide useless people.

SOME DISTANCE AWAY, MAL

approaches HARROW, who is indeed wearing a red sash. Harrow is upper-crust, an acute observer with a strong code of behavior. He doesn't immediately take to rough-edged Mal.

MAL
Beg pardon, sir. But would you be Mr. Warrick Harrow?

It's a bad start.

HARROW
Sir Warrick Harrow. The sash.

MAL
The sash.

HARROW
It indicates lordhood.

MAL
And it's, it's doing a great job.

Harrow moves a few steps away, dismissing Mal.

Mal has to follow.

MAL (cont'd)
Sir, my name is Malcolm Reynolds. I captain a ship, name of Serenity. I mention this because I have been led to understand you want to move some property off-world...

Mal is distracted as INARA AND ATHERTON DANCE NEARBY. No one makes eye contact, but Mal and Inara are very aware of each other. Harrow observes this.

MAL (cont'd)
...some property off-world, discreetly.

Harrow takes a closer look at Mal. Still not impressed.

HARROW
You're mistaken, sir. I'm an honest man.

MAL
Seems to me, there's nothing dishonest about getting your goods to people what need them.

HARROW
You're concerned about the poor. And yet, for what you're offering, you'd want money, I imagine.

MAL
Well, sir, I think you'll find that working with me is giving to the poor.

HARROW
Whom is it you represent?

MAL
"Represent" isn't exactly —

HARROW
Don't waste my time.

MAL
Fellow called Badger.

HARROW
I know him. And I think he's a psychotic lowlife.

MAL
And I think calling him that is an offense to the psychotic lowlife community. But the deal is solid.

Mal is startled by a touch on his arm. He turns, surprised to see Atherton there. Inara, unsmiling, is at his elbow.

ATHERTON
Sorry to interrupt.
(a greeting)
Sir Harrow. I know you from the club, I believe.

Harrow nods, coolly.

INARA
(resigned)
Captain, this is Atherton Wing. Atherton, Captain Mal Reynolds.

Atherton and Mal shake hands, sizing each other up.

MAL
Pleased to meet'cha. Inara, I didn't realize you were going to this party.

INARA
(icy)
It's the only party.

MAL
And I can see why. How 'bout that floating chandelier?

Atherton circles Inara's arm with his hand... a gesture that is both affectionate and possessive.

ATHERTON
How do you come to be here, Captain?

MAL
Oh I love a party. I was just telling that to my friend here.

ATHERTON
(to Harrow)
I didn't know you were acquainted.

HARROW
It is beginning to seem unavoidable.

Mal watches as Atherton's fingers shift on Inara's arm. We can see the white circle the pressure of his fingers has left. Mal sees that, makes a decision.

MAL
Ath. Can I call you Ath? Inara has spoken of you to me. She made a point of your generosity. Given that, I'm sure you won't kick if I ask Inara the favor of a dance.

Atherton hesitates, can't find a way out.

ATHERTON
Of course.

Atherton and Harrow end up standing side by side watching as Mal leads an angry Inara onto the dance floor.

HARROW
(to Atherton)
You're a brave man.

ATHERTON
(clipped)
I know what's mine.

Harrow scowls, disliking Atherton.

MAL AND INARA

On the dance floor.

INARA
Why are you here?

The music begins for their dance — it's a courtly and complicated dance, rather Regency England in style. Mal watches the other couples. It's easy at first, lots of walking around each other.

MAL
Business, same's you. I was talking to a contact about a smuggling job, and you came over to *me*.

INARA
You were staring at me.

MAL
I saw you, is all. You stand out.

The dance takes them apart for a few beats, bowing and curtsying to other couples.

Mal starts to make his curtsy mistake as in The Train Job, but he corrects it. They come back together and now dance palm-to-palm.

INARA
In this company, Captain, I believe you are the one who stands out.

MAL
Maybe I just like watching a professional at work, then. Is this the hardest part, would you say, or does that come later?

INARA
You have no call to try to make me ashamed of my job. What I do is legal, and how is that *smuggling* coming?

MAL
My work's illegal, but it's honest.

INARA
What?!

MAL
While this... the *lie* of it... that man parading you on his arm as if he actually won you, as if he loves you, and everyone going along with it. How can that not bother you?

INARA
"Going along with it"?

MAL
He treats you like an ornament. Other men look at you and discuss if you're worth the cost. The women talk behind their fans, picturing you with their husbands. And to your face, they're sweet as pie.

INARA
That's not true.

MAL
Well, I guess you'd know. It's not my world.

INARA
These people like me, and I like them. I like Atherton too, by the way.

MAL
Well, sure, what's not to like? I'm liable to sleep with him myself.

INARA
And he likes *me*, whether you see it or not.

MAL
(dismissive)
Of course.

INARA
He's made me an offer.

Mal didn't expect that.

INARA (cont'd)
You may think he doesn't honor me. But he wants me to live here. I would be his personal Companion.

MAL
<Wah!> [Wow!] That's as romantic as a marriage proposal. No wait, it's not.

INARA
It would be a good life, Mal. I could belong here. Call me pretentious, but there is some

appeal in that.

Mal reacts to the word "pretentious", startled by it. Beat.

MAL
I... You're right. I got no call to stop you.

Inara accepts that for the concession it is. Then:

INARA
I see Kaylee is here.

MAL
Girl was crying Cinderella tears. Shoulda seen her, when I said she could have that layer cake she's wearin'.

Inara relaxes a little.

INARA
I think she looks adorable.

MAL
Well, yeah, but I never said it.

KAYLEE

She's now surrounded by a group of gentlemen farmers, Murphy and his friends. Many of them are older, some young.

She's enjoying chocolate mints, talking with her mouth full. The men are laughing. The dialogue overlaps as they debate:

KAYLEE
I'm not saying the eighty-oh-four's hard to repair, it just ain't worth it.

OLDER FARMER
It's a fine machine, keep it tuned—

KAYLEE
<Tsai boo shr.> [No way.] The extenders ain't braced.

MURPHY
(re: older farmer)
We've been tellin' him buy an eighty-ten for years!

KAYLEE
(overlapping Murphy)
Those 'tenders snap off, it don't matter how good the engine's cyclin'.

YOUNGER FARMER
(jumping in quick)
Miss Kaylee, I wonder if I could request the honor of—

He's shouted down by the other men:

FARMERS
Dance later!/She's talking./Let her talk.

KAYLEE
(to Murphy)
By the way, the eighty-ten's the same machine. They changed the plating, hoped no one'd notice!

If you knew these machines, oh, you'd find this hilarious. The men laugh, urging her on.

MAL AND INARA

The dance gets more complicated now, some tricky footwork. Inara and all the other dancers do it easily. Mal stumbles. He catches himself with hands around Inara's waist. As the music ends, he straightens himself out, grins at her.

MAL
Possible you were right before. This ain't my kind of a party.

Inara can't help herself and she smiles. Atherton is suddenly there. He's seen enough. He takes her back roughly, hauling her by the arm.

MAL (cont'd)
Watch yourself there. No need for any hands-on.

Guests, including Harrow, look at the public display.

ATHERTON
Excuse me. She's not here with you, Captain. She's mine.

MAL
Yours? She don't belong to nobody.

ATHERTON
Money changed hands. Makes her mine tonight. And no matter how you dress her up, she's still—

Without warning, Mal hauls off and PUNCHES ATHERTON, lays him right down on the floor. Mal smiles and looks to Inara.

MAL
Turns out this is my kind of a party!

Harrow looks impressed, watching everything.

INARA
Oh, Mal...

MAL
What? Man was out of line —

ATHERTON
(as he rises)
I accept!

MAL
That's great. What?

GENTLEMAN
There has been a challenge!

Atherton is on his feet.

ATHERTON
I hope you're prepared, Captain.

MAL
You all talkin' 'bout a *fight*? Well, fine, let's get out of here!

INARA
It's not a fist fight, Mal.

GENTLEMAN
The duel will be met tomorrow morning, at Cadrie Pond.

MAL
Why wait? Where's that guard? He collected a whole mess a' pistols—

GENTLEMAN
If you require it, any gentleman here can give you use of a sword.

MAL
Use of a... s'what?

END OF ACT TWO

ACT THREE

INT. PARTY - CONTINUING

People are where we left them. Mal looks confused. Harrow, Inara and the ballroom full of people look on.

MAL
I laid the fellow out. Seems to me the transaction is complete. Also satisfying.

GENTLEMAN
Everyone, enjoy the party, please! There's no further action here.

The crowd disperses, including Atherton, who

moves away with an evil look at Mal. Kaylee separates herself from the crowd, moving in close to Mal.

KAYLEE
(to Mal)
What's going on?

MAL
Not rightly sure.
(to Harrow)
What's going on?

HARROW
Well, first off, you'll be put up in lodgings for the night, so you don't disappear. I wouldn't blame you, incidentally. Wing may be a spoiled dandy, but he's an expert swordsman. He's killed a dozen men with a longblade and you're the only one gave him a reason.

MAL
This is a joke.

INARA
And he'll need a second.

MAL
What's that?

HARROW
I'll take on the job.

INARA
He fights if you refuse—

ATHERTON (O.S.)
Inara!

ANGLE ON ATHERTON: Waiting impatiently. She hesitates.

ATHERTON
Come with me, please.

MAL
(to Harrow)
You takin' this on, being my second. Does this mean we're in business?

Harrow chuckles.

HARROW
It means you're in mortal danger. But you mussed up Atherton's face and that has endeared me to you somewhat. You might even give him a fight before he guts you.

ATHERTON
Inara!

Inara tears herself away, eyes still on Mal. Finally she turns, goes to Atherton. Mal watches her go.

KAYLEE
(apologetically helpful)
Up til the punching, it was a real nice party.

INT. SERENITY - CARGO BAY - NIGHT

Jayne is in the cargo bay, working out with those hanging rungs under the catwalk. His shotgun

leans against a wall nearby.

He's interrupted by a loud metallic BANGING.

Jayne crosses and opens the door (not the ramp, the door into the airlock), revealing Badger, holding a wrench. He's been banging on the door with it.

BADGER
(off-hand)
Your Captain's gone and got hisself in trouble.

TIME CUT TO:

INT. SERENITY - CARGO BAY - NIGHT

Badger stands near the infirmary end of the cargo bay. The assembled crew, Zoe, Wash, Jayne, Simon, Book, are gathered around, back to the closed ramp. (River isn't there.)

BOOK
A duel?

WASH
With swords?

SIMON
The Captain's a good fighter. He must know how to handle a sword.

Simon and Book look to Zoe hopefully.

ZOE
I think he knows which end to hold.

SIMON
All right. So now we just need to figure how to get him out of there.

BOOK
We have until the morning, correct?
(to Badger)
Do you know what lodging he's in?

BADGER
Oh, this is embarrassing. Some of you seem to be misapprehending my purpose in being here.

Zoe stands. It's suddenly clear that now, this is her ship.

ZOE
You're here to make sure we don't do what these men are keen on doing.

BADGER
Penny for the smart lady. Persephone's my home. I gotta do business with the people here. I don't want it known I brought someone in caused this kinda ruckus. We'll just settle in here til this blows over one way or t'other—

Jayne is suddenly there, at Badger's back, shotgun raised. Jayne points the gun at Badger's head.

ZOE
(calm)
Jayne. I wouldn't.

BADGER'S COSTUME

Costume designer Shawna Trpcic notes, "Originally, Badger was supposed to be played by Joss. So we designed it for Joss." However, Mark A. Sheppard wound up playing the role. "Mark was incredibly perfect for the role and fit Joss's clothes like they were made for him, so we just altered a little bit here and there. I love pink and when I bought my house, somebody put two sculpted pink flamingos out front as a welcome, and I adopted them as my mascots. I put my little pink flamingos touch on Badger for his second visit in 'Shindig', but the bowler hat, all that was from Joss. How he tied his cravat and those special touches — that was Mark. We had the cravat, we had the scarf, we had everything, but he added his own little style to it."

For sharp-eyed viewers, do Trpcic's flamingos turn up elsewhere in *Firefly*? "No. I was going to do a Jayne t-shirt with a pink flamingo on it as a print, but we got shut down."

JAYNE
Why not?

Zoe looks toward the doorway. Jayne follows the look...

ANGLE ON THE DOORWAY: FOUR OF BADGER'S LADS: all of them with guns. One of them has a scared Kaylee by the arm.

KAYLEE
(small)
Hi.

Jayne sags.

INT. LODGING - HALL AND ROOM - NIGHT

Inara slips quietly down a hallway, like a modern hotel hall, only with Chinese numbers on the doors. And, oddly, round SHALLOW HOLES INSTEAD OF DOORKNOBS (the holes don't go all the way through the doors). She stops at a closed door.

Now we get to see how a hotel key works. She is holding a small metal sphere with a small protruding round shaft. The sphere is about two thirds the size of a regular doorknob. She holds it near the hole in the door and magnets pull it in. THE SHAFT FITS INTO THE HOLE ON THE DOOR AND, THUS, THE SPHERE BECOMES A DOORKNOB! The mechanism hums and A SMALL LIGHT COMES ON. She turns it, unlocking and opening the door.

She enters quietly and we see the room, again, not too different from a modern hotel room. A sword lies on the bed.

Mal, suit coat off, shirt sleeves rolled up, stands, back to her, brandishing a second sword with ridiculous flourishes.

Inara makes a noise and Mal JUMPS. He spins to see her. His sword swings, hits the wall and the tip embeds in the plaster. The sword hangs there.

MAL
What are you doing here?

He tugs at the embedded sword, trying not to be obvious.

INARA
Atherton's a heavy sleeper, night before a big day. He's got the killing you in the morning, then a haircut later.

MAL
It's such a comfort having friends visit at a time like this.

Mal tugs the sword free. Inara looks around the room.

INARA
I knew the accommodations would be nice. Atherton doesn't skimp.

MAL
Don't s'pose I like being kept by him s'much as

others do. How come you're still attached to him?

INARA
Because it's my decision. Not yours.

MAL
Thought he made it pretty clear he's got no regard for you.

INARA
You did manage to push him into saying something, yes. Made a nice justification for the punch.

MAL
He insulted you. I hit him. Seemed like the thing to do. Why'd this get so complicated?

INARA
Well, it's about to get simpler. There's a back door. I have the desk clerk on alert. He'll let us out.

MAL
I'm not gonna run off.

Inara looks at him, surprised.

MAL (cont'd)
No matter what you've got into your head, I didn't do this to prove some kinda point to you. I actually thought I was defending your honor. And I never back down from a fight.

INARA
Yes you do! You do all the time!

MAL
Yeah, okay. But I'm not backing down from this one.

INARA
He's an expert swordsman, Mal. You had trouble with that wall. How will your death help my "honor"?

MAL
But see, I'm looking to have it be his death. 'S why I need lessons.

Mal picks the other sword off the bed and throws it to her. She catches it expertly.

MAL (cont'd)
Figure you'd know how. Educated lady like you.

INT. SERENITY - CARGO BAY

It's still a hostage situation here in the cargo bay.

Wash has his head down, trying to sleep. Book reads his bible and prays silently.

Badger leans against the wall, eating an apple.

Jayne, Simon and Zoe talk quietly, pretending to play cards. Kaylee is bending over to talk to them.

KAYLEE
...but he said not to do anything. He'll join us after he wins the duel.

JAYNE
And what if he don't win?

ZOE
It doesn't hurt to have a contingency plan, Kaylee.

Kaylee moves away, unconvinced.

SIMON
I'm thinking, since we're unarmed, we should take them by surprise all at once.

ZOE
Not necessarily. We could lure one or two of 'em away, say, to the infirmary, take 'em out, be on Badger 'fore he knows what happened.

ANGLE ON THE DOORWAY FROM THE INFIRMARY: River appears. She looks blank and aimless. No one sees her, and the discussion continues.

JAYNE
Only if his attention's elsewhere. We need a diversion. I say Zoe gets nekkid.

Wash, without raising his head:

WASH
Nope.

JAYNE
I could get nekkid.

SIMON/ZOE/WASH
No!

Book looks up and sees River. He winces, but keeps his reaction small. He gets up casually and makes his way over to Simon. Book puts a hand on Simon's back.

SIMON
What?

BOOK
(whispers)
Don't look now. In the doorway.

ANGLE ON: River. She's stepped over the threshold now...

Simon tenses, starts to stand up.

SIMON
I'll get her out 'fore he spots her.

Simon heads toward River. Badger doesn't look up. Simon is at her, hand on her arm...

ANGLE ON: RIVER AND SIMON

SIMON (cont'd)
(whispers)
River. You can't be here...

RIVER
(whispers)
There's things in the air in there. Tiny things.

SIMON
Come on...

SUMMER GLAU

One moment that really stands out for me is my scene with Badger in 'Shindig'. I love Mark Sheppard so much and he coached me through that scene. He took time out, on his own time, in a little café in Studio City, to coach me on my accent.

Simon tries to lead her back inside, but she pulls back, smiling a little, thinking it's a game.

RIVER
Pull, pull...

SIMON
River! Please!

BADGER (O.S.)
Who's this then?

Simon turns to see Badger, standing close. River avoids Badger's gaze, turning toward Simon for protection.

BADGER
Look at me. What's your story, luv?

River looks around, unfocused.

SIMON
She's just a passenger.

BADGER
(to Simon)
Yeah? Why ain't she talking? She got a secret?

SIMON
No, I'm sure not—

RIVER
(in Badger's accent)
Sure, I got a secret. More'n one.

River raises her head, looks Badger in the eye. She's completely sane, unafraid, and she sounds like she's from his home town. She's also kinda pissed.

RIVER (cont'd)
Don't seem likely I'd tell 'em to you, do it? Anyone off Dyton Colony knows better'n to talk to strangers.

She picks something off Badger's lapel, looks at it, wipes it back onto him.

RIVER
You're talking loud enough for the both of us, though, ain't you? I've known a dozen like you. Skipped off home early, minor graft jobs here and there. Spent some time in the lock-down, I warrant, but less than you claim. Now you're what, petty thief with delusions of standing? Sad little king of a sad little hill.

After a beat...

BADGER
Nice to see someone from the old homestead.

RIVER
Not really.

(to Simon)
Call me f'anyone interesting shows up.

BADGER
(to Simon)
I like her.

ANGLE ON: JAYNE and ZOE.

JAYNE
That there? 'Xactly the kind of diversion we coulda used.

INT. MAL'S LODGING - PRE-DAWN

The furniture has been pushed to the walls. In the center of the cleared room, Inara and Mal face off, holding swords.

INARA
Attack.

He attacks, swinging the sword. She slips out of the way.

INARA (cont'd)
How did I avoid that?

MAL
By being fast like a freak.

INARA
No. Because you always attack the same way, swinging from the shoulder like you're chopping wood. You have to thrust with the point sometimes, or swing from the elbow.

MAL
Swinging from the shoulder feels stronger.

She touches his arm, adjusting his swing, controlling it. It's an intimate touch.

INARA
It's also slower, Mal. You don't need strength as much as speed. We're fragile creatures. It takes less than a pound of pressure to cut skin.

MAL
You *know* that? They teach you that at the whore academy?

Inara backs away, breaking the contact.

INARA
You have a strange sense of nobility, Captain. You'll lay a man out for implying I'm a whore, but you keep calling me one to my face.

MAL
I might not show respect to your job, but he didn't respect you. That's the difference. Inara, he doesn't even *see* you.

INARA
Well, I'm sure death will settle the issue to everyone's satisfaction.

MAL
This <yu bun duh> [stupid] duel is the result of rules of your society, not mine.

She's angry now, waving her sword as she gestures.

INARA
Mal, you *always* break the rules. It doesn't matter which "society" you're in! You don't get along with ordinary criminals either! That's why you're constantly in trouble!

Mal backs away from her sword.

MAL
And you think following rules will buy you a nice life, even if the rules make you a slave.

Inara, turns away, frustrated almost to tears.

Then, Mal, avoiding her eye:

MAL (cont'd)
Don't take his offer.

Inara turns and stares at him.

INARA
What?

MAL
Don't do it. Because, in the case it comes up, that means he's the fella killed me. And I don't like fellas that killed me. Not in general.

He starts practicing again, unable to look at her.

MAL (cont'd)
I said before I had no call to stop you. And that's true. But, anyways... don't.

INARA
I need to get back. He'll be up early.

And she exits, leaving him alone. He swings the sword.

MAL
Right. He's got that big day.

EXT. PERSEPHONE - MORNING (DAY 3)

A grassy pond at dawn would be lovely. Eight spectators, all men, cluster around the duelling area. Among them are a couple of Badger's lads. The crowd shifts and CHATTERS with anticipation.

Mal and Harrow stand, heads together, to one side. Harrow is smiling, Mal looks intense, adjusting and readjusting his grip on his sword. He's still wearing his dressy suit.

Atherton and his Second, another young dandy, are at the other side, talking and laughing easily. Inara stands near them, but her eyes are on Mal.

He meets her look, holds it.

The gentleman who first announced the challenge steps to the center. He raises his hands, commanding attention. Gradually the crowd quiets. He clears his throat.

GENTLEMAN
Ladies and gentlemen, the field of combat is a somber place. A man will here today lay down his life. Let the duel begin.

The last sentence is given no special emphasis, and there is no sound from the crowd. Mal doesn't even realize the fight has begun until the gentleman blends back into the crowd and Atherton steps out, smiling and handling his sword casually.

Mal steps forward, uncertain.

HARROW has moved over by Inara. They exchange a grim look.

MAL AND ATHERTON

face off. Atherton attacks first, an easy swing that Mal parries.

Mal hits back, thrusting with the point of the sword. Atherton barely gets out of the way in time, in fact, his vest is nicked.

MAL
Best be careful, Ath. I hear these things are sharp.

HARROW AND INARA

HARROW
He thinks he's doing well, doesn't he?

INARA
He's being toyed with.

BACK TO THE FIGHT

Mal ducks to avoid a blow.

Atherton brings up his blade to deflect a blow. CLANG.

While Mal hesitates, Atherton tosses his blade in the air and catches it with the other hand, showing off.

Mal gets nicked on the arm.

Atherton parries a blow away with such force it throws Mal off-balance.

Atherton steps back, and PUTS HIS SWORD BEHIND HIS BACK.

HARROW
What's he doing?

INARA
(gritted teeth)
Don't fall for that.

Mal lunges. Atherton steps to the side, the lunge goes past him. Atherton strikes, as he had planned, attacking sideways with the sword from behind his back, stabbing Mal in the side.

Inara looks stricken.

HARROW
Well, this isn't going to take long, is it?

On Mal, looking down, shocked, at his wound.

END OF ACT THREE

ACT FOUR

EXT. PERSEPHONE - CONTINUING

The crowd is more active now, sensing the end is near.

Mal fights one-handed, his left hand staunching his wound. He's definitely losing now.

Atherton thrusts with the sword. Mal stumbles back clumsily.

Mal lunges. Atherton steps back. Mal lunges again. Atherton steps back again, laughing.

Atherton swings, cutting Mal's defensive arm.

HARROW
(to Inara)
We're coming up on the end, miss. You might not want to watch.

Mal thrusts. He sword CLASHES AGAINST Atherton's sword. MAL'S SWORD BREAKS. And the momentum carries Mal to one knee. Atherton's sword points at his chest.

INARA
Atherton! Wait!

Atherton hesitates, he may be about to get what he wants...

INARA (cont'd)
I'll stay here! Exclusive to you! Just let him live.

ON MAL, still down, as he registers what Inara's doing.

Mal lunges to his feet, catching Atherton under the chin with the hilt and throwing him back, face cut.

Atherton is regrouping, ready to move in for the kill again. He brings his sword arm back...

But Mal KICKS HIS BROKEN SWORD POINT OFF THE GROUND and up into his hand. He THROWS the broken sword point at Atherton like a dart!

Atherton takes the sword point in the shoulder. It sticks there, and Atherton, furious, reaches to pull it out.

Mal raises the hilt, still around his right hand, and brings it down like a gun butt, over Atherton's head. Atherton sprawls on the ground.

GENTLEMAN
He's down!

Mal scoops up Atherton's dropped sword off the ground and holds it, point at Atherton's heart. He freezes there.

HARROW
You have to finish it, lad. For a man to lie beaten and yet breathing, it makes him a coward.

INARA
It's a humiliation.

Mal pulls the sword back a little.

MAL
Sure. It would be humiliating, having to lie there while the better man refuses to spill your blood. Mercy is the mark of a great man.

Very quickly, offhandedly, Mal STABS Atherton!

MAL (cont'd)
Guess I'm just a good man.

He STABS him again!

MAL (cont'd)
Well, I'm all right.

Mal grins and tosses the sword aside. Inara goes to him.

Atherton gets up slowly. The crowd draws back, whispering behind their hands.

ATHERTON
Inara! Come here!

She ignores him.

ATHERTON (cont'd)
Inara!

Harrow puts a hand on Atherton's arm.

HARROW
You've lost her, lad. Be gracious.

Atherton shakes off Harrow's hand and staggers to Inara.

ATHERTON
You set this up, whore. After I bought and paid for you. I should have uglied you up so no one else'd want you.

MAL
(to Inara)
See how I'm not punching him? I think I've grown.

ATHERTON
(to Inara)
Get ready to starve. I'll see to it you never work again.

INARA
Actually, that's not how it works. You see, you've earned yourself a black mark in the client registry. No Companion is going to contract with you ever again.

HARROW
You'll have to rely on your winning personality to get women. God help you.

Inara and Mal start to walk away. Harrow joins them.

HARROW (cont'd)
You didn't have to wound that man.

MAL
I know, that was just funny.

HARROW
You willing to fight that hard to protect my property, I'll have it in your hold before midnight.

Mal nods. The deal is struck. Mal and Inara walk away, Mal a little unsteady.

MAL
(through pain)
Mighty fine shindig.

INT. SERENITY - CARGO BAY - DAY

Morning. Badger stands with his lads. Simon talks quietly to Book. Jayne pours coffee for Kaylee and Wash and Zoe.

JAYNE
(softly to Zoe)
Doc is filling the Shepherd in on the plan. We're ready to move on your signal. Doc's the diversion—

MAL (O.S.)
Did you ever see such a lazy crew?

CAMERA FINDS Mal and Inara in the doorway. Inara is helping hold him up, and he's still got a hand over his wound.

KAYLEE
Captain!

Kaylee runs to him. The others follow.

SIMON
You're hurt.

Badger approaches Mal.

BADGER
You get us a deal?

ZOE
(to Badger)
Back off, he's injured.

MAL
I got a deal. Now get off my ship.

Badger's heard all he needs to. He's a happy man.

BADGER
Ta very much for a lovely night then.

Badger exits. Inara and Simon guide Mal into a chair. The others gather around. Quickly:

BOOK
Are you badly hurt?

JAYNE
We was just about to spring into action, Captain. A complicated escape and rescue op.

WASH
I was gonna watch. It was very exciting.

EXT. SERENITY - IN FLIGHT - EFFECT

Serenity against a star field.

INT. SERENITY - DAY (DAY 4)

In the engine room, a grease-smudged Kaylee finishes installing a replacement engine part.

Humming, she wipes her hands on a rag and heads out...

Down the hall...

Down the ladder into her quarters...

She crosses to her Cortex screen. Kaylee's Cortex has no casing. The circuitry is exposed so she can tinker with it.

Kaylee hits some keys. Nothing happens. She frowns, presses a chip more firmly into place in the machine's guts.

TINNY DANCE MUSIC plays, like the kind at the party. This is what she's been humming.

PULL BACK FROM THE CORTEX

to find Kaylee, sitting on the bed, eating some of the CHOCOLATE MINTS from the party.

Pull further back to see she is looking at her party dress, which hangs from an exposed pipe.

INT. SERENITY - CARGO BAY - DAY (DAY 4)

Mal and Inara sit on the catwalk/balcony over the bay. Mal's midsection is bandaged. Inara wears another elegant kimono-type robe.

A bottle of wine sits between them and they drink from battered metal cups.

Inara sips her wine, makes a little face.

INARA
Thank you for the wine. It's very... fresh.

MAL
To Kaylee and her inter-engine fermentation system.

He raises his cup to toast, winces from the wound.

INARA
Are you in pain?

MAL
Absolutely. I got stabbed, you know. Right here.

INARA
I saw.

MAL
Don't care much for fancy parties. Too rough.

INARA
It wasn't entirely a disaster.

MAL
I got stabbed. Right here.

INARA
You also lined up exciting new crime.

MAL
It is good to have cargo. Makes us a target for every other scavenger out there, a' course, but sometimes that's fun too.

INARA
(beat, then)
I am grateful, you know, for the ill-conceived and high-handed attempt to defend my honor although I didn't want you to.

MAL
Gracious as that is, as I look back, I probably shoulda stayed outta your world.

INARA
My world. If it is that. I wasn't going to stay, you know.

MAL
Yeah? Why's that?

A little disingenuous:

INARA
Oh, someone needs to keep Kaylee out of trouble. And all of my things are here... Besides, why would I want to leave Serenity?

We ARM BACK to REVEAL

the cargo bay is full of mooing milling CATTLE.

MAL
Can't think of a reason.

BLACKOUT.

END OF SHOW

S A F E

Written by Drew Z. Greenberg
Directed by Michael Grossman

JOSS WHEDON

The idea was one that spoke to me and to [episode writer] Drew Greenberg very strongly, why was Simon so attached to his sister? So to show a world where he had the most genial and delightful father, and now he's stuck with this irascible, untrustworthy bastard [Mal]; and then, over the course of a series of flashbacks, to have him realize, as he has sort of always known, that his father is genial because everything is going his way. When the chips are down, he's nobody, and Simon has always been the only person there to look after his sister. However loving his parents may have seemed, he knew that, scratch the surface, and they'd scream and run away. And here he's confronted with a guy who is just everything he thinks is wrong about a person, who comes back for him when the chips are down because he's on his crew. To me, that's a *real* parent, and that is an extremely beautiful thing to get to, and I think it's very real. Having the 'she's a witch' thing was something we had planned to explore, because River had this power and she was a little strange and with the psychic, but we did want to show how backwoodsian people could become when they were

left to their own devices. But the most important thing about 'Safe' was that relationship. I will say, by the way, that that is a show that, again… this is why I love my crew and my actors and that whole experience so much. We needed to do a lot of reshooting on a lot of stuff and we came in short [the episode was not long enough for its running time] and I was worried that we weren't going to get a sense of them being off the ship and what that meant, so I literally said, 'Lock the show [do a final edit], give me thirty seconds here and twenty seconds there and I'm going to write two scenes.' And they were the scene of Jayne going through Simon's stuff and the scene of Jayne welcoming Simon back on board. And they're two of the best scenes we ever did on the show [laughs] — we literally had already locked the show, so Adam had fifteen props to pick up and a thirty-second monologue that he had to do to the second, with that precision, and be hilarious and true to character, and the precision with which he did both those little scenes was phenomenal. When you feel something like that, to be able to drop that in moments before it went to air — that's really fun.

TEASER

CLOSE ON:

Rich expensive BRANDY as it pours into a rich expensive snifter. Pull back to see:

INT. TAM ESTATE - DAY

The room, tasteful, lit by candlelight, feels warm. SIMON holds the snifter. He swirls the brandy around a bit to warm it, inhales the aroma, looks up and smiles.

SIMON
This is a joke, right?

We see Simon's father, GABRIEL, fifty, refined, used to having control, standing in front of him. At the moment, he seems warm and jovial.

GABRIEL
Yes. That's exactly right. Because brandy is funny.

SIMON
It's just, this is… this smells like New Canaan brandy.

Gabriel pours brandy for himself and for Simon's mother, REGAN, late forties, elegant.

SIMON (cont'd)
Aged New Canaan brandy. How much did you pay for this? I thought business was slow.

GABRIEL
Pierre owed me a favor. Seeing how it's a special occasion.

SIMON
Is it?

Simon tries to read his father's grin. Then:

REGAN
For god's sake, Gabriel. Just tell him.

Gabriel chuckles.

GABRIEL
Fine, spoil my fun.
(to Simon)
I had a talk today with Jerome Stuart. Seems he's about to take over as Head of Surgery at AMI. Said when you're done with your internship, there'll be an attending position waiting for you.

This is a huge moment for Simon. He's thrilled.

REGAN
(smiling)
Congratulations, son.

Simon stares into his glass, embarrassed.

SIMON
It's not a big deal.

GABRIEL
Oh. Well, all right then.

Playing along, Gabriel reaches for Simon's glass. Simon pulls it away, grinning.

SIMON
Okay, okay. It's an enormous deal. AMI, that's, I can really do good work there —

GABRIEL
Good work, good pay. There'll be an announcement at the term-end ceremony.

REGAN
We're so proud, sweetheart.

SIMON
Is River coming back?

Gabriel and Regan stare at Simon.

SIMON (cont'd)
For the ceremony. Did she say she'd be able to get away?

REGAN
We didn't…
(brightly)
We'll write to her immediately, tell her all about it.

GABRIEL
I doubt she'll come. You saw the schedule at that school of hers. I took one look at it, had one of those school dreams. You know, "I didn't study"…

Gabriel chuckles to himself.

SIMON
I just... I haven't heard from her in a while. I thought she'd come home sometimes, or at least send a wave, but there's only been the occasional letter, and half the time she doesn't sound like herself.

REGAN
She's changing. Finally starting to fit in. You should be happy for her.

Simon forces a smile.

SIMON
Of course.

GABRIEL
Your position will still be there for her to admire when she gets home, *Doctor* Tam. Come on... let's have a toast. I've been working on this all day.

The three of them rise and lift their glasses...

GABRIEL (cont'd)
May your future always be as bright as it is this very moment —

The three glasses meet... CLINK.

CUT TO:

EXT. JIANGYIN/CARGO BAY - DAY

Squish. Simon has stepped in cow poop on the ship's ramp. Future not lookin' so bright right this second.

SIMON
<Niou fun.> [Cow poop.]

JAYNE passes him, amused.

JAYNE
'Bout time you broke in them pretty shoes.

Jayne takes us further, showing us that the crew is off-loading the cows (from ep 3) into an open prairie at the edge of the woods. We're on Jiangyin, a planet heavy on the nature — woods and scrubby grazing ground.

Simon continues down the ramp, moving around cows, trying to keep out of the way of all the activity:

MAL leads a cow as Jayne SMACKS another steer on its rump, urging it to move.

JAYNE (cont'd)
Ha! Git along!

MAL
They walk just fine if you lead 'em.

JAYNE
I like smackin' 'em.

Simon looks down to see WASH AND ZOE, at the base of the ramp, where they are sending the cows off to the side, where BOOK directs them into a makeshift pen.

BOOK
Hope this corral's strong enough to hold them.

"Shepherd" is a purely figurative title, you know.

ZOE
Next time we smuggle stock, let's make it something smaller.

WASH
Yeah, we need to start dealing in those black-market beagles.

ANGLE ON: Simon again. He's made his way off to one side. He scrapes at his shoe with a stick. Mal approaches him.

MAL
What're you doing out here, Doc? Besides the scraping.

SIMON
I thought perhaps I could help. With the cows.

MAL
I'll let you know, any of 'em start complaining of palpitations. Til then, not much call for a doctor.

SIMON
(off Book)
But there is call for a preacher?

MAL
I was surprised myself, but turns out he's converted five of 'em. Not easy, neither. Seems they got this natural inclination toward Hinduism.

SIMON
Captain, my sister and I have been on your ship for more than two months. You've stopped collecting fare from us... no one's required my services in some time... I'm starting to feel a little —

MAL
Useless?

SIMON
Restless.

MAL
Ah.

SIMON
Is that your feeling? That I'm useless?

MAL
Well, Doc, useful man don't have to ask to be put to use. Usually just finds himself something to do.

SIMON
Sorry if my criminal instincts aren't as sharp as the rest of your crew.

EXT. TREETOPS - MOMENTS LATER

We move off them to find a man, STARK, staring from cover not far away. He scurries away to two other men.

STARK
Got a good look. They waitin' fer a payment. Somethin' there worth takin', too.

He turns to look back...

STARK (cont'd)
They got precious cargo.

On Stark's crafty look, we —

BLACK OUT.

END OF TEASER

ACT ONE

EXT. JIANGYIN/CORRAL - DAY

CLOSE ON RIVER and a cow. She's looking into one of its eyes and murmuring:

RIVER
Little soul big world. Eat and sleep and eat...

Jayne appears, bringing another cow, sees her communing with the bovine. She's reaching back toward the animals.

RIVER (cont'd)
Many souls. Very straight, very simple...

JAYNE
(calling, re: River)
Captain! This one's in the way!

Mal appears. On his approach, trying to get to her:

MAL
Cattle on the ship three weeks, she don't go near 'em. Suddenly, we're on Jiangyin and she's got a driving need to commune with the beasts?

River looks at Mal very seriously.

RIVER
They weren't cows inside. They were waiting to be, but they forgot. Now they see sky and they remember what they are.

MAL
Is it bad that what she just said makes perfect sense to me?
(reaching for her)
Come on, now. Let's move you clear of the work.

River recoils from him. He's not Simon. Now Simon appears, approaching. Sees River backing away from Mal. Some cows might get agitated by this.

SIMON
What's going on?
(off Mal)
What are you doing?

MAL
I was fixin' to do some business. Buyers'll be along soon. I can't be herding these steers and your sister, too.

SIMON
I'll keep her out of the way. But you don't need to say things like that in front of her.

MAL
Yes, I've clearly upset her.

River is looking at the ends of her hair now, completely tranquil. Jayne, still nearby, snorts. Simon bristles.

SIMON
She understands more than you think. Anyway — she didn't mean any harm.

RIVER'S COSTUMES

Costume designer Shawna Trpcic: "The first thought was, when she came on to the ship, that [once dressed] she would be wearing Kaylee's clothes. We got hippie-looking clothes, but in jewel-colored tones and in grays and blues, to make them kind of colder, to show that she was from a different world than the Serenity crew, and then we started to find her own look. In 'Safe', I lightened her up with pinks, but still staying with the garnet sweater, still staying with the jewel-like tones. We made the majority of the stuff, except for the classic hippie dress, and used boots to differentiate River from the softness of a normal girl in those kinds of soft fabrics. I like to contrast the really soft and flowing fabrics with the hardcore boots, because that's who she is — she's this soft, beautiful, sensitive girl, but with this hardcore inner character."

MAL
Never figured she did. But when a man's engaging in clandestine dealings, he has this preference for things being smooth. She makes things not be smooth.

SIMON
Right. I'm very sorry if she tipped off anyone about your cunningly concealed herd of cows.

MAL
You know, I'm starting to remember you asking if there wasn't something you could "do". Think now I got a notion regarding that. How about you take your sister for a little walk?

Simon looks startled, worried.

SIMON
A walk?

MAL
Yeah. Someplace... away.

SIMON
Probably best if we stay close. The Alliance has us marked as fugitives—

MAL
Closest Alliance is the Cruiser Magellan, hours out from here. And I promise you, they ain't coming to a backwater like Jiangyin.

SIMON
Still... I'm not sure it's such a wise suggestion.

MAL
Might not wanna mistake it for a "suggestion".
(off Simon's look)
Don't worry. We won't take off without you.

Mal continues with his back to Simon. Off Simon —

INT. "GENERAL SUPPLY" - DAY - LATER

A dusty local store. Mostly ranching supplies: feed and branding irons and horseshoes. Along one wall there are some local crafts. A bored-looking proprietor reads a Chinese-language newspaper at the counter.

KAYLEE and INARA browse among the crudely made items.

KAYLEE
Everything's dusty.

INARA
Does it seem every supply store on every border planet has the same five rag dolls and the same wood carvings of...
(looking at one)
What is this? A duck?

KAYLEE
That's a swan. And I like it.

INARA
You do?

KAYLEE
It looks like it was made with, you know... longing. Made by a person really longed to see a swan.

INARA
Perhaps because they'd only heard of them by rough description.

Kaylee holds up a little painted souvenir dish with painted Chinese characters on it.

KAYLEE
You think this'd make a nice gift?

INARA
A gift? For whom?

Kaylee just studies the dish.

KAYLEE
I just think it's nice. Kinda rich, you know.

INARA
Oh. For Simon.

KAYLEE
I didn't say that.

INARA
Well, you don't do a very good job of hiding your interest.

KAYLEE
He's just so <swai> [cute]. You wanna take a bite out of him all over, you know?

Just then, Simon and River enter. Simon is nervous about being out and visible, a little frazzled at having to watch River constantly.

INARA
(to Kaylee)
Careful.

KAYLEE
Did he hear? I don't think he heard.
(louder, maybe too loud)
Mornin', you two!

Kaylee's over-bright greeting just makes Simon more jumpy. He forces a smile, nods.

INARA
We don't usually see you two out and about planetside.

SIMON
(tense)
We're trying something different today.

River immediately goes to the farming equipment, starts touching things.

SIMON (cont'd)
River, careful with that, that's...
(helplessly to Kaylee)
What is that?

KAYLEE
That's a post holer. You dig holes. For posts.

SIMON
(to River)
It's dirty and sharp. Come over here.

He steers her over to the crafts section with the women. He picks up the little dish Kaylee was admiring.

SIMON (cont'd)
(reads the Chinese)
"Jiangyin, Prairie Paradise."
(then)
Good god. They ask money for this <go se> [crap]?

Kaylee flinches, but recovers.

KAYLEE
Hard to believe, ain't it?
(then)
I'm glad you're out.

He smiles absently, politely. His focus on River.

KAYLEE (cont'd)
Give you a chance to loosen up a bit.

Tiny delayed reaction to Kaylee's perfectly innocent comment.

SIMON
What's that supposed to mean? Loosen up?

KAYLEE
Nothing... I just... Well. You never seem to have any fun, is all.

His attention's split. He moves to take something breakable out of River's hand.

SIMON
Fun. Right. I consider this "fun". It's "fun" being forced to the ass-end of the galaxy, get to live on a piece of <luh-suh> [garbage] wreck and eat molded protein while playing nursemaid to my <boo-tai jung-tzahng-duh> [not entirely sane] sister. "Fun."

Simon may not have noticed how that all stung. Kaylee just stares at him. He glances at her. Sees her looking at him. A beat.

KAYLEE
<Luh-suh?> [Garbage?]

SIMON
Sorry?

KAYLEE
Serenity ain't <luh-suh> [garbage].

SIMON
I didn't mean...

KAYLEE
You did. You meant everything you just said.

SIMON
(trying to lighten things)
Well, no... actually I was being ironic. So in the strictest sense, I didn't really —

KAYLEE
You were being mean, is what. And if that's what you think of this life, then you can't think much of them that choose it, can you?

He's got nothing to say. She turns and heads for the exit. Inara falls in with her, walk out side by side. As they go:

INARA
(softly, to Kaylee)
You're getting better at hiding it.

Simon, already regretting the altercation, takes a beat, sighs a "god am I an asshole today" sigh. Then he turns to collect River.

SIMON
River?

But River is gone.

EXT. JIANGYIN/CORRAL - DAY

The ship's ramp is empty of cows now. But littered with that which cows leave behind. Mal stands at the base of the ramp, surveying the damage.

MAL
This is the last time. Last time with cows.

Zoe approaches Mal.

MAL (cont'd)
I heard there was some idea regarding beagles. They got smallish droppings?

ZOE
I believe so, sir. Also, the disreputable men are here.

THE OUTER PLANETS

Carey Meyer says that the production design for the outer planets "was based a lot on what we were able to find as a location to shoot. Obviously, once you start driving outside of Los Angeles, you end up with a real dirty dust-bowl feel and that's where a lot of the Western frontier town concepts started to play into it. There was a lot of discussion about, 'Do we really go with just a Western feel or do we try to recreate this concept in every episode or should we come up with a fully-realized design for each planet?' Our budget meant we had to go with a lot of existing locations. I think in the end the feel was that we wound up using a lot of places or exteriors that just felt too Western and we didn't necessarily want to go that way; but at some point, it just became the lesser of two evils — what could we actually create in three days?"

Mal turns to see the GRANGE BROTHERS standing near the makeshift corral, looking at the animals. Jayne stands nearby. Book is not far off, seeing to the fencing.

MAL
(to Zoe)
I better go take their money.

Mal heads toward the brothers. Zoe turns and heads into the ship.

ANGLE ON: THE GRANGE BROTHERS

There are two of them, shabby low-life types. They're looking over the cows critically now,

examining their hooves, eyes, teeth. Mal approaches.

MAL
Good morning, gents. You must be the Grange brothers. Hope you're hungry for beefsteak.

They say nothing. Continue to examine the cattle.

JAYNE
Attractive animals, ain't they?

OLDER GRANGE
They ain't well fed. Scrawny.

MAL
<Fei hua.> [Nonsense.] Hay and milk three times a day. Fed to 'em by beautiful women.

JAYNE
It was something to see.

YOUNGER GRANGE
They ain't branded.

MAL
You boys're hitting all the selling points. Unregistered. Claim 'em as your own.

The Granges continue to look sour.

OLDER GRANGE
Twenty a head.

MAL
That's an amusing figure in the light of you already agreed on thirty with Badger.

OLDER GRANGE
That's afore we seen 'em. They're atrophied, standin' 'round on a ship for near a month.

MAL
My comprehension is, less muscle, more tender the meat. Thirty.

The Grange boys step back to talk — they look nervous, casting looks toward Mal and Jayne, toward the surrounding woods...

Mal and Jayne eyeball them. A RUSTLING in the trees. Seems it could be the wind. Before Mal can take much note, Book approaches.

BOOK
(off the brothers)
Problem?

MAL
Nope. Minute from now we'll agree on twenty-five.

A NOISE. The Granges spin, hands go near their guns (they don't draw). WASH is on the loading ramp, dumping a bucket of water. The Granges relax. Wash re-enters the ship.

BOOK
They seem a mite jumpy to you?

Off Mal, watching the men, considering that...

EXT. "GENERAL SUPPLY" JIANGYIN - DAY

Simon, more than jumpy, standing in front of the store, just catches a glimpse of River's dress as she disappears around a corner. He dashes after her. He rounds the corner to see...

LOCAL COPS, a group of five, heading toward him with some purpose. He freezes.

But River is there, a block ahead of him. He bravely heads toward her. As he passes the cops:

SIMON
(comes out way too loud)
MORNING, OFFICERS.

The cops pass him harmlessly. We stay with him as he winces.

He continues on, spots River going around a corner. Follows.

EXT. JIANGYIN/CARGO BAY - DAY

Mal and Jayne are talking with the Grange brothers again. Book is visible in the b.g., tending to the corral fencing.

MAL
See, the problem we got with twenty-three is that it ain't thirty.

YOUNGER GRANGE
These cows ain't as young as you said.

JAYNE
They're babies. Half of 'em born on the trip.

OLDER GRANGE
I'm thinking maybe we walk away entirely.

MAL
I'm thinking you do that and we got ourselves trouble — morning, ladies...

Kaylee and Inara, returning to the ship, walk right past the group. The Granges' eyes follow the women. This isn't lost on Mal who steps into their purview with:

MAL (cont'd)
(without a break)
...serious trouble. Of the you-owe-us variety.

OLDER GRANGE
We can go to twenty-five.

Mal and Jayne exchange a look. The transaction is coming to a close.

MAL
Well, we'd be takin' a loss, but you seem like clean and virtuous boys... done.

The Elder Grange takes out a little cloth bag, starts counting money into Mal's palm. But freezes when he hears:

HEAD COP (O.S.)
Marcus and Nathaniel Grange!

CHINESE COINS

Prop master Randy Eriksen: "I got the Chinese coins for 'Safe' in Chinatown. There are a lot of Asian characters on the graphics, the money and the ships. Joss came up with the Sino-American Alliance, which was basically East meets West, and made the show quite visually interesting."

BANKNOTES

Prop master Randy Eriksen: "The number forty-seven appears on the banknotes because forty-seven is the most commonly occurring random number. It's been my lucky number since before high school. I was number forty-seven in the football team. It's kind of nonsensical but we try to work it in to most things. If you look at the notes in the canvas moneybag from 'Safe', it's on the money. You could probably go back to *Buffy* and find a bunch of forty-sevens. There's a whole forty-seven society on the Internet. It's funny, if you're looking for something, you find it. When you have a big hammer, pretty much everything starts looking like a nail."

SIMON

"How do I know you won't kill me in my sleep?"

Family. It's what truly drives the stories of *Firefly* and connects the disparate crew of Serenity. While Captain Mal and his crew may not be blood, they have evolved into their own kind of kin that squabbles, loves and protects just like any other. Yet, in the pilot of *Firefly*, a true brother and sister invade Serenity and their love and protection of one another ends up mirroring the relationships of those on the ship that takes them in. Dr. Simon Tam, a young man of privilege who risks his life and career to rescue his sister, River, from the Alliance, is a man with a lot to learn from the Serenity crew. Initially contemptuous of Mal and his people, Simon comes to learn that the eclectic personalities on board all have something to offer him and his wounded sister. It's certainly not the kind of sci-fi role an actor would expect to be offered and Sean Maher said during the press launch for *Firefly*'s cinematic reincarnation that that is what made him open to auditioning. He remembers getting the script from his agent and being told, "'Here's this Joss Whedon new sci-fi thing.' I was like, 'Hmm, sci-fi. I don't really know much about that.'"

Maher ended up reading for the part and while Simon Tam was interesting enough on his own, it was Whedon that sealed the deal for the actor. "Sitting down with him — he was just so intriguing. He's such a wonderful man and I'd just like to say it was love at first sight with him. When I met him, I wanted to do anything that he was part of."

Luckily, the entire cast felt the same way as Maher, and the legendary rapport among the cast and crew made for a chemistry and magic that the actor still marvels at. "Joss always says that in casting *Firefly*, he really looked for the person before the acting ability or the actor. Not that we're all not great actors, but that he just made sure that he connected with the person, and it was somebody that he really got a good vibe from — somebody with great energy. So then he just sort of put us all together,

and I think it was very quick, like right out of the gate, we all instantly bonded."

In describing the show from his perspective, Maher says, "The words 'science fiction' come to mind, but it's not actually science fiction. It feels more like a Western, like a post-apocalyptic Western. It's obviously set after there is no more Earth. Humans have colonized other planets. So it's a glimpse into the future. There's a huge Asian influence, more specifically a Chinese [influence]. Even on the set, little keyboards have American italics and also Chinese, so everyone is bilingual because of the meshing of the two cultures.

"Simon is picked up on Persephone," he continues. "He's looking for transport, so he picks Serenity because it looks disreputable and he tries to fly anonymously. The crew has stuff that they're hiding and they don't want the passengers to know about, because they are running goods illegally." It ends up being a match made in space as the denizens of Serenity all hold their own secrets as tragic and dangerous as the Tam's.

Yet despite that connection, Simon has a hard time conforming to Malcolm Reynolds' ship and his crew. "Simon has a huge contrast with the rest of the crew because he's definitely from a more privileged background," Maher says. "It's an entirely different level, an entirely different class of people. He's very well off. Simon is a very gifted doctor. He was a surgeon in the trauma centre on Osiris." It's through his profession that Tam finds a place amongst the Serenity crew and proves his worth to everyone, including himself. "When stuff goes down he turns out to be invaluable to the survival of a few people."

While Simon and Summer's path may have been hellish on *Firefly*, the actor says the experience of working on the series was incredible. As Maher told *TV Guide*, "Honestly, wherever Joss goes, I follow. And the cast, I would do anything with this group of people, whether it's television or film... even if we take a circus act on the road. I feel blessed to have been a part of this. The more and more it continues, it's overwhelming. We had this little show that could, you know?" ◒

They all turn to look — A COP, one of the ones Simon saw in town, stands nearby, gun drawn.

HEAD COP
You are both wanted in connection to the illegal killing of Rance Durban. You are bound by law to stand down!

The other four cops emerge variously about the scene. As Mal puts his hands in evidence, surrounded:

MAL
You know, I'm startin' to find this whole planet very uninviting.

Off that —

INT. CORRIDOR/INT. TENT - DAY

Simon enters a low ceilinged, long corridor/hallway. He catches a glimpse of River up ahead, she disappears around a bend in the corridor.

WITH SIMON

moving down the dark, scary corridor. Moving... River is nowhere to be seen, but Simon speaks to her anyway...

SIMON
River. Please...

He turns a dark corner which opens into —

TENT

An open, beautiful airy space. A decorated tent.

Music plays.

Local women fill the floor, dancing an intricate folk dance.

River stands on the edge of this, not seeing Simon. Never taking her eyes off the dancers.

EXT. JIANGYIN/CARGO BAY - DAY

The cops, guns drawn, are moving in on the scene. They disarm the Granges and also Mal and Jayne. Firearms are dropped into a neat pile on the dirt.

Another cop is rousting Book nearby. No gun.

MAL
Appears we have ourselves a situation...

HEAD COP
Who are you?

MAL
Just a bystander.

HEAD COP
This your beef?

MAL
No, sir.
(re: the Granges)
You're looking at the proper owners right there.

HEAD COP
Like to see some paper on that cattle.

The Younger Grange suddenly lunges at the cop who is frisking him. Wrestles the cop's gun away from him, turns to kill, but suddenly BANG!, the gun is shot out of his hand by —

ZOE

who is on the ramp at the ship, never far from her Captain's back.

And now all hell breaks loose. The Elder Grange pulls a concealed gun that the cops hadn't yet got to. More gunfire.

Mal and Jayne drop to the ground, reach for their guns from the pile...

JAYNE
Here we go.

MAL
It never goes smooth. How come it never goes smooth?

Now Mal notices — THE CLOTH MONEYBAG in the dust. Just a little more than arm's length away. Mal reaches for it, fingertips brushing the edge of it. Reaching... reaching... MAL grabs it —

— just as a BULLET kicks up dust. Mal rolls clear, but has the cash as

fire fight!

INT. TENT - DAY

River watches from the sidelines. She watches intently, studying. Simon tries to make his way to her. But she DARTS INTO THE DANCE.

SIMON
River!

She works her way into the pattern, mimicking the others' steps perfectly. She dances.

EXT. JIANGYIN/CORRAL - DAY

The fire fight continues. Mal and Jayne are on the ground between the other parties. The Grange boys fire at the five cops.

The cops return fire.

Mal and Jayne keep low, bullets sailing over them.

MAL
I hate it when this happens.

The Granges make a break for it, disappear into the corral. Still firing —

Mal looks back to Zoe on the ramp, she indicates where the Granges have gone.

Mal nods back. Mal and Jayne use the cows for cover as they do a mini-pincher move around the Grange boys —

INT. TENT - DAY

River continues to dance. As Simon watches, she throws back her head. We see what Simon sees: she wears a huge grin.

Simon notices, a look of amazement, wonder, on his face. He is in awe of her. Even Simon's starting to smile now, loosening up. The music continues, and so does...

EXT. JIANGYIN/CORRAL/INT. TENT - INTERCUT

The gun battle.

We're INTERCUTTING now. Between River as her dance gets more and more frenzied and...

...the gun fight. Chaos and confusion. The cops firing into the herd. The Granges firing back. And Mal and Jayne closing in on the Granges.

MUSIC

Composer Greg Edmonson says he was not responsible for the timing of the gunshots being percussively interspersed with River dancing with the villagers. "We used a traditional piece — 'The Sailor's Wife', I believe it's called — that I arranged for River's dance. The gunshots just happened — it's just the way they cut it together."

❖ Right: The hood that is pulled over Simon's head by the kidnappers.

IN THE TENT. River dances...

AT THE CORRAL. The Younger Grange is hit! He goes down, but he's only wounded. He reaches for his gun.

The Elder Grange comes to his aid, firing back at the cops. But suddenly —

— Mal appears, sailing at him, taking him down. The cops swarm in. None of them hit.

Mal sighs as the cops take the Granges into custody. He looks around. Reacts to something, as...

IN THE TENT. River stops dancing suddenly. Reacting to something as well. Sensing something terrible, as...

AT THE CORRAL. Mal and Jayne rush to find...

BOOK

on the ground. Hit. Blood blooms on his shirt. His eyes roll up. He blinks at Mal, confused. It's bad.

INT. TENT - CONTINUED

Simon grows concerned, seeing River through the undulating crowd. Sees she is caught up in one of her premonitions.

Simon strains to see her...

She is covered by the crowd, then revealed again, getting a bit jostled. Simon starts to move toward her when —

A HOOD is pulled down sharply over Simon's head. We reveal STARK and his two MEN — They spirit Simon off. Silent and fast. Off River, alone among the dancers —

BLACK OUT.

END OF ACT ONE

ACT TWO

EXT. JIANGYIN/CARGO BAY - DAY

Book lies in the dust of the corral, staring up at the milling cows. And also Mal, who is perched over him, trying to stem the blood flow. Jayne is there, too. Looking at something off screen.

MAL
Stay with me, Shepherd.

Book tries to focus, bleary-eyed. He looks down his body, tries to take it in...

BOOK
That's... that's quite a lot of blood, isn't it?

MAL
Just means you ain't dead.

BOOK
'Fraid I might be needin' a preacher.

MAL
That's good. You just lie there and be ironical.
(to Jayne)
Stretcher.

But Jayne's looking off toward —

— the COPS taking away what they came here for: the Grange brothers in rough custody.

MAL (cont'd)
Jayne.

JAYNE
They're goin'.

MAL
'Course. Got what they came here for.

JAYNE
(after a beat)
You get the cash?

Mal flashes him a look.

CUT TO:

INT. CARGO BAY - DAY

Mal and Jayne, along with Zoe carry Book onto the ship. Kaylee appears as they move through, toward the infirmary.

KAYLEE
What's going on — ?

She stops asking, sees it.

KAYLEE (cont'd)
Oh god, Shepherd! Shepherd can you hear me?

They carry the stretcher across the cargo bay toward the infirmary.

INT. SERENITY/INFIRMARY - DAY

They move Book from the stretcher onto the operating table. Zoe rips open Book's shirt, revealing the wound — gunshot high in the chest.

JAYNE
Don't look good.

Mal shoots him a look that says both "duh" and "shut the fuck up". Mal hits an intercom:

MAL
Wash! Get down to the infirmary! <Ma-Shong!> [Now!]

Mal moves with a purpose.

MAL (cont'd)
(to Zoe)
We gotta try and stop this bleeding.

Mal moves for the cabinet. As he does he tosses the cloth moneybag onto the infirmary counter — it leaves a bloody smear. He grabs more blood rags and bandages, like that.

Kaylee has drifted closer and closer to Book, tearing up.

KAYLEE
You don't worry now, Shepherd Book. Cap 'n Zoe got lots of experience with this kinda thing. Seen lots worse in the war.
(beat)
Shepherd? Shepherd Book?
(then, closer)
He ain't breathin'!

Book starts to CONVULSE VIOLENTLY.

ON KAYLEE, tears brimming as she backs away from the horror. Zoe rips open the package of a disposable stylette and hands it to Mal, who plunges it into Book's arm.

Finally the convulsions subside. Mal turns away

from the scene. Looks to Kaylee.

MAL
(calm down, be brave, I haven't the time)
He ain't dead. But he is bad off. Now we gotta see what we can do to help him.

Wash appears now. Takes in the sight before him.

WASH
<Lao-tyen, boo.> [Oh, god, no.]

MAL
Wash, I need you to go into town, see if you can find that <jing-tzahng mei yong-duh> [consistently useless] Doctor.

Wash nods, heads off. Mal rejoins Zoe at Book's side. Kaylee stares at her dying friend...

KAYLEE
Hurry...

EXT. WOODS - DAY

Simon is dragged through the woods by Stark and his men. Stark moves ahead, the Shabby Man drags Simon, stumbling, by the arm.

STARK
Faster. Gotta go faster. Wanna get there afore dark.

SIMON
Get where? Where are we going? Are you with the police?

STARK
Shut up.

SIMON
Please. If it's ransom you want, I... I can arrange something.

STARK
No talking.

SIMON
You don't understand. My sister...

Stark turns and shoves him hard and he falls. On impact —

INT. TAM ESTATE - NIGHT

Our second flashback. [Note: this scene takes place several weeks after the previous flashback, so wardrobe should change.] Simon stands facing his mother. It's tense.

REGAN
Your sister is fine, Simon.

SIMON
She's not fine. Didn't you look at the letters? Look at the letters!

Gabriel is at his desk, looking over a sheaf of papers. He stands up, bringing the papers with him.

GABRIEL
They seem perfectly normal to me.

Simon points at the pages frantically, pointing things out:

SIMON
She talks about last summer at the lake.

GABRIEL
So?

SIMON
We weren't at the lake, we were in the mountains.

REGAN
Oh honey, I'm sure there's a lake up there.

SIMON
No. These phrases... they don't sound like her. And look here — some of these words, they're misspelled.
(off parents' blank looks)
She started correcting my spelling when she was three. She's trying to tell us something. I think there's a code.

Regan and Gabriel share a look — that just sounded nuts.

GABRIEL
A code?

SIMON
Yes.

GABRIEL
Simon... have you talked to anyone about this?

SIMON
What? No. What do you mean? I'm talking to you.

GABRIEL
Good. Don't mention this to anyone outside the family.

SIMON
What?

GABRIEL
You don't hear what you sound like, Simon.

SIMON
I don't care —

GABRIEL
You should. Because it sounds insane.
(then)
Look, son, if your sister was in danger, we'd be right beside you. You know that.

SIMON
Then let's go and find out.

GABRIEL
Government schools don't allow visitors.

SIMON
And why do you suppose that is?

GABRIEL
You can't go charging in there ranting about

"spelling codes" and nonexistent lakes.

REGAN
It'll hurt your future at the hospital. It'll hurt River in the school.

GABRIEL
(then, not without affection)
I always thought it was River who was lost without her big brother... now I'm starting to wonder if it isn't the other way 'round.

Now Simon's less sure.

GABRIEL (cont'd)
I know you miss her.

SIMON
Yes...

GABRIEL
You want to see her.

He nods. Gabriel puts a paternal hand on his boy's shoulder.

GABRIEL (cont'd)
You will, son. Just be patient.

Simon, his anger dissipated, looks uncertain.

EXT. WOODS - DAY

SUNLIGHT GLARES through the trees. Simon squints against it as he is still being forced along in front of Stark and his men. He's a little dizzy from the earlier fall. He blinks through the glare up ahead... sees...

A FIGURE

Feminine, fragile, a nearly angelic vision up ahead.

SIMON

blinks again. Slows.

Stark gives him a mighty push that sends him stumbling ahead... but he doesn't take much note of the violence, he's still looking toward the figure that stands among the trees, looking at him now.

SIMON
No... Oh, no...

Stark and his men are noticing the figure now, too. It's River. And she's smiling.

SIMON (cont'd)
Oh, god...

The men exchange looks, grow wary —

RIVER
Found you!

SIMON
River! River, no! Run, RUN!

Her smile fades into confusion.

RIVER
Found you?

Simon manages to tear himself away by sheer force of will, the sight of his sister giving him sudden strength. He bolts toward her.

But Stark and his men chase him down. Simon is nearly to her, now. In desperation Simon PUSHES RIVER away roughly.

SIMON
RUN! GO!

River looks at him, tears in her eyes. She doesn't know why he pushed her.

And then one of Stark's men has her by the arms. She's caught too.

STARK
Bring her.

And now they're both being forced forward, Simon utterly defeated now as —

INT. CARGO BAY - DAY

Kaylee paces in the cargo bay. Inara and Jayne are nearby. They both react to the SOUND of the MULE. Kaylee perks up.

KAYLEE
(calling)
They're back! Doctor's back!

Mal appears from the infirmary area as Wash drives up in the Mule. Alone. The others register this. Wash parks the Mule, climbs off.

KAYLEE (cont'd)
Where's the Doctor? Why isn't he with you?

WASH
He wasn't in town. Wasn't anywhere.

KAYLEE
He was in town. We saw him there. Him and River. I can show you —

WASH
Town's not that big, Kaylee. Believe me when I say he wasn't there.

JAYNE
Knew it. Probably saw them cops, turned tail.

MAL
Doctor could be called a lot of things — coward wouldn't be one of 'em, though.

INARA
You don't think they were arrested, do you?

WASH
Worse than that, probably.
(then)
Looks like maybe they got snatched.

INARA
Kidnapped?

WASH
I went by the sheriff's office. Seems if we'd looked at the posted alerts for this rock we mighta known it. Settlers up in the hills take people sometimes. Usually tradesmen and the like.

MAL
And now they got themselves a doctor.
(then)

And we don't.

Mal moves to the controls that work the doors. Kaylee reacts as the ramp starts to rise, closing up.

KAYLEE
What are you doing?! What about Simon and River?

MAL
Forget them. We lost two people today. If I can help it, we won't lose a third.

THUNK! The ramp door closes.

MAL (cont'd)
Wash, get us in the air.

Wash obeys, heads off. Mal moves off, too. We hold on Kaylee, registering what's happening, surprised, devastated —

EXT. WOODS - DAY

As SERENITY RISES UP over some trees in the distance, then takes off heading for space — CAMERA TILTS DOWN TO...

SIMON

pausing in his trek, watching as he and River are left behind. Stark appears.

STARK
You just keep movin'.

And with a helpful shove from Stark, he does. He keeps moving. Moving and looking back for a moment, until the SOUNDS of Serenity hitting atmo and getting fainter cause him to

turn forward, stumbling toward whatever awaits him —

END OF ACT TWO

ACT THREE

EXT. SERENITY - EFFECT

The ship moves through space, fast.

INT. SERENITY - INFIRMARY

Book is laid out on the examining table, apparently unconscious. Zoe stands over him, cleaning the wound. He opens his eyes, watches her for a moment before she's aware he's awake. She looks grim.

BOOK
(re: her expression)
That bad?

She looks at him, a little caught.

ZOE
Battle wounds are nothing new to me, Preacher. Seen men live with a dozen holes in 'em that size.

BOOK
That right?

ZOE
It surely is. Knew a man with a hole clean

through his shoulder once. He used to keep a spare hanky in there.

BOOK
Where's the Doctor? Not back yet?

ZOE
We don't make him hurry for the little stuff. He'll be along.

Book's losing it, starting to drift away again.

BOOK
He could hurry a little...

INT. SERENITY - BRIDGE

Wash is piloting. Mal leans over his shoulder. They're looking at a star chart on a display.

WASH
Well, there's Greenleaf. They'd have med help there.

MAL
Too far, more'n ten hours. Man's worse off'n that.

Inara has just entered, overheard that last line.

INARA
You know where to find what you need.

MAL
Don't recall inviting you onto the bridge.

INARA
You didn't. Mal, you know where you can find a doctor. You know exactly.

MAL
Inara — he was dumb enough to get himself grabbed in broad daylight. Don't have the time to be beatin' the trees lookin' for him now. No assurance we'd find him. Or that he wouldn't need a doctor himself.

A beat as her pain and worry for Simon and River crosses her face, then, pushing on:

INARA
I'm not talking about Simon. I'm talking about medical facilities.

A beat as Mal realizes what she means, even if we don't at the moment. He turns away from her:

MAL
That's not an option. Nor is it a discussion I much want to have at the moment.

INARA
It doesn't matter what you want. He's dying.

He looks at her. Off that eye contact —

INT. SERENITY - INFIRMARY

Kaylee enters the infirmary, joining Zoe, who is watching Book — genuinely unconscious now. Kaylee makes a move to hold his hand.

KAYLEE
(re: holding hand)
Can I?

ZOE
Sure. He's out, though.

KAYLEE
He did this for me once. How's he doing?

ZOE
I cleaned it out, wrapped it up. Best I could do. I don't know.

KAYLEE
But we're headed for help, right?

ZOE
Captain'll come up with a plan.

KAYLEE
That's good, right?

ZOE
Possible you're not recalling some of his previous plans.

After a beat:

KAYLEE
We left 'em back there.

ZOE
Yeah.

KAYLEE
Don't seem right.

CUT TO:

EXT. WOODS/BACKWOODS SETTLEMENT - DAY

They come to a small community. Falling down gray wood shacks. A frontier town that lost the battle with the forest, and was overrun. The general look is Appalachian village.

A few beaten-looking people sit in front of the shacks: thin men cooking on crude clay ovens, grim-faced tattered women tending to dirty children in sack-dresses.

Stark pulls Simon roughly by the arm, out into the center of the cluster.

STARK
Look at what we got! It's a doctor! Got ourselves a doctor!
(proud, relieved)
A doctor. A real doctor.

Simon looks to Stark who suddenly seems less threatening — because he's smiling and not malevolently, but with a kind of relief.

Simon looks back to the village as more and more TOWNSFOLK begin to emerge...

STARK (cont'd)
(nudging him, sotto)
Stand up straight.

Simon does, as many of the townsfolk draw nearer, tentative, curious... some in awe...

INT. BRIDGE

Wash is looking with some awe himself at a thing just outside the cockpit window.

Mal looks less awestruck and more or less just grim.

WASH
You sure this is where you wanna be?

MAL
Oh, I'm fairly certain it ain't.

EXT. SPACE - CONTINUOUS

SERENITY moving (slowly now) through space. CAMERA PANS with Serenity, revealing just what it is she's moving toward...

AN ENORMOUS ALLIANCE CRUISER. A GRAPHIC comes up over this image: Alliance Cruiser, Magellan, Outer Rim.

INT. BACKWOODS SICKHOUSE - DAY

A DOOR is pushed open. Dusty SUNLIGHT pours into this dark place. Simon and Stark are silhouetted against it.

STARK
In here.

He ushers Simon inside.

STARK (cont'd)
Don't figure it's near as fancy as you're used to, but it's what we got.

River enters with them. Simon tries to make his eyes adjust to the dimness. It's dark in here, and there are eight or nine people inside, all ages. There are a few cots around the edges, but mostly people sit on the dirt floor. Everyone is thin, haggard, hopeless. They look at him with dead eyes.

SIMON
What... what is this place? Am I in prison?

INT. BRIDGE - CONTINUOUS

Mal and Wash looking out at the imposing Alliance Cruiser which fills the entire bridge window.

MAL
(to Wash)
Be sure to ask nicely.

Wash nods, he's already got his hand mic poised to speak into:

WASH
Alliance Cruiser Magellan, this is Firefly Transport Serenity, requesting permission for docking...

As Wash says this, Mal moves to exit the bridge, passing...

... Inara who stands there. He doesn't even look at her. Off Inara, and before Wash's request can be answered...

STARK (V.O.)
T'ain't a prison...

INT. BACKWOODS SICKHOUSE - DAY

The sad, dark place.

STARK
...it's the sickhouse.

There is some COUGHING and MOANING. Simon looks to River who gazes with sadness and compassion on those there. Stark calls out to a young woman, DORALEE.

STARK (cont'd)
(to Doralee)
Got yer doctor.

DORALEE
(joining them)
Praise the Lord!

STARK
Doralee here'll show you what's what.

Stark turns and exits. Simon looks around, moves closer to the patients.

DORALEE
What's your name?

RIVER
(appearing)
Simon.

Doralee looks over, sees River.

DORALEE
Well, hello there. Who're you?

SIMON
That's River.

River tries to move toward the sick people. Simon holds her back.

SIMON (cont'd)
River.
(indicates chair)
Just... sit down over there.

She does. Doralee looks to River; Simon looks to the assembled.

SIMON (cont'd)
(to Doralee)
Has there been... is there a sickness here?

DORALEE
Nothing especial. Just, people get sick. Or injured. Mostly people heal on their own, but sometimes...

SIMON
Sometimes you need a doctor.
(then)
Bring me light and any supplies you have.

As Simon rolls up his sleeves —

EXT. SERENITY - EFFECT

We dock with the huge ship Magellan.

INT. SERENITY - AIRLOCK

Mal and Jayne carefully lower Book onto a large crate in the cargo bay that's near the sliding airlock doors. Zoe starts rolling back the inner airlock doors.

ZOE
You sanguine about the kinda reception we're apt to receive on an Alliance ship, Captain?

MAL
Absolutely.
(then)
What's sanguine?

ZOE
Hopeful. Plus, item of interest, it also means bloody.

MAL
Well, that pretty much covers the options, don't it?

Mal moves to the smaller inner door on the ramp, hits a button — WHOOSH, it opens, and Mal finds himself facing a PHALANX OF GUNS held on him by Alliance soldiers.

INT. BACKWOODS SICKHOUSE - DAY

Doralee has brought a hurricane lamp and a wicker box presumably with medical supplies. Simon kneels in front of a child with a bandaged arm. He unwraps the bandage. As he examines the child —

SIMON
This all seems pretty minor. There's no epidemic? Nothing more serious? I was brought here just to tend to these people?

DORALEE
They need tendin', don't they? Last year, the place needed builders. Got two men. Five years ago, they decided they needed a teacher.

SIMON
So they... went and took one?

DORALEE
Went and took me.

Simon looks up from his work.

SIMON
You're... are you a prisoner here too?

DORALEE
I just live here now. Teach the children their sums, their bible lessons, how to live the Lord's way. Don't choose to leave.

SIMON
And you think they'd let you?

DORALEE
(shrugs)
Never thought to try. They needed a teacher. That's what I do. Teach.

Off Simon's incredulous reaction we return to...

INT. SERENITY AIRLOCK - CONTINUED

Mal, Zoe and injured Book face an array of guns. There are three soldiers, a COMMANDER in charge, and an ENSIGN.

Mal and Zoe are not wearing weapons and keep their hands in evidence as the Commander and his team moves into the cargo bay area. Regard the injured Book.

MAL
We're requesting aid. No other purpose.

ZOE
We got papers.

She carefully pulls a little folder of papers from her vest, hands 'em over to the Ensign. As he looks at them...

COMMANDER
What's your business?

MAL
We're a supply ship. Freelance. Had an accident this morning. Crewman got injured...

Mal indicates with his head — back toward Book.

ZOE
We need medical help.

Mal's getting twitchy — Book might be dying.

MAL
Fast'd be better'n slow.

The Ensign looks up from the papers. He hands them to the Commander. He looks at them.

COMMANDER
(to the Colonel)
Official seal's out of date, Captain...
(checks paper)
Harbatkin?

Book opens his eyes, looks up at the Commander.

MAL
We ain't been through a checkpoint in a while, sir. You gonna see to my man?

COMMANDER
How did this happen?

ZOE
He was —

MAL
(preemptively)
Bystander in a gun fight. Back on Jiangyin. You can check. Not he nor any of ours were the aggressors.

❖ Below: The ship's papers for Serenity.

❖ Opposite page: Book's ident. Note the issue number: 20 47 20, Randy Eriksen's lucky number makes another appearance!

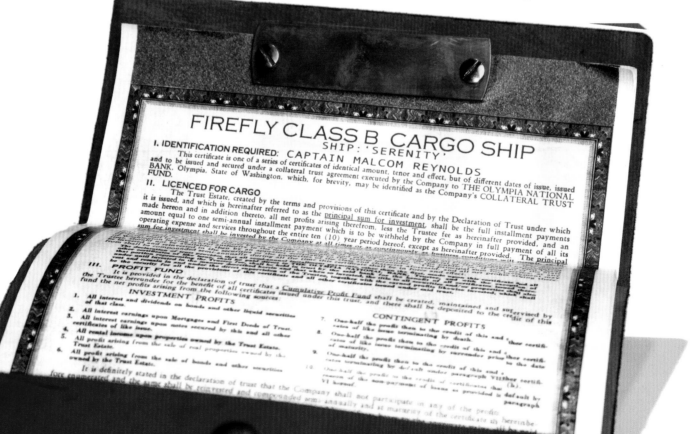

FIREFLY CLASS B CARGO SHIP
SHIP: 'SERENITY'
CAPTAIN MALCOM REYNOLDS

I. IDENTIFICATION REQUIRED:
This certificate is one of a series of certificates of identical amount, tenor and effect, but of different dates of issue, issued and to be issued and secured under a collateral trust agreement executed by the Company to THE OLYMPIA NATIONAL BANK, Olympia, State of Washington, which, for brevity, may be identified as the Company's COLLATERAL TRUST FUND.

II. LICENCED FOR CARGO
The Trust Estate, created by the terms and provisions of this certificate and by the Declaration of Trust under which it is issued, and which is hereinafter referred to as the principal sum for investment, shall be the full installment payments made hereon and in addition thereto, all net profits arising therefrom, less the Trustee fee as hereinafter provided, and an amount equal to one semi-annual installment payment which is to be withheld by the Company in full payment of all its operating expense and services throughout the entire ten (10) year period hereof, except as hereinafter provided. The principal sum for investment shall be invested by the Company at all times or as continuously as business conditions will...

COMMANDER
We aren't an emergency facility, Captain. Our services aren't simply available to any—

BOOK
(weakly)
Commander...

The Commander looks at Book, startled.

BOOK (cont'd)
My ident card... pocket...

Book tries to reach into his own pants pocket, winces...

The Commander nods to the Ensign. He helps Book, comes up with an ident card... a square of electronic paper.

Mal and Zoe watch with interest — weren't expecting this and don't quite know what to make of it.

The Ensign takes the card, slides it into a reading device (size of a credit card imprinter) which overrides its privacy code, and takes in secured information on it. He hands it to the Commander. WE CAN SEE information scrolling across the card. The Commander looks at it. Then, to the Ensign:

COMMANDER
(no nonsense)
Get this man to the infirmary at once.

The soldiers carry Book off to the infirmary. Zoe and Mal exchange a look.

INT. BACKWOODS SICKHOUSE - NIGHT

Simon has brought in even more light. Some of the people, having been treated, have left. The few remaining ones seem happier, livelier... Simon is making a difference.

Simon is treating a woman's infected hand when another woman approaches him. As Simon finishes treating the first woman, Doralee enters and approaches him. She has River with her.

DORALEE
I found her. She wasn't far.

SIMON
Thank you. She's... It's important she stay close.

River wanders to a corner of the room, sits among some small children.

DORALEE
She's not quite right, is she?

Simon finishes what he's doing...

SIMON
(to the patient)
You keep that bandage clean now, you understand?

Simon sits back and looks toward River.

SIMON (cont'd)
(to Doralee)
River's been through some trauma. She's recovering though.

DORALEE
She in a restful situation these days? Getting a chance to get better?

SIMON
Not... well. We're trying. But it's... difficult.

They watch as River looks at a little girl, age around seven, we'll know as RUBY. The little girl looks back at her, apparently unresponsive.

DORALEE
She won't get a good conversation out of Ruby, I can tell you that much. That little girl's mute.

SIMON
Do you know the cause? Was she born deaf?

DORALEE
No. She was fine until two years ago when she stopped talking.

ANGLE ON: River and the little girl.

DORALEE (cont'd)
Place like this might be good for your sister. Quiet, safe. Place where folks take care of each other.

SIMON
Yes, it seems like a lovely little community of kidnappers.

DORALEE

Costume designer Shawna Trpcic: "We had a lot of research about peasants from all around the world and whenever we went to a poor planet, we would tap into that. Doralee was very reminiscent of the Civil War period, of almost a Mammy, the kind, soft, helpful woman. We even put a little turban on her, which could be Hindu or it could be a classic turban or a scarf. Whenever we went to a planet, we always tried to blend the cultures and blend the influences, because that's the whole idea of pioneering, that you're taking people from all over the world and planting them in one spot together."

RIVER

"Two by two, hands of blue."

With her luminous eyes, dancer-lithe body and gentle spirit, it's hard to imagine anyone better born to play the character of River Tam than actress Summer Glau. In her first speaking role, Glau brought an amazing depth to her portrayal of the tortured, teenage lab experiment fleeing from the Alliance with her brother, Simon. It's under the protection of Captain Mal Reynolds and his crew that this wounded bird of a girl begins to heal from her traumatic past, and her story truly created the compassionate heart of *Firefly*. For the actress, her association with Joss Whedon and being cast as River signified the start of a new facet of her career, not to mention an amazing period of personal growth and discovery. Glau made her first impression on Whedon when she worked as a ballerina in his *Angel* episode, 'Waiting in the Wings'. When casting for *Firefly* took place soon after, Glau says it was that small role which opened the door for River. "I heard I was suggested as a good fit from that," she says. "Joss had me come in and work with him and the casting director, Amy Britt. He had to get me ready for the test because testing for a series is very intense. I had never done it before, or auditioned for a pilot. So I went in and worked with them and from that audition, I went straight to the test [for the network]. It was one of the most vivid days of my life; I remember everything about it. I remember when I did the read, it was in a very dark room with all these different faces, except that Joss was sitting in the front row and I remember looking at him afterwards and him smiling at me and looking proud, like he was happy with my read. He had called me after my audition, because he knew how nervous I was and how badly I wanted it, and told me that I did well.

"But they didn't want to cast me right away," she continues. "A lot of times they tell you a few days after or

even on the day, but in my case, because I was the youngest person in the cast and it was a smaller role, they wanted to focus more on Inara and Zoe, so I had to wait and wait and wait. Finally, it was Joss that actually called and told me I got the role, which was really special. He called me two weeks after and said, 'You're my girl!' I just cried and cried. I really believe that I got cast as River because I wanted the part more than any other girl."

While River might have been a major trial to decipher or understand for some actresses, Glau says she connected with the character from the start. "A lot of people ask me how I got inspired to play River because she is such a challenging, different person. It's funny, as soon as I read it, I knew exactly how I wanted to do it. I did. It was like we were meant to be together. I went in and I read for Amy and Joss and I was shaking like a leaf, I was so nervous. I always felt whenever I had to show someone a River scene, I had to go out on a limb. It was scary. But Amy looked at Joss when I was done and said, 'That's how you do it.' So it was just a fit, it felt right. I feel like my background and who I was before I was an actress helped me. I was really shy growing up, and dancing was my way of getting people to look at me and showing how I felt. You never talk in ballet and you are always so separated from everyone and there is a safety in that. River was a great transition for me because she was kind of distanced from the rest of the cast. She was in her own world, on her own stage, so I had a special relationship with her that way."

Of her first day Glau remembers, "The very first thing I did was go to the production office for a hair, makeup and costume test. Of course, they didn't have very much to do with River's hair. All we did was make it look dirty," she laughs. "The first person I met though was Jewel. I met her in the production office with Joss and instantly fell in love with her. She is so stylish and fabulous and fun and girlie and lovely and smelled so good. Her shoes were fantastic!

"Then I went down to get my hair done and they described her as the wacky, odd, sort of child of the group so they were trying all kinds of weird things with my hair. Of course, they had my hair stuck in some weird shape and in walks Sean. I was so awestruck and captivated by him," she blushes. "I couldn't even look at him for the first month, I just thought he was so fantastic. He treated me with care from the very beginning, just like Simon."

DORALEE
The Lord says "judge not".

SIMON
They took us off the street.

DORALEE
Life sometimes takes you places you weren't expectin' to go.

SIMON
Life didn't bring us here. Those men did.

DORALEE
You were on a transport ship, right? Takin' a journey? It's the way of life in my findings that journeys end when and where they want to. And that's where you make your home.

SIMON
This isn't our home.

DORALEE
If it isn't here, where is it?

We linger on Simon as he considers that, having honestly no answer.

INT. ALLIANCE CRUISER - INFIRMARY/ VIEWING ROOM

Mal, Zoe and Jayne in an observation room just off the big, hi-tech Alliance Cruiser infirmary. Within we see ALLIANCE DOCTORS working on Book. This has none of that E.R. urgency — it's all very staid and antiseptic.

JAYNE
This place gives me an uncomfortableness.

ZOE
So what do you figure — Shepherd's got some sort of Alliance connection?

MAL
Know what it looks like. Still — it'd surprise me if he did.

JAYNE
See, this is my whole problem with picking up tourists. They're never what they claim to be.

MAL
Does seem like everyone's got a tale to tell...

INT. BACKWOODS SICKHOUSE - NIGHT

Simon pulls a blanket over a patient who is asleep. He stands. Work done for the day. He turns. River is not there. Nor is little Ruby.

SIMON
River? River?

Doralee appears.

DORALEE
What's wrong?

SIMON
River's gone. So's the little girl.

DORALEE
Ruby —
(then, as she goes)
I'll check out back.

Simon nods. Doralee moves off. Simon moves to the entrance. He pulls open the door —

— and there's River. Alone. She's using her dress as a pouch for something.

SIMON
River, don't... what is that?

RIVER
For you.

She reveals a skirt full of BERRIES.

SIMON
Oh.

RIVER
I picked them.

He looks around for a bowl. He finds a wooden water bowl and she pours the berries from her skirt into it.

SIMON
Well, here... you'll stain your dress.

RIVER
You have to eat.

She feeds him one. He smiles. It tastes good.

SIMON
Blackberries. Do you remember when we found those giant blackberry bushes on the Cambersons' Estate... We thought they'd grown wild, but...
(his smile fades)
...long while ago.

He puts the bowl aside. River watches his bitter-sweet reverie.

RIVER
I took you away from there.

SIMON
No, no...

RIVER
I know I did. You don't think I do, but... I get confused. I remember everything, I remember too much and some of it's made up and some of it... can't be quantified, and there's secrets and ...

She's getting upset now, eyes welling up...

SIMON
It's okay...

RIVER
But I understand. you gave up everything you had to find me, and you found me broken and it's hard for you, you gave up everything you had —

SIMON
<Mei mei> [Little sister]... Everything I have is right here.

She feeds him another berry.

RIVER
You have to eat. Keep up your strength and we won't be here long, Daddy will come and take us home and I'll get better. I'll get better.

He clouds over at the reference to home and family, though he tries to hide it. Eats another berry.

SIMON
These are better than the Cambersons' berries.

RIVER
They are. Except they're poison.

He spits it out, horror on his face — and she laughs delightedly... He smiles, busted.

RIVER (cont'd)
He believed her, made a face.

SIMON
(genuinely happy)
You're such a brat.

Doralee appears with Ruby.

DORALEE
(relieved to see River)
You found her.

Ruby moves off to her makeshift bed, one of the many mats.

SIMON
Yes, she... there are berries.

DORALEE
Fruit of the ground. God's reward for a hard day's work.
(to Ruby)
You get to bed, now.

SIMON
(re: he and River)
We should probably think about doing the same. It's been a big day, what with the abduction and all.

DORALEE
Ya'll don't have to sleep here. There's a house set aside for you. We've been looking for a doctor for a good while. So things are ready.

SIMON
Really...

RIVER
(mouth full of berries)
Her sister got killed. Her mother got crazy. Killed the sister. That one lived.

DORALEE
Ruby talked to you, honey?
(to Simon, excited)
It's true what she's saying. Poor woman went out of her mind, tried to kill her two girls. Ruby lived.
(to River)
Sweetheart, you are an angel! No one's been able to get Ruby to speak even a peep! It's a miracle! That's what it is!

RIVER
Ruby doesn't talk. Her voice got scared away. I hear crickets.

DORALEE
I don't understand... if Ruby didn't talk, how do you...?

SIMON
My sister is... She's very good at —
(off Doralee's face)
What's wrong?

DORALEE
(reciting softly)
"And they shall be among the people, and they shall speak truths and whisper secrets... and you will know them by their crafts..."

SIMON
What are you talking about?

Doralee takes a troubled, horrified step backward...

DORALEE
"Thou shall not suffer a witch to live."

She runs into the night. Simon is, understandably, alarmed.

END OF ACT THREE

ACT FOUR

INT. TAM ESTATE - NIGHT

We're in Simon's third and final flashback. [Note: again, this is on a different night, new wardrobe.] We're in the same room. Regan looks out the window, alone. Face etched with worry, drink in hand. It's POURING RAIN outside. She hears the front door open O.S. Simon enters wearing an overcoat, walking briskly, followed by his father.

REGAN
Simon! Thank god! I was so worried.

SIMON
I'm fine.

REGAN
Then what were you doing in a police holding center?

GABRIEL
Your son was caught in a vice unit raid. Downtown, in a red-light tenement bar.
(to Simon)
Never expected I'd be dragged out of the house in the middle of the night for something like this, Simon.

SIMON
Weren't you even listening? I had to go there! It was the only place the man would meet me.

REGAN
Man? What man?

SIMON
Someone with information about the Academy. Someone with the contacts we're going to need. Other children have disappeared into that school, Mother. And the ones who do come out, they're... wrong... aphasic or psychotic...

She just stares. Gabriel looks more annoyed than worried.

GABRIEL
Can you believe this? This is what I've had to listen to for the last two hours.

SIMON
I've been working on her letters. There is a code. She says someone is hurting them.

Gabriel goes to the phone-screen, starts to make a call.

GABRIEL
I'll call Johan. He should be able to scrub this off his record, with a small transfer of funds...

Simon slams the shut-off, stopping the call.

SIMON
Dad! Forget my record! River is in trouble!

REGAN
River isn't here!

Simon looks like he's been slapped across the face. Stunned.

GABRIEL
We are. And we have to be careful how we act. This is a government school, Simon. People in our position... it's important that we show support for this government.

SIMON
You're talking about politics? This is about your daughter!

GABRIEL
This is about our lives.

Simon stares at them both for a beat, taking this in. Simon turns, heads for the door. Gabriel follows —

GABRIEL (cont'd)
Where are you going?

SIMON
To get her out.

GABRIEL
This isn't something you want to do.

SIMON
You're right. This isn't something I want to do. But if I don't, then no one will. So I'll do it. I'll take care of her. Just like I always have.

GABRIEL
That's <tsway-niou> [bullcrap]. We gave both of our children everything they could possibly want.

A beat as Simon stares at his father.

SIMON
(hardens, starts to turn)
Right.

GABRIEL
If you do this thing, they will find you, and they will put you away. And know this: when they do, I will not come for you. If you leave here, if you do this... I will not come for you.

Simon turns and walks away into the night.

EXT. BACKWOODS SETTLEMENT - NIGHT

Simon and River watch as Doralee rings the town bell. It's at the side of the little street, rigged to a pole. She pulls repeatedly at the cord that swings the clapper.

Townspeople, about a dozen, emerge onto the streets. Stark among them. Doralee yells to them as they appear.

DORALEE
Witch! The girl's a witch!

SIMON
This is lunacy. You're supposed to be the teacher here. What exactly is it you teach?!

An older man, an official known as the town PATRON, comes to Doralee, puts a hand on her arm, makes her stop ringing the bell. He's got a long coat over pajamas, an air of authority, and he seems completely rational and comforting.

PATRON
What's going on, woman? Why are you knocking us out of our beds this hour?

DORALEE
That girl, the new Doctor's sister... she read Ruby's mind. Saw things she couldn't —

River is clinging to Simon, confused and scared.

SIMON
River's not a witch. She's just a troubled girl —

The Patron smiles at the brother and sister.

PATRON
I'm sure that's true.
(to River)
You're not a witch, are you, <nyen ching-duh> [young one]? I'm the Patron here — do you know what that means?

RIVER
(to the Patron, pleasantly)
Yes. You're in charge. Ever since the old Patron died.

PATRON
That's right.

RIVER
He was sick and you were alone in the room with him.

The Patron slaps her across the face.

SIMON
No!

Simon makes a rush for him and is restrained.

PATRON
This girl reads minds and spins falsehoods! She has had congress with The Beast!

The Patron motions to two men who step forward, take River.

PATRON (cont'd)
We will purge the devil from her.

She KICKS... struggling to break free. This isn't delicate squirming, but an all-out fight.

She lets out a horrible long SCREAM — as if she's being killed. It's shocking. It doesn't help.

SIMON
No! She didn't mean anything!

PATRON
Bind her. She must be purged. With fire.

INT. SERENITY/INFIRMARY - NIGHT

We're back on Serenity. Book is on the recovery table. Comes around. Sees Mal hovering over him.

BOOK
Well. That's not a face I expect to see in heaven. Guess I survived.
(then)
Thank you, Captain. It was very resourceful of you.

MAL
Had no reason to think it'd work. Just took a chance.

BOOK
Reckon that's how you do lots of things.

MAL
Majority of the time it turns out bad. I may want to rethink my governing principle.

BOOK
Well, it worked out this time.

MAL
Yeah. They let us come and they let us go. What kind of ident card gets us that kind of reception and send off?

BOOK
I'm a shepherd. Folks like a man of God.

MAL
No they don't. Men of God make everyone feel guilty and judged. That's not what I saw. You like to tell me what really happened?

BOOK
I surely would. And maybe someday I will.
(then)
It's good to be home.

INT. SERENITY - INFIRMARY/COMMON AREA - CONTINUOUS

Jayne is seated at at little table, carefully drying money between little towels. He sets the last dried bundle in a tidy stack. Zoe enters from the cargo bay as Mal steps out of the infirmary.

ZOE
Badger just hailed us. Getting impatient for his share. Wants us to drop it to his men on the Kowlan Fed base.

JAYNE
Well, that'll be a hell of a lot eaiser to do without the "two most wanted" on board.
(excitedly)
Life would look to be simpler all round, us not carrying fugies.

Mal, and Zoe with him, go, neither wanting to say;

ZOE
He's right, you know.

MAL
Yeah. Simpler.

EXT. BACKWOODS SETTLEMENT - NIGHT

The villagers are constructing a witch-burning set-up... vertical pole, kindling... you know how it goes.

Men SCURRY UP TREES, like Stark before. They go into the high branches, drop down dry, dead kindling.

River, being held, is calm again. But Simon is losing it. Stark is there now, too, looking regretful.

SIMON
Don't do this. There has to be another way...

STARK
You asked for time, Doctor. The Patron give you that. But you don't offer him nothin'.

The men holding River spirit her over to the stake. They start to tie her to it. She doesn't struggle. They're piling kindling there. One of the men fires up a small TORCH.

SIMON
(to Patron)
Take me instead! Take my life for hers!

PATRON
The witch must burn. God commands it.

The man with the torch moves to the pile of kindling. Is about to light it.

SIMON
NO!

Simon manages to rip free, rush over, shoves that guy aside.

SIMON (cont'd)
Get away from her!

He gets hit. Hits back. More of the men come at him. He stands between them and River. Sees that he's woefully outnumbered. A few show up with old, rusty rifles pointed at him.

SIMON (cont'd)
She doesn't understand! Can't you see what you're doing? Please...

The mob just stares back, unmoved. Simon sees the odds. Nothing to do now. He turns, climbs up onto the pile of kindling —

STARK
That's not gonna stop us, Doctor.

He doesn't even look back to Stark. Looks at River.

RIVER
Post holer. For digging holes. For posts.

She smiles at him. Doesn't seem frightened. He smiles back, tries not to explode with the emotion. He looks at her bonds, at the mob converging. At the man with the torch. So he just wraps his arms around her. She rests her head on his chest. Then, all defiance, he turns to the mob.

SIMON
Light it.

SUMMER GLAU

In 'Safe', I got to dance. It was a really special episode that I remember very vividly. It's such a powerful image for me, being up on the stake — and it was cold. I remember the wind blew my hair up and it got stuck on the stake. Also the stake wouldn't stay in the ground: it kept tipping over so I would have to jump off of it.

The Patron nods to the man with the torch. He brings it up. Touches it to the pile of kindling. It starts to SMOKE and IGNITE. Simon holds on tight.

RIVER
(clear and still)
Time to go.

Then the wind picks up and it gets darker, as

SERENITY RISES UP

huge and gray. THUNK. The BOMB BAY DOORS open on the belly of Serenity and there's Jayne, hanging out of them, big ass rifle with a flashlight

strapped to it aimed down on those assembled. He could pick off any of them at any time.

THE VILLAGERS back away, stunned.

And into the clearing strides Mal, hero shot, big ass rifle in his hands, Zoe close behind. He speaks up, for everyone's benefit.

MAL
Well, look at this. Appears we got here just in the nick of time. What does that make us?

ZOE
Big damn heroes, sir.

MAL
Ain't we just. Sorry to interrupt, people, but you all got something of ours, and we'll be needing it back.

PATRON
This is a holy cleansing. You cannot think to thwart God's will.

MAL
Do you see the man hanging from the spaceship with the really big gun? Now I'm not saying you weren't easy to find, but it was kinda out of our way and he didn't wanna come in the first place. Man's looking to kill some folk, so it's really his will y'all should worry 'bout thwarting.

He moves past the Patron, addresses Simon.

MAL (cont'd)
Gotta say, Doctor, your talent for alienating folks is near miraculous.

SIMON
Yes, I'm very proud.

Mal turns to the Patron.

MAL
(to Patron)
Cut her down.

PATRON
The girl is a witch!

MAL
Yeah. But she's our witch.
(cocks his gun)
So cut her the hell down.

Off Mal's won't-take-no-for-an-answer look...

INT. SERENITY - INFIRMARY/COMMON AREA

Mal comes into the common area, glances into the infirmary, notes that it's empty. He turns

and there's Simon.

SIMON
I've moved him to his room.

MAL
How's he fairing?

SIMON
He's going to be fine. They took good care of him.

MAL
Good to know.

An awkward beat between them. Then:

SIMON
Finally a decent wound on this ship and I miss out. I'm sorry.

MAL
Well, you were busy trying to get yourself lit on fire. It happens.

Mal starts to go.

SIMON
Captain...
(Mal turns back)
...why did you come back for us?

MAL
You're on my crew.

SIMON
You don't even like me. Why did you come back?

MAL
You're on my crew. Why we still talking about this?
(his back to him, as he goes)
Chow's in ten. No need to dress.

As we hold on Simon:

INT. SERENITY/DINING ROOM - NIGHT

The crew gathered for supper. Everyone's there except for Book. Simon appears, ushers in River. She goes across the table, takes a seat in between Jayne and Wash.

Kaylee appears carrying a bread basket, sets it on the table. She glances at Simon. He smiles at her. She smiles back. He holds a chair for her. She sits.

There's lots of chatting and laughing and arguing.

WE FOLLOW the serving dish as it's passed around. Jayne takes a big hunk of bread, puts it on his plate, passes the dish. He looks back — the bread is gone. River's got it, is eating it.

Simon takes in the communal experience happening around him. And as we pull back on this milieu —

FADE OUT:

END OF SHOW

Some scenes in this episode changed quite substantially from the shooting script and some extra scenes were added in at the last minute. Here are those scenes as aired.

EXT. LARGE MANSION - NIGHT

Establishing shot. High-tech security fence surrounds the mansion.

INT. LARGE MANSION - NIGHT - CONTINUOUS

We're in a study or living room. Spacious, lushly appointed, a fire crackling in the fireplace.

Chyron reads:

TAM ESTATE, 11 YEARS AGO

Young Simon Tam sits on the couch doing his homework.

Young River Tam is playing behind the couch.

YOUNG RIVER
(peeping up from behind couch) We're in trouble. (beat) We got cut off!

YOUNG SIMON
Cut off from what?

YOUNG RIVER
Our platoon, Simon. We got outflanked by the Independent squad, and we're never gonna make it back to our platoon. (beat) We need to resort to cannibalism.

YOUNG SIMON
That was fast. Don't we have rations or anything?

YOUNG RIVER
They got lost. We're gonna have to eat the men.

YOUNG SIMON
Aren't you supposed to be practicing for your dance recital?

YOUNG RIVER
I learned it all. (re: his homework) That's wrong.

YOUNG SIMON
It's from the book, River.

YOUNG RIVER
No, the book is wrong. This whole conclusion is fallacious.

Simon smiles, puts his homework away. Turns to River.

YOUNG SIMON
So... how'd the Independents cut us off?

YOUNG RIVER
They were using dinosaurs.

YOUNG SIMON
(incredulous) <Jien tah-duh guay!> [Like hell!]

GABRIEL TAM enters the study.

GABRIEL
Language, young man.

YOUNG SIMON
Sorry, Dad. The Independents attacked us with dinosaurs.

YOUNG RIVER
Simon lost his head in the heat of battle.

GABRIEL
(chuckling) <Nah mei guan-shee.> [That has nothing to do with it.] Because there were dinosaurs involved, I think we'll let it slide.

YOUNG SIMON
Did you get my wave?

GABRIEL
I got it. Your text shorted. I got the whole thing during a board meeting. Thank you.

YOUNG SIMON
If I had a dedicated source box, it wouldn't short out. I lost half my essay.

GABRIEL
Yes, and you'd have access to any <tyen-shiao duh> [heaven knows what] that filtered in from the Cortex. I absolutely forbid it!

YOUNG SIMON
(pleading) Dad...

YOUNG RIVER
Dad...

GABRIEL
I will not have it in my house! (beat) But since your mother's already ordered you one, I guess I should give up the fantasy that this is my house!

YOUNG SIMON
Are you kidding?

GABRIEL
You will repay me by becoming a brilliant doctor. That's the deal. Dedicated sourcebox — brilliant doctor.

YOUNG RIVER
When do I...?

GABRIEL
(dismissive) Many years.

YOUNG SIMON
Dad, this is so <da bianhua> [big change]! It's really gonna —

GABRIEL
I know. You think I'd let you work with something second-rate?

YOUNG SIMON
Thank you.

GABRIEL
You're worth it. (beat) Now do you think it's possible for you two geniuses to give your tired old dad a couple minutes' quiet?

INT. SERENITY - COMMON AREA - CONTINUOUS

Back to the present. River is struggling and shouting.

Simon is attempting to calm her.

RIVER
(collapses onto couch) No! No, I don't wanna go back to the...

SIMON
It's okay. It —

RIVER
It's not okay! (beat) You can't just dig into me, shove twenty needles in my eyes and ask me what I see!

SIMON
I... we won't go in. Look. (shuts infirmary doors) No test today.

RIVER
No rutting tests? Stupid son of a bitch, dress me up like a gorramn doll!

SIMON
No tests, no shots... (beat) I'm, uh, I'm just gonna give you a smoother that'll...

River stands, takes Simon's case of medical supplies, and tosses it.

SIMON
River!

Mal is walking down the steps to the infirmary as this happens. None too pleased.

RIVER
(to Mal) You're not him? (beat) <Liou coe shway duh biao-tze huh hoe-tze duh ur-tze.> [Stupid son of a drooling whore and a monkey.]

River wilts and sits back on the couch.

Mal continues down the stairs.

MAL
So, she's added cussing and hurling about of things to her repertoire. She really is a prodigy.

SIMON
It's just a bad day.

MAL
No, a bad day is when someone's yellin' spooks the cattle. Understand? (beat) You ever see cattle stampede when they got no place to run? It's kind of like a... a meat grinder. And it'll lose us half the herd.

SIMON
She hasn't gone anywhere near the cattle.

MAL
No, but in case you hadn't noticed, her voice kinda carries. We're two miles above ground and they can probably hear her down there. Soon as we unload, she can holler until our ears bleed. (to River) Although I would take it as a kindness if she didn't.

RIVER
The human body can be drained of blood in 8.6 seconds given adequate vacuuming systems.

MAL
(to Simon) See, morbid and creepifying, I got no problem with, long as she does it quiet-like.

SIMON
This is paranoid schizophrenia, Captain. Hand-crafted by

government scientists who thought my sister's brain was a rutting playground. I have no idea what'll set her off. If you have some expertise —

MAL

(firmly) I'm not a doctor. And I'm not your gorramn baby-sitter, either. Gag her, if you have to. We got trade to be done.

Mal exits via the stairs. Simon sighs heavily.

EXT. PLANET - DAY

Establishing shot of Serenity landing on the planet's surface.

REVERSE camera to reveal three hill folk sitting in a copse of trees, all men.

One of the men is skinning a rabbit hung from a tree.

STARK

You see that? Fancy vessel such as that don't land here 'less they got something to sell. And if it's something we need...

He RIPS the skin off the rabbit in one move.

STARK (con't)

We take it.

BLACK OUT.

END OF TEASER

INT. TAM ESTATE - FLASHBACK - NIGHT

Forward in time from the last flashback. Simon is an adult now.

REGAN

Your sister is fine, Simon.

SIMON

She's not fine. Didn't you look at the letters? Look at the letters.

GABRIEL

Uh, I'm looking at letters.

SIMON

These phrases — they don't sound anything like her. Some of these words — they're misspelled. (off their looks) She started correcting my spelling when she was three. She's trying to tell us something. I think there's a code.

REGAN

A code?

SIMON

Yes.

GABRIEL

(chuckling) I always thought it was River who was lost without her big brother. Now I'm beginning to wonder if it isn't the other way around.

SIMON

Did you have a good time at the D'arbanville's ball this year?

GABRIEL

What are you...?

SIMON

River thought it was duller than last year. But since we don't know anybody named D'arbanville, I'm having trouble judging. (angrily) Did you even read these?

GABRIEL

Well, of course I did.

REGAN

It's one of her silly games. You two are always playing.

SIMON

She is trying to tell us something that somebody doesn't want her to say.

REGAN

Simon, this is paranoid. It's stress. If they heard you talking like this at the hospital, it could affect your entire future.

SIMON

Who cares about my future?

GABRIEL

You should.

REGAN

You're a surgeon in one of the best hospitals in Capital City. On your way to a major position, possibly even the Medical Elect. You're going to throw all of that away? Everything you've worked for your whole life?

GABRIEL

Being a doctor means more to you than just a position, I know that.

REGAN

A few months time, you'll turn around and there she'll be. Now, nothing is going to keep you two apart for long.

INT. SERENITY - SIMON'S ROOM - CONTINUOUS

Jayne is tossing Simon's room, stealing all the valuables he can find. He comes across a journal of Simon's, opens it up, reads to himself out loud:

JAYNE
(mock reading)
"Dear Diary, Today I was pompous and my sister was crazy."
(flips page)
"Today, we were kidnapped by hill folk never to be seen again. It was the best day ever."

Jayne tosses aside the journal and continues searching Simon's belongings. He finds some money, pockets it.

JAYNE (cont'd)
Now we're talkin'.

Jayne pulls out a fancy maroon shirt and shakes it out, holding it up as if sizing it.

JAYNE (cont'd)
Amazing we kept him this long.

INT. CAPITAL CITY PENITENTIARY - FLASHBACK - DAY

Gabriel Tam is waiting in a lobby. Simon is escorted in by a guard.

GABRIEL

Have you completely lost your mind?

SIMON

Pretty nearly.

GABRIEL

We got the wave at the Friedlich's. I had to leave your mother at the dinner table.

SIMON

(snidely) I'm sorry, Dad. You know I would never have tried to save River's life if I had known there was a dinner party at risk.

GABRIEL

Don't you dare be flippant with me. I just spent two thousand credits to get you out of here, and I had to walk through that door which goes on my permanent profile. (beat) Are you trying to destroy this family?

SIMON

I didn't realize it would be so easy. (beat) Dad, I — I didn't do anything.

GABRIEL

You were in a blackout zone!

SIMON

Talking! To someone who might be able to help River. And I'm going right back there.

GABRIEL

[Whispering in Chinese.] This is a slippery slope, young man. You have no idea how far down you can go, and you're not taking us with you.

SIMON

Meaning what?

GABRIEL

I won't come for you again. You end up here, or get mixed-up in something worse, you're on your own. I will not come for you. (beat) Now, are you coming home?

INT. SERENITY - SIMON'S ROOM

Close shot of Simon's bed. Someone's dumping a bagful of loot onto it. It's Jayne, hastily returning his ill-gotten gains. Jayne darts out of Simon's room into

INT. SERENITY - CORRIDOR - CONTINUOUS

Jayne's beating his retreat when he sees Simon walking past.

JAYNE

(looking guilty) Hey, there, Doctor. Glad you're back now on the ship.

SIMON

Thanks.

Simon keeps walking. Jayne bolts up the stairs.

COSTUME DESIGN

An interview with Shawna Trpcic

The original costume designer on *Firefly* was Jill Ohanneson; however, the vast bulk of the series' apparel was designed by Shawna Trpcic [pronounced "Trip-chick"]. Trpcic, who began her professional career by designing forty episodes of *Power Rangers* and went on to assist Albert Wolsky on the Costume Oscar-nominated *Toys*, had worked as Ohanneson's assistant designer on a show called *The First $20 Million Is Always the Hardest*. The duo got along well, so when Ohanneson got the gig to design the *Firefly* pilot, she invited Trpcic to work with her again; the job called for Trpcic to do the physical sketches of all the designs. "We pretty much designed the pilot together," Trpcic says. "When the series started, they asked her to come back, but she had gotten *Six Feet Under*, so she told them that she would

❖ Below: Designs for Mal as a civilian and as a soldier.

❖ Opposite: Costume design for Inara.

❖ Over the page: A selection of Trpcic's designs for Kaylee, Inara, Wash and Jayne, along with Rosie the Riveter (inspiration for Kaylee's look), and costume continuity photos.

design the first episode, but that they should hire me to do the rest."

Trpcic worked closely with *Firefly* production designer Carey Meyer. "We had a lot of the same styles. It's funny, because we have a lot of the same comic book collection," Trpcic laughs. "So when we walked in, the tone that we wanted was the same."

Firefly borrows from many different historical eras. Trpcic says especially influential periods for the look were: "World War Two and the Old West, 1876 and the American Civil War, 1861, mixed in with 1861 samurai Japan."

Regarding use of colors, Trpcic says, "If you look at Asian culture, with the red lamps and the colors they use to highlight emotions and feelings, I tried to do that with a brush stroke, with a deep red or a deep orange to constantly bring us back to the heart and the humanity of these people and the reality of their struggle, trying to separate them from the coldness of the Alliance. When we went to the hospital [in 'Ariel'], I wanted everyone to be wearing white and blue, and grey and purple, cold colors. Whereas, when you think of the Old West, you think of golden lights burning and coming home. I wanted people to feel at home with the characters, and to convey that with color."

Collaboration with the hair and makeup departments was also crucial, says Trpcic. "Sometimes I would get the character dressed and think, 'Oh, my gosh, I totally fell short, this isn't what I was trying to convey — what am I going to do?' And then they would go into hair and makeup and then come out, and I'd be like, 'That's what I was trying to do!' The hair and makeup people would complement the costume, or they would come to me with ideas, and then we'd go off of each other. They were an amazing group of incredibly talented men and women and I'm so grateful for them, because they would literally finish the idea I had in my head that I couldn't get out."

Some examples: "With Kaylee's ball gown [in 'Shindig'], I showed them the initial pencil sketch that I had done and they made Kaylee look so soft and so beautiful. And Inara — she would come out of hair and makeup looking drop-dead sexy gorgeous and I'm like, 'Yeah, the dress is doing what it's supposed to do.' Also, on 'Shindig', we dressed something like three hundred extras and I was just assembly-lining them, throwing these things together, trying to think of colors and shapes and

Firefly

Inara - ep6

Shavona Tropic - 02

We Can D[

WAR PRODUCTION CO-ORDINATING COMMITTEE

Kaylee ideas.

Paint

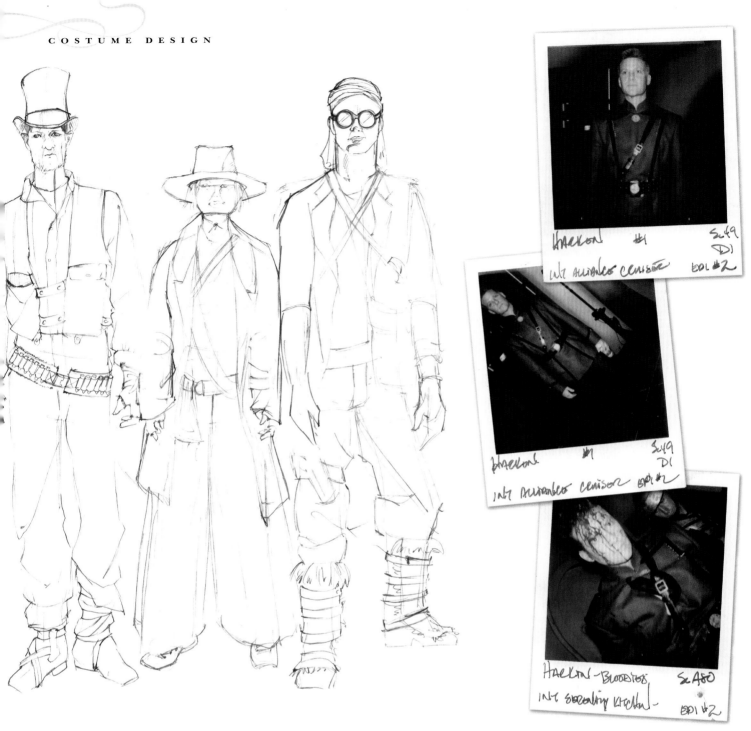

❖ Above left: Design sketches of Patience and her men from 'Serenity'.

❖ Above right: Continuity photos of Commander Harken from 'Bushwhacked'.

❖ Opposite page left: A design for an Alliance soldier.

❖ Opposite page right: A design for Simon.

going, 'Oh, this isn't working,' and then all the extras came out of hair and makeup, and they were beautiful! They looked like we had spent millennia planning this instead of just the few days that we had to do it."

When designing costumes for individual episodes, Trpcic says, "I took my cues off the script and then I would create boards of images. Say, for the mud episode ['Jaynestown'], I went to the library at Fox and talked to [Fox researcher] Brian, and said, 'I need people who farm mud, people who farm oil, people who farm different things from the earth.' And he would give me tons of images and I would put them on a board and send them to Tim or Joss, whoever was supervising that particular episode, and fine-tune the look for that planet. No two planets were ever the same."

The crew of Serenity and their adversaries had a tendency to get shot, which meant that their clothes got bloody. Wardrobe accommodated repeated takes of clothes getting gored by having multiple copies of costumes. "Up to six," Trpcic explains. "Sometimes, even that was not enough and we had to use a bloodied one over again and try to hide the blood or wash it really quick while they shot the last take. Squibs are the little explosions that look like a bullet hole, and sometimes they go off before the camera's rolling and we lose our shirts even before they catch it on camera. Sometimes, when they say there'll just be a small amount of blood, they will push the gage too quickly and there will be tons of blood. Most often, they want us to have a lighter-colored outfit to show the blood. I think with

Mal one time, it was a dark red shirt, so it didn't show a lot, but we just got it really wet so it looked really gooey."

It was also Shawna's job to costume the actors when the characters were supposedly naked. "We talk to them in the morning and say, 'What do you want to wear?' and we get the appropriate little pasties or G-strings or whatever it takes to make them feel comfortable with being in front of the crew."

Of the *Firefly* experience as a whole, Trpcic says, "Working with Joss is the dream job and doing *Firefly* was obviously a design dream job, because we were in a different universe every week. He's an incredibly gracious, humble, talented man who just has a gift for creating these worlds that are really fun to play in." ◉

OUR
MRS. REYNOLDS

Written by Joss Whedon
Directed by Vondie Curtis Hall

JOSS WHEDON

When I wrote 'Our Mrs. Reynolds', it was Tim who said, 'He's got to be married before the opening credits.' I'm like, 'I just don't think I can do that.' And then of course he was totally right. And then that episode — and I will never say these words again, and believe me, I wish to god I could — wrote itself.

❖ On-set prop master Skip Crank relaxing with the cast, while filming the teaser for 'Our Mrs. Reynolds'.

TEASER

EXT. RIVER IN WOODED GLADE - DAY

[NOTE: If a river is an impossibility, wagon in a glade will suffice. But water makes it cooler.]

A farmer in a broad-brimmed hat (Amish-ish) sits by his bonneted wife on the front of a flat-boat. There's a pole that sticks out to one side harnessed to a team of two horses. The boat is covered with a tarp, almost covered-wagon style.

We see it from a distance, through the trees — and in the foreground, horses snort and paw.

Someone else is watching as well.

A beat, and the riders — four of them — clear the woods and circle the boat (the river being shallow enough to ride in). The men are bandits, the main one (BANDIT 1) facing the cowed couple.

BANDIT 1
Pardon me for intruding, but I believe y'all are carrying something of mine.

The Farmer doesn't lift his head, barely whispers:

FARMER
T'ain't your'n.

MUSIC

Composer Greg Edmonson: "In the opening to 'Our Mrs. Reynolds', they're in a covered wagon. It wasn't specifically a Western, but this was near the end when they just said, 'Get rid of all the Western elements.' They called and said, 'Whatever you do, don't make this sound like *Little House on the Prairie*.' So as it fades from black, I had a sitar playing and then I had Chinese vocals, just purely to say, 'This is not a Western Western. It's a different Western, it's a different planet, it's a different universe.'"

BANDIT 1
(pissed)
You talking words to me? You <jung chi duh go-se dway> [steaming crap pile], you gonna mouth off after what you done? Did you think we wouldn't find out you changed your route? You're gonna give us what's due us and every damn thing else on that boat, and I think maybe you're gonna give me a little one-on-one time with the Mrs.

The Farmer lifts his head — it's JAYNE, smiling.

JAYNE
You might wanna reconsider that last part. I married me a powerful ugly creature.

MAL looks up from under his bonnet, shocked.

MAL
How can you say that? How can you shame me in front of new people?

JAYNE
If I could make you prettier, I would.

MAL
You're not the man I met a year ago.

Over this is the extreme confusion of Bandit 1, who finally gets pissed enough to go for his gun —

— and Mal and Jayne, in mid-spat, raise theirs first, targeting 1 and 2.

MAL (cont'd)
Think very hard. You been birddoggin' this township a while now, and they wouldn't mind a corpse of you. Now you could luxuriate in a nice jail cell but if your hand touches metal, I swear by my pretty floral bonnet I will end you.

A beat. The Bandits all look to each other —

Bandit 4 in the back raises his rifle — and a shot from the covered boat knocks him off his horse.

Then everybody's firing, Mal and Jayne dropping 1 and 2 as ZOE dives from the wagon, dropping 3

as she hits the water.

Much falling, much splashing and —

EXT. TOWN - NIGHT

Much celebration, the town gathered around a bonfire dancing, laughing… all the trimmings.

Mal walks through the celebration with INARA, who is dressed down (for her).

MAL
We'll head for Beaumonde in the morning, give you a chance to do some work of your own.

INARA
I appreciate it. This place is lovely, but —

MAL
Not your clientele. I'm wise. You got to play at being a lady.

INARA
Well, yes. So explain to me again why Zoe wasn't in the dress?

MAL
Tactics, woman. I needed her covering the back. Besides, them soft cotton dresses feel kind of nice. There's a whole air flow.

INARA
And you would know that because…

MAL
You can't open the book of my life and jump to the middle. Like woman, I am a mystery.

INARA
(laughing)
Best keep it that way. I withdraw the question.

MAL
Care to dance?

INARA
I've seen you dance.
(off his mock hurt)
Go enjoy yourself. You got hired to be a hero for once. It must be a nice change.

ANGLE ON: JAYNE: he sits by the fire, drunk as a butter-churn, as a townsperson, ELDER GOMMEN, hands him a big wooden stick filled with beads, that sounds like rain when you turn it over.

ELDER GOMMEN
It makes the rain come when you turn it. The rain is scarce, and comes only when needed most. And such it is with men like you.

Jayne's eyes fill with tears.

JAYNE
This is the most… you, friend. You're the guy.

He hugs the Elder hard.

JAYNE (cont'd)
I'll treasure this.

ANGLE ON: BOOK. He stands far off from the noise and light, by a sheet with four pairs of boots sticking out of it, silently reading last rites. Looks over and sees:

ANGLE: BOOK'S POV

Mal sits in a circle, next to Jayne. Book watches as a shyly pretty girl kneels before Mal and places a wreath on his head.

Book goes back to praying.

ANGLE: Mal — as the girl hands him a bowl of wine. Mal drinks and she smiles, moves off into the dance. Others draw Mal and Jayne into the dance as well, Mal finishing his wine sloppily and Jayne not letting go of his rainstick. Mal looks to Zoe, but she is making out with WASH like mad. These are three soused heroes.

Mal and Jayne join in the dance, noise and movement filling the frame, cutting to —

EXT./INT. SERENITY AIRLOCK/CARGO BAY - MORNING

The noise of the whirling engine coming to life — we pan from it to Mal and Elder Gommen on the ramp, as a couple of townsfolk load crates onto the ship.

MAL
Elder Gommen, thank you for your hospitality.

ELDER GOMMEN
We owe you a great debt. I'm sorry we have so little to pay it with. Though I hope our gifts will show our regard.

MAL
I don't think Jayne's ever letting go of that stick.

Zoe runs up to Mal from inside, whispers in his ear:

ZOE
Alliance patrol boat is heading into atmo right now.

Mal smiles at Elder Gommen as Zoe runs back up.

MAL
Well, we gotta fly.

He steers him off as Elder Gommen replies:

ELDER GOMMEN
We will pray for a safe voyage, and hope to lay eyes on you again 'ere too long, my friend.

MAL
Count on it. Bye now.

He runs back up, the ramp closing on the still waving Elder.

EXT. SERENITY

As she takes off and heads up.

INT. CARGO BAY - CONTINUOUS

As Mal is squaring away the goods he comes upon —

✤ Above and below: Before and after the Zoic effects have been added to the cargo bay scene.

MAL
Ahh!

— the girl from last night, huddled shyly in the corner between various boxes. She wears the same potato-sack shift she sported before, and sandals. And an expression of extreme subservient fear. Her name, we will learn, is SAFFRON.

MAL (cont'd)
Who the hell are you?

SAFFRON
What do you mean?

MAL
I think I was pretty clear. What are you doing on my boat?

SAFFRON
But you know! I'm to cleave to you.

MAL
To wabba hoo? You can't be here.

SAFFRON
Did Elder Gommen not tell you...

MAL
Tell me what? Who are you?

SAFFRON
Mr. Reynolds, sir... I am your wife.

We hold on his very stupid expression for a long, long time.

END OF TEASER

ACT ONE

INT. CARGO BAY - CONTINUING

Mal is still looking dumb for a while. Finally:

MAL
Could you repeat that please?

SAFFRON
I am your wife. That was your agreement with Elder Gommen, since he hadn't cash or livestock enough to —

MAL
I'm sorry. Go back to the part where you're my wife.

SAFFRON
(downcast)
I don't please you.

MAL
You can't please me. You've never met me.

Zoe and Jayne enter.

MAL (cont'd)
Zoe, why do I have a wife?

JAYNE
You got a wife?

ZOE
What's she doing here?

JAYNE
All I got was that dumb-ass stick that sounds like it's raining. How come you got a wife?

MAL
I didn't.
(to Saffron)
We're not married.

SAFFRON
I'm sorry if I shame you...

MAL
You don't shame me! Zoe, get Wash down here.

ZOE
(hits com)
This is Zoe. We need all personnel in the cargo bay.

MAL
All — I said Wash!

ZOE
Captain, everyone should have a chance to congratulate you on your day of bliss.

MAL
There's no bliss! I don't know this girl.

JAYNE
Then can I know her?

ZOE
(tough)
Jayne...
(sensitive)
Don't sully this.

MAL
Zoe, you are gonna be cleaning the latrine with your face, you don't cut that out.

Everyone is in now.

BOOK
Who's the new recruit?

ZOE
Everybody, I want you to meet Mrs. Reynolds.

ANGLE ON: INARA

True pain crosses her face.

SAFFRON

Costume designer Shawna Trpcic: "Saffron [Christina Hendricks] was a lot of fun. She had a challenging figure, because usually on TV, actresses are shaped like little boys and she was an incredibly shapely woman, so she was one of my favorites."

KAYLEE
(excited)
You got married?!

SIMON
Well, that's — congratulations...

WASH
We always hoped you two kids would get together. Who is she?

MAL
She's no one!

Saffron starts to cry.

KAYLEE
Captain!

MAL
(at a loss)
Stop that.

SAFFRON
I'm sorry...

WASH
You brute.

Kaylee goes up to Saffron —

KAYLEE
Oh, sweetie, don't feel bad. He makes everybody cry. He's like a monster.

MAL
I'm not a monster! Wash, turn the ship around.

BOOK
(to Simon)
Have you got an encyclopedia?

SIMON
<Dahng ran.> [Of course.]

He goes off. Wash and Mal are still talking throughout:

WASH
Can't.

MAL
That's an order.

WASH
Yeah, but can't.

MAL
What the hell is wrong w—

WASH
Alliance touched down the second we left. And there's already a bulletin on the Cortex as to the murder of a prefect's nephew — that's right, one of our bandits had some family ties. So unless you feel like walking into a gallows, I suggest we continue on to Beaumonde and you enjoy your honeymoon.

MAL
This isn't happening.
(to Saffron)
Will you stop crying?

INARA
Oh, for god's sake, Mal, can you be a human being for thirty seconds?

WASH
Speaking as one married man to another...

MAL
I am not married!
(to Saffron)
I'm sorry. You don't shame me, you have very nice qualities but I didn't ever marry you.

BOOK
(holding encyclopedia)
I believe you did. Last night.

Mal hesitates. As does everyone.

MAL
(to Jayne, quiet)
How drunk was I last night?

JAYNE
I don't know. I passed out.

BOOK
It says here, the woman lays the wreath upon her intended — which I do recall — which represents his sovereignty.

MAL
(to Saffron)
That was you?

BOOK
And he drinks of her wine. This represents his obeisance to the life-giving blood of her — I'll skip this part — and then there's a dance, with a joining of hands.
(closes book)
The marriage ceremony of the Triumph Settlers, been so over eighty years. You, sir, are a newlywed.

A beat.

MAL
So what does it say in there about divorce?

Saffron runs from the room, to the infirmary.

KAYLEE
<Nee boo go guh, nee hwun chiou.> [You don't deserve her, you fink.]

MAL
<Gwan nee tzi-jee duh shr.> [Mind your own business.]
(starts after her)
Everyone go back to... whatever.

ZOE
Really think you're the one to talk to her, sir?

MAL
Way I see it, me and her got a thing in common. We're the only ones who don't think this is funny.

His words ring true, and he storms out, passing Inara last, who doesn't particularly feel like laughing either.

INT. PASSENGER DORM - CONTINUOUS

Mal enters, finds no one. A quick look —

MAL
Hello? Woman-person?

He starts up the stairs.

INT. ENGINE ROOM - CONTINUOUS

Mal enters, finds Saffron huddled in the corner. She has been crying, but has stopped.

MAL
You all right?

SAFFRON
I thought last night during the ceremony... you were pleased.

MAL
Well, yeah, last night I was. I had some mulled wine, pretty girl gave me a hat made out of a tree, nobody said I was signing up to have and to hold...

SAFFRON
You don't have marriage where you're from?

MAL
Well, sure, we just... we do it different.

Awkward beat.

SAFFRON
Are you going to kill me?

MAL
What? What kind of crappy planet is that? Kill you?

SAFFRON
In the maiden's home, I heard talk of men who weren't pleased with their brides, who...

MAL
Well I ain't them. And don't you ever stand for that sort of thing. Someone tries to kill you, you try to kill 'em right back. Wife or no, you're no one's property to be tossed aside. You got the right same as anyone to live and to try to kill people. I mean, you know. People that are... That's a dumb planet.

SAFFRON
What will you do with me?

MAL
Not rightly sure. We're bound for Beaumonde, it's a decent kind of planet... might be able to set you up with some sorta work...

SAFFRON
I'll not be anyone's doxy.

MAL
I don't mean whoring, there's... factories and the like. Some ranches, if you're more for the outdoors... I don't know — near a week before we get there, we'll figure something.

Small beat.

SAFFRON
I'd be a good wife.

MAL
Well, I'd be a terrible husband. You got five whole days to figure that out.

SAFFRON
Five days, we'll be together?

MAL
We'll be together on the ship, not in any —

She stands, visibly cheered.

SAFFRON
That'll be fine, I'll do for you or not, as you choose.

MAL
Well, shiny. You hungry? Kitchen's just through there.

And she slips by him, excited.

SAFFRON
I'll cook you something!

MAL
No, I meant if you —

SAFFRON
I'm a fine cook, everyone says.

MAL
Yeah, but —
(she's down the hall)
Hold it!

She turns.

MAL (cont'd)
I ain't ever even —

SAFFRON
(smiling)
My name is Saffron.

And she goes. He stands there, bemused. Book appears from the infirmary hall. He has seen that nice moment between the two.

BOOK
Divorce is very rare and requires dispensation from her pastor. I can send him a wave, see what I can do.

MAL
I'd appreciate it. She's a nice girl.

BOOK
Seems very anxious to please you.

MAL
That's their way, I guess.

BOOK
(bright, casual)
I suppose so. If you take sexual advantage of her, you're going to burn in a very special level of hell. A level they reserve for child molesters and people who talk at the theater.

MAL
Wha — I'm not — Preacher, you got a smutty mind.

BOOK
Perhaps I spoke out of turn.

RON GLASS

There was no ad-libbing, but that was okay with me because I prefer not to have that kind of pressure. I like to come in and feel like the writer has written something significant enough and important enough that it needs to be said just as it was written. It worked out very well for me.

MAL
Per maybe haps, I'm thinking.

BOOK
I apologize. I'll make her up a room in the passenger dorm.

MAL
Good.

Book goes back. A beat and his head pops back in:

BOOK
The special hell...

And he's gone again. Mal sighs.

INT. DINING ROOM

Mal sits as Saffron places a plate in front of him, mostly mush (and a few bao), but well presented and aromatic.

MAL
Thank you.

Zoe and Wash enter as he tucks in.

WASH
Something smells good...

ZOE
Having yourself a little supper, Captain?

MAL
Well, Saffron insisted on... I didn't want to make her feel... It's damn tasty.

He can't figure out who to be careful around — so he just starts shoveling it in.

WASH
Any more where that came from?

SAFFRON
(downcast)
I didn't think to make enough for your friends.
(to Zoe)
But I've everything laid out if you'd like to cook for your husband...

Wash looks at Zoe for a microsecond of hope — her eyes narrow — and he laughs overcompensationally.

WASH
Ta-ha-ha— isn't she quaint? I'm just not hungry.

He sits, Zoe sitting as well. Her hilarious mood has abated. Saffron retires to the pantry.

ZOE
So, are you enjoying your own nubile little slave girl?

MAL
(mouth full)
I'm not... nubile...
(swallows)
Look, she wanted to make me dinner. At least she's not crying...

WASH
I might. Did she really make fresh bao?
(off Zoe's glare)
Quaint!

ZOE
Remember that sex we were planning to have ever again?

MAL
Y'all are making a big deal and I would appreciate it if one person on this boat did not assume I was an evil, lecherous hump.

ZOE
Nobody's saying that, sir.

WASH
Yeah, we're mostly just giving each other significant glances and laughing incessantly.
(to Mal)
Is that cider?

MAL
(finishing his)
By the stove.

WASH
(going for Mal's glass)
Yum. I'll give you a refill.
(to Zoe)
Hon?

Saffron is suddenly in frame, grabbing Mal's glass from Wash.

SAFFRON
That's for me to do.

She fills Mal's glass, places it by him. Everyone is quiet and uncomfortable as she stands by Mal, waiting for him to continue eating.

MAL
You know, you weren't lying about your cooking. If I hadn't just eaten...

SAFFRON
You don't want to finish.

MAL
No, I just, I have captain-y stuff I have to do, but truthfully, that's a fine meal. Thank you.

He rises.

SAFFRON
Do you need anything else?

MAL
(rising)
No, no. You just, you eat something yourself, I'm gonna go... captain.

SAFFRON
If you're done with supper, would you like me to wash your feet?

There is a pause. Mal exits.

Saffron goes back into the kitchen. A moment and Wash grabs Mal's plate, digging in. Zoe goes for it as well, elbowing in with a fork.

EXT. SHIP - LATER

Through space she floaty.

INT. INARA'S SHUTTLE - LATER

Inara is working her screen, talking to it as the graphics change accordingly.

INARA
Beaumonde, City of New Dunsmuir. Arrival, October 24, Departure...

Mal comes to the door.

MAL
Can I come in?

INARA
(touches screen to deactivate voice command)
No.

He does anyway.

MAL
See, that's why I usually don't ask.

INARA
What do you want?

MAL
I just needed to, um... hide.

INARA
So I take it the honeymoon is over?

MAL
She's a fine girl, don't misread — hell of a cook, too.

INARA
(pointedly)
I'm sure she has many exciting talents.

MAL
Do you ever, um, wash your client's feet?

INARA
(no)
It's my specialty. We'll be on Beaumonde at least two weeks, right?

MAL
Can't be exactly sure, but —

INARA
Well, I need you to be exactly sure, Mal. I can't make commitments and then not keep them. That's your specialty.

MAL
I'm sorry. Are you tetchy 'cause I got myself a bride or 'cause I don't plan to keep her?

INARA
I find the whole thing degrading.

MAL
That's just what Saffron said about your line of work.

INARA
Maybe you should think twice about letting go of "Saffron". You two sound like quite a match.

MAL
Maybe you're right. Maybe we're soulmates.

INARA
Yes. Great. I wish you hundreds of fat children.

MAL
(laughing fondly)
Can you imagine that? Me with a passel of critters underfoot? Ten years time, I could teach 'em to —

INARA
(standing)
Can you leave me alone for five minutes please?

Mal is surprised by the force of her outburst. He exits.

INT. CARGO BAY - CONTINUOUS

He calls back as he goes:

MAL
I wasn't looking for a fight...

Turns and sees Jayne standing with meanest looking future shotgun imaginable. He cocks it, stone-faced.

MAL (cont'd)
I always do seem to find one, though...

END OF ACT ONE

ACT TWO

INT. CARGO BAY - CONTINUOUS

JAYNE
Do I have your attention?

MAL
We're kind of going to extremes here, ain't we?

JAYNE
There's times I think you don't take me seriously. And I think that oughta change.

MAL
Do you think it's likely to?

JAYNE
You got something you don't deserve.

MAL
And it's brought me a galaxy a' fun, I'm here to tell you.

JAYNE
Six men came to kill me one time, and the best of them carried this. It's a Callahan fullbore autolock, customized trigger and double cartridge thorough-gage.

He holds it out to Mal.

JAYNE (cont'd)
It's my very favorite gun.

MAL
<Da-shiang bao-tza shr duh lah doo-tze> [The explosive diarrhea of an elephant], are you offering me a trade?

JAYNE
A trade? Hell, it's theft! This is the best gun made by man, and it's got extreme sentimental value! It's miles more worthy 'n what you got.

MAL
"What I got" — she has a name.

JAYNE
So does this! I call it Vera.

MAL
Well, my days of not taking you seriously are

certainly coming to a middle.

JAYNE
Dammit, Mal, I'd treat her okay...

MAL
She's not to be bought. Nor bartered, nor borrowed or lent. She's a human woman, doesn't know a damn thing about the world and needs our protection.

JAYNE
I'll protect her!

MAL
Jayne! Go play with your rainstick.

Mal heads downstairs. Jayne clearly not letting it go, but heading back up to his quarters.

Mal comes to ground level and runs into Saffron — he jumps a bit.

MAL (cont'd)
Gah! You do sneak about, don't you.

SAFFRON
You're a good man.

MAL
You clearly haven't been talking to anyone else on this boat...

SAFFRON
I don't wish to be wed to the large one. I'd rather... if I'm not to be yours, I'd rather have that work you spoke of. I could be useful on a ranch.

MAL
That's good work. My momma had a ranch, back on Shadow where I'm from. Ran cattle, mostly — wasn't nobody ran 'em harder or smarter. Used to tell me, don't brand the cattle, brand the buyer — he's the one likely to stray.

SAFFRON
She raised you herself?

MAL
Well, her and about forty hands. I had more family for a kid who —

He stops, looking at her.

MAL (cont'd)
Well, that is odd.

SAFFRON
What?

MAL
I just don't — I'm not one talks about his past. And here you got me...

SAFFRON
Does your crew never show interest in your life?

MAL
No, they're, they're... They just know me well enough to... What about you? What's your history?

SAFFRON
Not much to say. Life like yours, I fear you'd find mine terrible dull.

MAL
Oh, I long for a little dullness. Truth to say, this whole trip is getting to be just a little too interesting.

EXT. SPACE

Serenity passes a small (tiny) cracked moon. Zoom in to see a device webbed about the surface of the moon, with a dozen tiny camera faces all firing flashes one after another.

ANGLE: A COMPUTER

As a 3D image forms (fed by the camera's info) of Serenity. Pull back to:

INT. CHOP SHOP OFFICE

as two men, CORBIN and BREED, look at the screen. They are clearly disreputable, their outfits as hodge-podge and junky as the room they're in. Corbin is tough, strong, in charge. Breed is seedier, but also not to be underestimated. Bad guys.

BREED
It's a wreck.

CORBIN
No, no. This is good.

BREED
It's parts. A lot of cheap parts we'll never unload.

CORBIN
This is why you'll never be in charge, Breed. You don't see the whole. The parts are crap —

BREED
I said exactly that —

CORBIN
— but you put 'em together, you got a Firefly. Thing will run forever, they got a mechanic even half awake.

BREED
It's got no flash...

CORBIN
Some people ain't looking for flash. She's a good catch. She comes our way, you prep the nets.

BREED
Lotta effort we're going through here... hoped we'd hit a t-bird, at least.

CORBIN
Just keep complaining. The sound is soothing.

He's on his way out.

BREED
Kill the crew?

CORBIN
Save me the pretty ones. You know the drill.

IF POSSIBLE — This entire talk has been one slow pull-out from the screen, and now pull-out further, through the window, to see:

EXT. SPACE - FLOATING CHOP SHOP - CONT.

Which is basically a giant floating ring — the office sits on top like a giant crab, the rest of the ring made up of connecting tunnels and chambers, and mostly by ships and parts of ships. Some gleam enticingly, some are cannibalized. Electricity crackles silently along the rim, fired up at six key points (this, we will see, forms the net). Ten Serenities could pass through the ring at once.

A flash of electricity flares us out to:

INT. ROOM/PASSENGER DORM - LATER

Book is making up a room for Saffron, making the bed. He finishes smoothing it out, admires his work. We hold a still, wide frame as River enters and pulls the bed apart quickly and calmly and exits again, taking the pillow. Book sighs, starts out after River.

Simon is coming the other way, interrupts River. She takes him by the hand, turns back to Book.

SIMON
<Tzuh muh luh?> [What's going on?]

BOOK
Seems River doesn't want me making up a bed for our young guest. Or she's starting a pillow collection, I'm still collating data.

SIMON
I'm sorry. I'll take care of the room —

RIVER
It's not important!
(to Simon)
Tell him.

SIMON
Tell him what?

RIVER
(to Book)
We want you to marry us.

SIMON
What? We — no! What?

RIVER
Two by two. Everyone a mate, a match, a dopple. I love you.

SIMON
No, River, mei-mei, of course I love you too, but we can't be married.
(to Book, mortified)
She's... really crazy.

River kicks him in the shin.

SIMON (cont'd)
OW! I don't mean crazy — that's just not something brothers and sisters do. I mean on some planets, but only pretty bad ones.

RIVER
The Captain took a wife...

BOOK
Well, that's also complicated.

SIMON
I don't know where this is coming from...

RIVER
We'll take care of each other. I'll knit. You don't love me.

Mal enters with Saffron.

MAL
What's going on?

SIMON
I really couldn't say.

MAL
I was gonna show Saffron her quarters, did they get squared away?

BOOK
Once upon a time...

SAFFRON
I don't need anything, I'm really just fine —

RIVER
(turning)
You're a thief.

Slight beat as Saffron recoils from River's accusation. Book notices that she shrinks a bit toward Mal, who puts a protective hand to her back.

MAL
Well, ho, let's play nice here.
(to Simon)
Your sister's got some funny notions.

SIMON
That's not untrue.

SAFFRON
I'm sorry...

They all turn to her, surprised, as she pulls a packet of food from her dress pocket. River responds by stuffing her pillow under her shirt.

SAFFRON (cont'd)
(handing the packet to Mal)
I didn't know when I was to be fed, and I was afraid...

MAL
You made that fine meal, didn't eat nothing yourself?

SAFFRON
That was for you. Weren't but pot lickings left, so I took this for later, I didn't know she saw me.

RIVER
(to herself)
Didn't see you...

BOOK
Well, there's certainly no harm done...

MAL
(forcefully)
And I'd say there is. Good deal a' harm, and it's starting to tick me off.

Saffron is frightened, and Mal turns her to him.

MAL (cont'd)
Now, I got no use for people sneak around taking what ain't theirs.

BOOK
(wryly)
Yes, we frown on that here.

MAL
But what I got even less use for is a woman won't stand up for herself. Five days hence we're puttin' you in the world, and you won't last a day by bowing and sniffing for handouts. You want something, you take it, or ask for it. You don't wait to be told when to breathe, you don't take orders from anyone. Except me — and

that's just 'cause I'm the Captain, and people take orders from captains even in the world. But for the rest, damnit, be like a woman is. Not no petrified child. There's more'n seventy little earths spinning about the galaxy, and the meek have inherited not a one. Do you understand what I'm saying to you?

SAFFRON
(with quiet strength)
I do.

He tosses the food back to her. Looks to Book.

MAL
Shepherd, would you show Saffron her room please?

Mal exits, Book leading Saffron the other way. Simon is left with pillow-belly River.

RIVER
Now we have to be married.
(hands on belly)
I'm in the family way.

Simon cannot think of a response.

ZOE (V.O.)
She's clearly out of her mind.

INT. BRIDGE - LATER

Zoe and Wash in mid-conversation.

WASH
Well, she's led a sheltered life.

ZOE
Did you see the way she grabbed that glass from you?

WASH
Every planet's got its own weird customs. 'Bout a year before we met, I spent six weeks on a moon where the principal form of recreation was juggling geese. My hand to god. Baby geese. Goslings. They were juggled.

ZOE
Of course the man rushes in to defend her...

WASH
(huh?)
I'm talking about geese.

ZOE
Captain shouldn't be baby-sitting a damn groupie. And he knows it.

WASH
Okay, when did this become not funny?

ZOE
When you didn't turn around and put her ass back down on Triumph where it belongs.

WASH
Oh, hey, now it's even my fault! Is there anything else on your mind I should know about? There's all sorts of twists and cul-de-sacs, it's wild.

ZOE
She's trouble.

WASH
I'm getting that.

ZOE
I'm going to bed.

She exits.

WASH
I'm gonna stay here, where it's safe and quiet, and I'm gonna play with some of these dials and stuff.

He's watching her go, confused and unhappy.

WASH (cont'd)
I might, you know, steer.

She's long gone. He spins back around.

INT. JAYNE'S ROOM - LATER

Jayne sits on his bed, unhappily turning his rain-stick over and listening to it.

INT. FOREDECK HALL - NIGHTPHASE

It's empty as Mal starts down his ladder, we follow him into:

INT. MAL'S ROOM - CONTINUOUS

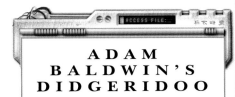

ADAM BALDWIN'S DIDGERIDOO

Prop master Randy Eriksen: "Adam Baldwin had a didgeridoo he brought down to the set that he wanted to use in the show, but Joss didn't like it. He was always playing it like 'Mmmoooo'. It was very cool."

CHRISTINA HENDRICKS

Christina Hendricks's upbringing likely helped her generally as an actress and more specific-ally as the nothing-if-not-multifaceted Saffron. "I was born in Tennessee," the actress says, "but I grew up all over — in Georgia, Oregon, Idaho, Virginia, New York — moving from city to city, very different kinds of places and things, seeing different kinds of people and how people deal with things in their own way."

How did Hendricks view Saffron? "I decided that Saffron is so good at what she does, and she does it so often, that she has to almost convince herself. So I never tried to play the secret — I just tried to play what was happening at that moment, because I think *she* believes it and she was so convincing. I tried to just be honest about each one of those people that she was, each time. I loved all parts of her. I like the little moments where she may do an eye-roll or a smirk behind someone's back, and they don't know it's happening."

Favorite scenes? "Well, clearly the seduction scene was fun," Hendricks laughs. "What a beautifully written scene — and I loved the reveal at the end of that, when Mal passes out. Running with Alan up on deck and then going into action mode was really fun, trying to seduce him and then knocking him out."

There's usually a difference between coming onto a series as a first-time guest actor and coming back but, Hendricks says, "less so on *Firefly* than on any other show. I mean, the cast on *Firefly* were so warm and just giving and immediately made me feel comfortable; whereas other casts — including the show that I'm on this week! — don't even speak to you. *Firefly* made me feel *so* comfortable. They showed respect for me as an actress immediately, so that was really, really nice."

Mal enters, pulls off his shirt. Tosses it in the corner, turning to see:

ANGLE: IN THE BED is Saffron. She is quiet, a bit apprehensive and more than a bit naked.

MAL
(jumps)
Wah! Yo— hey. You're, um... well, there you are.

SAFFRON
I've made the bed warm for you.

MAL
It, uh, looks warm.

SAFFRON
And I've... made myself ready for you.

MAL
Let's ride right past the part where you explain exactly what that means. Didn't you see you got a

room of your own?

SAFFRON
And... I'm to sleep there?

MAL
That's the notion. Assuming you're, yeah, sleepy...

SAFFRON
But we've been wed. Aren't we to become one flesh?

She is soo insouciently sexy. Mal looks up where his shipmates would be, resolve wavering...

MAL
Well, no, I think we're still two fleshes here. And that your flesh oughta sleep somewhere else.

SAFFRON
I'm sorry. When we talked, I'd hoped... but I don't please you.

BOOK

"Wasn't born a Shepherd, Mal."

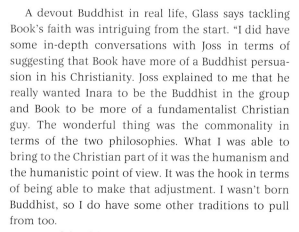

A respected, veteran actor with thirty years in the business appearing in such classic television series as *Barney Miller*, *All in the Family* and *Friends*, there were nevertheless a couple of genres Ron Glass hadn't explored in his career — until he was approached to play Shepherd Derrial Book. Called by his agent to take a look at the new series by Joss Whedon, Glass says he had his reserv-ations about taking a role in a space Western. "Before *Firefly*, I had always stayed away from science fiction and for that matter, Westerns too. I never made a point of seeking that kind of material once I got past ten years old," he laughs. "I had never seen much of Joss's work prior to that time. Of course, I read the pilot script... and fell in love with it. I loved all the characters, the story and the world and I especially loved the Book character. The thing that was galvanizing for me was the characters, so the environment was secondary. I was happy to see how Book would unfold in that kind of environment and it worked really, really well."

With his priest's collar and meager belongings, Book's physical presence was a strong reflection of the character right from the pilot. "Joss and the costumer had a pretty clear idea of how they wanted him to look," Glass says. "I concurred because it was really simple, but very definitive at a moment's glance. The only thing I had some curiosity about was whether that collar would be the only thing that he'd ever be seen in. As it worked out, there were some variations that I wore. For example, when I was working out and lifting weights and another time when we were playing Calvinball. I loved that huge coat that Book wore in the pilot episode.

"I used to tease Morena a lot because she has such a wide variety of costume changes. One time, there were bunches of people 'oohing and ahhing' over some new wardrobe Inara had and just to tease her, I walked around the corner and stepped back and said, 'Oh my gosh! What is this? A carnival act?' Everyone thought it was hysterical," he chuckles.

A devout Buddhist in real life, Glass says tackling Book's faith was intriguing from the start. "I did have some in-depth conversations with Joss in terms of suggesting that Book have more of a Buddhist persuasion in his Christianity. Joss explained to me that he really wanted Inara to be the Buddhist in the group and Book to be more of a fundamentalist Christian guy. The wonderful thing was the commonality in terms of the two philosophies. What I was able to bring to the Christian part of it was the humanism and the humanistic point of view. It was the hook in terms of being able to make that adjustment. I wasn't born Buddhist, so I do have some other traditions to pull from too.

"One of the things I was most delighted about as far as Book's character was concerned was that he was not a saint and he had not always been a preacher. Though rather mysterious, it was absolutely clear that he had had a very full life before he went off to the monastery and took on that responsibility. I loved the fact that he could save your soul but he could also kick your ass. That's a really great combination to play."

Remembering his first day on set, Glass says, "There was some commonality of the newness of the project for me as well as the newness of Book's experience, in terms of joining the crew of this ship that he also did not know. He was learning and unfolding in the script at the same time as I was learning and unfolding on the set. It was a happy circumstance that I was able to use real life experience to come to express what was happening on the page as well. On the first day I'm always a little tentative because you need to start picking up what the ground rules are, in terms of how the director is, if the director is going to be flexible or how much input you are going to have. It's part of the excitement and the learning process. I think the very first script and on one of the early days, I got to knock somebody out and at the same time have this wonderful, gentle experience with Kaylee, presenting her with the strawberry. In the same script, I also had this wonderful shared experience with Inara, explaining how conflicted I felt. It was a really full, dimensional exploration and really contributed to the feeling of great expectations." ◄

She says it shamefacedly, the covers slipping down as she sits naked before him.

MAL
Hey flesh! Look, Saffron, it ain't a question of pleasing me. It's a question of what's... uh... morally right.

SAFFRON
I do know my bible, sir. "On the night of their betrothal, the wife shall open to the man, as the furrow to the plough, and he shall work in her, in and again, 'til she bring him to his fall, and rest him then upon the sweat of her breast."

Beat.

MAL
Whoah. Good bible.

SAFFRON
I'm not skilled, sir, nor a pleasure to look upon, but —

MAL
Saffron. You're pleasing. You're... hell, you're all kinds of pleasing and it's been a while... a long damn while since anybody but me took a hold a' my plough so don't think for a second that I ain't interested. But you and me, we ain't married. Just 'cause you got handed to me by some <hwun dan> [bastard] couldn't pay his debts, don't make you beholden to me. I keep trying to explain —

SAFFRON
Let me explain.
(he waits, surprised at the grown up tone)
I lived my life in the maiden house, waiting to be married off for trade. I seen my sistren paired off with ugly men, vicious or blubberous, men with appetites too unseemly to speak on. And I've cried for those girls, but not half so hard as I cried the night they gave me to you.

MAL
(suddenly insecure)
Well, what — you — is there blubber?

SAFFRON
I cried for I'd not dreamed to have a man so sweet, so kind and beautiful. Had I the dare to choose, I'd choose you from all the men on all the planets the night sky could show me.

She stands, getting close to him.

SAFFRON (cont'd)
If I'm wed, I'm a woman and I'll take your leave to be bold. I want this. I swell to think of you in me, and I see you do too.

Mal looks down, embarrassed.

MAL
Well, that's just...

SAFFRON
Leave me at the nearest port, never look on me again, I'll make my way with the strength you've taught me... only let me have my wedding night.

They're inches apart. He's dying.

MAL
(looking up at the door)
I'm gonna go to the special hell...

She kisses him, slowly and sweetly. He pulls away, his face still close to hers, sad resolve in his eyes.

MAL (cont'd)
I really wish it was that simple, girl. But I just —

She kisses him again, and he gives massively in, putting his arms around her, their tongues intermingling...

He takes a step back, confusion on his face. Puts a hand to his lips.

MAL (cont'd)
Son of a —

He is already stumbling as he goes for his gun — it drops to the ground with the same lifeless thud as he does.

She looks at him a moment as he snores. The expression on her face, one we've not seen before, is sly triumph.

SAFFRON
Night, sweetie.

END OF ACT TWO

ACT THREE

INT. BRIDGE - NIGHT

Wash pilots alone. Saffron enters, tentatively — all shy girl (and dressed) again. Wash hears, turns —

WASH
Well, if it isn't the master chef. Not sleepy?

SAFFRON
Am I let to be up here?

WASH
Well, sure, why not. Not like anyone else is taking up space.

She enters, eyes on the window.

SAFFRON
I've never been off world before.

WASH
Beautiful, isn't it? Endless. You stare at it long enough, as long as I have, it becomes almost... preternaturally boring.

SAFFRON
(brow furrowed)
I don't think you're serious.

WASH
(smiling)
'Bout half. You stop seein' 'em after a spell, but they are your very first charts. Time and again, you look up from your screens and remember that.

SAFFRON
It's like a dream.

WASH
Planet I'm from, you couldn't see a one, pollution's so thick. Sometimes I think I entered flight school just so I could see what the hell everyone was talking about.

She smiles at him, her warmth enfolding his sweet reminiscence. A beat, and she moves to the door, quietly shuts it.

WASH (cont'd)
What are you doing?

She moves to the middle of the room, stands there, almost trance-like.

SAFFRON
Now we're alone. Us and the stars. No ship, no bellowing engines or crew to bicker at each other... look. Come look...

He's hesitant, but comes to stand next to her. They stare out at the brilliant black.

SAFFRON (cont'd)
Do you know the myth about Earth-that-was?

He can feel her closeness, her excitement — tries to be cool amidst the hard-on.

WASH
Not so much.

SAFFRON
That when she was born, she had no sky, and she was open, inviting and the stars would rush into her, through the skin of her, making the oceans boil with sensation, and when she could endure no more ecstasy, she puffed up her cheeks and blew out the sky, to womb her and keep them at bay, 'til she had rest some, and that we had to leave 'cause she was strong enough to suck them in once more.

Beat.

WASH
Whoah. Good myth.

She turns to him, eyes nearly moist with pleading.

SAFFRON
My whole life, I saw nothing but roofs and steeples and the cellar door. Few days I'll be back to that life and gone from yours. Make this night what it should be. Please...

Her face is inches from his.

SAFFRON (cont'd)
Show me the stars.

They're practically touching and she moves to kiss him, but he pulls away at the last minute.

WASH
<Wuh duh ma huh tah duh fong kwong duh wai shung> [Holy mother of god and all her wacky nephews] do I wish I was somebody else right

now. Somebody not married, not madly in love with a beautiful woman who can kill me with her pinky.

SAFFRON
I've been too forward.

WASH
No. Well, yes. But I actually like that in a woman. That's part of why Zoe and I are, as previously mentioned, married.

SAFFRON
I thought... she didn't seem to respect you.

WASH
Not everybody gets me and Zoe at first glance. Did it get very hot in here? I need airflow.

He moves to the door. She stops him with...

SAFFRON
You love her very much.

WASH
Yeah.

He turns to open the door. Saffron rolls her eyes with bored exasperation as he continues heading for the door —

WASH (cont'd)
I never did meet a woman quite like her. The first time we —

And Saffron sidekicks him in the back of the head, slamming his face into the door. He slides down, unconscious.

She pulls the door open, drags the body into the space before the stairs, hidden off to the side from view. Shuts the door again, locking it.

She moves to the console, hits the screens, working the nav like an expert. We see the course setting come up on the screen, see her change the coordinates and lock them in. Hits another screen and opens a channel to signal the new destination of arrival.

Just as swiftly and expressionlessly, she slides under the console, chooses a few wires and rips them out, sparks flying. Crosses a couple others (we see the nav screens wink out) and she's up, back at the door, opens it, looking to see she's alone.

She reaches under her dress and pulls a strip of tape from the hem, sticks it on the interior lock of the door and pulls off a layer, which causes a bubbling not unlike the burning glue of the pilot. As the lock begins to melt and fuse she slams the door shut, locking herself out of the bridge.

INT. CARGO BAY - MOMENTS LATER

She comes down the stairs, gets her bearings for a sec, then heads to the second shuttle. Opens the door and runs smack into:

INARA.

SAFFRON
Oh!

INARA
Are you lost?

Instantly she's subservient Saffron again, looking down. She backs up as Inara comes down a few stairs.

SAFFRON
I'm sorry. I thought the other shuttle was yours.

INARA
It is. I was on the Cortex and my screen shorted. This one's out too.

SAFFRON
Looking for customers?

INARA
What were you looking for?

SAFFRON
I don't mean to be rude... A Companion's life is so glamorous and strange... I wish I had the skill for such a trade...

By god, she's moving from subservient to seductive...

INARA
You'd like to please your new husband.

SAFFRON
Oh, he'll have none of me... For true I'm somewhat relieved... if I'm to learn of love, I'd want it to be at the hands of someone gentle... someone who could... feel... what I feel...

Their faces are close. Inara is as intimate in tone as Saffron:

INARA
But Mal said... you don't approve of my work...

SAFFRON
Sure and he said that to keep you from me... I was too curious about you, ever since I saw you...

They are face to face.

INARA
Come to my shuttle.

SAFFRON
You would... you would lie with me?

The alarm goes off, red lights spinning — Saffron looks around in innocent alarm, looks back to Inara, who drops the act.

INARA
I guess we've lied enough.

Saffron drops the act as well.

SAFFRON
You're good.

INARA
You're amazing. Who are you?

SAFFRON
I'm Malcolm Reynold's widow.

All the color drains from Inara's face. (Okay, not all the color, she's from Future-Brazil so she still has a hue, but she's upset, okay?)

Saffron punches, hard, but Inara blocks — a spinning kick from Saffron and Inara rolls out of the way, Saffron moving to the shuttle and slamming the door behind her.

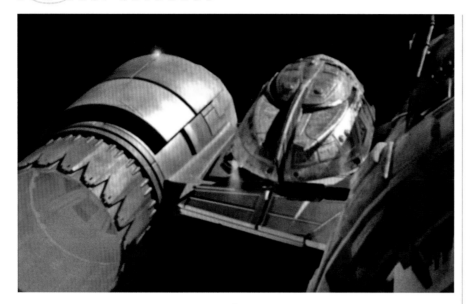

Inara is on her feet in a heartbeat, racing toward the foredeck hall...

INT. COCKPIT OF 2ND SHUTTLE - CONTINUOUS

Saffron pulls some chips from her dress and inserts them into the console, brings the shuttle to life.

EXT. SERENITY - CONTINUOUS

As the shuttle takes off and heads the opposite way.

INT. FOREDECK HALL - CONTINUOUS

Inara comes in as Zoe is at the entrance to the bridge, holding a dazed Wash. Jayne is trying to open the bridge door (it won't budge) as Kaylee is coming sleepily up out of her room. They all overlap:

ZOE
Baby wake up... He's bleeding...

JAYNE
There's nobody in there —

KAYLEE
What's going on?

Inara ignores them all, slams Mal's ladder in and drops down as fast as she can —

INT. MAL'S ROOM - CONTINUOUS

She finds Mal draped like the dead on the floor, rushes to him, fearing the worst —

INARA
Mal Mal Mal Mal —

She goes down, pulls up his head — and he moans — still alive. Unwanted wetness springs into her eyes as she gasps, relieved —

INARA (cont'd)
<Run-tse duh fwotzoo...> [Merciful buddha...]

And she kisses him, once, hard, then holds him to her, collecting herself — laying him back down and heading to the ladder as she calls out to above:

INARA (cont'd)
Get the Doctor! Mal's hurt... he...

She starts to sag. Puts a finger to her lips, recognizing the taste — she turns to Mal, scorn in her drooping eyes...

INARA (cont'd)
Oh, you stupid son of a —

And she collapses, unconcious, out of frame.

BLACKOUT AND FADE UP ON:

INT. - SAME - LATER

Fuzzy close on Mal awakening. Gets more focus as he looks about him, blinking.

MAL
Is it Christmas?

Reverse angle: The entire gang (minus River, Jayne and Kaylee) is staring at him. Simon closest, with his doctor bag, and Inara on his bed, propped up like a rag doll.

SIMON
Well, he's back...

ZOE
Yes, sir, it's Christmas. That special night when Nick the Saint comes down your chimney, changes your course, blows out the navcom, seals the bridge and takes off in your shuttle.

MAL
What happened about me...?

ZOE
Your blushing bride was a plant.
(re: him and Wash)
She took both of you out.

MAL
How did...

SIMON
A narcotic compound, probably spread over a seal on her lips. You get it on yours and pow.

ZOE
Lips, huh?

MAL
Well, no...

SIMON
We used to get a lotta guys brought in on the night shift at the E.R. — usually robbed and very groggy. Called it the "goodnight kiss".

ZOE
So you two were kissing.

BOOK
(pointedly, to Mal)
Well, isn't that special...?

MAL
(trying to change the focus)
Wash? How did —

WASH
Hey, I just got kicked in the head.

ZOE
My man would never fall for that <jien huo> [cheap floozy].

WASH
Most of my head wishes I had.

MAL
You guys don't understand...

BOOK
Seems pretty simple from here. You were taking advantage of a —

MAL
(standing clumsily)
I was the one being taken advantage of!

BOOK
My apologies, you were victimized, Wash was beaten and Inara found you here.

INARA
(defensively slurred and sleepy)
And then I fell. My head got hurt like Wash.

MAL
I don't get any of this.

INARA
I only fell is all.

MAL
What the hell is our status?

ZOE
We're shut down. Jayne and Kaylee are still trying to get on the bridge.

WASH
All we know is we're headed somewhere and it ain't Beaumonde.

Mal starts up the stairs, the others following. Hold on Inara, who says to Simon...

INARA
I'm fine. I don't need to be examined. I'm comfy.

INT. HALL - CONTINUOUS

As Mal and everyone files up (save Simon and Inara) to see Jayne firing up a blowtorch. Kaylee explains —

KAYLEE
She didn't just lock it, she fused it to something. Both entrances.

MAL
Why the big act? What the hell was she after?

BOOK
Besides molesting innocent captains?

MAL
You wanna stow it, Preacher? We're in some peril here.

ZOE
If she can fly this thing why just take the shuttle?

Simon is entering as well as:

WASH
Maybe she likes shuttles.

(off Mal's look)
Some people juggle geese...

RIVER
I told you.

They look at her.

RIVER (cont'd)
She's a thief.

A beat.

ANGLE: THE DOOR

as Jayne pulls it open.

INT. BRIDGE - LATER

Kaylee and Wash are lying side by side under the console, looking up at the wiring.

KAYLEE
She's a pro.

WASH
This is a masterful job of muck-up. See how she crossed the drive feeds —

KAYLEE
Yeah huh —

WASH
So we even try to reroute it'll lock down. <Jing tsai.> [Brilliant.]

KAYLEE
And she went straight for the thermal cap!

WASH
Yeah yeah! We're so humped!

They're starting just to admire it — a bit too much for Mal to take. He stands there with everyone else, waiting.

MAL
I'm glad you two are having a good time under there, you wanna progress to the making it right?

They poke their heads out.

WASH
That's not gonna happen for a good long while, Cap'n.

MAL
We don't have a good long while. We could be headed straight into a nice big solid moon for all we know, so hows about you get to work?

KAYLEE
Hey! You're the one whose big make-out session got us into this, sir.

MAL
I was poisoned!

INARA
You were drugged.

JAYNE
That's why I never kiss 'em on the mouth.

There is a moment for everyone's extreme silent horror.

MAL
Well, what CAN you do?

WASH
Give us some time we could get the Cortex and navcom back on line, at least see where we're headed.

MAL
That's fine, except for the part where I give you some time. What about steering?

INARA
What about stopping?

WASH
She humped us hard. We're gonna have to do a lot of —

MAL
Do it. It doesn't help me to see where I'm going if I can't change course.

KAYLEE
This girl really knows her ships.

INARA
That's not all she knows. She's well schooled.

SIMON
You mean the sedative? The Goodnight Kiss?

INARA
I only hit my head but Mal... went through that but no, I mean seduction, body language, signals... she had training. As in Companion, as in Academy.

BOOK
Our little Saffron's quite a wonder. I'm beginning to think she married beneath herself.

MAL
(to Inara)
How do you know? About the training?

INARA
She tried to seduce me too.

MAL
(trying not to sound too intrigued)
Really? Did she — did you —

INARA
You don't play a player. It was sloppy of her to try it, but I think she was in a rush.

MAL
But she had professional... so in my case, it was really...
(to Book)
You woulda kissed her too.

ZOE
Wash didn't.

MAL
But she was naked, and all articulate...

WASH
Okay. Everyone NOT talking about their sex lives, in here. Everyone else, elsewhere.

KAYLEE
Jayne, find me a splicer.

Jayne rummages through tools as everyone else save Book departs. Wash ducks back under with Kaylee.

WASH
Do you really think we have a hope in hell of fixing this?

KAYLEE
Not by talking 'bout it, darlin'.

INT. CHOP SHOP OFFICE - LATER

Breed is looking at a screen, call out of the room:

BREED
They're coming!

Corbin runs in.

CORBIN
How far out?

BREED
Ten minutes or so. Right on target, speed... a-1.

CORBIN
That girl is a wonder.

BREED
She gets it done. I'll tell the boys.

He starts out —

INT. BRIDGE - LATER

As Serenity's screens pop back to life:

WASH (O.S.)
YES!

He is looking at them, working them. Kaylee's still under the console, Jayne and Book at the ready.

Mal runs in.

MAL
You got it?

WASH
We got life. We got screens. It's a qualified "yes". A partial.

MAL
What about nav control?

Kaylee comes out to look miserable, shakes her head.

MAL (cont'd)
So where are we headed?

WASH
(working the screens)
Coordinates she entered... We're headed for something and it's not too far...

MAL
Did she signal anyone?

WASH
<Dung ee hwar...> [Hold on a second...] she did. Same coordinates, no I.D.

JAYNE
Who's out there...?

WASH
Let me see if her signal wave can translate to visual, there might be a — <Aiya!> [Damn!] Heavy ionization, electrical interference bouncing the signal all... Look at that... It's like a circle.

Mal gets it. He looks at Book, who also does.

MAL
It's a net.

JAYNE
I don't get it. Where are we headed?

BOOK
The end of the line.

Off their looks:

EXT. CHOP SHOP RING - CONTINUOUS

As the electricity fires up and does in fact form a powerful net.

END OF ACT THREE

ACT FOUR

INT. BRIDGE - MOMENTS LATER

The same gang are there, as the explanation begins.

BOOK
It's a Carrion House. Scrap shop, takes ships, pulls 'em apart or fixes 'em up.

WASH
Doesn't sound that scary...

MAL
That pattern you're looking at is a net. We fly into that we're more than helpless. It'll turn the ship into one big electrical conduit, burn us all from the inside out.

BOOK
Some of the newer ones'll just hold you, then the scrappers'll override the airlocks, pull the oh-two, or just gas you. They're not looking to deal with survivors.

JAYNE
One day you're gonna tell us all how a preacher knows so damn much about crime.

MAL
Kaylee.

KAYLEE
I'm trying, sir, but...

MAL
Well you stay on it. We can't fall into that net.

He's thinking fast, looks about him.

MAL (cont'd)
We need a plan B.

He hits the com.

MAL (cont'd)
(into com)
Zoe, get our suits prepped, now.
(to the others)
I figure we got one shot at this.
(to Wash)
Give me visual as soon as we're close.

WASH
Won't be long...

JAYNE
What do I do?

Mal turns to him, waits just a hair of a beat.

MAL
You go get Vera.

INT. CARGO BAY/AIRLOCK - LATER

Mal and Jayne are suited up, save helmets and gloves. Jayne is loading big-ass bullets into Vera while Zoe checks his suit and Simon hooks his encyclopedia to the com console with Book's help.

WASH (O.S.)
(over the com)
We are two minutes out...

JAYNE
This thing needs oxygen around it to fire, and we don't have a case.

MAL
We're gonna use a suit.

SIMON
Here. We got it.

They look over at:

ANGLE: SIMON'S ENCYCLOPEDIA

has a visual of the ring on it.

JAYNE
What am I aiming for. The window?

MAL
That might kill some folk, but it won't disrupt the net. See these six points where it's brightest? Those're the breakers. Hit one and it should short it out.

JAYNE
What do you mean, should?

INT. BRIDGE - CONTINUING

Kaylee slams her wrench against metal, near tears.

KAYLEE
If I just had a stupid conductor cap...

She pauses a moment, then races out of the room.

EXT. CHOP SHOP RING - CONTINUING

As we can see Serenity tiny in the distance.

INT. AIRLOCK - CONTINUING

Mal opens the door, and we see him suited up, with Jayne as well. Jayne is sitting, holding the gun. It's in a suit, Jayne holding it through the sleeves (which are duct-taped to his), the barrel

pointing out through the helmet. The butt of the gun is braced up against containers against the airlock doors.

Angle: their pov

through the door, of the approaching ring.

MAL
You see it?

JAYNE
Clear as day.
(then, softer)
You see, Vera? You dress yourself up, then you get taken out somewhere fun.

INT. COCKPIT OF INARA'S SHUTTLE - CONTINUING

As Kaylee rips some wires and parts from it.

She comes up and looks out the window, stops — mezmerized.

EXT. CHOP SHOP RING - CONTINUOUS

As the ship approaches, the net forms fully, electricity silently flaring in a spider's web of power.

INT. EXT AIRLOCK/SPACE - CONTINUING

Mal waits. Jayne waits.

Jayne FIRES, a silent burst blowing through the helmet, air rushing out as the breaker EXPLODES, the crackling web disintigrating —

— and Jayne continues firing, aims up at the office itself:

INT. CHOP SHOP OFFICE - CONTINUING

Corbin and Breed duck and cover as the bullets rake across the window. We hear it crack and

groan — they look at each other in horror —

EXT. CHOP SHOP RING - CONTINUOUS

and the window and all the contents of the office are blow out into space — pan down to see Serenity blow through the sparking but harmless ring, continuing on in the distance.

INT. BRIDGE - LATER

Kaylee, Mal, Zoe. Wash is at the controls. We hear things hummming to life.

WASH
We got it. It's not pretty, but we can steer enough to turn the hell around.

MAL
Nice work, Kaylee.

KAYLEE
(despondent)
Weren't soon enough to help.

MAL
Lot easier to pull things apart than to put 'em right. You're still the best mechanic floating.

He kisses her on the top of her head. She waves him away, but didn't hate the compliment.

WASH
Captain, don't you know that kissing girls makes you sleepy?

MAL
Sometimes I just can't help myself. Let's go visiting.

INT. HOTEL ROOM - DUSK

Can something be rustically plush? 'Cause that best describes this little suite.

Saffron sits on the bed, pulling on her boots. She is nothing like the girl we've seen, much more modern and cool (though she still wears a skirt). And she's packing a sidearm in a shoulder holster.

She stops a moment, listening to something.

The door flies open, Mal having kicked it in. Before she can draw, he has his gun to her head.

MAL
Honey... I'm home...

A beat. She knocks his gun aside, it fires as she draws hers but he is in close, they tussel — he wrenches her gun from her hand as they collapse onto the bed, him on top.

MAL (cont'd)
Looks like you get your wedding night after all.

She pushes him, they go tumbling to the floor but he's still on top and this time he's got his gun to her chin.

MAL (cont'd)
It's the first time, darlin'. I think you should be gentle with me.

She lets out a breath, smiles at him unfathomably.

SAFFRON
Are you gonna kill me?

MAL
Can you conjure up a terribly compelling reason for me not to?

SAFFRON
I didn't kill you...

MAL
You handed me and my crew over to those that would kill us, that buys you nothing.

SAFFRON
I made you dinner...

MAL
Why the act? All the seduction games, the dancing about folk — there has to be an easier way to steal.

SAFFRON
You're assuming the payoff is the point.

MAL
I'm not assuming anything at this juncture.

He sits, gun still well on her. She gets up on her elbows, below but facing him.

SAFFRON
How'd you find me?

MAL
Only a few places that shuttle could make it to from where you left. Happy to find it intact. You always work for Elder Gommen?

A beat, and he leaves.

INT. INARA'S SHUTTLE

As she is turning off her vidscreen. Mal knocks, enters after:

INARA
Come in.

MAL
We're back on course, should be on Beaumonde just a day or two late. Hope that's all right.

INARA
It should be fine, thank you. And does the vixen live?

MAL
If you can call it that. All's well, I suppose.

INARA
Yes.

MAL
You're a very graceful woman, Inara.

INARA
(surprised)
I... thank you.

MAL
So here's where I'm fuzzy: you got by that girl, came and found me, and then you just happened to trip and fall?

INARA
Wh— what do you mean?

MAL
Come on, Inara, how's about we don't play. You didn't just trip, did you?

She holds his look, and aquiesces.

INARA
No.

He smiles, nodding.

MAL
Well isn't that something. I knew you let her kiss you.

Her look changes to one of stupified disbelief. He exits, chuckling. We hold on her expression for a long, long time.

END OF SHOW

SAFFRON
I work with lots of folk. He's thrown me a few choice fish. What'll become of the dear Elder?

MAL
Oh, he'll be laying eyes on me soon enough. And to think I saved his town from vicious bandits.

SAFFRON
(smiling sexily)
You're quite a man, Malcolm Reynolds. I've waited a long while for someone good enough to take me down.

MAL
(also smiles)
Saffron... you even think about playing me again I will riddle you with holes.

Her smile goes. This is the closest we're gonna get to seeing what's inside her, and there ain't much to warm your hands by.

SAFFRON
Everybody plays each other. That's all anybody ever does. We play parts.

MAL
You got all kinds a' learnin' and you made me look the fool without trying, yet here I am with a gun to your head. That's 'cause I got people with me, people who trust each other, who do for each other and ain't always looking for the advantage. There's good people in the 'verse. Not many, lord knows, but you only need a few.

SAFFRON
Promise me you're gonna kill me soon.

MAL
You already know I ain't gonna.

SAFFRON
You know, you did pretty well. Most men, hell, they're on me inside of ten minutes. Not trying to teach me to be strong and the like.

MAL
I got one question for you. Just one thing I'd like to know straight up.

SAFFRON
Ask me.

MAL
What's your real name?

She looks at him... looks away, considering the question...

— and he slams the butt of his gun into her chin, knocking her out cold. He stands, regards her genuinely vulnerable form. Says with a kind of sadness:

MAL (cont'd)
You'd only've lied, anyhow.

THE OFFICIAL
COMPANION

VOLUME TWO

Features and Interviews by Abbie Bernstein, Bryan Cairns,
Karl Derrick & Tara DiLullo

STILL FLYING

An interview with Joss Whedon

What are some of your favorite incidents from filming?

I'm going to forget a bunch, but one that always comes to mind is the basketball game [in 'Bushwhacked']. Because I've always been extremely strict about how I shoot things and about how I write things. And Tim [who directed the episode] had written an entire scene, and I was like, 'But you're going to roll, right, and just let them mess around.' And we both knew instantly that we were not going to use any of our scripted dialogue. That was just [the actors]. I mean, a few of the gags were called upon, but mostly it was just 'Do what you can, have your fun.' And everybody was so socked into their characters, this being just the second episode, that the liveliness of that was something that I hadn't really ever allowed or been privileged to have from a troupe before. And then of course [in 'Serenity'], closing the doors on Mal and Jayne before they got in from the airlock was funny. I have to say, I argued strenuously against it, because I was terrified that something terrible would happen. I said, 'Let's close the doors a little earlier' and everyone was like, 'Don't tell them.' I'm like, 'But what if...' They're like, 'Dude, don't tell them. They'll be cool.' I'm such a wuss: 'I just don't know if that'll be cool...' And it was awesome [laughs], because everybody stayed in character. Jayne just pushed his way to the front. And most of my stories end up being about stuff like that. Nathan is hilarious and people are really fun to be around, but it was mostly about them bringing something, some energy or some moment or some piece of movement that I hadn't really prepared myself for. A show does unfold while you're shooting it. And watching

every actor get so specific and so focused that every time I looked at one of them, I'd be like, 'This is their story — there is nobody else.' And the camera moved to somebody else, and I'd be, 'This is *their* story, there's nobody else.' And it's not an incident, it's more a general feeling, but it's part of what made me fight for the show so hard.

One of the things I ended up doing was, we blocked a scene without the cameramen, which other shows have done, but I hadn't actually heard about it at the time. We gave the cameramen their general measurements and then sent them away so that we could rehearse the scene, so that the camera operators would have no idea who was talking next, just to keep them on their feet, just to keep things alive.

The best thing that ever happened was definitely during 'The Message'. I think for some reason it wasn't on the gag reel. It was possibly the best piece of acting I've ever seen, which is the three-sixty [360 degree camera rotation] that Tim [as director] did while everyone was listening to the farewell message from Tracey [played by Jonathan M. Woodward]. And Nathan is standing with Zoe, looking kind of stricken — this is his old friend — and the camera pans around to Kaylee — and Nathan's sitting next to Kaylee, looking kind of stricken in another way. And he managed to duck under the camera and get to every single member of the cast and just look really sad [laughs]. And some of them just could not keep it together and some of them did. But I've got to tell you — it's hard to describe. And then when it finally panned down to the body in the coffin, Nathan was lying in [Woodward's] arms, looking stricken. It was unbelievable — not only hilarious, but technically proficient. He really put some thought into it. But that's Nathan.

One other incident, definitely one of my favorites: a big executive came onto the big set, took a look at everything and gave me the words of encouragement that stayed with me throughout the run of the show. He looked around and said, 'Don't fuck it up' [laughs].

In the scripts, how much of the dialogue was to foreshadow or give exposition, and how much was just for the sheer pleasure of hearing the characters be the characters — for example in 'Serenity', when Mal asks Jayne what will happen if he's offered enough money to betray the crew and Jayne says, 'That'll be an interesting day'?

You're working both. The fact of the matter is, he said that, and as it turned out, it *was* an interesting day, but

❖ Opposite: Jayne and Mal: they aim to misbehave...

❖ Below: *Firefly* creator Joss Whedon.

that doesn't mean that it necessarily had to happen. What you do when you build a show is, you open as many doors as possible, and then don't look in all of them [laughs]. And that goes for not just the audience, but you yourself. You have to control it, because some shows will just build mysteries without knowing where they're going and suddenly you realize that that's what they're doing and they become unbearable. But you do want to open every avenue possible — romance, conflict, trouble, excitement, revelation — without deciding exactly what's going to happen, because the show's going to evolve; relationships are going to evolve; storylines are going to evolve. That's the way they work.

The relationship between Wash and Zoe and Mal was always very charged. 'War Stories' was like, 'Let's take a run at that.' It's good, primal stuff. One of the *key* things when the show was being picked up, or not being picked up, was when I got a call that said, 'We will pick up the show, but Wash and Zoe can't be married. Because we think that maybe the Captain and Zoe could have some tension from the script we read, from 'The Train Job'.' That was the moment where I said, 'You know what? Now we're talking about two different shows, and I don't want you to pick it up, because first of all, having a happily married couple is something that interests me, it's a different dynamic than I've been seeing. Second of all, what's more devastating: your husband will find out or your boyfriend will find out? So the stakes are just higher.' So that was important to me and something we knew was going to be exciting, and when we made 'War Stories', it was very much 'Let's give that marriage its moment.'

'Objects in Space' was 'Let's get away from the nu-nus-ba-boo-boo-ba-crazy and let's open up River a little bit.' Not because people were like, oh, they hate her, because nobody was *watching*, so it's not like we had all this feed-back, but just the feeling of, 'There's more there, let's start exploring that.' The thing is that every episode, you want everyone to shine. The 'Our Mrs. Reynolds' prin-ciple — the idea of having nine people in the show was so that you could just toss that pebble in the pond and the entire show could just be ripples. And everybody's take on something would be worth hearing about. That's why 'Out of Gas' and 'Our Mrs. Reynolds' are both key, because everybody's just being themselves, reacting to one extreme situation or another.

Did you run into problems with using the word 'humped'?

Never. I've always had it easy with language, because I'll always throw in a word that's not *quite* the word we're not supposed to use, but clearly means it. And I honestly don't think I ever had a language problem. I mean, I kept saying 'rutting' all the time and 'bunged', which if you really break it down, is even more impressive [laughs]. In the early days of *Buffy*, I used British terms. And on *Firefly*, I used British, but usually Elizabethan terms, or terms that were made up to be ever so slightly different, but never any that would actually raise alarms, because nobody actually really seemed to know what they *meant*. The one big restriction we had was, we couldn't say anything actu-ally really dirty in Chinese. Because they were like, 'Mm, if this goes overseas, people will be able to understand what they're saying, so you can't cuss.' Originally, we had them cussing like sailors in Chinese, but they were like, 'No, you have to say something that can be understood [with-out offending speakers of Chinese].' And then we found, because Chinese is so short — basically, it's the opposite of German or Japanese, there are no syllables of any kind — that we have to write monologues just for somebody to have a few syllables. That was a problem.

In the 'Serenity' teleplay, Mal has the line in Chinese, 'Fuck everyone in the universe to death…'

Yes. Probably changed. But we did have 'the explosive diarrhea of an elephant', which is apparently more acceptable.

With its somewhat existential subtext, does 'Objects in Space' break the fourth wall in any way?

It's not meant to. It describes the walls, but it's very much meant to be an episode of the show and to be what is real-ly happening in the lives of these people. Even though it contains elements of fantasy and some very strange

❖ Opposite top: Alan Tudyk and Jewel Staite prepare for a take.

❖ Opposite middle: Take 6 on the *Firefly* clapper board.

❖ Opposite below: Joss Whedon during filming.

❖ This page top: Nathan Fillion and Morena Baccarin on set.

❖ Middle: Sean Maher in front of the camera.

❖ Below: The Sino-American Alliance flag.

observations, it's all trying to live in a realistic world. I'm not a big fan of breaking the fourth wall, with very rare exceptions — on *Angel*, there was 'Spin the Bottle' and every now and then on *Buffy*, 'Dawn's in trouble — it must be Tuesday,' we'd do something like that. On a show like *Firefly*, which is in its infan-cy, we wouldn't go near that. Also, those shows [*Buffy* and *Angel*] take place in the modern world. Pop culture references, by their very nature, to an extent sort of break the fourth wall. *Firefly* was designed not to be able to *have* any pop culture references, so it would not be something I would be anxious to do. You spend so much time in a science-fiction show getting people to accept the world they're in, you don't want to mess with that.

Are there any episodes that you wanted to write and just did not have time to do?

Are you kidding? Here's the thing. There are episodes that I pitched to Nathan before we ever started shooting that burn up inside me, that I could spend three hours going over in my head meticulously, every moment, that

❖ Right: Mal and Wash on the bridge during 'Serenity'.

❖ Below left: The co-pilot's seat and steering yoke.

❖ Below right: One of Serenity's control panels.

though. The one good thing about being under constant threat of cancellation, as we were from the very beginning, is you make really good TV [laughs], because every time we thought, 'Here's an interesting idea — let's explore that somewhere along the line,' we'd get another smoke signal [that the show might be canceled] and we'd look at each other and go, 'We can't do this nice little idea. We have to punch everybody in the stomach. Right now, what's the most unbelievably cool thing we can think of — what's the most primal thing, what's the funniest, what's the most interesting?'

We were on our toes every second, because we figured, the one thing we had to fall back on was quality. That's all we had. And quite frankly, the first episodes wouldn't have been as strong, as frantic about trying to save it. And so, while I never got to make a lot of the episodes that I wished I had, I feel that the DVD box set is as strong as it is, pound for pound, partially for that reason. Which is not the way I'd *like* to live my creative life, but it did — we did make the best of it.

Was the storyline in *Serenity* — the *Serenity* movie rather than 'Serenity' the episode or *Serenity* the ship —

Or the battle.

Or the valley. Or the emotional condition. I think we've now exhausted them.

I believe there are the adult diapers.

we will never film. And there are more than a few. And that is again, part of how *Serenity* happened, because my desire to tell this story was overwhelming; but ultimately, TV and movies — a little bit different. And I knew if I made *Serenity*, I was not going to be telling those stories. Some of them are so dark, you can't believe it, and some of them are very beautiful. Most of them are both. But I had such paces to put these people through and never got the chance. I will say one thing,

Okay, or the diapers — were the elements of *Serenity* originally intended to eventually be part of *Firefly*, and if so, about where would they have come in?

My estimation was, towards the end of season two was going to be where we would find out about Miranda and the Reavers. This would not have led to any overthrow of the government, necessarily, but it would serve the uncracking of River's mind and rebuilding of her. I was giving it two seasons — could've ended up being one if we felt like we needed a little more momentum. But that was in the back of my head.

Would the Reavers ever have talked?

I certainly didn't intend them to. But I was still playing with different ideas about the Reavers. The idea that I used in the movie with the Reavers did not come right away. The idea of a planet being killed I had in my head. The idea that the Reavers had come from that, I didn't have until later in the process, until actually I was writing the movie. I think they would have been about the same [as they were in the film if they had been depicted on *Firefly*]. I had a whole thing worked out where Kaylee was going to go to a carnival and see one in a sideshow and then it was going to turn out to be a guy in a costume, because Mal explained that no Reaver would ever, *ever* let themselves be caught alive, that they'd eat themselves first. And I always wanted to keep that. It would have been a long damn while before we ever really caught sight of one. We had a lot of shows and ideas for shows, where we were constantly under threat of them, but they were in another ship, they were in another place, we didn't see them for a long while. And then once we saw them, oh,

the terrible, terrible things I was going to do. There are some things I won't say [laughs], because I will never give up on a story completely, but it wasn't going to be pretty.

What was in Inara's needle?

One of the things that I'm still going to keep for myself. It may be in the special edition once I finally wake up to reality. But my unreality occasionally opens in theaters, so...

How did you originally intend to end season one?

No idea. Because I really did think season two would be a good place to reveal River's troubles, so I didn't have anything in mind.

Can you talk at all about the episodes that you were prepping when *Firefly* got canceled?

❖ Above: Kaylee's room sign.

❖ Left: The galley set.

We really weren't [prepping anymore], because we had been given the order for three — we were filming the third when we got canceled — and we weren't concentrating on ideas. We had no impression that we were going to be told to make more. Now, had somebody said, 'Boom, you're on,' I'm sure we had some things floating around, but let me put it this way — I don't remember what they were.

We filmed 'Objects in Space' before we filmed 'Trash', 'The Message' and 'Heart of Gold'. There are in fact a couple of snafus. In 'Trash', River says, 'I can kill you with my brain', and in 'The Message', Jayne calls her 'a mind-reading genius', neither of which has been revealed until 'Objects in Space'. And we never aired those episodes ['Trash' and 'The Message'], we only aired 'Objects in Space'. But when we put them on DVD, we wanted 'Objects in Space' to be last, because it felt like more of a summing up, so you can look at those two things as kind of snafus, because originally they came after. But then they never came at all, at least not to network television.

While *Firefly* was airing in its first run, did you have any sense of how intense the fandom was?

Not huge [sighs]. I mean, there was a full-page ad in *Variety* before the show was canceled, trying to keep it on. I was aware that there was a fanbase, but at that point, the only thing that mattered to [the network] was, how big was it? Not how vociferous was it, how big. At one point, I was asked, 'Why should we keep this show?' and my answer was, 'You're going to have a fanbase that loves it like they don't love other things [laughs], and I believe it'll grow — if you ever air it.' The kind of shows I make start out this way and then the word spreads and they become part of people's lives — people who are more dedicated than anything — but the network was interested in opening-weekend mentality and they weren't going to listen to that. So I was aware of [the fandom] to an extent. I knew what we were doing, for one thing, I knew how good it was, and that may sound like I'm all up in me, but this was an alchemy that went way beyond anything I could have imagined when I first thought of the show. From every single crewmember, from every actor — *every* actor, and that's a lot of actors — the energy was just phenomenal and I knew the shows were reflecting that and I'd heard from fans who were amazed by it. But the thing with the Internet is, you can convince yourself the entire world's talking about you from three guys posting over and over and over [laughs]. You can't really put a number on that. And if you can't put a number on it, an executive isn't going to be interested in it — not the executives who ultimately have the power in this situation.

It's been widely reported that Alan Tudyk gave you the red button that recalls the crew in 'Out of Gas' when *Firefly* ended. Did you press the red button to bring the cast back when *Serenity* got greenlit?

You know, it doesn't work. It turns out it was just a prop. It was really cute that Alan gave it to me, but it's not connected to anything. Disappointing, really. No, I think like Mal, I passed out right in front of it. And then I woke up and used the telephone.

Is there anything else you want to say about *Firefly*?

So much and I can't really remember anything, because it's been a part of me for a long time. It was a part of me when it was just a story in my head and then it was the most beautiful experience I could have imagined, because it sprang fully armored from Zeus's head, like Athena. I mean, the casting process was nightmarishly difficult, but once they were put together, you just couldn't imagine that there would be such an extraordinary band, people that I would hold so dear, characters that I would love so much, a world that visually would excite me that much and a staff that would be that creative and exciting. I mean, I had grips

❖ Right: Joss Whedon on set.

❖ Below: Joss hugs Jewel Staite on the final day of filming.

❖ Opposite: The *Firefly* crew.

coming up to me saying, 'I've been in this business for twenty-five years and I've never had so much fun.' I don't know why the grips were having fun [laughs], but they were. There was no above and below the line [status division between cast and crew], there was no attitude. The troubles we had with the network, which were constant, only brought us together, only made us feel more like a unit, a platoon or a family. I saw people who were veterans, who have been in this game forever, and I saw people who were just getting their first break, and they were having the same emotion, they were feeling the same about what they were

doing. The connection was just extraordinary. And I realize, and I've said this before, that none of that matters if it doesn't make it onto the screen. But it did. The energy between those people, the work that went into those scripts, the ease that the crew worked with and the amount of care that went into all of these episodes, it *did* show up. So it *does* matter. It wasn't just a party that we happened to film, it was a really concentrated effort by a lot of extraordinary artists to make something and I'm just swimmingly proud of it. Like the nine actors, like the crew, like the episodes, like everything else, it was more than the sum of its parts. ✈

JAYNESTOWN

Written by Ben Edlund
Directed by Marita Grabiak

BEN EDLUND

Ben Edlund was known for creating the comic book and live-action satirical superhero series *The Tick* and had worked on the screenplay for the animated feature *Titan A.E.* before he was brought on board as a staff writer/producer on *Firefly*. His first credited episode was 'Jaynestown'.

Edlund says the idea for 'Jaynestown' came to him initially "when I was about to fall asleep, that there could be a way of reversing the Robin Hood myth: making everyone who took part in it seem like an utter piece of crap — starting with Jayne, of course. So the idea of there being a town that worshipped Jayne for all the wrong reasons, and how that might touch Jayne and also create problems for him, felt like a good story; when I pitched it to Joss, he was really happy with it.

"Jayne is such a bastard. And writing for a bastard is always fun. There were some abused/abusing childlike aspects to Jayne that you could almost sympathize with. He's a nightmare, there is something about him that makes you not want to see him succeed, but you don't want to see him fail, either. You don't want him gone, you just want him... punched."

Why are the planet's inhabitants farming mud? "I had read somewhere about high-tech ceramics. There were beginning to be quasi-synthetic ceramics in engine use and in other high-tech applications, so it made sense that there'd be a certain planet where there were valuable mineral sediment deposits. It just fit in with that frontier world and with the notion of fusing high-tech sci-fi with a really low-tech town of lumpen proletariat masses. I was trying, as always, to infuse ambient humor into an idea. There's something absurd about it, the whole culture of mud-

covered people with their own songs [Edlund wrote 'The Hero of Canton'], their own bar and their own history of attempts at rebellion, which were usually fairly small and uncoordinated. They were in a position where they would support the idea of a Robin Hood."

Inara's profession provided the subplot. "We were thinking there would be something for her to do on this planet. The organic part of it is that she would have a client who is this frontier, rich person, who was lording the wealth over all these people. I think we had just been fooling around with the notion of her relieving someone of their virginity, since that's so sci-fi," Edlund laughs. "At least when I was a sci-fi fan. I'm sure a story about having my virginity relieved was just what I was looking for when I was a kid — easily until I was twenty!"

As for River's freaked-out reaction to Book's hair, "I think I always had the 'snow on the roof' thing in my script. But when I was done with the first draft, it went to Tim and Joss. I know that Joss had some refinements. He was very pleased, as I recall, about the run where River is using her crazy intellect/lack of propriety to 'fix the bible'. That was something that helped cement some kind of interaction between River and Book through this episode. Also, about that period, Joss wanted to make sure that someone pointed out Ron's amazing crazy hair when it was undone, because it was a free special effect — we used as many of those as we could get!" Edlund laughs.

"I think 'Jaynestown' is about tone and maybe getting a sense that there was a lighter side to being on a spaceship with a bunch of freaks — there's something fun and almost familial about it."

TEASER

INT. SERENITY - COMMON AREA

KAYLEE and SIMON enter from the passenger corridor, walking slowly as they talk. Kaylee is aglow with warm flirtation.

KAYLEE
Come on, it's true. Admit it.

SIMON
No, I won't, because it's not. I use swearwords, like anybody else.

KAYLEE
Oh really? Never heard you. When is it you do all your cussin'? After I go to bed?

SIMON
I swear. When it's appropriate.

KAYLEE
(laughs)
Simon! Whole point of swearin' is that it ain't appropriate.

INARA walks toward them, heading for the stairs up to the shuttle catwalk. She's dressed with stunning elegance.

KAYLEE (cont'd)
Hey there, 'Nara. Heading off for some glamorous romance?

Simon turns, momentarily stunned by her elegance.

INARA
(a little laugh)
Let's hope so.

SIMON
You look... very... very...

INARA
(smiles, then heads upstairs)
That's my job, Doctor. See you two tomorrow. Don't let Mal get you into too much trouble while I'm gone.

KAYLEE
Bye now! Have good sex!

Simon turns to her, abashed. Kaylee is innocent sincerity:

KAYLEE (cont'd)
What?

Then Simon catches sight of something through the infirmary window, shouts, and makes his way around to the door.

SIMON
AAAA!

Kaylee follows. Simon stands in shock. The infirmary has been ransacked. The contents of the cabinets cover every surface. JAYNE sits on the examination table, quietly taping a SMALL HANDGUN to his bare mid-section with medical tape.

KAYLEE
Now see, this'd be the perfect time for a swearword.

INT. SERENITY - INFIRMARY

Simon enters, shrill with agitation. Jayne doesn't look up.

SIMON
What happened in here?!

JAYNE
Needed to find some tape.

SIMON
So you had to tear my infirmary apart?!

JAYNE
(looks up at mess)
'Parently.

Simon starts putting it all away, fuming. Kaylee helps him.

SIMON
My god, you're like a trained ape! Without the training. No, apes are noble creatures, you're some sort of man-ape-thing that went horribly wrong.

JAYNE
(nonchalant)
Keep that tongue waggin', little man, might just have to rip it out an' flush it down the freshener.

Jayne pulls a length of tape with a loud rip, biting it off with his teeth. MAL appears at the door, looking at the gun taped to Jayne's middle.

MAL
Jayne, I told you, we're puttin' down at the Canton

factory settlement on Higgins' Moon.

JAYNE
Yep. That you did.

MAL
Canton don't let you bring guns into their town.

JAYNE
Yessir. That's why I ain't strappin' one to my hip.

MAL
No, that's why you ain't strappin' one anywhere.

JAYNE
Listen, Mal, I was in Canton a few years back, and I might have made me a coupla enemies there-abouts.

SIMON
(sarcasm)
Enemies? You? No! How can it be?

JAYNE
(ignores Simon)
I just don't like the idea of goin' in empty-handed is all —

MAL
Why're you still arguing what's been decided?

Mal stares at him, and leaves as Jayne glumly pulls the tape off, wincing.

EXT. SERENITY - NEARING HIGGINS' MOON

Higgins' Moon below: small, muddy brown, no place to raise a kid. Serenity rakes back, her belly glowing red as she hits re-entry. She makes a controlled tumble into the atmosphere.

INT. SERENITY - BRIDGE - DAY

WASH pilots, hits switches in preparation for landing, then hits the ship's com.

WASH
Okay Inara, we're atmospheric. You're good to go —

INT. INARA'S SHUTTLE - DAY

Inara works her controls, heating up the shuttle's engine, disengaging from Serenity.

INARA
Thanks, Wash. Shuttle disengaging in three, two, one...

We hear LOUD METAL CA-THUNKS as Serenity's locks on the shuttle are released.

EXT. SERENITY - HIGGINS' MOON ATMOSP-HERE - DAY

Inara's shuttle disengages, peeling away.

EXT. CANTON - ESTABLISHING - DAY

ANGLE OVER MUD-BOG — which bubbles and farts in the FG. Beyond it, Serenity comes to rest on a landing field at the edge of a peninsula that

JAYNE'S COSTUMES

Costume designer Shawna Trpcic: "Your bounty hunter, your warrior, your guy just making it on the cusp. Anything from Robert De Niro's character in *Midnight Run* to every hardcore guy doing a thing — with the coats, again, we went to the past to define the future. It was a World War Two jacket, a World War One flight cap, modern-day army boots — pieces from a lot of different eras. I had a lot of fun with the graphics for Jayne's t-shirts. The costume production assistant was really good on the computer, and he and I were on the same page with our take on art. I would come to him with five or six different images and he would blend them all together on the computer and come up with a couple of different choices, then we'd show them to Joss and let him make the final decision. That was our way of making our tough guy a little more lyrical and a lot less of an echo of every other bad guy — with the goofy t-shirts. One of them did say 'soldier', but a lot of them said, 'fighting elves', all in Chinese. We had someone downstairs in the Fox library who could translate for us."

stretches out into the bog. Factory structures stand on the peninsula's far side.

EXT. SERENITY - CARGO RAMP - LANDING AREA - DAY

Mal walks down the ramp. Wash and ZOE stand at the bottom. Kaylee and Simon stand with BOOK and RIVER at the top of the ramp, looking around.

SIMON
Well. Canton really —
(breathes in)
— really stinks.

MAL
That's what makes it a great drop point. No one comes here that doesn't have to.

WASH
I vote we do this job really really fast.

MAL
Kessler's our man, he's holding the goods we're to deliver. We go in, we make contact. Easy peasy.
(turns to Zoe)
Zoe, you're holding down the fort. Call ahead to Bernoulli, tell him we'll have his merchandise there end of the week.

WASH
Don't I usually stay with the ship?

ZOE
I outrank you. Have fun.
(kisses him)

Zoe goes up the ramp.

SIMON
So, this is a place where they... they make mud?

KAYLEE
Yep. Clay, really. Be surprised how many things it ends up in.
(pats the ship)
Serenity's got more than a few ceramic parts in her.

SIMON
Really. Huh.
(looks out)
A mud-based economy. That's almost interesting.

KAYLEE
Cap'n...? Don't you think Simon should come with us?

SIMON
What? Kaylee, I don't think that's such a good —

KAYLEE
You said yourself this was an easy one. And he's got to get a little outlaw field experience sometime, if he's gonna be of any use 'cept doctorin'.

JAYNE
(snorts)
Fat chance of that.

Jayne stomps down the ramp, joining them. He's tying the flaps of his "thrilling heroics" hat under his chin. He pulls his goggles over his eyes. Wash sees his new look and raises his eyebrows. Book turns to Simon.

BOOK
You go on, boy. See the sights. I can watch over your sister. I believe we've been developing a rapport.

SIMON
I don't know. River can be —

BOOK
Go on. I'm a Shepherd after all. Should be able to keep my eye on a flock of one.

Book turns to River, who smiles at him sweetly, nodding.

MAL
We're not going far, Doctor. And you might maybe make yourself useful.

JAYNE
Come again?

Mal turns to Jayne, sees his hat/goggles, squints at him for a beat, then continues.

MAL
The management here don't take so kind to sightseein'. Which is why we'll be posing as buyers. And there isn't a one of us looks more the part than the good Doctor.
(looks Simon over)
The pretty fits, the soft hands, definitely a mon-eyed individual, rich and lily-white and pasty all over —

SIMON
All right. Fine. I'll go. Just, stop describing me.

Mal smiles and guides Simon into the lead of their party.

MAL
You're the boss, boss.

JAYNE
He's the boss now?
(growls to himself)
Day keeps gettin' better and better.

EXT. CANTON MUDWORKS - DAY

Oh, it's muddy all right. Mud encrusts everything; the WORKERS, the pipelines that feed out of the mud-bog, the crappy structures, and THE FORE-MAN who oversees it all. He wears hip-high rubberized boots, a MACHETE strapped in its sheath to one leg. Our crew passes through a chain-link fence which surrounds the area.

The Foreman sees them and turns. At his throat is a thin METAL COLLAR with two flat black discs, mounted over his larynx. He touches it, and his voice projects as if from a BULLHORN, gruff and confrontative.

FOREMAN
Area's employee-only! You best be headin' back to the Landing, 'less you got business here!

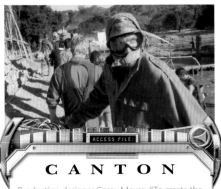

CANTON

Production designer Carey Meyer: "To create the large puddle of mud we used a big hole already at the location. We lined it with plastic and filled it with water and then added a chemical or a substrate to try to make it viscous. I remember the special effects guy, Bruce Minkus [also a *Buffy* alum], adding the stuff and saying, 'No, one gallon is going to make this whole huge pond super-viscous,' and ten barrels later, we were still adding and trying to come up with something that felt right.

"We created the interior of the bar, a little hole in the ground in the village, on stage. It's always an issue when you bring real dirt or products that can get airborne onto a stage. People get extremely wary and upset about it. We'd been through this issue a lot on *Buffy* — we were constantly in these environments that needed to look like dirt or mud or whatever. We decided, in this mud environment, to use actual dirt, just because it looks best.

"We had done some sketches for the sweat boxes and Ben Edlund thought they looked too rustic, and so he did a little sketch for us — he's actually a very good artist. We went with his design and found some of those dividers that they use on construction sites to direct traffic — they're plastic and they fill them up with water. We used them to create barriers. We put them together like puzzle pieces and created what looked like a square box that had a lot of intricate shape to it, and then painted it up like metal and created little hatch doors and propped them up on a little precipice in the middle of this swamp."

SIMON
(too loudly)
YES!
(Foreman puzzled)
We're, uh — I — Yes. I'm looking to buy some mud.

Mal trades a look with Wash over Simon's awkwardness. But the Foreman shuts off his bullhorn collar and steps forward, all salesman smiles now.

FOREMAN
Well, then. Came to the right place.

He claps Simon on the back, his glove leaving a dusty handprint of dried mud on Simon's jacket.

EXT. CANTON MUDWORKS - FURTHER IN - DAY

The Foreman leads Simon on a tour of the plant. The others follow a distance behind, and by their looks this has been going on a bit long. MUD WORKERS shamble by, bent under heavy loads of mud-bricks; clearly back-breaking work.

FOREMAN
...And a 'course we can handle any volume here, got over two-thousand workers, mostly indentured, pay 'em next to nothin', so's we can pass them savings directly on to you-the-customer...

SIMON
Savings. Excellent, that's — because as I said before, I'll be needing quite a bit of it... I — I'm a buyer.

Simon struggles to hold his cover, but the Foreman isn't listening closely enough to notice. He rambles on:

FOREMAN
Yup. Best of its kind. We mix it and brick it raw on the premises, but you add the right catalysts, kiln it proper, this stuff is stronger'n steel ten times over, at half the weight.

SIMON
Yes, I — I've heard good things about the mud... Lot of people are talking about the mud...

Now the Foreman turns to him, a little quizzical.

WASH
(to Kaylee)
What happened to Simon? Who is this diabolical master of disguise?

KAYLEE
He's learning...

MAL
(calls to Simon)
'Scuse me, boss? I'm sure the Foreman's got things need attendin'. Why don't we wander a bit, take a look at the operation, then you can figure on whether we'll set up our account here?

SIMON
Yes?
(playing up role)
I mean, I make the decisions around here, uh —

employee...
(to Foreman)
I employ him. He is a person I employ. I'm the boss.

The Foreman gives him a somewhat confused look.

FOREMAN
O-kay... So you'll be wantin' to —?

SIMON
Yes, I think we'll wander for a bit.

FOREMAN
Fair enough. You come see me when you're done.

He walks off.

MAL
All right, let's head to worker-town.

As they pass by Simon, he reads from their looks that he didn't handle things so effectively. But Kaylee falls in step with him, brushing the mud off his jacket, smiling.

KAYLEE
I thought you did great.

EXT. CANTON WORKER-TOWN - DAY

The crew walks down a muddy lane between two rows of MUD DWELLINGS. Jayne looks back at Simon.

JAYNE
(to Mal)
Boy's gonna get us killed. Let's just do the deal and git.

MAL
His disguise ain't half so funny as yours. What are you supposed to be, anyway?

WASH
You haven't been here in years, Jayne. You really think you need that get-up? No one's gonna remember you...

Mal, in the lead, stops, seeing something O.S. Deadpan:

MAL
Think it's possible they might.

Before them stands a life-size mud-clay STATUE OF JAYNE on a pedestal. It's posed heroically, staring down in proud defiance. Jayne stares, in shock.

SIMON
Son of a bitch...

END OF TEASER

ACT ONE

EXT. CANTON TOWN SQUARE - DAY

Jayne, Mal and the others look up at Jayne's statue, still stunned speechless. Mal steps up next to Jayne; both are transfixed by the statue.

MAL
Jayne?

JAYNE
Yeah?

MAL
You want to tell me how come there's a statue of you, here, starin' at me like I owe him somethin'?

JAYNE
Wishin' I could, Cap'n.

MAL
No. Seriously. Jayne? You want to tell me how come there's a —

Jayne shoots furtive glances all around, keenly aware of his current visibility. His voice is an urgent whisper.

JAYNE
(interrupting)
Look, Mal, I got no ruttin' idea. I was here a few years back, like I said. Pulled a second-story, stole a lotta scratch from the Magistrate up on the hill. But things went way south, and I had to high-tail it. They don't put you on a pedestal in town square for that —

MAL
Yeah, 'cept I'm lookin' at some fair compellin' evidence says they do. Or maybe there's more went down here than you're lettin' on?

JAYNE
(hand to breast)
On my mother, Mal. I don't got the faintest notion.

The others stare up at the statue. Simon is deeply disturbed.

SIMON
This must be what going mad feels like.

WASH
I think they've really captured him, though, you know? Captured his essence.

KAYLEE
He looks sort of angry, don't he?

WASH
Kinda what I meant.

A LOUD STEAM WHISTLE blows — Jayne jumps near a mile.

FOREMAN (O.S.)
(distant, bullhorn)
Shift four, on duty. Shift four, on duty.

A new shift of mud farmers starts coming out of their homes, trudging toward the factory area.

JAYNE
Hey, I got an idea — 'Stead of hangin' around playin' art critic until I get pinched by The Man, how's about we move the hell away from this eerie-ass piece-a-work and get on with our 'creasingly eerie-ass day? How's that!?

Mal stands, staring at the statue.

MAL
I don't know. This here's a spectacle might warrant a moment's consideration.

Kaylee sidesteps by behind him, looking up, unsettled.

KAYLEE
Wherever I move to, his eyes keep... followin' me.

Jayne stomps off, teeth gritted with fury.

JAYNE
Come on, gorramn it! We got a job, let's go do it an' get outta here.

Jayne stops and turns, a distance away from the statue. But they can barely pull their eyes off it.

JAYNE (cont'd)
I crossed the Magistrate of this company-town, understand? An' he's not exactly a forgivin' sorta guy —

EXT. HIGGINS' HACIENDA - DAY

Inara, escorted by a company man, walks across the lawn of the Magistrate's estate.

MAGISTRATE HIGGINS, late fifties, tall, powerfully built under a few decades of doughy excess, stands with his VALET, ready to receive her. She does a graceful curtsey.

INARA
Magistrate Higgins, I may presume?

HIGGINS
You may. But I only make the people I own use my title.
(chuckles)
Mr. Higgins will do fine.

INARA
And you can call me Inara, Mr. Higgins.

HIGGINS
It's a rare pleasure, your visit to my little moon. Journey wasn't too taxing?

INARA
Not at all. I am refreshed and ready. Shall we begin at say, six o'clock?

HIGGINS
Perfect.
(starts to go)
I have a feeling it will take all your arts to deal with this particular problem.

INARA
Every "problem", Mr. Higgins, is an opportunity in disguise...

INT. SERENITY - DINING ROOM - DAY

River sits at the dining table. Book's bible is open in front of her, and she scribbles furiously into it, crossing out words, writing in the margins. Book walks in, speaks from across the room.

BOOK
What are we up to, sweetheart?

RIVER
Fixing your bible.

BOOK
I — uh — What?

He starts moving over to her.

RIVER
Bible's broken. Contradictions, faulty logistics — it doesn't make sense...

Now Book sees what she's doing. His bible's all fucked up, and there's a small stack of torn-out pages next to it.

BOOK
No, no, you can't...

River's still scribbling away as she chatters manically.

RIVER
So we'll integrate non-progressional evolution theory with God's creation of Eden — eleven inherent metaphoric parallels already there...

Eleven, important number, prime number, one goes into the house of eleven eleven times but always comes out one —

BOOK
River, just take it easy. You shouldn't —

RIVER
Noah's Ark is a problem —

She flips a page back and forth, frowning at it.

BOOK
Really.

RIVER
(rapid nod)
We'll have to call it early quantum state phenomenon — only way to fit five-thousand species of mammal on the same boat.

She tears the page out of the book.

BOOK
Gimme that!

Book snatches the bible up, somewhat possessively.

BOOK (cont'd)
River! You don't fix the bible!

River looks up at him, sweet, sincere, deadpan:

RIVER
(holds up torn-out pages)
It's broken. It doesn't make sense.

BOOK
It's not about making sense. It's about believing in something, and letting that belief be real enough to change your life. It's about "faith".
(gets up)
You don't fix faith, River. It fixes you.

He smiles, trying to gently take the crumpled, torn-out pages from her hand. She tugs back. They have a short tug-of-war then Book relents.

BOOK (cont'd)
Why don't you, ah, you hang on to those then.

INT. CANTON TAVERN - DAY

The kind of dirty dive that's actually made of dirt. Rugged, simple furnishings, with a crowd of mud-crusted off-duty WORKERS hunkered over their beers. A LOCAL BUSKER strums a battered GUITAR in one corner. MEADOWS, a young Mudder, sweeps up the bar with a dust broom. He looks at Jayne with some interest.

Our crew sits around a table. Mal has his back against the wall, taking in the view.

There're several clay bottles of beer on the table. Jayne pours himself a drink, as do the others.

JAYNE
Can't be a statue a' me. No reason for it. Flies in the face of every kinda sense.

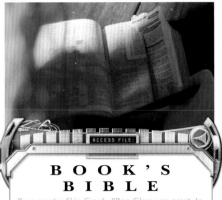

BOOK'S BIBLE

Prop master Skip Crank: "Ron Glass was great. In almost every script it said: 'Book enters with his bible.' It was a tiny bible that Joss had picked out. I'd hand Ron this bible and he'd say 'No, not the bible!' I'd reply, 'Didn't you read the script?'

"Summer went through the whole routine of destroying Book's bible. Ron was really happy as he thought he'd never have to see the thing again. Then, later in the episode, she gives it back to him! Summer insisted that she taped all the pages back in herself. She really did want to do the whole thing.

"On Randy's truck we had probably the biggest bible you've ever seen. It was like two phone books taped together. For a joke, I went to see Ron with it and said, 'You know River tore up your bible? Well, here's your new one.' He said, 'No Way!'

"After we were canceled, I presented him with his original bible, and he cried. It was really sad."

WASH
Won't argue with that —
(drinks, spits it out)
Gaah!<Je shr shuh muh lan dong shi!?> [What is this garbage!?]

JAYNE
They call it Mudder's Milk.
(takes a big gulp)
Got all the vitamins, proteins, and carbs of your Grandma's best turkey dinner, plus fifteen-percent alcohol.

WASH
It's horrific!

SIMON
Worked for the Egyptians.

Jayne downs his glass and exhales, turning to Simon.

JAYNE
Whazzat?

SIMON
The ancient Egyptians, back on Earth-That-Was. It's not so different from the ancestral form of beer they fed to the slaves who built their pyramids. Liquid bread. Kept them from starving, and knocked them out at night, so they wouldn't be inclined to insurrection.

KAYLEE
Wow, Simon... That's so — so historical.

JAYNE
(to Simon)
Tell me, Little Miss Big-Words — you see a pyramid sittin' out there?

SIMON
No —

JAYNE
(rests his case)
Neither do I.
(pours a beer)
So here, let me pour you a big frosty mug of "shut-the-hell-up".

Jayne shoves a mug of beer at Simon.

Mal narrows his eyes at a relatively WELL-DRESSED MAN across the bar, who seems to be watching them.

MAL
(to himself)
Now what's a gussied-up fella like you doin' in a place like this?

The man sees he's being seen.

A YOUNG BOY (maybe thirteen) stands a short distance away from the crew's table, staring at Jayne with intense interest.

JAYNE
Shake your head, boy. Yer eyes are stuck.
(boy still staring)
GIT!
(boy runs off)

The well-dressed man walks up to their table. He stops at Mal.

WELL-DRESSED MAN
You wouldn't be looking for Kessler?

MAL
Just having a brew.

JOSS WHEDON

A town where Jayne is the local hero because he gave to the poor because he was trying to get the hell away in his ship [laughs] — how do you not do that? That was a huge amount of fun and I also thought they did some great stuff with that muddy town visually, but it was just pure romp. There's some emotion that happens during it, but it really was just how ridiculous would this be, and everybody was at the top of their game. It was too good a premise not to do, basically.

The man sits, close.

WELL-DRESSED MAN
I knew a Kessler.

MAL
"Knew"?

WELL-DRESSED MAN
He was a good middle-man. Low profile, didn't filch. But last week, the factory Foreman and his Prod crew heard he was moving contraband through town and gave him a peck a' trouble for it.

MAL
What kind of a "peck" was that?

WELL-DRESSED MAN
'Kind where they hacked off his hands and feet with machetes and rolled him into the bog.

WASH
They peck pretty hard 'round here.

MAL
Listen, I got a client offworld waiting for his delivery. If the goods are gone —

WELL-DRESSED MAN
Not to worry, your man's merchandise is safe in Kessler's hiding place. We just got to figure out how to get it cross town without being seen by the Foreman and his Prods. I'd advise we all just lay low for the moment —

The Busker starts singing.

BUSKER
JAAAYNE! The man they call JAAAYNE!

Jayne hears his name and sits straight up, horrified.

JAYNE
<Yeh-soo, ta ma duh — > [Hay-soose-mother-of-jumped-up —]

With lightning reflexes, Kaylee slaps her hand over his mouth; the applause of the mud workers (for the busker) helps cover Jayne's outburst.

Thus begins 'The Ballad of Jayne'. The mud workers erupt into the opening chorus, swinging their mugs in joyful song.

CROWD
He robbed from the rich, and gave to the poor, stood up to The Man, and gave him what for / Our love for him now, ain't hard to explain, THE HERO OF CANTON! THE MAN THEY CALL JAYNE!

The crowd gives way to the Busker, who sings a verse:

BUSKER
Our Jayne saw the Mudders' backs breaking / and he saw the Mudders' laments / and he saw the Magistrate taking / every dollar an' leavin' five cents / so he said, 'Can't do this to my people' / 'Can't crush them under your heel'./ Jayne strapped on his hat, and in ten seconds flat, stole

everything there was fit to steal —

The crowd erupts again, REPEATING THE CHORUS. Over this, Mal and Jayne discuss this unsettling new wrinkle.

MAL
Umm... Jayne?

JAYNE
Yeah, Mal.

MAL
You got any light to shed on this development?

JAYNE
No, Mal.

Simon, seated by Kaylee, looks even more disturbed.

SIMON
No... This must be what going mad feels like...

He lifts up his beer and takes a deep drink.

The chorus ends and the Busker goes back to pickin', singing/story-telling another verse.

BUSKER
And here's what separates heroes / from common folk like you an' I. / The man they call Jayne, turned 'round his plane / and let that money hit sky. / He dropped it onto our houses. / He dropped it into our yards. / The man called Jayne,

'THE HERO OF CANTON'

Composer Greg Edmonson explains that it was 'Jaynestown' writer Ben Edlund who composed 'The Hero of Canton'. "The song had to be pre-recorded, so they had something to use during the filming of the scene." While he won't swear to it, Edmonson believes the actor singing lead in the episode is the same person singing on the soundtrack. "I'm pretty sure that they cast someone who could sing and he came in and sang. I know all the background singers were SAG singers who I use all the time; Craig Stull, who played on the main title, played guitar on that song. I didn't go to that recording session, because I was too busy trying to score another episode, so I think Craig called the singers that I knew and gave them instructions. I've worked with them all so many times before, I knew that it would turn out perfect, so I didn't have to sweat that one."

Edmonson did compose the music performed before the balladeer launches into 'Hero'. "The guitar music that precedes the song was just something that was meant to be played in a bar that really would just fit under the dialogue and not be too big a deal and would lead logically into the song."

THE HERO OF CANTON

Jayne.
The man they call Jayne...

He robbed from the rich
and he gave to the poor.
Stood up to The Man
and gave him what for.
Our love for him now
ain't hard to explain.
The hero of Canton,
the man they call Jayne!

Our Jayne saw the Mudders' backs breakin'.
He saw the Mudders' lament.
And he saw the Magistrate takin'
every dollar and leavin' five cents.
So he said, "You can't do that to my people";
He said "You can't crush them under your heel.
So Jayne strapped on his hat
and in five seconds flat
stole everythin' Boss Higgins had to steal.

He robbed from the rich
and he gave to the poor.

Stood up to The Man
and gave him what for.
Our love for him now
ain't hard to explain.
The hero of Canton,
the man they call Jayne!

Now here is what separates heroes
from common folk like you and I.
The man they call Jayne
he turned 'round his plane
and let that money hit sky.

He dropped it onto our houses
he dropped it into our yards.
The man they called Jayne
he stole away our pain
and headed out for the stars!

Here we go!

He robbed from the rich
and he gave to the poor.
Stood up to The Man
and gave him what for.
Our love for him now
ain't hard to explain.
The hero of Canton,
the man they call Jayne!

stole away our pain / and headed out for the stars.

The crowd has erupted again, REPEATING THE CHORUS. Jayne seethes, facts dawning on him:

JAYNE
I'll be gorramned! That's where the cash went!
(to Mal and the rest)
I stole that money from Higgins, like the song says. Lifted me one of his hover-planes, but I got tagged by anti-aircraft. Started losin' altitude — had to dump them strongboxes of money to stay airborne.
(takes a drink)
Sixty-thousand, untraceable, an' I dropped it square in mud-farmer central!

The CHORUS ENDS, and the Busker plays a final bit of guitar, crescendoing as the crowd APPLAUDS. Wash looks at them all in disbelief.

WASH
We gotta go to the crappy town where I'm a hero...

INT. SERENITY - BOOK'S BERTH - NIGHT

Book steps into his berth and pulls out the sink, starting his pre-dinner ablutions. He starts to untie his bun of hair...

INT. SERENITY - COMMON AREA - EVENING

River walks from the common area into the passage leading to Book's berth.

INT. SERENITY - BOOK'S BERTH - NIGHT

Book splashes his face, bent over the sink.

RIVER (O.S.)
Hello?

BOOK
In here, River.

River steps into his doorway, looking down at the crumpled pages in her hands.

RIVER
I'm — I tore these out of your symbol, and they turned into paper — but I want to put them back, so —

BOOK
Sorry? What's that?

His hair is like a corona of grey fire around his head. River looks up, sees him, and drops the pages.

RIVER
(highest-pitched scream imaginable)

She runs off.

BOOK
River —?

INT. SERENITY - CORRIDOR OUTSIDE BOOK'S BERTH - NIGHT

River runs by Zoe. Zoe hears Book inside.

BOOK (O.S.)
River — Come back —

ZOE
Book? What the hell happened to —
(as she turns, looks into Book's door)
AAA!

She startles at Book's hair.

INT. CANTON TAVERN - NIGHT

Jayne is hunched over his beer, looking ready to pop a nut. The crowd is lively and drunkish.

JAYNE
Captain, now they're off the subject of me, shouldn't we be gettin' the hell out of here?

MAL
I'd say that's a reasonable request, given the circumstance.

Jayne's up in a flash, stomping out. The others follow in his wake.

JAYNE
Ruttin' Mudders...

He pushes the front door open with a heave and stops dead:

EXT. CANTON TAVERN - NIGHT

The street in front of the tavern is filled with an affordable sea of MUD-WORKERS. At the front is the boy who Jayne chased off before. On sight of Jayne, they all cry:

CROWD
JAYNE!

Off Jayne and Mal's shocked expression, we BLACK OUT.

END OF ACT ONE

ACT TWO

EXT. CANTON TAVERN - NIGHT

A second after we left. Jayne stands, eyes aflame with alarm, as the crowd chants his name.

CROWD
JAYNE! JAYNE! JAYNE!

A beat of this, then Jayne turns, unceremoniously darting back into the bar. Wash turns to the others, mocking tremendous excitement.

WASH
I can't get enough of this local color!

INT. CANTON TAVERN - NIGHT

The crowd inside has stopped singing, confused. Meadows, the young man who's been sweeping the place, watches as Jayne pushes through them, bellying up to the bar, slams down his hat and goggles, desperate for drink.

JAYNE
Gimme some Milk.

The BARTENDER splashes a bottle of Mudder's Milk into a glass and Jayne takes a slug.

Meadows puts his broom down, stepping into the middle of the tavern behind Jayne, who's drinking down the Mudder's Milk.

MEADOWS
Don't you understand?! He's come back!
(crowd still lost)
It's Jayne!

Jayne's eyes dart like a wounded bull's in the ring. The bartender SLAPS the glass away from his lips.

JAYNE
What th —

BARTENDER
The hero of Canton won't be drinking that <shiong mao niao.> [panda urine.]

He pulls a dusty WHISKEY BOTTLE from below the bar and slams it down.

BARTENDER (cont'd)
He drinks the best whiskey in th' house.

Jayne, mystified, watches the bartender pour.

CROWD INSIDE BAR
(erupts into a CHEER)

They converge on him, slapping his back, shaking his hand. The brute has lost his connection to reality, just stands there as if in a strange dream.

Mal and the others push back into the crowded bar. The well-dressed man catches Mal by the sleeve, alarmed.

WELL-DRESSED MAN
'Hell is goin' on? This how people lay low where you're from?!

MAL
Not generally, no...

WELL-DRESSED MAN
Listen, friend, I came here to make sure a deal went down solid, not to get chopped up by the Canton Prod crew and fed to the bog!

Mal pulls the man's grasping hand from his arm, a touch riled by the contact. He's intuitively piecing out a new strategy.

MAL
Understand your concerns, friend. But this here is all part of our new plan.

KAYLEE
Captain? How exactly is this part of our —

MAL
(gritted teeth)
Still workin' the details...

MAL

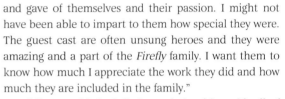

"No matter how long the arm of the Alliance might get... we'll just get us a little further."

While the casting of Nathan Fillion as Malcolm Reynolds seems like the most perfect connection of actor to character ever, Fillion laughs at the assertion and dispels that common misconception held among fans. "Malcolm Reynolds is a pained man and he's obviously closed off." The actor explains that, in reality, he is the polar opposite of Mal so taking on the role was an absolute stretch for him. "It's not so much that he's not like me, but that he was such a challenge to play. I felt it was important that Joss knew this. I said, 'Just so you know, I love this character and I want to play him — he's not me. This is not the kind of person I am. I'm a happy, very lucky, excited individual. Life has been very, very kind to me.' I just thought that the distinction was important."

Fillion says bridging the gap between reality and character in playing Mal really came so much more easily than expected due to the caliber of the cast around him. The usual stresses of being a series lead never materialized for the actor, who says, "I didn't feel immediately like, 'Oh there is a lot of extra pressure on me to do something in particular in terms of leadership.' I had been a fan of many of the people that were cast. Gina Torres — I loved her work. Ron Glass, of course. Adam Baldwin... are you kidding? Alan Tudyk, when I saw he was cast I thought, 'What is he doing here? He's a movie star! Why is he slumming with us?'" He laughs, then adds seriously, "There would be moments all the time, when we would be on set dealing with adversity, there would be a problem and they would say, 'How can we help?' It became apparent that these fun, easygoing, relaxed people, who were extremely talented, who were there to do a job, were also very passionate and interested that we were also there for each other. I'm only too grateful to know these people. I respect their talent. I admire them." After a thoughtful pause, Fillion lights up and adds passionately, "There were also a lot of guest cast that came to *Firefly* and became a part of it

and gave of themselves and their passion. I might not have been able to impart to them how special they were. The guest cast are often unsung heroes and they were amazing and a part of the *Firefly* family. I want them to know how much I appreciate the work they did and how much they are included in the family."

While Reynolds had distinct relationships with all of the members of the Serenity family, when asked whom Malcolm revealed himself most to, Fillion readily answers, "Shepherd Book. The characters would come to Mal with bits or ideas, and maybe Mal would listen or have his own ideas. But whenever Book says something to Malcolm Reynolds, Malcolm Reynolds listens. He's one of the few people Mal listens to. He'll listen to Zoe, but his call is *the* call. He doesn't listen to Zoe because she has a bigger heart than he does. Book is very knowledgeable about a lot of things. Mal holds a lot of his feelings within him. He doesn't say a lot or tell a lot of who he is or how he is or why he is, nor does Book. That is something that Malcolm sees and doesn't press him about. So if Malcolm had a guide, it was Book."

With the series long over and one last adventure captured on film for the big screen, Fillion still looks at his time playing Malcolm Reynolds as one of the highlights, not only of his career, but also of his life. "I fell in love," the actor says of the show. "I told myself in 1997, 'Don't fall in love. Do your best. Always give 110 percent. Always swing at what they throw at you, but don't fall in love.' I lost it with *Firefly*. I lost the plan and was so in love. It was hard. We fought a war and were in a battle and being crushed and I kept telling people, 'Don't worry. We are making a great show. That's our ace in the hole.' But it was taken away from me. The parallel between that and Malcolm Reynolds' experience is only too poetic."

Still touched by the loss to this day, Fillion is winsome but never bitter. With his signature smile, he offers, "I'm the biggest *Firefly* fan you will ever meet. I have a place in my heart for that program and that film like no other person could, except for Joss. But my one advantage over Joss is that I got to live it. To be a fan and the Captain is a real interesting and fortunate place to be."

INT. INARA'S SHUTTLE - NIGHT

Inara has laid out a complex array of bowls and china on a low table in the main area of her shuttle. She's preparing for the COMPANION TEA CEREMONY. She lights a candle, then flips open a pretty silver pocketwatch, nodding to herself as she checks the time. There is a knock at her O.S. door.

Magistrate Higgins steps into the doorway.

HIGGINS
Inara, allow me to introduce my son, Fess Higgins.

FESS HIGGINS, the Magistrate's twenty-six-year-old son, steps into the doorway. He's on the heavy side, but not unattractive, in his way. Inara smiles warmly.

INARA
Hello, Fess.
(to Higgins)
Mr. Higgins, this shuttle is a Place of Union. I'm sure you can appreciate —

HIGGINS
The lady said "hello", Fess. Don't just stand there looking at your shoes —

FESS
Dad —

Higgins forcefully guides Fess into the shuttle, stopping just short of the tea ceremony table.

HIGGINS
Get in there, son, make a man of yourself!

INARA
Mr. Higgins —

HIGGINS
(sees tea set-up)
What is this? I brought you here to bed my son, not throw him a tea party —

Inara is polite, but afire with firmness.

INARA
Sir, the Companion Greeting Ceremony is a ritual with centuries of tradition behind it. There are reasons for the way we do things.

HIGGINS
Listen, Inara, I called on you for one thing and one thing only. My son is twenty-six years old and he ain't yet a man. Twenty-six!
(looks at son with contempt)
And since he can't find a willin' woman himself —

Inara takes Higgins by the arm and starts gently but firmly guiding him out of the shuttle. He blusters but goes along.

INARA
Mr. Higgins, you are not allowed here.

HIGGINS
I — What?

INARA
As I said, this room is a consecrated Place of Union. Only your son belongs here.

HIGGINS
Well! This is — I —

She escorts him out the door. There's a WET SHLUP as Higgins' shoes hit the muddy ground.

INARA
Now you go on, and let us begin our work.

HIGGINS
Now you listen here, young lady —

Inara flashes a sweet smile and closes the door on him.

INARA
Goodnight, Mr. Higgins.

Inara resets an out-of-place hair, smoothes her countenance, and turns to Fess, now the portrait of hospitality.

INARA (cont'd)
Well. That's a bit more peaceful. Will you sit?

INT. CANTON TAVERN - NIGHT

Jayne leans against the bar, drink in hand, surrounded by adorers. He's starting to get into it. Meadows raises his mug.

MEADOWS
To Jayne —

CROWD
To Jayne!

They all drink. Jayne grins, despite himself, and swigs down his drink. The bartender fills it immediately. Jayne smiles wider, lifts his glass.

JAYNE
To the Mudders!

CROWD
To the Mudders!

They drink again.

Wash and Mal stand off to the side. Wash has a glass of whiskey in his hand. A MUDDER ELDER, in his sixties, finishes his drink and turns to Mal.

MUDDER ELDER
So, you're one of Jayne's men, eh?

Wash smiles. Mal's not pleased.

MAL
What? No —

MUDDER ELDER
Must be a heck of an honor, servin' under a man like that. Strong as a drafthorse, ain't he?

MAL
Listen, Mudhead, I don't —

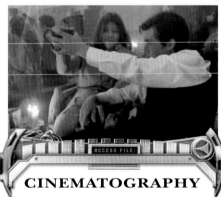

CINEMATOGRAPHY

Director of photography David Boyd: "I had made it known to Carey Meyer early on that I loved ceilings in sets. He totally agreed and built ceilings into everything that he constructed. In the Mudders' bar ceiling, we designed holes, as if this were subterranean, and stuck lighting down through it in the form of very spotty lights. We put fans in these holes which turned very slowly. So we built in the fact that this place needed to be ventilated for some reason on this planet, and that light came from these strange sources. No one could or wanted to explain what they were, but they landed at odd angles, not from a sun, but from some other thing."

MUDDER ELDER
An' a heart as big as all outdoors...

Wash CHUCKLES, patting Mal on the back.

WASH
Yup, we're just happy he lets us stay.

At a table, Simon and Kaylee sit, drinking. Simon's actually a little plastered, and Kaylee's having the time of her life, nestled next to him.

SIMON
(a little slurred — more reminiscing than bitter)
You know, I've saved lives. Dozens. Maybe hundreds. I re-attached a girl's leg. Her whole leg. She

named her hamster after me. I got a hamster. He drops a box of money, he gets a town.

KAYLEE
Hamsters is nice —

SIMON
To Jayne! The box dropping, man-ape-gone-wrong-thing, hero of Mudville.

Kaylee laughs and drinks his toast with him.

KAYLEE
You know, you're pretty funny, even without cussin'...

Simon takes another sip and smiles at her, seeing her in the drunken light which makes all things sublime.

SIMON
You know... you're pretty... pretty.

Kaylee's smile drops. She wants to make sure she heard right.

KAYLEE
What? What did you say?

SIMON
(drunk smile)
Nothing. Just that you're pretty... Even when you're covered with engine grease, you're — maybe 'specially when you're covered with engine grease, you're —

Mal steps in over them, unintentionally cutting Simon off.

MAL
It's time to get out of this nuthouse. Got some plannin' to work out.

Kaylee's nightmare: boy-in-gear, Captain wants to go.

KAYLEE
Now, Captain?! But things are goin' so well!

MAL
(not quite getting it)
Um. I suppose, Jayne's certainly feelin' better about life. But we —

Kaylee gives Mal a fierce look.

KAYLEE
I said things are goin' well —

MAL
(gets it)
Oh. "Well". Well... I tell you what. Jayne's stuck here with his adoring masses, how about you and Simon hang around, keep an eye on him for me?

Simon raises his glass, oblivious to any sub-text at this point, drunker by the minute.

INT. SERENITY - CARGO BAY - NIGHT

Book and Zoe are crouched, Book's magnificent hair still out of its cage. River is inside the bay's secret compartment.

RIVER (O.S.)
(to herself, rapid)
They say the snow on the roof is too heavy — They say the ceiling will cave in — His brains are in terrible danger —

BOOK
River...? Please, why don't you come on out...

RIVER (O.S.)
No. Can't. Too much hair.

BOOK
(surprised)
Is — is that it?

He turns to Zoe, who nods.

ZOE
Hell yes, Preacher. If I didn't have stuff to get done, I'd be in there with her...

Book gives Zoe a look of mild affront and starts tying up his hair.

BOOK
(to River)
It's the rules of my order... Like the book, it symbolizes —

ZOE
(cuts him off)
Uh-huh. River, honey... He's putting the hair away now...

RIVER (O.S.)
Doesn't matter. It'll still be there... waiting...

WASH (O.S.)
Honey, we're home!

Mal and Wash walk into the cargo bay. Zoe goes to them.

ZOE
Where you guys been? Mal, Bernoulli's chompin' at the bit. Says he wants his merchandise yesterday —

MAL
Yeah, well, we got a couple of wrinkles to work out on the deal.

WASH
(bit buzzed on drink)
Did you know Jayne is a bonafide folk hero? Got a song and everything.

ZOE
(as in "get out")
<Hoo-tsuh.> [Shut up.]
(eyes Wash)
You been drinkin', husband.

MAL
That he has. Don't make it any less the case.

ZOE
You're telling me Jayne is a —

MAL
(nods)
It's true. True enough to use, anyways. We've talked a few pillars of the Mudder community into havin' a little 'Jayne Day' celebration in town square tomorrow... That should buy us enough distraction to get those stolen goods out from under the Foreman and his crew a' Prods...

ZOE
You're really gonna have to start again.

They stop by Book.

MAL
Shepherd, everything goin' okay?

BOOK
I, uh, I'm working on it, Captain.

RIVER (O.S.)
We need a snow shovel...

INT. INARA'S SHUTTLE - NIGHT

Fess sits next to Inara at the low table, sipping his tea.

FESS
(looking into his cup)
It's just... my father's always been so in control, of everything, of me, of everyone... I could never be like him, no matter who he pays to —
(reddens, looks up)
I'm sorry... This whole thing, it is embarrassing. My father's right again, I guess. And to have to bring you here, to —

INARA
Your father isn't right, Fess. It's not embarrassing to be a virgin. It's simply one state of being. And as far as bringing me here — Companions choose the people they're to be with very carefully... For example, if your father asked me to come here for him, I wouldn't have.

FESS
Really?

INARA
Really, Fess. But you're different from him.

She turns to him, stroking his cheek, looking into his eyes.

INARA (cont'd)
The more you accept that, the stronger you'll become...

She leans in and kisses him gently on the lips.

INT. CANTON TAVERN - NIGHT

Jayne now has a WOMAN on one arm, clinging to him. She's somewhere between robust and plain, but with a Janis Joplin carnality that suits him. He speaks to Meadows, who looks at him adoringly.

JAYNE
So the Magistrate, he let you folks keep all that cash?

MEADOWS
He did. And it pained him, that's for dead sure. When he found out, he sent his Prods in to take it back from us... But the workers resisted.

JAYNE
Fought the law, eh?

MEADOWS
(nods)
If the Mudders are together on a thing, there's too many of us to be put down... So in the end, he just called it a "bonus".

JAYNE
(rueful laugh)
One hell of a bonus...

MEADOWS
And then, when we put that statue of you up in town square, he rolled in, wanted to tear it down. But the whole town rioted...

This, the idea of violence in his name, touches our drunken Jayne so deeply, a tear comes to his eye.

JAYNE
(drunken emotion)
You guys started a riot? On account of me? Oh... I am truly touched, truly, truly touched by that. I mean, all of this has been swell and all, but that, my very own riot...
(almost chokes up)
...That's just about the nicest thing I ever heard...

MEADOWS
I can't believe you're back...

He throws a big arm over Meadows, squeezing him warmly.

JAYNE
How could I stay away?

INT. HIGGINS' HACIENDA - NIGHT

Higgins paces as the Foreman comes in, led by a VALET.

FOREMAN
Magistrate Higgins —

Higgins is only vaguely listening, lost in his dirty hopes.

HIGGINS
M'son's out there, I pray to God losin' his cherry...

FOREMAN
There's a problem in worker-town, sir.
(Higgins listening)
Jayne Cobb's come back.

Whatever we can do to subtly imply that ancient, boiling hatred has just snapped a nerve in this Higgins' head...

EXT. CANTON PRISON FIELD - NIGHT

Out on the bog. A catwalk stretches out to an area dotted with rusted steel boxes (not unlike the hotbox from *Cool Hand Luke*). Airholes poke through doors in their fronts.

Higgins and the Foreman are at one of the boxes. The Foreman carries a beat-up duffel bag.

The Foreman fumbles through some keys and opens the door. Rank darkness inside. CAMERA PUSHES IN on the small dark doorway. We hear rustling inside, the scratch of uncut nails along a wall.

HIGGINS
Evening, Stitch.

STITCH (O.S.)
(hissing exhale)
What do you want with me?

HIGGINS
Nothing. You've done your time. Paid your debt. Time you were on your way.

STITCH HESSIAN'S face pushes out of the shadows inside, fast. Half of it is a mass of scar tissue; one eye is missing.

He slithers out of the box, dropping heavily to his feet on the catwalk. He's a tall, creepy son-of-Manson, long bedraggled hair and beard, scarred

all over his sinewy body.

Higgins nods to the Foreman, who throws the duffel at Stitch.

HIGGINS (cont'd)
Here. I believe these were your personal effects...

Stitch looks in the duffel, surprised to pull out a SHOTGUN. Higgins turns, starting to walk away, then stops.

STITCH
You keep me in that box four years and then give me a loaded gun?

HIGGINS
Got the urge to use it, no doubt. But I'm not the one that brought you in on that robbery. I'm not the one who partnered up with you and then turned on you when his plan went south. How high up was that shuttle when he pushed you out? Thirty feet? Jayne Cobb cost you four years of your life, plus a perfectly good eyeball. And here's the poetical portion: he's back in town. This very day.

Stitch's body tenses with hideous rage. He COCKS his gun.

HIGGINS (O.S.)
Best of luck in your new life.

END OF ACT TWO

ACT THREE

INT. CANTON TAVERN - MORNING

The morning after. One or two MUDDERS lie passed out. Camera finds Kaylee and Simon. They're tangled up in each other, asleep. Kaylee has her hand on Simon's chest, under his shirt, which is half-unbuttoned. She wakes groggily, sees Simon next to her, and smiles, soaking him in.

Then Mal is above her. She turns and smiles at him, too, still half-asleep.

KAYLEE
(dreamy)
Hiya, Captain...
(snaps out of it)
Captain!!

This wakes up Simon, who gets his bearings quickly.

❖ Left: The lantern Higgins is carrying when he releases Stitch.

SIMON
Wha — ? Kay — ? — Mal! Mal, I, uh...

He starts untangling himself roughly from Kaylee's embrace.

SIMON (cont'd)
Captain, nothing happened — There was some drinking, but — We certainly didn't — I mean, I would never — not with Kaylee, I — I assure you, nothing inappropriate took place —

KAYLEE
What do you mean, not with me?

Kaylee, getting pissed, helps him untangle with a strong shove. Mal is uninterested.

MAL
Uh-huh... Where's my hero?

JAYNE
(singing)

He robbed from the rich, and gave to the poor, stood up to The Man, and gave him what for...

Jayne descends the stairs into the tavern from the rooms above. His arm around the woman from last night.

JAYNE (cont'd)
The living legend needs eggs!
(gives it thought)
Or another Milk, maybe...

MAL
No. The living legend is comin' with us. He has a little appearance to make.

JAYNE
He does?

MAL
That's right. This job here has gone way past long enough.

JAYNE
(to the woman)
You go on, now. Got me important hero-type stuff to do.

Kaylee follows them to the door. Simon gets up, to fall in line, but Kaylee turns on him.

KAYLEE
Where you goin'?

SIMON
What? I'm coming with y —

She pokes him in the chest, miffed enough to not want him around for a bit.

KAYLEE
I don't think so. No, maybe you ought to stay here. It's about the time for a civilized person to have his breakfast. That's the sorta thing would be appropriate, don't you think?

Simon turns to Mal, who shrugs. It's clear Simon is only an honorary member of the club; Kaylee outranks him. They turn and go, leaving Simon alone in the tavern.

SIMON
Mal...
(as they walk out)
Guys?

MAL
See you on the ship, Doc.

Simon shakes his head, still groggy, and sits down. After a beat, he turns to the bartender.

SIMON
Excuse me... Could I see a menu?

BARTENDER
(laughing snort)
"Menu"...

INT. INARA'S SHUTTLE - MORNING

Fess lies next to Inara in bed.

INARA
You're very quiet.

FESS
I'm sorry — I'm just — I just thought I'd feel... different, after... Aren't I supposed to be a "man" now?

INARA
A man's just a boy who's old enough to ask that question. Our time together, it's a ritual, a symbol. It means something to your father. I hope it was not entirely forgettable for you...

FESS
Oh, no, it was...

INARA
But it doesn't make you a man. That you do yourself.

This seems to sink in with Fess. We hear a loud RAPPING at the shuttle door.

HIGGINS (O.S.)
Fess! Fess Higgins, get out here!

EXT. CANTON BACKSTREET - DAY

Mal and Jayne walk along the lane of shanties we used once before. Kaylee walks a distance behind.

MAL
So that's where the little "Jayne" celebration we planned comes in... Should give us time to move the goods back onto Serenity...

JAYNE
I dunno. I mean, do you think we should be usin' my fame to hoodwink folks?

Mal stops, turning.

MAL
You better laugh when you say that.

JAYNE
No really, Mal. I mean, maybe there's somethin' to this — The Mudders... I think I really made a difference in their lives. Me, you know? Jayne Cobb.

MAL
I know your name, jackass.

JAYNE
Did you know they had a riot on my account?

Mal turns as Wash drives up on the MULE, with Zoe.

WASH
Morning, kids.

ZOE
Is that Jayne? Is that really him? Wash — pinch me, I must be dreamin'!

Mal hops on the Mule, as does Kaylee. He turns to Jayne.

JAYNE
Hell, I'll pinch ya.

MAL
Just get on over to town square, Jayne. Your fans are waiting.

They drive off.

EXT. CANTON WILDS - DAY

Wash drives the Mule to a deserted back area of Canton, and they all dismount.

They clamber through the reeds, and come upon a steep earth-cut. Down in it we see a pile of CRATES, covered with a mud-colored CAMOUFLAGE TARP.

MAL
Here we go...

INT. INARA'S SHUTTLE - DAY

Fess is sitting down in the shuttle. Inara is cleaning up tea stuff.

INARA
A criminal hearing?

FESS
My father's ordered me to attend. See, there was this man... It happened when I was growing up here. He stole a ton of money from my dad, and gave it to the poor, to my father's workers. And he's become kind of a folk hero in Canton.

INARA
Go on.

JEWEL STAITE

I remember the most riding of the Mule that we had to do was in 'Jaynestown'. It was in this dusty desert part of California, and was just gross. There was sand everywhere, in my mouth and in my eyes and it was just so unbelievably hot, we were all just drenched and trying to hang onto the Mule with sweaty hands. It was always pretty precarious. It was like a dirt bike, but much larger. Alan was always behind the wheel, which made me totally nervous, because he'd decide to slam on the gas and take us for a spin. It was difficult to hang on — I was so paranoid of falling off that thing. I'd broken my collarbone about a year before, falling off something else, and my doctor had told me that it would only take the slightest fall for it to re-break. That was the worst pain ever. I was hanging onto the back going, 'I'm going to wipe out and break my collarbone again, I just know it...' Gina said, 'Just grab onto me.' So I'm hanging on in the back, and Joss says, 'Why are you clutching Gina's can? It's weird — we can see it in the shot. Don't do that!'

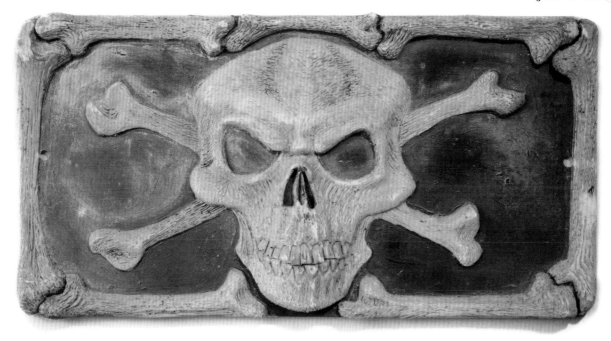

THE MULE

Production designer Carey Meyer: "We had a little ATV, an all-terrain vehicle, a four-wheel job, and really, it was just the cheapest thing that we could come up with [laughs] that we could actually have an actor drive. We created a little wagon that could connect to it and drag stuff around, and then of course we tried to art-direct it and make it feel like Serenity; but there wasn't a big process in the design to that end, it was very much an ATV that we could get quite inexpensively and then dress up and it actually worked. However, everybody felt cheated that we went with that concept and that's why, in 'Heart of Gold', we created the floating car for the main character."

❖ Above: The Mule's license plate.

FESS
Well, he's back. Apparently he landed here yesterday.

INARA
Yesterday.
(sighs, to herself)
Oh, no.
(to Fess)
I know this man. He's — he just has this idiotic sense of nobility, you know? He can never just let things be — He thinks he's this hard-hearted criminal, and he can be unrelenting... but there's a side to him that is so...

FESS
You mean you actually know Jayne?

You could knock her over with a feather.

INARA
Jayne? Jayne Cobb? You're talking about Jayne Cobb.

FESS
Yes. Jayne Cobb, the Hero of Canton. The only person I ever saw who stood up to my father.

INARA
I — wha — nnn?

FESS
My dad traced him back to his ship. He had Port Control put a land-lock on it. Jayne'll get back and find out he's grounded. I sort of hate the idea of his getting caught.

INARA
(still thrown)
Yes. That would be bad.

INT. CANTON TAVERN - DAY

Simon picks through a plate of MUDDER FOOD, nose wrinkling at every greasy item on it.

SIMON
Uh... Ahem, could I just get the — the check, please?

Then he sees that the bartender is gone. The door SLAMS open. Stitch Hessian stands in the doorway, backlit.

STITCH
Heard tell you run with Jayne Cobb...

Simon, squinting into the daylight, with Stitch's shadow falling over him.

SIMON
Excuse me?

STITCH
You're gonna take me to that dirty low-down shingle of a man...

Stitch strides toward Simon, who bristles, somewhere between affronted and afraid.

SIMON
Listen, "sir", I don't know who you think you —

Stitch backhands Simon across the face with vicious force, slapping him to the floor.

STITCH
Sir!? Look at me, ya' pantywaist idjit!

He kicks Simon in the guts, hard.

STITCH (cont'd)
I just spent the last four years steamin' in a hotbox and you're sirrin' me?

He kicks him again, then reaches down and lifts him up with one hand. Simon reaches desperately for a clay beer bottle off a table as Stitch talks.

STITCH (cont'd)
Folks say you're part a' Jayne's team. So —

Stitch pulls a SWITCHBLADE from his belt and flicks it open alongside Simon's face.

STITCH (cont'd)
Where is that no-good reptile hidin' hisself? You tell me, boy, or I'm a' cut off every last bit a' your good looks.

Simon brings the bottle up and smashes it against the side of Stitch's head. Stitch SLASHES THE KNIFE ACROSS THE BACK OF SIMON'S FOREARM! Simon drops the jagged bottle neck.

SIMON
Aaagh!

Stitch slams his fist into Simon's face, dropping him.

STITCH
(low chuckle)
Not done yet, youngin'... That's gonna cost you an eye.

Stitch whips his head around as he hears an O.S. chanting, down the street:

CROWD (O.S.)
Jayne! Jayne! Jayne!

He hauls Simon toward the door.

STITCH
Come on.

EXT. CANTON STREET - DAY

The Mule drives by, as its riders witness the MASS OF MUDDERS thronging in the distance.

EXT. CANTON SQUARE - DAY

Jayne stands before his statue, arms upraised, amid a throng of MUDDERS, who chant his name.

CROWD
Jayne! Jayne! Jayne!

The Foreman and his PRODS stand in a tight snarl of hip-boots and truncheons. The Prod turns to the Foreman.

PROD
Come on, sir, let's just get in there and —

FOREMAN
No. Magistrate says no, so we hold position. Understand me?

The Prod and his ilk are chomping at the bit.

INT. SERENITY - CARGO BAY - DAY

ACCESS FILE:

THE MUDDERS

Costume designer Shawna Trpcic says that the biggest costume challenge in all of *Firefly* were the 'Jaynestown' Mudders. "We had to cover about 350 extras in mud each day and then collect those clothes at the end. We couldn't really wash them; we were able to anti-bacterialize the inside, so they could at least put clean clothes against the body. But it was pretty gross and muddy and really dirty. The mud is what we call 'clean mud' — it's a mixture that we made ourselves from a lot of different materials — and we splattered the clothes before the people came in. I had an ager, Julia Gombert, and she aged all the clothes and came out with us to the set and finished the job while people were wearing them so it looked more natural. We tried to use as much cotton as possible, mainly because a lot of it was rented, so we wanted to use something we could shake off and throw into the washing machine to save on the dry cleaning costs; also, to make sure we didn't destroy any fabrics, because we really had to respect our renters. So the costumes were cotton and wools — wools are pretty easy to clean, although they're not as easy to throw in a washing machine — and rubber, of course. Some of the stuff was from the movie *Waterworld*, which was supposed to be wet and gooey, so that was perfect, because it was already aged and it was rubber or plastic or something that could handle it."

Mal, Zoe, and Wash haul crates of STOLEN PROP up the ramp (off the Mule?) sweating from the honest labor of lifting. Mal slaps the top of the last crate with finality, breathing easy for the first time in a day.

MAL
Zoe, pack down this cargo. Wash, you heat up Serenity. We're blowin' this mess inside a' half an hour.

Wash heads off for the bridge.

WASH
Already there.

MAL
(to Kaylee)
Let's go get our wayward babes.

He turns and starts heading back out the door. Kaylee follows.

EXT. CANTON SQUARE - DAY

Meadows finally manages to quiet the townfolk. Meadows cries out.

MEADOWS
Speech!

CROWD
Speech! Speech!

A wave of public-speaking anxiety sweeps over Jayne, but he succumbs to the will of the people.

JAYNE
I'm no good with words. Don't use 'em much, myself...
(crowd chuckles)
But I want to thank y'all, for bein' here, and for thinking so much of me... Far as I see it, you people have been given the shortest end of a stick ever offered a human soul in this crap-heel 'verse... But you took that end, and you, you know... Well... You took it. And that's... I guess that's somethin'.

Jayne nods. The crowd APPLAUDS. Kaylee and Mal have just arrived.

KAYLEE
Wow... That didn't sound half bad...

MAL
I'm shocked, my own self.

The applause halts as A SHOTGUN BLAST EXPLODES.

Stitch stands there, shotgun pointed skyward and smoking, Simon, bloody, held up by the scruff. He hurls Simon forward, he pitches into the dirt, barely conscious.

JAYNE
(moment of disbelief)
Stitch Hessian...

STITCH
Hey there, Jayne. Thought I'd make ya watch

while I butcher me one a' your boys.

Jayne looks down at Simon. He covers for him.

JAYNE
Ain't one'a mine, Stitch...

Stitch looks at Simon, then at Jayne, skeptical.

JAYNE (cont'd)
(mirthless chuckle)
Where you been hidin'? You gone and got yourself lookin' mighty hideous...

STITCH
(laughs at it)
Yeah...

Stitch walks past Simon, squaring off with Jayne, about twenty feet between them.

The Prods and the Foreman look on. The Prods are jumpy, but they see that the Foreman is smiling.

FOREMAN
Yep. Now Jayne gets his...

Kaylee gets to Simon and gathers him up into her arms.

SIMON
Kaylee — ?

KAYLEE
Aw honey...

STITCH
So what's this 'bout the "Hero a' Canton"? Was I hearin' that right? Four years' lock-down can play tricks on the ears...

Jayne looks around at the crowd, their scared eyes, remembering suddenly he has an audience.

JAYNE
Ain't no hero, Stitch. Just a workin' stiff like your-self...

STITCH
(fit of cackling)
Whoo! Yessir! Now that is funny...
(to the crowd)
Yep. He's right, Jayne is. Fact, we used to work together, he an' I.

The crowd looks to Jayne, who seems to redden a bit. Mal gets to the front of the crowd, about ten paces from Stitch; he's too tuned in. He swings his shotgun at Mal, covering him.

STITCH (cont'd)
Now you let ol' Stitch speak his piece.

Mal raises his hands slightly. Instinctively, Mal knows he's dealing with a cold and deadly son-of-a-bitch.

MAL
(slight nod)
Go on, then.

STITCH
Whole lotta money inna Magistrate's safe, weren't there, Jayne?
(to crowd)
Got away clean too. But then our plane took a hit, an' we were goin' down. Dumped the fuel reserve, dumped the life support, hell we even dumped the seats. Then there was Jayne, the money and me. And there was no way he was gonna drop that money...

MEADOWS
He did! He dropped it on the Mudders!

STITCH
By accident, you inbred dunghead! He tossed me out first. We run together six months and he turned on me 'fore I could scream.

JAYNE
You'd'a done the same.

STITCH
Not ever! You protect the man you're with — you watch his back! Everybody knows that — 'cept the "Hero of Canton".

JAYNE
You gonna talk me to death, buddy? That the plan?

Meadows turns to Jayne, eyes imploring him. Jayne looks away. Jayne's hand is sliding up his side, reaching for the hilt of his knife.

STITCH
This is the plan.

Stitch lifts up the shotgun, cocking it in the same motion, and fires, square at Jayne.

Meadows hurls his body in the way, taking the blast full in the chest.

END OF ACT THREE

ACT FOUR

EXT. CANTON SQUARE - DAY

Meadows falls, dead. Jayne throws his knife.

Knife whizzes through the air and catches Stitch dead center in the chest. He staggers back, and throws the spent gun to the side. He and Jayne charge each other, ROARIN' LIKE BULLS.

Jayne catches him, they struggle. Jayne spins Stitch, shoving him (he's beginning to flag from the knife) back.

Jayne gets to his statue and starts smashing the back of Stitch's head against it. Over and over. As much as is showable, he Peckinpahs Stitch's sorry ass.

The crowd, Mal, our crew, the Prods, everyone is silent. Jayne rears up from the O.S. bloody mess of his ex-partner, and turns to Meadows' body, which lies in the mud near him. He starts to pick him up, but the man flops, lifeless.

JAYNE
Get up you stupid piece-a — Get up!

Jayne looks down into Meadows' open, dead eyes.

The YOUNG BOY (thirteen, from the end of Act One) stands over Stitch's body. He reaches for the knife...

JAYNE (cont'd)
(still to Meadows)
What'd you do that for? What's wrong with you? Didn't you hear a word he said? I'm a mean, dumb sommbitch!

(drops the body)
An' you don't take no bullets for a dumb somm-bitch, you dumb sommbitch!

Jayne turns back to the crowd.

JAYNE (cont'd)
All of you! You think someone's just gonna drop money on ya, money they could use? There ain't people like that! There's just people like me.

Jayne turns to the boy, who holds his bloody knife out to him. Jayne takes it, seeing the unabated reverence in his eyes.

Jayne's eyes go wild for a beat. He walks past the boy, to his statue.

With a MIGHTY HEAVE he pushes it back, top-pling it, continuing on out, the others following.

INT. SERENITY - CARGO RAMP - DAY

They jog up the ramp, Kaylee helping Simon. Jayne stalks in after them, head down, silent. He just keeps walking. Mal hits the ship's comm.

MAL
Wash, we're in. Get us the hell offa this mud-ball.

WASH (O.S.)
(over intercom)
Uh... yeah... I'm — uh — workin' on that.

INT. SERENITY - BRIDGE - DAY

Wash's screens all flash: "LAND-LOCK"!

WASH
(to himself)
<Goo yang jong duh goo yang.> [Motherless goats of all motherless goats.]

He hits switches all over, trying to override it. Inara walks into the bridge.

INARA
Hello, Wash. Has there been any problem with

take-off — ?

WASH
Is there a problem? Is there a problem?!

The "LAND-LOCK" message changes to "LAND-LOCK RELEASED". Wash sits up, calms down.

WASH (cont'd)
Uh, no. We're fine.

Inara just smiles as we hear the ENGINES START TO WARM UP.

EXT. HIGGINS' MOON - LANDING AREA - DAY

Serenity takes off, leaving this ugly-ass moon behind.

INT. HIGGINS' HACIENDA - DAY

Fess sits at the dining room table. His red-faced, furious father looms over him, barking. Fess smiles, relaxed.

HIGGINS
You did WHAT!?

FESS
I sent an override to Port Control. Lifted the land-lock on Serenity.

HIGGINS
I ought to tear that smile off your head! How dare you defy me! You — You —

FESS
You wanted to make a man of me, Dad. I guess it worked.

INT. SERENITY - PASSENGER DORM

River sits, reading intently — and ripping a page out, setting it beside her. Book passes, coming from his room with his taped together bible. He moves to speak —

RIVER
(not looking up)
Just keep walking, Preacher-man.

He does.

KAYLEE (O.S.)
You got to be steely.

INT. SERENITY - SIMON'S ROOM

It's darkish in here — intimate, as it's near bed time. Simon sits on his bed, a bandage on his cut forehead, a bit of a bloody eye. Kaylee touches his face, gently, as she talks.

KAYLEE
Can't be letting men stomp on you so much.

SIMON
Wasn't exactly a plan...

KAYLEE
You ain't weak — You couldn't beat him back? Or would that not be "appropriate"?

SIMON
You're never letting go of that, are you?

KAYLEE
Well you confound me some, is all. You like me well enough, we get along, and then you go all stiff.

SIMON
(misunderstanding)
I'm not — I didn't —

KAYLEE
See? You're doing it right now! What's so damn important about bein' proper? Don't mean noth-in' out here in the black.

SIMON
It means more out here. It's all I have. My way of being, polite or however — it's the only way I have of showing you that I like you. Of showing you respect.

A beat as she takes this in.

KAYLEE
So when we made love last night —

SIMON
(ack!)
When we what?

KAYLEE
(laughing)
You really are such an easy mark.

INT. SERENITY - CARGO BAY - NIGHT

Jayne stands looking at his knife on the catwalk above the bay. Mal walks in, Jayne sees him, sheaths the knife. Mal rests his hands on the rail by him. Then, after a long beat.

JAYNE
Don't make no sense.
(beat)
Why the hell'd that Mudder go an' do that, Mal? Jumpin' in front a' that shotgun blast. Weren't a one of them understood what happened out there — hell, they're probably stickin' that statue right back up.

MAL
Most like.

JAYNE
Don't know why that eats at me so...

MAL
It's my estimation that every man ever got a' stat-ue made of him was one kind of sommbitch or another. Ain't about you, Jayne. 'Bout what they need.

Beat as Jayne takes this in. Neither man moves.

JAYNE
Don't make no sense.

END OF SHOW

THE BALLAD OF SERENITY

The Firefly Theme Song

JOSS WHEDON

I think you can sum up the compromise we made with the network in terms of the theme song, which has kind of a pumped-up orchestration for what it is. It's a very downbeat song. It should have been one guy and a twangy acoustic guitar, really dampened, and instead, it's almost like the theme for an action show. It's got all these instruments and all this momentum; it's a little bigger than that song actually should be. It's well-done, it's well-produced, it's not a dig. Quite frankly, I thought they were going to make me throw it out [laughs] — I was amazed they let me do it at all. But we were worried and there was some talk about, 'Well, we want to make sure that it's peppy.' Because it was written as a very downbeat number, before the pilot. The day I sold the idea of the show to the network, I came home and wrote that song, then started work on the pilot. It's a song of life in defeat, and that's kind of what the show is about. It's about people who have been either economically or politically or emotionally beaten down in one way or another and how they cling to each other and how they fail each other and how they rebuild themselves. I wrote it so that it could be sung as a Civil War lament, and yet — 'Take me out in the black' could be space, could be death. It's basically a way of saying, 'We've lost.' Which is not usually what you come in humming in most of your shows.

GREG EDMONSON

Composer Greg Edmonson: "I did the arrangement and called all the players and got them in and we just worked it out as best we could. The vocalist was Joss's pick. He found this really interesting guy, Sonny Rhodes. Very famous people wanted to sing this, but Joss found Sonny and stuck with him. We had Charlie Bischerod on fiddle; Lee Sklar, who's very famous, on bass, John Goux and Craig Stull played guitar, and Brad Dutz played percussion. There are no drums, per se — it's a guy beating on found percussion — a hubcap, a can. We were trying to make music with what we had. We did cheat on the guitars, because we needed to tune them up a little bit, but that was the approach, not some big bombastic pop song.

"I think Joss always saw this as a lone black man sitting on the front porch, kind of like Leadbelly, singing this post-apocalyptic song. However, the network envisioned this as an action series and so they wanted a theme song [he imitates driving action music], 'Tonight on *Firefly*!' And so the final theme song was as much of a compromise as could be done and Joss still be able to live with it. And you can hear that if you listen. You can hear it in the way it flows and in the way it could have been one single black man with an acoustic guitar singing this song." Although, there are some swirling fiddles in there. "Well, there are *now*," Edmonson laughs. "That was the compromise."

The Ballad of Serenity
By Joss Whedon

Take my love
Take my land
Take me where I cannot stand
I don't care
I'm still free
You can't take the sky from me

Take me out
To the black
Tell 'em I ain't coming back
Burn the land
And boil the sea
You can't take the sky from me

Have no place
I can be
Since I found Serenity

But you can't take the sky from me

PRODUCTION DESIGN

An interview with Carey Meyer

Thanks Loni!

❖ Above: A photo of the original concept model of Serenity, which Carey Meyer gave to Loni Peristere.

❖ Opposite: This model of Serenity was formed using a rapid-prototyping method, by computer-guided laser from layers of laminated paper. It has the apparent density of wood and is finished in grey primer spraypaint. It was used to envision scenes involving the ship during the planning stages of an episode.

Production designer Carey Meyer was no stranger to Joss Whedon when he was tapped to work on *Firefly*. "I had been designing *Buffy the Vampire Slayer* for about five years," Meyer explains. "I'd come on as the art director in the first season and stayed on as the designer for the subsequent seasons after that. Joss asked me if I would like to work on *Firefly* and if I could put forward some concept art in terms of the design of the spaceship. He gave me a couple of pointers on what he was thinking, and so we started doing some concept boards. From that I was able to convince him that I could do it. This was in mid-December and we really needed to get a jump on it, because our shoot date was early February."

The design of Serenity was the chief concern, Meyer says. "Joss wanted it to have an insect feel, an ugly duckling feeling, a really battered, run-through-the-wringer feel. Also, he had very strong ideas about how the ship was constructed and put together spatially. He wanted the spaceship to be another character in the show."

There were a lot of discussions between Meyer, Whedon and Loni Peristere of CGI firm Zoic, Meyer relates. "We created illustrations from the concept model. From that, it went directly into somebody working on a computer, and going back and forth between myself and Loni and Joss, and that started to dictate how the exterior looked. We did build some of the exterior, mainly the landing gear and the faces of the two large jet engines, and so once they

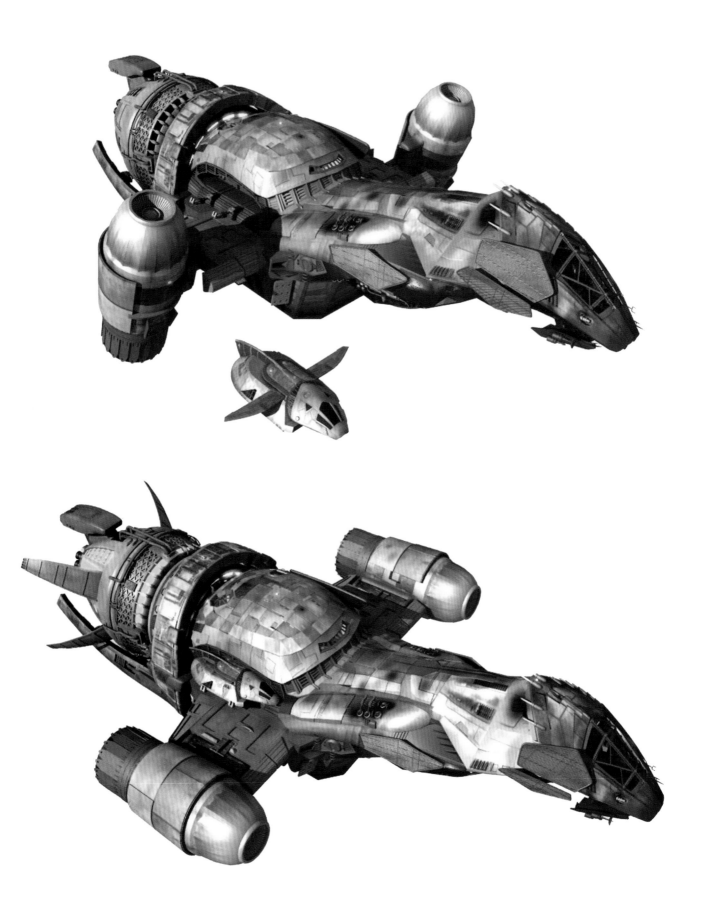

were actually finished in the design process in the CG environment, we were able to reverse-engineer that and construct a match to it on the exterior of the ship — where you had to have the cargo bay door that comes down and lands on the ground, the two large engines and the two feet that land in front.

"We ended up taking some very large pieces of landing gear and two arms that were extremely heavy from an airplane junkyard. Once we had located that large piece of landing gear, we were able to go back to the CG guys and say, 'Well, this is what we're going to use and we can add this, based on the design that you guys are working with, but this has to change a little bit to match what we've got...' It just went back and forth until we all locked in on something. So what did actually exist on the set were those two large arms that came out of the side of the ship and then came down to two large feet that were on the ground. We mostly hid them underneath set dressing, bushes or snow, wherever we were, because they didn't really look anything like what the feet of the landing gear looked like in the CG environment.

"We ended up filming pretty much only the interior," Meyer continues, "although we did build the exterior of what we coined 'the tortoiseshell', the very middle top of the ship, which was the dome over the galley. We built that, and the windows that looked into that room, for an episode ['Objects in Space'] where we really needed to isolate in-camera photography, where you had a lot of actors on the exterior of the ship.

"We completely built the interior and it mostly had breakaway walls, although, because it's such a very tight and complicated space, there were several areas where it didn't break away; it was not like an ordinary set, where you just have four walls and each wall can be removed."

It was Whedon's idea, Meyer says, to build one contiguous set for Serenity's lower deck and another for the upper deck. "Joss always said he wanted to try to go from point A to point B, from the front of the ship all the way to the back. I think even in the pilot, we tried to go from the upstairs all the way to the cargo bay in one shot.

❖ Opposite: A 3D mesh render of Serenity by Sean Kennedy.

❖ Above: The Serenity exterior on the *Firefly* set.

❖ Left: The design for the exterior of the ship.

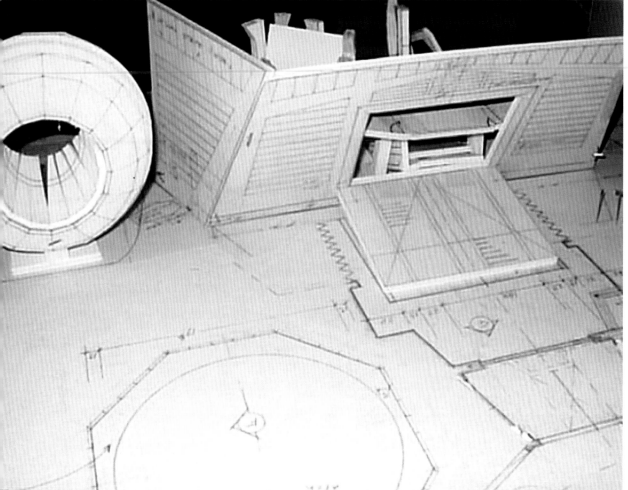

FIREFLY MODEL 01
REFURBISHED THROUGH HANG CHI YARDS

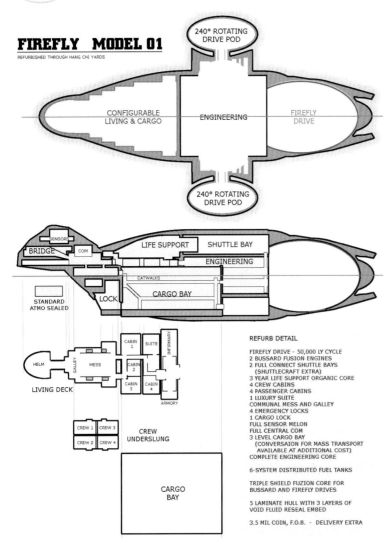

240° ROTATING DRIVE POD

CONFIGURABLE LIVING & CARGO | ENGINEERING | FIREFLY DRIVE

240° ROTATING DRIVE POD

SENSORS

BRIDGE COM LIFE SUPPORT SHUTTLE BAY

ENGINEERING

CATWALKS

LOCK CARGO BAY

STANDARD ATMO SEALED

HELM GALLEY MESS CABIN 1 SUITE INFIRMARY

CABIN 2

CABIN 3 CABIN 4

LIVING DECK

ARMORY

CREW 1 CREW 3

CREW 2 CREW 4

CREW UNDERSLUNG

CARGO BAY

REFURB DETAIL

FIREFLY DRIVE - 50,000 LY CYCLE
2 BUSSARD FUSION ENGINES
2 FULL CONNECT SHUTTLE BAYS
(SHUTTLECRAFT EXTRA)
3 YEAR LIFE SUPPORT ORGANIC CORE
4 CREW CABINS
4 PASSENGER CABINS
1 LUXURY SUITE
COMMUNAL MESS AND GALLEY
4 EMERGENCY LOCKS
1 CARGO LOCK
FULL SENSOR MELON
FULL CENTRAL COM
3 LEVEL CARGO BAY
(CONVERSAION FOR MASS TRANSPORT
AVAILABLE AT ADDITIONAL COST)
COMPLETE ENGINEERING CORE

6-SYSTEM DISTRIBUTED FUEL TANKS

TRIPLE SHIELD FUZION CORE FOR
BUSSARD AND FIREFLY DRIVES

5 LAMINATE HULL WITH 3 LAYERS OF
VOID FLUID RESEAL EMBED

3.5 MIL COIN, F.O.B. - DELIVERY EXTRA

❖ This page clockwise from the top: A diagram of the interior of a Model 01 Firefly; part of the exterior of Serenity; the corridor leading from the bridge to the galley; the infirmary looking towards the door.

❖ Opposite page top: The design for Inara's shuttle.

❖ Opposite page below: The design for the Reaver ship.

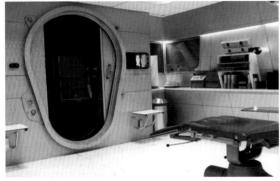

Obviously there was a cut, because we had to go from the upper-floor stage to the lower, but we tried to make it a seamless cut and make it feel like it was all one continuous set. That went along with the whole concept of trying to feel the space and not to break walls away, to try to light from within the existing space. It became an overall approach for everybody."

It was certainly the approach adopted by *Firefly* director of photography David Boyd, Meyer notes. "David was very interested in trying to shoot the space as it was and trying not to break the walls away for camera and/or lighting. David and I had a very similar approach in that sense. We both wanted to not only see but also light and shoot the space as it was. He went out of his way to work within the confines of the space, and to let the camera feel that. He went with Arriflex cameras, which are smaller, and he did a lot of handheld, so they weren't on a dolly — which takes up a lot more room and requires a lot more mechanics to move the camera around. So when you see scenes inside Serenity, a lot of it is handheld. That was a conscious choice, not only because it helped give it a more visceral feel and a documentary feel, but also because it really enabled you to feel the space a little bit more realistically."

Asked to sum up his *Firefly* design experience, Meyer concludes, "It was *the* most challenging project I've ever worked on and to that extent, the most fun I've ever had designing anything, and certainly the most fun TV show that I've ever worked on." ◉

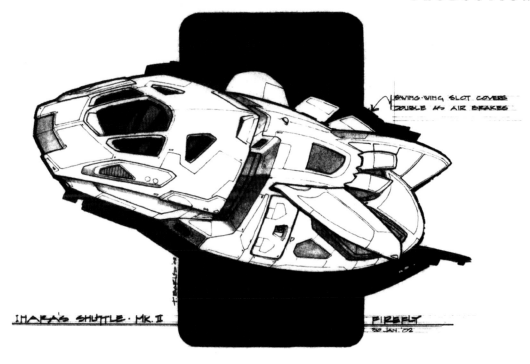

INARA'S SHUTTLE · MK. II

SWING WING SLOT COVERS
DOUBLE AS AIR BRAKES

FIREFLY
30 JAN '02

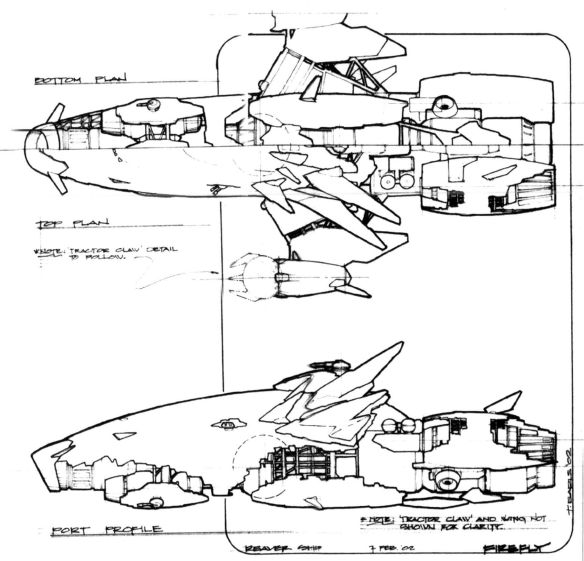

BOTTOM PLAN

TOP PLAN

NOTE: 'TRACTOR CLAW' DETAIL
TO FOLLOW.

PORT PROFILE

NOTE 'TRACTOR CLAW' AND WING NOT
SHOWN FOR CLARITY.

REAVER SHIP   7 FEB '02   FIREFLY

OUT OF GAS

Written by Tim Minear
Directed by David Solomon

TIM MINEAR

"It's my favorite," Minear reveals. "It was a really hard episode to break. I remember it took us days to figure out what it was. Joss had this notion of them running out of gas. He wanted to do an episode where they just got stuck in the middle of nothing. I remember initially his idea was that they would come across another ship that could be them, not literally, but another ship of possibly pirates. And to show what makes our people different from your average ship of pirates: that was what the story was going to be. I was having a lot of trouble with it. I thought it wouldn't go anywhere and it would turn into a play and I wasn't that interested. I remember we were having dinner, which we often did when we couldn't figure stuff out. We would go eat! Joss said, 'Can it start with Mal being gut-shot?' I'm like, 'Cool! Now, I'm interested... How did that happen?' We started talking about flashbacks and how it would be flashbacks to the core crew and how they came on board. It was that simple, and once we figured that out, it was pretty easy to figure out what the beats were."

The episode also reflected Mal's deep connection with and love of his ship. "His love affair with Serenity was in other episodes, so it's not like it was a new thing in that episode, but it's the way it starts and the way it ends. He is shot, and he's remembering the first time he brought Zoe onto the ship and talking about what it means: freedom, a life, tomorrow — it's everything. The fact that he won't abandon the ship,

Inara mistakes it for some kind of old sea captain chivalry, but that really wasn't what it was. It was, 'If the ship goes down, then I go down anyway. I'm not leaving it, not when there is a chance of saving it.'

"I've heard people say 'Out of Gas' should have come sooner, but I disagree. I don't think it would have resonated because you didn't know the crew yet.

"It's not that thick on plot. If you think about it, the story is really simple. As far as the flashbacks go, again they feel like they are moving the story forward, but it's in a very elliptical, poetic way. I do remember when we sent it to the network they didn't like it. They wanted it in chronological order and I had to try to explain to them: 'If you think you are confused, wait until you try to put this in chronological order. There is no chronological order! It's jumping around all over the place and it makes sense the way it's structured.' Basically, what I told Joss was that if they force us to do this thing, 'I quit. I'm done.' He said, 'I support you.' And then they didn't ask us to change it; I think at that point they didn't care enough about the show to fight it. My feeling was that if they don't get this, they'll never get it. We weren't canceled yet, but we were seeing the writing on the wall. We made a web commercial of Mal sending out a mayday for people to watch the show. We made that when making 'Out of Gas'. It gave us the idea to do the mayday actually."

TEASER

EXT. SPACE

Serenity in the Big Black of space. She might seem a bit cock-eyed to us at the moment. No engine movement. She's less floating and more just kind of hanging there. Either near dead — or hurt real bad. Reserve emergency power gives it just a flicker of life. As we nose closer, we peer into the bridge. No sign of anyone...

INT. SERENITY - UPPER DECKS

Various shots of the ship. Quietly holding silent images.

The cockpit: empty.

Looking down the body of the upper decks — no one in sight.

The dining area — evidence of recent habitation. A dinner party was in progress, but seemingly cut short. The table is askew. Dishes and an uncut cake have all crashed to the floor. But not a soul here.

The engine room. The entrance and walls are

scorched. The big turbine sits silent. No movement.

INT. SERENITY - BELOW DECKS

It looks like a tornado blew through here. In the common area: debris is everywhere, furniture is upturned, caught up against walls. But no sign of anyone anywhere. The ship seems eerily abandoned. Until finally we go to —

INT. SERENITY - CARGO BAY

More debris. More strewn cargo. And then —

MAL

falls INTO FRAME, landing hard on the floor of the cargo bay. Sweating, pale, somewhat delirious. And alone.

(We may or may not notice a piece of an engine part lying nearby.)

He struggles to stay conscious; it's a struggle he's not winning at the moment. As we PUSH IN closer to his feverish face, we start to HEAR what HE HEARS... VOICES IN HIS HEAD:

SALESMAN (V.O.)

Yep. A real beauty, ain't she? Yessir. A right smart purchase, this vessel. Tell you what, you buy this ship, treat her proper, she'll be with ya for the rest of your life.

Mal smiles weakly at the memory — or possibly the irony. Now the SOUND of the AIRLOCK DOORS, KER-CHUNK! A sliver of DAYLIGHT hits him in the face. The light UNFOLDS, growing, blinding him. He squints against it, as —

INT. SERENITY - CARGO BAY

THE AIRLOCK DOORS open, revealing two FIGURES, SILHOUETTED by sunlight, BLUE SKY behind them. (The ramp is down, and it seems we're planetside someplace.)

The figures step onto the ship — and now we see that it's Mal and ZOE. They enter the cargo bay. They might look slightly different than we're used to, because it's now a few years earlier.

Zoe steps deeper into the ship, takes it all in, as if for the first time. In fact, this is the first time she's set foot on Serenity. Mal watches for her reaction.

They are the only two here. The cargo bay itself is

now TOTALLY EMPTY. Big, empty and echoey. And everything's covered with a thick layer of dust.

MAL
Well?

ZOE
(after a good long look)
You paid money for this... On purpose?

MAL
Come on, Zoe. Serious. Whaddya think?

ZOE
Honestly, sir. I think you were robbed.

MAL
Robbed? What, no! What do you mean?

ZOE
Sir, it's a piece of <fei-oo.> [junk.]

MAL
<Fei-oo?> [Junk?] Okay. So she won't win any beauty contests, that's true enough. But she's solid. Ship like this, be with ya til the day you die.

ZOE
Yessir. Because it's a deathtrap.

MAL
That's not... You are very much lacking in imagination.

ZOE
I imagine that's so, sir.

MAL
C'mon. You ain't even seen most of it. I'll show you the rest.
(as they go)
Try to see past what she is, on to what she can be.

ZOE
What's that, sir?

MAL
Freedom, is what.

ZOE
(pointing)
No, I meant — what's that?

He looks down, sees something we don't need to see, something he was about to step in.

MAL
Oh. Just step around it. I think something must've been living in here.

As they move off:

MAL (cont'd)
I tell ya, Zoe, we find ourselves a mechanic, get her running again. Hire on a good pilot. Maybe even a cook. Live like people. Small crew, them as feel the need to be free. Take jobs as they come — and we'll never be under the heel of nobody ever again. No matter how long the arm of the Alliance might get... we'll just get us a little further.

ZOE
Get her running "again"?

MAL
Yeah.

ZOE
Sooo... not running now?

MAL
Not so much.
(then)
But she will.

He moves deeper into the ship, back toward the common area/infirmary. She follows. We don't, we stay in the cargo bay and let them move off.

MAL (cont'd)
I even know what I'm gonna call her.
(they're OFF SCREEN by now, fainter)
Got a name all picked out...

That last bit trailing off as their footsteps recede. We assume he's telling her the chosen name, but

now they're too far away for us to make it out. We do, however, hear a BURST of LAUGHTER from off-screen Zoe.

As the LAUGHTER echoes and fades, CAMERA BOOMS DOWN to a TIGHT FACE in the FORE-GROUND...

...Mal, back in the present day, curled up on the cargo bay floor, wincing in his pain... CAMERA MOVES down his body, and now WE SEE the wound... gut-shot. Blood, almost black, bubbles at his abdomen.

A thick drop of Mal's blood drips through the grating on the cargo bay floor...

...and falls into —

BLACKNESS

END OF TEASER

ACT ONE

INT. SERENITY - CARGO BAY

Where Mal's breathing is coming in sharp, painful gasps. He reaches for the fallen engine part that lies nearby. Grabs it and starts dragging himself back toward the infirmary. Above him, echoey GROUP LAUGHTER from somewhere in the ship.

CAMERA moves off the crawling Mal, RISES, passing through darkness, moving toward the sounds of joviality, the LAUGHTER becoming more present, until we are:

INT. SERENITY - DINING AREA

Mid LAUGHTER BURST from the assembled. A communal dinner. Or what's left of it. Gathered are: Mal, Zoe, JAYNE, KAYLEE, SIMON, RIVER, INARA and BOOK. Book has been telling them a story and they're all in stitches.

ZOE
(laughing so hard it hurts)
No, no, no. That is not true.

BOOK
I swear it is!

INARA
(catching her breath)
Surely one of you must have told him!

RON GLASS

The scene was that we were all supposed to be sitting around the table where we ate. It was supposed to open with everybody responding to a joke I had told, so they were supposed to be laughing really, really hard. The first time we did it, they said, 'action' and I started this laugh and I started to look around and get everybody to join in and they were all looking at me like I was nuts. So, of course, it takes a moment to hit that it's a practical joke. It became clear that Nathan has told everybody, 'Let's not laugh!' That was really fun and funny. It helped keep a certain kind of camaraderie and good spirits on the set. It's not in my nature. I'm not a practical joker. I can appreciate them but I don't do them.

BOOK
No! There wasn't one among the brethren had the heart to say anything. He was so proud of it!

LAUGHTER. WASH enters from the bridge, the guy who missed the joke. He smiles/laughs clueless along with them.

WASH
What? What was he proud of? Who he?

BOOK
(tears from the laughing)
Looked rather natty, truth be told!

Another explosion of laughter. It's contagious. Even for Wash, who's still anxious to be let in on the joke.

WASH
(as he sits)
I want to hear about the natty thing.
(reaches for serving bowl)
What was natty?

Book gets his laughter under control, takes a drink, waves Wash away with a "nothing, nothing" gesture.

KAYLEE
Shepherd Book was just tellin' funny stories about his days at the monastery.

WASH
Monastic humor. I miss out on all the fun.
(sees serving bowl is empty)
And all the food, too, apparently...

ZOE
Now just who do you think you're married to?

Zoe lifts a napkin off a plate piled with food.

WASH
I love my wife.

He kisses her. They sit close, a couple, easy and relaxed. He digs in.

MAL
So we got a course set?

WASH
We do. Took a little creative navigating, but we should make it all the way to Greenleaf without running afoul of any Alliance patrols. Or a single living soul, for that matter.

MAL
Good. Way it should be.

WASH
'Course, what should be an eighteen hour trip's gonna take the better part of a week by this route.

MAL
We're in no rush. I like an easy, languorous journey.

Kaylee rises, picks up some plates.

KAYLEE
What would that be like, I wonder?

SIMON
(moves to assist)
Let me help you with that —

KAYLEE
Not a bit. In fact, it's your turn.

SIMON
(clueless)
My turn...?

KAYLEE
Shepherd told a funny story 'bout bein' a preacher. Now you tell a funny story about being a doctor.

SIMON
Funny story...

JAYNE
Yeah, 'cos sick people are high-larious.

SIMON
Well, they can be...
(chuckles)
In fact, I remember there was this one time I was working the E.R. and this fellow, very upright sort of citizen, comes in complaining of...

JAYNE
(interrupts)
Now Inara — she's gotta have some real funny whorin' stories, I'd wager.

INARA
Oh! Do I ever! Funny and sexy! You have no idea!
(then, deadpanny)
And you never will.

Zoe SNORTS with laughter. She likes the dissing of Jayne.

INARA (cont'd)
I don't discuss my clients.

JAYNE
Aww, come on 'Nara. Who'd know?

INARA
You.
(then)
Anyway, a Companion doesn't kiss and tell.

MAL
So there is kissing?

She shoots him a look — and a half smile. He smiles back.

ZOE
Hey, Doc?

He looks at her. She's nestled nice and close to her hubby.

ZOE (cont'd)
(nods behind Simon toward:)
I think maybe our Kaylee could use your help after all —

He turns and is surprised to see her carrying aloft a sweetly pathetic ship-made birthday cake with miss-matched candles ablaze.

KAYLEE
Care to make the first incision, Doctor Tam?
(then)
Happy birthday, Simon.

EVERYONE
(variously)
Happy birthday! Yeah, many more. Happy birthday, son.

Simon reacts, taken aback. It's clear they all knew.

SIMON
Well this is... I didn't... How did you know?
(glances to:)
River, did you — ?

RIVER
"Day" is a vestigial mode of time measurement. Based on solar cycles. Not applicable.
(then)
I didn't get you anything.

WASH
I'm afraid it was me who ratted you out, Doctor.

SIMON
You?

MAL
Seems a fresh warrant for your arrest come up on the Cortex. Had your birth date attached right to it.

SIMON
Oh. I see. Well. That's...
(worried)
Really?

KAYLEE
(re: the cake)
Hope you like it. Couldn't get a hold of no flour, so it's mostly protein. In fact, it's pretty much what we just had for supper. But I tried to make the

frosting as chocolatey tasting as possible.

He looks at Kaylee. It's very warm and wonderful.

SIMON
Thank you. I'm really very deeply moved.

Kaylee beams her Kaylee-ness right back at him.

JAYNE
Well deeply move yourself over there and blow out them candles so we can try a slice.

SIMON
Right...

KAYLEE
Come on, Doc. Give a good blow.

He does a slight take. She's sort of poker-faced. He smiles, nods, leans forward, is about to blow out the candles, when... something makes a ghastly noise deep inside the ship. A GRINDING back near the engine. The power DIMS and FLICKERS, the engine stops...

A beat. They all pause at this pregnant moment. Then the familiar HUM of the engines again.

JAYNE
What the hell was that?

KAYLEE
Maybe just a hiccup. I'll check it out.

She sets down the cake on the counter. Starts to move off.

WASH
(rising)
I'll take a look at the helm.

Now he heads off toward the bridge. River is staring at the cake.

RIVER
Fire...

Simon glances at her, then back to the cake. The candles.

SIMON
Right. Okay, okay...

He leans in to blow out the candles and —

Kaylee is stepping up to the door that leads to the aftdeck hall —

BOOOOM! A horrific EXPLOSION from the back of the ship, at the engine room.

Zoe is on her feet in an instant. She lunges for Kaylee as —

— a giant BALL OF FIRE roils from the back of the ship, filling the aft corridor. Zoe shoves Kaylee clear of the doorway, but the big ass FIREBALL bursts at the doorway. Zoe is knocked back hard by the concussion of the blast, her body glancing off the dinner table, then hitting a wall — god-damn hard. Wash comes running back from the

foredeck hall —

WASH
Zoe!

Everyone's a bit disoriented. Wash flies to his wife's side. Inara and Book move to Kaylee, who was shoved out of the way pretty damn hard.

Mal has run over to the aftdeck doorway. Feels another ERUPTION coming —

ANOTHER FIRE BALL growing down there, exploding toward us. Mal forces the big metal door shut, latches it just before it hits. He's knocked back by the blast that impacts on the other side of the closed door.

RIVER
Fire... fire...

Mal turns, sees that Simon is already with Wash at the downed Zoe.

WASH
Zoe, honey, talk to me — you gotta talk to me, baby...

Mal passes Jayne as he hoofs it toward the bridge, pausing only long enough to say:

MAL
Seal off everything that leads below decks. Do it now.

Jayne moves to do that. Mal runs to the bridge —

INT. SERENITY - BRIDGE

Mal works some controls on the console —

EXT. SPACE

As the ramp lowers into space, while —

INT. SERENITY - ENGINE ROOM

The fire rages —

INT. SERENITY - DINING AREA

Wash is beside himself, has his wife's limp hand pressed between his. Simon's feeling for a pulse.

WASH
She gonna be okay?

SIMON
I need my med kit.

Simon rises, turns toward the aftdeck, sees that the door is shut.

KAYLEE
(shakes her head)
We got fire.

He turns, moves to the foredeck, steps up to —

FOREDECK DOOR

Jayne is just coming up from around the corner where he's sealed off that exit.

JAYNE
Where you think you're going?

SIMON
Zoe's badly hurt. I need my medical supplies.

JAYNE
Sorry, Doc. Nobody leaves.

SIMON
If you don't let me through, she could die.

JAYNE
I let you through — and we all die.

Off this stand off —

INT. SERENITY - BRIDGE

Mal continues to work the ship's controls, as —

INT. SERENITY - CARGO BAY

The AIRLOCK DOORS open, revealing the black of space and now —

INT. SERENITY - ENGINE ROOM/ AFTDECK/ STAIRS

The fire becomes a SNAKE as it is sucked down toward the lower deck, toward the vacuum of space, making sharp, violent turns —

INT. SERENITY - COMMON AREA/INFIRMARY

As the SNAKE OF FIRE races down the stairs, whips past the infirmary, furniture and not-nailed-down items getting sucked along with it, and into —

INT. SERENITY - CARGO BAY

The pillar of fire goes ROARING through the cargo bay and, along with some loose cargo, is spit out into space —

EXT. SPACE

As the snake of fire shoots out of the cargo bay, dissipating in cold space.

INT. SERENITY - BRIDGE

Mal watches through the bridge window as the fire shoots out, extinguishing itself in the void. He sighs.

INT. SERENITY - CARGO BAY

As the ramp closes and the airlock doors close. The storm is over.

CUT TO:

INT. SERENITY

Mal ENTERS from the cargo bay, staggering down the steps, every step more laborious than the last. CAMERA LEADS HIM as he reaches the bottom of the steps, turns towards the infirmary.

CAMERA ANGLES DOWN past Mal's face, down his chest to his midsection, where his bloody hand clutches at his stomach wound. Blood seeps through his fingers. He holds the catalyzer in his other hand.

He struggles to make it to the closed infirmary doors. He reaches to open the doors, and as they start to slide open —

CUT TO:

INT. SERENITY - COMMON AREA/INFIRMARY

BAM! The infirmary door is shoved open and Mal, Wash and Jayne carry in the unconscious Zoe, place her on the examination table. Simon gets right to work.

Everyone else is close at hand, variously in the infirmary and lingering outside in the common area.

SIMON
No sign of burning. Must be internal. I'll have to do a scan.

He starts hooking her up to his equipment. Wash at his side, concern etched on his face. Mal fades back, away from the activity there, to...

COMMON AREA

Kaylee is hovering just outside the door of the infirmary in the common area. Mal approaches her.

MAL
Kaylee. Kaylee.

She's in shock. Staring.

MAL (cont'd)
Look at me.

She does.

MAL (cont'd)
I need you up in the engine room, figuring out what caused this.

KAYLEE
(feeling it)
She ain't movin' —

Mal glances from spacey Kaylee to Zoe through the glass. His attention is drawn back to Kaylee by:

KAYLEE (cont'd)
Serenity's not movin'.

Mal realizes she meant the ship, not Zoe. Nods, keeping cool.

MAL
I know it. Which is why we gotta suss out what it was happened so we can get her going again, right?

She nods. Tries not to cry.

MAL (cont'd)
Think you can do that?

KAYLEE
Yes, Cap'n.

MAL
That's a good girl.

Kaylee gathers herself, heads off. Mal turns his attention back to:

INFIRMARY

Simon works on Zoe. Wash is at his wife's side, inches from out-of-his-mind with distress.

WASH
Come on, baby. Stay with me. You're strong. Strongest person I've ever met. You can do this.

JAYNE
She gonna make it?

SIMON
Please. I need to work.

Mal appears at the door.

MAL
Wash.

Wash won't look away from his wife.

MAL (cont'd)
Wash, I need you on the bridge.

WASH
Zoe's hurt.

MAL
And the Doctor's gonna do everything he can. Meantime, I gotta have you on that bridge. We need to know how bad it is.

Wash laughs grimly to himself, under his breath.

WASH
(turning on him)
How bad? It's bad, okay, "sir"? My wife may be dying, here. So my feeling is it's pretty damn bad.

MAL
Wash...

WASH
I'm not leaving her, Mal. Don't ask me again.

MAL
(no joy in this)
I wasn't askin'. I was tellin'.

WASH
(without looking back)
<Chur ni-duh.> [Screw you.]

Mal sighs. Reaches in, grabs Wash by the shirt, swings him around, shoves him up against a wall.

For all the physicality of that, Mal is calm, cool.

MAL
You're gonna get to the bridge and get us on our feet, because if we can't do for Zoe here, you're gonna have to be the one that saves her.

Well, yeah there's tension right about now. Simon continues to minister to Zoe. No one else says a word. Mal eases off. Wash's back is now to the infirmary door. A beat.

He goes, just totally fucking torn up inside. Mal looks back to the faces looking back at him, then he exits, too.

INT. SERENITY - BRIDGE

We're looking at Wash's pilot's chair. Empty at the moment. CAMERA moves off that to find... Wash on his back, examining the cockpit innards. His face is somewhat obscured from us.

He's speaking to someone who is O.S., also he seems much calmer than he did moments before.

WASH
Oh, yeah. This is all very do-able.

Wash slides out — and the first thing we notice is the big, bushy moustache. He stands and now WE SEE, outside the cockpit windows, BLUE SKY. We're parked someplace in the day again.

WASH (cont'd)
Shouldn't be a problem at all. A few modifications, get some real maneuverability out of this boat. You'd be surprised.

Mal and Zoe stand at the cockpit door as Wash looks the vessel over.

MAL
So you'll take the job, then?

As Wash sits into the pilot's chair, gives it a little swivel.

WASH
Might do, might do. Think I'm startin' to get a feel here.

MAL
Good. Well, take all the time you need. Make yourself at home. Fiddle with them dials. We'll be nearby.

Wash swivels away from them. Fiddles with dials.

MAL AND ZOE

moving away from the cockpit, down the foredeck, toward the dining area as they confer —

MAL (cont'd)
He's great, ain't he?

ZOE
I don't like him.

MAL
(taken aback)

CINEMATOGRAPHY

Director of photography David Boyd: "For the flashback sequences, we shot color reversal film, Fuji Velvia, to give it that very contrasty, old look, almost like our own kind of 'flash-backs'. If we look at our old home movies in Kodachrome, it would give it that idea. It's a white-white and a black-black, and the colors are very saturated, very vibrant and colorful."

What?

ZOE
Something about him bothers me.

MAL
(losing patience)
What? What about him bothers you?

ZOE
Not sure. Just... something.

MAL
Well, your "somethin'" comes up against a list of recommendations long as my leg. Tanaka raved about the guy. Renshaw's been trying to get him on his crew for a month. And we need us a pilot.

ZOE
I understand, sir. He bothers me.

MAL
Look, we finally got ourselves a genius mechanic, now it's about time we hired someone to fly the damn thing.

A BUFFED, SURFER-ISH DUDE, BESTER, passes through frame.

BESTER
(nodding "excellent!")
"Genius". No one's ever called me that before. Shiny.

Zoe doesn't even register that Bester passed by. She's musing on Wash in the distance.

ZOE
(musing on Wash)

Just bothers me.

INT. SERENITY - INFIRMARY - HEART MONITOR

Starts to BEEP AN ALERT. Zoe's hooked up to the equipment now. Simon reacts.

SIMON
Her heart's stopped...

INARA, BOOK AND JAYNE

looking on, helpless. Nervous.

BOOK
Maybe someone should get her husband down here...

MAL
No.

They see Mal has appeared. He moves into the infirmary. Simon's racing around the infirmary, grabbing things.

MAL (cont'd)
What do you need, Doc?

As Simon chooses a vial of something from several —

SIMON
(pointing)
Top cabinet —

Mal pulls it open. Sees a large hypo. Big needle.

SIMON (cont'd)
That's the one.

He hands it to Simon who doses it up.

INARA
What is it?

SIMON
Pure adrenaline —

Simon readies himself, poises the needle right

Adrenaline

| 35 ml syringe | Reorder no. 9662 w1886 | CAUTION! Sterile Destroy after single use! 急诊用时 | 药 | 小心 | Adrenaline Adrenaline Injection BP Adrenaline Acid Tartrate BP eq. to Adrenaline 1.0 mg/mL | 肾上腺素 | Reorder no. 9662 w1886 | 35 ml syringe | 小心 |

← PEEL AT TAB ← PEEL AT TAB ← PEEL AT TAB ← PEEL AT TAB ← PEEL AT TAB

❖ Above: The label on the adrenaline hypodermic needle packaging.

over Zoe's heart. Ready for the *Pulp Fiction* moment? 'Cause that's always funny.

Inara turns away.

Simon plunges the needle in. Zoe's body JOLTS and we

HARD CUT TO:

INT. SERENITY - INFIRMARY

MAL HOWLS in pain. He's alone in the infirmary, sitting on the edge of the examination table, wrapping a bandage around his midsection, it's quickly filling with blood. He breathes hard, then tries to rise. He nearly passes out merely from that.

He manages to steady himself, moves to the counter, rummages around in some of Simon's supplies — comes up with the big ass needle that we saw Simon shoot up Zoe with. He injects himself. Has violent reaction.

CLOSE — MAL

His eyes wide, wide awake. He blinks, fueled with the stuff. Now he moves to the engine part that we saw him dragging. It's near the door. He picks it up, but looks toward the infirmary door, as:

KAYLEE (O.S.)
Cap?

INT. SERENITY - INFIRMARY/COMMON AREA

Earlier that day. Mal turns away from the table where Zoe lies. Now the medical monitor beeps a constant, steady rhythm. The crisis seems past. Mal moves to Kaylee at the infirmary door. She looks pale, worried. Bad news a'comin'. They step into —

COMMON AREA

KAYLEE
Zoe gonna be okay?

MAL
You let the Doctor worry about Zoe. Tell me what you know.

KAYLEE
Catalyzer on the port compression coil blew. That's where the trouble started.

MAL
I need that in Captain Dummy talk, Kaylee.

KAYLEE
We're dead in the water.

MAL
Can you fix it?

KAYLEE
I could try...

MAL
Just get us to limpin'. That's all I need.

She looks at him. Nearly staring. Nods. He senses more...

MAL (cont'd)
What? What is it?

KAYLEE
Well. It's worse'n just the coil.

MAL
How can it be worse?

KAYLEE
Main life-support's down on account of the engine being dead.

MAL
Right. But we got auxiliary —

KAYLEE
No. We don't. It ain't even on. Explosion musta knocked it out.

MAL
So what are we breathin'?

KAYLEE
Whatever got pumped into the atmo before the explosion shut it all down.

Jayne has overheard part of this, joins them.

JAYNE
Mosta that oxygen got ate up by the fire when it went out the door.

KAYLEE
Whatever's left is what we got.

Mal takes a beat, weighing his very slim options —

MAL
How long?

KAYLEE
Couplea hours, maybe.

Now Simon appears, emerging from the infirmary.

SIMON
She's stabilized. I think she's out of the woods.

Off Mal, Kaylee and Jayne, not quite ready to celebrate —

BLACK OUT.

END OF ACT ONE

ACT TWO

INT. SERENITY - AFTDECK/ENGINE ROOM

Stillness for a beat, then... the ENGINE PART (which we will soon come to know as the catalyzer) is slammed down before Mal.

He's forcing himself up the stairs and around the corner into the aftdeck corridor.

INJURED MAL moves into the engine room, PAST LENS. We HOLD FRAME, looking (from the engine room POV) down the empty aftdeck. A beat, then...

...MAL APPEARS advancing from the dining area,

coming down the aftdeck toward the engine room. He's uninjured Mal.

MAL
Bester!

And WE ARE:

INT. SERENITY - ENGINE ROOM

— in a different time. Mal's looking for his mechanic (the handsome mechanic we saw earlier).

MAL
What's this I been hearin' 'bout yet another delay?

As Mal moves closer to the engine room, we can make out BESTER'S ARMY BOOTS sticking out from under the engine. Presumably doing his grease monkey thing.

MAL (cont'd)
You were supposed to have that engine fixed and us up and...
(as he sees:)
What in the name of <suo-yo duh doh shr-dang...?> [all that's proper...?]

Bester's shorts are... well, down around his army boots. He's having the sex with an unseen FEMALE. There is energetic humpage. Mal's a bit scandalized. Casts his glance away from the action. Might clear his throat.

MAL (cont'd)
Bester.

Much with the dirty humping. Mal gives it a beat.

MAL (cont'd)
Bester.

They seem to be, uh, finishing.

MAL (cont'd)
BESTER!

Bester climbs out, mostly still naked, yanking up his shorts.

BESTER
What?

Bester just looks to Mal. Innocently inquisitive. There is some deadpan staring on Mal's part. Oh, yes there is. Then:

MAL
You do realize we been parked on this rock near a week longer'n we planned?

BESTER
Yeah, but... there's stuff to do.

MAL
As for example that job we got waitin' for us on Paquin. When we landed here you said you just needed a few days before we were space worthy again and is there somethin' wrong with your bunk?

BESTER
What?

More impatient staring, then Bester gets it finally: right. The naked girl behind the engine. Bester laughs.

BESTER (cont'd)
Oh! No. Cap!
(leans forward "confidentially")
She likes engines. They make her hot.

MAL
Bester. Get your prairie harpy off my boat and put us back in the air.

BESTER
'Kay. But... can't.

MAL
Whaddya mean "can't".

BESTER
No can do, Cap. Secondary grav boot's shot.

KAYLEE (O.S.)
No it ain't.

Kaylee pops up, getting dressed. The men look at her.

KAYLEE
Ain't nothing wrong with your grav boot. Grav boot's just fine.
(to Mal)
Hello.

She drops down again, out of view. Mal glances at Bester. Bester's a bit flustered.

BESTER
(to Mal)
She don't... That's not...
(to Kaylee)
No it ain't!

KAYLEE
(reappearing)
Sure it is. Grav boot ain't your trouble. I seen the trouble plain as day when I's down there on my back. Your reg couple's bad.

BESTER
(clueless)
The... the what?

KAYLEE
Reg couple. Right here. See?

BESTER
No.

KAYLEE
This.
(Bester is still of the blank expression)
I'm pointin' right at it.

She rolls her eyes, sighs, reaches in, breaks off a part of the engine.

BESTER
Hey!

KAYLEE
Here.

She plunks the part in Bester's hand. She reaches back in, tinkers.

KAYLEE (cont'd)
Don't really serve much of a purpose anyway. Just tends to gum up the works when it gets tacked.
(re: a nearby wrench)
Hand me that, will ya?

JOSS WHEDON

Did Joss Whedon and/or Tim Minear always know what the characters' back-stories were going to be, or did they come up with the various histories when 'Out of Gas' was being created? "Pretty much came up with them," Whedon says. "I had a vague idea that Wash is the kind of guy who would just be hired, who wouldn't have an adventure; and we'd made jokes about the idea that Jayne had been trying to rob them when they hired him. I worked on this — not to take away from Tim — he wrote; David Solomon directed, did an amazing job — but the two of us worked out the back-stories together. Kaylee's — I don't know if I'd thought of that before and had it in my pocket, but it just seemed like such a delightful thing. Although, a lot of people were very upset: 'Why did they make Kaylee a whore?' they said. And I was like, 'I don't recall her being *paid* at any point.' She's just havin' sex. She's Kaylee. But, you know, a television audience is very... interesting. The Inara one was pure Tim. I wasn't really sure how to make that work at all and, god, I love that scene so much. The ironic thing is, I watched the second season première of *The West Wing* and they did the flashbacks, the origins, and I was like, 'It's a little early in the show to be doing this.' And then I ended up doing it in episode seven of season one. But we didn't start with the flashbacks. The idea was simply, what happens if we run out of gas? And the idea of doing the three-tiered structure, that was really Tim, of Mal trying to get the thing in and then save himself and then everything falling apart and everybody coming on board — we felt like in order for the emotion of the thing to be as great as we felt it was, we wanted to show what drove all of these people. It is my favorite episode — and that includes the ones that I directed — because I just think it's so beautiful, and it just *kills* me. And, of course, Mal's introduction to the ship, starting with 'The ship will stay with you for life' and then finding out it's not the ship that's being pitched to him. Which some people didn't get. But no, no, no, you don't go to a salesman and have him point out a ship. You see it across a crowded room, like Tony and Maria [from *West Side Story*]. And that's probably the most romantic introduction of them all."

(he does)
So I figure, why even have it? Better to just plug your g-line straight into the port pin-lock and that should...

She's done. WHIRRR the turbine starts to turn.

KAYLEE (cont'd)
There.

She shoves it in Bester's hand. Fiddles with the engine.

BESTER
What'd you do?

MAL
She fixed it.

KAYLEE
Well, it wasn't really broke.

Bester looks at the part in his hand.

MAL
Where'd you learn to do that, Miss?

KAYLEE
(shrugs)
Just do it, that's all. My daddy says I got a natural talent.

MAL
I'd say you do at that.

BESTER
(re: the part)
We don't need this?

KAYLEE
Not 'specially.

MAL
You work for your daddy, do you?

KAYLEE
When he's got work. Which lately ain't been too often.

MAL
And have you had much experience on a vessel like this?

KAYLEE
Never even been up in one before.

MAL
You never been... How'd you like to?

KAYLEE
(points skyward)
You mean...?

MAL
Sure.

KAYLEE
For how long?

MAL
Long as you like. Long as you can keep her in the sky.

KAYLEE
(getting it now)
You offering me a job?

BESTER
What?

MAL
Believe I just did.

KAYLEE
Just gotta ask my folks!

She pulls her hastily assembled wardrobe about

THE ENGINE ROOM

Prop master Randy Eriksen: "On the ship, Serenity, we pretty much got away with murder. I'd say, 'Okay, we need a box and some wires.' You know, Kaylee's up there fixing it, so we'd get some crummy hinged-lid metal box and some electrical wires. We used the same stuff over and over. I had these little blinky lights which were actually earrings, I guess. For the first couple of episodes there was blinky stuff all over the place; then, by episode ten, as the batteries ran down and the budget ran down, we'd look around and say, 'Look, there's one, over there', if we happened to spot one still working! David the DP [director of photography] was really great. He was hand-holding stuff and lighting stuff real loose. He liked the blinky things. If you had it, he'd use it."

her, pushes past Mal and a stunned Bester.

KAYLEE (cont'd)
Don't leave without me!

Mal watches Kaylee go, tickled. Bester just blinks, stunned.

BESTER
Mal. Whaddya need two mechanics for?

MAL
I really don't. Pack your things.
(then)
She got a name?

INT. SERENITY - ENGINE ROOM

MAL
Kaylee!

Mal has entered the engine room. He looks off screen, a little annoyed to see —

Kaylee is just sitting there. Forlorn. She's holding the same piece of equipment that Mal was dragging in here. But the one she's got is twisted and melted and screwed up. She stares at it.

MAL (cont'd)
Kaylee, what are you doing?

KAYLEE
I'm sorry, Captain. I'm real sorry. I shoulda kept better care of her.

KAYLEE (cont'd)
Usually she lets me know when something's wrong. Maybe she did and I wasn't paying attention.

MAL
(patiently)
I cannot be having this from you right now. We got work to do. <Dong-ma?> [Understand?]

KAYLEE
(re: the warped engine part)
Catalyzer's broke. Gonna need a new one.

MAL
There is no new one. You gotta make do with what you got.

KAYLEE
It's broke.

She just sits there. He gently makes her stand up.

MAL
Come on. This the part?
(she nods)
Well that don't hardly seem like nothing at all. Where does it go?

She shows him the spot in the engine.

KAYLEE
Here. But it won't fit no more.

He tries to install it, no go.

MAL
Then you gotta figure a way to make it fit.

KAYLEE
Tried. Sometimes a thing gets broke, can't be fixed.

MAL
Engine don't turn without this?

She shakes her head "no".

MAL (cont'd)
Engine don't turn, life support won't function, we don't breathe. You want to keep breathin', don't you?

She nods.

MAL (cont'd)
So do I.
(then)
Will you try again?

She looks at him. Doesn't want to disappoint. Nods. He smiles. Puts his hand on the back of her neck. Off this moment —

INT. SERENITY - COMMON AREA/INFIRMARY

Simon checks the still unconscious Zoe's vitals. Inara appears at the infirmary door.

INARA
How is she?

SIMON
Still unconscious. But her vitals are strong. She won't know it, but as long as her condition remains like this... she'll outlive us all.
(then)
She's using less oxygen.

He moves into the common area. Sits. She joins him.

SIMON (cont'd)
I always thought the name "Serenity" had a vaguely funereal sound to it.

INARA
I love this ship. I have from the first moment I saw it.

SIMON
I just don't want to die on it.

INARA
I don't want to die at all.

SIMON
Suffocation's not exactly the most dignified way to go. The human body will involuntarily —

INARA
Please, I don't really require a clinical description right now.

SIMON
I'm sorry. I just...
(after a beat)
It was my birthday.

He smiles wistfully. She smiles back. Puts her hand over his. Off this moment...

INT. SERENITY - BOOK'S QUARTERS

Book sits at his little table. We can see he's scared. Reading from the Psalms. Trying to find comfort in those ancient words.

RIVER (O.S.)
Don't be afraid.

He looks up, a bit startled to see River haunting his doorway.

RIVER
(re: his bible)
That's what it says. Don't be afraid.

BOOK
Yes.

RIVER
But you are afraid.

BOOK
Yes.

RIVER
You're afraid we're going to run out of air. That we'll die gasping.
(then)
But we won't. That's not going to happen.

He looks at her. Taken by her utter certainty. He finds a kind of comfort there. Well, that is until:

RIVER (cont'd)
(flatly)
We'll freeze to death first.

CUT TO:

INT. SERENITY - BRIDGE

Wash is at the helm. He's torn up with worry and anger. He's seething a bit. Mal enters. Wash doesn't even turn.

MAL
You get that beacon sent?

WASH
(much with the resentment)
Yeah, it's sent.

MAL
Good.

WASH
(under his breath)
Pointless.

MAL
What was that?

WASH
Nothing, sir. It's a brilliant plan, I'm sure we'll all be saved.

MAL
Getting a little weary of this attitude, Wash.

WASH
Are you? Well I'm very sorry about that, sir. I guess the news that we're all gonna be purple and bloated and fetal in a few hours has made me a little snippy.

MAL
It's possible someone might pick up the signal.

WASH
(pissed)
No, Mal. It's not possible. Nobody's gonna pick up the damn signal. You wanted us "flying under the radar", remember? Well, that's where we are: out of range of anyone or anything.

MAL
Then make it go further.

WASH
What?

MAL
Make the signal go further.

WASH
Can't make it go further.

MAL
Not if all you're gonna do is sit here and whine about it, no.

WASH
What do you expect me to do, Mal?

MAL
(building)
Whatever you have to. And if you can't do it from here, then you put on a suit and get out on the side of the boat and...

WASH
(voice rising)
And what? Wave my arms around?

MAL
Wave your arms around, jump up and down. Divert the nav sats to the transmitter. Whatever.

WASH
Divert the...? Right. Because teenage pranks are fun when you're about to die!

MAL
Give the beacon a boost, wouldn't it?

WASH
Yes, Mal. It'd boost the signal, but even if some passerby did happen to receive, all it'd do is muck up their navigation!

MAL
Could be that's true.

WASH
Damn right it's true! They'd be forced to stop and dig out our signal before they could go anyplace!

A beat as Wash let's what he just said sink in. He snaps:

ZOE

"Okay people, if it moves, shoot it."

At the heart of all the bickering and capers that take place on *Firefly*'s ship, Serenity, are the captivating characters and their dysfunctional family dynamic. One such character is warrior and second-in-command, Zoe Washburne. As one half of the only married couple on board the ship, Zoe and her husband, Wash, frequently draw emotional strength from one another while providing a fresh perspective.

"I have to say that I consider their marriage a very healthy one," offers Gina Torres. "At its core you have two people that really love each other and are getting to work jobs they both love and excel at. And Zoe can be vulnerable and silly with Wash. Their marriage is a part of the show that allows the audience to relax because they are so completely themselves with each other."

Nonetheless, that doesn't mean there aren't disagreements or jealousy. During 'War Stories' Wash looses his cool over his wife's professional history with Malcolm Reynolds, and her tendency to follow his orders blindly. Torres explains, "Finding that kind of unconditional love, support and understanding with someone is very rare. Zoe managed to find it twice [in both Mal and Wash]. I guess you can't blame Wash for wanting to be the only one."

At the beginning of the episode 'The Message' the characters briefly revisit their Unification War days. Torres remarks, "I suppose we could have gone on talking about the war, but actually seeing it was far more effective. "

That episode features a figure from Zoe and Mal's military past. When former ally, Tracey, betrays them and goes to shoot Wash, Zoe doesn't hesitate to take him down. "She loves her husband and will not stand for her family being threatened," states Torres. "That part is not at all complicated. I promise you Zoe slept great that night. Her former 'comrade' was always a screw-up with a gift for 'self-preservation', if you will."

Another key moment for Zoe came in 'War Stories' when Mal and Wash are taken prisoner by the sadistic Niska, and Zoe has to rescue the two most important men in her life. "At the risk of repeating myself, she loves her husband!" declares Torres. "And the rescue was great, mostly because we got to enlist the help of the other crewmembers, and not all of them were very comfortable with weaponry."

Despite the drama and intense emotions of 'War Stories', it is 'Out of Gas' that Torres pinpoints as her favorite episode. The story finds the ship in crisis mode, while flashbacks detail Mal amassing together his crew. "It's all that back-story interwoven with Mal's fight for life," Torres explains. "It gives us an insight into him, how he cares about and needs us. And it also contains some of the funniest writing we had on the show."

While playing Zoe, Torres had to endure much physical hardship fighting the enemy but as she recalls, it was her sweltering costumes that caused her the most discomfort. "The toughest challenge I met was shooting in the desert in 110 degree weather wearing our costume of boots, trench coats, leather and wool. Not fun. The space suit created its own claustrophobic set of challenges as well."

There's no doubt the talented cast gave 100 percent to *Firefly* yet they knew how to laugh too. Torres smiles, "At the end of every week, around six p.m., no matter what we were shooting, and particularly if it involved Ron, Jewel and Sean, a case of the giggles would overwhelm us. Finishing a sentence would become damn near impossible because anything and everything could set us off."

Dedicated viewers were devastated when their beloved *Firefly* was canceled so prematurely, and they weren't the only ones. Torres remembers that day well: "I was on the set like everyone else, putting in my day's work, when Joss came down to deliver the news. Of course there was the immediate anger and sadness but I also felt relief. We had been working for a few weeks not knowing whether we were going to live or die. I didn't realize how stressed I was feeling about it until the axe finally fell. I could breathe again. Unfortunately it was a mournful breath."

Thankfully, *Firefly*'s cult status continued to grow when its DVD sales rocketed. The sci-fi series proved to be a memorable experience that really resonated with fans. "I like to think that people connected to other people, not entirely unlike themselves, who were able to step up and sometimes achieve great things, and other times just survive in what were pretty impossible situations," concludes Torres. "That can be inspiring for some."

WASH (cont'd)
Well, maybe I should do that, then!

MAL
(snapping back)
Maybe you should!

WASH
Okay!

MAL
Good!

WASH
Fine!

JAYNE
HEY!

Jayne has appeared, forces himself between the two of them.

JAYNE (cont'd)
What the <guay> [hell] do you two think you're doing?! Fightin' at a time like this.

A moral lecture from Jayne. They both ease off. Cool down.

JAYNE (cont'd)
(as he turns and goes)
You'll use up all the air!

WAAA! WAAA! WAAA! A KLAXON SOUNDS and WE ARE:

INT. SERENITY - ENGINE ROOM

Where the ALARM originated. Mal, gut-shot, listens to the ship warning him that:

SERENITY (V.O.)
Life support failure. Check oxygen levels at once.

Then the same ALERT repeats IN CHINESE.

SERENITY (cont'd; V.O.)
<Jeo-shung yong-jur goo-jang. Jien-cha yong-chi gong yin.> [Life support failure. Check oxygen levels at once.]

Mal's bleary-eyed, fumbling with the ship part, trying to install the catalyzer into the failed compression coil. But he's having a fuck of a time.

He wipes sweat from his brow with the back of his hand — leaving an ugly smear of blood. He blinks it back. It's in his eyes. Shit.

The KLAXON continues to sound. The ship's message repeats in English again.

Mal nearly has the part installed... but it slips from his bloody fingers and drops into the engine. Lost to him.

He can't believe that just happened. And the alert continues to sound —

BLACK OUT.

END OF ACT TWO

ACT THREE

EXT. SPACE

Dead Serenity just hanging there.

INT. SERENITY - COMMON AREA/INFIRMARY

Everyone sits huddled together. They're wearing coats and blankets. It's cold. Mal stands before the assembled, grim. He's a bit distracted, tries to keep focused. A combination of the situation and the thinning of the air.

MAL
Well. As you're all keenly aware... seems we, uh, run into a... bit of a situation. Engine's down. Life support's on the fritz. And I got nine people here all wanting to breathe.
(tries to be light)
Could take turns, I suppose.
(thud)
But that doesn't really appear to be an option. Truth is... ain't got a whole lot of options at this juncture.

A beat. They all look back at him. Watch him as he casts a glance up at Serenity. Runs his hand along a bulkhead or wall. Then gives it an affectionate pat. Continues —

MAL (cont'd)
So now instead of focusing on what we don't got — time to talk about what it is we do. And what we got are two shuttles. Short range. Won't go far. But they each got heat, and they each got air. Last longer than what's left in Serenity.

SIMON
Long enough to reach someplace?

MAL
No.

BOOK
So... where will we go, then?

MAL
Far as you can get. We send both shuttles off in exact opposite directions — betters the chance of somebody being seen, maybe getting picked up.
(then)
Shepherd Book, Kaylee and Jayne'll ride with Inara in her shuttle. Doc, you and your sister will go with Wash and Zoe — seein' as Zoe still needs some doctorin'.

KAYLEE
What about you?

MAL
Four people to a shuttle. That's the arrangement. Even's the odds.
(then)
I'm staying with Serenity.

KAYLEE
Cap'n —

MAL
We sent out a beacon. Even managed to boost it a little. Now, if by some chance we do get a response, there's gotta be someone here to answer.

That hangs there for a moment. Nobody believes that's going to happen.

MAL (cont'd)
Let's get those shuttles prepped.

Wash stands, starts moving to the stairs near the infirmary.

MAL (cont'd)
Wash — shuttles are that way.

WASH
I know. But like you said — someone might answer the beacon. And when they do, I want to make sure you're able to call us all back. Won't take me a minute.

Mal nods. Wash moves off.

MAL
Jayne, get shuttle II ready. I'll see to Inara's.
(to everyone else)
Let's get moving.
(as he goes)
Take only what you need.

Mal moves off. Everyone's a bit stunned. Inara moves to follow Mal.

INT. SERENITY - CARGO BAY/CATWALKS

Mal heads up to the catwalks, moving toward Inara's shuttle. She appears, following.

INARA
Mal...

MAL
You fly smart, don't push too hard, shuttle life support should last you a good long while.

INARA
Mal, this isn't the ancient sea. You don't have to

go down with your ship.

MAL
She ain't going down. She ain't going anywhere.
(then)
Jayne'll be worth something if you run into trouble. But don't trust him, and don't let him take
over. You're paid up through the month. It's still
your ship.

INARA
Mal...

MAL
But so far as your security deposit goes... that I
think I might have to owe you.

He enters her shuttle. She follows —

INT. INARA'S SHUTTLE

Inara steps through first. She's wearing different
clothing. Mal steps in behind her. The shuttle is
either empty or dressed differently. Mal's showing
her the "property".

MAL
Well, here she is.

She glides in, takes in the space for the first time.

MAL (cont'd)
Nice, ain't she?

INARA
Smallish...

MAL
Not overly. How much space you really need for
what you do, anyway?

She ignores that, still considering the shuttle. She
moves into the cockpit. Blue sky outside the windows. Mal follows.

MAL (cont'd)
Got a surveyor and his wife interested in renting
it. They're just waiting to hear back.

INARA
What's her range?

MAL
Standard short. She'll break atmo from a wide
orbit. Get you where you need to go, bring you
back home again.

INARA
This shuttle — it seems newer than the rest of the
ship.

MAL
My understanding is this airlock was added some
years back. Certain modifications and improve-
ments been made over the course of the years.

INARA
Mmmm.

MAL
But she's space worthy. Like the rest of Serenity.

INARA
No need to sound so defensive, Captain.
(sliding past him)
I prefer something with a few miles on it.

He watches her as she moves into the main chamber, looking it over. Looking her over...

INARA (cont'd)
Were we to enter into this arrangement, Captain
Reynolds, there are a few things I would require
from you. The foremost being complete auto-
nomy. This shuttle would be my home. No crew
member, including yourself, would be allowed
entrance without my express invitation.

MAL
You'd get your privacy.

INARA
Good. And just so we're clear, under no circumstances will I be servicing you or anyone who is
under your employ.

MAL
I'll post a sign.

INARA
That won't be necessary. The other thing I would
insist upon is some measure of assurance that
when I make an appointment with a client I'm in
a position to keep that appointment. So far as
such assurances are possible on a vessel of this
type.

Mal blinks at all that for a beat, letting it register,
then:

MAL
That's an awful lot of caveats and addendums
there, Miss.

INARA
As I stated, I just want to be clear.

MAL
Well. I'll be sure and take all of that into consideration when I review the applications.

INARA
Don't be ridiculous. You're going to rent this
shuttle to me.

MAL
Am I?

INARA
Yes. And for one quarter less than your asking
price.

MAL
(like hell)
That a fact?

INARA
It is.

MAL
And you figure you'll be getting this discount...
why exactly?

INARA
You want me. You want me on your ship.

MAL
Do I?

INARA
Yes. Because I can bring something that your "surveyor" or any of the other fish you might have on
a line can't — a certain respectability.

MAL
Respecta —

INARA
And based on what little I've seen of your... operation... I suspect that's something you could use.

MAL
Fine. Let me ask you this: if you're so
"respectable", why are you even here? I mean, I
heard tell of fancy ladies such as yourself shipping
out with the big luxury liners and the like. But a
registered Companion on a boat like this? What
are you running from?

INARA
I'm not "running" from anything.

He looks at her. Doesn't believe her.

MAL
If it's Alliance trouble you got, you might want to
consider another ship. Some on board here fought
for the Independents.

INARA
The Alliance has no quarrel with me. In fact I supported Unification.

MAL
Didja? Well, I don't suppose you're the only whore that did.

She looks at him. Smiles, won't let this guy rankle her.

INARA
Oh — one further addendum. That's the last time you get to call me a "whore".

She walks past him.

MAL
Absolutely. Never again.

INT. INARA'S SHUTTLE

Mal moves about the cockpit, checking gages, dials, etc.

MAL
Keep everything set as low as possible. Don't waste what you got.

She pushes him out of the way, takes over.

INARA
Let me do that. You never could operate this thing.

He lets her take over. Gazes down at her. Now she looks at him. So much to say. He sees that. Feels similarly.

MAL
And try not to talk. Talkin' uses up air. There ain't no need for it.

INARA
Mal... come with us.

MAL
Can't. Four to a shuttle, Inara. Four.

INARA
One more person. You know it can't make a difference. Not now.

MAL
I'm not leaving Serenity.

INARA
Mal — you don't have to die alone.

MAL
Everybody dies alone.

WE hold on their look to each other, we PRE-LAP the horrible SOUND of the KLAXON SOUNDING —

CUT TO:

INT. SERENITY - AFTDECK/ENGINE ROOM

Gut-shot Mal fishes out the part to the compression coil. Works to fit it into the damaged engine. It takes some work, but he does it.

He fires it all up — the turbines start to spin. It works. The BLARING ALERT stops. Power restored. Life support functioning again. He starts dragging himself toward the bridge —

INT. SERENITY - BRIDGE

We're in Mal's POV, moving toward the seemingly empty bridge — but Wash appears in the doorway.

WASH
Everything's set and ready.

REVEAL — MAL (uninjured-Mal) moving toward the bridge.

MAL
Good.

WASH
I linked the nav systems of both shuttles into the helm, here.

Wash points out a LARGE, DISTINCTIVE BUTTON on the navigation control panels.

WASH (cont'd)
When your miracle gets here, you just pound this button once. It'll call back both shuttles.

Mal nods. Wash wants to say something. Everything's all fucked up. He's about to speak, but before he can:

MAL
Go see to your wife.

Wash takes a beat. Then exits.

INT. SERENITY - CARGO BAY

Mal walks with Jayne. Jayne has a duffle and some guns slung over his shoulder.

JAYNE
I went ahead and closed off all below deck vents. Diverted what there is to the bridge. It ain't much. So my advice, seal off everything tight behind you when you go back up. Might buy you some time.

Mal nods. He's looking up to —

MAL'S POV

Of the upper catwalks. To the left, Wash and Simon carry a stretcher with unconscious Zoe into the second shuttle. River follows.

Mal looks to his right —

Book and Kaylee enter Inara's shuttle. Inara stands at the doorway, looking down at him.

JAYNE (cont'd)
And I prepped a suit for you. It's hanging in the foredeck. When the time comes, you can just...

MAL
(cuts him off, though not angrily)
I won't be needing it, but thanks.

JAYNE
Okay. Well.

Jayne takes a beat. Then he moves off, heading up the catwalk stairs.

WASH at the door to shuttle II. He slides the door shut.

JAYNE reaches the top of the catwalk. Motions for Inara to go inside. A beat. Her eyes on Mal. Then she disappears inside. Jayne follows, shuts the door. Mal stands alone in the big, empty cargo bay, as...

EXT. SPACE

The two shuttles detach from Serenity, go their separate ways, off into space.

INT. SERENITY - CARGO BAY

Mal moves through the door leading to the infirmary, shuts up the door behind him.

INT. SERENITY - UPPER DECK

Mal closes off the door to the aftdeck. Moves through the dining area, moves into the foredeck, slides that door shut behind him.

INT. SERENITY - BRIDGE

Mal closes off the bridge. He sits into the pilot's seat. Sighs. And WE SEE his FROZEN BREATH misting. He sits alone. Staring out into the empty vastness of space.

The air is thin and he starts to get drowsy. Each breath is COLD MIST. The MIST getting thinner and thinner. He shivers. His eyes start to close —

EXT. SPACE

Serenity. Silent. Alone. Not moving.

INT. SERENITY - BRIDGE

Some time has passed. Mal looking half frozen and unconscious in the pilot's chair. He doesn't react

to the SOUND of a SIGNAL as it starts to come through on the console...

CLOSE — MONITOR (INSERT)

THE SIGNAL on the console. A FUZZY IMAGE. A MAN'S FACE through the mostly STATIC. Barely discernible.

CAPTAIN (V.O.)
(filtered)
Firefly Serenity... This is the private salvage S.S. Walden. Receiving your distress beacon, do you read?

We're only getting about a third of that as it's trying to break in on Serenity's wounded half-powered system. It continues to repeat and CRACKLE.

Mal sits motionless. Not hearing it. Maybe dead.

More STATICKY SIGNAL. More CRACKLING. But now Mal starts to stir slightly. A few more WORDS of the DISTRESS REPLY crackle through...

Mal forces his heavy-lidded eyes open just as... The transmission ends. No more signal.

Mal tries to orient himself. Did he hear something? His head lolls as he looks to the now silent monitors. Could have been a dream. His bleary eyes shift up to the window —

ANOTHER SHIP

TWICE THE SIZE OF SERENITY rises up there, right the fuck in front of the window. Which is as good a place as any for —

BLACK OUT.

END OF ACT THREE

MUSIC

Composer Greg Edmonson: "That was a terribly emotional episode. The main thing I remember about the music is that even during the opening scene everything is still and everything is quiet, because the ship's dead at that point. And so the music needed to convey that feeling. There were lots of scenes, once everyone left, of Mal walking through the ship. There's a scene when he does everything he can do, nothing works, and he finally goes to his cabin to prepare to die. He is prepared to die — he's going down with his ship. So the music wasn't meant to do anything but just be part of that."

ACT FOUR

EXT. SPACE

The S.S. Walden nose-to-nose with the smaller Serenity.

INT. SERENITY - BRIDGE

Mal on the bridge. WE SEE the IMAGE of the CAPTAIN of the Walden on the vid monitor. A serious sort; Mal without the funny. Mal does his best to keep up, but lack of oxygen and the extreme cold aren't helping.

CAPTAIN
I'm sorry for your troubles, Captain. They sound many. But you do understand I can't invite you on board my vessel. I got folks here to consider. They depend on me to make the right choices. And I don't know you.

MAL
I'd do the same myself, were the situation reversed. 'Course, one of my idiot crew'd probably talk me into changing my mind... You got idiots?

CAPTAIN
No.

MAL
Well I'm not looking for a ride, Captain. Just a little push is all.

CAPTAIN
Right. Your mechanical trouble. Compression coil, you say?

MAL
It was the catalyzer.

JEWEL STAITE

I thought that was one of our strongest episodes. Joss came up with some amazing philosophical ideas for that one. I think it's really poignant, especially the scene where Mal tells us to get into the two different shuttles and split up and there's that shot of the ship alone and the two shuttles flying away in opposite directions. I cry every time I watch that episode. I love it.

CAPTAIN
Not even the coil? Catalyzer's a nothing part, Captain.

MAL
It's nothing til you don't got one. Then it appears to be everything.

CAPTAIN
It is possible we might have something that'd do you. We just come from a big salvage job off Ita Moon. Picked the bones'a half a dozen junk heaps not unlike the one you're sittin' in.

MAL
Mmmm.

CAPTAIN
I suppose we could dock, take a look around, see if there ain't some way we might come to terms. That's if we have the part —

Captain looks off screen, presumably at some unseen person speaking to him.

CAPTAIN (cont'd)
I'm told we do.

MAL
I would appreciate it.

CAPTAIN
Trouble is... how can I know for certain your story's true? Ambush could be waiting for me and my people on the other side.

MAL
You can plainly see both my shuttles been launched, just like I said. And I'm sure by now you scanned me. You know I got no life support.

CAPTAIN
(muses, then)
I don't expect to see any weapons when we board.

MAL
And I do expect to see that engine part before I open the door.

CAPTAIN
(smiles)

I feel like maybe we can do business.

FZZZT. The Captain's face disappears from the monitor.

EXT. SPACE

As the S.S. Walden's airlock attaches to that of Serenity...

INT. SERENITY - CARGO BAY

Mal, breathing very shallow, waits near the standing airlock door controls.

The Captain appears at the airlock doors. He holds up the catalyzer at the window. Mal activates the airlock doors.

As the doors open, there is a tremendous RUSH OF AIR from the other side — blessed oxygen. Mal nearly passes out from the drinking in of it. He closes his eyes for a beat, just sucking down as much as he can. When he opens his eyes again —

The Captain and his FOUR PEEPS have their guns raised and aimed at him. Mal's hands go up instinctively.

CAPTAIN
Check him.

One of the Captain's crew moves in, frisks Mal as —

CAPTAIN (cont'd)
(to another flunky)
Search the ship. Start in the cockpit, work your way down.

MAL
This what you meant by "ambush"?

CAPTAIN
(smiles)
We're just verifying your story.
(to flunkies)
You find anyone on board not supposed to be — you shoot 'em.

The Captain was hoping that last bit would elicit a reaction from Mal. It doesn't. As the lackeys go —

MAL
Thought we were gonna be reasonable about this?

MARCO
Reason?

No, that wasn't a typo, because suddenly we are:

EXT. SERENITY - RAMP/CARGO BAY - DAY

On the open ramp of Serenity and it's Mal and Zoe in an armed stand off with another gang — THREE PRICKLY BANDITOS, a grizzly fellow called MARCO their leader.

MARCO
(to his partner)
He's gonna talk to us about "reason", now.

JAYNE
Yeah. That's a joke.

Oh, yeah — Jayne's one of the members of the rival gang.

MAL AND ZOE — a brief, sotto exchange:

MAL
Which one you figure tracked us?

ZOE
The ugly one, sir.

MAL
(long beat)
Could you be more specific?

THE OTHER GANG

MARCO
Do we look "reasonable" to you?

MAL
Well. Looks can be deceiving.

JAYNE
Not as deceiving as a low down dirty... deceiver!

MAL
Well said. Wasn't that well said, Zoe?

ZOE
Had a kind of poetry to it, sir.

JAYNE
You want I should shoot 'em now, Marco?

MARCO
Wait until they tell us where they put the stuff.

JAYNE
That's a good idea. A good idea. Tell us where the stuff's at so I can shoot ya.

MAL
Point of interest? Offering to shoot us, don't work so well as an incentive as you might imagine. Anyway, we've hidden it. So if you kill us, you'll never find it.

JAYNE
Found you easy enough.

MAL
Yeah. Yeah you did, actually.
(then)
How much they paying you?

JAYNE
Wubba — huh?

MAL
I mean, let's say you did kill us. Or didn't. There could be torture. Whatever. But somehow you found the goods. What would your cut be?

JAYNE
Seven percent, straight off the top.

MAL
Seven? Huh.

Mal makes a "wow, that's pathetic" grimace. Jayne squints.

JAYNE
What?

MAL
Mmm? Nothing. Not a thing. Just...
(to Zoe)
That seem low to you?

ZOE
It does, sir.

JAYNE
It ain't low...

MARCO
Stop it.

JAYNE
Seven percent, that's standard.

MAL
Who told you that?
(re: Marco)
Him?
(then)
Okay. Zoe, I'm paying you too much.

JAYNE
Why? What does she get?

MARCO
Knock it off.

MAL
Look, forget I said anything. I'm sure you're treated very well. You get the perks. Got your own room...
(off Jayne's reaction)
No? You share a bunk?

JAYNE
(re: the other guy)
With that one.

MAL
Really.

MARCO
Jayne, this ain't funny.

JAYNE
Yeah, I ain't laughin'.

MAL
You move on over to this side, we'll not only show you where the stuff's at — we'll see you get the share you deserve. Not no sad "seven".

JAYNE
Private room?

MARCO
Jayne!

MAL
Your own room. Full run of the kitchen. Whole shot.

MARCO
Jayne. I ain't askin' —

POW! Jayne shoots Marco in the leg and instantly drops the other bandito (who was just barely starting to turn on Jayne) without really looking.

JAYNE
Shut up.
(to Mal)
How big a room?

Off that —

INT. SERENITY - CARGO BAY

The Captain with his gun trained on Mal. Now the others start to return to the cargo bay.

LACKEY #1
Ship's clear, Captain.

CAPTAIN
You check the engine room?

LACKEY #1
(nods)
It's like he said. Catalyzer's blown. That's all he needs.

MAL
Now anything that's worth anything's really right

ZOE'S COSTUMES

Costume designer Shawna Trpcic: "Zoe wore the same straight pants as Mal toward the beginning of the series and then we tightened them up and made them a little bit sexier as we got a little more freedom. But same idea — she's a warrior. She's not Xena, but we wanted to highlight her figure and her strength and her poise with really clean lines. So the leather vest fit tight and could resemble a bulletproof vest and actually acted as one in the pilot, 'Serenity'. So she was from the same background as Mal, but obviously different."

here in this cargo bay. You take a look around, decide what you think's fair.

CAPTAIN
Already decided.

BOOM. The Captain shoots Mal in the gut. It happens suddenly and without passion.

CAPTAIN (cont'd)
We're taking your ship.

Mal's eyes go wide and he sinks to his knees. Topples onto his back. The Captain coolly instructs his crew. Tosses the catalyzer to one of his men.

CAPTAIN (cont'd)
Billy, get this plugged in. Jesse, call Stern over here. You and him'll pilot this pile of <go se> [crap] out of here.

MAL'S POV

Looking up under Jayne's workout bench where there is a gun taped to the underbelly.

RESUME

CAPTAIN (cont'd)
We'll get it as far as —

He stops short as he hears the sound of a GUN being COCKED —

CAPTAIN'S POV

Looking down the barrel of Mal's gun.

MAL
(eyes on Captain)
Jesse, don't call Stern. Billy, leave the catalyzer.

CAPTAIN
(nervous, nods)
Do as he says.

The lackey with the catalyzer sets it on the cargo bay floor.

MAL
(to Captain)
Take your people and go.

CAPTAIN
You would have done the same.

MAL
We can already see I haven't.
(then)
Now get the hell off my ship.

And now the Captain and all his men back away to the airlock doors. Mal, through sheer force of will, rises to his feet, keeping the gun on them, moves to the airlock door controls. Hits the button as they step through. The doors shut.

And Mal collapses on the cargo bay floor. Exactly where we first found him.

EXT. SPACE

As the larger salvage ship detaches from Serenity and heads off.

INT. SERENITY - VARIOUS

The cargo bay floor, blood there.

The common area, infirmary, and the trail of blood left behind by the wounded Mal.

The engine room, the turbines turning with the restored part.

The aft and foredeck corridors, the trappings of the interrupted party... and the tell-tale trail of blood.

INT. SERENITY - BRIDGE

We find Mal. He's dragging himself to the bridge. He reaches for the button to call back the shuttles. But before he can touch it... he passes out.

BLACKNESS.

UP FROM BLACKNESS

VOICES. Familiar voices. Growing more present as Mal wakes in —

INT. SERENITY - INFIRMARY

Mal blinks as he sees —

Simon, Book, Inara, Jayne... then River, then Wash, and finally even Zoe, who's sitting up nearby. No

one (save maybe Zoe) is directly facing him. Various backs to him. They're in conversation, though since we're in Mal's POV we can't quite make out what they're saying. Zoe's the first to notice that Mal's come into consciousness.

ZOE
Welcome back, sir.

The others follow her look, see he's waking up.

MAL
(disoriented)
I go someplace?

BOOK
Very nearly.

INARA
We thought we'd lost you.

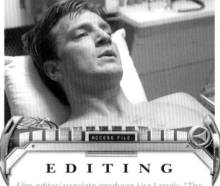

EDITING

Film editor/associate producer Lisa Lassek: "The order of the flashbacks and the transitions between them were really well thought out. It was just like a puzzle, and all the pieces only fitted together as it was written. People always say, 'Oh, the editing is so great in that episode,' and I have to reply, 'Well, it was actually written perfectly to begin with.' David Solomon directed that episode, so not only was it really well conceived in the script form, it was beautifully directed; so that when it came to the editing, it was completely easy. In post we discovered how far to push the color in those flashbacks. We started with what we thought was a little too much and then we kept going," Lassek laughs, "until the color was really stylized.

"Sometimes Joss would see something in the footage, at the editing stage, that you would never expect, that you'd never got a glimpse of in the script. He said on 'Out of Gas', 'Why don't we have a sound montage before Mal wakes up?' It was a brilliant idea and so fun for an editor. I went through the whole show and grabbed little sound bites that could have many meanings, and interwove them over black after Mal passes out, and then he wakes up in the infirmary. I did try to represent everybody, I really did. And I was also thinking — again, this is the joy of working for Joss, you can think, 'Oh, what would Mal care about?' or 'What would he be recalling?' Although you want it to be a dream, where it's just random and it's not meaningful, because that's how dreams really are," Lassek laughs, "but I did get a chance to think about bigger things."

SUMMER GLAU

I loved 'Out of Gas'. It's really sentimental for all of us. A lot of people in the cast and crew, even Joss and Tim, consider it their favorite episode, because it's the story of where everybody came from and how we all ended up on the ship — and how we stick together and come back. It still makes me cry every time I watch it. It's really important to all of us and I think it's our best episode.

I remember the night we were shooting the scene where Mal wakes up and we were all there, we were so tired and were getting really punchy and laughing so hard we were crying. It was probably one of my very favorite days we ever had shooting. We were picking on each other and laughing and crying and it's how I feel about us — we are a family. It's the story of who we are, I think.

MAL
(disconnected)
Been right here.

Mal notes Wash hooked up to an IV — he's giving Mal a transfusion. Mal, in his out-of-it-ness doesn't quite understand that.

MAL (cont'd)
Wash, you okay?

WASH
(amused)
Yeah, Mal. I'm fine.

MAL
Got a thing in ya.

WASH
Yeah.

SIMON
(to Mal)
Try not to speak. You're heavily medicated and you've lost a lot of blood.

MAL
Oh.
(then, realizing)
Thought I ordered ya'll off the ship?

The others exchange looks. Jayne glares at Inara.

JAYNE
(under his breath, accusatory)
Told ya.
(points to Wash)
It was them! They come back first! Their shuttle was already here when we docked.

MAL
(to Wash, trying to remember)
I call you back?

WASH
No, Mal. You didn't.

ZOE
I take full responsibility, Captain.

SIMON
That decision saved your life.

ZOE
It'll never happen again, sir.

MAL
(to Zoe)
Good. And thank you. I'm grateful.

JAYNE
(huh?)
You are?

Zoe smiles, nods.

ZOE
My pleasure, sir.

They hold the look between them. The original two. A special connection. Jayne observes that exchange.

JAYNE
Hey! That ain't... We'da been here first! But there's something wrong with 'Nara's shuttle! She done somethin' to it, Mal. Smells funny.

INARA
(heard this all day)
I've told you — that's incense.

JAYNE
Whatever.

Kaylee enters. Sees Mal's awake.

KAYLEE
(brightly)
Captain! You fixed the ship!
(then, a serious professional assessment)
Good work.

MAL
Thanks.

SIMON
All right. I have to insist. The Captain needs to rest.

MAL
(nodding off)
Yeah. I think maybe Doc's not wrong about that. Just for a few...
(forces himself not to drift)
You're all gonna be here when I wake up?

BOOK
We'll be here.

Mal allows himself to close his eyes.

MAL
(eyes closed, smiles)
Good. That's good...

As we PUSH IN closer to his face, which, if I can say, exhibits a kind of serenity. We start to HEAR what HE HEARS... VOICES IN HIS HEAD:

SALESMAN (V.O.)
Yep. A real beauty, ain't she? Yessir. A right smart purchase, this vessel.

EXT. USED SPACESHIP LOT - DAY

SALESMAN
Tell you what, you buy this ship, treat her proper, she'll be with ya for the rest of your life.

The Used Ship SALESMAN giving Mal the hard sell.

Now WE SEE that they're standing in front of a totally different ship. Not Serenity at all.

SALESMAN (cont'd)
Son? Hey, son?

The Salesman notices that Mal doesn't seem to be paying a bit of attention.

SALESMAN (cont'd)
You hear a word I been sayin'?

He hasn't, really. Because he's looking across the lot at something else...

MAL'S POV

Across the lot sits Serenity, dirty, a bit broken down... and silently speaking to Mal. Off that —

BLACK OUT.

END OF SHOW

YOU CAN'T STOP THE SIGNAL

Firefly Fans

Firefly fans tend to feel they have a lot in common with the Browncoats — in fact, that's what most of the fans call themselves. Like Joss Whedon's creations, the fan Browncoats have fought against impossible odds in the face of a dream-squelching bureaucracy. However, in the fans' case, the outcome has been lot better. First (and most important), nobody actually died. Second, fans helped raise *Firefly* from the ashes of cancellation into the feature film *Serenity*, arguably through Internet visibility and a letter-writing campaign and inarguably through purchasing the *Firefly* DVD box set in quantities that caused the project to be taken seriously.

There is even a fan-made documentary, *Done the Impossible*, narrated by Adam Baldwin and featuring interviews with many *Firefly* personnel, chronicling the history of *Firefly* fandom and the support for the nascent *Serenity*.

Jeremy Neish, one of *Done the Impossible*'s producers/directors, reckons that organized *Firefly* fandom may have begun with the *Firefly* Immediate Assistance program. "A couple of months before the show was canceled, they organized write-in campaigns to both the network [Fox] and its advertisers, raised funds for an ad in [the show business publication] *Variety*, organized fan viewing parties and invited the local press to them. From that point on, the fandom has grown. Though I wouldn't go so far as to call the cancellation of a TV show a tragedy, I would say that the sense of mourning created a powerful bond between complete strangers, who in turn directed their energy to not letting such a wonderful work of art die. Considering how shockingly good *Firefly* was in so few episodes, can you imagine how stunning it would have been by season three or four? I don't think any of us wanted to give up that dream — most of us still don't."

One example of what makes *Firefly* fans distinctive is an event known as the Backup Bash. It's not that something like this *couldn't* happen in other fandoms, but so far, it hasn't: a sold-out *Firefly* convention in December 2006 in Burbank, California, is canceled the day before it was it was scheduled to begin. Rather than stay home, the California Browncoats — spearheaded by Adam and Karla Levermore-Rich, Arielle Kesweder, Louise Du Cray and James Riley — organize within hours, find a new venue and the result is a three-day celebration with about three hundred attendees, many of whom have flown in from out of state or overseas for the original event, despite rumors of cancellation, having a great time. At various points throughout the weekend, Nathan Fillion, Adam Baldwin, Alan Tudyk, Morena

SUMMER GLAU

I have one little fan that I see when I go to England. She is just so special to me. She has been my loyal pen pal and tries to make it to everything that I do in the U.K. The last time I was there, she dressed in River's dress, when she fights the Reavers, and she had her sword and her axe. There was a costume contest and everybody walked across the stage. When she got to the middle, she knelt down in River's pose from the European poster. It was the most precious thing, and I was thinking, 'Oh my gosh! People are practicing that pose!' It is really amazing that she loves River and wants to dress up like her.

A D A M   B A L D W I N

Funny, what I found in my initial delving into the message boards is the intellect level of the fans of the show was inspiring. Their kindness flowed through it as well and that fascinated me. I have nothing but the highest appreciation for all of those people who participated in it and have taken the time to build up fan sites, fanzines, and everything that went along with it. It is really interesting stuff.

❖ Clockwise from opposite page: Summer Glau, Jewel Staite, Joss Whedon, Nathan Fillion and Ron Glass at the 2005 Flanvention; Christina Hendricks at the Backup Bash; Adam Baldwin at the Backup Bash; Nathan and Joss answering questions from fans at the 2005 Flanvention; Alan Tudyk, Mark A. Sheppard and Nathan Fillion enjoying the Backup Bash.

Baccarin, Ron Glass, Christina Hendricks, Michael Fairman, Mark A. Sheppard and Jonathan M. Woodward variously sign autographs, pose for pictures and just hang out with fans, as does *Firefly* executive producer (with Joss Whedon) Tim Minear, 'Trash' episode and *Firefly* comics writer Brett Matthews, composer Greg Edmonson, costume designer Shawna Trpcic, *Serenity* actors Yan Feldman and Rob Lee and *Serenity* graphics designer Geoffrey Mandel. Even actors from *Buffy* are on hand, including Clare Kramer — whose husband Brian Keathley opened his La Cantina Restaurant on Hollywood Boulevard to the Bash's Saturday night shindig — Camden Toy, James Leary and Robia LaMorte; while Corey Bridges talked about *Firefly*'s future as a licensed Massively Multiplayer Online game from Multiverse.net, beta-launching in 2008.

Amy Mayrhofer, one of the fans who traveled cross-country even after learning of the original event's cancellation, says, "We still wanted to come because the fans are such a great family and we heard that the California Browncoats were going to throw a great party no matter what, and it's so kind of the actors to come and donate their time."

Mark A. Sheppard says, "We love to have a good time, and the idea of canceling something is not a good time, so we'll do everything that we can to make it a good time."

Jonathan M. Woodward says he enjoys the vibe the fans create in each other's company. "I did a four-day shoot in 2002. I had no idea that it was going to become such a family, such a group, such a commitment and such a blessing. I just like being around people who are so excited to see each other."

"It was so amazing to see the sheer joy on people's faces when [the actors and creative personnel] showed up," says Backup Bash organizer Adam Levermore-Rich.

N A T H A N   F I L L I O N

When we got canceled I wrote in a blog to say, 'Hey, if you ever see me on the street I know you want to come up to me and say, "Why did your show get canceled, it shouldn't have gotten canceled, I think this and blah blah blah."' And I said, 'You know what, it's a little close to my heart. You don't have to say all that. If you see me on the street, all you have to do' — and one guy did it, it was awesome — I said, 'is nod and say, "Captain".'

"The fact that there are so many people willing to step up within twenty-four hours, just the outpouring of support and a willingness to look out for each other is just inspiring."

"*Firefly* attracts people like this," says *Done the Impossible*'s Tony Headlock. "It took somebody like Joss Whedon and something like *Firefly* to bring us out of the woodwork. And it turns out that [*Firefly* fans] are not just good people, they're some of the best people I've ever met."

ARIEL

Written by Jose Molina
Directed by Allan Kroeker

JOSE MOLINA

Writer Jose Molina says, "Joss wanted to do a story where Simon hired the crew to rob a hospital so that he can get River onto a machine and look at her brain. Ben Edlund was waist-deep in 'Jaynestown', so Brett Matthews, Cheryl Cain and I holed up in my office to break 'Ariel', and every few days, Joss would come around and hear what we had."

In the sequence where Mal, Zoe and Jayne are trying to memorize the spiel Simon gives them, Molina says, "A good chunk of that was the actors, especially Nathan, just being completely in character. A couple of times, he ad-libbed — he screws up at one point and goes, 'shiny'. But most of the screw-ups were carefully scripted. It's a testament to how good those guys are that they made it look as natural as they did."

Showing Simon saving the dying patient, Molina explains, "was to show how proud River was of Simon and to play out the tragedy that he was not being what he could have and should have been, because of her."

How was it decided that Jayne would try to sell out Simon and River? "What we didn't have in the original premise was a huge personal stake. We kept going back to the drawing board and trying to figure out what was missing. Then one day we came up with this brilliant idea. I called Tim and said, 'Jayne betrays Simon and River'. Joss was in the middle of directing 'Spin the Bottle' for *Angel*, so we pitched him what we had on the big hotel stage at *Angel* between takes. Joss being Joss, he had more good ideas in an hour than we had come up with in a couple of weeks. So after about two hours of that, we were done. Ben and I went and put the outline together on a Thursday night, so I had from Thursday night to Monday morning to hand in a draft.

"The idea of Mal punching Jayne because he realized what had happened was either me or Brett, but on the beat sheet was the idea that Mal just hits him over the head and knocks him unconscious. Ben said, 'What if, instead of tying Jayne up and forcing him to confess, Mal throws him into the airlock, and opens the ramp so Jayne's got thirty seconds before he's going to die.'

"It evolved out of Jayne's betrayal in 'Serenity'. There's a moment between Mal and Jayne where they talk about the fact that Jayne's loyalty lies with no person but with the payday. Mal asks what's going to happen when the money is too good, and Jayne says, 'Well, that'll be an interesting day.' So the idea of the interesting day was something that we talked about constantly in the writers' room and this was the interesting day.

"By making Mal so definitive, I painted the guys into a corner where Jayne has to say something really valid to save his own life. Being typical Jayne and offering money and trying to bribe him, trying to lie, wasn't going to work. But actually showing that he is a human being, that he realizes he messed up and that maybe he does deserve to die for his mistake and that he is truly, honestly sorry at the moment where he believes he's going to die, was the only way to get Mal to close the ramp. So it came from the characters just being themselves and not out of any master plan, just out of wanting to show Jayne's humanity."

TEASER

EXT. SPACE

Serenity in space.

INT. SERENITY - DINING AREA

JAYNE sits at the table, in his Blue Sun shirt, cleaning a pistol. At the coffee table, KAYLEE and INARA play a kind of two-person mah jong. In the kitchen area, SIMON takes a pot from a burner and spoons a sludgy gumbo into one bowl for himself and one for RIVER. She wrinkles her nose at it.

RIVER
I don't want it.

SIMON
River, you have to eat. It's good, it tastes like —
(tries it, it's awful)
It's good.

JAYNE
Smells like crotch.

KAYLEE
Jayne!

JAYNE
Well, it does.

They sit across from Jayne to eat, River mostly stirring her food around, her eyes often drifting to Jayne. WASH and ZOE enter, mid conversation —

WASH
We don't even have to do anything fancy. We'll just go to a park or something, feed the pigeons.

ZOE
Sure. We'll feed the pigeons... probably get the firing squad for littering.

WASH
Come on, it's not that bad.

ZOE
Yes, it is. It's a Core planet. It's spotless, there's sensors everywhere, and where there ain't sensors, there's feds. All the central planets are the same.

WASH
(to Inara)
Could you please tell my wife the fun she's missing out on.

INARA
Ariel's quite nice, actually. They have some beautiful museums, not to mention some of the finest restaurants in the Core.

WASH
But not all boring like she made it sound. There's, uh...

He kicks at Simon's chair: help.

SIMON
There's... there's... hiking. You can go swimming in a bioluminescent lake.

ZOE
I don't care if it has sunsets twenty-four hours a day, I ain't setting foot on that place.

MAL
(entering)
No one's setting foot on that fancy rock. I don't want anyone leaving the ship. Come to

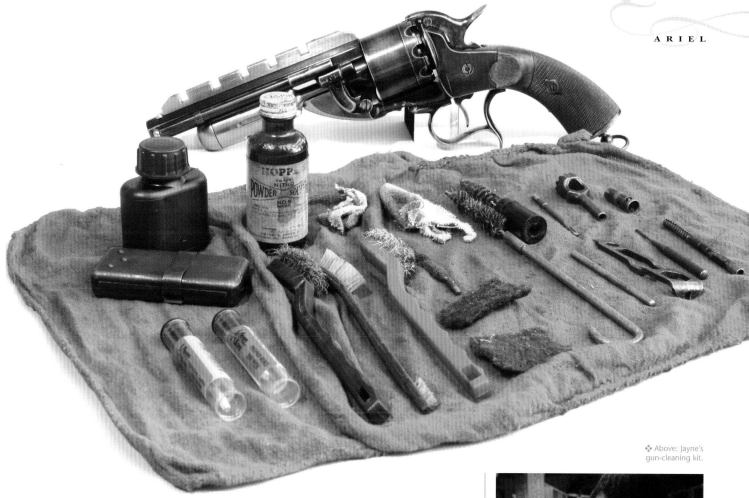

❖ Above: Jayne's gun-cleaning kit.

think of it, I don't want anyone looking out the windows. Or talking loud. We're here to drop Inara off, that's it.

JAYNE
What's the point of coming to the Core if I can't even get off the boat?

MAL
Could've gotten off with Shepherd Book at the Bathgate Abbey. You could be meditating over the wonders of your rock garden right about now.

JAYNE
Better'n just sittin'.

WASH
(you idiot)
It is just sittin'.

Jayne grumbles, puts away the pistol, starts cleaning his knife.

ZOE
(to Inara)
How long you going to be planetside?

INARA
Shouldn't be more than a day or two.

WASH
Big stop just to renew your license to Companion... Can I use "Companion" as a verb?

INARA
It's Guild law. All Companions are required to undergo a physical exam once a year.

Jayne spits a large glob of saliva on his blade, wipes it on his shirt, shining it.

SIMON
Could you not do that while...
(beat)
...ever.

Jayne looks him square in the eye, then does it again. Simon moves down the table. River gets up and goes to the kitchen. Wash resumes his train of thought —

WASH
So, two days in a hospital, huh?
(Inara nods)
That's awful. Don't you just hate doctors?

SIMON
Hey!

WASH
I mean, present company excluded.

JAYNE
Don't be excluding people, that's just rude.

A blur. Suddenly something's coming at Jayne. It's River with a kitchen knife. She attacks, slashing at his Blue Sun t-shirt. Jayne barks, he's cut. SMACK! He reflexively backhands her

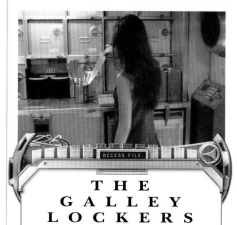

THE GALLEY LOCKERS

Prop master Skip Crank: "In the galley there were these aircraft lockers. Often a character had to open them and take stuff out. I'd always put severed heads and hands in them to freak them out. Gina would want to make tea, so I'd tell her the tea was in this locker — but I'd put a head in there too. Pretty soon they'd be like, 'What's in there today?'"

across the room. Bedlam ensues, and all of this happens in an instant: Simon and Inara rush to River's side, Mal, Zoe and Kaylee to Jayne's; mah jong tiles spill, food falls from the table, as the following overlaps —

MAL SIMON
Jesu — River, no — !

ZOE INARA
It's deep — Oh, god, honey...

KAYLEE
He's bleedin'.

SIMON
(shocked)
River...

RIVER
(matter-of-fact)
He looks better in red.

INT. SERENITY - INFIRMARY

Mal and Jayne talk as Simon stitches up the shirtless Jayne. Jayne is rightfully irate.

JAYNE
Gorramn freak's completely off her axel.

SIMON
I'm sorry about this. I don't know what she —

JAYNE
Shut it. I ain't talking to you.

(to Mal)
She's gotta go. Both of them's gotta go. Ariel's as good a place to leave them as any. Might even pick us up a reward for our troubles.

Simon shoots Jayne a nasty look. Jayne couldn't care less. Simon continues what he's doing.

MAL
No one's getting left.

JAYNE
She belongs in a bughouse. You don't pitch her off this boat right now, I swear to you...

MAL
What? What do you swear, Jayne?

JAYNE
They don't get gone... you better start locking up your room at night. Next time lil' sister gets in a murderin' mood, might be you she comes calling on.
(beat)
Maybe Kaylee. Or Inara. You let 'em stay... we're gonna find out.

Simon glances to Mal, wants to say something. Mal doesn't even look at him, his eyes on Jayne.

MAL
Finish your work, Doctor.
(to Jayne)
This is my boat, and they're part of my crew. No one's getting left. Best you get used to that.

Jayne steps off the table, not happy. He moves for the infirmary door, addressing Simon without turning —

JAYNE
You owe me a shirt.

Simon's about to speak, but Mal beats him to the punch.

MAL
She's to stay confined in her room at all times, no exceptions. You want to take her to the kitchen, the infirmary, whatever — you ask me first. You understand?

SIMON
I do.

MAL
When I took you and your sister in, the deal was you keep her in check. You can't hold up your end, we're gonna have to revisit that deal.
(after a silent beat)
She's getting worse, isn't she?

SIMON
Yes.

Off Simon, the admission killing him...

EXT. ARIEL - DAY

Serenity flies over the cityscape of the obviously wealthy Core city of Ariel, sweeps past, lands on a tarmac in the FG.

INT. SERENITY - CARGO BAY

Kaylee walks with Inara towards her shuttle. Below, Mal, Zoe, Wash and Jayne toss horseshoes.

KAYLEE
Look at the bright side, maybe you'll meet a young, handsome doctor and he'll ask you out and —
(beat)
What's Companion policy on dating?

INARA
It's... complicated.

KAYLEE
Figures.

Inara smiles, kisses Kaylee on the cheek —

INARA
Stay out of trouble.

— and heads into her shuttle.

KAYLEE
You too.

THE HORSESHOE TOSS

JAYNE
How're we gonna find a job if we don't leave the ship?

MAL
Alliance territory. Ain't any jobs worth havin'.

WASH
Nor the last three places we been.

JAYNE
My pop always said anyone who can't find work ain't looking hard enough. We ain't even looking at all.

SIMON
You can stop looking.

Actually, they all stop and look at him. Kaylee has drifted down here by now.

SIMON (cont'd)
There is a client. Me.
(then, to Mal)
I have a job for you.

Off everyone's reactions —

END OF TEASER

ACT ONE

INT. SERENITY - CARGO BAY

Right where we left off. Mal and the others looking at Simon.

MAL
You got a job for us?

SIMON
One that'll pay for itself ten times over.

JAYNE
Forget it. We ain't that desperate.

Simon pulls a vial out of his pocket.

SIMON
Do you know what this is? It's a common immunobooster called isoprovalyn. Street value for a dosage this size, fifty platinum, maybe twenty credits.
(another vial)
Propoxin, maybe eighty.
(another)
Hydrozapam, two hundred. And these are just from the med kit I had with me when I came on board. At a hospital like the one in Ariel City, they'd have shelves of this stuff. Whatever the take, more than enough payment for what I have in mind.

WASH
So the medvault's not the job?

SIMON
That's the payment. I tell you how to get in, get out, and what's worth taking. If you help me get River into the hospital's diagnostic ward.

MAL
What's in the diagnostic ward?

SIMON
A 3-D neuroimager. If I can get River in there, I

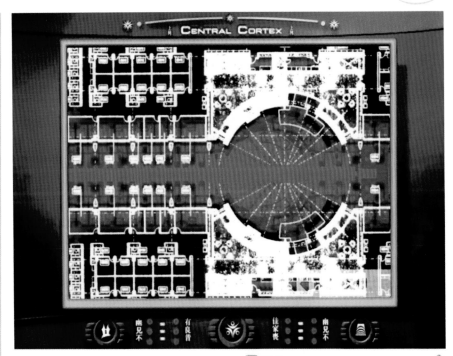

might be able to figure out what they did to her at the Academy.

MAL
So we get you and your sister into the whatchathing, you tell us how to clean out the hospital?

SIMON
Yes.

KAYLEE
Not to be negative — but don't the hospital need that medicine?

ZOE
Government run facility. They'd have it restocked in a matter of hours.

SIMON
She's right. They'll never miss it.

MAL
And folks on the rim could use it.

WASH
You know, it's very sweet — stealing from the rich and selling to the poor. But we are talking about breaking into a highly secure Alliance facility. How do you plan on getting around security?

SIMON
It's not easy, but it can be done.

Simon starts to pace, laying it all out...

SIMON (cont'd)
Like all Core hospitals, St. Lucy's has its own dedicated security force...

INT. SERENITY - DINING AREA

Continuing the movement. SIMON paces into FRAME...

SIMON
...A small battery of local Alliance federals, sub-stationed here.

The dining area has been turned into a war room, with a portable Cortex screen on the kitchen table, and assorted diagrams and schematics scattered around. Simon pauses occasionally to indicate on the Cortex —

SIMON (cont'd)
Every floor, every doorway, every room is equipped with sensors. And at all points of entry: patient ident scans. However, once clear of those checkpoints, movement within the facility itself should be relatively unhindered. The standard layout should put the medvault somewhere...

MAL
Back up to the ident scans. You and your sister are tagged fugitives. How you figure we're gonna get you in the building?

SIMON
Through the front door.

(off their looks)
Believe me, Captain — getting the two of us in is going to be easy. The rest of you... that's going to be the real trick...

More pacing.

SIMON (cont'd)
We'll have to procure a few items off ship. I've made a list. Given my status as a fugitive, someone else will have to...

Kaylee, Wash and Jayne all instantly thrust their hands in the air. Mal and Zoe just look at them.

SIMON (cont'd)
We have some volunteers... good. Before we ever make it to the front door, we're going to have to breach the perimeter. Only official vehicles are allowed in. So, we'll need one.

EXT. JUNKYARD - DAY

BIG SHINY CITYSCAPE. Tilting down to find, on the edge of the city —

SIMON (V.O.)
Obviously, we can't steal what we need. Any illegal activity in the planning stages could end this thing before it starts.

DECREPIT SANDLOT. Kaylee and Wash in the junkyard — every corner is littered with engines, carburetors, rusted out shuttles, carts, etc.

SIMON (cont'd; V.O.)
Ariel City Hospital contracts with a local municipal dumpyard for its large disposals.

KAYLEE
Figures... first time on the Core, what do I get to do? — dig through trash. Why couldn't he send me shopping at the triplex, or —
(sees something)
Ooh, synchronizers!

As Wash starts looking around...

SIMON (V.O.)
Big hospitals mean big waste. We shouldn't have any trouble.

Wash waves Kaylee over to where he is — he's found something. He points to —

— a highly crappy, broken down and discarded body of an old AMBULANCE SHUTTLE.

INT. SERENITY - DINING AREA

Simon's still pacing...

SIMON
We'll have to look like we belong.

EXT. CITY STREET - DAY

Jayne loiters at a PUBLIC VIDPHONE. He sees a PARTICULARLY DRESSED MAN moving his way. He's carrying a PAIR OF BUNDLES under his arm. As he passes the vidphone "booth", he reaches out and picks up an ENVELOPE that is sitting on a lip near Jayne.

SIMON (V.O.)
That means uniforms, ID badges...

He keeps walking. A few steps, and he drops the bundles, never losing stride. Jayne walks over and sweeps up the bundles, heads off.

INT. SERENITY - COMMON AREA

Jayne dumps the bundles from the street onto the common area table. He picks out a PHOTO ID from amidst the stash — which includes EMT uniforms — looks at the ID. An Asian man is pictured. Jayne starts cutting out the picture.

SIMON (V.O.)
All of these items are easy to obtain.

INT. SERENITY - DINING AREA

Simon stops pacing. Looks to the group.

SIMON
They'll get us up to the door. Now in order to get in...

CUT TO:

INT. SERENITY - INFIRMARY

Simon sits on the examination table, Mal, Zoe and Jayne gathered around him. Mal is mid-spiel —

MAL
The patients were cynical and not-responding and we couldn't bring 'em back.

SIMON
So they were cyanotic and non-responsive and you were unable to resuscitate. Good. Which methods did you use?

ZOE
We tried the, uh, pulmonary stimulators and the cardiac, um...

SIMON
Infusers. Right. What about the cortical electrodes?

This asked of Jayne. He hesitates.

JAYNE
Um... we forgot 'em?

SIMON
Let's try that again.

INT. SERENITY - CARGO BAY

Wash screws open a plastic panel, pulls out a motherboard, starts fussing with the parts. A CLICK and a WHOOSH and he turns to see Kaylee brandishing a lit blowtorch.

INT. SERENITY - INFIRMARY

As before —

MAL
Pupils were fixed and dilapidated —

SIMON
Dilated.

MAL
Dilated, dilated — <ching-wah TSAO duh liou mahng.> [frog-humping sonofabitch.]

INT. SERENITY - CARGO BAY

VARIOUS SHOTS

— Wash untangling a mess of wiring, straightening them out and connecting one part to another.

— Kaylee welding two metal plates together, a rain of sparks around her.

— Wash manning a paint gun, spraying white paint over a smooth metal surface.

INT. SERENITY - INFIRMARY

And one more time —

MAL
By the time we got there, the patients were cyanotic and, uh... non-responsive. We tried, but we couldn't revive them — resuscitate them — despite our best efforts.
(beat)
They kicked.

SIMON
Yes. Which methods did you use?

ZOE
We used the pulmonary stimulators and cardiac infusers.
(beat)
Or is it cardiac stimulators and pulmonary infusers?

SIMON
You had it right the first time. What about cortical electrodes?

This, once again, asked of Jayne —

JAYNE
We, uh, used them electro... magnetic... Hell, I don't know, if I wanted schooling, I'da gone to school!

Simon reacts — it'll have to do.

INT. SERENITY - CARGO BAY

TRACKING WITH SIMON as he enters the cargo bay, a pleased expression on his face.

SIMON
That's amazing.

We don't yet see what he's looking at as he's joined by Kaylee and Wash.

SIMON (cont'd)
You two did an incredible job.

Now we see what they're looking at — the broken down shuttle has been retro-fitted to look just like a shiny new Ariel City Hospital ambulance.

KAYLEE
And the finishing touch —

Out of the ambulance emerge Mal, Zoe, and Jayne dressed in EMT uniforms, complete with clipped-on IDs and keycards, looking very much the part.

SIMON
If I didn't know better, I'd say you're ready to save

❖ Above (clockwise): False IDs for Wash, Jayne, Mal and Zoe.

some lives.

MAL
Now all we need's a couple of patients.

SIMON
Corpses, actually. For this to work, River and I will have to be dead.

JAYNE
I'm startin' to like this plan.

PRELAP —

SIMON (V.O.)
We're going to be asleep.

INT. SERENITY - RIVER'S ROOM

River sits on her bed, Simon at her side, explaining.

SIMON
Captain Reynolds and the others will have to pretend that we're dead to sneak us into the hospital, but once we're inside we'll wake up and everything will be fine. You understand?

RIVER
You're going to suspend cerebral, cardiac and pulmonary activity in order to induce a proto-comatose state.

Simon reacts — of course she'd get the science.

ACCESS FILE:

THE ARIEL AMBULANCE RESCUE GROUP

The ambulance began life as a mock-up of a helicopter fuselage, which was used in Hollywood films. Carey Meyer rented the fuselage from Mark Thompson's Aviation Warehouse and the *Firefly* crew modified and repainted it to become the ambulance. After 'Ariel' was filmed, the ambulance was returned to the Warehouse, which later sold it to the El Dorado Aircraft Supply Co. Ltd, who kept it in their scrap yard in Mojave, California. Scott S. Atkins discovered it in Spring 2005, and reported the find in his LiveJournal. After a phenomenal online fan response, the Ariel Ambulance Rescue Group was formed by Adam Whiting, and they purchased the ambulance on 6 May 2006 (dubbed 'Ariel Ambulance Day'). The ambulance is being gradually restored and has been outfitted with props from the movie *Serenity* donated by The Prop Store of London, including: an Alliance Lab Assistant costume, an Alliance medkit prop, and a bank heist money display. The intention is for the ambulance to travel around to conventions, stopping off at museums in between. Its first highly successful visit was to WorldCon64 in August 2006 where Loni Peristere, Jane Espenson and Tim Minear signed it!

❖ Clockwise from the top: The Ariel ambulance backstage; signatures on the inside of the restored ambulance; Jane Espenson with the ambulance; Adam Whiting, Tim Minear, Loni Peristere and Scott S. Atkins with the ambulance; Scott S. Atkins having his 'Wash moment'.

SIMON
That's right.

RIVER
I don't want to do it.

SIMON
I know.

RIVER
I don't want to go to that place. I don't want to die.

SIMON
No one's going to die. It's okay. The others will take care of us while we're asleep and when we get back —

RIVER
(on and on)
No, no, no —

SIMON
Shhh... it's okay. River. River.
(she calms)
This could be what we've been hoping for. When this is over... I'll be able to help you. I'll be able to make the nightmares go away. Okay?

Very much not okay, River nods.

SIMON (cont'd)
Okay. Lie back.

She does. Simon preps his syringe.

SIMON (cont'd)
It's time to go to sleep.

He injects her.

INT. AMBULANCE - NIGHT

Jayne, Mal and Zoe all huddled in the M.A.S.H.-like medi-shuttle. We're IN FLIGHT but it's all tight and interior.

MAL
We speak only when spoken to, we avoid any unnecessary contact and we stay together until we reach the morgue. Understood?

ZOE
Yes, sir.

Jayne doesn't reply — he's mouthing his lines. Trying to get them right.

JAYNE
(really just muttering)
Applied the cortical electrodes. Unable to get a neural reaction...

MAL
Jayne?

JAYNE
Yeah, yeah I got it.

MAL
Are we gonna have a problem?

JAYNE
I know what I gotta do.

MAL
That's not what I'm talking about. Am I gonna have a problem with you and Simon?

JAYNE
That's up to him.

MAL
Look. You got a little stabbed the other day, that's bound to make anyone a mite ornery. So I figure...

JAYNE
(cuts him off)
It's a good plan.

MAL
What?

JAYNE
Doc did good, coming up with this job. Don't mean I like him any better... but nothing buys bygones quicker'n cash.
(then)
Maybe I'll give him a tattoo while he's out.

MAL
You let him do his thing, then you get them out. No messing with him for a laugh.

JAYNE
Don't worry about me. Long as I get paid, I'm happy.

As Jayne goes back to muttering his script...

EXT. HOSPITAL - E.R. LANDING STRIP - NIGHT

The ambulance lands in front of the hospital, a pair of body bags attached nacelle-like to the side of the ambulance. [NOTE: the body bags are hard, silver shells without a discernible zipper.]

Mal, Zoe, Jayne and Wash (in his EMT uniform) spill out of the ambulance, unhook the bodybags.

ANGLE: THE PAVEMENT

as the wheels of a retractable gurney hit the ground.

WIDER — The casket-like body "bags" are now on wheels. As Mal, Zoe and Jayne start to move off with them —

WASH
We got just a few hours before the morning shift.

MAL
Won't be an hour.

And they're moving —

EXT. HOSPITAL - GANGWAY - NIGHT

Mal, Zoe and Jayne wheel the gurneys towards the door.

ARIEL

Production designer Carey Meyer: "I think we shot the junkyard on stage and pretty much the entire environment, short of a couple of foreground pieces, was practical. We brought in several pieces of junk and created essentially a foreground area for Wash and Kaylee to walk into, and then the heaps and piles of junk beyond it were a matte painting or a CG front.

"We created the ambulance for that sequence as well, where it comes in and lands at the end of that long gangway outside the hospital. We rented a fake fiberglass helicopter body and added parts to it to make it look like the CG version. We completely mocked up the interior as well, for the interior set. All the movement was CG — although it was moved from the exterior to the stage and was filmed inside the cargo bay. So it moved, but not on camera.

"The hospital interior was a white building out in Valencia that used to be called Skunkworks, where they created a lot of jet engines and military engineering. I think we used the exterior to some extent as well. It was a location that we had known during *Buffy* and relied on a lot. You often go back to places you know, because you already know the practical details and what's already there and what you're able to create. I can't stress enough how in television production, just to get to the end of the day and still be alive is a huge challenge [laughs] — and you really need to be creative. That location played perfectly. We did a lot of built-in scenery to tie into scenery that we created on the stage, namely a long hallway that led up to the operating room. The lab and the hallway that led up to it were on stage, but as the characters came out of an elevator into that hallway, the interior of the elevator and the hallway on the other side of the elevator were at Skunkworks."

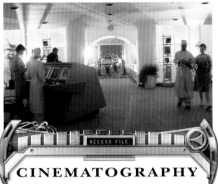

CINEMATOGRAPHY

Director of photography David Boyd: "'Ariel' is one of the times when I began to put motion picture lights into the frame. In other words, we would photograph [the lights]. There's a scene in the hospital lobby and the lighting that's seen outside those windows is actually our own lighting, which played as kind of a klieg light out of the windows there, which I thought was tremendously effective. There were times when we'd get flared out by them, where the frame just gets obliterated by the light, but by hiding them behind things and seeing them occasionally at oblique angles, we got away with that pretty well."

INT. HOSPITAL - RECEIVING CHECKPOINT - NIGHT

Mal, Zoe and Jayne wheel in the body containers toward a NURSE and a RECEIVING DOCTOR.

RECEIVING DOCTOR
What have you got?

MAL
Couple DOAs. By the time we got —

RECEIVING DOCTOR
(abruptly)
Take them down to the morgue.

The doctor waves a beeper-like device over the body bags and the bags go from silver to black —

Mal, Zoe and Jayne just sort of blink. Receiving Doctor goes back to whatever it was she was doing. Jayne isn't about to go without blurting:

JAYNE
We applied the cortical electrodes but were unable to get a neural reaction from either patient!

The Receiving Doctor just looks up blankly. She didn't ask. A beat and our people move off. And they're in.

INT. HOSPITAL - MORGUE - NIGHT

Mal, Zoe and Jayne wheel in the gurneys. Jayne takes in the many blue-tinged bodies on slabs and examination tables, many of them in various stages of post-mortems. He'd rather be anywhere but here.

MAL
Let's get 'em out.

Jayne and Zoe pull a tab on each body bag and they slide open neatly, parting down the middle. They pick up Simon and River and lift them onto a pair of nearby examination tables. Another pull on the tab and the body bags close, retaining their shape.

Mal pulls a hypo out of his med bag, injects Simon and River.

MAL (cont'd)
That should bring them out of it in a few minutes. As soon as they're up, get them to the imaging suite, let Simon do his thing, then haul it back to the roof. Fifty minutes.

JAYNE
Got it.

Mal and Zoe wheel their gurneys back out.

JAYNE (cont'd)
I'll just... sit here.

And he does. For a beat. Creeped out by all the dead people. Another beat, then Jayne peeks out the door before moving out into —

INT. HOSPITAL - RECOVERY WARD - NIGHT

Jayne walks down a corridor, stops at a Cortex terminal. He swipes a card on the terminal, and in a moment a face appears on the Cortex screen — this is AGENT McGINNIS.

JAYNE
I'm in.

AGENT McGINNIS
Do you have the fugitives?

JAYNE
You got my reward?

AGENT McGINNIS
Yes. Just like we talked about.

JAYNE
Then I got your fugitives.

AGENT McGINNIS
Good. We'll see you shortly. Congratulations. You're about to become a very rich man.

Off Jayne —

END OF ACT ONE

ACT TWO

INT. HOSPITAL - MORGUE - NIGHT

Jayne slips back into the morgue, where Simon and River still lie unconscious. Now that he's alone, Jayne is even more spooked by this place. Especially the quiet.

Behind Jayne (and unseen by him) River SITS UP INTO FRAME. She's just woken up and is a bit dazed, disoriented. She's inches behind him as she says —

RIVER
A copper for a kiss.

Jayne jumps — she startled the hell out of him.

JAYNE
Jesu — ! What — what did you say?

River falters — even she's not sure what just came out of her mouth.

In the BG, Simon now bolts awake with a CHOKED GASP. Jayne jumps again. Simon goes into a coughing jag, every cough causing him noticeable pain.

JAYNE (cont'd)
What's the matter with you?

SIMON
Nothing, just after-effects from the drugs.
(coughs, it hurts)
I'll be fine, just give me a second.

JAYNE
(you weenie)
Your sister seems okay.

From behind Jayne comes the sound of River throwing up. Jayne looks behind him, sees the mess — yuck. He turns back to Simon and tosses him a bundle of clothes.

JAYNE (cont'd)
Get dressed. We gotta move.

INT. HOSPITAL - CORRIDOR - NIGHT

A pair of elevator doors open and Mal and Zoe push their gurneys down a quiet corridor.

MAL
Two rights, two lefts and we're there. You see

anyone, smile.

ZOE
I don't think people smile in hospitals.

MAL
'Course they do. It's the Core, everybody's rich and happy here. Why wouldn't they smile?

From O.S., a voice calls to them —

OFFICIOUS DOCTOR (O.S.)
'Scuse me —

Mal turns, sees an OFFICIOUS DOCTOR.

MAL
(big smile)
Hi!

OFFICIOUS DOCTOR
(unsmiling)
Where are you taking those bodies?

MAL
Just downstairs to the morgue.

OFFICIOUS DOCTOR
(pointing behind them)
Downstairs is that way.

MAL
Right. Must've got turned around.

OFFICIOUS DOCTOR
Let me see your badge.

Mal hands it over.

INT. HOSPITAL - RECOVERY WARD - NIGHT

Simon and Jayne wheel River down a corridor in a wheelchair. She's in a hospital gown, Simon is in scrubs, Jayne still wears his EMT uniform.

RIVER
We're doing it backwards. Walking up the down slide.

JAYNE
Keep her quiet.

Simon leans in close to River as he walks, as soothing as ever —

SIMON
This is the recovery ward. This is where patients come to get better.

RIVER
They're going to die.

SIMON
No one's going to die.

RIVER
(indicates a patient)
He is.

Simon looks where River's indicating. A fortysomething PATIENT lies in bed, a cocky YOUNG INTERN tending to him.

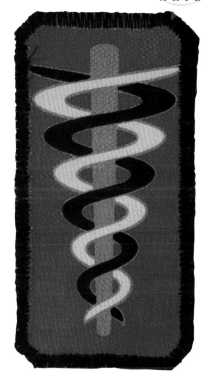

❖ Above: A patch from one of the EMT uniforms worn by the crew.

SIMON
No, he's not. That man standing next to him is his doctor, he's going to help him.

RIVER
He's not going to help him right.

SIMON
River, the doctors here are the best in the system. This is one of the top hospitals in the Core or anywhere else.

RIVER
Where you should be.

Simon does his best to not react to that. River grabs the wheels on the wheelchair, effectively slamming on the brakes. She starts to get up; Jayne won't let her.

JAYNE
Uh-uh. No wandering off.

RIVER
(to Simon)
You have to help him.

SIMON
River, we don't have time to —

RIVER
(loud)
He's killing him!

The monitors by the patient start BEEPING, alarms going off. And now River is struggling against Jayne, trying to get up out of her chair.

YOUNG INTERN
Code blue!

NURSES converge on the trauma area. Simon sees them working frantically, knows he can help —

SIMON
(to River)
Stay here. Don't move.

With a look to Jayne that says "watch her", Simon jumps into the fray. This is FAST —

SIMON (cont'd)
What do we have?

YOUNG INTERN
Forty-two-year-old, double bypass post-op. Prognosis was positive —

CRASH TEAM NURSE
BP sixty over twenty, pulse is thready.

Simon rips the patient's gown open, listens to his heart.

YOUNG INTERN
(to Simon)
Who are you?

CRASH TEAM NURSE
He's crashing —

SIMON
(to Nurse)
Get the cart.

She moves to get the crash cart; that's when a long, constant BEEEEEP starts coming from the EKG —

CRASH TEAM NURSE
We have flatline —

YOUNG INTERN
We gotta crack him —

SIMON
(stern, to Intern)
We're not cracking a post-op.
(to the Nurse)
Get the infusers and point-four of atropine.
(to Intern)
What did you give him?

YOUNG INTERN
Just twenty of alprazaline push.

Simon gives him a look — whatever that means, it means the Intern fucked up.

The Nurse hands Simon a hypo and a pair of pen-like devices. (These are cardiac infusers, and they look not unlike a pair of tire pressure gauges.) Simon puts the hypo between his teeth, applies the infusers to the patient's chest —

SIMON
Clear —

PHUMP! A blip on the EKG, then back to flat-line —

SIMON (cont'd)
Clear —

PHUMP! A blip on the EKG, this time it keeps blipping, but another ALARM SOUNDS. Simon gives the infusers to the Nurse.

YOUNG INTERN
(an accusation)
He's going tachy.

Simon takes the hypo from his teeth —

SIMON
(dismissive)
But his heart's beating.

— plugs it into the IV, pushes in the atropine. Instantly, the alarms stop. A beat, then the EKG blips become slower and more regular.

Everyone breathes a sigh of relief, especially the Intern.

YOUNG INTERN
(willing it)
He's okay...

Simon gets in his face, genuinely pissed —

SIMON
Explain to me how you justify administering a vasoconstrictor to this patient?

YOUNG INTERN
Alprazaline's a painkiller, not a —

SIMON
Unless you combine it with dilavtin, which any first year should know is the standard prep medi-cine your patient was taking before his surgery. Your patient should be dead. And you'd be stand-ing here scratching your head as to why.

YOUNG INTERN
I — I'm... sorry, Doctor.

SIMON
Good.

Simon moves back to River and Jayne. River's practically beaming. Jayne's not unimpressed.

SIMON (cont'd)
Let's go.

INT. HOSPITAL - CORRIDOR - NIGHT

Mal and Zoe and the Officious Doctor, moments after we left them. The Doctor examines Mal's ident badge carefully.

OFFICIOUS DOCTOR
(moving towards a vidphone)
Walk with me a minute.

Mal gives Zoe a look — better do something. She sidles over to a crash cart.

MAL
Where we going?

The Doctor stops, actually seems offended at the question. He holds up his ident card.

OFFICIOUS DOCTOR
You see this badge? It says "Doctor". I say walk with me, you walk with me.

Mal stays put — he already hates this guy.

MAL
Yeah, but... Where we going?

Now the Doctor is pissed —

OFFICIOUS DOCTOR
You must be new.
(Mal doesn't deny it)
Don't get comfortable; your type doesn't last long here. When your supervisor hears about the rude and disrespectful attitude you just —

PHUMP! The Doctor collapses to the ground. Zoe stands behind him, a pair of cardiac infusers in hand.

ZOE
Clear.

INT. HOSPITAL - IMAGING SUITE - NIGHT

Simon and Jayne push River into the suite, Jayne hanging back and looking both ways out the door before shutting it.

Simon crouches next to River, as soothing as he can be —

SIMON
Ready?

Although clearly apprehensive, River nods.

INT. HOSPITAL - ANOTHER CORRIDOR - NIGHT

Mal and Zoe push their gurneys down the corri-dor, stop at a door.

MAL
Twelve-oh-five. This is it.

He looks around, makes sure the coast is clear, then swipes his keycard through the scanner. A RED LIGHT flashes on the scanner — the door won't open. He tries again. Again, red light.

BEN EDLUND

I think the show is actually at its strongest when it discusses the tension between the fron-tier and the Core worlds. That's why 'Ariel' strikes me as one of the strongest episodes, because you get both. You get the dirty, unwashed real people coming back to this plastic utopia. That mix — not that it should be in every episode — was something very important.

MAL (cont'd)
Zoe.

Zoe tries her keycard. Twice. Same thing: the light blinks red.

ZOE
They must've been de-mag'd.

Mal pulls the tab on one of the bodybags — it opens to reveal the Officious Doctor, who is MOANING but unconscious. He snatches his keycard, slides it through the scanner. The door opens.

MAL
His works.

INT. HOSPITAL - IMAGING SUITE - NIGHT

Simon helps River onto the steel table and she leans back, her eyes staring straight up. This place clearly scares her.

Simon moves to a podium-like control column, wheels it over close to River. He inserts a PLASTIC TAB into the column, then presses a few buttons, turns on the machine. The entire room starts to make a WHIRRING SOUND.

River closes her eyes. Jayne simply watches.

INT. SUPPLY VAULT - NIGHT

This is thief heaven. Simon was right — the shelves are lined with vial upon vial of medicine. Mal dumps the Officious Doctor on the floor, and he and Zoe start filling the body bags with drugs.

In a series of JUMP CUTS, they quickly, efficiently clean out the room, cramming as many vials as they can into the body bags, reading labels and tossing away the worthless ones before sealing the jammed packed body bags again.

INT. IMAGING SUITE - NIGHT

The WHIRRING is a little louder now. Simon works for a moment longer before —

SIMON
River... I'm going to start the scan now. You okay?

River is trying very hard to keep her shit together; she's on the brink of freaking. Her lips are moving fast, but no words are coming out.

SIMON (cont'd)
River?

RIVER
(snapping)
Just do it.

Simon works the controls and a HOLOGRAPHIC IMAGE APPEARS, a three-dimensional scan of her brain floating above her like a bizarre rain cloud. Numbers and wave-graphs flank the central image of her brain.

INT. HOSPITAL - CORRIDOR - NIGHT

Just outside the supply vault. Mal and Zoe push the gurneys back out into the corridor. Mal shuts the vault door with the Doctor still inside.

INT. IMAGING SUITE - NIGHT

Jayne sits in a corner, watching Simon work at the control column. (An LCD window on the column reads DOWNLOADING DATA.) Simon mans the controls like the professional he is — rotating the image, punching up new numbers and scans. He's riveted by the flood of information, stares at the images before him in disbelief.

SIMON
<Yen guo duh hwai dan.> [Castrated bastards.] How anyone could do this to another person... She's seventeen...

Jayne remains impassive, not wanting to be drawn into this. Nonetheless, Simon turns to him —

SIMON (cont'd)
They opened up her skull. Look —

Using the controls, he highlights (Madden-like, but slicker) a straight line drawn across River's frontal and temporal lobes — an incision line.

SIMON (cont'd)
That's a scalpel scar. They opened up her skull... and then they cut into her brain.

Curiosity gets the best of Jayne —

JAYNE
Why?

SIMON
The only reason to make an incision in someone's brain is to lobotomize them — you go in to remove damaged tissue. Why someone would cut into a healthy brain...

He lets it hang there — the answer is beyond him.

SIMON (cont'd)
They did it over and over.

The downloading window switches to DOWNLOAD COMPLETE. Simon absently takes the plastic tab out of the machine, pockets it. A moment, as Simon looks at something else.

SIMON (cont'd)
They stripped her amygdala...

JAYNE
(growing discomfort)
Her what?

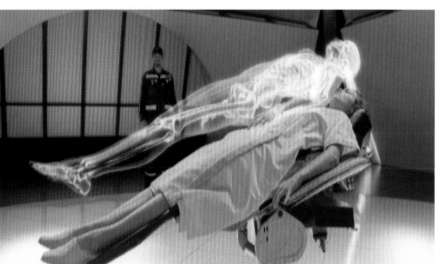

WASH

*"I can be terse. Once, in flight school,
I was laconic."*

Many have theorized that *Firefly* fell victim to being too far ahead of its time, and maybe just a little too smart for what television was ready for. Shedding the conventional trappings of what science fiction on film looks like, and using the Western metaphor literally, made the show externally unique, but at its heart, the series was always about the dynamic personalities that lived together on Serenity. Alan Tudyk thinks that's the key to what attracted so many diehard fans to the show — the common threads humanity will always exhibit through space and time. "My description of *Firefly* is this: it is set in space, but the great thing about it is that it brings the human condition to space. People argue, people get hungry and don't like the food they are eating. It's not like other shows, which I'm not going to mention, where they can just order up their food in a little processor and go 'beef sirloin' and they have it. We have these protein cakes, which are kind of moldy. We don't have much cash. Sometimes I make mistakes flying, like you do when you're driving

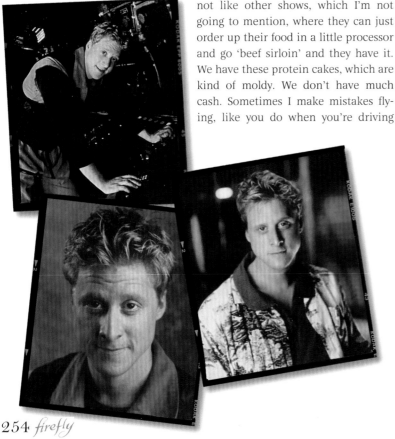

and you miss an exit. I can miss a whole planet if I'm not paying attention!"

No one can argue that the rapport between characters and amongst the actors also infused the series with an intimacy that was a great attraction for viewers. Tudyk says that connection was real and it made the show live. "The cast all bonded over the material. I think we knew going in that Fox was already having problems with the vision of the show and the minute any kind of noise like that happens, you look to the person beside you, grab hold and say, 'We're in this together. We are going to fight this out!' Very quickly, we became a tight knit family. It's really fortunate when it works out that you enjoy working with the people that you are spending fourteen hours of the day with."

Like his fellow cast, Tudyk is the first to say that a lot of that bonding stemmed from Nathan Fillion. "Nathan is so perfect as the Captain because he really is a leader himself. When things were screwing up like they do on any TV show, like the lighting was wrong or you can't get something, there was never a complaint from him. Actually when I first read the script, the Captain was a very important role and I was like, 'Who did they get to play the Captain?' They told me the name and I didn't recognize it. I was like, 'I hope this works; I hope they got a good guy.' The first day I walked in, I was like, 'God dangit, he's so not right! He's not right for the role, just by looking at him, they screwed up, god this is going to tank!' So I was like, 'Hi, hi' and we introduced ourselves and I said, 'Wow, so you're the Captain?' and he replied, 'No, no! I'm the Doctor.' It was Sean," he laughs. "It's true! And then I met Nathan and I was like, 'Oh good, that's going to work out fine.'"

Tudyk's other favorite connection was with actress Gina Torres, who played his better half, Zoe. "I love Gina," the actor enthuses genuinely. "She's the greatest. We got to have a post-coital scene in the series. We did some making out, which was fun. We did some fighting together and she saved me. I don't think I ever saved her — that would be fun! For me to save her and be the bad ass for once would have been fun." ⊙

SIMON
You know how... you get scared. Or worried, or nervous. And you don't want to be scared or worried or nervous, so you push it to the back of your mind. You try not to think about it. The amygdala is what lets you do that — it's like a filter in your brain that keeps your feelings in check.
(beat, disturbed by this)
They took that filter out of River. She feels everything. She can't not.

That's as perturbing to Jayne as it is to Simon, but he's not going to get drawn into River's problems.

JAYNE
That's fascinating.
(grabs the tab, puts it in Simon's coat pocket)
We should get moving.

SIMON
(looks at a wall clock)
We still have twenty minutes.

JAYNE
Wrong. Plan changed when you were out. We're meeting out the back way in five.

RIVER

Her eyes snap open.

THE HOLOGRAM

Images begin to change furiously as River's brain starts firing, going berserk. Greens go to red, levels spike, warning lights flash. Simon has his back momentarily turned, addressing Jayne.

SIMON
I could use another couple of minutes. I'm sure if we contact Captain Reynolds —

JAYNE
Captain gave his orders. We play it by the book.

River lets out an ear-splitting SCREAM OF TERROR.

Simon turns, sees the hyperactive hologram. He shuts off the machine and rushes to River's side. She's in full freak-out mode now; her dialogue overlaps with everyone else's.

SIMON
River — it's okay, you're okay.

JAYNE
Get her in the chair and let's go.

RIVER
No, no, no — they come out of the black. They come when you call.

SIMON
It's okay, it's over.
(looks at Jayne)
We're leaving.

River fixes Jayne with a look — like she sees right into him. It's wigging him a bit.

RIVER
Your toes are in the sand.

JAYNE
(defensive)
And your head's up your —

SIMON
Hey! Back off.

JAYNE
Just make sure she keeps her mouth shut. We don't need her screeching while we're trying to make a quiet getaway.

Jayne goes to the door, looks around outside, then looks back at Simon and River. She's in hysterical tears, her hands clutching his shirt. He's stroking her hair, cooing, trying to calm her. Off Jayne... is he starting to feel guilty?

CUT TO:

INT. HOSPITAL - RECOVERY WARD - NIGHT

Jayne leads the way as Simon pushes River in her wheelchair. Her lips are again moving soundlessly.

SIMON
(quietly, to Jayne)
You should've let me know when the plan changed.

JAYNE
I told you when you needed to know.
(off Simon's look)
What are you griping about, you got what you came for.

They turn a corner into —

INT. HOSPITAL - ANOTHER CORRIDOR - CONTINUOUS

The reach the back exit doors, are about to push through when River puts the brakes on the chair.

RIVER
No... can't go back, don't want to go back...

SIMON
Shh, it's okay. We're just going back to the ship. We're almost home.

River reluctantly allows herself to be pushed through the doors to —

EXT. HOSPITAL - BACK EXIT - CONTINUOUS

The doors aren't even shut behind them when SPOTLIGHTS spark to life, pinning Simon, River and Jayne in their crosshairs.

AGENT McGINNIS (filtered)
Federal Marshals — don't move.

They shield their eyes... just enough to see that they're surrounded by armed feds. Lots of them, and moving cautiously towards them, rifles raised.

AGENT McGINNIS
River and Simon Tam. By the authority of the Union of Allied Planets, you are hereby bound by law.

Off their reactions —

BLACK OUT.

END OF ACT TWO

ACT THREE

EXT. HOSPITAL - BACK EXIT - NIGHT

As we left them. The feds come up to Simon and River, who offer no resistance as they're patted down and cuffed, their hands behind their backs.

AGENT McGINNIS
Take them to processing.

The officers start ushering Simon and River away, another comes to cuff Jayne, who plays along, takes a slow step towards McGinnis —

JAYNE
(sotto)
So... you gonna take me away for questioning now, or how d'ya wanna play it?

AGENT McGINNIS
You're under arrest for aiding and abetting federal fugitives. Better get a lawyer.

Jayne almost laughs. McGinnis doesn't.

JAYNE
You're kidding, right?

McGinnis says nothing.

JAYNE (cont'd)
(through his teeth)
Where's my rutting money?

AGENT McGINNIS
You mean my money? For apprehending the three fugitives? I expect I'll be getting it soon.

With that, McGinnis walks away. Jayne realizes he's been double-crossed. He yanks free of the fed

---

A D A M   B A L D W I N

On Jayne's good intentions for turning Simon and River over to the Alliance: "Well, he wasn't betraying anyone; he was doing it for the crew. Jayne came at it from the angle that he was helping them out, and if he makes a little money along the way, great. It wasn't like he was betraying the crew. They had some weird passengers on their heads, too. I like the scene where they describe the blue hands, and those little wands that make people's heads explode from the inside."

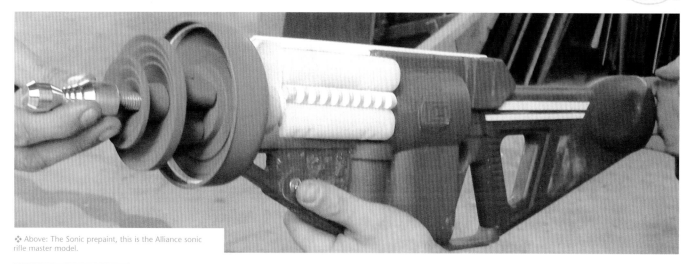

❖ Above: The Sonic prepaint, this is the Alliance sonic rifle master model.

cuffing him (one cuff on, one off), he starts to lunge at McGinnis, when —

A FED

swings around with his SONIC RIFLE. We're LOOKING DOWN THE BUSINESS END as a wave of compressed sound DISTORTS THE AIR and slams into Jayne like a wrecking ball, sending him FLYING hard into a wall.

EXT. HOSPITAL - E.R. LANDING STRIP - NIGHT

Mal and Zoe trot the gurneys out towards the ambulance shuttle. Wash hops out and helps them strap the body bags to the outside of the shuttle. He reacts to the weight of the bags. (They're essentially filled to the brim with liquid.)

WASH
How much did we get?

Zoe smiles at Wash — it's a lot. Mal downplays it.

MAL
Enough to keep us flying.

ZOE
(psyched)
Can we fly somewhere with a beach?

WASH
Maybe a naked beach.

Wash and Zoe kiss.

MAL
Cut it out. Job ain't done til we're back on Serenity.

ZOE
Sorry, sir. Didn't mean to enjoy the moment.

MAL
(to Wash)
Where are the others?

INT. HOSPITAL - SECURITY SUBSTATION - RECEPTION - NIGHT

FED #1 escorts Jayne, Simon and River into the reception area. Simon whispers to the defeated-looking Jayne:

SIMON
I appreciate what you tried to do out there.

JAYNE
(defensive)
I didn't do nothing.

SIMON
More than I did.

They are herded over to a bench, shoved onto it. Jayne is in between Simon and River.

They eyeball McGinnis in the near distance, talking to FED #2, prepping paperwork.

SIMON (cont'd)
If those officers hadn't been armed, I think you'd have had a chance.

JAYNE
Guy shoved me, I shoved back. Not like I was trying to mount a rescue.

SIMON
Still. I appreciate you trying.

JAYNE
You know what I'd appreciate? If you'd stop flapping your pretty mouth at me. I'm trying to think of a way out of here and I can't do it with you yammering.

RIVER
They took Christmas away.

JAYNE
What the hell now?

RIVER
Came down the stairs for the shiny presents, but they took the tree and the stockings. Nothing left but coal.

JAYNE
(to Simon)
Shut her up.

RIVER
(to Jayne)
And don't look in the closet, either. That's greedy. It's not in the spirit of the holiday.

JAYNE
(very harsh)
Shut. The hell. Up. Right now. Or so help me I will shut you up.

INT./EXT. AMBULANCE SHUTTLE - NIGHT

Mal, Zoe and Wash.

MAL
Time.

ZOE
Ten minutes past rendezvous.

MAL
Something happened.

Wash opens a communication channel with Serenity.

WASH
Kaylee, are you linked?

INTERCUT:

SUMMER GLAU

'Ariel' was, for me, the hardest episode to shoot. The scenes in it were very emotional and I had to say a lot of things that I didn't understand. I found it very complicated, emotionally. However, I am really proud of the way it turned out. I love that episode. We were up in this old apartment building; it was really creepy and such a challenging shoot. Sean and I were working so much, that whenever I sat down in my chair I would just fall asleep.

INT. SERENITY - BRIDGE - NIGHT

Kaylee's on the bridge, in the pilot's seat. She taps a few buttons and the Cortex pops up on the helm screen.

KAYLEE
I am now. What do you need?

WASH
Find out if there's been any kind of security alert in the hospital.

KAYLEE
Hang on...

As Kaylee works —

ZOE
Could be they're just late.

MAL
Not this late. Jayne would've sent up a flag.

Kaylee gets what she's looking for.

KAYLEE
Nothing from hospital security. Nothing on local pipeline, either. Although I'm getting some weird chatter on the official two-six-two. Sounds like they're talking about... ducks?

ZOE
(to Mal)
Code?

MAL
(nods)
Feds got 'em.
(to Wash)
Have her bring up the hospital schematics on the Cortex. Find me a way into the security substation.

Zoe ducks into the ambulance, tosses Mal his gun. He tucks it in his vest; she lifts up her pantleg and straps her shotgun to her calf with bandage tape.

WASH
Wait a minute, you don't even know for sure they're in there —

Now Zoe places an earwig in her ear, hands one to Mal, who does the same.

MAL
Gonna find out.
(presses the earwig into his ear)
Check.

ZOE
(re: her earwig)
Coming in clear.

WASH
So you're just gonna walk in through the front door?

MAL
No. You're gonna find me a way round the back.

They shut the ambulance doors and move off.

INT. HOSPITAL - SECURITY SUBSTATION - RECEPTION - NIGHT

McGinnis approaches the bench where Simon, Jayne and River sit (armed feds in evidence).

AGENT McGINNIS
(to Simon)
Get up.

SIMON
What's going to happen to us?

AGENT McGINNIS
I said get up.

McGinnis grabs Simon by the arm; he yanks himself free.

SIMON
Agent McGinnis, I'm certain you're working under a superior who's keeping close tabs on this case. I'm certain of that because important people don't do field work. I'm also quite certain your superior wants me and my sister alive. I'm not going to move from this spot until one of two things happen: you answer my very simple question, or you shoot me.

McGinnis bristles, but has little choice but to answer.

AGENT McGINNIS
We're transferring you to a holding area until you can be retrieved.

SIMON
Retrieved... by whom?

AGENT McGINNIS
By people who want you alive. People not me.
(to the feds)
Take 'em.

PRELAP the sound of a BUZZER and —

CUT TO:

INT. HOSPITAL - SECURITY SUBSTATION -

HOLDING AREA - NIGHT

A security door opens and two feds escort Jayne, Simon and River through the holding area. The feds usher the prisoners around a corner and towards a cell.

River and Simon file in, as does Jayne. As Fed #2 goes to shut the door, Jayne springs — SLAMMING HIS HEAD into Fed #2's nose and shattering it, knocking him out.

Fed #1 raises his rifle, but Jayne rams into him shoulder first, practically lifting him off the ground and CRUSHING him against a wall. The impact is such that both men go down, the rifle skittering away. Jayne quickly wriggles his cuffs past his feet. His hands are in front of him now. He grabs Fed #1 with both hands, one hand on his mouth, the other on his throat.

The following is dirty, ugly and almost completely silent:

Jayne squeezes hard, crushing his windpipe. The fed tries to pry Jayne's hands off him, but Jayne's too strong. So the fed bites down on Jayne's hand; blood streams down, but Jayne keeps his hold on both mouth and throat.

Simon goes to help Jayne, but hears Fed #2 stir — he's coming to. Simon moves to him, kneels on his throat. He won't make a sound.

Still wrestling on the ground, Fed #1 gouges at Jayne's eyes, gets him pretty good, causing Jayne to look away and allowing the fed to flip Jayne on his back. Fed #1 straddles him, proceeds to SLAM Jayne's head repeatedly on the marble floor. (Jayne should get a forehead welt in all of this that we carry to the end of the show.)

River watches the violence.

INT. HOSPITAL - RECOVERY WARD - NIGHT

Mal and Zoe.

MAL
Wash, a little direction, please.

INTERCUT AS NEEDED:

INT. AMBULANCE SHUTTLE - NIGHT

Wash talks into his transmitter —

WASH
Working on it...

Then into the com —

WASH (cont'd)
Kaylee, whaddya got?

INT. SERENITY - BRIDGE

Kaylee's looking at the hospital blueprints on the Cortex.

KAYLEE
Tell them to make a left when they get to cryo. They'll see a door —

INT. HOSPITAL - RECOVERY WARD - NIGHT

Mal and Zoe, moving fast —

WASH
Go through that door and down to green level.

Mal and Zoe go through the door and into —

INT. HOSPITAL - PURPLE STAIRCASE - NIGHT

They descend the steps, taking them two and three at a time. As they do —

MAL
This is exactly what I didn't want. I wanted simple, I wanted in-and-out, I wanted easy money.

ZOE
Things always get a little more complicated, don't they, sir?

MAL
Once, just once, I want things to go according to the gorramn plan!

They reach the bottom of the steps, head for the door, when —

WASH (V.O.)
Um, guys... you might want to hurry.

MAL
Is there a problem?

INT. AMBULANCE SHUTTLE - NIGHT

Wash looks out the window, sees an ominous-looking shuttle descending towards City Hospital and landing on its roof.

WASH
I think the reinforcements are here.

Off Wash's dread...

INT. HOSPITAL - SECURITY SUBSTATION - HOLDING AREA - NIGHT

Back to the ugly, quiet fight at the substation.

Simon continues to put pressure on Fed #2's throat.

Jayne knees the fed in the nuts — it's enough to try to flip on top of him. They roll around, Jayne repeatedly taking punches as he tries to squeeze the life out of this bastard.

Finally the fed goes limp. Jayne gives him a few squeezes and shakes for good measure. Lets the body drop. He takes the keys off the dead fed. Moves to Simon, who is expressionless, standing over the unconscious body of Fed #2. No remorse from Simon at what Jayne has just done. Maybe even a bit impressed. Jayne uncuffs him, then moves to do the same for River.

Simon picks up the fed's sonic rifle. Jayne turns back to him just as Simon tosses the rifle to Jayne.

SIMON
Come on.

Simon starts to move to an intersecting corridor. Jayne is going back toward the front door. Simon turns to him —

SIMON (cont'd)
What are you doing?

JAYNE
Going out the way we came in.

SIMON
There's at least four armed feds out there.

JAYNE
Six.
(holds up the rifle)
I know.

SIMON
(re: a corridor)
We run.

JAYNE
You got no idea where that goes.

SIMON
We'll find our way.

JAYNE
I ain't chancing that. I can handle the feds.

RIVER
Doesn't matter.

Jayne and Simon turn to her. She's hugging her arms to her body as if cold... actually, she's just terrified.

RIVER (cont'd)
They're here.

INT. HOSPITAL - SECURITY SUBSTATION - RECEPTION - NIGHT

McGinnis can be seen with his back toward reception, talking to one of his men who is doing paperwork. Another of his men approaches him, whispers something to him. Something like, "they're here". McGinnis turns, registers recognition as he spots someone over at reception that we DON'T YET SEE. As McGinnis crosses toward the unseen newcomers:

AGENT McGINNIS
Gentlemen. That was prompt. We're almost finished here. Prisoners'll be out in a minute. Let me get the paperwork together for you.
(to one of his men, re: paperwork)
Bobby, bring all that over here.
(looks to unseen men)
Not that it's gonna mean much. The men were tight lipped. And the girl was just spewing gibberish. We got it all down, for the good it'll do.

REVERSE — TO INCLUDE TWO MEN

Relatively non-descript, except for the blue gloves they wear. (They will henceforth be known as the BLUE GLOVES.)

JEFF RICKETTS

Jeff Ricketts, along with Carlos Jacott, Andy Umberger and Jonathan Woodward, is one of Joss Whedon's four 'hat-trick' actors, who have appeared on all three Whedon series: *Buffy* (Ricketts played one of the Watchers chasing Faith in 'Who Are You?'), *Angel* (same Watcher in 'Sanctuary', plus the sewer monster in 'Sacrifice') and *Firefly*, as one of the sinister Blue-Gloved Men in 'The Train Job' and 'Ariel'.

What was Ricketts initially told about the Blue-Gloved Men? "I think the words were, 'Futuristic CIA'. It was a teaser at the end of 'The Train Job', the Colonel comes in and says, 'Yes, sir, we've been expecting you,' and my line is, 'We didn't fly eighty-six million miles to open a box of band-aids, Colonel.' How much better can you tantalize someone? I was ready to do it arch, taste every word, and Joss, who directed that episode, said, 'Just say it. Less acting.' Which is great fun.

"In the beginning, I didn't know what to expect. He seemed like a suit and tie, office-type character, a little bit self-consciously bureaucratic, but of course in 'Ariel', we're making people bleed from their orifices," Ricketts laughs, "so I think I'm a little bit more than one of Kafka's bureaucrats.

"It felt like, this is a new universe. I can't even describe it, other than obviously the design felt more open, a new squeaky-clean feel to it, and yet there was a little more anxiety in the *Firefly* world. Maybe it was because the characters we were playing were so squeaky-clean, but horrible, horrible people, too.

"I took the bureaucrat thing very seriously. When they're holding River for us, Federal Agent McGinnis is instructed not to speak to the prisoners. From the Blue-Gloved Man's point of view, you just have a few orders: 'Get the prisoner, don't speak to her, hold her for us.' And McGinnis violates this one thing. Since I'm a very nit-picky bureaucrat, if you do one little thing that I told you not to do, then we have to take out this instrument which makes you bleed from your eyes. So I'm very fastidious about the rules. It was Dennis Cochran, Blue-Gloved Man Number Two, who had to handle that instrument. Somehow, he managed to endow it with a supernatural property.

"The blue gloves were the subject of some debate," Ricketts recalls. "By 'Ariel', the exact shade of blue was being debated offstage." This was partly because blue screens are used in special effects. "'The Chromakey won't deal with this shade of blue.' Also, they didn't want them to look like we were about to go do dishes," Ricketts laughs.

FIRST BLUE GLOVE
You spoke to the prisoners?

AGENT McGINNIS
Well, yeah. Had to process 'em. There was no kind of interrogation, if that's what you mean.
(lightly)
Didn't do your job for you.

The SECOND BLUE GLOVE reaches in his suit pocket, pulls out a thick rod-like device. He squeezes it and a thin spicule extends from each end.

SECOND BLUE GLOVE
Did your men also speak with them?

AGENT McGINNIS
Much as they had to.

A trickle of blood drips from McGinnis' nose. He feels it, dabs at it with his hand, sees it's blood.

ANGLE: HIS HAND

as he turns it over... revealing his fingernails. Blood is seeping from under them. He brings his hand up closer to his face... We FOLLOW his HAND to his FACE, revealing —

His eyes have gone red, bloodshot through. And blood is already streaming down his cheeks as he BLEEDS OUT.

He SCREAMS... Whatever is happening to him is excruciating...

THE BLUE GLOVES

watch. Impassive. McGinnis's SCREAMING takes us to —

BLACK OUT.

END OF ACT THREE

ACT FOUR

OVER BLACK.

The SOUND OF SCREAMING.

INT. HOSPITAL - SECURITY SUBSTATION - HOLDING AREA

Jayne, Simon and River react to the SCREAMS. First it's just the one. Then more — all in the same agony as McGinnis when he died.

JAYNE
What the hell is that?

Simon shakes his head, doesn't venture a guess. River's breathing is coming quicker now. She knows what's out there and it fills her with terror. She's backing away, moving away... Simon sees this.

RIVER
(muttery)
Two by two, hands of blue. Two by two, hands of blue.

She keeps moving backward, stumbles, is nearly running now. Simon starts after her.

Jayne is left listening to the nearby carnage. A beat. He follows the others.

INT. HOSPITAL - SECURITY SUBSTATION - RECEPTION

ON McGINNIS

as we left him, very much dead. Then, CAMERA DRIFTS through the reception area... FINDING another fed. Also dead, also bleeding out of many orifices. CAMERA CONTINUES TO DRIFT... finding another fed. Same thing. And another. And another. Every fed we've seen lies dead in a pool of blood.

CAMERA CONTINUES TO DRIFT... finding the Blue-Gloved Men walking through the carnage, completely unaffected. They walk up to the separator door, walk through.

INT. HOSPITAL - STEEL ROOM - NIGHT

River leads Jayne and Simon into the guts of the hospital. This space is more industrial, less pristine. She keeps moving fast, Simon and Jayne following.

JAYNE
Where the hell's she goin' —

SIMON
There must be some sort of an exit this way.

INT. HOSPITAL - SECURITY SUBSTATION -

❖ Left: The prototype rod weapon for the Blue-Gloved Men.

HOLDING AREA - CONTINUOUS

The Blue-Gloved Men walk in, past the separator door and into the cell area. There, they find the two laid out feds Jayne took out. First Blue Glove takes the pulse of one, Second Blue Glove the pulse of the other.

FIRST BLUE GLOVE
Dead.

First Blue Glove looks in the direction Jayne and the others went.

SECOND BLUE GLOVE
This one's alive.

Second Blue Glove takes out The Device from his pocket.

INT. HOSPITAL - STEEL ROOM - NIGHT

JAYNE
I don't see any exit, and I got no intention of running around like a rat in a maze til we're dead. We're going back.

Jayne starts to go. He pauses at SCREAMING from somewhere above. Maybe best not to go back thataway...

INT. HOSPITAL - SECURITY SUBSTATION - HOLDING AREA - NIGHT

The Blue-Gloved Men step over or past the now BLED-OUT fed, moving ever forward, as...

INT. HOSPITAL - HUM ROOM - NIGHT

River runs down the steps, Jayne and Simon following.

RIVER
Almost there. Almost there.

She reaches the bottom of the steps, keeps running, Simon and Jayne gaining... then she finally stops at a large steel door.

RIVER (cont'd)
There.

Jayne tries the door — locked. A faint TAP-TAP-TAPPING can be heard in the distance. Jayne looks in its direction — fear starting to become evident in his face.

JAYNE
Stand back.

He takes aim at the door with the sonic rifle, BLASTS IT! In these echoey halls, it makes an ENORMOUS REVERBERATING BOOM! But it does nothing to the door. When the sound subsides, the TAP-TAP-TAPPING starts to get closer.

JAYNE (cont'd)
(under his breath)
<Shee-niou> [Cow sucking] high-tech Alliance crap.

Jayne looks towards the tapping sound... about to

freak... turns the rifle around, starts wailing on the lock with the rifle butt. WHAM! WHAM! Nothing. WHAM! WHAM! Nothing.

Simon looks back the way they came. If possible, maybe the SHADOWS of the APPROACHING BLUE-GLOVED MEN nearing the doorway.

Jayne continues to POUND on the locked door with the butt of the rifle.

RIVER
(under her breath)
Hurry...

Then — BLAM! That's the sound of a shotgun blast ripping through the lock from the other side.

The blasted door drifts open... and there stand Mal and Zoe, guns in hand, Zoe's shotgun pluming a bit of smoke.

Jayne reacts, never so relieved to see anyone, as...

REVERSE

HUM ROOM ENTRANCE

As the Blue-Gloved Men appear. They react to —

THEIR POV — of only a little smoke hanging at the empty door. Off that —

INT. SERENITY - CARGO BAY

The ramp is in the process of opening as Kaylee comes down the stairs from the bridge, runs into Inara coming out of her shuttle. She peers out the ramp as she addresses Inara —

KAYLEE
Hey, 'Nara. How was your checkup?

INARA
(dismissing it)
Same as last year.
(re: her peering)
What's going on here?

KAYLEE
Well, let's see. We killed Simon and River, stole a bunch of medicine, and now the Captain and Zoe are off springing the others got snatched by the feds.

Inara's jaw drops. Before she can ask any questions —

KAYLEE (cont'd)
And here they are now!

The ambulance shuttle flies in. As soon as it touches down, Mal, Zoe, Wash, Jayne, Simon and River spill out. Kaylee and Inara join them on the floor, Kaylee moving to the control panel to close the ramp.

MAL
Tell me we weren't followed.

WASH
Nothing in the rearview the whole way back.

MAL
(to Wash)
Take us out of the world. The quicker, the better.

WASH
We'll be out of atmo in five minutes.

Wash books towards the bridge, Zoe in tow.

MAL
Hey. How was your thing?

INARA
As advertised. Lots of needles and cold exam tables. I heard you had some excitement.

MAL
Nothing much. Lots of running around. A little gunplay.
(beat)
Couple of needles.

JAYNE
Next time we come to the Core, I'm staying with the Preacher.

MAL
(nonsense!)
You hadn't come, you wouldn't be getting your big pay day.

Jayne looks to Mal — is there something behind that seemingly innocuous statement? Mal just turns to Simon.

MAL (cont'd)
Did you get what you needed?

SIMON
I think I did. I have the information I downloaded from the imager. I just have to go over it and...
(pauses, hint of a smile)
I'm hopeful.

Kaylee notes the injuries to Jayne's face.

KAYLEE
What happened to your face?

JAYNE
Nothin'.

SIMON
He was amazing. I can't begin to tell you... We wouldn't be standing here if it weren't for him.
(to Jayne, means it)
Thank you.

JAYNE
Hey. You're part of my crew.

MAL
I think I might cry.
(then —)
Jayne, help me with the cargo. Everyone else... make yourselves useful. You got jobs, go do 'em.

Everyone disperses but Mal and Jayne, who unload the body bags from the ambulance, haul them over to the smuggling hold. As they work —

JAYNE
Gotta be one of our best takes ever.

MAL
Doc had a good notion. Boy's got a decent criminal mind.

Jayne kneels by the hold, stowing the goods.

JAYNE
What're you buying with your cut?

WHAM! Without warning, a WRENCH WHIPS Jayne across the temple, knocking him out. Mal drops the wrench by his inert form.

EXT. SERENITY - DAWN

As she takes off and shoots towards the atmosphere.

INT. SERENITY - CARGO BAY/AIRLOCK - DAY

Jayne comes to in the airlock. Trapped between the closed ramp and the double airlock doors. He stands, sees Mal through one of the windows.

JAYNE
The hell are you doin'?!

MAL
(via intercom)
Job's done. Figured it was a good time for a chat.

M U S I C

Composer Greg Edmonson: "I don't remember too much about the music during the airlock scene. I was doing piano. What I thought was amazing about that scene was this was when you begin to see the humanity of these characters, because Jayne really doesn't want them to know what he did. There's a part of him that's ashamed. It's a human moment. I can only tell you how I saw the scene. I just watched it and did music that I thought worked. In other words, I didn't have to lead anybody, I didn't have to punch it up — it was all on screen. It would have worked had I done no music to it. That's the anomaly of this show — it worked because the writing and the acting were so magnificent. I got to be part of the fabric without having to think that the music made something work."

He works the controls, cracks the ramp open. The airlock area fills with WIND. Jayne reacts to that...

MAL (cont'd)
Seems to me we had a solid plan. Smooth, you might say. What I can't figure is what you were doing 'round the back exit.

JAYNE
What? I couldn't make it out the front, I had to improvise. Open the damn door!

MAL
You called the feds.

JAYNE
(indignant)
What — I got pinched!

MAL
Kind of thing that happens when you call the feds.

JAYNE
(selling it well)
I would never do that. My hand to God, may He strike me down where I stand.

MAL
You won't be standing there long. Minute we break atmo, you'll be a lot thinner, you get sucked out that hole.

A loud KLAXON BLARES, a RED ALARM LIGHT goes on — Jayne SLAMS his fists against the airlock doors —

JAYNE
Mal! C'mon! This ain't no way for a man to die. You wanna kill me, shoot me! Just let me in!

MAL
Heard tell they used to keelhaul traitors back in the day. I don't got a keel to haul you on, so...

JAYNE
Okay! I'm sorry, all right?!

MAL
Sorry? What for, Jayne? Thought you'd never do such a thing?

JAYNE
The money was real good — I got stupid. I'm sorry.

Mal says nothing.

JAYNE (cont'd)
Be reasonable. Why you taking this so personal? It's not like I ratted you to the feds.

MAL
But you did. You turn on any of my crew, you turn on me. And since that's a concept you can't seem to wrap your head around, means you got no place here.
(then)
You did it to me, Jayne. And that's a fact.

The fight goes out of Jayne. Jayne takes a long moment, looking at the ramp. He really thinks he's going to die here. Mal starts to go, when —

JAYNE
What are you gonna tell the others?

MAL
About what?

JAYNE
'Bout why I'm dead.

MAL
Hadn't thought about it.

JAYNE
Do me a favor...

❖ Above: Mal and Jayne's coms. These are found items made from obsolete firefighter's distress signal units.

(beat, genuine)
Make something up. Don't tell them what I did.

A long beat.

Then Mal hits the controls and the ramp starts to close.

MAL
Next time you decide to stab me in the back... have the guts to do it to my face.

With that, Mal goes, leaving Jayne between the ramp and the airlock doors. Jayne doesn't bother calling after Mal; he knows he's lucky to be alive. He simply sits. Someone will come let him out... eventually.

INT. SERENITY - RIVER'S ROOM

River sits at a table, scribbling on a pad. Simon enters, a hypo kit in hand.

SIMON
Hi.
(sees her scribbling)
What are you doing?

RIVER
Drawing.

Simon looks at her pad — she's drawn a very well-rendered sketch of a matryoshka (a nesting doll), each layered doll lined up from big to small.

SIMON
That's really good.

RIVER
(re: the hypo kit)
What are you doing?

SIMON
Oh, I... brought some medicine. You remember why we went to the hospital?

River nods.

RIVER
Is it time to go to sleep again?

SIMON
No, mei mei. It's time to wake up.

Off Simon, hopeful...

BLACK OUT.

END OF SHOW

JOSS WHEDON

When we got to episode eight, we had something totally wrong, and I remember thinking, 'Simon. We've got to make Simon cooler. He's got to hire them to do a job,' and Jose worked out all that beautiful hospital stuff. And it seemed like a good time for Mal and Jayne to have a confrontation. At first, I was kind of like, 'Wow, that's a lot of plot.' I was worried about it. And then Tim and I started talking about what we refer to as 'the Jesus Corleone speech', where he says, 'You do it to any of my people, you do it to me!' and that, we knew, was such an essential piece of who Mal had become and was so hard, but at the same time so extremely decent, that we knew it was necessary. And it was Nathan who said, 'Let's use these little intercoms so I don't have to yell through the window and then we can have some blocking,' and it was Adam who said [meek voice], 'Can I come in now?' while we were rolling, both of which helped the scene enormously. We could have held out for it [to have happened later in the season], but again, we were going, 'Okay, let's make sure we are primal. This guy has a lot of threat to him. Let's make good on our threat, because we want people to be galvanized by what they're seeing and not just vaguely intrigued, because we don't have time for vaguely intrigued [laughs].'

CINEMATOGRAPHY

An interview with David Boyd

❖ Left: Scenes from 'Objects in Space'.

❖ Below: Lighting the bridge.

❖ Opposite page top: Lighting the galley.

❖ Opposite page below: Wash steers the ship during 'The Message'.

David Boyd started his college education majoring in physics before falling in love with film, changing universities and becoming a cinematographer (recent credits include TV shows *Deadwood* and *Friday Night Lights*). He believes his passion for Westerns helped him get the *Firefly* gig.

Meeting Joss Whedon for the first time at the job interview for *Firefly* director of photography, Boyd says, "For some reason, we had a fantastically great study of the John Ford film *The Searchers*. We ended up just saying the dialogue to each other, because we'd memorized the scenes," he laughs. "When I said, 'As sure as the turnin' of the Earth,' I think I had that job. My enduring remembrance of *Firefly* was working with Joss Whedon. He's just plain great."

While it is common for television series to build sets with removable walls, Boyd was against this for *Firefly*. "When we play tricks on audiences, they know it. If we use a lens that's a little too long a focal length for the space that the audience knows we're in, I think they sense it. So I was adamant that we would never pull a wall. We would always stuff ourselves in a corner with some camera and get what we could. And what we couldn't see in that frame, we would just cover in some other way. So it would truly be as if we were way out in the universe somewhere. And outside was so dangerous."

There were some unique aspects to *Firefly*'s filming style, Boyd adds. "I love [light] flare. I started off *Firefly* with a lens that was very expensive and very well designed. It had tremendously good coding on it, but this thing would not take a flare. So I quickly got rid of it," Boyd laughs, "and found the cheapest lenses out there I could, which gave us the best flares."

Boyd and production designer Carey Meyer were in constant communication with one another. "I think the hardest task for me probably was having lighting concepts incorporated into the design of the ship that would allow it to be believable," Boyd notes. "That took an awful lot of care and time in the pre-production process as the set was being built. Carey Meyer was so helpful in designing recesses or corners or headers around which I could put lights, or something that would be behind a grid-like material that could mask what it was, but making sure that it would put light in the right places and could be flexible, so that when a character walked one way or another, I'd be able to illuminate that person. In the bridge, Carey put in these wacky goose-neck lights that came across the console. I

knew we couldn't point those things at the actors' faces, so I stole some square aluminum heat pads from the galley set, took them up to the bridge and taped them to the console. We would shine these goose-neck lights into these square aluminum pieces of metal. You'd see the pads in shot. You don't really question what they are, but the light from the lamps bouncing off the heat pads is actually illuminating their faces.

"Strictly from a cinematographer's point of view, *Firefly* was huge," Boyd continues. "In terms of the distance that light was thrown, in terms of the spaces on a stage that needed to be lit appropriately, and the size and weight of the things that got moved around. Before and after, I haven't done anything that big. If we did flying shots outside the bridge, we'd move a big crane around much faster than it was ever intended to be moved around because it had a light on it and this would approximate the roll and yaw of the ship. With a camera on the bridge, and the moving around of this very big light outside the bridge so quickly, you could get a fast bank or a big turn going. To make that stuff happen takes an awful lot of planning ahead of time and also takes a lot of skill on the part of the grips and electricians and camera people to pull it off."

The work has paid off in people's memories, Boyd points out. "People that I've run into since then have said, 'My god, you shot *Firefly*!' Here on *Friday Night Lights*, people want to know about it and they want to learn about it — they want to know how it was done. There's still tremendous interest for that project. Other shows go and never come back. No one wants to know about them. This one endures."

WAR STORIES

Written by Cheryl Cain
Directed by James Contner

CHERYL CAIN

A former assistant production coordinator for *Buffy*, writer Cheryl Cain returned to Whedon's universe as a staff writer for *Firefly* in 2002. 'War Stories' was her first credited episode for the series. Talking about the episode's origins, Cain remembers, "The idea was, what would happen if Zoe had to choose who to save — her husband, Wash, or Mal. I remember Joss and I talking about it in my initial interview. I went, 'Well, she'd have to save Mal.' And he said, 'No, she'd have to save Wash! Because she knows that Mal can save himself and she doesn't trust that Wash would be able to save himself.' It was such a brilliant way to deal with the characters, because there is so much more conflict.

"By the time we got to my episode, it had gotten pretty crazy because Fox wanted the episodes fun and lighthearted. So Brett [Matthews], Ben [Edlund] and I would be working on that and then they would say they wanted it dark instead, and we'd have to scrap ideas. So we started the first day of prep going, 'Crap, we don't have anything!' Joss, being brilliant, came in with, 'Hey, remember we were talking about that triangle idea? Let's do this and this and go back to Niska and see what happens from that.' He gave us a lot of material and we sat down and broke it. Since we had such a collapsed time schedule, we all had our hands in it, just to get it done. I did the initial work on the outline and the rough, rough draft and then we all went in to deepen it. I feel really blessed I have my sole name on something that really had everybody's hands in it. It kept the essence of these people, who were a family and were willing to

do anything to save family. The core was about family.

"The violence was quite a crank up, as was the many ways that we killed people. This was probably the most violent episode. We just mowed through people to save Mal. Fox came back to us and there was one comment about when the guy is melting — to turn away from him. Otherwise, their big thing was that we couldn't have two women kissing on screen. We were like, 'We can kill people in multitudes of ways on screen, but heaven forbid we have two women kissing?' Joss, god love that man, just said, 'Forget it.' And he could say that. We probably cut back on it a little bit, but we were able to keep it.

"I love the moment where Zoe has to go back to that triangle and choose who she is taking out."

Cain reveals Jayne's now trademark line, "I'll be in my bunk", wasn't from her pen. "It either had to be Joss or Ben. Jayne was always the fun guy to write for.

"I loved Inara and Mal. One of the things when I interviewed with Joss that we were both really interested in was, what if Mal and Inara sleep together? He said, 'Would that ruin it?' I'm like, 'No! Then you know that Mal would never be able to be with her because he could never get over his own demon.' How cool would it be for them to sleep together? They have that beautiful moment together and then he fucks it up. I would have loved to see that. They had such chemistry on screen."

TEASER

ANGLE: A reading of River's brain — shown on a screen in the infirmary. Information runs past it — information gathered in 'Ariel'.

BOOK (O.S.)
Have you ever read the works of Shan Yu?

INT. SERENITY - INFIRMARY/COMMON AREA - DAY

SIMON is studying the data. BOOK is as well, though not as close or intently.

SIMON
Shan Yu, the psychotic dictator?

BOOK
Yep. Fancied himself quite the warrior poet. Wrote volumes on war, torture... the limits of human endurance.

SIMON
(absorbed in the screen)
That's nice...

BOOK
He said, "Live with a man forty years, share his house, his meals, speak on every subject. Then tie him up and hold him over the volcano's edge.

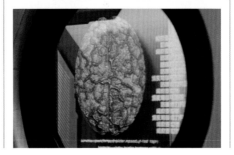

And on that day you will finally meet the man."

SIMON
(looking at his notes now)
What if you don't live near a volcano?

BOOK
I expect he was being poetical.

SIMON
Sadistic crap legitimized by florid prose. Tell me you're not a fan.

BOOK
I'm just wondering if they were. The people who did this to River.

Simon actually looks up at that.

SIMON
The government did this to her.

BOOK
A government is a body of people, usually notably ungoverned.

SIMON
Now you're quoting the Captain.

BOOK
I'm just wondering if they put her through this just to see how much she could take. To "truly meet her", as Shan Yu would have said.

SIMON
No. The more I see, the more I think their purpose was very specific.
(he shows a readout)
Look at that. The pattern. Besides, if all they cared about was hurting River, they wouldn't still be after her. This isn't my specialty, but whatever they were doing, I gotta figure they were close to succeeding.

BOOK
But she's doing better?

SIMON
I've tried a couple of different medications. She's sleeping better, but nothing really stable.

We see a shelf full with pills and liquids.

SIMON (cont'd)
I'll keep trying — certainly got enough drugs on hand...

BOOK
Yes, I'd forgotten you're moonlighting as a criminal mastermind now. Got your next heist planned?

SIMON
No, but I'm thinking of growing a big black moustache. I'm a traditionalist.

On that last line, RIVER and KAYLEE run through the background, from the passenger rooms toward the cargo bay. They are laughing, having kid fun as River flees from Kaylee, holding an apple aloft.

KAYLEE
You give that back! I mean it!

INT. SERENITY - CARGO BAY - CONTINUOUS

The girls rush in and start dodging about the crates.

MAL and INARA are up at the catwalk, in mid-conversation. They look down, but continue on topic:

MAL
I said yes already. Where's the outstanding issue?

INARA
The Councilor is an important political figure and a very private person. I wouldn't —

MAL
So he visits you here instead of you going to his place. Fine. Is the ship not clean enough?

INARA
I just want the Councilor to feel comfortable. And when I say comfortable I mean totally alone.

The cries of "that is mine" and "you gotta get it" and the like that have been accompanying the running about downstairs finally get Mal's attention.

MAL
(smiling)
Ah, the pitter patter of tiny feet in huge combat boots.
(to the girls)
SHADDAP!
(to Inara)
There's nobody sets foot on my boat that I don't meet 'em. Don't worry, I won't start any sword-fights. I'm over that phase.

INARA
Well, I'd appreciate it if you would keep the others from ogling.

The girls, who have failed to shut up in any way, have come up the stairs, headed for the bridge. Mal stops them with:

MAL
One of you is gonna fall and die, and I'm not cleaning it up.

They are breathless, laughing:

KAYLEE
She took my apple!

INARA
Jayne bought a crate of them.

KAYLEE
And that one's mine!

RIVER
Not anymore —

And they're off again, up the stairs —

INT. SERENITY - FOREDECK HALL/DINING ROOM - CONTINUOUS

Into the foredeck hall and then to the dining room. ZOE and WASH sit at the table, Wash eating an apple and Zoe picking one out of a bowl as the girls pass and pitch into the couch area, where they wrassle until Kaylee gets her apple back, holding it victoriously aloft.

KAYLEE
No power in the 'verse can stop me!

She takes a big ol' bite as River goes over to the table to get her own. Wash looks at River affectionately.

WASH
How you doin'?

She smirks, curtsies, takes a bite. Zoe has a knife out, begins methodically cutting her apple into wedges before eating them.

ZOE
These really are the genuine article. I could get used to being rich.

WASH
It's Jayne being so generous with his cut that

confuses and frightens me.

ZOE
It does kind of freeze the blood.

KAYLEE
Zoe, how come you always cut up your apples?

WASH
You do?

KAYLEE
Her an' the Captain both, whenever we get fresh fruit you never just munch on 'em.

ZOE
Do you know what a Grizwald is?

JAYNE
(entering)
It's a grenade.

ZOE
(shows with fingers)
'Bout the size of a battery. Responds to pressure. Our platoon was stuck in a trench outside New Kasmir during the winter campaign... More'n'a week, completely cut off, and the Alliance entrenched not ten yards away. We even got to talking with 'em, yelling across insults and jokes and such, 'cause no ammo to speak of, no orders, what are you gonna do? We mentioned we were out of rations and ten minutes later a bunch 'a apples rained into the trench.

WASH
And they grew into a big tree and they climbed up the tree into a magical land with unicorns and a harp. Honey, there are children present.

RIVER
Tiny helpless children...

KAYLEE
Blew off their heads, huh?

ZOE
Captain said wait, but they were so hungry. Don't make much noise, just little pops and there's three guys kinda just end at the ribcage.

Mal enters over:

WASH
But these apples are good and healthsome.

JAYNE
(dryly)
Yeah, grenades cost extra.

As Mal speaks, he takes an apple, unthinkingly cuts it up.

MAL
We're about 20,000 miles from our last drop, people. Then we can take a break, think about spending some of this money.

A smattering of yays and applause. River looks queasy a moment, shakes it off.

WASH
Could've made more...

MAL
It wasn't a bad idea, Wash, but eliminating the middleman is never as simple as it sounds.

Wash looks surprised — looks to Zoe, who looks busted.

WASH
So you heard about my —

MAL
'Bout fifty percent of the human race is middlemen, and they don't take kindly to being eliminated. This quadrant, we play nice. Got enemies enough as it is.

EXT. SKYPLEX

To establish.

INT. NISKA'S TORTURE ROOM - DAY

NISKA casually watches his TORTURER, a creepy, lethal-looking man, whip what looks like rusted barbed wire into the chest of an almost unconscious hanging victim.

NISKA
(to the Torturer)
Hold, please.
(to the man)
So. Now we are past the... uh... the preliminaries. The little questions — why you skim from the

protection fund, how you could betray my trust — this we are past.

The Torturer hands him a horrible looking knife. A beefy minion, DALIN, enters.

NISKA (cont'd)
Now we get to the real questions. About you. About who you truly —

DALIN
I'm sorry, sir.

NISKA
Ach! I get to the heart of the matter and always interruptions.

DALIN
One of our long ranges picked up a read on the other side of the world. Might be Serenity. Malcolm Reynolds' boat.

NISKA
Oh! Oh, this is exciting news! Malcolm Reynolds, I must see him again!
(to the man)
If it's any consolation, what I'm going to do to Captain Reynolds will make this seem like a bris.
(to Dalin)
Send a team. Bring him here to me. Very exciting.

DALIN
Yes, sir.

Dalin exits, Niska turns back to his man. Comes closer to him.

NISKA
Now. We get to spend some time finding out about your true self, yes. Tell me —

He digs in the knife offscreen — the man gasps in pain, unable to scream...

NISKA (cont'd)
Are you familiar with the works of Shan Yu?

END OF TEASER

ACT ONE

EXT. SERENITY - EZRA - DAY

Serenity coming to land on an arid-looking desert planet.

INT. SERENITY - BRIDGE - DAY

As Wash brings her in and shuts her down, he continues a conversation with Zoe that she doesn't much wanna have. Wash's tone is dryly humorous, but he is not actually amused.

WASH
So when you said you didn't get a chance to tell the Captain my idea...

ZOE
(little voice)
Yeah-huh?

WASH
What you actually meant was that you told him my idea, he rejected it out of hand, and you didn't argue the point or even give it another thought.

ZOE
I gave! Honey, I...

WASH
And then came the lying to me about it, which for me is sort of the highlight of this little adventure.

ZOE
Is there any way I can get out of this with honor and dignity?

WASH
You're pretty much down to ritual suicide, lambie-toes.

ZOE
I didn't want to upset you.

WASH
What did you think of it?

ZOE
Of what?

WASH
My idea. Call the local MDs, forget the fence and go to the source. Better prices, and we know the drugs get to the right people.

ZOE
Captain thinks it'll get back to someone, just

cause trouble.

WASH
<TAI-kong SUO-yo duh shing-chiou doh SAI-JIN wuh duh PEE-goo> [All the planets in space flushed into my butt] was I ever not asking what the Captain thought.

ZOE
Well, I tend to agree with him.

WASH
Tend to? Or have to? I love that you two are old army buddies and have wacky stories with ribcages in them but could you have an opinion of your own please?

ZOE
(a bit pissed)
You're losing the high ground here, sweet-cakes.

WASH
I'm sure you and Mal will take that hill and fortify it with the bodies of —

ZOE
I thought your plan was too risky. I. Thought.

WASH
Then tell me! I'm a large, semi-muscular man, I can take it. Don't hide behind Mal 'cause you know he'll shoot it down for you. Tell me.

ZOE
Right, 'cause what this marriage needs is one more shouting match.

WASH
No, what this marriage needs is one less husband.
(beat)
Right now it's kind of crowded.

He exits, leaving her to stew.

INT. SERENITY - RIVER'S ROOM - DAY

Simon enters to find River shaking, very sweaty, sitting on the bed.

SIMON
Whoah! Mei mei, how are you doing?

RIVER
I threw up.

SIMON
I'm sorry, it's a side effect... We just have to find the right treatment for you. How do you feel now?

RIVER
Going. Going back, like the apple bits coming back up. Chaos.

SIMON
But you felt okay this morning...

RIVER
(smiles)
Played with Kaylee, the sun came out and I walked on my feet, heard with my ears...
(crumbling)
I hate the bits, the bits that stay down and I work,

I function like I'm a girl. I hate it because I know it'll go away, the sun goes dark and chaos is come again. Bits. Fluids.
(really crying now)
What am I?

He takes her in his arms, calms her shaking.

SIMON
You're my beautiful sister.

A beat.

RIVER
I threw up on your bed.

SIMON
Yep. Definitely my sister.

She smiles a little.

INT. SERENITY - CARGO BAY/PASSENGER DORM - DAY

Mal and Inara wait near the airlock. Kaylee and Jayne are peeking out the doorway to the passenger dorm. Book sits with a book (not the bible) on the couch.

BOOK
Didn't Inara express a wish for privacy?

KAYLEE
Oh, we gotta see who she's got! I bet he's handsome.

JAYNE
You gonna give him a lecture on the evils of fornicating?

BOOK
Astonishingly enough, I have other things on my mind.

KAYLEE
Do you think he'll bring her flowers?

Inara shoots a very disapproving look at Kaylee, who shoots her a big grin and a thumbs up.

INARA
Honestly, Mal —

She stops as a tall, handsome MAN in a suit, wearing sunglasses, comes up the ramp.

MAL
Seems a respectable sort.

ANGLE: KAYLEE

KAYLEE
Ooh! There he is!

Book pops up, cranes to look from the bottom of the stairs.

The man walks around the cargo bay, checking everything. Mal holds his hand out to the man.

MAL
Welcome aboard. I'm Capt —

The man turns away, depresses a mike in his ear.

MAN
We're all clear here, Councilor.

ANGLE ON the ramp as a beautiful, composed woman, the COUNCILOR, thirties, comes up the ramp. Inara walks over to her smiling, takes the woman's hands in her own in greeting. Mal doesn't move.

MAL
Huh.

Inara links her arm through the Councilor's, leads her toward the stairs.

ANGLE: THE OTHERS

are surprised.

BOOK
Oh my.

KAYLEE
Well, gosh, I knew she took female clients but... They look so glamorous together...

A beat, as they all watch.

JAYNE
I'll be in my bunk.

Jayne turns, goes back toward the aft stairs.

❖ Left: Shawna Trpcic's costume designs for the Councilor.

front

Concilor

BACK

INT. SHUTTLE II - DAY

Zoe and Mal are getting her ready to go. Zoe is having trouble working the controls. Mal is securing the crate o' drugs.

MAL
Bolles is ready and waiting. Lucrative as this stuff is, I'll be glad to see the last of it. Kinda makes us a target —

ZOE
(interrupting)
Did River get in here, start playing around? Ignition sequence is completely turned about. I can't even —

WASH
(entering)
I can.

MAL
Get it set, okay? We got to be moving.

WASH
Here's a funny twist: no.

MAL
No what?

WASH
No sir.

ZOE
You changed the sequence?

WASH
(to Zoe)
Didn't want you taking off without me. In fact, didn't want you taking off at all. Thought maybe I'd take this run instead. Me and the Captain.

MAL
The Captain who's standing right here telling you that's not gonna happen?

WASH
Well, it's a dangerous mission, sir, and I can't stand the thought of something happening that might cause you two to come back with another thrilling tale of bonding and adventure. I just can't take that right now.

MAL
Okay, I'm lost, I'm angry, and I'm armed. If you two have something to work out —

ZOE
It's all right. We've dealt with Bolles before, shouldn't be a problem. I wouldn't mind sitting this one out, sir.

Beat, Mal looking at both of them.

MAL
This is a <FANG-tzang FONG-kwong duh jie> [knot of self indulgent lunacy] but I don't have time to unwind it. Wash, get her started. Zoe, the ship is yours.

Wash and Zoe pass each other. She's pissed, but not overly so. They're about on a par, actually, but

he smiles at her.

WASH
Bye hon. We promise not to stop for beers with
the fellas.

She shuts the door behind her. Mal moves into
the copilot seat as Wash whirrs her up for lift off.

WASH (cont'd)
So. You wanna sing army songs, or something?

EXT. SERENITY - DAY

As the shuttle lifts off, it crosses over Serenity,
taking the camera to the first shuttle, on which
we zoom...

INT. INARA'S SHUTTLE - DAY

Inara massages oil onto the naked back of the
Councilor, who's lying on her stomach on Inara's
bed, eyes closed with pleasure. Filmy sheets cover
what needs to be covered. Inara's in an off-the-
shoulder silky dress, tied at the shoulder with a
ribbon.

COUNCILOR
That feels amazing. Oh, right there. Perfect.
(sighs)
I should've done this weeks ago.

INARA
(flirty)
I wouldn't have been here weeks ago.

COUNCILOR
And that would've been a shame.

INARA
For me as well... You have such beautiful skin...

The Councilor turns on her side, looks at Inara.

COUNCILOR
There's no need for the show, Inara. I just need to
relax with someone who's making no demands
on me.

The Councilor starts to lay back down again. Inara
stops her with a hand on her shoulder. The
Councilor sits up, facing Inara, curious.

INARA
Most of my clientele is male, do you know that?

COUNCILOR
No...

INARA
If I choose a woman, she tends to be extraordinary in some way. And the fact is, I occasionally have the exact same need you do. One cannot
always be one's self in the company of men.

COUNCILOR
Never, actually.

INARA
So no show. Let's just enjoy ourselves.

Beat. The Councilor raises her hand, caresses
Inara's face.

COUNCILOR
(hushed)
You are so lovely...

Inara smiles, leans into her. The Councilor kisses
her; a soft, sexy kiss. Inara deepens it by placing
her hand behind the Councilor's head.

The Councilor reaches up to the ribbon on Inara's
shoulder, unties it. We see from the back as

Inara's dress slithers down...

EXT. EZRA - DAY

Shuttle II soars over the barren terrain. Cool
desertscape passing by below them.

INT. SHUTTLE II - CONTINUOUS

Wash flies. Mal in the seat next to him.

WASH
So, not a man?

MAL
Not so much.

A beat.

WASH
Damn.

MAL
I mean, I knew her clientele was... varied...

WASH
Yeah, but, I mean, you know... damn.

MAL
Yeah.

Beat.

MAL (cont'd)
Look, this thing with you and Zoe —

WASH
Really not looking to talk on that topic.

MAL
Hey, I let that <NIOU-se> [cow dung] trick of
yours slide 'cause this is a milk run. But I go on a
mission, I'm taking Zoe and that's the drill. You
know that. Suppose we get into a situation here.

WASH
Hey, I've been in a firefight before. Well, I was in
a fire. Actually, I was fired, from a frycook opportunity — I can handle myself.

MAL
And you understand what Zoe's job entails.

WASH
I'll learn as I go.

TIME CUT TO:

EXT. EZRA - RIDGE - DAY

The ship behind them, Mal and Wash are walking
down the ridge, Wash carrying the crate of drugs.

WASH
So, now I'm learning about carrying.

EXT. EZRA - MOMENTS LATER

At the bottom of the ridge, Mal and Wash meet up
with a large man, BOLLES, their contact. He has
two men flanking him.

BOLLES
That it?

MAL
As described. The money?

BOLLES
Open it first.

Wash pries open the box. Bolles looks in, sees the medicine.

BOLLES (cont'd)
Nice to know you're still trustworthy.

MAL
Not so trustworthy that I don't want to see that money you promised me.

Bolles reaches into his jacket, pulls out a pouch. Tosses it to Mal.

BOLLES
(shaking his head)
Can't believe you knocked over an Alliance hospital. The pair you have.

MAL
Stuff legends are —

Mal stops because there's a red laser dot on Bolles forehead.

MAL (cont'd)
<Tzao-gao!> [Damn it!]

WASH'S COSTUMES

Costume designer Shawna Trpcic: "Wash's look was taken from Harry Dean Stanton's character in *Alien*. That was one thing that Joss threw out there. We created our own variation with the flight clothes, but the Hawaiian shirts, that's very Harry Dean Stanton. Wash's character is more lyrical and he's a lighthearted guy, and so we tried to use colors, oranges and greens, that weren't as intense or earthy as Zoe and Mal."

A SHOT rings out, and Bolles drops, dead. Just as Mal drags Wash to the ground, two more dots appear on Bolles' men's foreheads. BANG. BANG. They drop, also dead.

Mal and Wash lying on the ground. Their bodies covered in laser sights as several men in desert camouflage, holding rifles, approach. Wash looks over at Mal, a bit freaked.

WASH
Now I'm learning about scary.

Off Mal's look.

END OF ACT ONE

ACT TWO

INT. SERENITY - CARGO BAY - DAY

Book works out at the bench press. Jayne stands over him, spots him. Jayne's attention wanders at the sound of GIGGLING. He glances over to see —

INARA AND THE COUNCILOR

have emerged from Inara's shuttle. They look like bestest buddies, laughing and giggling together as they descend the stairs. Inara's showing her out. Jayne can't take his eyes off this, his imagination fueled.

Book's struggling a bit with a heavy loaded dumbbell. Jayne's looking off as —

Inara kisses the Councilor sweetly on the cheek. The women embrace. The Councilor exits.

Inara turns back, catches Jayne's eye, then moves off.

Book struggles with the weights. Without looking, Jayne easily grabs the bar, deposits it in the holder.

JAYNE
I'll be in my bunk.

He turns to go. But now Zoe appears.

ZOE
Jayne — grab your weapon.

Book gives a raised-eyebrow look that says, "Funny you should put it that way." The double entendre goes right past Jayne.

JAYNE
Why? What's going on?

ZOE
Maybe nothing. Maybe trouble.

JAYNE
The drop?

ZOE
(she nods)
They're late. Shoulda been back more'n an hour ago.

BOOK
You try to radio them?

ZOE
(shakes her head "no")
Errand such as this, Captain always orders radio silence until the deal's made. If there was trouble... he shoulda been the one to break it.

JAYNE
That's if he could...

That hangs there.

ZOE
(to Jayne)
We go by ground. We'll take the Mule.

Jayne nods, starts to go, but pauses as Book says to Zoe:

BOOK
I'll go with you.

ZOE
No offense, Shepherd — but I sure as hell hope they don't need a preacher.

BOOK
Three sets of eyes'll be better'n two. Might see something you don't.

Zoe and Book hold a look. Finally, Zoe nods.

ZOE
Let's move.

CUT TO:

EXT. EZRA - DROP SPOT - DAY

Shuttle II can be seen sitting up on the ridge. We PULL BACK... the Mule is parked down here. Now, in the foreground, Zoe turns over a DEAD BODY. It is:

ZOE
Bolles.

Jayne turns over another body.

JAYNE
None of 'ems ours.

Book examines one of the dead men.

BOOK
This is precision work. Sharpshooters. From the look of these wounds, I'd say a 54R sniper rifle. Laser sights.

Jayne looks at Book, suspicious/curious.

JAYNE
You do a lot of shootin' at the abbey, Shepherd?

BOOK
Rabbits.

JAYNE
For stew. Sure.

ZOE
Whoever did this... they weren't after the goods.

She knows this because she's indicating the spilled box of stolen meds.

BOOK
No. They were after our people.

JAYNE
(indicates terrain)
Laid in wait. Patient under this sun. Triangular formation. Probably trenched in — there. Maybe...
(sees something)
— there.
(then)
We ain't gonna find 'em here. They're off planet already.

Book and Zoe join him — look where he's looking: down a ridge to a BLACKENED SCORCH MARK in

the distance.

JAYNE (cont'd)
Only one kinda transport I know leaves that kinda mark.

ZOE
Fast burn rocket shuttle.

BOOK
Craft like that wouldn't commonly be part of a ship. More likely we're looking at —

ZOE
A space station.
(then)
I know who's got them...

CUT TO:

EXT. NISKA'S SKYPLEX

Shuttles dock, ships fly around this busy skyplex.

INT. NISKA'S TORTURE ROOM - DAY

BAM! Mal and Wash, blindfolded and hands tied, are shoved with force into the torture room by some GOONS. The GOONS exit, shutting the heavy door behind them. After a beat.

MAL
You okay?

WASH
I think I've been kidnapped.

MAL
Yeah.

WASH
You see where we are?

MAL
No.

Wash listens, tries to get a bead.

WASH
It's not a ship. I don't think we're traveling.

MAL
Good to know...

WASH
What in the name of god is that smell?

MAL
(lies)
Could be anything. Try not to think about it.

WASH
Okay. I'll just... I'll stop breathing. Mal, what the hell is going on?

MAL
Not sure exactly.

WASH
But you've got some theories.

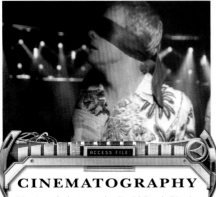

CINEMATOGRAPHY

Director of photography David Boyd: "Again, Carey Meyer put together a set that was eminently shootable. Through the slits in the walls, I could put lights in a ring and have the flare that makes, I think, those scenes believable. Also, the vast majority of it was done with two hand-held cameras, using very light-weight zoom lenses made out of plastic that actually picked up the flare of those lights more than a glass lens would. Then we hung our strong overhead lights over their faces, straight down, as if in the old movies where someone's being interrogated by the Nazis, and then played the rest in shadow. We introduced smoke to that environment to pick up the very bright lights from outside."

MAL
Still working it through.

WASH
I don't want you to spare me, Mal. If you think you know what's happening, then you tell me. You wouldn't spare Zoe if she were here with you, would you?

MAL
Well...

WASH
That's right. You'd be conferring and planning and plotting and possibly scheming. So whatever Zoe would do in this instance is what I want to do. And you know why?
(before Mal can speak)
Because no matter how ugly it gets, you two always come back. With the stories. So I'm Zoe. Now. What do I do?

MAL
Probably not talk quite so much.

WASH
Right. Less talking. She's terse. I can be terse.

Once, in flight school, I was laconic.
(beat, nothin')
If I'm not gonna talk, then you have to. What else?

MAL
Just gotta keep our heads.

WASH
Right. Keep our heads. That way we'll be able to, you know, keep our heads. You and Zoe been in plenty of situations like this before, right?

MAL
Many a time.

WASH
Many a time. You and Zoe...

MAL
Once we know who it was took us...

WASH
Zoe and you. Together in a tricky... Mal, she's my wife.

MAL
Huh?

WASH
What gives you the right to put her in a dangerous situation like this?

MAL
I didn't.

WASH
You did!

MAL
She ain't here, Wash.

WASH
No, but she would have been!

MAL
Okay, but...

WASH
It never really hit me until... Well until I got hit. And blindfolded and kidnapped and this smell is burning my nostrils...

MAL
Wash...

WASH
I mean, I'm the one she swore to love, honor and obey!

Mal's about to fire back, but does a take with:

MAL
She swore to obey?

WASH
Well, no. Not... But that's my point! You she obeys! She obeys you! There's obeying happening right under my nose!

MAL
Zoe and I have a history. She trusts me.

WASH
What's that supposed to mean?

MAL
Don't mean a thing. You're making out like Zoe just blindly follows my every word, and that ain't true.

WASH
Sure it is.

MAL
Not so. There've been plenty of orders of mine she didn't obey.

WASH
Name one!

MAL
She married you.

Wash does a take, looks over at Mal. Well, turns his head at any rate, what with the blindfold thing.

They both react now as the door opens. They hear someone entering. Mal's blindfold is ripped off — he reacts to the sight of —

NISKA

standing there. Grinning. It's your basic "oh, shit" moment.

MAL (cont'd)
<TAH-mah-duh hwun-DAN.> [Mother humping son of a bitch.]

WASH
(still blindfolded)
What?

INT. SERENITY - DINING ROOM - DAY

Money of varying denominations being dumped on the table. Book, Simon and Inara are there, all pitching in. Zoe is gathering it up, shoving it all into a canvas bag. Kaylee appears, adds her share to the kitty.

KAYLEE
Here's all I got left.

ZOE
Thanks.
(calling)
Jayne!

BOOK
How do you know he won't just grab you, as well?

ZOE
Don't think that's like to happen, I walk in there unarmed, make the offer. Niska has his own code, twisted as it may be. Very excited about "reputation". He'll see reason.

INARA
Reason? He's a gangster. The money he paid you for that other job, it was already returned to him.

ADAM BALDWIN

'War Stories' was probably my favorite to shoot and watch, or at least in my top three. I always loved the scene with Mal, Wash and Niska. I always loved Niska. There is something cool about the way we charged down that hallway in a good action scene, and the stray bullets that will get you. That episode also had one of my favorite lines: 'Could be he's harboring some resentment at us for putting his man through our engine.'

JAYNE
(appearing)
Could be he's harboring some resentment at us for putting his man through our engine.

Jayne tosses some money onto the table. Zoe glances at it, grabs it up, then looks to the others.

ZOE
Wait a reasonable amount of time... But if you don't hear back, you take Serenity and you get out of this quadrant. This don't play out right, there's no guarantee he wouldn't come looking for the rest of you.

INT. NISKA'S TORTURE ROOM - DAY

Mal and Wash are both strapped to semi-vertical torture boards, their shirts ripped open and electrodes attached to their skin. The Torturer presides. Niska is there.

As we come into the scene, Mal's body seizes in pain as ELECTRICITY surges through him. Niska nods to the Torturer who turns down the dial. Once the latest surge subsides:

MAL
(with some difficulty)
I'm not... gonna say it...
(turns to Wash)
...again. Shipboard romance complicates things.

WASH
For who? For you?

MAL
For everyone.

WASH
Yeah? Well, what about lo —
(electric surge)
...VEAAAAHH!

MAL
(fighting the pain)
Ain't against it as a rule. But in a situation such as ours, tends to cause problems. Splits loyalties.

WASH
(hmmmph)
Know what I think?

MAL
What?

NISKA
I hire you to do job...

Niska nods. Another jolt for the both of them.

NISKA (cont'd)
Job does not get done...

Wash is totally dazed by the pain. Mal strains to see him, get him to focus. Ignores Niska totally.

MAL
(prodding)
What? What do you think, Wash? 'Cause I'm interested.

WASH
Huh?

NISKA
You make lie of my reputation...

MAL
(to Wash)
You were gonna say something to me. What was it?

WASH
(woozily)
Wha — ? Oh. This "policy" you got against shipboard relationships... that's just you projecting your own intimacy issues onto everyone else.

NISKA
I show you my reputation is no lie. Is truth —

MAL
Yeah? Well that's just downright insightful. It surely is.

Niska nods to Torturer — big ZAP. Wash coughs (maybe some blood?). Looks for a second like he doesn't know where he is.

MAL (cont'd)
Or, could be it's a mite simpler than that. Could be I just don't think you're good enough for Zoe.

WASH
(finally registers)
I don't give a good gorramn what you think.

MAL
Don't you?

WASH
No.

MAL
See, I think you do care. Think you care quite a lot.

WASH
You're wrong.

Niska nods. Pains ensues. Wash blinks helplessly and confusedly at Niska and Torturer. Mal presses on:

MAL
You know me and Zoe got a history — and I figure you gotta be asking yourself some fairly fundamental questions about the nature of that history...

Wash laughs weakly to himself, isn't buying it.

WASH
You never slept with my wife.

MAL
You know that for a fact, do you? You ever ask her?

More electricity. Mal rebounds. Wash not so much.

MAL (cont'd)
We were together a good long time before you come around, Wash. And she is a damn fine lookin' woman.

Wash rallies enough sass to respond, despite his weakening condition:

INARA

"Every well-bred petty crook knows — the small concealable weapons always go to the far left of the place setting."

While Inara's position as the beautiful, refined Companion who entertained an elite clientele (while providing a certain air of legitimacy to the ship) often kept her inside her shuttle, she nevertheless played an essential role in the dynamic of the Serenity crew. "Inara was sort of the heart of the ship," says Morena Baccarin. "Kaylee could also lay claim to that title because she had feelings for everyone, but Inara bridged the gap between them all. In a sick and twisted way, Mal and Inara were like the momma and papa of the ship. They were the parents who don't really want to be parents but they can't help but take care of people. She cared a lot about everyone on Serenity and she offered a level of experience and intelligence they weren't quite familiar with. Everybody had their function but she tied them together. She's very selfless. Inara doesn't let anyone worry about her feelings. She sees what is happening and does her best to keep the harmony.

"I think the reason everyone was cast the way they were is because none of us had to struggle to create those characters. It sort of just fitted. I imagined Inara in my head from what Joss had given me, and we never had arguments about how she would say this or that. A couple of times I would say, 'This line is a little too Western, a little too like the guys' talk, Inara would keep herself removed from that,' and he would agree and change it."

The relationship between Mal and Inara was one of the most intriguing aspects of the show; although they bickered constantly, the chemistry between the two characters was unmistakable. "It is funny," laughs Baccarin, "we would have these little jokes on set where any time I got to do a scene with Nathan during rehearsals and Joss was there, I would just turn to Nathan and say, 'I love you. I hate you. I love you.' That was basically their relationship. They have this intense connection and this love for each other but so many things get in their way — pride being the number one thing. Who knows what would happen if they actually got together? I don't know if they could sustain a relationship. They have such strong ideas and are so pig-headed about them.

"I have several favorite moments between them. I really loved in 'Our Mrs. Reynolds' where I wake up, everyone is in the room, and I'm worried that Mal is going to figure out I kissed him. And then at the very end of the episode, he says, I get it. I know what happened. 'I knew you let her kiss you.' Inara thinks he knows she kissed *him*. I love that they are constantly not getting it."

Firefly was Baccarin's inauguration into television, and naturally she learned a lot from all the talent that surrounded her. "From Nathan, I learned you don't have to memorize anything until you get to the make-up room," she explains. "I was always amazed. He would have pages and pages of dialogue, just read it once, and would know the whole thing. He is a really hard worker and so am I. I was trained classically in theater where you are taught to be really disciplined. He did it with such pleasure, so I learned how to have fun with Nathan. Do your work to the best of your ability but don't take it too seriously. It was all a lesson to me just in terms of the technical stuff and dealing with a camera in your face."

The series has left an everlasting impression on Baccarin. "I believe the last thing we shot was the group of us walking towards the weird aluminum house in 'Heart of Gold'," she recalls. "Or was it? It is so hard to remember because there were so many goodbyes. It was very tearful and really sad. We felt cheated and robbed and were just trying to make the best of it. Everybody felt it was very special and I know, for me, it was a huge lesson in how I want my career to go. I don't want to settle for anything less than that."

WASH
Never happened... Know how I know?

MAL
How. Tell me, Wash.

WASH
The whole "captain" thing isn't Zoe's trouble. It's the guy-she-never-slept-with thing. Hell, Mal — I wish you had slept with her! Then at least she'd be over it!

MAL
You want me to sleep with her? That make you feel better?

WASH
It might!

MAL
Imagine it'd do wonders for her, too.

WASH
Screw you!

MAL
Get in line.

ZAAAAP! Wash starts to go. He's cracking, starts to pass out, maybe never to come back.

MAL (cont'd)
Okay. Gonna do it, then. Wash? Wash! First thing, we get back — I'm taking your wife into my bed. Gonna get me a piece 'a —

Wash's eyes SNAP OPEN he lets out a PRIMAL YELL. Mal relaxes — then Mal is screaming too as the VOLTAGE SURGES. Off their screams —

EXT. NISKA'S SKYPLEX

Shuttle II pulls into the skyplex, begins to dock.

INT. SHUTTLE II

Zoe pilots the shuttle as it lurches, indicating that it has latched onto the skyplex.

Zoe steels herself, rises, moves to the door/airlock. Pushes open the door revealing —

INT. SKYPLEX - CORRIDOR

Goons and guns. Lots of them. Zoe's already got her hands in the air, one of them holding the canvas bag. Even as Goons rush her —

ZOE
I'm unarmed.

They frisk her. Take the bag, look at it.

ZOE (cont'd)
I want to talk to Niska.

Off that —

INT. NISKA'S TORTURE ROOM

SCREAMS. Niska watches with pleasure. Mal and Wash both breathing hard from the pain of the last bit of torture. It's a pause in the action. Dalin appears, whispers something to Niska. Niska listens, motions for the Torturer to hold. Nods to Dalin, who exits.

NISKA
(to Mal)
You will not mind if I pause to do a little business?

MAL
Knock yourself out. No, really.

INT. SKYPLEX - CORRIDORS

The armed henchmen escort Zoe through the skyplex. Zoe paying close attention to every detail of her surroundings. The corridor has large windows along the side that look out onto the factory.

They arrive at Niska's door, where a couple more armed henchmen await. A henchman slides A KEYCARD near the door, opening it. WE MOVE INTO —

INT. NISKA'S TORTURE ROOM

We're in Zoe's POV as the full horror of it is revealed. She sees Mal and Wash both there, restrained and in pain. She tries to stifle her reaction. They don't notice her yet: Mal is whispering something to the droopy-eyed Wash.

Dalin has given the bag of money over to Niska, who looks at it. Takes in the amount. Now Wash blinks through his haze, seeing Zoe there. Mal follows his look to her —

WASH
(muttering)
No, no, no... run, run...

She ignores him, looks away, to Niska.

ZOE
It's five times what you paid us for the train job.

NISKA
Yes. You have had, you say it, good times... I see that.

ZOE
Should be more than enough to buy back my men.

NISKA
This is your opinion, is it?

ZOE
It is.

NISKA
They are perhaps damaged now. Are they worth so much to you?

ZOE
Yes.

NISKA
And to me... they are worth more. I think it is not enough.

Zoe clenches her jaw muscles. Fucker's not going for it.

NISKA (cont'd)
Not enough for two. But sufficient, perhaps, for one.

She looks at him. Sees where this is going.

NISKA (cont'd)
So you now have a question to make an answer. It is for you, pretty lady, and only you, now to ch —

ZOE
(cuts him off)
Him.

She points at Wash. Niska's a bit thrown.

ZOE (cont'd)
I'm sorry. You were going to ask me to choose, right? Didja wanna finish?

Off Niska, open-mouthed, still back at the not-being-able-to-get-his-sentence-out moment —

END OF ACT TWO

ACT THREE

INT. NISKA'S TORTURE ROOM

WASH FALLS INTO FRAME, dropping hard onto his knees in front of Zoe. She helps him shakily to his feet. Niska eyes the money. Waves a dismissive hand at them.

NISKA
He is yours. We are ended now.

WASH
(whispers, desperate)
Mal...

He tries to look over at Mal. Zoe takes him gently by the chin, turns his head back to her.

ZOE
(in his eyes)
Shhh. Start walkin'.

INT. NISKA'S OFFICE - CONTINUOUS

Zoe and Wash move through Niska's office, away from the sound of Mal's continued HOWLING. The door to the torture room slides shut, only slightly muffling the sound. They exit.

INT. SHUTTLE II

Zoe and Wash enter. The moment the door closes, Wash basically collapses. Zoe manages to guide him down to his knees. And she sinks right along with him. He's stunned, staggered, his mind still back in that room. She looks at him with a mixture of relief, worry and, goddamn it — love.

WASH
He's insane.

ZOE
I know it.

WASH
I mean... you've told the damn stories. Saved you in the war. But I... I didn't know...

ZOE
You mean Mal?

Wash nods.

WASH
He's crazy.

She looks at him, not sure if he's in shock or making any sense at all.

WASH (cont'd)
He wouldn't break, Zoe. And he kept me from... I wouldn't have made it.

She tries to hold it together. Touches his face.

WASH (cont'd)
Niska's gonna kill him.

ZOE
He'll make it last as long as possible. Days, if he can.

A look of stoic resolve crosses Wash's face. He rises shakily but surely to his feet —

WASH
Bastard's not gonna get days.

— and moves to the pilot's seat of the shuttle. Off Zoe, watching her pilot husband fire up the shuttle —

INT. SERENITY - CARGO BAY

Zoe and Wash emerge from the shuttle. Wash in the lead.

BOOK
Thank God you're safe.

SIMON
(to Wash)
Let me take a look. How bad is it?

He obeys. She turns to go, leading Wash.

NISKA
A moment, please. This money...

Zoe stops, turns — are they going to have a problem now?

NISKA (cont'd)
There is too much. You should have some small refund.

ZOE AND WASH

Film editor/associate producer Lisa Lassek: "The relationship of Wash and Zoe is one of my favorite things in the show. And that was something that was really important to Joss. In fact, the entire episode of 'War Stories' comes from the moment where Zoe decides to choose Wash; that decision being so instantaneous is something that tells you so much about their marriage. That moment to me is a signature of *Firefly*, but, more importantly, a signature of the larger questions that are in *Firefly*. It shows that the relationship between Zoe and her husband is so different to the relationship between Zoe and Mal. It's what Joss loves to do: switch things on your expectations. It's a big dramatic moment where somebody has to make a decision, and Joss takes that completely away. And it makes perfect sense. You see Zoe's decision comes from a place of love. I mean that's just where you are when you're in that relationship."

ZOE
(tries to move)
Keep it.

NISKA
No, no, no. I insist.
(to Torturer, in Czech)
They have enough for a slice.
(to Zoe, in English)
I wouldn't want the talk to be that Adelai Niska is a cheat.

The Torturer has picked up a knife, moved to Mal — and SLICES Mal's ear clean off. Mal SCREAMS in agony. Niska produces a handkerchief from his pocket. The Torturer places Mal's ear in the handkerchief. Niska then hands it to Zoe, who remains impassive, despite Mal's ROARS OF PAIN.

NISKA (cont'd)
Now we are ended.

Dismissed, Zoe and Wash move for the door, their backs turned to Mal, as his SCREAMS REVERBERATE in the small room.

MICHAEL FAIRMAN

"In 'War Stories'," Niska's alter ego Michael Fairman recalls with a laugh, "I spend the entire episode torturing the Captain." His reaction on first reading the script was, "'Oh my god, this man is being tortured for an hour.' I wondered how that would play, since the only reason Niska is torturing Mal is because he messed up the job. Well, the other reason is to send a message, but there's no real active reason; I'm not trying to get information or make him do something — it's just retribution for him having crossed me. So I had to find different re-actions, different approaches to it. The choice I made was sexual. I mean, Niska is psychotic. I was trying to communicate a perverse sexual pleasure — not so that it would hit people over the head, but so that it was just sort of delicious for me. Even though I mention in 'The Train Job' I have a wife, I didn't make too many choices about what went on with her — but I do know that when I had to torture Mal, it was a sexual delight."

Unlike the *Firefly* regulars, Fairman didn't have to speak Chinese — instead, he had a line in Czech: "There was a woman on the set, one of the people behind the camera, and she was Czech. She wrote it out phonetically for me — 'Cut off his ear'. I pretty well butchered it; as I recall, I made a motion with my hand."

At the end of the episode Niska is still alive. Fairman reminds us, "I scurry away like the rat I am. Which was very good. My heart sang when that happened because I thought, 'Oh, I'm going to come back and do this again!' I couldn't believe it when they canceled the show."

KAYLEE
You okay? What happened?

WASH
(pulling away from Simon)
I'm fine.

INARA
Where's Mal?

ZOE
Niska wouldn't let him go.

Wash pushes past everyone, still steely-resolve guy, heads for the stairs.

INARA
Is he alive?

ZOE
For now.

She moves to follow Wash. As she goes, she hands Simon the handkerchief with the ear.

ZOE (cont'd)
Take that to the infirmary, put it on ice.

KAYLEE
What is it?

SIMON
It's his ear.

Inara, Kaylee and Book recoil, noticeably sickened. Simon looks at it, his head tilted.

BOOK
(pissed)
<Huh CHOO-sheng tza-jiao duh tzang-HUO!>
[Filthy fornicators of livestock!]

ZOE
We're getting him back.

JAYNE
What are we gonna do, clone 'im?

SIMON
(re: the ear; clinically)
It's a clean cut. With the right equipment, I should be able to reattach it.
(looks at them, also clinically)
That's assuming there's a head.

But Wash and Zoe aren't there anymore to answer that. Off the perplexed and worried looks, with emphasis on Inara, whose mind is racing —

INT. NISKA'S TORTURE ROOM

Mal grits and bears the pain. The Torturer is near him, working at his body somewhere BELOW CAMERA. What he's doing is left to our imagination.

NISKA
Do you know the writings of Shan Yu?

MAL
We're starting a book club? What? Are you trying to torture me?

The Torturer reapplies his torment sporadically as they speak.

NISKA
Yes, today I meet you... and you are quite a man.
(Mal cries out again)
An extraordinary man. Yes. But these are not times for extraordinary men. Business is not war. Heroics, they are unseemly. They complicate.

Niska walks across the room to a standing cart, starts wheeling it towards the Torturer.

NISKA (cont'd)
For you I have special machine. Very precious.

The Torturer reaches in, pulls out a thick mechanical hose with an opening like a lamprey's mouth at the end.

The Torturer hands the device to Niska, who holds it close to Mal's face so that he can see its many sharp metal teeth. It's a rather nasty, ugly-looking device. Niska practically strokes it.

MAL
And they say people don't look like their pets...

Niska hands the device to the Torturer, who moves to attach the mouth to Mal's chest.

NISKA
Let's see if we can't learn more about you.

The device WHIRS TO LIFE. The mouth attaches itself to Mal, writhing metallic tendrils shooting out from its jagged teeth, burrowing under his flesh, creeping outwards from the skin on his chest down to his nether regions and up to his head. As Mal SCREAMS —

CUT TO:

EXT. COUNCILOR'S HOUSE - NIGHT

A country house, to establish.

INT. COUNCILOR'S HOUSE - NIGHT

Inara waits in the foyer of this opulent home, uncomfortable about being here. The Councilor is sitting, a bit blindsided by Inara's presence. Imperious — but also a bit nervous.

COUNCILOR
This is an unwarranted imposition. You are in my home. It belittles both our stations to —

INARA
A man will die, horribly, if I do not act. I apologize for my conduct, but as a member of the World Council you cannot be unaware of what Adelai Niska is.

COUNCILOR
His skyplex is beyond our jurisdiction. I really must ask that —

HUSBAND (O.S.)
Sweetie, we're looking for Maynard's elephant...

The Councilor's very vanilla HUSBAND enters with a young boy, their son. The husband sees Inara as he kisses the Councilor on the head. He regards Inara with benign irritation.

HUSBAND
We're taking solicitors at the house? I thought you promised...

The Councilor blanches, moves to speak —

INARA
Forgive me. I imposed on a mutual acquaintance

for the audience. I appreciate your position, Councilor. Goodnight.

Inara, now getting the Councilor's coldness, exits.

EXT. COUNCILOR'S HOUSE - NIGHT

Inara descends the steps to the house.

COUNCILOR (O.S.)
Inara —

Inara stops as the Councilor approaches.

COUNCILOR
You had me in an awkward situation, you didn't press your advantage.

INARA
I'd never take advantage of a client's confidence.

COUNCILOR
I... I appreciate it. I'm just sorry I can't do more to help you.

INARA
(temper rising)
Then do more — help me. The Council can claim jurisdiction over Niska's skyplex —

NISKA'S TORTURE SPIDER

Chris Calquhoun of Applied Effects explains the origins of the Torture Spider. "I got a basic sketch. They wanted it tripod-like but kind of 'nurnified'. I designed it in Solidworks, a 3D CAD program, then printed out the files on our 3D wax printer. The printer is a rapid prototyping machine which will produce a 3D model in wax. Then I made silicone rubber molds of the pieces and poured urethane resin parts." The flexible, lightweight tubing coming from the back of the device is what Applied's crew calls 'Ridley-Flex', after Ridley Scott's *Alien*.

Chris made a fully functional, spring-loaded hero prop. "I made up some little bronze pins to act as catches and hold the sprung legs in the closed position. The hexagonal section on top is spring-loaded in the up position and the catches click into little recesses in the top. When the spider is pushed against someone's body, the hexagonal cap is depressed, the catches pop out of the recesses and the legs spring out. The resin was gray in color, so I sprayed the finished prop black and added silver dry-brush on the surface to pick out the detail and make it look old and used.

"We made a really light foam version of the spider with pin-backs, like earring-retainers, on the feet. This was clipped to the henchman's shirt for the sequence where Mal attacks him with his own device and he runs around screaming. There was a really detailed hero version too, where you could see the detail on the inside, and another which they glued to Nathan."

❖ Above: Niska's Torture Spider.

COUNCILOR
A year ago, maybe, but Niska's become... He's bought off most of the Council. I'd be in the minority and on my way to the grave. I wish —

INARA
(leaving)
I haven't time to wish.

COUNCILOR
I thought Companions weren't allowed to take lovers.

Inara stops one last time.

INARA
He's not my lover.

COUNCILOR
He must be an extraordinary Captain, then.

INT. SERENITY - DINING AREA

A stash of weapons — guns, knives, grenades — is laid out on the dining room table. Zoe and Wash are strapping on as many as they can. Jayne leans against the doorway, watching this lunacy.

ZOE
Here. Six shots, then just drop it. Keep moving.

He nods, adds it to his arsenal. Wash is still recovering, but ignoring any lingering shakiness — he's all about the resolve still.

JAYNE
This here's suicide. You do know that, right?

Wash picks up a knife —

WASH
Worth taking?

ZOE
(chooses a different one)
I'd go with something like this.

He takes her choice. Sheaths it.

JAYNE
You really think you can mount a two-man frontal assault on Niska's skyplex and live?

WASH
Technically it's a one-man/one-woman assault. A unisex.
(to Zoe)
Grenades?

ZOE
Oh, yes. Thank you, dear.

He hands her some flash grenades. She puts them in her belt.

ZOE (cont'd)
(to Jayne)
They won't be expecting it.

JAYNE
Right. 'Cause they ain't insane!

Kaylee enters from the bridge —

KAYLEE
Just got a wave from Inara. No luck with the... Councilor...
(to Jayne)
What're they doing?

JAYNE
Fixin' to get themselves killed.

ZOE
We're goin' to get the Captain.

KAYLEE
Oh. Good!
(then, aside to Jayne)
Can they do that?

JAYNE
No.

WASH
There's a certain motto Jayne. A creed among folk like us, you may have heard it: "Leave no man behind."

JAYNE
Suicide.

INT. SERENITY - SIMON'S ROOM

Simon sits on his bunk. River appears at the door.

RIVER
You're not responsible. It's not your fault.

SIMON
What?

RIVER
You think because it was your idea to steal that medicine, and because it happened when he was out there trying to sell it, that's why he got took.
(confused beat, trying again)
Taken.
(no, beat)
Abducted. The Captain was abducted.

There, she got the grammar right. She smiles at him, looking for his approval. He smiles back.

CUT TO:

INT. SERENITY - CARGO BAY

Zoe leads Wash into the cargo bay.

ZOE
Got a good look at the layout on my way in last time. You let me lead, cover my... back.

Zoe trails off when she sees Kaylee, Simon and Book at the already open weapons locker. All of them arming themselves.

ZOE (cont'd)
What's this?

SIMON
We're going with you.

KAYLEE
If it were any one of us, Captain wouldn't hesitate.

Book holds up a large rifle.

BOOK
This should do.

ZOE
Preacher, don't the bible got some pretty specific things to say about killing?

BOOK
Quite specific. It is, however, somewhat fuzzier on the subject of kneecaps.

Zoe shakes her head, but she's touched.

ZOE
All right, then. If you're looking for me to talk you out of it...

CHUK-CHUK. From above, the sound of a large gun being cocked.

The gang looks up in unison — on the catwalk stands Jayne, Vera in hand, an assortment of guns and knives tucked into every available nook and cranny in his clothing. He's like Space Rambo. They all stare. He's a bit self-conscious.

JAYNE
What?

Zoe smiles.

ZOE
Let's go get the Captain.

Off this triumphant moment:

INT. NISKA'S TORTURE ROOM

The screams have stopped. The Torturer pokes limp Mal twice. Poke, poke. No response. He turns to Niska.

TORTURER
Yep. He's dead.

BLACK OUT.

END OF ACT THREE

ACT FOUR

INT. SKYPLEX - NISKA'S TORTURE ROOM

CLOSE UP ON two CARDIAC INFUSERS as they press into human flesh and fire with buzzing voltage — QUICK TILT UP to Mal's face as his body bucks, convulsing back to life.

Eyes still closed, Mal's head lolls as consciousness returns. He's been taken down from the steel plank he was shackled to, and lies out on a table. The Torturer puts the infusers down and touches two fingers against Mal's neck, checking his pulse.

Niska stands nearby, sipping whiskey from a glass. The Torturer turns to him and nods.

NISKA
Good, good...

The tendril device has been removed from Mal's chest. The Torturer gives its toothed nozzle a

shake, and Mal's blood spatters off it. He goes to the array of TORTURE DEVICES, looking them over.

Niska steps up to Mal, dips his fingers into his whiskey and flicks the alcohol at the flat hell of Mal's severed ear.

NISKA (cont'd)
Mr. Reynolds.

Mal stirs at the pain, coming-to a little bit more, though his eyes stay closed through all the following dialogue:

MAL
[weak groan]

NISKA
You died, Mr. Reynolds.

MAL
(groggy)
Seemed like the thing to do.

The Torturer holds up a DEVICE. Niska shakes his head.

NISKA
When you die, I can't hurt you anymore. And I want two days at least. Minimum.

The Torturer holds up another WICKED IMPLEMENT, and Niska shakes his head.

NISKA (cont'd)
I think many people know the name Malcolm Reynolds. Many know he crossed Niska. They must know what happened after that.

The Torturer holds up another IMPLEMENT, and Niska nods.

NISKA (cont'd)
They must know that business is still running.

Mal looks up, sees the implement, and closes his

eyes again, turning away slightly. He's losing his fight, bit by bit.

EXT. NISKA'S SKYPLEX

Serenity cruises into frame, a black silhouette heading for the skyplex. The ship's lights are out, and its engines are dead.

INT. SERENITY - BRIDGE

Wash sits in the pilot chair, his arms crossed. Jayne and Zoe stand behind him. It's dark in the bridge too. The only light comes from the skyplex, which grows larger in their windows.

JAYNE
Think this'll work?

WASH
Well, except for the com static I'm piping out on all frequencies, we've been completely powered

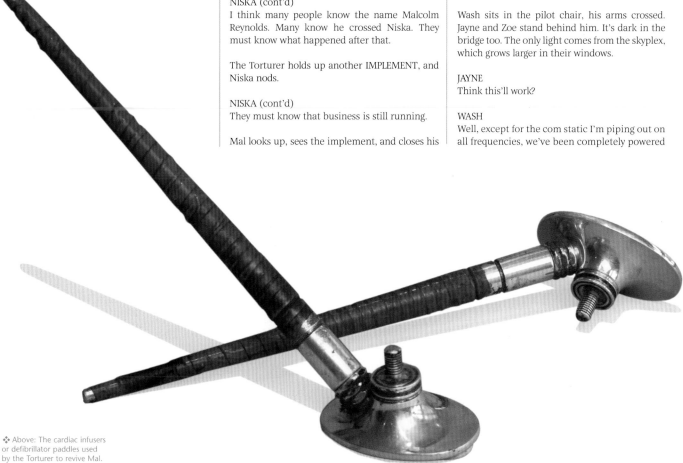

❖ Above: The cardiac infusers or defibrillator paddles used by the Torturer to revive Mal.

down since I fired our attitude thrusters half an hour ago — We should come up on their screens as a radar glitch, if they aren't looking too close...

JAYNE
And what if they're lookin' too close?

WASH
(shrugs)
Hell, I'm just glad we're on course.

JAYNE
(unsatisfied grunt)

ZOE
It's like throwing a dart, Jayne — and hitting a bull's eye six thousand miles away.
(smiles at Wash, puts a hand on his shoulder)
That's my man.

WASH
You guys should get down to the bay. We'll be at their front door in less than a minute.

Wash starts hitting switches, getting ready to power up. Jayne exits. Zoe leans in and kisses Wash on the cheek.

WASH (cont'd)
I'll be right behind you, baby.

INT. SERENITY - CARGO BAY

Powered down; dark. By the light of a lantern, Book finishes affixing some kind of gas tank to the front of the MULE, which is positioned in the middle of the cargo bay, facing the door. Zoe and Jayne enter the bay from above.

ZOE
Book, you good?

BOOK
Yes ma'am. Ready when you are.

ZOE
Kaylee, how we doing on that over-ride sequence?

Kaylee is by the ramp door, working on a BAT-TERY-POWERED KEYBOARD wired into a control pad on the wall. Simon holds a flashlight on her.

KAYLEE
Pretty sure this will pop their airlock doors, if Wash can make a seal on his first try...

JAYNE
You know, I'm smellin' a lot of "if" comin' offa this plan.

Zoe smiles at Jayne — she knows he's in this for the whole haul.

ZOE
Coulda stayed in your bunk.

JAYNE
(smiles back)
Coulda, woulda, shoulda...

He cocks a shell into Vera's chamber, as the LIGHTS COME ON and we hear Serenity POWER-ING UP.

Wash comes running down into the bay, carrying his gun.

WASH
We're set —

Simon and Kaylee lift up SMOKE CANISTERS, ready to pull their pins.

ZOE
Okay, people —
(cocks her gun)
If it moves, shoot it.

KAYLEE
Unless it's the Captain.

ZOE
(nods, all business)
Unless it's the Captain.

INT. SKYPLEX - ENTRY ROOM

It's the same spot where Zoe entered earlier. Niska's radar operator reads a magazine, feet up on his counter. His MONITOR SCREEN flashes with static, until it doesn't, and we see the front of Serenity filling the screen, hurtling forward.

A PROXIMITY ALERT buzzes, and he sits for-

❖ Right: The small lantern used by Book to work by.

ward, just as his booth rocks with the impact of Serenity. On his screen we see the first set of air-lock doors slide open. PAN OFF HIM to the air-lock, through his windows. The cargo ramp begins to fall open, as SMOKE BELCHES OUT of it, into the airlock, obscuring his view. He hits an ALARM.

INT. SKYPLEX - NISKA'S TORTURE ROOM

Niska looks up at the ALARM. Mal, in pain, looks up too.

MAL
Listen, if you got guests, I can come back later —

INT. SKYPLEX - AIRLOCK/ENTRY ROOM

The ALARM still blares. THREE OF NISKA'S MEN arrive, guns out, just as the airlock door opens. The smoke has settled somewhat, and rolls out in a hip-high blanket. An O.S. MOTOR REVS and the Mule ROARS down the hazy ramp toward them. Niska's men OPEN FIRE on the Mule, their bullets hitting the tank strapped to its front, which EXPLODES, taking out the men.

Zoe, Jayne, and Wash come out from either side of the cargo door and march down the ramp. Wash is wincing, walking stiffly, still pained by his tor-ture session.

Inside his booth, the radar man pulls a gun out from under his counter. Jayne swings Vera at him and fires. The GLASS separating the radar man

JOSS WHEDON

I think the torture device was inspired by the machine that goes 'Ping!' in *Monty Python's The Meaning of Life*. You use electricity because it makes big sparks and people can scream and you don't actually have to do anything and there's no blood.

from the airlock SHATTERS and he sails back, caught by Jayne's shot.

More of NISKA'S MEN pile through the lefthand door leading out of the entry room. Zoe levels her rifle and fires. The lead guy drops and the other three back into the cover offered by the doorway. Zoe pulls a GRENADE from her belt, arms and tosses it.

It bounces off the doorway's edge into the corridor beyond and EXPLODES. One of the two men hiding there falls out into the entry room, CHARRED and SMOKING.

Zoe hits the wall next to the doorway, Jayne rolls to its far edge, covering the curved corridor with Vera.

ZOE
Second team!

Book, Simon, and Kaylee come down the ramp, weapons out.

ZOE (cont'd)
Hold this position. We lose this ground, we lose it all.

She nods to Wash and Jayne, who move into the corridor, taking cover behind struts.

She's about to go, but turns and eyes Kaylee, Simon, and Book for a quick beat. They sure as hell ain't soldiers.

ZOE (cont'd)
You're going to hold this ground, understand me? That's an order.

The far door opens and one of NISKA'S MEN storms for them, gun raised. In a flash, before even Zoe gets a bead on him, Book fires from the hip, hitting the guy in the KNEECAP.

He pitches forward with a SCREAM, his face smashing into the side of the Mule — out cold.

Book turns to Zoe, calm and ready.

BOOK
Understood.

ZOE
(nodding)
Okay then.

INT. SKYPLEX - CURVING CORRIDOR

Zoe strides forward, past Wash and Jayne, who cover her from either side. A group of GUNMEN run around the curving corridor towards them, the front two blasted back by Zoe's rifle. Zoe dashes to the side as the rest return fire.

INT. SKYPLEX - NISKA'S TORTURE ROOM

Mal looks unconscious again. Niska and the Torturer turn from him, looking toward the office, listening to the O.S. FIREFIGHT. Niska hits an intercom.

NISKA
Dalin — What is this? Dalin —

Mal opens his eyes, seeing their backs.

The Torturer, looking on as Niska hits the intercom button again, suddenly arches his back, SCREAMING. We hear the SOUND OF THE TENDRIL DEVICE firing its tendrils out. He claws at his back — turning to show us that the tendril device has sunk its teeth into him, through his jacket (so we don't need any prosthetics).

He drops out of frame, revealing Mal, on his feet. Niska shrinks back in surprise.

Mal BACKHANDS him across the face. The old man crumples onto the steps up to his office, mouth bloody, arm up, defending feebly. Mal shuffles toward him, in pretty bad shape, but standing.

MAL
(low, burning rage)
Looks like business ain't running so much as crawling away...
(deadly)
You wanna meet the "real me" now...?

INT. SKYPLEX - CORRIDOR

Zoe, Jayne and Wash continue their firefight, pressing forward down the corridor. A bullet GRAZES Jayne's side.

JAYNE
(just pissed)
Ow, gorramn it —

Zoe (who is BLEEDING from a few FLESH WOUNDS herself) empties a rifle into the guy who shot Jayne. She drops it, and rolls behind the cover of a corridor strut. She pulls twin HANDGUNS from cross-strapped shoulder holsters and pivots back into the fray, firing.

INT. SKYPLEX - ENTRY ROOM

Book covers the door to the entry room; he's got A GUNMAN pinned down with his fire, a distance down the corridor. He peers out and Book shoots, hitting the guy's hand. He screams, dropping his gun.

SIMON
Book — We, uh —

Simon and Kaylee cover the opposite door, and Simon starts firing as GUNMEN head down it toward them. Book rushes over and shoots too.

Kaylee, however, holds her gun shakily, unable to fire. She backs away, wincing as gunmen pitch to the floor under the hail of Simon and Book's fire.

She can't do it.

More GUNMEN come, through the door Book was covering before he went to Simon's aid. They fire at Book and Simon, who manage to dodge into the corridor, using the return of the doorway as cover, but are now pinned between two groups of men.

Kaylee lowers her gun, backing towards the ramp, terrified, paralyzed.

Simon and Book have their hands full, firing down the corridor at two remaining GUNMEN.

JEWEL STAITE

On Kaylee using a gun: "I don't think Kaylee had seen much violence, other than the stuff she'd seen on the ship. It was probably an incredibly terrifying thing to face. I imagined it as the scariest moment in her life, and she felt like she was going to die until River came in and grabbed the gun and saved her."

Staite had no gun training for the episode. "They made sure I didn't," she laughs. "So it looked like I had absolutely no idea what I was doing. The sweet part is, Kaylee's willing to do whatever she can to be a part of it, save her ship and help save the crew. In the movie, it was nice to see her get a little gutsy and fight along with the rest of them, but I like that innocence in her."

JAYNE'S KNIFE

Prop master Randy Eriksen: "Adam is a prop actor, he likes props. He always wanted more and different ones and was always adding his own touches. His character needed the knives and the guns. He had this whole arsenal in his room. Jayne's knife is a found item, it's a coffin-handled Bowie [a model 225, 'Patrick Henry Liberty Bowie' made by Roughrider]. I think we molded it and made some rubber ones. The leather sheath with the star was also found."

❖ Left and below: Jayne's stunt knife and leather sheath, used throughout the series.

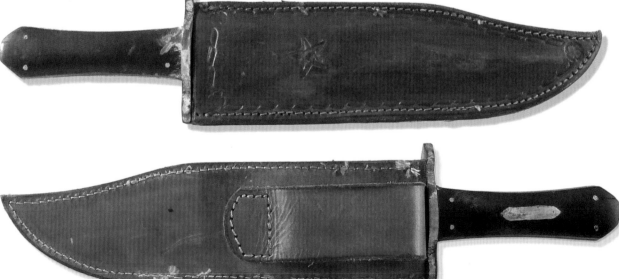

Others slink in through the opposite door. Book fires on them, and they scatter, firing back. Book has to take cover.

THREE OF THEM see Kaylee on the ramp and fire on her, moving in towards Serenity. She darts behind the cover of the cargo bay doorway, as bullets SPARK off its metal hull.

INT. SERENITY - CARGO BAY

Kaylee stifles sobs, clutching the gun to her chest as the gunmen stalk cagily toward the ramp in the background.

And then suddenly River is there, standing before her, with a slight, compassionate smile on her lips. Kaylee startles. River reaches out and takes her gun, Kaylee too surprised to stop her.

River peeks out from behind the cargo bay doorway. The men are on the ramp. They fire as River swings back behind the cover.

RIVER
(flat, unreadable)
Can't look. Can't look.

She closes her eyes, and spins out into the doorway firing three shots, eyes closed, pop pop pop — machine-like. This is from Kaylee's POV.

Kaylee looks out onto the ramp, where the three men lie dead. River, holding the smoking gun, turns to her.

RIVER (cont'd)
No power in the 'verse can stop me.

Off Kaylee's horrified look —

INT. SKYPLEX - NISKA'S OFFICE

Mal backhands Niska again (they've moved up into Niska's office) and Niska hits the floor, scrabbling backward. Mal slowly shuffles after him.

The Torturer enters behind Mal, brandishing the barbed-wire whip from the teaser. Mal is too focused on Niska to notice.

The Torturer jumps him from behind, brings

the whip around, clotheslining Mal and pulling him backwards.

As they struggle, Niska staggers away.

INT. SKYPLEX - ENTRY ROOM

Book and Simon stop firing; the coast is clear, except for the piles of thug BODIES that surround them. They exchange a look.

INT. SKYPLEX - NISKA'S OFFICE

Mal and the Torturer struggle. Mal bends forward, lifting the strangling Torturer onto his back, then hurls them both backward, smashing through one of Niska's windows —

INT. SKYPLEX - FACTORY SHAFT

Mal lands on the Torturer, slamming into a steel balcony that overlooks the abyss of the factory shaft. The Torturer releases his grip on the whip, and Mal pulls it from his throat — the Torturer ain't out though; he starts getting up, and they square off again. Mal's strength is all but gone.

MAL
(spent sigh)
Haven't you killed me enough for one day?

INT. SKYPLEX - CORRIDOR

Dalin's body rocks as he takes several bullets and falls back. Zoe pushes forward, trailed by Jayne and Wash.

She drops to one knee, frisks Dalin's corpse

quickly and comes up with a KEYCARD.

INT. NISKA'S OFFICE

Zoe, Jayne and Wash come in. They rush to the open window, see Mal fighting the Torturer on the edge of the factory shaft precipice. Jayne lifts his gun, takes aim... about to plug the Torturer. Zoe grabs his arm.

ZOE
This is something the Captain needs to do himself.

Jayne lowers his gun.

MAL
(calling back to them)
No, it's not —

ZOE
Oh.

As one, Zoe, Jayne and Wash raise their weapons and OPEN FIRE on the Torturer, filling him with as many holes as standards and practices will allow. The Torturer's bullet-ridden body falls into the blackness below.

EXT. DESERT PLANET

Serenity is parked amongst the dunes, much as it was in Act One.

INT. SERENITY - CARGO BAY - DAY

Inside, Simon repacks some high-tech MEDICAL DEVICE into a METAL CASE. Book and Inara stand nearby. Mal enters.

Kaylee sits on one of the stairways, a distance from them, arms hugged across her body.

Mal gingerly touches at his ear, which has been re-attached. A faint line of fresh scar circles it.

MAL
Sure this thing's gonna stay on?

SIMON
This dermal mender creates an excellent tissue bond. It should be fine... Just don't fiddle with it.

MAL
(to Inara)
Be sure to thank the Councilor for me. Awful nice of her to pull strings and lend us this equipment.

INARA
It was the very least she could do. I just wish you'd killed the old bastard.

MAL
I got regrets on that score my own self.
(to Book and Simon)
I'm told ya'll took up arms in that little piece of action back there.

Book nods. Simon looks uncomfortable.

SIMON
Yes, I — Yes.

MAL
How you farin' with that, Doctor?

SIMON
I don't know... I never shot anyone before.

Book smiles and claps Simon on the shoulder.

BOOK
I was there, son. I'm fair sure you haven't shot anyone yet.

Mal chuckles, heading for the stairs. As he passes by Kaylee, he rests his hand on her hand tenderly. She smiles up at him. He exits up the stairs.

Kaylee turns back and catches sight of River standing at the far end of the bay, on an upper catwalk. She goes cold.

River looks down at her, face blank. After a beat she turns, and disappears into a dark doorway.

INT. SERENITY - DINING AREA

Zoe has just finished making soup for her husband, who sits at the table. She puts it down in front of him. We see that her wounds from the firefight are bandaged.

WASH
Mmmm. Wife soup. I must have done good.

ZOE
(kisses the top of his head)
Yes, dear. You done good. But this is a one time thing, so I suggest you savor it.

Mal enters.

MAL
Did you tell her?

WASH
Tell her what?

MAL
(to Zoe)
Your husband has demanded that we sleep together.

ZOE
(looking at Wash)
Really.

WASH
What? Mal, come on —

MAL
He seems to think it would get all this burning sexual tension out in the open. You know, make it a fair fight for your womanly affections —

WASH
No — That was just the torture talking...
(looking at Zoe)
Remember? The torture?

Mal steps over to Zoe and holds her hips.

Wash pushes his chair back, and winces to his feet.

She puts her hands on his shoulders, and they stare into each other's eyes, play-acting. Jayne enters, also bandaged. He catches this display.

MAL
Sergeant, it's a difficult mission — but you and I have to get it on.

ZOE
I understand. We have no choice. Take me, sir. Take me hard.

Jayne looks at them for a beat.

JAYNE
Now somethin' about that is just downright unsettlin'.

Wash cuts in, takes Zoe by the hand and pulls her away.

WASH
We'll be in our bunk.

They exit. Jayne looks down at the table.

JAYNE
Hey. Free soup.

BLACK OUT.

END OF SHOW

EDITING
FIREFLY

An interview with Lisa Lassek

If you ask film editor Lisa Lassek if there was anything different about working on *Firefly* compared to other TV shows she replies, "Everything. First off, *Firefly* was a special case because I've never been so involved in a show. I was an a.p. [associate producer], so I supervised all the editing, and then mixed all the episodes and supervised the visual effects on all the shows besides the ones that I was personally editing."

Firefly had two other editors, J.P. Bernardo and Sunny Hodge, in addition to Lassek. Lassek cut 'Serenity', 'Our Mrs. Reynolds', 'Out of Gas' and 'Objects in Space'. "That's how the rotation fell, but I worked on all the episodes. I would oversee the first versions of everything and then pass them on to Joss; and then I did all the mixes, the sound effects, the music and things that we put in at the last minute. So I was living and breathing *Firefly*. I feel like *Firefly* is by far the most ambitious show I've ever worked on, because not only is it tackling the politics of a whole new universe, and the social commentary on our own world, but the characters were much richer and there are more stories to tell with them than we ever got a chance to tell, unfortunately. I remember being on the set one day and Joss and Tim running up to me, like they couldn't contain themselves, to tell me the story that was eventually going to be 'Out of Gas'. Not only are the creators engaging in dialogue with everybody all the time, but they were so excited about this episode they had just been breaking that they couldn't wait to tell me about it."

Firefly was edited on three Avid computer systems, though Lassek feels her film school training, physically handling film, helped teach her the importance of the individual frame. For her, editing is a very organic process. "When you're in the act of editing, it's so intuitive. You can go back [in hindsight] and say, 'Oh, the effect of this was to achieve this.' But when I'm doing it, it's whatever feels right."

Lassek experienced many challenges in creating a new universe, not least when it came to soundeffects: "We had a heck of a time coming up with beeps that weren't beeps, so we called them 'chones' — somewhere between a chime and a tone. The guns couldn't sound like regular guns — they had to have a little bit of something extra. We had an amazing sound team [at post-production facility] Todd-AO. The harder things were when we were creating sounds for the first time, like, what does the airlock sound like, and what sound does every single ship make?

"There will be nothing like *Firefly* again in my life," says Lassek, who went on to edit *Serenity*. "After it was canceled, we finished those last three episodes with the same amount of love that we did the other episodes, but we knew that that was it. We were in denial and then eventually we got around to acceptance, but we really were grieving. Except for Joss, who I feel never got past the denial phase," Lassek laughs. "Our grief hit us in the heart, we felt like we were slain, and we tried to pick up the pieces. The end, the finality of the end and that grief that you have never happened for Joss, so he never gave up and in his mind, he was like, 'This show has got to go on.' He never lost that passion to make it happen. That's how *Serenity* the movie got made, Joss's inability to accept that *Firefly* was over. The day they finally announced that Universal would green-light it was the greatest joy, because it was so unexpected. It's hilarious that one of the catch-phrases for the show is, 'done the impossible', because it couldn't fit more perfectly."

❖ Left: Jayne's flash-back scene from 'Out of Gas'.

❖ Below: Mal, Zoe and Wash on the bridge during 'Objects in Space'.

"I CALL IT VERA"

Jayne's Weapons

"Callahan fullbore autolock, customized trigger and double cartridge thorough-gauge." She really does sum up Jayne's character very nicely: big, awkward, entertaining, clunky and very, very dangerous.

This prop has become one of the icons of the show. If you talk to Browncoats anywhere and mention Jayne, it isn't long before Vera pops up. Vera was made in Mike Gibbons of Gibbons Ltd's shop and is based on a Saiga 12 automatic shotgun, made in Russia and designed on the Kalashnikov assault rifle.

"Randy Eriksen would call from time to time asking for something different for an episode. You know, different looks or something completely new. I forget exactly how it was scripted but he wanted a world-beater — a big, nasty weapon for Jayne. They didn't have a huge budget for it. I remembered I had this bad guy weapon from the De Niro/Murphy movie *Showtime*. Randy, Larry, my gunsmith Jim Bolland and myself all sat round and put our heads together to come up with the modifications Randy wanted. You know, the cartridges in the buttstock, the different types of scopes, the flash-hider on the muzzle. We put it together basically from what was already here. I think the only pieces we actually custom-made for Vera were the flash-hider, the scope mounting rail and the cartridge holder in the stock. Of course, this is on top of what we'd already done for *Showtime*."

Although Vera never actually fired in *Firefly*, she was seen to 'shoot' at the energy web in 'Our Mrs. Reynolds'. Mike admits, "She never really fired. That was a gag that Special Effects came up with." The script called for Vera to be inside a space suit. There was a second flash-hider made which was attached to a gas-gun rig in the suit. A gas gun is a tube, a reservoir of gas and a solenoid valve which allows the gas to be released through the tube in controlled bursts. A pilot light on the side of the flash-hider ignited the gas as it came out of the tube. The result is a gas flare which looks very much like a large muzzle flash but without the noise and percussion of a blank. "We decided that using shotgun blanks and actually firing Vera would have destroyed the space suit. On the *Showtime* gun Vera is based on, the actual barrel length is around six inches. To make the gun work properly the blanks were pretty horrendous. They were very powerful

in order to develop the pressure required to cycle the action. Close range work with those things was out of the question. The noise, the flash and the concussion were too much. In fact, the director of *Showtime* described them as 'evil'."

Vera's construction is unusual. The Saiga 12 has been chopped down to a simple receiver block and short barrel with all the other machined parts bolting on. In the original *Showtime* configuration, the guns were designed to operate either folded or unfolded. Folded meant the buttstock and barrel both hinged up and collapsed onto the top of the gun. Vera's additional parts mean she can no longer be folded without removing the scopes, the scope mounting rail, the flash-hider, the cartridges and cartridge holder in the buttstock. In *Showtime*, the guns were firing live shotgun blanks, and Vera has a magazine and adapter which will accomodate these. She also has a

VERA'S VITALS:

Length: 90cm
Height, top of scope to bottom of mag: 45 cm
Width: 7 cm at widest point
Capacity: 12 rounds
Caliber: 12 gauge
Construction: CNC machined aluminum alloy components anodized in lilac, blue and gold. Some steel parts and phenolic-impregnated, laminated wood grips.
Weight: Around 12.69 kg (28 lbs) depending

second magazine which carries the huge, brass-cased dummy rounds used in *Firefly*.

In the hands, Vera has a tendency to feel a little top-heavy and there isn't a great deal of room for your hand on the forward grip. However, she's an extremely charismatic prop and an iconic piece of television history. Vera represents an ideal pairing of character and hand prop. You really can't imagine Jayne without her, or vice versa. Vera also pays tribute to the creative people behind *Firefly*, proving you can do great work on a limited budget. As Jayne himself says, "This is the best gun made by man... I call it Vera."

The man they call Jayne is a bit of a character. It's only fitting that his weapon of choice would be too. Jayne's sidearm was made at Gibbons Ltd's Burbank workshop (Gibbons supplied all the weapons on *Firefly* with the exceptions of the Alliance sonic rifles and Mal's pistol). Mike Gibbons remembers the prop well: "When Randy Eriksen first came in and we were looking at stuff for the show, we had some replica, but live-firing, Civil War Le Mat revolvers. These are unusual in that they are a nine-shot revolver and they have a short shotgun barrel in the middle of the cylinder, under the main barrel. Randy had seen some of the guns we'd done for the Jet Li movie *The One* and thought something like that might be good, so some of the influences for the Jayne pistol came from there. The *Firefly* production loved that Le Mat. They designed lots of stuff to go on it. It's a big, ugly Western-style revolver, but they fell in love with it. We made two Hero guns for Jayne."

The base gun is a live-firing reproduction of a Civil War Le Mat Cavalry model. Very few changes were made to convert the Le Mat into Jayne's gun. A crenellated top-rib was machined out of steel to fit along the top of the barrel. The front sight was removed and a small, flat, steel piece made to fit in the now-empty dovetail in front of the new rib. The shotgun barrel was removed and an assembly of machined parts made to replace it. The cylindrical assembly comprises three parts — inner barrel, outer barrel and end cap — all held firmly in place with recessed socket head Allen screws. The retainer ring for the original shotgun barrel was left in place and the machined parts are assembled around it. All in all, a very strong arrangement. The only other addition was a turned steel stem, with a sphere at the end. This replaces the original loading ramrod — an essential tool for the black powder shooter but not required in the future.

There's a scoop-shaped fairing slung under and in front of the cylinder. Its purpose is to change the lines of the Le Mat and make it look a little more sci-fi. The scoop is

retained in place by a spring-loaded press stud. To disassemble the piece the stud is depressed allowing the scoop to swing down into the open position. The whole section forward of the cylinder will now unscrew. The barrel and the machined section move as one piece. The pistol can be seen disassembled for cleaning on the mess table in 'Ariel'. If you look closely at the disassembled gun on the table, you can see that there are nine brass cartridges in a line next to it. As supplied, the Le Mat is a black powder weapon requiring each cylinder to be loaded with powder, wad and ball — like a miniature cannon. Mike says, "The base gun was a black powder weapon converted to fire cartridges. There are several reasons for doing the conversion: it's safer, no horsing around with loose black powder; you don't have to worry about chain-fires (several cylinders firing at once); you don't have all the grease and the goo and the wads flying out the front; it's much safer and it saves the production money because reload time is much shorter and reliability is much better. Since the Le Mats were converted to cartridge long before *Firefly* came along, we sleeved down the existing shotgun barrel in the middle of the cylinder to .38 caliber so we could fire it on screen with a blank, should the need arise."

In the hand, Jayne's pistol dives, nose first, toward the deck at an alarming rate. The total lack of balance is a little worrying until you put your second finger onto the trigger guard spur. It all suddenly makes sense. The base weapon was designed for a cavalry officer and, on horseback, a steadying influence is required for a sure aim. The second finger provides this, and the gun settles into balance quite nicely. It's still very hefty, at 1.96 kg (4.32 lbs) unloaded, but it doesn't feel ungainly. Jayne's gun fits snugly into Joss Whedon's *Firefly* universe. It's a fusion of the old and new, past and future. Initially it seems rather contradictory and a bit of an oddball. But it grows on you.

TRASH

Written by Ben Edlund & Jose Molina
Directed by Vern Gillum

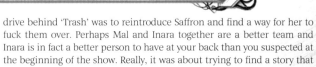

BEN EDLUND

Ben Edlund reflects: "'Trash' to me, because it was more, say, sci-fi ambitious, didn't have quite the focus as a story that the others [Edlund's 'Jaynestown', Molina's 'Ariel'] did. It wasn't as much a story about *Firefly* and about those people as it was telling more about Saffron and building her up as a romantic foil in the series. It was more a puzzle piece for a larger puzzle than it was a fully formed episode, in my opinion. If that had been allowed to go its way over a couple of seasons, my guess is that Saffron would constantly come back, always fuck them over, but almost affectionately. Saffron and Mal would appreciate each other for their bombastic, crazy misdeeds, and there would be a relationship that would tease itself along through the episodes, so that there could be moments where Inara would be actually jealous of Mal and Saffron. I think primarily the drive behind 'Trash' was to reintroduce Saffron and find a way for her to fuck them over. Perhaps Mal and Inara together are a better team and Inara is in fact a better person to have at your back than you suspected at the beginning of the show. Really, it was about trying to find a story that would highlight the dynamics between those three characters."

There's also some resolution between Jayne and Simon and River. "I think that there were some things that had to be addressed a couple of times in terms of the crap that Jayne pulled in 'Ariel'. You want to feel like everything has its impact, that there were feelings that would be festering and had to be dealt with over time. This was organic to where those characters would be and gave them something to go through in the course of that story."

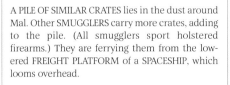

TEASER

EXT. WASTELAND - DAY

SLOW CAMERA PAN across a flat vista of shattered rock. Barren. Lunar. PAN ONTO a MAN, seated a short distance away on the ground. His side is to us, and he is BUCK NAKED. It's MAL REYNOLDS. He lifts his head, nodding to himself as he takes in his surroundings.

MAL
(flatly)
Yep... That went well.

CUT TO BLACK:

TITLE APPEARS: "SEVENTY-TWO HOURS EARLIER..."

EXT. DUST PLANET - NIGHT

A LARGE CRATE slams down onto the ground, hard. The two SMUGGLERS who were hefting it straighten, turning to go. WIDEN to see that Mal stands close by, arms crossed.

A PILE OF SIMILAR CRATES lies in the dust around Mal. Other SMUGGLERS carry more crates, adding to the pile. (All smugglers sport holstered firearms.) They are ferrying them from the lowered FREIGHT PLATFORM of a SPACESHIP, which looms overhead.

MONTY (O.S.)
Malcolm Reynolds!

A VERY LARGE MAN steps off a ladder that goes up from the platform to the belly of the ship, beaming at Mal.

He's a big, gut-toting bear of a man. Not pretty. Not in the least. Think of a greasy Brad Garrett with bad teeth.

MONTY
Y'old son-of-a — Com'ere!

MAL
Oh hey Monty —

He sweeps a mildly protesting Mal up into a bear-hug, lifting him off his feet for a beat.

MAL (cont'd)
(wheezes)
How — you — do — in'?

Monty releases him, one mitt still clapped on Mal's shoulder, shaking it with rough welcome.

MONTY
They didn't tell me you were picking up this leg of the run.

MAL
Yeah, things were a little slow. Figured to do a little honest smuggling 'tween jobs.

MONTY
(scans desert)
Where's that sorry-ass ship a' yours?

As they speak, Monty's ND CREW continues off-loading the crates, passing in and out of frame.

MAL
Monty, two boats like ours meeting on an empty

JOSE MOLINA

Due to an ever-more-demanding schedule, Jose Molina says the *Firefly* writing process became an increasingly joint effort. "When 'Ariel' was done, Cheryl Cain did a full draft of 'War Stories'. After that, everything was a lot more collaborative in the scripting stage. 'Trash' and 'The Message' were the two additional episodes that the network ordered, so when people were sent off to script, we had caught our breath a little bit, but not enough that one person could go off and crank out a script at a fast enough pace. So on 'Trash', Ben Edlund and I were sent off together to write two acts each.

"The Macguffin came to be what it was after 18,411 things were eliminated," Molina semi-quips. "For a while, the Macguffin was going to be *Sgt. Pepper*'s, but we couldn't get the rights. I had the idea that

it would be a globe of Earth-That-Was, which is something that had been referred to a lot of times, but we'd never seen it. I called Ben and he thought that was very cool. By the time we got into work on Monday, Joss had already had the idea that he wanted it to be the first laser gun. The ultimate argument was that a big fat ball wouldn't fit down the trash chute and it would look a little ridiculous if Mal was trying to hide a big globe. He'd look like pregnant Mal!"

Who came up with the idea of the opening? "Joss," Molina laughs. "The idea of starting with naked Nathan in the middle of the desert at five in the morning, when it's freezing cold in the middle of Lancaster [California], I think just appealed to Joss too much to not figure out a story to go with it."

---

rock like this, it just screams contraband to the fed. Or have you forgotten that time you got pinched on Beylix?

MONTY
(points to his own temple, nodding)
Always thinking, ain't ya. Smarts. That's what you got. Smarts.

MAL
(shrugs)
Okay.
(looks closer at Monty)
Something's different.

MONTY
(smiles proudly)
Yup.

MAL
You look — there's something —
(Monty strokes his chin)
The beard! You shaved off the soup-catcher!

MONTY
Yup.

MAL
I thought you were gonna take that ugly chin-wig to the grave —

MONTY
(chuckles)
So did I. But she didn't much like my whiskers...

MAL
She — ?

MONTY
(calls out)
Bridgit!
(to Mal)
What the hell am I thinking, I got to introduce you to the missus!

MAL
Monty! You've fallen from our noble bachelor ranks?

MONTY
Wasn't looking to, but she kinda swept me off my feet. Bridgit!

A woman hurries to them obscured by the smuggly bustle.

MAL
Well she must be a rare specimen indeed.

MONTY
That don't begin to cover it. Mal, I want you to meet my Bridgit.

And she steps out from behind Monty, smiling — until she recognizes Mal. A beat as he and SAFFRON look at each other.

Saffron sweeps a foot under a smuggler's leg, tripping him forward, pulling his gun from its holster as he falls, and pirouetting over his body as he hits the dirt, coming out of the spin with the gun locked on Mal's head, just as Mal's gun is flashing from his holster, locked on hers — a Woo-off. They are frozen, Monty right in the middle, nonplussed.

MONTY (cont'd)
So... you guys have met.

BLACK OUT.

END OF TEASER

ACT ONE

EXT. DUST PLANET - NIGHT

Right where we left off. Mal and Saffron sidestep, guns trained, slowly circling, very intense. Monty stands nearby, brow knitted with confusion.

MONTY
Mal — why you got a piece trained on my wife?

MAL
She ain't your wife, Monty —

MONTY
Huh? I married 'er, didn't I?

MAL
Yeah, so did —

Mal's cut off before he can finish, because in the

instant Mal's eyes flick toward Monty, Saffron scissors up a high kick, knocks the gun out of Mal's hand. She has the drop on Mal for an instant, but doesn't fire. Mal lunges, sweeping her arm to the side, catching her wrist in his grip and squeezing hard. She drops the gun. Saffron throws her head forward, smashing into Mal's nose painfully.

MAL (cont'd)
Gaaah!

MONTY
Bridgit!

Mal staggers back, buffeted by a series of punches from Saffron. Mal fires one punch back, catching her on the chin and knocking her to the ground.

MONTY (cont'd)
Mal!

She lands on her back, mostly unfazed, and instantly rolls for the gun a short distance away. Just as she almost reaches it, Mal sails in on top of her, tackling her flat.

SAFFRON
Get OFF!

She swings an elbow back, hits the side of Mal's head hard. He reels, she rolls on top of him, hands around his throat. He does the same, and now they're strangling each other. They do this for a vicious beat, until —

MONTY (O.S.)
(roars)
Gorramnit! That's enough!

Monty's big hands drop into frame, lifting them both off the ground and pulling them apart. They're both breathless, Mal's got a BLOODY NOSE.

MONTY
Now what the hell is goin' on here? Whaddya mean she ain't my wife?

MAL
She ain't your wife... 'cause she's married to me.

SAFFRON
(also huffing)
Don't listen to him!

MAL
It's true. Half-a-year back, out at the Triumph Settlement. Didn't call herself "Bridgit" then. It was "Saffron". Hitched me by surprise, got on my ship, and tried to steal it out from under me... She's as cold as ice and dead crazy on top of it.

SAFFRON
You're a liar, Malcolm Reynolds!

MONTY
Oh, he's a lot of things. But a liar he ain't. All the terrible thick we been through, he ain't never lied to me, not even once.
(pointed to Saffron)
And I never got to telling you his name.

MAL'S COSTUME

Costume designer Shawna Trpcic: "The direction from Joss was American, go back to the frontier and pioneer of the land. We researched World War One and Two pilots and Civil War and frontier characters and, out of all those different images, we came up with five or six different types of sketches and Joss picked them out. It was pretty much Civil War pants and a Civil War jacket, but made out of leather like a frontiersman. It was a mishmash of a bunch of different things and a little Han Solo thrown in — because we like him [laughs]! The Han Solo influence is in the holster and the gun belt, which isn't a copy at all, that's where the design came from — slung over the side like a cowboy."

NATHAN FILLION

Fillion says finding Mal was a challenge, since his own life is so different from the character's, but Whedon's attention to detail, even down to costuming, helped him assume Mal's skin. "Joss was very specific in his vision. I didn't look at my Mal Reynolds costume and say, 'You know what this needs?' or 'You know what sucks about this?' No, I was very happy about it. I looked like a mean Charles Ingalls [Pa on *Little House on the Prairie*]. I really liked that — the frontierism of what we were doing. I loved that we weren't wearing silver jumpsuits or jumpsuits of any kind. I was very excited about that."

Saffron drops all pretense — the jig is up.

SAFFRON
Oh, hell. Fine. Be like that.

She pulls away from Monty and starts neatening herself up, brushing back her hair, wiping the dirt from her face.

MONTY
(hurt)
You said you loved me for me...

Mal looks at Monty, saying with tender frankness:

MAL
Believe me, Monty, she says that to all the boys.

Off of Monty's crestfallen face we CUT TO:

EXT. DUST PLANET - NIGHT

MONTY'S SHIP as its engines FIRE UP, whipping a small cloud of dust around the tiny figures of Saffron and Mal. [Note: the design of this ship must be such that it can take off without its engines incinerating what is directly beneath it.]

SAFFRON stands with her arms crossed, looking up irritably, lit by the O.S. glare of the ship's lights. Mal is in the BG, with the crates. He dabs at his bloody nose with a white kerchief. Monty's voice echoes down over the SHIP'S

LOUDSPEAKER, choked with hurt.

MONTY (O.S.)
Damn you, Bridgit! Damn you ta Hades! You broke my heart in a million pieces! You made me love you, and then y — I SHAVED MY BEARD FOR YOU, DEVIL WOMAN!

SAFFRON
Whatever.

After a beat, a DUFFEL BAG drops into frame from above, SLAMMING into the ground. The O.S. ship pulls away with a burst of engine thrust, the light from it fading.

SAFFRON (cont'd)
<BUN tyen-shung duh ee-DWAY-RO.> [Stupid inbred stack of meat.]

She moves to the duffel bag, crouches, unzips it, and roots around inside. The barrel of Mal's pistol enters frame, pressing against her temple.

MAL
You're goin' to wanna pull your claw out of that bag, nice and slow.

SAFFRON
Relax. I'm not going for a gun or anything.

She slowly pulls a small cylinder out of the bag, and shows it to him, cranking it. It's lipstick.

SAFFRON (cont'd)
Just freshening up.

She's about to apply it when Mal snatches it and hucks it out into the O.S. desert.

MAL
You and lipstick is a dangerous combination, as I recall.
(gestures with gun)
Now get up and turn around.

She does so, with some impatience. Mal moves in and frisks her, trying to be businesslike, but she responds in a way that crackles with sexual tension.

SAFFRON
Oh... Yeah... Just like old times.

MAL
We don't have any old times. I just don't want you pullin' a pistol out of... of anywhere...

She writhes into him a little as he finishes frisking her.

SAFFRON
(super sexy)
Mmmm. You missed a spot...

Mal gives her a rough shove and she stumbles forward a step.

MAL
Can't miss a place you never been.

She am freaky — turns to him not with anger, but with practiced emotion — playing to Mal as if they have a troubled, but real marriage.

SAFFRON
Marriage is hard work, Mal. I know it... But that doesn't mean we have to give up...
(moves closer to him)
Sure, we've had our spats. Maybe I made some bad decisions along the way.

MAL
Oh, you're a tweaked one, you are.

SAFFRON
(smiles)
But face it, hubby. I'm really hot.

MAL
Uh huh.
(waves gun at her)
Start walkin'.

SAFFRON
Walking? Walking where?

MAL
Pick a direction. Just don't turn around.

SAFFRON
Come on, Mal.

MAL
This is my scrap of nowhere. You go on and find your own.

SAFFRON
You can't just leave me here, on this lifeless piece-of-crap moon...

MAL
Sure I can.

SAFFRON
I'll die.

MAL
Well, as a courtesy, you might start getting busy on that, 'cause all this chatter ain't doin' me any kindness.

Saffron sits down on her duffel bag with a defiant pout. But she seems done with the full court press, more herself now.

SAFFRON
Why don't you just go ahead and shoot me, then?

MAL
I dunno.
(thinks on this)
Why didn't you shoot me? Back there, when I took my eyes off you for a split? Shamed to say it, but I gave you the window.

SAFFRON
(condescending sigh)
You and Monty, you fought in the war together, right?
(he nods)
I could smell that. The war buddy bond is a tough one to crack. I knew if I shot you I'd lose Monty anyway. You just had a better hand of cards this time.

MAL
It ain't a hand of cards. It's called a life. I've got a better life than you. And that's just barely, and just 'cause I don't spend my every waking hour pissing all over it, like some folks I'm holdin' a gun on...

Saffron flashes a tight, insincere smile.

SAFFRON
Touché, mon amour.
(as she stands)
Seriously, Mal. You have to give me a ride.

MAL
(bitter laugh)
Woman, you are completely off your nut.

SAFFRON
I won't make trouble. You can stick me in one of those crates if you like. Just don't leave me he —

Mal SHOOTS. A bullet kicks up the dust about three feet from her. A beat. She sticks out her tongue. ANOTHER BULLET kicks up dust, two feet away. Another beat. She bends, lifting one strap of her heavy bag. She starts dragging it off, struggling. Then she stops and turns again.

SAFFRON (cont'd)
This was all your fault, you know. I had a perfect crime lined up.

MAL
Sure. You were stealing a man's beard.

SAFFRON
No, you <HOE-tze duh PEE-goo!> [monkey's ass!] A million-square job. The big time. I was going to cut Monty and his crew in, but you screwed that royal.

MAL
(raises gun again)
Odd, but I don't think I'll be losing sleep over it.

SAFFRON
I've got the layout, entrance codes, believe me, this thing practically robs itself.

MAL
Bye now.

SAFFRON
I'm handing you a fortune on a gold platter, sweetheart! Don't you even want to hear the details?

Mal considers that for a beat, then looks at the kerchief, BLOODIED from his nose. He raises his gun again.

INT. SERENITY - CARGO BAY - NIGHT

JAYNE stands by the cargo bay door, pulling on leather work-gloves. Behind him, BOOK, SIMON, KAYLEE, and ZOE stand at the ready.

JAYNE
Sure you're up to liftin' this stuff? Crates are fair heavy, I gather.

The engines are HUMMING, and the bay ROCKS a bit as Serenity sets down. Kaylee nods, enthusiastic.

KAYLEE
I can handle it.

JAYNE
Wasn't talkin' to you.

Jayne smiles at Simon, who mocks a pained expression. Jayne hits a button — the airlock opens, and the ramp beyond it starts to lower.

The lowering ramp reveals Mal, standing in front of the pile of crates, alone. He doesn't look too happy. He has a wadded up TWIST OF TORN KERCHIEF in each nostril, to stem the blood.

JAYNE (cont'd)
Woah there, Cap... Tell me you didn't get into a fight with Monty.

KAYLEE
Really? But I thought we loved Monty!
(to Zoe, sincere question)
Don't we love Monty?

ZOE
Sweetie, if he had a tussle with that sasquatch, we'd be in the dirt right about now, scoopin' up the Captain's teeth.

Mal stomps up the ramp, holding them all in an

even glare.

ZOE (cont'd)
Ain't that so, sir?

MAL
You know what? I don't particular want to talk about it. Now we got work. Let's shut up and do it.

Zoe looks from the Captain to the others, then back, eyebrows raised. WASH comes down the cargo bay stairs closest to the bridge, stops by Mal.

WASH
Inara was asking for you. Wanted to —

Mal walks away.

WASH (cont'd)
So later with the talking then.

Wash walks down toward camera, mouthing words to Zoe and Book, who carry one of the crates up the ramp.

WASH (cont'd)
(mouthed silently)
"What happened?"

EXT. SPACE

Just a stock shot of Serenity for transition please.

INT. SERENITY - INARA'S SHUTTLE

Mal enters INARA's chamber —

MAL
Heard you were looking for me?

— to find her seated, preparing tea. Her whole attitude is formal, yet inviting...

INARA
I was. Care to sit?

He does, slowly.

INARA (cont'd)
I was hoping to talk a little business. Would you like some tea?

He stands again, less slowly.

MAL
Okay, what's the game?

INARA
I offered you tea.

MAL
After inviting me into your shuttle of your own free will, which makes two events without precedent and which makes me more'n a little skittish.

INARA
Honestly, Mal, if we can't be civilized and talk like —

MAL
I'm plenty civilized. You're using wiles on me.

INARA
I'm using what?

MAL
Your feminine wiles. Your Companion training, your some-might-say uncanny ability to make a man sweaty and/or compliant, of which I have had just about enough today.

INARA
Maybe this isn't the best time.

MAL
(sitting again)
It's a fine time. Just talk plain, is all.

INARA
I'm not sleeping with you, Mal.

Beat.

MAL
Uh, no, I think I would have noticed if you were. My keenly trained... senses would have...

INARA
You're not my lover. Neither are you my mother my house mistress or anyone who has the

slightest say in how I conduct my affairs.

MAL
Well enough. So?

INARA
So let me conduct my affairs!

MAL
Who's keeping you from —

INARA
I haven't had a client in three weeks. Backwater moons, slums, frontier planets without so much as a temple built —

MAL
We go where the work is!

INARA
There's all kinds of work, Mal.

MAL
And ours is the kind the Alliance shuts you down for. I opt to stay off the radar —

INARA
There's plenty of worlds where both of us could work. We used to visit them, remember?

MAL
<EE-chee shung-hoo-shee.> [Let's take a deep breath.] Are you saying I'm doing this deliberate on account of you? There's some reason I don't want you on the job?

INARA
Is there?

MAL
(sighing, pacing)
Well this is one of the crazier things I've heard today and when I tell you about the rest of my day, you'll appreciate —

INARA
Mal, I'm not accusing you of anything, it's just —

MAL
Hey, no, we'll set course for Planet of the Lonely Rich and Appropriately Hygienic Man. I'll just tell Wash, we can park there for a month.

INARA
(rises as well)
Not all of your work is illegal. And the —

MAL
What, you're trying to get me off the job now?

INARA
And the best job you ever pulled was on a central planet!

MAL
How about I stay out of your whoring —

INARA
That didn't take long —

They're right in each other's faces now, goin' at it.

❖ Below: Inara's teapot.

MAL
And you stay out of my thieving. I know my business plenty well, thank you.

INARA
Right. You're a criminal mastermind. What was the last cargo we snuck past the Alliance to transport?

MAL
We made a perfectly good piece —

INARA
What was the cargo?

MAL
They were dolls!

INARA
They were little geisha dolls with big heads that wobbled!

MAL
People love those!

INARA
And what exactly was our net profit on the famous wobbly-headed doll caper?

MAL
"Our" cut? You're in the gang now?

INARA
Well, since I can't seem to find work as a Companion, I might as well become a petty thief like you!

Beat. Oops. The air goes out of both of them.

MAL
Petty.

INARA
(backtracking)

I didn't mean petty.

MAL
What did you mean?

INARA
(meekly)
<Suo-SHEE?> [Petty?]

MAL
That's Chinese for petty.

INARA
No, that's a narrow... there's nuances of meaning that...

MAL
Maybe you shoulda stuck with your wiles.

INARA
Don't put this all on me, Mal. You know you haven't been after serious work in a —

MAL
Serious work? You wanna know what I —

He stops himself.

INARA
What?

MAL
Nothing.

INT. SERENITY - CARGO BAY - SOON AFTER

Mal, alone, descends the stairs into the cargo bay. He goes to the crates, scanning over them for a moment, finding one that has TWO BULLET HOLES in its lid. He pries it open, pulls the lid away and looks in.

MAL
All right. Tell me more about this job a' yours.

OVER HIS SHOULDER INTO CRATE

Where, frowning with discomfort, wedged kinda sexily into a shipment of PROTEIN PACKETS, lies Our Mrs. Reynolds...

CUT TO BLACK.

END OF ACT ONE

ACT TWO

INT. SERENITY - DINING AREA

Jayne, Zoe, Wash and Kaylee are all gathered at the dining room table. Presently they're staring a bit open-mouthed at — MAL AND SAFFRON standing variously before them as Saffron makes her pitch. She's sort of in the middle of it:

SAFFRON
The mark's name is Durran Haymer. Maybe one of the biggest collectors of Earth-That-Was artifacts in the 'verse. Guy's got warehouses full of stuff. But his prize piece is sitting in his parlor — an antiquity of unspeakable value: the Lassiter. The original hand-held laser pistol. One of only two known to still exist. The forerunner of all modern laser technology. Haymer got lucky, picked it up during the war for nothing.

MAL
But it wasn't just luck.
(then)
Tell them.

SAFFRON
Haymer's Alliance. Bio-weapons expert during the war. He'd target neighborhoods with valuables, wipe out every living soul without ever damaging the goods. Go in, take whatever he wanted.

MAL
He's living fat on a private estate on Bellerophon.

Saffron tosses some future computer disks onto the table.

SAFFRON
I managed to get ahold of his schedule for the next eighteen months — the layout of the estate grounds... and every security code for the place.

No one moves to touch them.

MAL
Saffron's got a notion we can just walk in — take the Lassiter right off his shelf.

More with the staring. Finally Wash speaks:

WASH
I'm confused...

SAFFRON
(ahead of him)
You're asking yourself if I've got the security codes, why don't I just go in and grab it for myself — why cut you in?

WASH
No. Actually... I was wondering...
(to Mal, suddenly)
What's she doing on the ship!? Didn't she try to kill us?

SAFFRON
(rolls her eyes)
Please. Nobody died the last time.
(suddenly unsure)
Right? Where's the old guy with the hair?

WASH
We're in space. How'd she get here?

MAL
She hitched.

WASH
I don't recall pulling over...

MAL
Look. Point is, there's more'n one of us here wouldn't mind sticking it to a <Chiang-BAO HOE-tze duh> [monkey raping] Alliance bastard. Besides that, this could be a very lucrative venture for all of us. This ain't no wobbly-headed doll caper. This here's history.

Jayne's been thinking hard. Raises his hand.

JAYNE
Okay. I got a question. If she's got the security codes, why don't she just go in and grab it for herself — why cut us in?

A beat as they stare. Then:

SAFFRON
Good point. Getting through the door and putting our hands on the Lassiter is easy. Getting out with it... that's the tricky part.

MAL
It's tagged and coded. Second it passes through the door — alarms, security, feds.

SAFFRON
This isn't a one-woman operation. To do this right, I need...

INARA (O.S.)
Idiots.

They turn. Inara has entered the room.

SAFFRON
Partners.

INARA
Dupes. And that's what you'll all be if you trust her.

MAL
Could be that's so. Lord knows ain't none of us "criminal masterminds". So if you got something better, Inara — something not "petty" — we'd sure be willing to hear it.

A beat as Inara and Mal hold the look between them. Saffron doesn't hate the tension that's evident there. Finally:

INARA
(turns and goes)
<Nee-mun DOH shr sagwa.> [Idiots. All of you.]

MAL
(looks back to gang)
Okay. So the question remains — how do we get the artifact out without setting off the alarms?

KAYLEE
You don't. Not through the door, anyway.
(reaches for the disk)
This the layout?

SAFFRON
Full blueprints of the entire grounds.

KAYLEE
Could be we look hard enough, we find a way.

Mal smiles, that's what he likes to hear.

MAL
You dig into that, little Kaylee.

(looks to Zoe)
Zoe. You ain't said a word. Time to weigh in.

ZOE
Take sounds ripe enough. That's assuming we can fence it.

SAFFRON
I know a guy on Persephone. He's already got half a dozen buyers on the bid. The split is gonna be sweet.

ZOE
But Inara's not wrong —
(eyes on Saffron)
— she can't be trusted.

MAL
I ain't asking you to trust her. I'll be with her on the inside the whole time.

SAFFRON
See there? Only one thing you gotta do if you want to be a rich woman, hon — and that's get over it.

ZOE
Mmmm. Okay.

POW — Zoe hauls off and slugs Saffron in the mouth. She goes down on her tush. Everyone's a little astonished.

ZOE (cont'd)
You, too. Hon.
(then, to Mal)
I'm in.

Off nobody offering to help Saffron up —

INT. SIMON'S ROOM - DAY

Jayne is dumping off a bunch of food and water packets, talking to Simon and RIVER.

JAYNE
Captain says you're to stay put. Doesn't want you runnin' afoul of his blushin' psychotic bride. She figures out who you are, she'll turn you in 'fore you can... say... "Don't turn me in, lady".

SIMON
The bounty on us just keeps getting more exciting.

JAYNE
(busying himself)
Well, I wouldn't know.

RIVER
(looking at Jayne)
She's a liar.

JAYNE
That don't exactly set her apart from the rest of us. And the plunder sounds fun enough.

RIVER
She's a liar and no good will come of her.

JAYNE
Well, I say as a rule that girlfolk ain't to be trusted.

RIVER
Jayne is a girl's name.

JAYNE
Well Jayne ain't a girl.
(to Simon)
She starts on that "girl's name" thing, I'm a show her good an' all I got man parts.

SIMON
I'm trying to think of a way for you to be cruder. It's just not coming.

JAYNE
I just heard enough ab —

SIMON
(wearily dismissive)
<KWAI chur hun-rien duh di fahng.> [Go far away very fast.]

JAYNE
And I WAS gonna leave you a deck of cards...

He goes, shutting the door behind him.

SIMON
Great. Another exciting adventure in sitting.

RIVER
Afraid.

SIMON
We'll be okay. Why the Captain is trusting that <BOO hway-HUN duh PUO-foo> [remorseless harridan] is beyond —

RIVER
Not her. Jayne.

SIMON
(amused)
Afraid? Since when?

RIVER
Since Ariel.

Simon is no longer amused.

RIVER (cont'd)
Afraid we'll know.

INT. SERENITY - CARGO BAY - CATWALKS

Zoe is headed up the catwalks from the cargo bay, Inara comes down the stairs leading from the bridge, heading to her shuttle.

ZOE
We should be on Bellerophon by oh-six. I figure the job should be —

INARA
Please. I really don't wanna know.

ZOE
Least it's your kind of world. You got appointments made?

INARA
The minute we hit atmo, I'm gone. I've booked a few choice clients, should help me get my mind

JOSS WHEDON

"I think basically we wanted to do another caper show," Whedon says, "and Saffron always was charming and sexy and kept you off-balance and we could have another 'This is how the rich live and we're going to have a caper on a floating island and garbage,' and have a lot of fun with that, but still turn things around, still play Mal and Inara's tension. It was an idea of having a good time and not being bottled up in the ship, opening it up a little bit. The idea that the first laser pistol is an antique helps with the timeline, too, it helps tell you how these people live."

Was it also desirable to show Inara doing something useful as a member of the team? "Always a good thing and difficult to do," Whedon notes, "because she's not a bank robber." But she can get down and dirty when she needs to? "Well, she wasn't that dirty," Whedon points out. "She was sitting on a high wall."

off Mal's descent into lunacy —

ZOE
(curious)
What happens if you got an appointment coming and you ain't finished the one you're at?

INARA
Overbooking is a cardinal sin. Clients must feel the experience is timeless. Only thing worse is a badly faked fall.

ZOE
See, that's where me and Companionship part ways. I never could work the notion of pretending a man was gettin' it done when he wasn't.

INARA
So you've never pretended to fall.

ZOE
Well, never is a strong word... sometimes it's easier.

INARA
What about with Wash?

ZOE
One time. Poor boy was bone-tired...

INARA
And?

ZOE
He knew. Son of a bitch called me on it.

INARA
That's the one you marry.

ZOE
Damn right.

Zoe starts to leave.

INARA
Zoe. Don't let Mal trust her.

ZOE
Thought you didn't care about the job.

INARA
I really don't. I just want there to be someone around to pick me up when I'm done.

ZOE
<FAHNG-sheen.> [Don't worry.] I got his back.

Captain starts thinking with his <JAN-doh duh ee-KWAI-ro,> [dangly piece of flesh,] I'll step in.

INARA
The man's a moron. Everything Saffron is, is a lie. She'll get the drop on him — which as far as I'm concerned is what he richly deserves.

ZOE
Ain't sayin' it ain't risky. Don't count Mal out, though. He just knows the estate is —

Inara holds up her hands.

INARA
No details. I meant that. Just be careful.

ZOE
See you when we're wealthy...

They split up, Zoe heading up toward the bridge, Inara going into her shuttle.

ANGLE: SAFFRON — has been eavesdropping from above, near the second shuttle. Mal steps out —

MAL
You give me a hand in here. No wandering about, remember? Or I'll stick you back in your crate.

WASH (V.O.)
(from the com)
Cap'n?

Mal keeps his eye on Saffron as he hits a nearby button.

MAL
Yeah?

WASH (V.O.)
We think we got something...

INT. SERENITY - DINING AREA

Mal, Zoe, Jayne, Wash, Kaylee and Saffron are gathered around the table. Kaylee has the portable display (seen in 'Ariel') with the estate schematics. It gets passed around as she and Wash speak:

WASH
Bellerophon Estates... Home to the rich and paranoid... gracious living... ocean views...

EXT. BELLEROPHON - DAY

Ocean as far as the eye can see. Floating above the blue expanse are enormous manors — estates hovering a mile above the water, complete with greenery, landscaping, etc.

WASH (V.O.)
...and state-of-the-art security, including local patrols, and multi-code-keys needed at all entrances and exits...

INT. SERENITY - DINING AREA - CONTINUOUS

SAFFRON
Which we have —

WASH
Right. You and Mal will split off in Shuttle II as we make our approach...

EXT. BELLEROPHON - DAY

SERENITY zooms into the shot (continuing CGI shot from before). Shuttle II splits off from Serenity, veering slightly up. CAMERA STAYS WITH SHUTTLE II as it approaches the floating estate, other flying vehicles coming and going.

WASH (V.O.)
There's a landing port just south of the main house.

INT. SHUTTLE II - DAY

Mal at the helm.

MAL
Prepped for landing. You ready?

Saffron appears from the back, two ENORMOUS FLOWER ARRANGEMENTS in her arms.

SAFFRON
Ready.

EXT. FLOATING ESTATE - DAY

The well manicured grounds. SHUTTLE II lands in the distance. CAMERA PANS to find various DOMESTICS bustling about who carry covered trays, carts loaded with fine china, a BARTENDER setting up an outdoor bar, etc.

WASH (V.O.)
Haymer's throwing a big party this weekend, so you should have no trouble blending with the hired help who'll be there setting up.

CAMERA FINDS Mal and Saffron carrying the flower arrangements, now moving through all of this.

WASH (cont'd; V.O.)
All you gotta do is get through the back door.

EXT. FLOATING ESTATE - BACK ENTRANCE - DAY

Mal and Saffron arrive at the back door. Saffron pulls out a punch-pad and small round "enabler". Attaches the small cylinder to the door, taps in

her code, the cylinder LIGHTS —

MAL (V.O.)
Shouldn't be a problem, unless someone's been less than truthful —

The DOOR CLICKS open, Saffron looks to Mal, smiles...

INT. SERENITY - DINING AREA

Saffron's looking to Mal, here, too.

KAYLEE
The parlor with the Lassiter's on the ninth floor. You'll have to disable the display. Won't be any trouble. 'Course, once you got your hands on the goods, you can't take it out the front door, nor the back door, nor any door. Every piece of pretty is tagged for the scanners.

SAFFRON
Right. So what do we do?

KAYLEE
(to Wash)
You wanna tell them?

WASH
(waves it to her)
It was your genius idea.

KAYLEE
(proud)
You chuck it in the garbage.

Saffron stares at her, unimpressed.

INT. FLOATING ESTATE - CORRIDORS - DAY

Mal and Saffron move through the interior estate still carrying their flower arrangements. They pass a YOUNG HOUSEKEEPER as she moves past with a garbage bag.

KAYLEE (V.O.)
All the estates on Bellerophon use an automated garbage drone system.

Mal and Saffron exit further into the estate. WE STAY WITH the Housekeeper who moves to a chute opening. She dumps the bag down, then moves to a panel on the opposite wall.

KAYLEE (cont'd; V.O.)
You hit one little button, and the drone whooshes off with the trash.

The Housekeeper touches the panel. Words appear ONSCREEN: "READY FOR DISPOSAL. YES. NO." She touches "Yes".

INT. SERENITY - DINING AREA - CONTINUOUS

SAFFRON
(not really)
Brilliant.

KAYLEE
Thanks.

SAFFRON
Oh, except it's idiotic. Those drones take the disposal bins straight to reclamation. Thirty seconds after we hit the button, the booty'll get incinerated.

KAYLEE
Not if we reprogram the bin. Give it new co-ordinates.

EXT. UNDERNEATH THE FLOATING ESTATE - DAY

Underneath the floating estate, a futuristic dumpster (lined with computer panels) is latched onto the body of the estate. We hear the low THUD of the bag landing inside.

KAYLEE (V.O.)
Once I override the standard guidance protocol, I can tell the disposal bin to go wherever we want.

A flying GARBAGE DRONE GLIDES INTO FRAME, flies towards the dumpster, and its forklift-like claws clamp onto the dumpster with a loud METALLIC KLANG.

JAYNE

"I'll be in my bunk."

Firefly featured an eclectic rag tag crew of survivors ranging from two fugitives to a space prostitute and a holy man, yet the grumpiest of the lot was Jayne Cobb, a man who often only had his own welfare in mind. Nonetheless, somehow Jayne emerged as one of the series' fan favorites. "Jayne is the handsomest and strongest," laughs Adam Baldwin. "You have to ask people why they like him. I think it goes back to the fact that, at first glance, you see him as this ugly duckling bad guy with a gruff exterior — who turns out to be saying what is really on your mind. 'We don't have to do that. We can do this. It's quicker.' He's the poseable action figure. You make him run, jump, scream, yell, shoot, holler, get into fights, and leer at girls. It's all the stuff you don't get to do in real life."

Jayne had an attitude that didn't always make him a team player. He often came into conflict with other crewmembers, most notably River and Simon. "Well, River's crazy!" exclaims Baldwin. "Jayne felt Simon wasn't fit for the job; that he wasn't tough enough to be out there; that he was raised in too cushy of an existence to belong. He felt they were excess baggage. And I remember Simon's line describing Jayne as 'man ape gone wrong thing'. Yeah, Simon felt like he needed to lash out and call me names. Maybe there was some sort of underlying homo erotica or subtext Joss was trying to build there..." he laughs.

Though Serenity had no shortage of beautiful females on board, Jayne never managed to hook up with any of them. "I had an ongoing battle with Joss Whedon because

I always felt the perfect woman for Jayne would have been Inara, because she wouldn't be there in the morning," recalls Baldwin. "The perfect relationship for Jayne — but Joss never let me get that far. It is so hard to speculate on what could have been... but that's one of Jayne's little secrets I came up with, to keep things interesting.

"For me, the oddest relationship Jayne had was with Zoe, because they were portrayed as physical equals, although I could have kicked her ass," he continues. "She was tough, so that was a respectful relationship. Obviously, she didn't respect me because she thought Jayne was dumb, but she wanted me around in a fight. That was the toughest one to figure out. River was just crazy, and Kaylee was more of the little sister who I'd try to protect."

Jayne always seemed to be throwing a punch or getting into trouble. "I had a really great fight scene in 'Ariel' with the guard, who was played by our stunt coordinator," recalls Baldwin. "It was fun to try and fight with handcuffs on behind your back! And I liked dangling on the wire and going down to the train through the hole [in 'The Train Job']. I love doing that stuff. As far as I'm concerned, movies and television are entertainment, so you jump in there and get some action going, and have some popcorn! I think some people take themselves too seriously when they are doing this stuff. It is hard work and you are trying to tell a story, but don't tell it by pretending to be more important than you are."

If clothes maketh the man, then Jayne's tight t-shirts, baggy army pants and outrageous hats certainly make a loud statement. Baldwin comments that his *Firefly* threads were "Brave. Daring. Dirty. Practical. Functional. And had a lot of pockets." He continues, "The hat originally was for jumping into the train and not getting blown away in the wind. Then it just became a running joke. Whenever we could, we'd grab a hat. The last episode we shot was 'The Message', and it had a knitted hat with a pompom on it. It's become this nice souvenir that folks have knitted quite a few of, and you see them frequently at conventions. I still have that hat. I am getting my eBay sale ready..."

With credits such as *Predator 2*, *Independence Day*, *The X-Files* and *Angel*, Baldwin has become a sci-fi staple. However, he maintains *Firefly* was his dream role. "I've been fortunate to have had a few 'gigs of a lifetime', but this is my favorite so far," he says. "I realized it right away. I knew that this guy and group of people was something special. And I had learned from *Full Metal Jacket*, which I did when I was twenty-three, that you need to appreciate what you are doing while you are doing it, and not look back ten years later and wish you had appreciated it then. I actually did come to work every day looking to keep it special, positive, and fun. We were under the gun pretty much from the get go and I think we all appreciated how fleeting it can be and how much of a risk you are taking with making television. That is why the work came out so well and at such a high level."

The dumpster shudders with the impact, then detaches from the structure and the drone whisks it away. Another dumpster drops into place where the other one was.

INT. SERENITY - DINING AREA

SAFFRON
And where would that be?

WASH
The loneliest piece of desert we can find. Here. Isis Canyon. Drone dumps the bin, we claim the goods when we're all together again.

SAFFRON
How do you plan on getting to the bin to re-program it?

KAYLEE
You get to the loot — we'll get to the bin.

EXT. SERENITY/UNDERNEATH THE FLOAT-ING ESTATE - DAY

WIDE — CGI. Serenity RISES INTO FRAME, hovering steadily a few feet below the dumpster. Bright sunlight and wind whipping up here.

CLOSER — THE HATCH opens and Jayne emerges. He's wearing goggles, his thrilling heroics hat and a harness with cable (which dangles at the moment).

He pulls himself out of the hatch and crawls carefully up the hull and attaches the safety latch of his cable to a rung on the ship.

Now from the hatch, Kaylee emerges, also wearing goggles and protection from the wind and cold. She hands up the end of her safety harness to Jayne. He clips it. She hands him out a tool kit. He takes it, then helps her up onto the top of the ship. She crawls toward him on her belly. They're under the bin now.

He makes her lie flat, one arm over her protecting her as he pulls out his com, speaks into it, yelling over the ROARING WIND —

JAYNE
Okay! We're planted!

INT. SERENITY - BRIDGE - DAY

JAYNE (V.O., FILTERED)
Take us up —

Wash white knuckling it. Zoe at his shoulder. He pulls back on the controls, as...

EXT. SERENITY/UNDERNEATH THE FLOAT-ING ESTATE - DAY

Jayne and Kaylee still lying flat. Serenity rises up. Jayne and Kaylee look up as the bottom of the estate looms closer.

JAYNE
(into com)
That's good! Hold 'er there.

Kaylee, still face down, pops open her mobile tool kit, hands an electric (space age?) screwdriver to Jayne. Jayne gets to his feet with great care — reaches up to the control panel side of the trash bin. It's all very precarious now as he sets to work on the panel, removing

the face of it...

INT. FLOATING ESTATE - CORRIDOR - DAY

Mal sneaks down a corridor, Saffron standing watch at the other end of the hall. She's keeping an eye on Mal — specifically, on his ass. Mal turns to her —

MAL
Clear.

She trots down to him, looks at a Palm-like device which displays the house's blueprints.

MAL (cont'd)
Which way?

SAFFRON
Left.

They continue on.

EXT. UNDERNEATH THE FLOATING ESTATE - DAY

Jayne pulls off the front panel of the control mechanism, sets about removing the innards, hands the motherboard down to Kaylee, who begins work on it.

INT. FLOATING ESTATE - CORRIDOR - DAY

Mal and Saffron move down another corridor — one that opens into a larger room. Saffron peeks at her Palm as Mal peers into the room,

addresses him in a whisper —

SAFFRON
This should be it.

Mal holds up a finger. The sound of VOICES in the other room slowly drifts away. Then he nods and they walk into —

INT. FLOATING ESTATE - PARLOR - DAY

They ENTER into a room that defines opulence. Beautiful furnishings, expensive art on the walls. Memorabilia of Earth-That-Was fills the room. This room alone cost millions to decorate.

MAL
<Shun-SHENG duh gao-WAHN.> [Holy testicle Tuesday.]

And, on the mantel, in the proper place of honor: a Buck Rogers lookin' laser gun. It is to phasers what those huge old clunky cell phones were to modern ones.

Mal and Saffron set down their flower displays, move to it. She reaches out. He stays her hand. Holds up a small aerosol-looking can, sprays and a FORCE FIELD becomes visible for a moment. Mal reaches into his flowers, pulls out a mini-tool kit.

MAL (cont'd)
Let's get to work...

EXT. SERENITY/UNDERNEATH THE FLOATING ESTATE - DAY

Kaylee hands the jerry-rigged motherboard back to Jayne.

KAYLEE
Okay! She's set!
(yelling over roar of wind)
Careful! It's hot!

Jayne nods, starts to replace the innards. Serenity rises up a few inches, closing the distance between the bottom of the estate and Jayne's head.

JAYNE
(sharply into com)
Gorramn it, Wash! Hold it steady!

INT. SERENITY - BRIDGE

Wash and more with the white knuckles.

WASH
Sorry...

Wash eases off...

EXT. SERENITY/UNDERNEATH THE FLOATING ESTATE - DAY

As Serenity dips ever so slightly, Jayne gets a bit more "head room". Continues to work. Kaylee reacts as she watches:

❖ Above: Kaylee's reprogrammer

KAYLEE
Jayne! No! The dyna-ram's live!

He can't hear what she's saying over the ROAR. Glances at her, annoyed —

JAYNE
What?

KAYLEE
(worried)
Don't touch the dyna —

ZAP! A BLUE BOLT of energy jumps out of the bin control innards, zapping Jayne and knocking him out. He falls and lands hard on the top of Serenity and starts sliding, out like a light. Kaylee instinctively grasps for the tether as Jayne's body slides and rolls, the tether taught. This all happens very fast and off Kaylee's SCREAM!

INT. FLOATING ESTATE - PARLOR - DAY

Mal uses a space-aged allen wrench as he digs into an open panel under the Lassiter.

MAL
Where's the trash chute?

SAFFRON
We passed it in the vestibule.

FOOTSTEPS...

SAFFRON (cont'd)
Someone's coming...

Mal quickly shuts the panel, moves away just as — DURRAN HAYMER, the master of the house, enters the room, freezing both Mal and Saffron. He looks from one to the other, in shock.

DURRAN
(to Mal)
You...

Mal waits.

DURRAN (cont'd)
You found her...

He takes Saffron in his arms.

DURRAN (cont'd)
Oh, god, you've brought back my wife!

Off Mal, in jaded awe...

BLACK OUT.

END OF ACT TWO

ACT THREE

INT. FLOATING ESTATE - PARLOR - DAY

Durran holds Saffron close to him... His face is away from Mal's, hers toward Mal. She looks vexed, though she hugs him back.

DURRAN
Oh, my dear...

Mal mimes hitting the guy. Saffron shakes her head slightly, no.

DURRAN (cont'd)
Oh, my own sweet Yolanda...

Mal mouths "Yolanda?" amused. Durran holds her at arm's length.

DURRAN (cont'd)
I thought I would never see you again.

He's fighting welling emotion. To Mal:

DURRAN (cont'd)
Forgive me... I don't mean to make a show...

MAL
Please. I'm the one intruding.

DURRAN
Not at all. I owe you a great debt of thanks.

MAL
Just gave the lady a lift.

DURRAN
You did much more than that. You returned to me the only thing I truly treasure.

MAL
Well, then, this is a day I'll feel good to be me.

DURRAN
Do I owe you any —

MAL
No. Trip weren't even out of our way.

SAFFRON
I promised him 800 square.

MAL
But, no, I never agreed to —

DURRAN
Please. I'd be embarrassed not to make some recompense... In my study, I... Are you hungry? You both look so tired, there's food, or... Yolanda, I'm babbling like a moon brain...

SAFFRON
Hush. We'll both have plenty to say by daybreak.

DURRAN
Six years...

SAFFRON
Is that all?

DURRAN
From the day we found your shuttle —

SAFFRON
They set on me at Parth, these awful men...

MAL
That wasn't me, though. I don't know those men.

SAFFRON
They said they wanted ransom, but they... they sold me... to slavers...

MAL
Also unknown to me...

DURRAN
(ashamed)
At first I thought — well, you disappeared the same day as Heinrich —

SAFFRON
Heinrich?

DURRAN
The security programmer. And he was young, and I'd seen you two talking, and I thought — but after they found his body...

MAL
They killed Heinrich. Guess he wasn't useful anymore.

DURRAN
(to Saffron)
I never stopped looking.

SAFFRON
I knew you wouldn't.
(tears and all)
That's the thought that kept me alive.

They kiss passionately. Mal looks around, at his nails, at the wall...

SAFFRON (cont'd)
(seductively)
We have so much time to make up...

MAL
Well, that's my cue to skedaddle...

DURRAN
Let me get your money.
(to Saffron)
You won't disappear again?

SAFFRON
Never.

He goes. A beat, as her loving look hardens.

SAFFRON (cont'd)
We gotta move fast.

As Mal returns to the dismantling of the force field with his space-aged allen wrench...

MAL
Yeah, he might come back and hug us in the act.

INT. SERENITY - FOREDECK HALL - BELOW HATCH, LOWERING

Zoe (who's wearing goggles and anti-wind-clothing) and Book struggle to lower the dead weight of an unconscious Jayne into the ship. Zoe is halfway up the ladder, using Jayne's tether to guide him down to Book. She wears a tether harness vest now.

KAYLEE (O.S.)
Zoe?

ZOE
(calls out of hatch)
I'm comin', Kaylee —
(down to Book)
Book — You got him?

BOOK
I got him — I got hi —

Zoe unhitches his tether line and Jayne's full weight topples toward Book. He staggers back, pinned against the wall of the corridor by Jayne's bulk.

BOOK (cont'd)
(wheezes)
Lord — this boy weighs — a solid ton —

He lowers Jayne to the floor. Simon appears, having been summoned. Zoe hitches the tether line to her vest.

ZOE
Doctor, you got yourself a patient to see to.

Simon nods, face clouded with subtle darkness.

SIMON
Yes. I'll take care of it.

Simon moves to assist Book. Zoe hauls herself up out of the hatch.

INT. FLOATING ESTATE - PARLOR - DAY

As Mal continues his dismantling...

SAFFRON
You don't know him. He's everything I said he was.

MAL
Oh, he's a killer of men. Why I'll bet he eats up babies.

SAFFRON
You're wasting time.

He's actually being very efficient while continuing.

MAL
But let's take a breath here, Yolanda. You're sneaking into a place you could walk into as welcome as glad news. What's the math on that?

SAFFRON
The math is you not adding up that Durran Haymer would as soon cut your throat as —

MAL
You would?

SAFFRON
If possible.

MAL
No. That ain't it at all. You'da knocked him on the brain, were that the case. You don't want him knowing the truth. Unlike all the — I'm gonna go with hundreds — of men you've married, you actually want this one to think well of you after you've gone.

A FLASH and WE SEE the FORCE FIELD appear then DISAPPEAR. Mal reaches in easily, grabs the Lassiter.

MAL (cont'd)
My god... Could it be that I've just met your real husband?

She has backed up to her flower arrangement, whips out a small gun at him, furious.

SAFFRON
Congratulations, anything else you want on your tombstone, you piece of crap?

DURRAN
Now I'm intruding.

She puts the gun down, genuinely upset that Durran has busted her.

SAFFRON
Durran... This isn't what it looks like...

MAL
Unless it looks like we're stealing your priceless Lassiter, 'cause that's what we're doing. Don't ask me about the gun, 'cause that's new.

As he says this, Mal has elegantly moved past Durran, dropped the Lassiter into the trash chute just outside the door, hit the button.

DURRAN
Well. I appreciate your honesty. Not, you know, a lot, but —

SAFFRON
Durran, you don't know what he's forced me to —

DURRAN
Stop. Yolanda, please just stop.

There is terrible sadness in his voice. And a frantic misery in hers:

SAFFRON
Durran... Don't look at me like that...

A beat. She whips the gun at him.

SAFFRON (cont'd)
I said don't look at me like that!

She might just shoot him as we GO TO:

EXT. UNDERSIDE OF FLOATING ESTATE - DAY

Kaylee teeters on precarious tippy-toe, straining to plug a piece of HARDWARE into the top part of the control panel on the dumpster. Zoe steadies her, heels dug in, one hand gripping Kaylee's tether.

KAYLEE
Almost... done... Just have to plug the interface strike-plate back... in...

There's a CLACKING of machinery from the dumpster, and a BEACON LIGHT begins flashing.

ZOE
That's the pick-up call — they must have dropped the Star... How we doing?

Kaylee strains but can't quite reach.

KAYLEE
(growls)
Can't reach it —

Zoe looks to —

ZOE'S POV — of A [CGI] GARBAGE DRONE in the distance, taking a hard turn towards them, like a shark nosing toward its prey.

Zoe speaks into her com.

ZOE
Wash — we need a little more altitude — now —

WASH (O.S.)
Working on it, dear —

ZOE
Kaylee —

Kaylee fumbles with the plate as Serenity lurches up another foot or two.

ZOE (cont'd)
KayleeKayleeKaylee —

Kaylee snaps the strike-plate into place.

KAYLEE
Got it!

Zoe pulls hard on Kaylee's tether —

GARBAGE BIN

as Kaylee is yanked hard down OUT OF FRAME, just as the drone SLAMS into place, right where Kaylee had been a micro-second before. It attaches to the dumpster with a DEAFENING BONG.

ZOE AND KAYLEE

lay prone on the top of the ship, exchange a look. Start to scurry forward out of frame and we GO TO:

NATHAN FILLION

It was no secret that Christina Hendricks was extremely talented and super-attractive. She has a real way about her. She played two characters in this episode exceedingly well. It's another case of how other people do my job for me. I don't have to worry about how I react to Saffron's seductions because all I'm doing is standing there getting some love from Christina Hendricks. I loved it!

INT. SERENITY - BRIDGE - DAY

Wash pilots hard as Zoe's voice crackles in over the com.

ZOE (O.S.)
We're in! Go! Go!

WASH
Copy that —

Wash pulls back on his controls.

EXT. UNDERSIDE OF FLOATING ESTATE - DAY

Serenity drops away from the underbelly, peeling into a dive and sailing off, as the drone detaches the dumpster and flies off in the opposite direction.

INT. FLOATING ESTATE - PARLOR - DAY

Mal inching his way around from the door; Saffron staring down Durran, gun pointed at him...

MAL
Whoa, whoa, let's not get worked up here —

SAFFRON
(to Durran)
Are you really so naive? Do you really think your life is anything to me?

Mal is next to his flower arrangement — whip-quick he pulls his own gun from it, is drawn and pointed at her in a heartbeat.

MAL
Okay, we're not killing folk today, on account of our very tight schedule. So why don't you drop that pistola, Yo-Saf-Bridge, and we'll be about our —
(suddenly as fierce as a cop)
DROP IT NOW.

He comes at her as he shouts it, his whole attitude wrought with controlled fury, putting the gun to her head. She drops hers to the floor, knowing he means business, but never takes her eyes off Durran. They play everything to each other, even when talking to Mal. (Mal retrieves her gun, pockets it.)

SAFFRON
Did you think I was a princess? That I would stay locked up here in the tower? With you?

DURRAN
I hoped.

SAFFRON
You're a rutting fool.

MAL
Saffron, you wanna finish the damn job? We're short on minutes here. I'm sorry mister —

DURRAN
How long have you been with him?

MAL
Oh we're not together.

SAFFRON
He's my husband.

MAL
Well who in the damn galaxy isn't?

She starts working.

DURRAN
I feel so bad for you.

SAFFRON
Bad for me? I'm not the patsy getting stole from. You had half a brain you'da called the feds the minute you saw me.

DURRAN
Oh, I did.

They stop. He points to his ring. It's modern, with a stone like a button. That is a button.

DURRAN (cont'd)
Emergency signal. For kidnappings and the like. I love you, Yolanda, but I couldn't think for a second you were actually here for me.

The sound of approaching cops, etc.

DURRAN (cont'd)
That would be them now.

A beat, as Mal and Saffron fume.

SAFFRON
Men.

EXT. FLOATING ESTATE GROUNDS - CONTINUING

As a trio of POLICE CRUISER-SHIPS descend on the estate, sirens blaring, lights flashing.

END OF ACT THREE

ACT FOUR

INT. FLOATING ESTATE - DAY

We hear the SIRENS and POLICE ANNOUNCING their arrival. Saffron sidles desperately up to Durran...

SAFFRON
Durran, peaches, just call them off. Tell 'em it was a mistake.

DURRAN
You need help, Yolanda.

SAFFRON
I'll do whatever you want... You know how I can make you feel...

DURRAN
Please. You're embarrassing yourself.

She punches him into unconsciousness.

SAFFRON
I'm embarrassing? Who's the dupe on the floor?

She spits on him as Mal comes up, grabs her arm.

MAL
I hate to bring up our imminent arrest during your crazy time, but we gotta move.

He tugs at her and they take off.

EXT. FLOATING ESTATE - GROUNDS - DAY

COPS (armed with those SONIC RIFLES we saw in 'Ariel') at the doors, speaking into a COM.

POLICE SERGEANT
...Police. Responding to emergency call code. Request entry, all points.

A BEAT, then the doors BUZZ as the locks give. The cops race inside...

INT. FLOATING ESTATE - CORRIDOR - DAY

Mal and Saffron hoofing it out of here. A COP comes around the corner, heading right at them. The cop is more surprised than they are — Mal takes him down with a few well-placed moves. Saffron reacts as —

TWO MORE COPS — appear coming the other way. One of them is raising his SONIC RIFLE.

SAFFRON
<Wahg-ba DAN duh biao-tze.> [Son of a mother's whore.]

Mal drags her along, over the fallen cop. They round the corner just as BOOM! from the sonic rifle.

INT. FLOATING ESTATE - BACK ENTRANCE - DAY

They bolt down the glass corridor, the way they came in. Cops appear, coming after them. They push through the door, end up —

EXT. FLOATING ESTATE - BACK ENTRANCE - DAY

Saffron beelines for the security panel, hooks her device onto it, starts working. Mal braces himself against the door.

MAL
What are you doing?

SAFFRON
Shut up and stand back.

Mal backs away from the door just as her enabler BEEPS.

INT. FLOATING ESTATE - BACK ENTRANCE - DAY

A cop reaches for the door — but it pulls AWAY FROM him. We hear a KA-CHUNK as the door locks.

EXT. FLOATING ESTATE - BACK ENTRANCE - DAY

SAFFRON
Let's go!

She runs off. Mal regards the door and the POUNDING from the trapped cops for a tiny beat.

MAL
(impressed)
Good security.

He turns to join her as —

SAFFRON (O.S.)
Mal!

TWO MORE COPS, armed with sonic rifles, coming at them. Saffron is already spinning and kicking at the first one. Mal takes on the second one, hand-to-fist-to-face.

SAFFRON
(calls to Mal, as she fights)
Can I have my gun back now, please?

MAL
No!

He lays out the cop he's fighting. Then reaches down and grabs the fallen sonic rifle. Spins on Saffron and the cop she's still engaged with:

MAL (cont'd)
Move!

She dives out of the way as Mal fires a [CGI] SONIC BLAST. Second cop is down for the count. Mal tosses the sonic rifle aside. Saffron goes to grab it. Mal grabs her, yanks her from it.

MAL (cont'd)
Nope. Let's go.

And they do.

INT. FLOATING ESTATE - BACK ENTRANCE - DAY

One of the cops is trying to work the security code pad. No luck. The Sergeant calls into his COM.

POLICE SERGEANT
Subjects have exited the residence and are on the grounds. Does anyone have visual?

Off the Sergeant's frustration —

EXT. FLOATING ESTATE - DAY

Shuttle II flies away, unpursued.

INT. SHUTTLE II - DAY

Mal pushes buttons, engages autopilot (either burned in graphics or a voice saying as much), and heads into the back as he straps on his holster, back to normal.

Saffron sits on a crate, facing away from him, sullenly ignoring the welling in her eyes.

MAL
That must've been tough.

SAFFRON
Yeah, have yourself a great guffaw.

MAL
I mean it. Six years, you knew he was holding such treasures, you didn't move on him. I gotta figure that's a job you told yourself you'd never take. Til times got hard enough, and the one line you hadn't crossed...

SAFFRON
(turning, fierce)
My name's not Yolanda.

MAL
Never entered my mind that it was.

She looks away again. Her tone at first is worldly, bitter — but there is clearly more underneath.

SAFFRON
I tried. I actually tried. I thought, "This is a decent man. The genuine article."

MAL
A working man, struggling to get by with the barest necessities on his private floating island...

SAFFRON
Yeah, he had money. I thought it would help. That if I had everything... I wouldn't want...

MAL
Heinrich the Security Programmer?

SAFFRON
You know, I'd forgotten his name.

MAL
Addressing the itch of curiousness, you marry him too?

SAFFRON
No. I didn't kill him either.

MAL
I don't reckon you've killed many. Just put 'em in a position to die easy.

SAFFRON
I should've killed Durran.

MAL
Right. The one guy that don't have it coming. The man who knows you and still loves you, treachery and all. Can't have him walking about.

She does start crying now, balled up, not making any move toward Mal.

SAFFRON
You must be loving this.

MAL
Little bit. I seen you without your clothes on before. Never thought I'd see you naked.

She looks up at him with genuine pleading in her eyes.

SAFFRON
Can people ever change?

MAL
Depends on the person. I'm guessing the pain of this fades away, you'll just go back to being what you are.

SAFFRON
(small voice)
What is that?

He squats before her, takes her chin in his hand.

MAL
(not unkindly)

A brilliant, beautiful, evil, double-crossing snake. Cheer up, weepy: you've earned yourself a boatload of hard cash today. You can question the meaning of life on a floaty island of your own for a while.

SAFFRON
You won't tell anyone about me breaking down?

MAL
I won't.

SAFFRON
Then I won't tell anyone how easily I got your gun out of your holster.

He looks down.

MAL
I take that as a kindness.

They rise, her with the gun pointed at his belly.

SAFFRON
You just may be the most gullible fool I have ever marked. And that makes you special.

MAL
You can riddle me with holes, Yolanda. Won't make what I just saw anything but truth.

SAFFRON
(almost convincing)
I played you. From minute one.

MAL
You got me at barrel's end, who am I to argue. What's your move?

SAFFRON
We'll be settling down in the desert. Leave you to set a spell. Oh, and speaking of naked...

MAL
No, now that's just low.

SAFFRON
Kinda evens things out, don't you think? Pants.

She cocks the hammer, he starts undoing his trousers.

MAL
Don't really see the benefit in all this. However I slip, you're not gonna catch my crew with their trousers down.

INT. SERENITY - BRIDGE - DAY

Wash at the controls. Zoe and Kaylee enter.

ZOE
We still clear?

WASH
Nobody's following.

ZOE
Good. Time to turn around. Bin'll be dumped by now. Let's get there before anyone else does.

Wash nods. Pulls on the ship controls. Frowns.

WASH
Can't.

ZOE
What?

WASH
Can't... turn.
(still trying)
Not getting any tug from the aft alternator —

KAYLEE
What? That don't make no sense...
(realizing)
Unless...

She turns and runs out, toward the —

INT. SERENITY - ENGINE ROOM

Kaylee goes right for the engine, Zoe and Wash following. She only has to look for a second before knowing what's up —

KAYLEE
Yep. <Tah-shr SUO-yo DEE-yure duh biao-tze duh MAH!> [She's the mother of all the whores in hell!] The filament in the grav-dampener's stripped.

WASH
Now, who could've possibly done that?

KAYLEE
I can fix it, but she must've put a timer on the motivator and wetwired the dampener with —

ZOE
What does that mean, Kaylee?

KAYLEE
We ain't gonna make the rendezvous. We have to land. Now.

Off their reactions, PRELAP —

MAL (O.S.)
That dirty, dirty whore...

CUT TO:

EXT. WASTELAND - DAY

MAL'S FACE staring up into the sky as CAMERA CRANES UP, the engines of the departing (yet unseen) shuttle whipping wind and dust around Mal.

As CAMERA CONTINUES TO PULL BACK, we see that Mal is very much naked. And standing in the wasteland where we first saw him in the opening. Mal stares at his bare feet and shakes his head as if to say "shoulda seen it coming".

EXT. MOON - DAY

A different wasteland-y part of the moon. The disposal bin sits near Shuttle II, its lid open. From inside the bin, we hear —

SAFFRON (O.S.)
Blaerghchh!

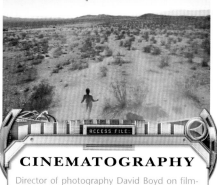

CINEMATOGRAPHY

Garbage comes flying out of the bin.

INSIDE THE BIN —

— is Saffron, digging through the trash, rummaging through moldy fruit, eggshells, and assorted sticky, wet rubbish. Her hair is matted — basically, she's covered in shit and doesn't look happy about it.

SAFFRON
Where the hell is it...

She keeps digging. Diggy, diggy, diggy — then she stops, throws her hands up in defeat.

SAFFRON (cont'd)
It's not here.

INARA (O.S.)
Looking for this?

She looks up to see Inara perched on the wall of some nearby ruins, beautiful as always, in her veil and bare midriff ensemble. She points to the Lassiter.

INARA
Wonder if it works?

Pulls the trigger. Nothing.

INARA (cont'd)
Ah well. Still worth a fortune.
(as she raises a Lugar)
Anyway, this one works fine.

(then)
Honey, you look horrific.

SAFFRON
What are you doing here?

INARA
Oh. Just my part of the job.

SAFFRON
What part of the job?

INARA
(matter of fact)
You know, I put on this big act and storm away in a huff, then I fly off, wait for you to doublecross Mal, beat you to the rendezvous spot and grab the loot before you can get to it.
(beat)
What, you didn't see it coming?

Saffron makes a move; Inara points her Lugar.

INARA (cont'd)
Uh-uh.
(beat)
You know, I'm a little disappointed. Some of the crew's performances weren't quite as nuanced as they could've been. I thought they might tip the fact that we were playing you from the second Mal took you out of that crate.
(beat)
Oh, well. Guess not.

As she's said this, she's set aside the Lassiter and picked up a small REMOTE CONTROL. She aims it at the bin, presses a button — and the lid SLAMS SHUT on Saffron.

SAFFRON
Wait a minute, wait, you can't —
(SLAM! the lid shuts)
— mmmf mmfff ni ffmm do hmf!

INARA
You're not going to die, you big baby. The authorities will be here in a few hours to dig you out.

INT. SERENITY - INFIRMARY

Jayne fuzzily comes to, looks around. Simon is quietly notating some things, his back to Jayne.

JAYNE
Wuh guwwunoh?

SIMON
(not looking around)
You got knocked out.

JAYNE
Dih we gedda payoff? Dih we make the money?

SIMON
Can you move your arms and legs?

Jayne looks suddenly worried. Tries — cannot move anything below his neck.

JAYNE
Dah nod movin'!

SIMON
Do you want to know why?

He turns to Jayne, eerie calm on his face.

SIMON (cont'd)
Your spine. You hit it pretty hard when you fell.

JAYNE
(worried)
'Pine?

SIMON
Yes. So I gave you something to knock out your motor functions so you wouldn't wrench it when you came to. Should wear off in half an hour. You'll just be bruised.

JAYNE
'Pine okay?

SIMON
How much did they offer you to sell out me and River on Ariel?

Jayne pauses. Now he's worried.

JAYNE
Das crazy talk.

SIMON
Then let's talk crazy. How much?

JAYNE
(looking beyond Simon, calls out)
Is anybody there?

River leans in from the doorway, looks at him calmly. It's not comforting.

JAYNE (cont'd)
(quieter)
Anybody else?

SIMON
You're in a dangerous line of work, Jayne. Odds are, you'll be under my knife again. Often. So I want you to understand one thing very clearly. No matter what you do, or say, or plot... No matter how you come down on us, I will never ever harm you. You're on this table you're safe. I'm your medic, and however little we may like or trust each other, we're on the same crew. Got the same troubles, same enemies and more than enough of both. Now we could circle each other and growl, both sleep with one eye open but that thought wearies me. I don't care what you've done. I don't know what you're planning on doing, but I'm trusting you. I think you should do the same, 'cause I don't see this working any other way.

He exits. We hold wide on Jayne, thinking on what Simon has said, as River's head pops in the doorway at the other end of frame.

RIVER
Also, I can kill you with my brain.

She pops back out, leaving Jayne to contemplate even more.

EXT. WASTELAND - DAY

ON MAL, who sits naked on a sheared-off stump of stone. He lifts his head, and utters the now familiar:

MAL
Yep... that went well.

REVERSE TO INCLUDE Inara, who has emerged from Serenity's open ramp and is now standing a few feet from Mal. The line is addressed to her.

INARA
You call this "going well"?

MAL
We got the loot, didn't we?

INARA
Yes, but —

MAL
Then I call it a win. What's the problem?

He stands, starts casually walking back to Serenity

NAKED MAL

Costume designer Shawna Trpcic: "Nathan was an incredible sport about having to be buck-naked in the middle of the desert surrounded by crew, because there was nothing we could do to cover him up — he just had to be all out there."

with Inara, who does her best to not glance at his naughty bits.

INARA
Should I start with the part where you're stranded in the middle of nowhere, or the part where you have no clothes?

MAL
All according to plan.

INARA
Really? I thought the plan was for me to act as a failsafe in case everything else went wrong. Like, for instance, if Saffron disabled Serenity and left you for dead.

MAL
Nonsense. You had a key role to play in this. How sad would you have been if you hadn't gotten to play it?

INARA
Heartbroken.

MAL
See? All according to plan.

They reach Serenity, where Zoe, Wash and Kaylee await. As Mal moves up the ramp —

MAL (cont'd)
Wash, take us out of the world. Zoe, contact

Brennert and Ellison, see if they're interested in fencing a priceless artifact for us.

Zoe and Wash just stand there, staring at his nakedity. Yes, I said nakedity.

MAL (cont'd)
What?

Zoe and Wash mutter "nothing", "I'll get right to work", etc., as Kaylee smiles at Mal, not at all thrown.

KAYLEE
Good work, Cap'n.

MAL
Thanks.

Kaylee goes off as Mal closes the ramp. As the ramp rises, Mal looks out at the wasteland with a certain fondness.

MAL (cont'd)
Good day. Good day.

The ramp shuts and we —

BLACK OUT.

END OF SHOW

FIREFLY-THAT-WASN'T

Unused Story Ideas

Jose Molina recalls: "When we started assigning the scripts, Ben had an episode that was called 'Blue Sun Rising' that we spent a couple of weeks breaking. The basic story is, our guys land in a junkyard on this planet, because a piece of the ship has broken, and this mom-and-pop operation helps them get back on their feet. It turns out Blue Sun is trying to build a freeway over their planet and want them off, but the planet's residents won't leave, and so Blue Sun send the Blue-Gloved Men after them — and the Blue-Gloved Men kill everything and everyone. So we knew what these guys were in terms of their job within Blue Sun and we knew that we wanted to introduce that Darth Vader sort of menace to the universe. Ben [Edlund] wrote a really cool, detailed beat sheet, about thirteen pages long. He had come in a couple of weeks earlier with this crazy idea about 'Jaynestown', with the whole beginning, middle and end, but because of the writer rotation, he was going to write 'Blue Sun Rising' and I was going to write what became 'Jaynestown'. Joss and Tim then decided that 'Blue Sun Rising' was maybe a little too heavy on mythology or maybe too dark. We decided to put a pin in 'Blue Sun

Rising', and so Ben inherited what should have been his in the first place and wound up writing 'Jaynestown'."

Any other unmade stories? "There was one that I actually pitched to Tim a few times when we were running low on ideas, which was where Kaylee had to go undercover in a heist as a Companion, and so Inara has to train her to be a girly girl. The idea was that our guys get caught in the middle of a robbery and thrown in jail and will be executed, and the only way of getting them out was for Kaylee to do what Inara did in 'The Train Job'.

"I remember Brett Matthews and I were talking about doing this episode which we loved and pitched to Joss. It was the first time that I've actually seen Joss go, 'That's too dark.' It starts with a standoff gone wrong and one of the members of the opposite posse is a pregnant woman. She draws on our guys and our guys, to save their own lives, have to kill her. Simon, being the excellent doctor that he is, saves the baby. Our crew is left to play out *Three Men and a Baby*, until we figure out what we are going to do with this baby. Well, we are who we are, so let's sell the baby. Then of course, we find a great home for the baby, but we've killed the mother and we've sold him for a profit. And Joss, I think wisely, went, 'that is really too bleak for our gang of marauders'. There were limits. If we'd gone a couple of seasons and the show was doing well and the network was giving us free rein, I think we would've possibly done that at some point,

because Brett and I were very gung-ho on it. I remember having a conversation with him about a year after the show ended, he was about to do the *Firefly* comic book, and he was still interested in doing that story. So it's something that neither of us let go of, because it had such darkness and such heart."

Ben Edlund remembers some ideas for *Firefly* episodes that didn't make it to the screen: "I didn't have any that I had written. We were really burning our engines to just meet the demands of production as it occurred over every week, so there wasn't a lot of material ahead of us. I remember an idea for an episode — when we were talking about 'Trash', we had actually been, for some time before then, discussing a different episode, which may have eventually been used in one form or another. It was about going to a planet that was surrounded by mines left over from the war, and having the ship get caught by the Alliance. Basically, the feel-

ing was that Mal had survived the war, and then they were flying by some Podunk [small-town] planet and they actually get clipped by a mine, ten years after the war has ended, and the ship goes down. Then they're stuck on this junked planet that's been kept completely isolated because no one's come by to clean out the mines, and they find a whole adventure there. That was going to bring us about as close to a monster as we had gotten up to that point — some genetically-altered soldiers that had been store-housed in an underground complex. That was going to be kind of interesting, but ultimately, I think, too big and too off-character for the period that we were chronicling at that point. Maybe something from that story might have gotten into a later episode, but mostly we were just burning the midnight oil trying to figure out what story would fit *now*, to keep the train moving — the constant challenge in television production." ◗

❖ Opposite: Some of the scripts that *were* produced, signed by cast and crew.

THE MESSAGE

Written by Joss Whedon & Tim Minear
Directed by Tim Minear

JOSS WHEDON

'The Message' was simply an idea we liked with a nice Act Two twist that also showed a little bit more of Mal and Zoe and the war, which is interesting to us. We managed to get a funeral scene that really sort of makes you feel a little bit of something when it's basically the funeral of a guy we don't trust and don't like and haven't known before this episode. We got to throw somebody in Simon's way with Kaylee, which is always nice. But there's a very emotional thing about people who are in a war together. And when somebody betrays that and it ends up killing them — that whole scene with Tracey at the end with Mal and Zoe, to me, that's what makes the whole thing work.

It was the last episode we filmed and therefore the funeral scene was incredibly funereal. [It was when the *Firefly* company was] in the middle of filming that episode that I was told we were canceled. [Prior to the filming of 'Trash', 'Heart of Gold' and 'The Message',] we were given an order for two or three more, instead of the back nine, which was not a good sign; and then right before Christmas, Tim was directing 'The Message' and I came on set and told the crew. We all went home. The next thing we had to shoot was the scene of Zoe and Mal laughing their asses off, talking about their friend who was dead, and in a way, there couldn't have been a more appropriate scene and they couldn't have been better in it, because we all had a friend who was dead. But the joy we got from it was so worth laughing about.

TEASER

EXT. SPACE BAZAAR - DAY

(Black, space-y day.) Ships land and take off from this decrepit but inviting old structure, clearly clapped together from several different ships and stations. We hold on it, silent but for a bit of intro music and a sudden, booming voice:

BARKER (O.S.)
We are not alone!

INT. BAZAAR - CONTINUING

It's a giant flea market/food court/carnival/bar/post office/whatever the hell anybody needs out here station. We see the scope of the place as we push in (low angle) towards a BARKER, standing in front of a small, curtained off space. He's talking from the top, very fast, selling hard.

[NOTE: This is not a large build — it's the size of a large closet, curtained off on all sides, with but one display.]

BARKER
Forget what you think you know. Forget what your mother told you when she tucked you in at night, forget the lies of our oppressive, cabalistic Allied governments! Behind this curtain lies the very secret they don't want you to see — the most astounding scientific find in the history of humanity. Proof! Of Alien life. Yes, go ahead and laugh, sir, but what you see inside this room will change your life forever! It will haunt your dreams and harrow — YES — your very soul. For six bits you can unlock — this lady wants to go, I cannot allow her to be near such wonder, such thrilling horror, unescorted! Who will go with her? Who will see the unholy

truth, the only captured specimen — in existence — of Alien life!

INT. BARKER'S BOOTH - CONTINUING

Hold a still frame on SIMON and KAYLEE, staring intently at something in a big jar that we can't see very well. Wait a beat.

SIMON
Yep. That's a cow fetus.

KAYLEE
Guess so... Does seem to have an awful lot of limbs...

SIMON
It's mutated. Most of the breeding on the outer planets was done by shipping DNA scrip instead of animals. The first herds were grown in labs, then

set loose. Every now and then...

KAYLEE
But cow? How do you figure?

SIMON
It's upside down.

She cranes her head upside down, looks. Nods, sagely...

KAYLEE
Okay, then. Cow.

SIMON
And I'm out twelve bits. I really know how to show a girl a... disgusting time.

KAYLEE
Oh, it's sweet. Poor little thing never even saw the

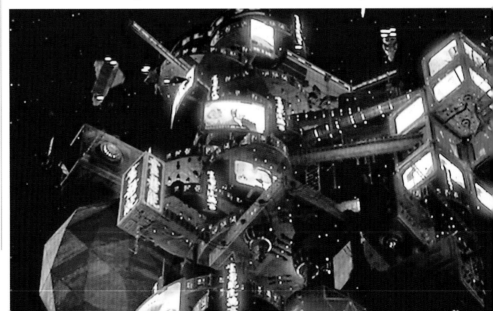

light of day, now it's in show business!

He looks at her admiringly.

SIMON
You manage to find the bright side to every single thing.

KAYLEE
(coming closer)
Also, we get the booth to ourselves for five whole minutes...

SIMON
(glances at jar)
We are not alone, remember?

KAYLEE
(taking his hands)
He won't squawk. Tell me more good stuff about me.

SIMON
(smiles)
Well, you're kind of a genius when it comes to machines... you always say what you mean, and your eyes...

KAYLEE
Yeah? Eyes, yeah?

SIMON
I don't know how to...
(joking)
Plus, every other girl I know is either married, professional or closely related to me, so you are more or less literally the only girl in the world.

Those famous eyes of hers darken considerably. She draws back.

KAYLEE
That's a hell of a thing to say.

SIMON
I was joking...

KAYLEE
No, no, I get it. Back on Osiris you probably had nurses and debutantes crawling all over you. But down here at the bottom of the barrel, there's just me.

SIMON
That is not even —

KAYLEE
Well, I'm glad I rated higher than dead bessie here. <Nee GAO-soo NA niou, TA yo shwong mei-moo?> [Why don't you tell the cow about its beautiful eyes?]

She is storming out just as WASH and ZOE are coming in. Simon watches Kaylee despairingly.

WASH
Oh my god, it's grotesque! Oh, and there's something in a jar.

He ogles the fetus as Zoe comes up to Simon.

ZOE
Scared her away again, did you?

SIMON
This may come as a shock, but I'm actually not very good at talking to girls.

ZOE
(not unkindly)
Why, is there someone you ARE good at talking to?

WASH
(in the background, to the jar)
Do not fear me. Ours is a peaceful race, and we must live in harmony...

INT. BAZAAR - CONTINUING

MAL and INARA walk through, talking.

INARA
Struck out again, did you?

MAL
It's like something from a fable! I've got a priceless artifact, the biggest score of my unseemly career, and no one will touch it.

INARA
The Lassiter is universally known, Mal. Fencing it has to be like... like fencing the Mona Lisa.

MAL
The Mona who?

INARA
You're out of your league. You should think about my offer —

MAL
I done that thinking, and you're to stay clear.

INARA
I know people in the highest ranks of —

MAL
Jabber jabber, I ain't listening. Just 'cause you helped on the job don't make you a crook, and I don't want you jeopardizing your career over this.

INARA
The career you abhor and look down on?

MAL
I don't want you in the way a' trouble. Take it as you like.
(calling out)
Amnon, how've you been?

They have reached a more official-looking section of the bazaar, with a sign reading: POST, FREIGHT and HOLDING.

AMNON DUUL, the postman, wears a sort of combination of a postal uniform and Hasidic wear. He

TIM MINEAR

Tim Minear is fuzzy on the actual inspiration for the episode, "I think Loni Perestere showed me this ice planet footage that he had acquired and I said, 'Can we do a thing where Serenity is flying through these snowy mountains?' and that may actually be where the idea for the episode came from. We just built the whole thing around that so we could do that chase. Loni had the material so we could afford to do it.

"That episode was harder in many ways. We started shooting and we didn't really have the script finished. The battle scene in the top of Act One wasn't written. Joss was supposed to write it and I was like, 'When are you going to write this thing?' He said, 'I'll get around to it.' And I said, 'But I'm shooting it!' To be honest, I was more focused on directing. I'm

not sure what I was trying to say except I was just trying for it not to be boring. My favorite thing was Mal's line, 'Someone's carrying a bullet for you right now, doesn't even know it.'

"It was kind of a spare parts episode in some ways. There were things we wanted to do and we built set pieces around the episode. The whole space mall was built from spare parts from every set we had done so far. We also talked about going to real snow, doing a location thing, but then we didn't and we ended up with fake snow on the stage."

The episode also introduced Jayne's now infamous hat from his mother. "We knew we were going to make him wear a stupid hat when we wrote it. Adam was all about the hat!"

is decent and more or less unflappable, and happy to see Mal.

AMNON
(shaking his hand)
Malcolm, an old friend's face is a balm in this age.

MAL
It's been too long.

AMNON
No, just about the right amount. Too much of you is less of a balm.
(to Inara)
I'm disappointed to see you haven't found a better berth by now.

INARA
I'm a little confused myself.

MAL
I read your wave. You're holding post for us?

AMNON
Got yourself a haul this time. You can sign for everyone?

MAL
Sure.

Amnon goes into a back room as Mal starts filling out a form.

BOOK arrives, with RIVER in tow. They both hold short sticks that dangle strings off the end. Each string runs through the middle of a ball of ice cream that is supported by a bowl shaped cookie attached (under the ice cream) to the string. They're sort of like little mace and chains, and eating them is not altogether convenient, since they swing a bit.

BOOK
Any packages for me?

MAL
Don't know yet.

RIVER
My food is troublesome.

JAYNE arrives, toting a couple of boxes of ammo.

JAYNE
Girl's a mind-readin' genius, can't figure out how to eat an ice-planet.

MAL
You get everything?

JAYNE
They didn't have rounds for the Buhnder, but we're ammoed up pretty good. Got a discount, too, on account of my intimidating manner —

Amnon returns, wheeling in a man-sized crate. He tosses a couple of smaller packages on the counter.

AMNON
This one's addressed to you and Zoe, Mal.

MAL
I don't remember ordering any parts...

He gives Amnon a hand, settling the crate and starting to open it.

AMNON
The little one's for Cobb.

Jayne hurriedly puts the ammo on the counter and takes the small package.

JAYNE
I got post?

BOOK
Might we all want to step back a few paces before he opens that?

INARA'S COSTUMES

Costume designer Shawna Trpcic: "Inara was taken from a lot of different cultures. I went to the past once again to find pictures of a lot of women in lingerie; I took from a lot of different periods, all the way back to Grecian times and all the way up to modern-day geishas. So we combined a bunch of them, and then I just took Morena Baccarin's body and designed on it. She was my Barbie doll, she has this incredible body; I had this little figure, and I would draw on it and just use my imagination, and then we'd collect amazing fabrics from all different sources and blend them to try to come up with her look."

JAYNE
Haw haw. It's from my mother.

During this, Inara finds a small package, squarish, addressed to her. She smoothly slips it beneath her outfit without anyone noticing, turns to see Kaylee arrive, looking glum.

INARA
(to Kaylee)
So, do aliens live among us?

KAYLEE
One of 'em's a doctor. No post for me?

Amnon shakes his head. Inara puts her arm around Kaylee, Kaylee putting her head on Inara's shoulder as Jayne tears open his package and pulls out a letter.

Zoe and Wash wander up with Simon trailing behind as Jayne reads, with the classic toneless hesitation of a slow reader:

JAYNE
"My dear boy. I hope you are well and that you get this soon in your travels."

AS JAYNE CONTINUES: Mal motions for Zoe to help him.

MAL
You order equipment?

ZOE
No sir.

JAYNE
"Thank you for the credits you forwarded, they have helped as Matty is still sick with the Damplung. He waves hello, and so does your father. He is in good spirits and there was layoffs but the foreman said no one can weld like a Cobb so he has employment still. I made you the enclosed" —

He digs in the box —

JAYNE (cont'd)
Ooh! Enclosed!

He reaches in and pulls out a woolly knitted hat with earflaps and a pompom. He is clearly moved. He puts it on, continues reading.

JAYNE (cont'd)
— "the enclosed to keep you warm on your travels. Hope to hear from you soon, love, mother."

He closes the letter, proudly adjusting his hat.

JAYNE (cont'd)
How's it sit? Pretty cunning, don'tchya think?

It's faintly ridiculous, but are you gonna tell him that? Anyway, Kaylee likes it, wistful as she is.

KAYLEE
I think it's the sweetest hat ever.

BOOK
Makes a statement.

JAYNE'S HAT

Costume designer Shawna Trpcic explains the genesis of Jayne's hat: "He had a World War Two pilot's hat in 'The Train Job' — it's a green canvas cap with flaps. I went to the production coordinator in the office — I saw her knitting something for her mom for Christmas — and I said, 'Look, I need a hat for Jayne.' My thing is the ombre — ombre is a way of dyeing something where you start dark and it gets lighter and lighter. That's the idea that I wanted. Elyse, the girl who sewed it for me, brought me different yarn samples, and we put it together from there, and she knitted it from the pattern using that World War Two fighter pilot's hat. And of course, it had to have a pompom on top. Joss said it shouldn't look really stupid, like we're trying too hard, but it should look like a labor of love. So I went to my grandmother's slippers that she used to make me every Christmas — they are goofy because they're these knit slippers with this giant pompom on them, but I love them, because they're from her. That was how we were supposed to see Jayne's hat. You can tell that he loves it because it's from his mom, and he doesn't even think about the fact that here he is, this hired killer, wearing a pompom on his head."

JAYNE
Yeah, yeah!

WASH
A man walks down the street in that hat, people know he's not afraid of anything.

JAYNE
Damn straight.

Mal and Zoe are just finishing unlocking the crate, trying to pry it open.

MAL
Well I hope we got us some fun hats too.

As he's saying it, they pry the lid off and we see the corpse of a young man lying, arms folded, inside.

Mal and Zoe look at him with somber recognition. Everyone goes very quiet, looking inside.

The last to bother is Jayne, who cranes his head into frame, hat still perched proudly, looking quizzically at the body.

JAYNE
What'd you all order a dead guy for?

As Mal and Zoe look at each other:

END OF TEASER

ACT ONE

INT./EXT. BUDDIST TEMPLE - NIGHT

Just inside the temple we see TRACEY, who is a green but gutsy private. Right now he's sweaty and tense. He looks out over the remains of a wall slowly, looking for enemies.

Light from the occasional explosion or far away burst of gunfire gives us a better view of the place — it's being held by about six Independents, all looking out in different directions.

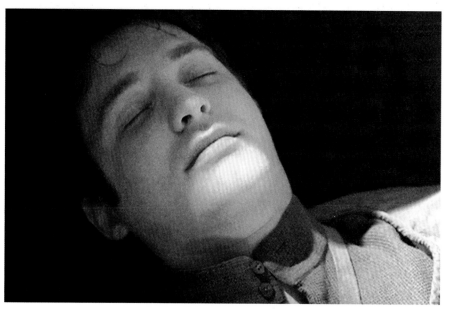

Tracey sees nothing. He takes a moment and lays down his weapon. Reaches into his bag and pulls out a can of beans. As he does, we see an Alliance soldier creeping towards him from the other side of the wall. Tracey doesn't see —

— til the guy's foot hits a rock — Tracey moves, scrambling for his rifle — too late as the Alliance soldier raises his —

CLOSE ON: The Alliance soldier — as Zoe calmly appears behind him and draws a knife across his throat.

ANGLE ON: Tracey — as a few blood splatters hit his face.

Zoe drops the soldier and enters, taking the extra rifle.

TRACEY
Thanks. Didn't know you were there.

ZOE
(stone cold)
That's sort of the point. Stealth, you may have heard of it.

TRACEY
I don't think they covered that in basic.

ZOE
Well, at least they covered "Dropping your weapon so you can eat beans and get yourself shot."

TRACEY
Yeah, I got a badge in that.
(off her look)
Won't happen again.

ZOE
It does, I'm just gonna watch.

TRACEY
Anything interesting out there, you don't mind my asking?

ZOE
(indicating)
'Bout thirty troops behind those buildings. Mortars, but no rollers yet. I expect they plan to pick at us a spell before they charge. They had two scouts sniffin', about ten yards out, but I took 'em down.

TRACEY
(impressed)
I didn't hear a single thing.

ZOE
First rule of battle, little one. Never let 'em know where you are.

Mal runs in, screaming and firing behind him, and dives over a wall for cover, lands nearby, bullets zinging over his head.

ZOE (cont'd)
Of course, there's other schools of thought...

Mal scrambles over to them, laughing.

MAL
Oh! That was bracing. They don't like it when you shoot at them. I worked that out myself.

ZOE
Did you find Vitelli?

MAL
Vitelli's out of it. That bumblebee laid down arms at the first sign of inevitable crushing defeat. Can you imagine such a cowardly creature?

TRACEY
Northwest quadrant's open, then?

MAL
Tracey. Ain't you been killed yet?

TRACEY
(looking sheepishly at Zoe)
No fault of my own, I promise.

MAL
(disappointed)
I really wanted your beans.

ZOE
They're gonna be coming right through here. They got rollers?

MAL
They got every damn thing. How's the Lieutenant?

TRACEY
He started screaming. All of a sudden. About his arms, where was his arms. We hadda go back and

find 'em.

ZOE
What the hell hap —

TRACEY
He ain't even hurt! Got ten pretty fingers like the most of men, but he's screaming they're gone, crying. Then he ain't said a word in two hours.

MAL
(mournful anger)
These kids...

ZOE
Sir. Do we hold?

TRACEY
(breaking a bit)
I don't want to die here. Forgive me saying, but this rock ain't worth it. Not our lives.

MAL
Everybody dies, Tracey. Someone's carrying a bullet for you right now, doesn't even know it.
(smiles)
The trick is to die of old age before it finds you.

ZOE
We can still cut through to the 22nd at the school system. Make a decent stand there.

MAL
We can't do any good here. And I sure as hell ain't laying down arms. Zoe, you heard the Lieutenant give the order to join up with the 22nd?

ZOE
I did.

MAL
Round 'em up, then.
(to Tracey)
You also heard the Lieu —

TRACEY
I wouldn't rat you out, Sarge, hell I —

MAL
Ain't me I worry on. Lieutenant gets his mind back in order, he shouldn't have this on his record. Weren't his fault he couldn't take it.

TRACEY
That's more'n he woulda done for —

Mal raises a hand, intense, for quiet. Tracey doesn't get it, doesn't hear the growing whine of —

ZOE
SEEKER!

Things happen very quickly (or very slowly, depending on Mr. Minear). Zoe dives for cover as Mal pulls a flare from his belt that activates the moment he touches it, hurls it above his head —

— and a tiny missile zooms at the group, suddenly turning up, hitting the flair thirty feet up —

The explosion lights up the air, Mal also diving over Tracey as shrapnel rains down —

TRACEY
AAGH!

Mal is hit in the back and arm. He rolls off Tracey, who's taken it in the leg pretty badly.

TRACEY (cont'd)
Is it bad? Is it bad?

MAL
(ignoring his own wounds)
It's glorious.
(calls out)
We gotta move!

TRACEY
I can't...

MAL
Time to run!
(to Zoe)
Zoe! Get the Lieutenant!

TRACEY
Sarge, I really can't run here.

MAL
Well, you know the old saying...

He hoists Tracey over his shoulder and runs just as a tank bursts through the wall —

SMASH CUT TO:

INT. BAZAAR - CONTINUING (PRESENT DAY)

Close up of that same Tracey, all stiff and dead and blue.

After a moment, Mal slides the lid back over him.

MAL
This don't make any kind of sense. Zoe?

ZOE
I got nothing. But it's definitely Tracey.

WASH
You know this guy?

INARA
Is this a warning of some kind?

AMNON
(quietly)
Listen, Mal, you gotta get this thing out of my station.
(Mal starts to object)
Human transport on a postal route is very very illegal. Anybody even knows I took a corpse in, I'll lose my franchise.

MAL
Well who sent it to you?

AMNON
No return.

ZOE
How long has it been here?

AMNON
Near a week, that's why I waved you. If I'd known...

JAYNE
He don't smell.

MAL
I know. He's been decently preserved.
(to Zoe)
Give me a hand.

JAYNE
We're taking him on board?

MAL
We are.

JAYNE
Don't figure the percentage in that.

MAL
Don't strain your brain trying, then. Might break something.

Mal and Zoe haul the box up, start walking. Book moves to help —

ZOE
(stony)
We got him.

They cart him off, the others folding in behind, quietlike. Simon approaches, oblivious, hoping to win Kaylee into a conversation.

SIMON
What's going on? Did we get something fun?

A glare for Simon. River passes him, ice cream swinging —

RIVER
You are such a boob.

INT. SERENITY - CARGO BAY - A BIT LATER

The box is open again. Everyone is about.

JAYNE
How do we know he ain't plague-ridden or some such?

ZOE
We know.

WASH
We don't, actually. I mean, I respect you guys have a history, but... What are you doing?

Zoe is reaching in, pulling something from the corpse's folded hands.

KAYLEE
He's so young...

SIMON
(to Mal)
If you want me to do a proper autopsy —

KAYLEE
Cut him up?

MAL
Not just yet, thank you Doctor.

KAYLEE
(muttering)
Robot.

Zoe produces a FUTURISTIC DEVICE! That is a tape recorder — of the FUTURE! [Someone design this please.]

MAL
What do you got?

She turns it on. The voice stops them all. It is hesitant at first, and weak, as though the talker were straining for breath, but it soon settles into a rhythm...

TRACEY (V.O.)
Uh. Okay. Um, recording... Hi, I guess. It's me. Tracey. This is a message for Zoe, and for Malcolm Reynolds, and I really hope you all are the ones listening to it. Or, I guess I don't. I guess I hope I'm upright and telling you this tale myself, and we're laughing about how stupid I am, but that don't look likely.

EDITING

Film editor/associate producer Lisa Lassek: "*Firefly* has the best gag reel of any show I've ever worked on, and it's because of Nathan, he is hilarious. You could just give Nathan a camera and turn him loose and craziness would ensue. That *Firefly* gag reel is priceless. In 'The Message', where they're all standing over the corpse in the coffin and they're playing the tape that Tracey recorded, Nathan was everywhere. That was one of the best gags ever, because it was shot exactly as the shot was for the episode, which was a pan of everybody reacting. In one take, Nathan stayed ahead of the camera, so as it pans around Nathan is with everybody. And in every single one, he's got a different expression. It's the funniest thing ever."

We move over everyone as they listen soberly.

TRACEY
No, it's more probable I've gotten myself dead, which is a shame if you're me. I'll spare you the boring details, falling in with untrustworthy folk, makin' a bunch of bad calls... All that matters is I expect to be shuffled off, and you two are the only people I trust to get me where I'm going. Which is home. I'd like my body to be with my folks on St. Albans. We got the family plot there, and my mom and dad deserve to know I died. If you can come up with some heroical lie as to the how, I'd be... no. I'd just like to be able to lie with my kin, and for them to know that's what I wanted. It's funny. We went to war never looking to come back, but it's the real world I couldn't survive. You two carried me through that war. Now I need you to carry me just a little bit further. If you can. Tell my folks I wanted to do right by them, and that I'm at peace and all. When you can't run anymore, you crawl, and when you can't do that... well, you know the rest. Thanks, both of you. Oh. Yeah. Make sure my eyes is closed, will you?

A moment, and the tape ends. Everyone is quiet.

Wash rises, heads to the stairs —

MAL
Wash?

Wash turns back.

WASH
St. Albans ain't two days ride, we burn hard enough.

A moment, and Mal nods. Wash continues up and Mal turns to replace the lid again, says to Inara:

MAL
This might make your schedule a little —

INARA
It's all right.

He nods again, not much with the verbal thank yous right at this moment. He and Zoe lift the top together —

ANGLE: FROM INSIDE THE BOX as they cover it.

EXT. SPACE BAZAAR - MOMENTS LATER

Silent but for music, we see Serenity gently lifting off. It passes another ship — a slightly larger, ALLIANCE SHORT RANGE ENFORCEMENT VESSEL. It's basically an oversized, beat up squad car. As it lands right near where Serenity took off, the music changes to indicate this might not be wonderful.

INT. BAZAAR - MOMENTS LATER

We TRACK BEHIND three men as they stride through the bazaar. If they're cops, they're detectives, since they have no uniforms to speak of. The man in the middle is called WOMACK. He's

been around the block, and likely beaten up everybody on it. The other two, FENDRIS and SKUNK, aren't much different, but they clearly defer to Womack.

They make their way through the place with purposeful indifference. Pass the Barker:

BARKER
That's right, gentlemen, you've been told tales all your life, but Alien races exist among us, the proof is right inside, you'll be amazed and astounded. What is the government not telling us? Alien life! Six bits!

WOMACK
(to the others, an ugly growl)
It's fake. I seen it. It's a pig or some such.

ANGLE ON: Amnon. He is going through papers behind his counter. He arranges them carefully —

ANGLE ON: his papers

— as a badge is dropped on top of them.

Amnon looks up to see Womack standing right in front of him. Amnon hesitates, and before anything can happen Skunk is already going in his back room to search. Fendris is behind Womack, checking his rather large pistol and watching out for pain-in-the-ass innocent bystanders.

AMNON
Can I help you...?

WOMACK
You are an ugly-looking little quim, you know that?

AMNON
If there's a problem —

WOMACK
So you have to be asking yourself, ugly as you are, how repulsive-looking the guy that makes you his lady friend is gonna be. I mean, prison is a lonely place, and you sure as a hundred moons ain't gonna be pitching, so what kind of sorry-ass troll is gonna get blue enough to grapple with you? Shudder to think.

AMNON
I've broken no law.

WOMACK
Transportation of human cargo — especially dead cargo — through the Allied postal system is punishable by five to ten years on a penal moon. Plus, you don't know this yet, but you resisted arrest.
(off Amnon's terror)
Where's my body?

AMNON
I didn't... I don't...

WOMACK
The dead guy. He got shipped here.

Skunk comes out, shakes his head no.

WOMACK (cont'd)
And shipped back out, I guess. Where?

AMNON
I never saw a body. But there was a crate big enough for one. I did hand that over just a while ago.

WOMACK
Lovely. Who got it?

Amnon hands over the register, points to a name.

WOMACK (cont'd)
Malcolm Reynolds. And where would you suppose he's off to?

AMNON
I swear on my soul I don't know. But he just left. He captains a firefly, you should be able to capture them if you leave now.

WOMACK
Are you telling me to leave?

AMNON
No, no...

WOMACK
Relax, you've been great. I was only bluffing with that stuff about arresting you. Who needs that kind of paperwork? Skunk. Light him on fire.

Skunk sprays Amnon with lighter fluid he keeps in a cool container in his jacket. With swift, graceful motion, he holds up a suddenly lit match. Amnon backs into a huddle in the corner, utterly terrified.

Womack stands next to Skunk, over the cowering postman.

WOMACK (cont'd)
Tell anyone we were here, warn
(looks at the register)
"Malcolm Reynolds" that we're coming, and you'll wish we'd burned you. <Dong ma?> [Understand?]

Amnon nods frantically.

WOMACK (cont'd)
Boys... let's go find us a corpse.

He blows out Skunk's match.

END OF ACT ONE

ACT TWO

INT. SERENITY - ENGINE ROOM - NIGHT

Kaylee lies in her hammock, listening to the recording of Tracey's voice. She clearly has been doing this for a while, and has gotten awful misty about the lad.

TRACEY (V.O.)
All that matters is I expect to be shuffled off, and you two are the only people I trust to get me where I'm going. Which is home. I'd like my body to be with my folks on St. Albans. We got the family plot there, and my mom and dad deserve to know I died.

INT. SERENITY - AFT HALL - CONTINUING

Simon comes up, looking for Kaylee. He stops outside the engine room door. Sees her, hears the recording...

THE LITTLE HAN

Prop master Skip Crank: "The little Han in Carbonite was something I had. I started putting it in every shot. It's in the engine room twice, but it's most prominent in the galley. He's a big *Star Wars* fan; *Star Trek* too — he does the best Bill Shatner impression."

TRACEY (V.O.)
If you can come up with some heroical lie as to the how, I'd be... no. I'd just like to be able to lie with my kin, and for them to know that's what I wanted.

Simon slowly slips away, realizing with regret he is unwanted.

INT. SERENITY - CARGO BAY - CONTINUING

Book stands at the head of the crate/coffin, bible in hand, head bowed. WIDEN to see that during his little silent service, Jayne is busily lifting weights. Jayne replaces the barbell in its holder, the metal noisily clattering. Book looks around.

JAYNE
Hey, I'm sorry, Preacher. Makin' too much noise?

BOOK
No, no, I was just... saying a few words. Don't know the boy's denomination, but...

JAYNE
It's good. Lord should oughta look after the dead.

Over the following, Jayne pats himself down with a towel — he's quite sweaty. Really been going at it.

JAYNE (cont'd)
You wanna do a set? I'll spot you.

BOOK
Not so terribly in the mood.

JAYNE
Most people is pretty quiet right about now. I guess the Captain and Zoe were summat bonded with the kid.

BOOK
It would appear.

JAYNE
Me, I see a stiff — one I didn't have to kill myself — I just get, you know, the urge to do stuff. Work out, run around, get some trim if there's a willin' woman about... Not that I get flush from corpses or anything. I ain't crazy.

BOOK
Makes sense. Looking to feel alive, I would venture.

JAYNE
For psychology, that ain't half dumb. My kind of life don't last, Preacher. So I expect I'm invested in making good sport of it whilst I can.
He puts on his hat as he says it.

As they continue talking, we come around to see River in the background, crawling gracefully onto the coffin. She stretches, catlike, moving her head about in an odd fashion, as though listening, then lies flat on her belly, arms out to her sides.

JAYNE (cont'd)
You gonna read over me when I'm taken down, Shepherd?

BOOK
Oh, I suspect you'll be around long after we're all —

JAYNE
(noticing River)
What the hell is she —
(at River)
What the hell are you doing?

BOOK
Oh. River, that might not be the best place to...

RIVER
I'm very comfortable.

They consider pulling her off... hesitate...

BOOK
(to Jayne)
I guess we do all have different reactions to death.

SMASH CUT TO:

INT. SERENITY - DINING ROOM - CONTINUING

Mal and Zoe are laughing their asses off. We widen to see Inara is with them, laughing as well. They've all had a few drinks, and continue to drink as they talk:

MAL
I really thought I was gonna die.

INARA
How could he possibly have even...

MAL
The Colonel was dead drunk. Three hours pissing on about the enlisted men, "They're scum, they're not fighters" — and he passes right out. Boom.

ZOE
We couldn't even move him. So Tracey just snipped it right off his face.

KAYLEE

"Bye now! Have good sex."

Jewel Staite says that *Firefly* creator Joss Whedon and show-runner Tim Minear have somewhat different styles as directors. "Joss is really specific. He has his vision mapped out and he gives great direction. I think Tim likes to go with the flow and see what happens and what we come up with. They're both really cool."

Minear directed a scene that Whedon has cited as being among his favorites: the partially improvised basketball game in 'Bushwhacked'. Staite is fond of it as well. "That was hilarious. We didn't really know what we were doing and we were running into each other. We were genuinely having a lot of fun and it didn't require much acting."

Of all the various relationships between the *Firefly* characters, did Staite have a favorite to play? "I would say the relationship with Book, because Kaylee was the first person that he met before he came onto the ship and they had this instantaneous bond. They're always really sweet to each other. I think everybody felt a little unrestrained with Book. He's full of great advice and he's such a strong, sage character; he's very experienced and I think Kaylee felt like she could really trust him."

In which episode do we learn the most about Kaylee? "I would have to say 'Out of Gas'. Because the revelation of how Kaylee got the mechanics job surprised even me. I had no idea they were going to do that until I read the script a couple of days before we were going to shoot it. I was totally shocked — but I loved that it was really shocking. Kaylee was this seemingly sweet and innocent girl and really, she's this very sexual being and totally unashamed of it. I thought that was really great. I had asked when I was first cast, 'What are her parents like, how did she get on the ship?' And they said, 'Oh, you'll see, we're going to do an episode about that,' so I just went with the flow, but never really knew

how naïve to play her. I started out thinking she was *really* innocent and she's not at all," Staite laughs.

Staite finds it difficult to narrow down her favorite experiences on *Firefly*. "If he ever finds this out, he's going to gloat about it, but I loved working with Nathan so much, because he makes me laugh so hard. But at the same time, I don't break character with him. He really does bring the best out of me somehow.

"I had to keep my weight up to play Kaylee for the series, and that was fun. I had to raid the craft service table about twenty times a day just to make sure I kept the extra twenty pounds on me.

"The cast in general, just being friends with them and being able to hang out off-set and really bond. I've worked on a lot of series and I never really had that with another cast — you get close and you become friends and say you're going to keep in touch, but no one ever really does. We actually did. That is one of my absolute favorite things."

Whedon announced *Firefly*'s cancellation during the shooting of 'The Message', "It was in the scene where Tracey has me in his grip just outside of the bridge. Alan was there and Gina and Nathan and poor Jonathan Woodward and me. Joss came up and told us all then. We still had another four days left to go and we had to buck up and just get over it, keep shooting. We all had been really stressed. It was a daily obsession: seeing the numbers and how many people were watching. It was just excruciating. So I was relieved that we finally had an answer. Even if it was a 'no', at least we knew it was a 'no', and we could move on now and figure out a plan B. But I don't remember the shooting of that episode being particularly sad. I remember us goofing off like crazy. We knew that they weren't going to fire us, because we were already canceled, so there was a lot of laughter and a lot of fun on that one."

Summing up, Staite says, "I had such a special experience on that show that everything I do, ever since the end of *Firefly*, I compare to that experience. And I don't think anything will ever be like that again. It's kind of this indescribable thing. It was a sort of bond that we had, and we knew it was really special, we all felt that way. But when we were filming *Firefly*, I had absolutely no idea that it would be one of those things that I don't think will ever really go away." ◀

MAL
And you never seen a man more proud of his moustache than Colonel Obrin. In all my life I will never love a woman the way this officer loved that lip ferret.

ZOE
Giant walrussy thing, all waxed up...

INARA
Did he find out?

Another burst of laughter from Mal and Zoe.

MAL
The next morning, he wakes up, and it's gone. He's furious, but he can't actually say, you know, "Someone stole my moustache". So he calls out all the platoons —

ZOE
I thought he was gonna shoot us —

MAL
And he's eyeballing the men something fearsome, not a word, and he comes to Tracey... and Tracey is wearing the gorramn moustache on his face.

ZOE
He glued it on.

MAL
Staring the old man down, wearing his own damn... Oh god...

The laughter falters, Mal looking into his drink a moment. Inara looks at him sympathetically, tries to jump start the conversation again:

INARA
Well, the Colonel must have said SOMETHING to —

The SHIP ROCKS with the force of an explosion. They all start out of their chairs.

ZOE
Are we hit?

MAL
Too damn close —

And they are racing to the —

INT. SERENITY - BRIDGE - CONTINUING

Where Wash is piloting intently.

WASH
They're behind us. Fired over the port bow.

MAL
Warning shot?

WASH
They coulda hit us...

ZOE
Feds.

The screen comes to life, Womack's face on it.

WOMACK
This is Lieutenant Womack of Allied Enforcement. You are in possession of stolen goods and are ordered to cut thrust and prepare for docking.

MAL
The Lassiter.

ZOE
That was quick.

INARA
Think Saffron tipped them off?

Mal hits the screen com:

MAL
This is Captain Reynolds. I think there's been a mistake.

WOMACK
There's been a lot of mistakes, Captain. The latest of which is you taking that crate.

He looks at the others. "Crate"?

MAL
(to Womack)
We took in a lot of inventory today. If something got mixed in, we'll sure hand it back, but I don't think we're your men. Let me check through the cargo — is it marked at all?

WOMACK
You might wanna think twice about playing games with me. I will blow you into fragments.

MAL
You do that, your precious crate's gonna be in bitty shards. Now I got deliveries to make, Officer, so you just lock onto my trajectory and I'll see if there's anything here fits your description.

He turns off the screen.

WASH
Police procedure has changed since I was little.

MAL
They call back, you keep them occupied.

WASH
What do I do, shadow puppets?

BOOK
We'll take care of it.

ZOE
I don't get this. They're after Tracey?

MAL
Or there's something else in that box.

INT. SERENITY - CARGO BAY - MOMENTS LATER

Tracey's body lies on the floor as Mal, Zoe and Jayne go through both the crate and the box, looking for something. The others including Simon, Inara and River (minus Wash and Book) look on.

MAL
Anything?

JAYNE
(smashing planks)
Not unless this crate's made a' magical, wish-granting planks.

MAL
(to Zoe)
Check his pockets.

KAYLEE
That ain't right...

MAL
Neither's being blowed up. There's nothing about this sits well with me.

ZOE
Empty.

MAL
Well, they want this body for something, and I'm guessing it ain't a proper burial.

Looks around. No option. Looks to Simon:

MAL (cont'd)
Well, Doctor... I guess you are doing an autopsy.

INT. SERENITY - INFIRMARY - LATER

Mal, Zoe and Jayne watch as Simon prepares to open up the now naked (but sheet covered) body.

ZOE
You really think there's something in there.

MAL
Using corpses for smuggling is a time-honored repulsive custom.

JAYNE
Maybe it's gold!

ZOE
And maybe this was a friend of ours, and you wanna show a little respect.

JAYNE
I got respect. But I'm just saying... gold...

SIMON
He's been opened before.

MAL
How's that?

SIMON
It's good work. The scar's nearly invisible, but...

He traces his finger all the way down the chest.

MAL
Well, let's see what's in there.

He looks at Zoe, hating this. A tense moment. Simon takes his scalpel and starts cutting.

And Tracey SCREAMS.

END OF ACT TWO

ACT THREE

INT. SERENITY - INFIRMARY

Where we left off. Everyone backing away from the SCREAMING Lazarus. Tracey looks with horror to his bleeding chest, then to the man who holds the scalpel — Simon. Simon sees the blood, makes an instinctive move to see to the wound. All Tracey sees is the knife. He gives a PRIMAL CRY as he lunges off the table at Simon. They struggle, knocking shit over. Mal and Zoe jump into the fray. Mal calling to Jayne:

MAL
Get hold of him!

JAYNE
Spry for a dead fella!

Mal pins him to the floor, ends up sitting on top of him.

MAL
SETTLE! That's enough!

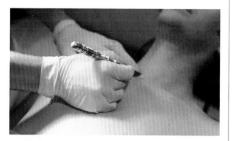

TRACEY
He was cuttin' on me, Sarge!

MAL
I know it! I told him to!

TRACEY
You told him to! What for?!

MAL
You were dead!

TRACEY
(coming back to him)
Hunh? Oh. Right. Suppose I was.
(sees Zoe)
Hey there, Zoe.

ZOE
Private.

MAL
You feeling a mite calmer now?

TRACEY
Yes, Sarge.

TRACEY (cont'd)
(then)
Sarge?

MAL
What?

TRACEY
I think I'm nekked.

A beat. Mal's straddling a naked man.

MAL
Okay. We're gonna get up off this floor, you're gonna stand like a person, cover yourself, and the Doctor's gonna tend to that gash.

Tracey nods. Mal gets off of him. He rises. Looks a bit sheepish. Pulls the sheet up around his waist as he sits on the edge of the table. As Simon starts to tend to the wound:

TRACEY
Sorry for jumping on you the way I did. I was a little confounded.

SIMON
Emerging from that state can be disorienting. Was it byphodine?
(clarifying)
The drug you took to make it appear as though you were dead. Do you remember what it was called?

TRACEY
Never did ask.

SIMON
(puts gauze to wound)
Hold that there.
(casually, to Jayne)
Bring that pan, please.

Jayne, not knowing why, brings a bedpan over. Simon positions Jayne's hand with pan in front of

Tracey without explanation, then moves to his med supplies.

TRACEY
Fella sold it to me said I'd be under a week or more. He told me I wouldn't dream. But I did. Dreamt of my family.

Simon has moved back to his patient, reaches out, repositions the bedpan as Tracey suddenly HEAVES forward (leaning forward so all spew is sound fx). Jayne reacts. Simon doesn't, was expecting it. Gives Tracey a shot:

SIMON
This should take the edge off the nausea.
(to grossed-out Jayne)
You can take that.

Simon goes about checking Tracey's vitals, hooking him up to the scanners and reading the monitor in the BG.

MAL
All right. Now you care to explain why it is you got yourself all corpse-ified and mailed to me? What're you running from?

TRACEY
Running to, not from. Just want to get home is all. That's all I ever wanted. 'Cept there's them took exception to that. To me leaving... while I's in possession of their property...

MAL
What'd you boost, Tracey? More important, who'd you boost it from?

SIMON
Captain... Captain, I don't mean to... I think we may have a medical emergency here...

They all look at him; he's looking at the monitor.

SIMON (cont'd)
This man... He appears to be in cardiac arrest...

MAL
What? Tracey, you having a heart attack?
(to Simon)
Don't look like he's having a heart attack...

TRACEY
(laughs)
Don't pay no attention to your machines, Doc. They'll fib to ya. Heart's just fine. Better'n fine. Runs a bit hotter'n normal, is all.

SIMON
(off monitors)
My god... it's not just the heart muscle... it's everything...

TRACEY
All the movin' parts. That's what I took, Mal. And that's what they want back.

MAL
Tracey — you want to explain what in the <TYEN shiao-duh> [name of all that's sacred] you're talking about?

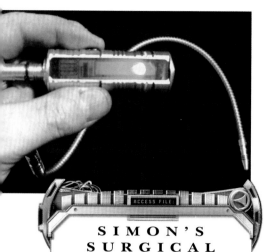

SIMON'S SURGICAL INSTRUMENTS

Prop master Randy Eriksen tasked Applied Effects with the job of making Simon's surgical instruments for the pilot show. Applied's Chris Calquhoun explains: "We were just told: 'medical tools', a scalpel and a bullet-grabber. A year after the first *Star Wars* movie came out I customized an X-Acto hobby knife handle, and I used to make all kinds of cool little tools and stuff that were based on the look I came up with like a zillion and a half years ago. I've incorporated the look into a couple of props since then, but never so prominently as in Simon's medical instruments. This is me 'going off' on the lathe. As well as the lathe work, there are some little milled parts too. The scalpel was originally designed with a laser cutter as shown in the design artwork, but was later changed to a more traditional blade." The colored bands are sections of silicone sleeving stretched over the handles. It is a more durable surface than paint and stands up to on-set rigors far better.

The scalpel and bullet-grabber were first, then the laser probe device was ordered: "I picked a style and made it fit in with the other instruments. I turned some aluminum tube and made an end-cap and fitted an LED, some batteries and a little switch on top. The graphic on the display is a 'geekness' flow chart — so you can tell how geeky you are in comparison to other sci-fi fans! It's too small to read on TV and I put it in just for fun."

Randy Eriksen on Simon's surgical tools: "Applied Effects made Simon's surgical tools, which were totally awesome. They were inspired by desperation. I was standing in Applied's shop talking to Chris and I noticed his X-Acto knife. I said that it was cool and we should just do them like that. We had a scalpel, a scope and a grabber. They are so good and you didn't really see them on the show much. They look much better in real life than they do on the screen. Then again, they *would* focus on something that we didn't pay any attention to and was awful and kind of embarrassing. Oh, you'd see that!"

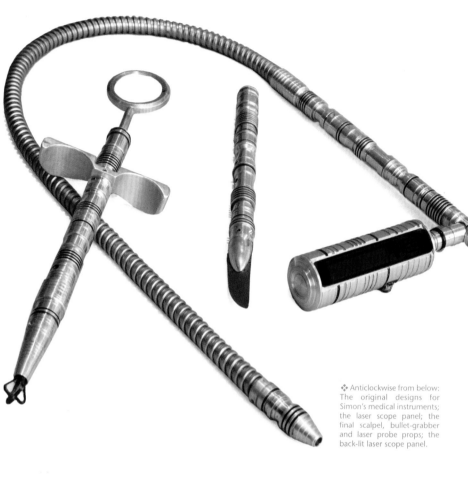

❖ Anticlockwise from below: The original designs for Simon's medical instruments; the laser scope panel; the final scalpel, bullet-grabber and laser probe props; the back-lit laser scope panel.

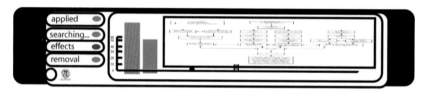

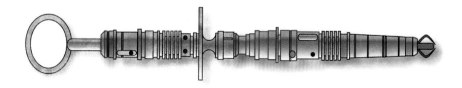

TRACEY
(distracted)
Sure, Sarge... sure...

Now the MONITOR really starts to go nuts, Tracey's heart beating ever faster. The others look from the monitor to him, then follow his gaze to...

KAYLEE stands in the doorway, staring at the man come back to life. They hold the look between them.

INT. SERENITY - COMMON AREA - (SHORT TIME) LATER

Mal, Zoe, Jayne, Simon, Kaylee and Tracey. Kaylee brings Tracey some water. They will have a silent connection throughout the following.

TRACEY
Thank you.

She smiles at him, takes a seat.

MAL
So your innards... ain't your innards?

TRACEY
Mine got scooped out, they replaced every bit.

JAYNE
Why'd you wanna go and do that?

TRACEY
For the money. They're paying me to transport what they stuck in.

ZOE
You're smuggling human organs?

TRACEY
But not from a person. I wouldn't do a thing like that. Grown in a lab. Only way they can be moved is in a person. Not sure why.

SIMON
Because the technology's not ready. The blastomeres are unapproved. Likely unstable. You're not just a carrier — you're an incubator.

TRACEY
Whichever. It ain't strictly legal, I can tell you that. I was supposed to be at the drop spot two weeks ago. A clinic on Ariel. They were to open me up, take the goods and put back my own workings.

ZOE
And you believed them? That they'd put you back together?

TRACEY
Sure. They want you to make as many runs as you're able. Hell, I met a fella, he's on his third already.

MAL
So what happened?

TRACEY
Well, truth is I had a —

SIMON
Change of heart?

A beat. Simon's amused. No one else is. Tracey continues:

TRACEY
A better offer. Another buyer, willing to pay three times the going rate. Enough I could get my folks off that rock they been forced to live on, set them up someplace nice, someplace warm, maybe one of the central planets.

MAL
But your "better offer" went south...

TRACEY
Got myself into a bit of a pickle, Sarge. The folks I was working for... they musta got wind what I was planning. When I showed up... my new buyer was dead. There was men there, waitin' for me.

KAYLEE
But you got away.

TRACEY
Only just. I knew they'd never stop looking for me so long as I was alive. Thought my chances'd be better if I weren't.

MAL
So you "died" and figured then they'd stop looking?

TRACEY
Yeah.

A SUDDEN BLAST from outside. The ship ROCKS with the impact. Tracey reacts with fear. As Mal rises —

MAL
Think maybe you figured wrong.

EXT. SPACE - CONTINUING

The police cruiser is behind Serenity, pacing. It lets loose with another ELECTRONIC BLAST.

INT. SERENITY - BRIDGE - CONTINUING

Wash and Book on the bridge. As Mal and Zoe and Jayne enter behind them:

WASH
I think they're about done being stalled, Ca —
(as he swivels)
GAHHHH!

He's just laid eyes on Tracey, who stands in the doorway with Kaylee. Book takes in the sight with interest.

WASH (cont'd)
Mal, your dead army buddy's on the bridge!

ZOE
He ain't dead.

WASH
Oh.

MAL
How close're we to St. Albans?

WASH
Five from atmo.

MAL
Pull up the terrain specs. Kaylee, take him out of here. And strap in.

Wash brings up terrain maps on the nav monitor. Mal starts paging through the maps on the screen as he grabs the radio mic, speaks.

MAL (cont'd)
This is Captain Reynolds —

WOMACK (ON VID)
Reynolds, I'm a dangerous-minded man on a ship loaded with hurt. Why you got me chattin' with your peons?

MAL
(shuts off mic)
Tracey, you go on below. Let us handle this —
(back into mic:)
Just seein' to some technical difficulties, Officer.

WOMACK (ON VID)
Not interested, Captain. I stepped over a lot of bodies to get to that one you got in your hold. You play this right, and yours won't have to be among them.

TRACEY
(scared)
Sarge...

ZOE
Private, the Captain ordered you off the bridge.

KAYLEE
Come on.

She starts to lead him away. Mal pages through maps.

MAL
We'd love to let you boys dock, but that last pop you give us knocked out our fore-couple. We're gonna have to park it if you want the tour.

FOREDECK HALL — Tracey heard that, turns back. Kaylee gently tugs him her way.

KAYLEE
It's okay. Captain'll take care of it. You'll see.

They have arrived at the door to her bunk, she pulls it open. Gives him a little push forward. He looks at her, unsure. But the total, guileless faith in her face persuades. He starts down the ladder to her bunk. She follows as —

BRIDGE

WOMACK (ON VID)
All right, Captain. We can do this on the ground just as easy.

Womack FITZES out. Mal looks at the blank screen.

THE CHASE

Visual effects supervisor Loni Peristere: "I loved working with Tim Minear on 'The Message'. We had discovered a new software program called Terragen that created virtual landscapes. It was so realistic that we thought it would be an interesting idea to show a demo of a fighter plane flying through a landscape to Joss and Tim, so they could maybe write it into an episode. We came up with this cat and mouse game, which was chasing down Serenity in a snowfield."

MAL
(to himself)
Yeah. Easy.
(clicks off, points to map)
There. Think you can do it?

WASH
Watch me.

Mal clicks over the feed on the mic, now when he speaks it's an internal SHIP PA.

MAL (AMPLIFIED)
Attention all crew. Sit down and hang on to something...

EXT. SPACE/ATMO - CONTINUING

As Serenity, followed by cops, dips down, heads for a PLANET.

SERENITY

breaking atmo, speeding up, taking a dive, as...

INT. SERENITY - KAYLEE'S BUNK - CONTINUING

Kaylee is coming down the ladder into her room. As the ship heads into the dive, she is sent into Tracey's arms. He catches her. Holds her. They look at each other as —

INT. SERENITY - BRIDGE - CONTINUING

Jayne has great sea legs, he walks back onto the bridge (he stepped out during that intercut) with three guns. Starts prepping them, just in case.

Book is over at a secondary radio station, checking monitors. Zoe steps in by him.

ZOE
What is it?

BOOK
Just a little strange. There's a fed station near here, but our friends haven't made a transmission since they broke atmo...

As Zoe considers that...

Wash is all concentration, heading for —

EXT. PLANET - DAY

Serenity banks off now, heading for —

MOUNTAINS in the distance... the police cruiser banks easily, dogging them as —

INT. SERENITY - BRIDGE - CONTINUING

Wash grits his teeth —

WASH
Get ready for hard burn —
(leans on controls)
They'd be crazy to follow us in here.

Everyone hangs on, as

EXT. ICE CANYONS - CONTINUING

Serenity racing into the mountain range, then diving into snowy canyons. As the walls of the canyons start to close in and things get tight —

— the police cruiser pulls up sharply, leaving Serenity to go it alone.

Serenity thrillingly zooms through the twisty canyons.

INT. SERENITY - BRIDGE - CONTINUING

Wash lets out a breath.

WASH
Not behind us anymore —
(then, glancing up)
Oh. Didn't think of that...

EXT. ICE CANYONS - CONTINUING

Cops follow placidly just above the canyon, pacing. BELOW, Serenity is having a tougher time of it as it maneuvers through the ever precarious canyons.

INT. SERENITY - KAYLEE'S BUNK - CONTINUING

As before. Tracey holds Kaylee.

TRACEY
You okay?
(she nods, their faces close)
So I can let go now?

KAYLEE
(only if you want)
You can...

They start to separate and another lurch throws them, they go to the bed, sitting, bracing. Tracey looks momentarily queasy.

KAYLEE (cont'd)
All this hard banking — when the gravity drive and actual gravity start working against each other, it tosses your lunch about a bit.

TRACEY
Your pilot's pretty wild.

KAYLEE
Oh, he could thread a needle with this bird. He's the best.

TRACEY
Good to know.
(tentative foray:)
So you two are —

KAYLEE
Sweeties?
(laughs)
Hell no, I got no... I'm not with any...
(too forward)
He's married to Zoe.

TRACEY
Zoe got married? I can't even get my mind around that. Next you'll be telling me she smiles and has emotions.

KAYLEE
She must have been such a stone-cold <SHIONG-tsan SHA-sho> [ass-kicking killer] during the war.

TRACEY
Nobody EVER messed with her. I think the Sarge was even a little afraid of her. And she got married. It's good. People making a life for themselves.

KAYLEE
What about you?

TRACEY
Mostly —
(another LURCH)
— stuff like this. Sorry to bring you all into it.

KAYLEE
Oh, danger is pretty much our business.

TRACEY
Still, if you got put in a bad spot at all, Kaylee... I think I'd be real unhappy.

Bing! Moment.

INT. SERENITY - BRIDGE - CONTINUING

Wash pilots, swinging the ship from side-to-side as he navigates the terrain.

WASH
Whoo! This kind of flyin' really wakes up a guy —

MAL
(teeth gritted)
Awake helps —

The ship SHUDDERS — one side brushed up against a mountain, as we can tell by Wash's

hard turn —

WASH
Whoa! Baby!

MAL
(nervous)
Wash —

WASH
Just a love tap —

EXT. ICE CANYONS - CONTINUING

Serenity goes behind a curve, disappears for an instant, reappears, then disappears again... then doesn't reappear.

The police cruiser circles, looking. No sign.

EXT./INT. ICE CANYONS/CAVE - CONTINUING

As Serenity backs into ice cave.

INT. SERENITY - BRIDGE - CONTINUING

Wash sets the ship down, starts flipping switches and the ship POWERS DOWN to dashboard light.

WASH
There. Now, I shut down main power, they might not read our auxiliary under all this.

MAL
And if they come down here and try to get a visual?

WASH
(looks around)
Well... she's not a small ship.

INT. SERENITY - KAYLEE'S BUNK - CONTINUING

TRACEY
(nervous)
We're not moving. Why aren't we moving?

KAYLEE
Probably part of some genius plan to give the feds the slip.

TRACEY
Yeah. Probably.

BOOM! A concussion ROCKS the ship. Tracey reacts, spooked.

TRACEY (cont'd)
What was that?

INT. SERENITY - PASSENGER DORM - CONTINUING

Simon and River sit, looking a bit nervous.

RIVER
Thousand-one, thousand-two, thousand-three —

SIMON
River?

RIVER
Shh. Counting between the lightning and the thunder. See if the storm is coming or going... Thousand-eight, thousand-nine —

INT. INARA'S SHUTTLE - CONTINUING

Inara is strapped into the pilot chair of her shuttle. She takes out the small SQUARE PACKAGE she picked up in the teaser, looks at it. Whatever's in it sits heavy with her.

ANOTHER BOOM shudders the ship, her shuttle with it. She's scared, but keeps her courtly manner about it.

INARA
That's enough, thank you very much — !

EXT. ICE CANYONS - CONTINUING

Where WE SEE the police cruiser drop a CONCUSSIVE DEPTH CHARGE.

INT. SERENITY - BRIDGE - CONTINUING

ANOTHER BOOM.

ZOE
Sounds like full-yield mag-drops.

WASH
I think they picked up a little triangulation in cop school —

MAL
Options?

WASH
Well, we're only good as long as the roof holds out. Direct hit above us, ship's electrics'll be fried. We'll have to climb out.

JAYNE
Or be dug out.

ANOTHER BOOM!

ZOE
Gettin' closer.

Book steps in by the Captain.

BOOK
Captain, there is another way.

They look at him.

INT. SERENITY - KAYLEE'S BUNK - CONTINUING

A L A N   T U D Y K

The last episode we shot was 'The Message'. I'm flying and trying to lose this cop and he has a better spaceship than me. If you watch that sequence you can see that, because the show was canceled, we abandoned the whole Wash calm thing and, in fact, that was closer to me in real life. I was totally Jerry Lewis. I went completely, 'Whoa! Wow! Whoa!'. Joss came on set that day and went over to Tim and said, 'So, the calm pilot thing... that's gone?' Tim was like, 'Yeah, that's gone. We're going for the funny.'

BOOM! The room shudders with the impact. Tracey moves to the ladder.

KAYLEE
Captain said to stay put.

TRACEY
I just want to see what's happening.

INT. BRIDGE - CONTINUING

BOOK
We're cornered, outgunned and it's only a matter of time before they find us — or what's left of us. Let's not wait for that to happen.

ZOE
What are you saying, Preacher?

BOOK
I'm saying we make good on what we said we were going to do. We call them, fly out of this canyon — and let them board.

During this we have CUT TO A SUBJECTIVE POV moving toward the bridge from the FOREDECK HALL.

JAYNE
Give ourselves up?

BOOK
It's our only choice.

MAL
We let them walk on this ship, we're taking an awful chance. These boys ain't playin', Preacher.

BOOK
Yes. I'm aware of that.

BRIDGE

Mal and Book hold a look between them. Mal is weighing this advice. Reading some world experience in Book's certainty.

The moment is interrupted by yet another, and much closer, CONCUSSIVE BOOM. This time ICE and ROCK rain onto the front window. They look up, react, as —

REVEAL

What they don't see behind them — TRACEY is at the door; he's heard it all. He looks ashen, betrayed... and now his gaze falls to —

— one of JAYNE'S newly loaded GUNS, within arm's reach.

Tracey's face clouds over.

END OF ACT THREE

ACT FOUR

INT. BRIDGE - CONTINUING

Sweat-beaded brows, a beat of nervous silence, held breaths. Then from above a rolling

THUNDEROUS BOOM. The bridge vibrates with the O.S. explosion's force. A cascade of ICE CHUNKS clatters over the windshield and the nose of Serenity.

Wash lets out his breath, checking some of his dash monitors.

WASH
<Wuo duh MA.> [Mother-of-Jesus.] That one was really close...

Jayne turns from the debris still falling to the others. He's extra sweaty, falling prey to his cowardly side.

JAYNE
That tears it. I'm with the Preacher. I ain't gettin' snowed-in permanent on account of some jack-ass kid —

ANOTHER BOOM FROM ABOVE — throughout this scene, the depth charges are a slow, regular drum beat, adding rhythmic percussion to the tense-ness.

BOOK
(quiet conviction)
It's the only option, Captain.

Mal turns to Zoe. They exchange a look. Zoe gives a slight nod — "Can't think of anything else to do". Mal nods back.

MAL
Wash... Call the cops. Tell them we give up.

Wash nods and flicks the RADIO ON, preparing to call.

TRACEY (O.S.)
No.

ANOTHER BOOM.

Tracey edges the barrel of a gun into the FG, holding it on the others on the bridge.

MAL
Tracey, what are y —

TRACEY
I said NO! Those bastards up there are gonna pull this million-credit meat outta me and leave me bleedin' —
(turns gun on Wash)
Now turn off that radio!

Another depth charge EXPLODES, closer, louder. Jayne braces himself as more ICE SHARDS rain down on the ship.

JAYNE
Ruttin' twerp's gonna get us —

TRACEY
(loud, arresting)
Don't you move! No one move!
(gun back to Wash)
Power up! We have to run! NOW!

Book takes a slow step toward Tracey. Tracey

swings the gun at him, the model of panicky-guy-with-gun-in-over-his-head-and-ready-to-go-postal.

BOOK
Put that thing down, boy. You got no idea what —

TRACEY
Shut it, Shepherd! I swear to God I'll shoot you dead if you don't.
(manic, bitter laugh)
Sarge — Zoe — Why you listening to this bible-thumper?

ZOE
We've seen the man fight, Trace. Seen him think. And we trust him on both counts.

TRACEY
Yeah, well, you two were always lookin' for someone to spend your trust on... Didn't exactly get your war won, did it?

He turns to Mal, whose hands are slightly raised, eyes boring back at Tracey. ANOTHER BOOM.

MAL
Wash. Call the cops.

Wash's eyebrows raise; he points gingerly at Tracey's gun.

WASH
Um —

TRACEY
(to Mal, re: Wash)
I'll kill him. I'll put a hole right through him.

MAL
You mailed your ugly business to Zoe and me, Tracey, cash-on-delivery. I'll go to hell before I watch you turn and bite us for the favor —

ANOTHER BOOM, even closer. Ice, clatter, scary.

MAL (cont'd)
Wash, you call them up. Tell them we'll meet 'em topside.

TRACEY
No —

MAL
Do it.

Wash does that funny-under-pressure nod of his, turns to the radio, reaches for the switch —

TRACEY
NO!

Tracey swings his gun off Mal and fires a SHOT at the radio console. He misses, and it RICOCHETS off the railing above it, grazing across Wash's temple, throwing his head back.

Tracey stands, mouth open. For a moment we think he can't believe what he's done. But now we realize it's for another reason, this look of surprise... He looks down, and the camera tilts down, to his chest, where a BIG RED HOLE gapes. Fresh blood blooms there. He looks up at —

Zoe, who holds her gun at him, having got her shot off the instant he moved to fire on Wash.

TRACEY (cont'd)
You sh — You shot me...

Zoe cocks her gun, sending the spent shell flying.

ZOE
Damn right.

ANOTHER BOOM. A little dazed, but still standing, Tracey backs out of the bridge. Zoe covers him as she glances to Wash.

ZOE (cont'd)
Wash — ?

Wash dabs a finger at the bullet graze.

WASH
Ow?

It ain't critical.

INT. SERENITY - FOREDECK - CONTINUING

Tracey backs down the stairs into the foredeck, gun covering the door to the bridge.

ANOTHER DEPTH CHARGE shakes the ship.

Kaylee appears, emerging from her room.

KAYLEE
What happened!? I heard —

MAL
Kaylee! Get out of here!

Tracey turns on her, swings an arm around her, pulling her against him as a shield. Mal is at the bridge door, gun out.

TRACEY
Gorramn it, Mal.

He fires a wild shot toward the door, Mal ducks. Tracey herds Kaylee toward the exit to the cargo bay stairs —

INT. SERENITY - STAIRS/CARGO BAY

As Tracey pushes Kaylee down the stairs, her arm in his white-knuckled grip.

TRACEY
Kaylee, I'm sorry... I don't want to scare you... I just —

She sees the blood pouring down his shirt front.

KAYLEE
Blood...!

TRACEY
They shot me. They want to turn me in...

KAYLEE
No — they wouldn't —

ANOTHER BOOM.

TRACEY
Come on, Kaylee... You've got to fly me out of here. We'll take a shuttle and go —

They get to the catwalk, and he drags her toward Shuttle II's airlock.

TRACEY (cont'd)
They want to sell me off... You won't let 'em do it, will you? I mean, I thought — I thought we had a moment back there —

Kaylee digs in her heels at the shuttle's entrance.

KAYLEE
Tracey —

TRACEY
Didn't we have a moment back there?

ANOTHER BOOM.

KAYLEE
(scared but firm)
Tracey, take that gun offa me...

TRACEY
Kaylee, please —

KAYLEE
I ain't goin' anywhere with you.

MAL
Nobody's going anywhere, Private.

Mal walks down the stairs from above, gun trained on Tracey.

KAYLEE
Captain, what's happeni —

He pulls Kaylee back into shield position, gun now raised to her head. He's nothing but panic in a pair of pants now.

TRACEY
Don't make me do it.

ANOTHER BOOM. Mal gets to the catwalk, angry, but cool as cucumber slices. Zoe moves slowly down the stairs behind him.

MAL
Far as I can see, nobody's made you do anything. You brought this onto yourself. Got in over your head with these stone cold gut-runners, then you panicked, and then you brung the whole mess down on all of us...

As he was speaking, we saw Jayne, easing himself onto the catwalk across the bay, gun in hand, quiet like a kitty.

TRACEY
That ain't how it happened —

MAL
Oh yes, that's how it happened. And I'm startin' to think that trail of bodies Womack was talkin' about, I'm thinkin' some of that trail was left by you...

TRACEY
And you ain't left a trail of bodies, work you do? 'Cause your rep speaks elsewise.

MAL
Weren't bodies of people helping me out —

TRACEY
Oh, you're helping lots! 'Cause I needed a chest wound...

MAL
That can be seen to —

TRACEY
You think I'm stupid?

MAL
In every way possible.

TRACEY
You know why I picked you and Zoe? 'Cause you're saps. You're repped out as stone killers, but I still remember old Sarge with his stories and his homilies, honor and glory...

MAL
Maybe you shoulda listened.

TRACEY
What are you now? What are we now?

Mal looks up, around, then back to Tracey.

MAL
See there? Hear that quiet? Means the call's already been made.

TRACEY
(breaking up)
You — That call —
(sobs, gun at Kaylee's head)
That call means you just murdered me.

Mal flicks his eyes towards Jayne, who responds by LOUDLY COCKING HIS GUN. Panicky-panic, Tracey spins, trying to see where the sound came from, as Kaylee wrenches free. Mal FIRES, hitting him in the chest, inches from the first wound.

MAL
You murdered yourself, son.
(as Tracey sags, eyes wide)
I just carried the bullet for a while.

Tracey drops the gun, slumps to the catwalk floor. Zoe and Mal move briskly toward him, holstering.

WASH (O.S.)
Captain, they say we got two minutes before they start shelling again —

MAL
Get us up there!

Kaylee heads off.

KAYLEE
I'll get the Doctor.

Zoe and Mal look at Tracey, then at each other, eyes speaking: "There's no way in hell he's gonna make it."

EXT. PLANET - DAY

Serenity parked nose-to-nose in front of the cop ship, on a plain of glacial ice.

INT. SERENITY - CARGO BAY - DAY

The airlock doors slide open — the blinding glare of sun on snow — out of that, Womack and his

two men emerge, walking up the ramp into the cargo bay, guns drawn.

Womack stops, confronted by Jayne, who stands in the middle of the bay, BIG GUN trained on Womack's head.

WOMACK
Well now... Somebody left their dog off the leash...
(cold low growl)
I been shot too many times to be scared by a gun, boy.

JAYNE
(keeping aim)
I hear you. Most ever'body I know's been shot least once. S'no big thing.

A voice trails thin from above.

TRACEY
Womack...

Womack looks up, sees Tracey propped up against the catwalk railing, sees the BLOOD dripping down through the grates.

WOMACK
Smith? You squirrely little piece a' go-se, that you?

TRACEY
(delirious chuckle)
I think I... I think I broke your junk...

Mal appears over the railing, gun on the cops as well.

MAL
Little problem during shipping.

Simon is by Tracey up on the catwalk, but there's nothing he can do.

WOMACK
Don't think I need to tell you folk the trouble you're in. Wetware smugglin', resistin', fleeing an officer a' the law... an' I'm sure a search of your ship'll come up with another few felonies.

Book walks out from behind some crates and stuff.

BOOK
You won't be searching the ship, Womack.

WOMACK
That so?

BOOK
It is. You won't be taking us in. Nor that boy who's dying up there. You're going to turn around, and just fly away.

WOMACK
You know, I'm authorized to kill as I like, Shepherds not withstandin'.

Book is so cool here it's making my hands sweaty.

BOOK
There's nine armed and dangerous desperados on this ship. You count in at three. Why is it you

didn't call in for back-up?
(Womack skips a beat)
There's a fed station eighty miles from where you're standing.
(walks closer)
You got your command stripes at the Silverhold colonies. Puts you about eight solar systems away from your jurisdiction...

WOMACK
Listen here, Preach —

BOOK
And since you're running this job on the side, you took pains to keep your presence here secret. I don't imagine it'd bother anyone if we laid your bodies to rest at the bottom of one of these canyons.

Zoe cocks her gun from above. The cops lower their guns.

Womack looks up at the dying Tracey, at the various guns trained on him, crunching the numbers. Finally, he spits on the ground.

WOMACK
Damaged goods, anyhow.
(to his men)
Let's go, boys.

They start backing out of the bay. Jayne and Book slowly follow them, Jayne still aimed rock solid on Womack's face. As they get past the open airlock doors:

CINEMATOGRAPHY

Director of photography David Boyd: "That was done right out the back of the cargo bay, on a stage. Carey Meyer found a backing in the Fox library that I'm sure hadn't been unrolled for four decades, and it was just beautiful. I learned that day that artists back then made these things so not only could you front-light them, which I thought was all you could do with these painted backings, you could backlight them, too. They painted [the backings] so that you could actually make a sunrise. The paint used for the horizon, the land, was opaque, and the paint used for the sun, or the skyline, was translucent. And so here we had a snowstorm at a transitional time of the day, and we put up this wonderful backing, probably a hundred-and-twenty-feet long and forty-feet high, and made for this wonderful look, which was soft snow falling in a cool light and a far distant horizon. That was a great day."

WOMACK (cont'd)
Hat makes you look like an idiot.

This, oddly, hits Jayne. He frowns with affront.

Book hits the airlock button and the doors SLIDE SHUT.

JAYNE
You either spent a lotta time dealin' with bad cops... or bein' one.

BOOK
Maybe both.

Up on the catwalk, Tracey's life ebbs fast. He looks up to Mal as Zoe enters frame, crouching by him.

TRACEY
So... That was the plan?
(Mal nods)
That —
(coughs)
That was a good plan.

MAL
I think so.

He looks to Kaylee, then to all gathered there.

TRACEY
You weren't far off about me bein' stupid... Never could get my life workin' right, not once since the war...

TRACEY (cont'd)
Sorry, Kaylee. Didn't mean to...
(scared)
Sarge?

MAL
Right here.

TRACEY
That stupid message of mine, trying to play you guys... and now I'm... You'll do it? Get me home?

ZOE
Yeah.

MAL
You know the old saying...

Zoe brushes his hair from his face gently.

TRACEY
(sad little laugh)
"When you can't run anymore, you crawl... and when you can't do that — "

Coughs again, this time a trickle of blood falls from his lips.

ZOE
"You find someone to carry you."

Tracey nods, his eyes fluttering, dying.

Head slumps. Dead. Sad.

EXT. SNOWY HOMESTEAD - DAY

THE SNOW

Production designer Carey Meyer: "There were several different areas that got snow. We shot at the Universal backlot for one portion of that sequence. It was a small, English-looking town. First you go in with a crew and put cotton down on all the little horizontal surfaces and then, on the day of the shoot, you come in and spray foam, like soap suds, everywhere in the background. For the foreground of your shot, you actually have a truck that comes with huge blocks of ice. They chop them up into what looks like snow, and spread that around where you might have somebody walking, so you can really see their footprints. On stage, it's essentially the same processes, but you try to control it a little bit more so you don't have as much water — ice, actually — in your environment.

"For falling snow, if you're at an exterior that is environmentally sensitive, you end up using potato flakes or a cornstarch product, usually something that is biodegradable that you can get away with washing down a drain. If you're on stage, something like a synthetic plastic tends to hang in the air a little bit better and so that's usually what it is on stage."

Tracey's body is carried down the ramp by Mal and Zoe, the others in attendance. Before them is a homestead, a large EXTENDED FAMILY stands there awaiting their dead son.

ANGLE ON: Mal, Zoe and Kaylee (in particular) as they hand the body over. The coffin is open, the mother over it, fussing with Tracey's hair. Kaylee hands the tape recorder to the father. As they stand over the body...

TRACEY (V.O.)
Uh. Okay. Um, recording... Hi, I guess. It's me. Tracey.

END OF SHOW

MUSIC

Composer Greg Edmonson: "I got to make a musical comment, because there was no dialogue and so the music was free to tell a story that was not being told any other way. The end of 'The Message' had everybody together. They were all at the funeral and were bonding. Little moments — Simon stands and he takes Kaylee's hand, Jayne takes his hat off. There weren't too many moments in the show where you had all the characters together in a poignant scene like this. I didn't write that music for the Tracey character, I wrote it to say goodbye to the *Firefly* characters, who I desperately loved and didn't want to say goodbye to, but who I had to say goodbye to. The music was maybe too emotional for what the Tracey character deserved, but I didn't really write it for him."

MUSIC
An interview with Greg Edmonson

Greg Edmonson says of being hired to score *Firefly*, "It's really a miraculous tale. Everyone wanted to work with Joss. His track record is so good and he's so creative. For whatever reason he responded to the CD I sent in. So we had a meeting, and there you have it. It never normally happens that way. You usually have to jump through a lot more hoops, a lot of it happens because somebody is somebody's brother's cousin — in other words, the hiring decision is almost never made on the basis of music."

Filming had already begun at the time Edmonson came aboard, so the music team had to work hard and fast. "It was primarily a synth [synthesizer] show, for budgetary considerations and also time constraints. Probably about eight players on every show were live: the woodwinds, the guitars, the percussion, the violin, and when we used a cello, that was live. So the overdubs were live. That's fairly common in television."

Edmonson credits Whedon for much of *Firefly*'s unique sound. "One of the great joys of *Firefly* was that because Joss had created such a diverse universe, almost any kind of music could be appropriate, depending on the scene. It was a cultural melting pot, so almost anything could work. If there was a directive, it came from Joss and was, 'Let's not sound like every other TV show.' In the television world everyone always says that, and then most of them run away from the idea. Certainly there are common elements — we all have a limited number of musical instruments to choose from. But I so admire Joss's willingness to not just do what everyone else does. Sometimes, a producer or a writer might have a vision and then the studio gets scared and goes, 'We want it to be like this other show, because this is successful.' And you don't have the power to fight it. Joss had the power to make it be what he wanted it to be, and he did."

Some shows require music to fill in emotional holes; Edmonson says this was never the case with *Firefly*. "The acting and the writing were so good on this series that it didn't need music to tell the story.

❖ This page clockwise: River about to grab Kaylee's gun during 'War Stories', Inara during the pilot, the Reaver ship.

❖ Opposite: Tracey's funeral in 'The Message'.

Sometimes people go, 'Well, this scene was supposed to be like this, but it didn't really work out, so we need you to lead people by the nose with the music, so they come to the right conclusion.' *Firefly* was never like that. The writing, the directing and the acting were all spectacular. It felt like you were working on a feature every week."

Did the characters or Serenity herself have specific musical themes? "There was no reason for that," Edmonson replies. "Rather than a theme, we would use sounds. For instance, every time you saw Serenity in space, the one thing we *weren't* going to do was French horns going [makes a majestic noise], because that's like *Star Trek*. So any time you had a space shot, it was dobros, fiddles, those kinds of things, which gave it a unique character. For River we used a lot of ambient stuff, because we never knew what was going on in her mind, so she got lots of atmospheric piano and tinkly bells. For Inara's room, there was some Asian theme, because Inara was essentially a Buddhist. So it was more just specific instrumentation."

As for the metallic sound that introduced the Reavers, Edmonson says, "One of the things I think Joss was doing was making the anti-*Star Trek*. So the enemy ships were not necessarily some high-tech, gleaming piece of looks-like-a-shark; this was a rag-tag, very dangerous-looking thing. There was something on the temp music track used in editing, not like what I did, but something that made me think of it. When I heard this thing, it seemed to match the ship that we were looking at. It seemed more evil to do this than to play music that had some dark, horrific melody."

Edmonson had a unique perspective on the scenes; he saw everything before the music was added. "While composing the score I would watch the same scene over and over. I picked up nuances, and I was never disappointed. I would just look at a scene and say, 'What can I do to rise to the same level as the acting and the directing?'"

One of the most satisfying pieces of music Edmonson composed was also one of the saddest — Tracey's funeral in 'The Message'. "That little sequence meant a lot to me, because I was saying goodbye to these people. In fact, I wept at the end of that. I really put my heart into it. I wasn't putting my heart into it as opposed to not doing so on other things, it's just that my heart was desperately involved with *Firefly*.

"I've got to tell you, of all the things I have ever done in my life, nothing has ever lived on like this show has. I've never worked on a project that I've cared as desperately about as this one. It's amazing to me that it's still alive; it's amazing to me that people love something that I loved, and that's given me an even greater love for it." ✺

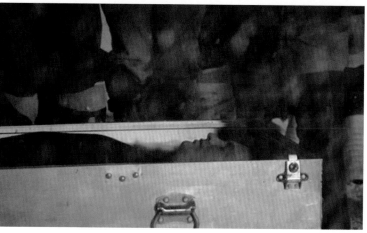

HEART OF GOLD

Written by Brett Matthews
Directed by Thomas S. Wright

BRETT MATTHEWS

Comic writer Brett Matthews (*Spider-Man*, *Daredevil*) made his television-writing début with 'Heart of Gold'. Matthews explains the episode's origin: "I originally pitched a Reaver-centric story that Joss really liked, and saw as a Christmas episode. But when the time came to do it, he decided he didn't want to overexpose the Reavers as they'd already featured heavily in 'Bushwhacked', and would again figure in the original pilot. Long story short, we needed a different episode and we needed it yesterday.

"It took a long time to settle on what story we were going to tell to fill a rapidly approaching slot. A lot of different ideas were bandied about before pulling 'Heart of Gold' out of the drawer, so to speak. It was the stock, Western-heavy episode we had always talked about doing — the crew of Serenity as *The Magnificent Seven/The Seven Samurai*. It may literally have been pitched in the writers' room on day one. The decision was eventually made that now was the time, and we got to work.

"As soon as we got the script to a point it could shoot, it was shooting," he remembers. "We're talking a matter of days, not weeks. The lion's share of the changes came afterward, in post, when Joss and Tim and the episode's editor, Sunny Hodge, had a little more time. A couple of things were shot and added to the episode at that point.

"The shadow puppet origin of the 'verse was something I got maybe too into, to the point where I actually scripted the entire thing, knowing it would ultimately be 'lost in translation'. Still, we tacked it on to the end of the script as an addendum and had the whole thing translated

and read underneath the scene. You don't hear much of it, but it's there if you want it. If memory serves, Alan was the one constantly joking he wanted to find a place in the show for Balinese Puppet Theater. And, lo and behold, Joss took it to heart and did.

"Jayne in a whorehouse is pretty much fish in a barrel. One of my favorite little things — and I actually indicated this in the script — is that he doesn't let his favorite girl kiss him on the mouth when they start to go at it. You'll see the way Adam goes out of his way to avoid it and shakes his head. It's an in-joke, but I loved that *Firefly* was so specific and consistent that way. Like all of Joss's shows, it gives meaning to the canon.

"Morena really cried her guts out in the scene where Inara breaks down. She really got to that place. It was hard to watch in person, but beautiful.

"A couple of rooms in the Heart of Gold brothel set were wallpapered with old newspaper. I'm not sure if this reads onscreen, but it struck me as a neat idea and very much of the world. The stunt guys used full blank rounds for the scene in which the brothel gets shot up. They were beyond loud, and the splintering wood you see when they go off is not so much an effect.

"I really like the last scene, how wounded and blindsided and gut shot Mal gets by Inara and the way Nathan played it. A lot of actors wouldn't have surrendered to it the way he did, especially when playing a male lead. That moment was a bombshell, and is vintage Joss. Every one of his series delivers them."

TEASER

EXT. HEART OF GOLD BORDELLO - DAY

A plain but stately-in-its-own-way multi-storied wood-frame structure, alone and secluded on this pleasant moon.

A PRETTY GIRL (late teens) and PRETTY BOY (same age) are currently out front, hanging the laundry. Sheets. They giggle and laugh. Picture perfect country tranquility. They react to the SOUND of POUNDING HORSE HOOVES...

THROUGH THE BILLOWING SHEETS...

HORSES on the horizon. Coming up fast over a rise. And now, in between them, bouncing up INTO VIEW — A HOVERCRAFT, a badass SPACE JEEP, zooming over its buffeting hover-current.

The BOY AND GIRL register recognition. React —

PRETTY GIRL
Nandi! NANDI!

A BEAUTIFUL WOMAN, early thirties, NANDI, the madam of this concern, appears from the house. Sees the trouble approaching in the distance.

NANDI
Get inside.

But they are frozen to the spot as the riders and hovercraft get closer. Some other GIRLS are appearing variously at the door and windows. All of them are varying degrees of pretty — prostitutes.

NANDI (cont'd)
GO!

The frightened girl and boy head in. Nandi mentally runs through her options. There is only one: stand tough. The horses gallop up. She is immovable.

NANDI (cont'd)
We ain't open for business. It's the Sabbath. We don't do no trade on the Sabbath.

The HOVERCRAFT glides to a stop. Piloting it is RANCE BURGESS. A handsome, fancified imperious GENTLEMAN. But he's anything but gentle...

BURGESS
Shut up, whore.

NANDI
And you we don't trade with at all, Rance Burgess. You're no longer welcome in this establishment. You been told that.

BURGESS
Been told a great many things. I'm here for what's mine.

NANDI
Ain't nothing here belongs to you. You don't get gone, we'll be well within our rights to drop you.

BURGESS
Only rights you got are the ones I give you.
(to his men)
Find her.

The horsemen move to the door, push their way in.

NANDI
She ain't here. Girl left this moon more'n a month ago. It was you chased her off.

BURGESS
I got information says different.

Nandi is poker-faced. Some SCREAMING and CRYING from inside. Crying he recognizes. He smiles at the stone-faced Nandi.

BURGESS (cont'd)
We'll look to dealing with your prevaricatin' ways another time.

Rance's men now hustle a struggling GIRL out through the door — young PETALINE. She'd be the picture of scrubbed wholesomeness — except for the fact that she's very, very pregnant. 'Bout ready to pop. She's terrified. They force her to her knees.

BURGESS (cont'd)
Petaline. Good thing you didn't leave with my baby.

PETALINE
This baby ain't yours!

BURGESS
So you've been saying.

He nods to his men, who rip open Petaline's dress, exposing her belly. Rance pulls a FUTURISTIC HYPO DEVICE from his coat, plunges it into her belly. She winces and gasps in sudden pain. He brings the device away from her.

MUSIC

Composer Greg Edmonson: "The very last episode that I scored was 'Heart of Gold'. I put the music together for the opening sequence, and also the vocals, which are Indian. I didn't specifically record the vocals — I took vocals that I had access to and made it work. Again, the whole fun of this show, the opening shot — there's an establishing shot of a planet, and then we see this air glider racing across the desert, and then the whorehouse. So what are you going to do? The whole idea here is to say, 'We have a multi-ethnic world.' So as I looked at the scene, I thought, this is the perfect place — because we don't have a lot of big [dialogue or sound effects] things to fight — for the vocals to say, 'We're just in another place.' The reason for using vocals and making it sound ethnic was specifically to say, 'Even though we have a whorehouse, which might be interpreted as a Western thing' — and girls looking like this could have been out of a Western — 'I'm just trying to say, it's not exactly that.' And the foreign vocals are a real good way of putting some identity on it.

"The last scene in this episode was Inara telling Mal that she's leaving and then she walks off; that was the last *Firefly* scene that I got to write music for."

❖ Above: Burgess's DNA test device.

BURGESS (cont'd)
If this DNA is a match to mine — know I'll be back for my child.

Rance climbs on his hovercraft, his men to their horses.

BURGESS (cont'd)
And if you decide to close your legs for once in your life and that baby hasn't been born by the time I'm ready — I'll cut it out of ya.

They go. Nandi and some of the other girls move to Petaline, who's quietly sobbing. Help her to her feet.

NANDI
Shhh. Quiet, now. It's all gonna work out.

Among the whores helping to steady Petaline are CHARI, a petite and refined prostitute, maybe the prettiest one here, and HELEN, a more hardy whore. They watch the men leaving.

CHARI
He'll do it, too. He'll do what he says.

NANDI
No, he won't. We won't allow it.

HELEN
How we gonna stop him, Nandi?

NANDI
We'll get help. That's how.

CHARI
Help? There's not a soul on this moon'd go up against Rance Burgess.

HELEN
She's right. Ain't nobody strong enough. And even if there was — who'd help us?

CUT TO:

INT. SERENITY - DINING ROOM

MAL

in a wicked-cool CLOSE UP whips his gun at us with a stylish rack to the barrel. He's cleaning and checking it, looking casually heroic. Spread out on the dining room table are an assortment of his best guns and such.

INARA enters behind him. He doesn't hear her.

INARA
Hi.

MAL
BWAAA!

INARA
Sorry. I didn't mean to startle.

MAL
You didn't.
(repeating, as if he meant to, points gun)
BWAAA! That's a kind of a warrior... It's a... Strikes fear into...
(nothin')
Bwaa?
(then, fuck it)
You know, it ain't altogether wise, sneaking up on a man when he's handling his weapon.

INARA
I'm sure I've heard that said. But perhaps the dining area isn't the place for this sort of thing?

MAL
What do you mean? Only place with a table big enough.

INARA
Of course. In that case...
(rearranges guns)
Every well-bred petty crook knows — the small concealable weapons always go to the far left of the place setting.

Mal bridles at the term "petty crook". Before he can speak, WASH enters from the bridge.

WASH
Got a distress call coming in. Some folks asking for help.

MAL
Really? Folks asking for help? From us petty crooks?

WASH
Well...

MAL
(at Inara)
Maybe I should take that right away.

Mal makes to do that, but Wash stops him with:

WASH
Well, it's for her.

MAL
Huh?

WASH
They didn't ask for you, Mal. Call's for Inara.

INARA
I'll take it in my shuttle.

WASH
I'll send it back there.

MAL
This distress wouldn't be taking place in someone's pants, would it?

She throws a look, goes one way; Wash goes the other. Mal is left alone. A beat.

As Mal whips his gun back up into a heroic frame.

MAL (cont'd)
(all cool)
Bwaa.

BLACK OUT.

END OF TEASER

ACT ONE

EXT. SPACE

Serenity gently moving through the big black.

INT. INARA'S SHUTTLE - DAY

Inara sits at her Cortex screen, where WE SEE the live image of NANDI.

NANDI
Can't say I'm not a little ashamed, Inara, this being the first contact we've had since we parted in Sihnon.

INARA
Nonsense.

NANDI
I been meaning to answer the last few waves you sent. It's just... things do get a mite chaotic.

INARA
It's perfectly understandable.

NANDI
And now here I am, calling on you for a favor like this. Imposing on a past friendship.

INARA
It's not past. Never past. I want to help, Nan... I do. I just don't know if there's any way...

NANDI
Just speak to your people. That's all I ask.

INARA
Yes. Yes, I will. But so you know... they're not actually "my people". I'm a tenant. I just rent a shuttle on the ship.

NANDI
(after a beat)
You'll speak to them?

INARA
Yes.

NANDI
I'll wait to hear from you.
(then)
<TZOO-foo nee, mei mei.> [Blessings on you, dear sister.]

INARA
And you.

Inara touches the screen. Nandi's image FREEZES there. Inara sits there quietly contemplative for a beat. Then:

INARA (cont'd)
I suppose you heard most of that?

Mal appears, peeking around the corner at the entrance.

MAL
Only 'cause I was eavesdropping.
(then, no bullshit)
Your friend sounds like she's in a peck of trouble.

INARA
She is. There's no authority on that moon she can turn to. They're totally alone.

MAL
Some men might take advantage of that.

INARA
One man.

MAL
And she's lookin' for someone to come along and explain things to him?

INARA
That's essentially it, yes.

MAL
A whole house full of Companions... How they fixed for payment?

INARA
They're not Companions.
(then)
They're whores, Mal.

MAL
Thought you didn't much care for that word?

INARA
It applies. None who work for Nandi are registered with the Guild. They're —

MAL
Independent?

INARA
Yes.
(then)
If you agree to do this, you will be compensated. I'll see to it. I've put a little aside...

MAL
You keep your money. Won't be needing no payment.

INARA
Mal. Thank you. I'll contact Nandi at once.
(he smiles; she turns away)
But you will be paid. I feel it's important we keep ours strictly a business arrangement.

Her back's to him now, so she doesn't see the stung look.

MAL
I'll speak to the crew.

INARA
Good.

She never looks back. Off Mal, waiting a beat before he goes —

INT. SERENITY - CARGO BAY

Mal has EVERYONE assembled (except Inara). He's letting ZOE brief the troops. He's to the side, the silent commander.

ZOE
Those who have a mind are welcome to join. Those who just as soon stay on the ship can do that, too.

JAYNE
Don't much see the benefit in getting involved in strangers' troubles without an upfront price negotiated.

BOOK
These people need assistance. The benefit wouldn't necessarily be for you.

JAYNE
S'what I'm sayin'.

ZOE
No one's gonna force you to go, Jayne. As has been stated — this job's strictly speculative.

JAYNE
Good. 'Cause I don't know these folks. Don't much care to.

MAL
They're whores.

JAYNE
I'm in.

MAL
(moving off)
Wash — plot a course.

EXT. PLANET - DAY

Serenity lands amidst cover.

INT. BORDELLO LOBBY - DAY

Our gang files into the lobby. The girls are all hanging about, some making a bit of a show of themselves, draped about as if for customers; some more earnest or just curious. Inara is in the process of coming towards Nandi for a great big hug. Mal is behind her, waiting, as is Zoe.

As for the rest, they politely nod and greet the whores, Kaylee guilelessly, Simon politely, Book kindly, Jayne grinningly, Wash uncomfortably, River inquisitively. Much ad-libbing from them as have speaking parts. (Chari and Petaline are not present.)

INARA
Nandi, darling.

NANDI
It's so good to see you, mei mei...

INARA
You look wonderful.

NANDI
And you look exactly the same as the day I left. How do you do that out here?

MAL
Sheer force of will.

INARA
Nandi, this is Malcolm Reynolds.

NANDI
I appreciate your coming.

She shakes his hand, firmlike.

MAL
Any friend of Inara's is a strictly businesslike relationship of mine.

The dig is not lost on Inara, nor is her reaction lost on Nandi.

MAL (cont'd)
This is my first mate, Zoe. I'll introduce you to the rest in a bit. They're good folk.

JAYNE
(calls out from across the room, no 'tude)
Can I start getting sexed already?

MAL
Well, that one's kind of horrific.

Jayne has Helen by the shoulder, is pointing at her...

JAYNE
This one could sex me okay...

NANDI
He good in a fight?

MAL
'Bout the best.

NANDI
(calls out)
Helen, why don't you show our new friend what a
Palastinian Somersault is.

Helen giggles. Jayne looks confused and excited.

JAYNE
Is that good?

ZOE
(ugh)
Can we talk business?

NANDI
(indicating lounge)
In here.
(to the others)
Rest of you, there's food and some liquor at the
sideboard, make yourselves to home.

The four exit. We stay with the others.

JAYNE
(to Helen)
Just let me get a drink in me, and then we'll get to
that Panatarian... thing you do.

Kaylee nudges Simon and Wash, indicates the two
young men.

KAYLEE
Look, they got boy whores! Isn't that thoughtful?
Wonder if they service girlfolk at all.

WASH
Let's not ask.

SIMON
Isn't there a pregnant woman I'm to examine?

WASH
(to Kaylee)
You'd really lie with someone being paid for it?

KAYLEE
(pointedly forlorn)
Well, it's not like anyone else is lining up to, you
know, examine me...

JAYNE
(joining them)
Man, my John Thomas is gonna pop off and fly
around the room, there's so much tasty here.

WASH
Would be you get your most poetical about your
pecker.

Chari brings Petaline up to them.

CHARI
You'd be the Doctor?

SIMON
Yes. And this is Petaline?

PETALINE
Yes sir.

CHARI
She's feeling a mite weak right now.

SIMON
Well, let's get you lying down, take a look at you.

JAYNE
Now that's a plan!

He goes off with Helen, Simon goes to the back
room with the two girls, River trailing.

We see Book making up a sandwich — he is
approached by LUCY and EMMA.

EMMA
Shepherd —

BOOK
No thank you!

They smile a bit.

EMMA
We were hoping we might have a prayer meeting?

LUCY
We ain't had one in months, 'cept what Emma
here reads out on Sunday.

EMMA
Last Shepherd to come by was springtime. He

only read the one passage, and he took it out in
trade off both of us.

Book has no response.

Kaylee watches the girls chat up Book...

KAYLEE
Everyone's got somebody...
(wistfully)
Wash, tell me I'm pretty...

WASH
Were I unwed, I would take you in a manly
fashion.

KAYLEE
'Cause I'm pretty?

WASH
'Cause you're pretty.

KAYLEE
Thank you. That was very restorative.

INT. BORDELLO - LOUNGE – DAY

Mal, Zoe, Nandi and Inara. Mid talk.

MAL
So I take it reason doesn't enter into this?

NANDI
Not with Rance Burgess. The man is a taker.

ZOE
You think the kid is his?

NANDI
(firm)
I think it's Petaline's.

INARA
But the blood test...

NANDI
Well, he did favor Petaline pretty exclusively, but
she had others. Fifty-fifty, not that it matters. The
man ain't fit to raise a cactus plant. His barren
prairie shrew can't bear him an heir, so he takes
it into his head to pull it outta us. That's not
gonna happen.

MAL
(likes her strength)
I see that's the case.

NANDI
He means to burn me out, Mr. Reynolds. Besides
the matter of his child, this is one of the few
establishments around he doesn't own.

MAL
He sounds like a fun guy. I'd like to meet him.

NANDI
This won't be solved with talk.

MAL
I'm gonna fight a man, it helps to size him up.

NANDI
Well, he'll be at the theater tonight, that's a certainty.

MAL
Then so will I. Inara, think you could stoop to being on my arm?

INARA
Will you wash it first?

He smiles at the light dig, turns to Zoe.

MAL
Zoe, start getting the lay of the place: fortifications,

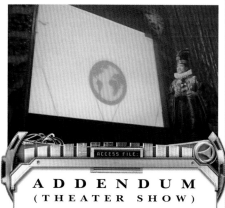

ADDENDUM
(THEATER SHOW)

A CIRCULAR SHADOW representing Earth-That-Was fills the frame.

NARRATOR (Chinese)
<Man, man di, ren lei yong jin le da di de zi yuan. Huang wu le, ta wu ke gong yin.> [Little by little, the tribes used the Earth up. Barren, she had little left to offer them.]

Silhouetted shapes appear. SPACESHIPS. They radiate out from the shadow sphere, scatter in all directions. Leave it behind.

NARRATOR (continuing)
<Lue duo ze, man zai er chu. Chuang si ji, can shen de da di, shou du gan dao gu li.> [Swollen of her, they left. And for the first time since the Great Burn that birthed her, she was alone.]

The ships are gone now. A wisp of SMOKE wafts off the sphere, creates a snake of shadow.

NARRATOR (continuing)
<Di qiu wei ren lei de rou lin er tong ku liu lie, suan ku de lei shui, man liu le yi shi ji.> [The Earth cried, and terrible were her tears. Acid and caustic, the spawn of the tribes' rape. They flowed a century.]

The smoke INTENSIFIES, becomes shadowy FLAME.

NARRATOR (continuing)
<Hui mie zhi huo, ru tien jiang fu zhong yu lai dao.> [The fire that finally came did so as a blessing.]

The sphere SMOLDERS now, bits of it breaking up and disintegrating under the intense heat.

weak spots and whatnot. I'll slip into my Sunday best, and see what passes for entertainment in this town.

INT. THEATER - NIGHT

A CIRCULAR SHADOW representing Earth-That-Was FILLS THE FRAME. Silhouetted shapes appear. SPACESHIPS. They radiate out from the shadow sphere. We're witnessing some form of Balinese Puppet Theater. A nattily attired NARRATOR (speaking in Chinese: see addendum) presides before the backlit gauze screen across which the shadows play. It's the story of the destruction and fleeing of Earth-That-Was.

WIDER — Well-heeled PATRONS mill about as the show continues on a small stage in the BG. The theater itself is upscale, ornate in its own particular way. Asian and Pacific influences abound.

Mal and Inara enter, arm-in-arm. They're dressed to kill.

MAL
I'll never understand rich folk. All that money, this is what they do with it.

INARA
It's art.

MAL
It's puppets.

INARA
It's puppet art.

A waiter passes with a tray of strangely-colored drinks. Mal grabs one, takes a sip. His face immediately contorts.

MAL
<LAN-dan JIANG!> [Weak-ass sauce!] I swear to you, it's like money and good taste are inversely proportional.

INARA
That might make you the most tasteful man I've ever met.

MAL
Funny.

He swirls his colored drink. Eyeballs it.

MAL (cont'd)
Maybe you drink enough of this stuff, the puppets start makin' sense.

Inara smiles, enjoying him. It fades as her eyes lock on something beyond Mal. Off her reaction:

MAL (cont'd)
Found our boy?

Inara nods, and Mal turns to find Burgess lording over a particularly influential crowd. He's holding court, his guests laughing with disturbing frequency and force. On Burgess's arm is his wife, BELINDA. Pale and slight, she's dressed a cut above most every woman there, fiscally speaking.

Conservative excess.

MAL (cont'd)
I've a sudden itch to see how the other half lives.

Mal offers his arm to Inara, she takes it and they stroll up to where a conversation is in progress.

BURGESS
(midstream)
...So I explained to the boy: you take a clean woman's virtue, you take the woman. And that's for life. Boy said his vows right then and there. Took very little persuading on my part.

Burgess pats his laser pistol which hangs conspicuously on his belt. LAUGHTER from the assembled. And now Mal is among them, laughing LOUDER and LONGER than any of them. Finally everyone's staring at him.

MAL
Nice to know there's some places left in the 'verse where old-fashioned values still mean a thing.
(to Inara)
Isn't that right, dear?

INARA
(forced smile)
Mmmm.

BURGESS
I don't think I know you...

MAL
(hand extended)
Name's Malcolm. Malcolm Reynolds.

Burgess takes Mal's hand. They shake. Mal doesn't let go as he leans in a bit closer, says:

MAL (cont'd)
And might I just say? She is quite a beauty.

Mal releases Burgess's hand. Burgess looks at him.

BURGESS
Thank you.

He unholsters his laser gun, offers it up to Mal.

BURGESS (cont'd)
You ever have an occasion to handle one, Mr. Reynolds?
(offering it)
Silk trigger active return bolt laser.

Mal takes the laser pistol, looks it over.

MAL
Lighter than it looks. Thought it'd have more heft to it.

BURGESS
Don't let that fool you. Won't find technology like that short of Alliance. And even their issues don't yet have the auto-target adjust. Had that one crafted special.

MAL
Didn't think firearms such as this were generally

legal — for a private owner, I mean.

BELINDA
My husband makes a distinction between legality and morality, Mr. Reynolds.

Mal glances over at Belinda, holds her eyes for a beat.

MAL
I've said that myself.

BURGESS
Bending one unjust law is a small thing when it comes to protecting one's family.

MAL
I think I understand you.

BURGESS
(smiles)
And as you say — she is a beauty.

MAL
She sure is.
(hands it back)
'Course, I was referring to the lady.
(nods to Belinda)
Ma'am.

Mal steers Inara away. The others watch them go.

Now Burgess's FUTURE CELL PHONE BEEPS. He takes it out of his pocket, his eyes still on the retreating Mal —

BURGESS
Yes?

EXT. TOWN - NIGHT

Mal and Inara exit the theater hastily. Mal walks quickly, looking to put distance between himself and the theater.

INARA
Well?

MAL
Well what?

INARA
You said you wanted to look him in the eye. You've done that. So what's the plan?

MAL
Plan is — we get back to Serenity and we get off this rock just as fast as we can.

Mal hasn't slowed his pace. Off Inara, surprised —

INT. THEATER - NIGHT

Burgess is in a private-ish corner speaking on his future cell phone. Belinda joins him, expectant.

BURGESS
(into cell)
And there can be no mistake? Good.

Beat. Burgess snaps the cell shut. Mulls.

BELINDA (O.S.)
Rance?

BURGESS
The DNA matches. The child's mine. And Belinda — it's a boy.

PUSH IN on Belinda. Registering that.

BELINDA
A son... A son.
(then)
Come first light, you ride over there... and you get me my boy.

BLACK OUT.

END OF ACT ONE

ACT TWO

INT. BORDELLO LOBBY - NIGHT

Mal stands in the center of the bordello's lobby, his finery from the previous scene taken down a notch. The crew and the staff of the Heart of Gold surround him.

MAL
We run.

Nandi takes this with stoic calm, but some of her girls GASP with surprise.

MAL (cont'd)
Math just don't add up. Our weapon store ain't exactly overpowerin' at the moment, and I don't much like what we'd be up against...

The Serenity crew looks a bit surprised by this as well.

MAL (cont'd)
Nothing worse than a monster who thinks he's right with God. We might turn Burgess away once, but he'll keep comin' — won't stop til he gets what he thinks is his. So we —

NANDI
Captain Reynolds, I understand. You have your people to think of, same as me. And this isn't your fight.

MAL
Don't believe you do understand, Nandi. I said "we run".
(Nandi gives no response)
We. My people. Your people. And whatever bits of precious you got in this place you can't part with. We load up Serenity and leave Burgess in the dust.

Nandi steps closer to Mal, all strength and resolve. Despite the audience of listeners, she and Mal talk with intimate intensity, as if they're the only ones there.

NANDI
Captain Reynolds... It took me years to cut this

piece of territory out of other men's hands. To build this business up from nothing.

MAL
Nandi —

NANDI
It's who I am. And it's my home. I'm not going anywhere.

MAL
He'll kill you.
(re: her people)
Kill every last one of them, it comes to that. And he'll sleep well that night.

NANDI
And how well will you sleep, Captain?

Mal has no answer for that. Nandi holds her stare on him as she calls to her staff.

NANDI (cont'd)
Any of you want to take up the Captain's offer, you do it, with my blessing.

Behind her, much head shaking by the whores. No one's going anywhere. Nandi turns to Petaline, voice gentle.

NANDI (cont'd)
Petaline, that means you, too.

Petaline sits in an overstuffed chair, sweating, clearly uncomfortable. Simon takes her pulse.

PETALINE
No, Miss Nandi. I ain't leavin' the Heart of Gold. Ain't leavin' you...

Nandi turns back to Mal.

NANDI
Rance Burgess is just a man... And I won't let any man take what's mine. I doubt you'd do different, in my position.

Eyes still locked on each other, a stalemate of personal cool, until Mal shakes his head slightly.

MAL
Well, lady, I must say —
(admiring smile)
You're my kinda stupid.

He turns to Zoe and the rest of his crew.

MAL (cont'd)
Y'heard my points of contention with this thing. But I got a lifetime of good night's rest to consider, so I'm goin' back on that.
(glances at Inara)
There's still money in the job, for them that want to throw in —

Jayne, arm around Helen, shrugs.

JAYNE
Hell, he ain't expectin' much of a fight. We might catch him with his drawers low.

MELINDA CLARKE

I remember doing *Firefly* at Halloween, because I missed Halloween when my daughter was two [laughs]. Somehow I always end up getting these characters who are madams or dominatrix [recurring character Lady Heather on *C.S.I.: Crime Scene Investigation*] or in science-fiction. Ultimately, these women are not stupid; they're businesswomen and they're highly evolved in their way of thinking and don't make excuses for what they do. In a society where people might look down on that kind of position as abnormal, the writers always kind of revere them as being much more intelligent than your average female.

I have no idea why I get these roles. Maybe it's my eyes or the way I look, but it's the furthest thing from the real me. It's interesting that people consider me sexy or very strong, because my husband would say that I'm a wimp and looking pretty haggard every morning [laughs].

Lady Heather and Nandi, they're like mothers, taking care of their girls; I think it's just an intuitive thing that happens, that women will do naturally.

You always hope that every show is going to be full of amazing people, but I've got to say that *Firefly* had some of the *most* amazing people and was one of the most harmonious sets I've ever seen. They really, truly loved being at work and laughed hysterically at every moment and appreciated each other. It was really a joy to see how much they loved working together.

Mal raises his eyebrows. Zoe checks the chamber on her gun, cocks it.

ZOE
(nods)
He'll probably ride in by daylight, but I figure a three point watch, say, four hour shifts, be on the safe side.

WASH
(nods, mock expertise)
Three-point, four-hour, should do it.

Mal gives a slight smile, then Book steps up.

BOOK
I'm fair handy with a hammer, Captain.

MAL
That so, Shepherd —?

BOOK
Been following the footsteps of a carpenter for some time now. I think I can do something about our fortifications.

Mal looks over the rest of his people, Kaylee smiles and nods, Simon looks up from Petaline, then back to his task. We feel Mal take understated pride in knowing them.

MAL
Okay then...

His strategy wheels start turning, as UNDER-STATED "GET SHIT DONE" MUSIC starts to build.

MAL (cont'd)
We start shootin', they'll most like try to burn us out, save their sweat and bullets. Nandi, what's the water supply here?

NANDI
Underground well. Pump that draws it up's antiquated, but it don't break down.

Quietly, off to the side of the action, Petaline stops with a jolt. She puts a hand to her belly.

MAL
Kaylee — think you can swing an upgrade for

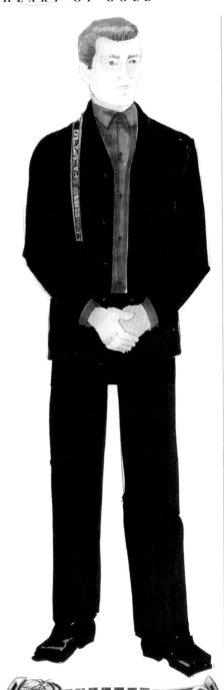

BOOK'S COSTUME

Costume designer Shawna Trpcic: "We went through a few different designs trying to come up with our nondenominational and yet recognizable preacher. He was more like a pastor than, say, a Catholic priest, but we wanted people to recognize him because at one point Book says, 'I thought the outfit gave it away,' about what he does. So we ended up with a blend of a lot of different religious leaders. The grey was to echo the Alliance colors. And when I could, I showed off his body, I threw a t-shirt on him, because the guy is in incredible shape."

their waterworks?

Kaylee moves closer to him, beaming happily.

KAYLEE
I'll talk to Serenity, see what she's got we might use.

MAL
Good. And we'd better find some —

River is suddenly at their side.

RIVER
It's starting.

Kaylee gives a little STARTLED JUMP, unseen by Mal.

MAL
That's a sure fact. But time is on the enemy's side, so —

PETALINE
(pained yelp)
Dr. Tam — !

Mal sees Petaline, who Simon helps to her feet as she pants with contraction.

MAL
Oh — It's starting — Okay.
(a little panicky)
It's starting! — No one panic — It's gonna be fine —

Simon leads Petaline toward the bordello's back room, nodding to Mal.

SIMON
I got this one, Captain.

Mal looks around at everyone else, they smile, at the brink of chuckling, at his display. He CLAPS his hands, resuming his heroical authority:

MAL
Come on, people! Let's get to work.

INT. BORDELLO LOBBY - BALCONY - DAY

Book wields a hammer, boarding up windows. Lucy and Emma, the "church" whores, assist.

EMMA
The girls and I've been talkin', Shepherd.

He stops, turns to face her.

EMMA (cont'd)
We've been discussin' what we'd like said over us if we should happen to fall —

BOOK
No.

Book reaches out, places a hand on her.

BOOK (cont'd)
I only bury the dead, child. And no one here is going to die. Not a one of you.

He smiles and the tension disappears. Lucy returns it.

SMASH TO:

INT. BORDELLO - UPSTAIRS ROOM - DAY

JAYNE
Now, there's people gonna die.

Jayne sits in front of a large window, its field of view panoramic. Across from him, Helen sits attentively.

JAYNE (cont'd)
Ain't no way 'round that. And with people dyin' comes guts and screamin' and that can bring on all sorts of screwed-up behaviors, a person's not used to it. When the time comes, most important thing is you keep your wits about you. Clear?

Helen nods. Jayne reaches over to a nearby table strewn with weapons and ammunition.

JAYNE (cont'd)
These here are my favorites, and you're to keep 'em comin' til there ain't no more to be had. I shoot, I run out, you just hand me the next biggest and so on. Is there an understanding here?

HELEN
Yes.

JAYNE
All right, then. Let's get to work.

Giggling, Helen hops on top of Jayne, straddles him. She plants wet kisses all over. Jayne craning his neck to keep his mouth out of reach.

EXT. BORDELLO - DAY

Wash sweeps a pile of dry earth over a wood-and-rope contraption, securing and camouflaging the device.

WASH
All I'm saying is we're living pretty deep in the rough and tumble, and I don't see that changing any time soon.

Zoe rises behind him, a large spool of wire in her hands.

ZOE
Nor do I.

She crouches, begins to wind the wire between one of two stakes buried deep in the ground, some fifteen feet apart.

WASH
Well, I'm not sure now is the best time to bring a tiny little helpless person into our lives.

Wash lies flat, secures the wire to the stake. He takes a pair of WIRECUTTERS and cuts the wire.

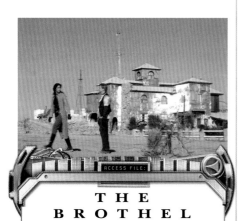

THE BROTHEL

Production designer Carey Meyer: "We needed to find this brothel out in the middle of another deserted planet and we ended up with a location that was great for shooting. We found this house — we'd been getting a lot of feedback from Joss and the studio that this whole Western concept wasn't really playing as well as anybody had hoped and so we had been given a directive to try to make it less Western. We ended up covering the entire house with something that looked like tin foil, essentially, which were those silver space blankets — you know, the little packages that you might keep in the glove box if you were in danger of getting stranded in your car, to keep your body warm. The blankets were very thin, silver, reflective Mylar sheets. It felt a little bit like the Apollo spaceships, they were covered in a lot of that sort of material.

"We also had this laser gun, because it was at this point they decided they had to have lasers in our world as well, and a floating hovercraft. So we completely sheathed this whole house in this tin foil material and had explosives behind it, so that when the laser whipped across the house, a large streak of flame would be blown up on the side of the house. It just ended up being a little comical, and I remember Joss referring to it as 'the Jiffy-Pop mansion'. It was very funny."

ZOE
That excuse is getting a little worn, honey.

WASH
It's not an excuse, dear. It's objective assessment. I can't help it if it stays relevant.

Zoe stands, starts kicking dirt over the lines of their trap.

ZOE
I don't give a good gorramn about relevant, Wash. Or objective. And I'm not so afraid of losing something that I won't try havin' it. You and I would make one beautiful baby. I want to meet that child one day. Period.

WASH
And this beautiful baby of ours, you don't mind that it's going to grow up on a spaceship?

ZOE
Worked fine for me.

Beat. Wash considers, nods.

EXT. TOWN - DAY

Burgess stands in the street, jacket swept back behind his holstered LASER PISTOL, tumbler of whiskey in one hand. He takes a swig then FAST DRAWS, firing THREE SHOTS from his laser. Just before the third, we CUT TO:

ANGLE ON TARGET DUMMY

A stuffed burlap dummy, tied to a rough wood tripod. The last LASER BEAM sears into its head, IGNITING IT. HOLD ON the dummy as it bursts into FLAMES.

INT. BORDELLO - NANDI'S ROOM - EVENING

Mal looks out the window. We can't see what he sees, but we hear a cluster of gunshots, followed by the barking of Jayne:

JAYNE (O.S.)
That ain't nothin'! Y'all are pulling, not squeezing like I said. Next one doesn't hit that board is giving up a special treat, <dong-MA?> [you understand?]

Mal closes the window, smiling a little.

MAL
That man is gonna use up all our credit 'fore we've earned it.

NANDI
Well, after you've saved our lives you can do some chores, maybe.

She is getting a box from her bottom drawer. As they talk she lays it on the bed, pulls out a few fancy looking pistols.

MAL
I'm a fair hand with a mop.

NANDI
So your legend tells.

(chuckling)
Truth is, I expected a whole lot more of you to be taking payment in our trade.

MAL
Well, we're an odd conglomeration. Got a preacher, a married fellah, and the Doctor... Well, he'd have to relax for thirty seconds to get his play, and that'd be more or less a miracle.
(re: guns)
These are fetching little pieces. They work at all?

NANDI
Don't got many rounds for the Chaplain there, but the rest'll be of use.
(picks one up)
This is my favorite.

MAL
What's its history?

NANDI
Violence and crime, sad to say. What about you?

MAL
Similar.

NANDI
No, I mean, when are you planning to avail yourself of some of our trade? My girls is clean and kind-spirited.

MAL
Well, I got the job in mind. After, I'm sure I'll... trade. They're a fine bunch.

NANDI
You ain't looked at one of 'em as long or as lovin' as you looked at those pistols. You're not sly, are you? 'Cause I got my boys...

MAL
(totally comfortable with the question)
Sly? No. I lean towards womanfolk. Just one thing at a time. Never like complications.

She smiles, knowingly.

NANDI
I'm certain of that.

MAL
Something to be smiling at?

NANDI
I trained as a Companion, remember? I read people pretty well.

MAL
Well, that's nice for you.

He's examining the weapons, deliberately.

NANDI
She's a hell of a woman, ain't she?
(off his look)
Inara.

MAL
(casual)
Oh. Yeah. She's a cherry-blossom, no denyin'.
(still looking at gun)

SIMON

"Well, my sister's a ship, we had a complicated childhood."

At the time he auditioned for *Firefly*, Sean Maher was something of a Fox television veteran: he had had the title role in the teen cop series *Ryan Caulfield: Year One*, which was pulled off the air after episode two; he played Neve Campbell's boyfriend in seven episodes of *Party of Five*; he was on the short-lived financial drama *The $treet*. But the Pleasantville, New York native says he hadn't done science fiction before, partly because it hadn't interested him. However, Joss Whedon and the *Firefly* universe won him over: "Joss made my character and this universe so unique. That is the first thing I was attracted to when I read the pilot. It was like nothing I had read before. It was so unique and like a world of its own. Everything about it was so complete and well thought out, so that it was this altered world — there was no element that was missing. Everything about it... The characters were so rich and flawed. I was always drawn to the relationships between them and their dynamics because it was so fresh. Someone was asking me the other day about what archetype I would compare Simon to and I really couldn't think of anything. In that regard, each character, Simon included, is a character of their own."

Maher found his close relationships with his fellow cast members very helpful to him in his portrayal of Simon Tam: "Initially, as an actor, there are times when you read a script and you worry you will never draw parallels between yourself and this character. It sort of happens with me that when I start rehearsing and working with the other actors I discover those similarities. My love for my sister after working with Summer, and the crush I have on Kaylee after spending a lot of time with Jewel. In this particular project, the dynamics of the characters were all attributed to the other actors, and that is when I started finding all the similarities between myself and Simon." As much as he enjoyed playing Simon,

Maher concedes there's another *Firefly* character he would have liked to play: "Jayne!"

When Zac Hug (www.BrilliantButCancelled.com) asked Maher how he felt about the cancellation, he said at the outset, things were somewhat mysterious. "We were not told much. I think we were strung along for a little while, because they were on the fence about what to do with us. We all took it really hard. It was a big blow; it was awful."

Like many of his *Firefly* colleagues, Maher says the dedication of the fans to the show came as a welcome surprise. "We would not be here without them. That's how important they are. I always say, 'Why are we here? — Joss Whedon and the fans.' There was support from the very beginning. They were always there. There was always a small group and it just grew and grew and grew. It was inspiring to us and it kept driving us. It was nice to know that someone was out there actually getting what we were trying to say."

Maher feels that the movie *Serenity* is a rightful continuation of the series *Firefly*. "The tone was very similar in terms of the wit and the humor, and the lightness of the dynamics between the characters. There's an overwhelming sense that the stakes have been raised. Summer had to be even more tormented than she was before, in the series, in questions of her sanity and how she reacts to everything, so I just built off of what she gave me. It was really a lot of reacting to her and wanting to keep her character safe. There was a greater sense of urgency for me to figure out what was going on with her and to put an end to this pain that she was in."

Zac Hug asked Maher if he would want to be part of a continuation of *Firefly*, "If there's a sequel, or anything these people want to do, I'm there. We always joked about taking the show on the road, as a side show act: 'Let's drive cross country and do *Firefly* episodes on stage!' It's a wonderful group of people."

What would Maher like to see happen if Simon and Co. have more adventures? "If Joss takes requests — I think Kaylee should be barefoot and pregnant, shaving Simon's head, telling him he just looks too pretty." ⊖

'Spect you know her better'n I do, comin' up together and all.

NANDI
Imagine I do. She ever tell you why she left Sihnon?

MAL
Never asked.

NANDI
Yes you did, and I don't know my own self. I was gone long before. And I'll tell you, it was a shock, her leaving. She was special. There's forty women in House Madrassa and you'd pick her out in a second. Coulda been House Priestess, few years time.

MAL
Is that right.

NANDI
Had her eyes on it, too. Very focused. She's like you, more than a little.

MAL
And how exactly is that?

NANDI
She hates complications.

A moment between them. A small understanding.

MAL
They do crop up though, don't they?

NANDI
Such is life.

INT. BORDELLO - BACK ROOM - NIGHT

Petaline is in bed, letting out an impressive YELL. She's sweaty and breathing hard. Inara is by her side, mopping her brow supportively.

Simon is at the foot of the bed, looking under the tent of sheet they've rigged up. River looks over his shoulder, completely agape.

SIMON
You're not completely dilated yet. Should be pretty quick but don't try to force it. These contractions are still preliminary.

PETALINE
What's he saying?

INARA
It's gonna be a little while, sweetie.

PETALINE
But it hurts! Child wants to be born, I know it.

SIMON
(to Inara)
Can you grab the green vial from my bag. We can dull the pain some.

Inara crosses, pausing by Simon, whispers —

INARA
How many babies have you actually delivered?

SIMON
As the primary? This would be the first. You?

INARA
My first too.

RIVER
(looking even closer)
Mine too.

They look at River a moment.

SIMON
Gonna be a long night.

Inara gives him a peck on the cheek for luck.

INARA
You'll do great, Doctor.

RIVER
(still staring)
Who do you think is in there...?

Petaline huffs and puffs...

DISSOLVE TO:

INT. BORDELLO LOBBY - NIGHT

Book is standing with his bible, about half the whores standing or kneeling before him.

BOOK
...Forgive us our trespasses, as we forgive those who trespass against us, and lead us not into temptation, but deliver us from evil, for thine is the kingdom, the power and the glory, Amen.

WHORES
Amen.

They rise, some squaring away tools and weapons and such.

BOOK
Not much more we can do tonight. I think it best we all get some rest. Is there... is there a room I can lay down in?

EMMA
(sweet but sly)
Alone?

They all look at him, guilelessly sexy. He waits perhaps a bit much of a beat.

BOOK
Alone.

They laugh, and he smiles along with them.

BOOK (cont'd)
Thank you.

INT. BORDELLO - NANDI'S ROOM - NIGHT

It's very late, and Mal and Nandi are on the couch. He throws back a shot. They've both been drinking a while.

NANDI
It was the dulcimer.

MAL
The dulcimer drove you out of Sihnon. What, did you kill a dulcimer in a terrible passion?

NANDI
(smiles)
Actually, yes.

MAL
And that dulcimer's family is looking to get even. I get it.

NANDI
I was at practice. You never stop practicing, you know, not a true Companion. Some baroque piece, and the instructor keeps saying "You're playing it, not feeling it". And the fifth time he said it I took the damn thing and smashed it into kindling. And that's when it occurred to me that a Companion's life might just be a little too constricting.

She crosses to the dresser to pour two more shots.

NANDI (cont'd)
So I trucked out to the border, learned to say "ain't" and came to find work. Found this place.

MAL
It's a nice place.

NANDI
It was a dungheap. Run by a pig who had half the girls strung out on drops. There's no Guild out here; they let men run the houses, and they don't ask for references. We didn't get along.

MAL
Where's he at now?

NANDI
(sitting)
Let's just say he ain't playing the dulcimer any-more either.

They clink glasses. Knock 'em back.

MAL
You are a remarkable woman, you don't mind my saying.

NANDI
Long as it's you saying it, and not my fine rice wine.

MAL
It takes more'n a few drinks to render my judgement blurry. What about you? Am I getting any prettier?

NANDI
By the minute.

She is so sweetly seductive that they hold on each other a moment. Then he breaks it, all conscience.

MAL
(rising)
I should check the barricades, make sure everyone's ready to —

NANDI
Everyone's asleep. Well, them as can, night before a fight.

She heads for the dresser, to pour again.

NANDI (cont'd)
Can you?

MAL
What?

NANDI
Sleep?

Another beat, as that loaded question settles in. Mal's reply is intimate in tone as well, as he steps forward.

MAL
Miss Nandi, I have a confession to make.

NANDI
Maybe I should get the Shepherd.

MAL
Well, I ain't sinned yet, and I'd feel more than a little awkward having him here when I do.

NANDI
You expect to accomplish something sinful then, do you?

MAL
If I'm overstepping my bounds, you let me know.

NATHAN FILLION

Melinda Clarke in 'Heart of Gold', another amazing casting job. She's an amazing actress. I loved learning more about Malcolm Reynolds through other characters, and Nandi was a big one. It was the first time Malcolm could actually feel along the lines of something he needed to feel for so, so long. Of course, it was a little bit misguided not being Inara and all. He's a human being and it's hard for him to let himself be a human being.

NANDI
<jen mei NAI-shing duh FWO-tzoo> [Extraordinarily impatient Buddha], Malcolm, I been waiting for you to kiss me since I showed you my guns —

They're kissing. It's soft, but not without heat. He pulls away, looks at her.

NANDI (cont'd)
You okay with this?

MAL
I'm just waiting to see if I pass out. Long story.

NANDI
I want you to bed me.

MAL
I guess I mean to.

A small beat, as he strokes her hair.

NANDI
I ain't her.

MAL
Only people in this room is you and me.

She hands him one of the newly filled shotglasses, takes one herself.

NANDI
So, my child... How long has it been since your last confession?

MAL
Longer than I care to tell.

NANDI
You gonna remember where everything goes?

MAL
Let's just say I plan to take it real slow.

They drink. They kiss. They sink to the bed.

INT. BORDELLO - NANDI'S ROOM - NIGHT

It is later, and they are in the act. They are both naked, him sitting up at the foot of the bed and her astraddle, sheets pooled about the lower portions of them and clever camera work concealing the more interesting details of the upper. Their movement is slow, deliberate — and not quite so rhythmic as to be entirely specific. They are drenched in sweat.

He runs his hands along the side of her head, his thumb sliding indelicately into the corner of her mouth, Nandi biting down lightly, eyes closing, then opening again, near startled, as his hands slip to her hips and they look at each other with something resembling need.

She brings his head to her breast, still moving, eyes wet with tears not spilt.

EXT. TOWN - NIGHT

BURGESS
So the whore's got herself a champion, has she?

He is standing in the light of a couple of torches, on the balcony of a two-story building, couple of his men behind him. He looks over the railing a moment, amused. Looks back to the person he's addressing.

JOSS WHEDON

There's one more edict of the network — 'For god's sake, no Western.' And then we saw the dailies from 'Heart of Gold' and went, 'Oh, we're in trouble. Oh, we're in so much trouble.' We did a lot of re-shoots on 'Heart of Gold' just to explain why it was so Western because we thought the network was going to kill us. The network *was* going to kill us, but we didn't know that it was going to happen right away at that point. 'Heart of Gold' really was, let's *do* a Western — let's do *Rio Bravo*, let's do the siege, and let's let poor Mal get some play and see how that affects Inara. It was again throwing everybody into a different kind of situation — 'Let's help a bunch of nice whores and get ourselves into kind of a classic Western scenario.' Then we realized that we were being told not to make a Western, and we weren't really sure what to do about it.

BURGESS (cont'd)
This great man got a name?

REVERSE to see CHARI is the one feeding him info. Why, she's a TURNCOAT!

CHARI
Reynolds. Malcolm Reynolds.

BURGESS
(thoughtfully)
Yes, I've met the man. How many does he have with him?

CHARI
Just a few, and only two real fighters besides his-self. But they got the girls stirrin' for a battle.

BURGESS
Well, I certainly wasn't counting on a battle.

He turns out over the railing, addresses his men.

BURGESS (cont'd)
Seems the Heart of Gold has got itself a few mercenaries. I guess we'd best call the whole thing off!

As he says this, the camera pans over to take in the view of the men — and they number at least thirty, many on horseback, all total bad-asses. A ROAR of laughter meets Burgess's statement.

Burgess grins, turns back to Chari.

BURGESS (cont'd)
Earned yourself quite a bag of silver, little kitten. Got a few more chores in mind afore you get it, though.

CHARI
I'm ready.

He motions for her to come closer, puts his arm around her as he addresses the men.

BURGESS
Now Chari here, she understands a whore's place, don't she?

General assent and applause.

BURGESS (cont'd)
But Nandi, and those others, they spit on our town. They've no respect for the sanctity of fatherhood, for decency or family. They got MY CHILD held hostage to their decadent ways and

that I will not abide!

More cheers.

BURGESS (cont'd)
We will show them what power is! We will show them what their position in this town is! Let us all remember, right here and now, what a woman is to a man!

He turns to Chari, no longer smiling.

BURGESS (cont'd)
Get on your knees.

She looks startled. Looks out at all the men watching. But Burgess is unwavering, and she hesitantly sinks out of frame.

ANGLE: THE MEN

There is a pause. Then an uproarious cheer.

END OF ACT TWO

ACT THREE

EXT. BORDELLO - DAWN

The sun creeps over the horizon. The MORNING OF.

INT. BORDELLO - NANDI'S ROOM - DAWN

Mal and Nandi are asleep together in a tangle of sheets, in a tangle of limbs. Content.

Sunlight streams in from the horizon, cutting her across the eyes. She blinks awake. She looks at him sleeping awhile.

INT. BORDELLO LOBBY - MORNING

Mal is coming quietly out of Nandi's room, doing up his shirt, just as Inara is coming from the back hall. He stops, totally busted.

MAL
Um...

INARA
Well.

She is startled, but doesn't seem shocked. That doesn't stop Mal from excusifying:

MAL
I was just, um, I had to tell Nandi about the... It's near time to... Big fight today.

INARA
Mal. Please.

MAL
Hey, no, I've got, I've been up thinking...

INARA
(sincerely)
So you took to bed with Nandi. I'm glad.

MAL
Thinking and pondering the — Glad?

INARA
Yes! She's a dear friend, and probably in need of some comfort about now.

MAL
Well, I...

INARA
(amused)
One of the virtues of not being puritanical about sex is not being embarrassed afterwards. You should look into it.

MAL
Well, I just... didn't want you to think I was taking advantage of your friend.

INARA
She's well worth taking advantage of, I sincerely hope you did.

MAL
So you're okay. Well, yeah. Why wouldn't you be?

INARA
I wouldn't say I'm entirely okay. I'm a little appalled at her taste.

Smiling, she turns and exits, leaving him come-backless.

INT. BORDELLO - UPSTAIRS ROOM - MORNING

The sun's a mite higher now. Jayne stirs, stretches, as does Helen. Then he rolls over and goes back to sleep.

INT. BORDELLO - BACK ROOM - MORNING

We see Petaline, having dozed off. Track across the room to find Inara sitting on the floor in the corner. Sobbing her eyes out.

EXT. PLAINS - MORNING

Wash and Kaylee trek toward Serenity, which looms in the distance (for one — and only one — shot). Wash sips coffee from a lidded MUG. He has a PISTOL holstered at his side.

Mal's voice comes in over Wash's RADIO HANDSET.

MAL (O.S.)
Wash — are we there yet?

Wash pulls his radio off his belt and answers.

WASH
All but. Nice day for a last stand, innit?

MAL (O.S.)
Nope. Plan to make a healthy few stands after this one. Just hopin' for some air support from your quarter, is all.

WASH
(nods)
Couple of low fly-overs, engines tipped earthward at full blast, should give our guests something other than killin' you to think about.

MAL (O.S.)
What I like to hear... Out.

Wash clicks off his radio and clips it back to his belt.

KAYLEE
Captain seem a little funny to you at breakfast this morning?

WASH
Come on, Kaylee. We all know I'm the funny one.

INT. BORDELLO - MORNING

Mal walks behind some of the women, who stand in position at the bottom floor lobby windows, holding rifles. He himself is now armed for battle. He wears a RADIO EARWIG.

MAL
You ladies all locked and loaded?

LUCY
Yes, sir.

MAL
Good. Remember, shoot the man, not the horse. Dead horse is cover, live horse is a great pile of panic.

He stops as a TRANSMISSION crackles in over his earwig:

JAYNE (O.S.)
(lewd chuckle)
Whoa now, girl, that's just plain dirty —

He holds a finger up to the women, and hits the transmit switch.

MAL
Jayne — You aware your radio's transmittin'?

INT. BORDELLO - UPSTAIRS ROOM - MORNING

CLOSE ON RADIO HANDSET — which sits in a twist of bedspread. Jayne's hand enters frame, fumbling for it.

MAL (O.S.)
'Cause I ain't feelin' particular girlish or dirty at the moment.

Jayne picks up the radio and speaks into it as he untangles himself from Helen. He's dressed for war. She, not so much.

JAYNE
Oh, uh, just up here waitin', Captain. Ready one-hunnert-percent.

He grabs his weapon and looks out his window.

MAL (O.S.)
Better be.

Jayne gives Helen a sharp, businesslike nod, and she nods back.

EXT. PLAINS - ELSEWHERE - MORNING

A beat of quiet. Then the FAR-OFF SOUND of horses as a cloud of dust rises on the horizon. SMASH CUT TO —

— MID-THUNDER with the MERCENARY HORSEMEN surging forward at full gallop, flanking Burgess's hovercraft.

Burgess pilots the hovercraft, expressionless, behind stylish mirrored goggles. Over his face, PRE-LAP Petaline's SCREAM OF PAIN —

INT. BORDELLO - BACK ROOM - MORNING

CLOSE ON Petaline, who writhes in the throes of a contraction.

PETALINE
(continued scream)

Her legs are up and spread apart, concealed by a sheet. Inara holds her hand.

Inara leans in toward Petaline's face.

INARA
You're stronger than this thing, honey. I can feel it in your grip...
(Petaline SCREAMS again)
Petaline, look at me —

Petaline looks up at Inara, who catches her eyes in an intense, almost hypnotic stare.

INARA (cont'd)
This is just a moment in time... Step out of it and let it happen...

Nandi enters, stopping at Inara's side.

NANDI
How is she, Doctor?

Simon speaks from a counter a short distance away, as he fits a VIAL OF MED into his HYPO-GUN.

SIMON
She's at ten centimeters. Not long now.

Nandi turns to Inara. They share a subtle exchange of looks. This should be cut to show they're communicating via expression alone — Companions wordlessly reading each other.

Nandi smiles sadly, rests a hand on Inara's shoulder. Inara turns to Simon, sees he's still engaged, then quietly:

INARA
Nandi, believe me, I'll be fine.

❖ Below: Burgess's hovercraft.

They share a look and Nandi exits.

EXT. BORDELLO - MORNING

BINOCULAR POV — of Burgess and his riders, charging forward in the distance, trailing a plume of dust.

INT. BORDELLO LOBBY - MORNING

Mal, now standing on the interior balcony, lowers a slim pair of BINOCULARS. He is not at all pleased.

MAL
Zoe, Jayne — you seein' this?

JAYNE (O.S.)
Gotta be thirty men out there.

ZOE (O.S.)
Confirm that. Plus a mounted gun on that hover-craft.

JAYNE (O.S.)
What's that you said about runnin' for it?

Mal takes a moment, visibly adjusting to the new odds. He lifts up his RIFLE.

MAL
All right, folks — We got no shortage of ugly ridin' in on us. But that don't change the plan.

Nandi climbs the stairs, gun in hand, addressing the whores.

NANDI
Anybody here goes down, you drag 'em to the back, then get back to shooting. Only way to help them is to finish this.

She cocks her rifle then turns to Mal, smiles at him sweetly for a quick beat.

NANDI (cont'd)
Morning.

Mal smiles back.

INT. SERENITY - CARGO BAY - DAY

Kaylee and Wash enter through the SMALL

DOOR. Kaylee closes the door behind them; something's not right — She scans the bay as they start for the stairs. Mal CRACKLES IN over Wash's radio:

MAL (O.S.)
Wash — gonna be tradin' injuries in under two minutes. Like my sky a little less empty —

WASH
Copy that, Mal. We —

Kaylee sees SHADOWY FIGURES on the catwalk above, and tackles Wash just as GUNFIRE rains down at them, SPARKING off metal.

Wash slams down behind some metal crates, Kaylee on top of him. The radio skitters off into open floor; unreachable. But they have cover for the moment. Wash looks up into her face.

WASH (cont'd)
I told you, Kaylee — I'm a married man —

Kaylee knits her brow at him as another SHOT ricochets off their cover.

KAYLEE
(flatly)
You ain't all that funny.

EXT. BORDELLO - DAY

The hovercraft HUMS forward, just ahead of the horsemen.

Lead horse SNAPS A TRIPWIRE, and the ROPE springs up out of the dirt, singing taut, catching THREE RIDERS in the throats and pitching them off their horses. The other riders duck, some slide sideways in their saddles, clearing the line.

Burgess calls back to KOZICK, the man on the craft's large MOUNTED GUN.

BURGESS
Open her up, Kozick —

Kozick nods, cranks back a lever and starts shooting — MASSIVE MACHINE GUNFIRE flares.

INT. BORDELLO LOBBY - CONTINUING

Mal sees it coming and swings behind his shielding.

MAL
Cover!

The women do the same, just as a HAIL OF MACHINE GUNFIRE rips through everything that isn't fortified.

MAL (cont'd)
(into earwig)
Jayne — I believe that's our first hurdle. Think you might —

EXT. BORDELLO - CONTINUING

Kozick, FIRING AWAY, is plugged in the chest and FLIPS BACKWARD off the hovercraft.

INT. BORDELLO - UPSTAIRS ROOM - CONTINUING

Jayne pulls his eye away from his sight long enough to speak into his radio:

JAYNE
Think I might, Cap.

INT. BORDELLO LOBBY - CONTINUING

Mal calls to his troops.

MAL
Fire!

They all swing out and unleash a BARRAGE OF FIRE from their positions. One WHORE is caught by a shot and falls.

Nandi sees this and bristles, aiming another shot —

NANDI
<Wang bao DAHN — > [Dirty bastard sons-of —]

She FIRES.

EXT. BORDELLO - CONTINUING

A HORSEMAN takes it in the neck and flops off his horse.

INT. SERENITY - CARGO BAY - DAY

Wash and Kaylee under fire. Wash is trading shots with his pistol as THREE OF BURGESS'S MEN work their way along the upper catwalk. Wash and Kaylee fall back behind different crates, finally getting close to the door that leads to the COMMON AREA.

WASH
GO!

Kaylee darts out, Wash behind her, fires a FLURRY OF SHOTS to cover their exit.

They get through the door.

The men race down the stairs after them. CAMERA FINDS the radio.

MAL (O.S.)
Wash — Where the hell is my spaceship!?

EXT. BORDELLO - CONTINUING

Horsemen criss-crossing, SEVERAL get hit by GUNFIRE from the whorehouse, dropping from their steeds.

A HORSE GOES DOWN, crashing into the FG and throwing its rider.

The REST RETURN FIRE.

Burgess angles the hovercraft, flying parallel with the house front, still a ways off. He lifts his laser and FIRES a CONTINUOUS BEAM.

The BEAM sears along the front of the house, wavering between the second-storey windows and the eaves of the roof, which already started SMOKING.

INT. BORDELLO LOBBY - CONTINUING

As the LASER BEAM traces a RED-HOT LINE along their barricade, FLASHING through the gun-slits as Mal and the others hunker away.

Mal looks up, where he sees SMOKE pouring in from a TORN UP PATCH OF CEILING.

MAL
Ruttin' lasers —
(into earwig)
Book — Zoe — Second hurdle —

EXT. BORDELLO - CONTINUING

FIRE HAS BROKEN OUT on the front facade of the whorehouse. PAN/TILT to what looks like a PILE OF BARRELS AND TARPS on the ground in front of the house.

ZOE (O.S.)
Copy that, sir —

The tarps are thrown away, revealing Zoe and Book. Book holds the hose, Zoe covers his back with her rifle. He starts up the hose, and A HISSING JET OF WATER sprays up toward the wall.

A HORSEMAN turns toward them, leveling his gun at Book. Zoe FIRES, taking him out.

BOOK
Thank you —

Book catches sight of a PAIR OF RIDERS behind Zoe, taking aim. He swings the hose around, BLASTING them off their horses with its powerful stream.

ZOE
Don't mention it —

INT. BORDELLO LOBBY - CONTINUING

Mal, Nandi, and the others continue BLASTING AWAY. Petaline's SCREAMING comes in from the back room.

INT. BORDELLO - BACK ROOM - CONTINUING

Simon is in position, Petaline is bearing down hard and SCREAMING between breaths. River is fascinated and smiling.

PETALINE
(screams again)

SIMON
That's it, Petaline, one more push —

She bears down.

SIMON (cont'd)
That's the shoulders... Good —

EXT. BORDELLO - CONTINUING

The horsemen are in chaos now, riderless and wounded horses stymie their efforts to fire on the house. Our guys are kicking ass!

INT. BORDELLO LOBBY - CONTINUING

Up on the balcony, Mal talks into his earwig as he scans the battlefield.

MAL
Jayne — I lost visual on Burgess —

JAYNE (O.S.)
Same here —

A BOY WHORE falls away from a window down the line, bloodied by a gunshot. Mal RETURNS FIRE.

INT. BORDELLO - SIDE OF HOUSE - CONTINUING

Burgess's hovercraft is up close to the house, and he's leaping off it to the ground. A BULKHEAD CELLAR DOOR swings open. Chari is there, and ushers Burgess inside.

INT. SERENITY - DINING AREA - CONTINUING

The three mercenaries move through the dining area, grim-faced, covering it with their guns, cursorily checking its nooks and crannies for their prey.

A DOOR LOCKING SHUT calls their attention to the aft corridor.

They see Wash at its end and raise their guns.

WASH
(that weird Robert Mitchum "hoot!" from *Night of the Hunter*)

Wash darts into the engine room, narrowly missed by their FIRE as they move into the AFT CORRIDOR.

Kaylee pops out of a CLEVER HIDING PLACE and swings the door shut behind them, then locks it.

INT. SERENITY - AFT CORRIDOR - CONTINUING

Before they can react, Wash swings the ENGINE ROOM DOOR shut as well, locking it. The passage leading off from the middle of the corridor is BARRED BY ITS DOOR [which we have not seen yet in the series — a Carey issue]. They're trapped.

INT. SERENITY - ENGINE ROOM - CONTINUING

Wash peers in through the thick glass porthole, issuing adrenaline-charged laughter.

WASH
Got you, you <niao SE duh DOO-gway.> [piss-soaked pikers.]
(laughs again, then realizes he's trapped in the engine room)
Nobody's going any... where...

He massages the headache his brilliant scheme has occasioned.

INT. BORDELLO - BACK ROOM - DAY

Simon lifts up a SWADDLED BABY, purple, newborn, squealing. Inara and River look on. Petaline is near delirious from childbirth.

SIMON
It's —

RIVER
It's a boy. Healthy.

A DOOR behind Inara opens, and Burgess is there, laser covering them.

BURGESS
Mornin', Petaline...

INT. BORDELLO - LOBBY - CONTINUING

Nandi hears PETALINE'S SCREAM first:

PETALINE
Rance! NO!

Mal is caught in the ebbing FIREFIGHT, but Nandi races down the stairs, toward the rear hall.

INT. BORDELLO - REAR HALL - CONTINUING

Burgess backs out of the back room, where Petaline screams. He's got the BABY in one arm, laser pistol in the other. Nandi appears behind him, entering from the lobby, confronts him.

NANDI
Most of your men are dead, dyin', or run off, Rance.

BURGESS
Don't matter none. Got what I came here for.

NANDI
Ain't leaving here with it.

BURGESS
This is my blood, woman.

Burgess gestures toward the baby with his pistol.

Suddenly a slim arm snakes a nasty curved RAZOR in under Burgess's chin from behind, digging its tip into the side of his throat, DRAWING BLOOD. It's Inara, accompanied by two ND whores, as cold dead serious as we've seen her.

INARA
(re: blood dripping down his neck)
No. This is your blood.
(nods to a whore)
Now you give over that child nice and slow, or I'll spill more than you can spare.

Burgess complies, wincing at the wound, handing the baby over to a whore, who backs out of the scene to safety.

As this happens, Burgess takes the pause to ELBOW Inara hard in the stomach. As she staggers back, he FIRES his laser from the hip, searing straight through Nandi's chest.

Mal gets to the lobby end of the hall, just as she drops, dead.

END OF ACT THREE

ACT FOUR

INT. BORDELLO - REAR HALL - DAY

The WHORES shout in alarm. They can't believe Nandi has fallen. Even Burgess seems surprised at what he's done. Mal moves to the fallen Nandi — as Burgess turns and runs for a side door, escaping.

Mal touches Nandi. She's stone dead. He shares a look with Inara, there's murder in both their eyes. He hears the O.S. THRUM of the hovercraft

❖ Below: Inara's knife.

starting up and turns for the front door.

EXT. BORDELLO - CONTINUOUS

ANGLE ON FRONT DOOR

The front door slams open and Mal stalks out, eyes forward.

Without dropping a beat, Mal PLUGS a horseman off his horse, and swings up into the saddle just as the man finishes falling.

Burgess's hovercraft rumbles out from behind the house, heading out for the plains.

Mal spurs the horse hard, and it tears off —

MAL
Hyah!

EXT. OPEN LAND - DAY

A WIDE LANDSCAPE SHOT of Burgess speeding away in his hovercraft and Mal in pursuit, his horse kicking up dust as he whips and spurs it into a breakneck gallop.

Burgess sees Mal behind him and stands in his craft, steering with one hand as he turns back. He FIRES his laser —

The LASER BEAM cuts the air by Mal's head. Mal whips a burst of speed out of his horse as another BEAM sears past him.

Mal is closing in on the hovercraft, an easy shot. Burgess takes careful aim, and pulls his trigger. We hear a RAPID BEEPING. Burgess checks the display screen on his gun —

LASER GUN

The LCD screen flashes "CHECK BATTERY".

Burgess GROWLS, looking up just as Mal flies from his horse, tackling Burgess off the hovercraft.

They slam into a hard roll on the plain as the hovercraft drifts off aimlessly in the BG.

Burgess has had the wind smashed out of him and writhes on the ground. Mal ain't much better, but drags himself to his feet using sheer force of will.

He grabs Burgess's shirtfront and hauls him up, pulling his pistol from his holster, bringing its barrel up to Burgess's head.

MAL
You're gonna pay for what you took.

BURGESS
(still out of breath)
She was a whore.

Mal seethes with vengeful fury, he's about to pull the trigger, but then — he flips the gun in his hand and smashes the butt across Burgess's face. Burgess collapses, unconscious.

❖ Above: Burgess's laser pistol battery read-out.

MAL
That don't enter into it.

CUT TO:

EXT. BORDELLO - DAY

Mal and Zoe watch as Inara finishes tying the kneeling Burgess's hands behind his back.

THREE MEN CRASH INTO FRAME, as Jayne dumps the bruised and bloodied Serenity-crashers before the bordello steps, Kaylee and Wash close by. Burgess's other men are also tied up.

BURGESS
(calling out)
PETALINE! YOU BRING MY BOY OUT, RIGHT NOW! YOU HEAR ME? I WANT TO SEE MY SON!

Petaline appears at the bordello door, the baby nursing at her breast. All eyes watch as she descends the steps and approaches Burgess.

PETALINE
Rance... this is Jonah.

(beat)
Jonah, say hello to your daddy.

BURGESS

smiles like a proud papa. He's actually moved at the sight of his son.

Petaline raises her free hand in which she holds Nandi's favorite gun. She aims it at Burgess's head.

PETALINE (cont'd)
Say goodbye to your daddy, Jonah.

Burgess blanches.

CLOSE PETALINE: Camera looking up the business end of the gun, she fires.

Petaline looks up from Burgess's dead body, icy —

PETALINE (cont'd)
Anyone else wanna try and take what's mine?

She scans the rows of Burgess's bound men; every last one avoids eye contact.

PETALINE (cont'd)
Go on, then. Go home. Next time I see any of you... you best be coming to get your wick wet. You pay up front from now on... and for god's sake, tip a girl once in a while — especially you, Milo.

Milo nods quickly: whatever you say, Petaline. The men start rising to their feet. Petaline indicates Chari —

PETALINE (cont'd)
You go with 'em. You got no place here.

Chari is about to speak, before she can:

PETALINE (cont'd)
You let 'em in the back door, Inara seen it, now go.

CHARI
You can't just make me —

CLICK. Petaline cocks the hammer of her pistol. Chari shuts up, breaks eye contact, falls in step with Burgess's men as they walk away.

Mal approaches Petaline, indicates Burgess's body —

MAL
We'll dispose of that for you.

PETALINE
Thank you, Captain.
(beat)
Emma?

Emma (Book's churchy whore) appears at Petaline's side.

PETALINE (cont'd)
Get the spade from the shed.
(beat)
Our Nandi's gonna be buried proper.

HIGH ANGLE

As the crowd disperses, we HOLD for a long moment and PRELAP:

LUCY (V.O.)
(singing)
Amazing Grace, how sweet the sound...

EXT. HILLTOP - DAY

LONG SHOT: A score of mourners have gathered around a makeshift cross beneath a large oak. This is a fusion of BUDDHIST and CHRISTIAN ceremony. A number of mourners are dressed in

white robes, with Tibetan prayer beads draped over their clasped hands.

Lucy sings in a simple, quiet voice. (Think Margo Timmins.)

LUCY
That saved a wretch like me/ I once was lost, but now am found/ Was blind but now I see...

Lucy continues to sing. One by one, Nandi's staff step up to the wooden cross marking her grave. At its foot is a low Asian-looking table, on which sits a bowl of smoking incense. They bow as they drop pinches of incense into the bowl.

SIMON AND RIVER

Alongside a couple of the girls, their faces a solemn mask.

LUCY
'Twas Grace that taught my heart to fear...

ZOE, WASH AND JAYNE

Zoe and Wash hold hands. Jayne looks at his feet.

LUCY
And Grace my fears relieved/ How precious did that Grace appear...

BOOK

holds the bible to his chest, a tearful Emma with her hands wrapped around his arm.

LUCY
The hour I first believed...

PETALINE

Baby in her arms, the stolid look of one who's been to war on her face.

LUCY
Through many dangers, toils and snares/ We have already come...

INARA

steps up to the small table, dressed in a white shawl, beads draped, and drops a pinch of incense into the bowl. She bows to it and turns away.

MAL

His arm paternally around Kaylee's shoulder, comforting, as tears roll down her face.

Inara takes in the entire gathering now: the unit that is Serenity's crew standing side by side with the bordello gals. She stands slightly apart from all of them.

LUCY
T'was Grace that brought us safe thus far...

Lucy's singing continues as we —

CUT TO:

MORENA BACCARIN

I love the scene in 'Heart of Gold' where I tell him I'm leaving. It is the first genuine moment between them when they're *honest* with one another, because she is going to go. When I first read it, I remember running to Joss going, 'What is this scene — I'm leaving the show?' but he said, 'Don't worry.' I think, had we gone on, they were planning to do something where they would show me in the Companion training house, like they did in the movie.

EXT. SPACE

Serenity exits atmo and glides silently into the black.

LUCY (V.O.)
And Grace will lead us home...

INT. SERENITY - CARGO BAY - NIGHT

Mal and Inara stand on the catwalk outside her shuttle. They are contemplative, subdued.

MAL
I think those girls'll do all right.

INARA
She taught them well.

MAL
Yeah.

A beat.

INARA
I'm... I'm glad that you were with her. Her last night. I am.

MAL
I ain't. Hell, I wish I'd never met her. Then I wouldn't've failed her.

INARA
That wasn't the way of it.

MAL
It's a kindness, but nothing you say'll convince me different.

INARA
Well, I'm still glad.

A small beat.

MAL
So you weren't before?

He's looking at her direct. She looks away.

MAL (cont'd)
Inara, I ain't looking for anything from you. I'm just feeling kind of truthsome right now. Life is too damn short for ifs and maybes.

INARA
I learned something from Nandi. Not just from what happened, but from her. The family she made, the strength of her love for them. That's what kept them together. When you live with that kind of strength, you get tied to it, you can't break away. And you never want to.

They're getting closer to each other, Mal's eyes locked on hers.

INARA (cont'd)
There's something that I... that I should have done a long while ago. And I'm sorry — for both of us — that it took me this long.

A beat.

INARA (cont'd)
I'm leaving.

Another moment, and she goes past him into her shuttle.

He doesn't move.

END OF SHOW

VISUAL EFFECTS

An interview with Loni Peristere

From the beginning, Joss Whedon had a unique vision for how he wanted to portray space in *Firefly*. He wanted it to be a character, as alive and complex as Mal and as ephemeral and daunting as River — it was to be an equal with the cast, enfolding Serenity into its limitless, black embrace. Finding a visual effects team to 'get' that vision would seem difficult in theory, but Whedon just turned to the team that he'd already been working with for six years, Loni Peristere and Zoic Studios, to get it absolutely right.

Peristere was brought onto the project even before a script had been written, and he vividly recalls how Joss pitched him this new series. "It was just before Christmas time, several months before we were to go to pilot. He said, 'After the break, I am going to start working on this pilot and I think you are going to like it. It's set in the future, but it's centered around characters out of our past and the present. It takes place on a spaceship and I think that might interest you.'" Detailing the concept, Loni remembers Joss said, "'I really want to do something different with space. I want to get away from placid, calm imagery and I want to use space as a character, and the ship as a character. I need to feel the camera is always important in the story, when we are inside the ship *and* outside the ship. With that in mind, think about 3D in a different way. When you are designing the sequences for my show, I really want

❖ Right from top to bottom and below: Scenes from 'The Message'.

❖ Opposite page left: A scene from 'The Train Job'.

❖ Opposite page right: The green screen before and after shots of Mal and the Torturer during 'War Stories'.

❖ Opposite page bottom: Serenity arrives in Ariel City.

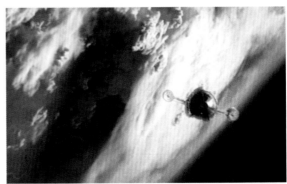

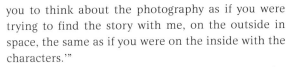

you to think about the photography as if you were trying to find the story with me, on the outside in space, the same as if you were on the inside with the characters.'"

With that concept driving him, Peristere says he threw himself into finding the look of the show's effects shots, which was to be a revolutionary departure from the sedate, measured style of the past. "I started taking a look at voyeuristic ways of looking at exteriors and objects in motion. I started watching things like NASCAR and air shows, documentaries about science and space exploration, anything where

there wasn't a plan for photography. I decided that that was going to be my approach to pitch to Joss. So instead of having cameras in these magical places that just happen to be there to catch the spaceship, I thought we should have rules. The main rule should be: if you are photographing a spaceship, you should know where you are shooting it *from*. If you are the 'camera spaceship', you can be just like a helicopter, you can fly around the ship and there must be an operator that tries to keep the ship in frame, if that is important. So there is always a camera operator in space, and there is always a placement for a camera on the ship, with options that would mirror options you would have using aerial photography in real life.

"So I made a compilation for Joss where I literally took every single space scene I could think of from

movies and TV series, put them all on one DVD and called it 'Firefly Research'," Peristere continues. "We sat down and watched it and Joss said, 'You had so many cool things on there and some things I hadn't seen in a long time — but that's not what the show is about,'" he laughs. Then Peristere showed him some documentary footage, with its whip pans and crash zooms, as an example of the style he was aiming for. "Joss just said, 'I have no idea what you just showed me, but I'm sure it will look good!'" And with that, Whedon entrusted Loni and his team with the task of making his ideas translate to the screen.

"I did illustrations, storyboards or animatics so Joss got a better idea of what I was talking about," Peristere remembers of the initial stages. Whedon was soon giving him a lot of latitude when it came to ideas for shots. "We'd had such a great partnership for such a long, long time, but I had always wanted to participate more. He knew I was hungry, and with *Firefly* he was happy to give me this fun gift to design some really cool sequences. He gave me the keys to the car, and I was very excited to have that opportunity. Joss would really challenge us every episode to do something that seemed impossible. When I got the script, he would write things like, 'a great space battle ensues', which was very curt; and then sometimes put, 'Loni will think of something cool here.' In every instance, he would write it knowing there would be a solution that we would have to come up with to make that show work, and that's what we expected. He knew he should always be pushing us, or it wouldn't be fun."

Peristere says the Reaver chase scene in the pilot was the key moment when he knew he had achieved the right look for *Firefly*. "When I got the script, I immediately ran rampant with our shot designer Neil Smith and we put together the animatics of the Reaver chase sequence. I showed the sequence to Joss, Lisa Lassek, David Solomon and David Greenwalt and they all said, 'That's awesome!' It was a great feeling, because it let us know that we were on the right track. Solomon even said, 'You are going to win an Emmy!' and he was right!" Zoic Studios won a richly deserved Outstanding Special Visual Effects Emmy in 2003 for *Firefly*, which forever sealed the series' place in television effects history. ◉

❖ Above: Serenity takes off towards the end of 'Heart of Gold'.

❖ Opposite page top: Serenity in space.

❖ Opposite page middle: The Ariel City junk yard.

❖ Below: A sequence from the Reaver chase during 'Serenity'.

OBJECTS IN SPACE

Written & Directed by Joss Whedon

JOSS WHEDON

"The most difficult villain for me in *Firefly* was Jubal, and the most rewarding. That whole thing was the best experience I could ever have had. I had been trying to break the story, and it was about River, and her powers discovered, and, oh, the not-very-interesting stories we were going back and forth on. I called Tim in desperation and he said, 'Well, can't you just have Bobba Fett?' [Minear mispronounced Boba Fett, of *Star Wars* fame.] And I said, 'Who's Bobba Fett, first of all? And you call yourself a nerd? And second of all, thanks. Bye.' Because it just clicked. And when I got to 'Objects in Space', I had the idea of this character, and I had the idea of River and what I had to do. I said, 'This will write itself. Like 'Our Mrs. Reynolds' did. I'll just be sitting here waiting for it to write itself. Any minute now, it will start to write.' And then I realized that I was in... Hell [laughs]. I had a couple of things that helped me. One of them was *The Minus Man*, which is a movie that I think has an extraordinary portrait of a serial killer, just the main character's comical observations. The other was — and this has worked for me on all my shows when things are hard — walking the set. I went one weekend, just walking the set and doing everything that River did and everything that Jubal did, climbing up on the ladder, standing on the railing. The physicality of the thing clued me into his *perception* of the physicality of the thing and ultimately what the episode was going to be about: the ecstasy of being, the idea of imprinting meaning on objects and that two people who really step out of the norm are very similar, but because what they bring emotionally is completely opposite, they ultimately are very different. That came from physically being there in the space, and once it unveiled itself, it was an extraordinary experience — but it was a long time coming."

Did Whedon expect the audience to respond to 'Objects' on an existential level? "Well," he replies, "ultimately, you try to reach people on the level of, 'Ooh, this is entertaining, this guy's a badass — ooh, he's menacing Kaylee, oh, he's got a cool outfit and wait a minute, *is* River the ship?' Because it's science-fiction — we don't *really* know the parameters — we found out she's psychic and that's weird. Is it possible that she's the ship. It was, 'Let's have as much fun as possible, and let's bring the team together as a family.' Beyond that, the meaning that it had was extremely important for *me*, and I know it was extremely important for a lot of the people who watched it, but I am sure there are equal if not greater numbers of people who just said, 'Ah, it was a fun one.' If people come out feeling that you've written an essay, then you have made bad TV. I do these things because there's something I want to say or feel and I make sure that not only is the show entertaining, but that what is entertaining about it is wrapped up in whatever it is I'm trying to say."

TEASER

EXT. SPACE - NIGHT

Not just 'cause it's dark in space, but because it's evening cycle for those in Serenity, which happens to glide into frame. We are above and behind it, and we glide with it a bit, keeping pace.

CLOSE ON: the top of Serenity as the camera goes THROUGH it, into the labyrinth of wires and pipe and spaceship innards, moving about rabbit-fast, twisting and turning, ending up looking down through a grating at:

INT. RIVER'S ROOM - EVENING

RIVER, sleeping.

Cut to EXTREME CLOSE UP on River's closed eyes. There is talk, chatter from every shipmember, like static in her head, rising slowly. The noise builds until —

A MAN'S VOICE
We're all just floating...

Her eyes snap open. That voice could've been in the room with her.

She rises, sits on her bed. She wears a dress, no shoes, seems to be in a slightly dreamlike state. (No huge change there, but we may do something with the lens occasionally to accentuate that.) Laughter pulls her from her room.

INT. PASSENGER DORM - CONTINUING

She moves slowly, finds KAYLEE and SIMON on the couch. Kaylee is lying with her legs (her feet are also bare) over the sitting Simon, innocently intimate. Laughing.

KAYLEE
You couldn't possibly have!

SIMON
I wish I was lying. I just — we'd all just made surgeon, that was it. We were the elite, the world was ours, you know —

KAYLEE
So you had to be naked.

SIMON
Naked, yes, and on top of the statue of Hypocrates, and — Can you just picture me?

KAYLEE
Naked? I'll have to conjure up — it'll be tough.

He smiles at her, and she taps his chin with her toes playfully.

KAYLEE (cont'd)
So the feds came?

SIMON
There were no feds. Until I started singing.

KAYLEE
(laughing)
Oh no! What'd you sing?

SIMON
This is not funny. This is a morality tale about the evils of sake.

River has been watching them the whole time. They suddenly turn to her, the laughter draining from their faces.

SIMON (cont'd)
(to River)
I would be there right now.

There is coldness in his voice, and Kaylee looks at her with an expression that matches.

And then, oddly, there's a JUMP CUT to the two of them laughing again, as though that moment never happened.

River looks mildly confused, then starts up the stairs.

SIMON (cont'd)
It was either that or the national anthem. Reports vary.

KAYLEE
Do you remember any of it?

SIMON
I remember talking them out of telling my father... or paying them out of telling my father. I'm fuzzy on aspects...

INT. AFT HALL/DINING ROOM - CONTINUING

River comes into the hallway, touching the walls as she goes, looking at her hands. She finds BOOK and JAYNE, also in mid-conversation. Jayne is cooking scallion cakes on the griddle. Book is at the table.

JAYNE
So, like... never?

BOOK
Well, no.

JAYNE
Not ever never?

BOOK
Some orders allow Shepherds to marry, but I follow a narrower path.

JAYNE
But, I mean, you still got the urge, right? They don't cut it off or nothing...

BOOK
(smiles)
No, I'm more or less intact. I just direct my energy elsewhere.

JAYNE
You mean like masterbatin'?

BOOK
I hope you're not thinking of taking orders yourself...

JAYNE
That'll be the day.

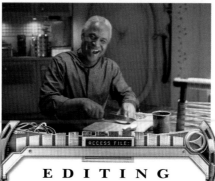

EDITING

Film editor/associate producer Lisa Lassek: "Joss and I often talked about getting inside River's head. In 'Objects in Space', the entire opening of the show is from her perspective. We gently increased that feeling, so at the beginning you're in reality just watching Simon and Kaylee talk, so that when it jumps into what River's perceiving, and then jumps back out, you're surprised. As she moves through the ship, it gets more and more surreal and we get more and more into her head. We did the same thing with the sound design. It started out normal and then we got progressively more into her space. One of the most tantalizing clues about Book's background is in what he says, because it seems to come out of left field, something like, 'I don't care if you're innocent or not.' We get a clip of what he's thinking; we've never seen Book be so aggressive and scary. This is a perfect example of something laid almost in the background that, if you watch the entire series and then the movie, ends up becoming really meaningful."

During all this, River wanders unnoticed right between the two of them. She turns to look at Jayne, who looks back guiltily.

JAYNE (cont'd)
I got stupid. The money was too good.

She turns, looks at Book, who is in her face, fiercely angry.

BOOK
I don't give half a hump if you're innocent or not! So where does that put you?

JUMP CUT back to reality — the men are laughing, Book still sitting, and River has walked between them unnoticed. She heads to the foredeck hall as the men continue:

JAYNE
It ain't impossible! Saint Jayne, it's got a ring to it.

BOOK
I'm just trying to remember how many miracles you've performed.

JAYNE
I once hit a guy in the neck at five hundred yards with a bent scope, don't that count upstairs?

BOOK
Oh, it'll be taken into consideration...

JAYNE
Well, you make that sound kinda ominous...

INT. FOREDECK HALL/BRIDGE - CONTINUING

River moves into the foredeck hall, is about to turn right when she sees WASH and ZOE on the bridge. The door is half shut and they are a ways away, but she is suddenly awash in their energy.

Which is different than anyone else's, seeing as how Zoe is sitting on Wash's lap, facing him, smooching him. Their clothes are on (it's the bridge, already), but though they are playful, their energy is intense, their eyes locked.

We see them as River feels them, VERY CLOSE up, wide angle lens roving around them, sweat and smiles and the sound of the ocean, waves breaking as River nearly staggers back with it, suddenly perturbed to be in that intimacy.

She moves away, hugging the wall, down into:

INT. CARGO BAY/INARA'S SHUTTLE - CONTINUING

And now she's coming down the steps as MAL and INARA are in quiet conference at the entrance to her shuttle.

INARA
I've put out a few waves to some old acquaintances — I may even be able to find something in New Melbourne, if you need the shuttle free.

MAL
Only thing you're gonna find in New Melbourne is fish and fish related activities. Unless you got

an overwhelming urge to gut sturgeon — and who hasn't, occasionally —

INARA
But it's a layover point for almost every planet this side of the system, and I could... I just don't want to draw this out.

MAL
You decided when you're gonna tell the others?

INARA
I... no. I appreciate your not saying anything.

MAL
I don't. So make up your mind.

River stops near the entrance. Inara looks at her, says:

INARA
I'm a big girl. Just tell me.

Pan over to Mal, who is looking away from us.

MAL
None of it means a damn thing.

That ocean noise again, and River looks pained,

nothing is as it should be here. She stumbles down the steps in a jumbled series of jump-cuts...

She walks along the floor of the cargo bay, steps on something.

ANGLE: HER FOOT

steps on a branch. She gingerly steps off it, then bends over to look at it, her head coming into frame, staring.

ANGLE: FROM HIGH ABOVE we see the entire cargo bay floor around her is littered with branches and leaves.

She picks up the branch. It's smallish, curved to fit well in her hand.

She studies it, uncertain.

RIVER
Just an object.
(looks up)
It doesn't mean what you think...

She smiles comfortingly —

Jump-cut to reality — Simon and Kaylee are standing in front of her, yelling — Mal yelling as well from above...

SIMON
River you know that's not to be touched!

KAYLEE
Everybody just be real calm already —

MAL
Get it away from her —

SIMON
Just put it down!

River looks confused at the sudden cacophony. Looks down at her hand — and there is a BIG DAMN GUN in it. Pointed at Simon and Kaylee, the latter of whom looks shit-scared.

River lowers the gun, looking grouchily confused, as Simon comes to take it from her. She looks

over at Kaylee, who fades out to the passenger dorm, unable to deal.

RIVER
Kaylee...?

SIMON
What were you thinking? Where did you get ahold of this?

Mal is down with them by now, takes the gun from Simon, checks it.

RIVER
It was in my hand...

MAL
Fully loaded, safety off. This here's a recipe for unpleasantness, does she understand that?

She turns to him.

RIVER
She understands. She doesn't comprehend.

MAL
Well, I'm glad we've made that distinction. No touching guns, okay?

RIVER
No touching.

She moves off, quickly.

SIMON
River —

RIVER
It's getting very very crowded!

And she's out. Mal looks at Simon.

MAL
Thought she was on the mend.

SIMON
The medications are erratic: there's not one that her system can't eventually break down, and you have to recalibrate —

MAL
I want a lot of medical jargon thrown at me, I'll talk to a doctor.

SIMON
You are talking to a doctor.

MAL
Yeah, okay — point is, coulda been you she mighta shot just then. The doctor, as you just made note of. And who exactly could fix you? Not nobody. We're still in deep space, Doctor, corner of No and Where. You take extra care with her. 'Cause we're very much alone out here.

EXT. SPACE - CONTINUING

Serenity continues on, as the camera comes around to see that there is another, smaller vessel RIGHT behind and above it. Sleek, quiet.

They're not so much alone out here.

END OF TEASER

ACT ONE

EXT. SPACE - CONTINUING

We move in on the smaller craft as it hugs Serenity's wake. Move in closer to see the windshield, and a single figure inside the cockpit. (It's way too small to be called a bridge — if Serenity is a family van, this is a Harley.)

INT. EARLY'S SHIP - CONTINUING

He's called EARLY, and for the next while, he will say not a word. He merely goes about his business with quiet, intense efficiency. His business is hunting.

He watches the ship below him as readouts come over the windshield "screen". Among them:

— Serenity heat-scanned with infrared, showing a small model of the ship with heat signatures indicating where everyone is.

— A blueprint of Serenity that shows her layout, names the rooms, shows points of egress, lists components and operating systems.

— A graph of two lines coming together that then flashes: TRAJECTORY SYNC COMPLETE. LOCKED ONTO FLIGHT PATH.

While he works the controls beneath these readouts, the camera pans over to see a picture stuck to the hull near his head. A picture of River — the one the Blue Hands sported in 'The Train Job'. Around it are a warrant showing River with the legend, FUGITIVE, and at the bottom, REWARD 200,000 CREDITS, Alliance Bond Standard. WANTED ALIVE.

There's also a picture of River and Simon, and a beat up picture of an older black woman with a dog on a lawn.

Early takes the first picture of River off the wall, stares at it a moment, returns it. Then slips out of his seat.

INT. BRIDGE - EVENING

Wash is at the helm, Zoe beside him. He's talking, but also concentrating on his readouts.

WASH
Little River just gets more colorful by the moment. What will she do next?

ZOE
Either blow us all up or rub soup in her hair, it's a toss up.

WASH
I hope she does the soup thing. It's always a hoot and we don't all die from it.

ZOE
That poor kid...

WASH
(looking at screen)
Yeah, she's definitely... got... funny.

ZOE
Something wrong?

WASH
I'm just getting a weird heat bounce off our wake.

ZOE
Engine flux?

WASH
Sensor probably got turned around. I'll climb up top when we hit land.

Over this last exchange, Jayne and Mal enter, talking.

MAL
The lockers were sealed. We both know —

JAYNE
I don't leave my guns around, Mal. And I don't leave 'em loaded.

MAL
Well, somehow she got her hands on your hardware. Suppose she took up something with hull-piercing bullets?

JAYNE
Bullets is soft lead, Mal. Even Vera could barely breach hull and she's the best I got! Anyhow, let's direct this conversation in a not-Jayne's-fault direction. I didn't make her crazy. Hell, I didn't want her on the damn ship.

MAL
(in his face, quiet)
Is that the direction you want this conversation to go in?

Jayne looks guilty, covers...

JAYNE
I just don't like taking a lashing for what I ain't the cause of.

ZOE
Where's River at now?

MAL
In her room, which I'm thinking we bolt from the outside from now on.

WASH
That's a little extreme, isn't it?

JAYNE
Anybody remember her coming at me with a butcher's knife?

WASH
(remembering fondly)
Wacky fun...

JAYNE
You wanna go, little man?

WASH
Only if it's someplace with candlelight.

ZOE
Sir, I know she's unpredictable, but I don't think she'd harm anyone.

JAYNE
("Hellooo...")
Butcher's knife...

ZOE
Anyone we can't spare. I mean, far as we know, the girl's never even picked up a gun before.

KAYLEE
That ain't so.

She's standing in the doorway, looking upset. They give her their attention.

MAL
Kaylee, you got something to say?

She looks at him, not sure where to start.

EXT. SPACE - LATER

We are close on Early's ship, near the bottom as a door slides open and he glides out. Pushes a few keys as it shuts, then looking down, steadies himself a moment —

And pushes off, floating down toward Serenity. We pull out wide to show the three objects: the big ship, the smaller ship, and the tiny man floating rapidly from one to the other.

Close on the top of Serenity as he hits the top, landing gently as possible. He walks, slowly and deliberately, pulling his feet up with the slight effort of disconnecting magnets. Walks to the window. Very slowly, looks in.

INT. DINING ROOM - CONTINUING

We see his head — briefly — by the fore window, looking in at the group that contains everyone save River.

KAYLEE
It was when... when the Captain and Wash got took by Niska.

MAL
Ain't like to forget that any time soon.

KAYLEE
Well, we all went in, me too... Didn't make much account of myself, I'm afraid.

CINEMATOGRAPHY

Director of photography David Boyd on filming actors in 'space': "Sometimes we'll overcrank the camera, and so that's slow-motion; sometimes the actors, in conjunction with that, can move a little slower, a little more controlled. We also had the shots in wide of the character arriving onto the outer shell of the ship, and that's just done with wires; the speed of that and the way that it is done physically sells the fact that there's weightlessness out there. To have that going on as part of the work day is just plain fun, because all of those things have to come together in a perfect way for it to be believable."

MAL
(touches her head)
I got no problem with the notion of you not killin' nobody, Kaylee. Take it as my own fault that you were put in such a spot.

SIMON
What's this got to do with River? She wasn't even in that fight.

KAYLEE
Well, no, she was. I got pinned down, there was three guys and I couldn't... and then River comes up and she looks out, sees 'em all. They was spread out, you know, had some cover, but she just looked for a second and... She took my gun. Closed her eyes. Killed 'em.

SIMON
She shot them?

KAYLEE
All three dead in an instant. With her eyes still closed.

JAYNE
Well that's <FAY-FAY duh PEE-yen.> [a babboon's ass-crack.] You saw it wrong.

KAYLEE
Not a jot. And it weren't autofire, or luck... She just... She just did the math.

ZOE
You understand how that sounds...

JAYNE
What? She killed them with mathematics. What else could it have been.

KAYLEE
You couldn't've done it, Jayne. Nor you, Captain; not nobody can shoot like that that's a person.

SIMON
So River's not a person?

As they continue, the camera moves suddenly down to the floor, THROUGH the floor, pipes and wires visible, to the ceiling of:

INT. CARGO BAY - CONTINUING

Where River is standing directly below them, feet on the railings of the catwalk, ear as close to the ceiling as she can get, hearing every word. Or sensing them.

KAYLEE (O.S.)
Please don't be mad...

SIMON (O.S.)
I just want to understand what you're saying here. I thought River was your friend.

INT. DINING ROOM - CONTINUING

KAYLEE
She is. But Simon... the way she... right after, she looked at me and smiled, like nothing was wrong. Like we were playing.
(to the group)
Scared me.

There's a moment, as the group takes this in.

BOOK
Could be she saved your life, Kaylee.

KAYLEE
I'm all aware of that, I'm not trying to —

SIMON
She probably didn't even know what was going on! Thought it was a game.

JAYNE
Later on you can explain to me how that's a comfort. Might have to use some'a that math we been hearing about...

MAL
(running over Jayne)
What we got here to deal with is the larger issue. And the larger issue is we got someone on board this ship might be a danger to us.

Now the camera moves UP, again through pipes and wires, through the hull, to:

EXT. TOP OF SERENITY - CONTINUING

Where Early kneels, holding a listening device to the hull. The voices are coming through, somewhat static-y.

MAL (O.S.)
It's not a question of whether we like her... some of us have grown attached...

INT. DINING ROOM - CONTINUING

MAL
Kaylee, I know you have or you'd've spoken up sooner, which by the by you should have. I find River pleasant enough myself. But she's got an oddness to her, and it ain't just her proficiency with fire-arms. Girl knows things she shouldn't. Things she couldn't.

JAYNE
Are you saying she's a witch?

WASH
Yes, she's a witch, Jayne. She has had congress with the beast.

JAYNE
She's in congress?

WASH
How did your brain master human speech? I'm just so curious.

INARA
<BEE-jway, neen hen BOO-TEE-TYEH duh NAN-shung!> [Shut up, you inconsiderate schoolboys!] This isn't a joking matter. This is about your — about our lives. And River's.

MAL
Thank you.

SIMON
She's deeply intuitive, it's true she has a —

MAL
I don't think she's just intuitive, Doctor. I think she's a reader.

ZOE
Psychic?

WASH
Is that even remotely possible?

MAL
(to Simon)
You tell me. You been studying what they did to her.

SIMON
They've definitely altered the way she reacts to things, even the way she perceives... but I'm not...

WASH
Psychic, though? That sounds like something out of science fiction!

ZOE
You live in a spaceship, dear.

WASH
So?

JAYNE
(suddenly more uncomfy)
Back up a sec. You're saying she might really read minds?

MAL
Or near enough. Am I the only one thinking along those lines?

BOOK
No.

JAYNE
I don't like the idea of someone hearing what I'm thinking.

INARA
No one likes the idea of hearing what you're thinking.

BOOK
The Alliance could have any number of uses for a psychic. Any government would.

ZOE
A psychic or an assassin...

SIMON
She's just a kid.

His voice is quiet, but it stops them.

SIMON (cont'd)
She just wants to be... a kid.

MAL
I wish it were that simple.

JAYNE
Yeah, and if wishes were horses we'd all be eatin' steak. What do we plan to do about this?

MAL
Well, that's the question.

SIMON
I don't think she'd ever hurt any of us.

MAL
Maybe you're right.

He looks around, at all of them.

MAL (cont'd)
Well, I ain't making a decision on anything til I've thought on it awhile. It's late.

Looking at Inara:

MAL (cont'd)
We hit New Melbourne in three days time. We'll see who... We'll think of what to do by then. Let's get some rest.

Simon turns and goes quickly out the back. Kaylee follows.

INT. AFT HALL - CONTINUING

He is rounding the corner as she stops him.

KAYLEE
Simon —

SIMON
I gotta go check on my assassin.

KAYLEE
Simon please don't be mad at me. I had to say something.

He turns to her.

SIMON
I'm not mad at you. I just... She loves this ship. I think it's more home to her than any place she's been.

KAYLEE
What about you?

SIMON
I'm... I thought the hospital was home. I was really making a difference there... and embarrassingly large stacks of money, and I could've... I would be there now if she hadn't... if they had just left her alone.

KAYLEE
Is it so bad here?

SIMON
I don't even know if the Captain'll let us —

RIVER

"Also, I can kill you with my brain."

Of all the actors on *Firefly*, Summer Glau was the only one without any previous acting experience. With wide-eyed wonder and sheer terror, Glau admits the early days of the series were an intense learning curve for her. "I was very, very nervous. The first table read where we worked as a group, I didn't know what a table read was! I barely knew how to follow the script. They send you rewrites all the time and you have to put them into your original script and I didn't know how to do it!"

Part of her comfort with the role and her new vocation came from her rapport with Whedon. Taking the actress under his wing, Glau admits he helped push her creatively to trust her instincts and her talent. "Joss was so good at coaching me and getting a performance out of me," she smiles. "I need a lot of reassurance. I'm the kind of actress that comes on set every day thinking, 'What am I doing here? I have no business being here.' Joss is so good at bringing out the best in me. He never would give a lot of direction before a scene. He wanted to see what I would do with it and then he would talk me through it, finding things that would inspire me or get me going in the right direction. I think that everyone would probably say about Joss, that he sees things in his head exactly how he wants them. He is such a strong leader. You go on set and things go so quickly because he is really good at getting us on the right track. Also, our chemistry as a cast and a team has been incredible from the beginning. We were just meant to be together. Everybody has such strong ideas about their characters and I think from the pilot everyone was bringing so much to the table."

Over the season, Glau says discovering River's history was incredible to portray. "Everything was shocking. Whenever we got a script, it would usually be late at night when we were working on another episode. It would be so hard to focus on finishing out the episode we were on because we were all dying to know what would happen to us in the next script! River was just shocking every week: I got to dance in 'Safe'; in 'War Stories' I ended up

shooting people; and in 'Objects in Space' I fly somebody else's ship. It was spectacular. I got to do so many things that I never dreamed I'd do in my life."

With only half a season produced, Glau says the cancellation of *Firefly* was a devastating reality check about Hollywood, but also an incredible introduction to the tenacity of Whedon's fanbase. "When we were doing it, we were in our own world. Afterwards, when we got canceled, I went home to Texas for Christmas. It was just gone and over, all of a sudden. My mom went online to look at the message boards and I thought, 'Nobody is going to be on them anymore.' But they were just flooded with people saying, 'We are going to save this show, we aren't going to let go, and we are going to petition and riot!' This is when I realized it's powerful to be part of Joss's universe. The things that he creates are so special and beloved. His fans are so dedicated and I couldn't believe how they kept us alive. I think they made our movie. Joss created miracles all along and it was a miracle that he wanted to stay behind us, because god knows he could have moved on ten times over. But our fans love him and what he creates so much and it's a really special thing to be part of."

Now years after cancellation, Glau is still in awe of the support of those fans and what they give to her personally. "I'm constantly touched by the fans and the things that they've gotten for us or written to us. I get a lot of mail from people who suffer from depression or have schizophrenia or some kind of other mental illness and River has brought them comfort. I think the show as a whole teaches you about family and loving things unconditionally and being part of a team. River fights so hard to contribute to her family. Simon always said, 'River loves this ship. She just wants to stay here and be a part of this.' If the series continued, you would have seen more of what you saw in the film, which was River defeating the demons and things that haunt her mind and being able to go back to the people that care about her — her new family on Serenity. I think that is why people love the story and want more of it. It's a story about love and loving something that doesn't make sense. Mal is always looking at River and asking himself why he is keeping this liability on board when she isn't part of his family or his crew, yet he can't walk away from her. I hope that's what people remember about our story and keep with them."

KAYLEE
No, but, isn't there anything about this place you're glad of?

He looks at her. Something passes between them, something that draws them closer —

BOOK
G'night, you two.

He passes right through the moment and blows it completely. Simon and Kaylee go back to being awkward.

SIMON
Uh, I —

KAYLEE
No, yeah —

SIMON
Good night.

KAYLEE
Don't let the space bugs... bite...

He goes. She looks after him, feeling like the queen of Lame-donia. A beat, and she heads into the engine room, muttering:

KAYLEE (cont'd)
Space bugs...?

INT. DINING ROOM - NIGHT

It's later, and the Captain sits alone. He thinks a moment, then exits, killing the lights.

INT. FOREDECK HALL - CONTINUING

He goes to his door and kicks it in, starts climbing down. The camera moves away from him to the exterior hatch Simon and River used in 'Bushwacked'.

It opens.

Early comes quietly down, looking about him. Pulls off his helmet. And pulls out his gun.

END OF ACT ONE

ACT TWO

INT. RIVER'S ROOM - NIGHT

River is lying in her bed. She senses something, pulls the covers over her head.

INT. FOREDECK HALL - CONTINUING

Early looks around the hall. No one around. He holsters his gun, moves back to the hatch, puts his helmet in there and seals it shut.

He comes back into the hall and bumps into MAL, who's headed back to the dining room. Mal is completely taken by surprise — and Early is a blur, a little bit ninja as he pops Mal in the throat to keep him from screaming, gets in close and punches a nerve cluster in Mal's back. Mal pushes

him off and swings, connects only glancingly —

INT. WASH AND ZOE'S ROOM - CONTINUING

Zoe stirs — is something going on upstairs?

INT. FOREDECK HALL - CONTINUING

Early slams his foot into Mal's face, slamming the back of his head into his own ladder, Mal starts to drop — and Early shoots forward, GRABS him by the shirt, keeping him from falling.

INT. WASH AND ZOE'S ROOM - CONTINUING

Zoe rolls over. Nothing.

INT. MAL'S ROOM - CONTINUING

Early lowers Mal gently into the room, letting him drop the last of the way, unconscious. Closes the door from above.

INT. FOREDECK HALL - CONTINUING

He goes to the com and locks the rooms from the outside — this involves punching buttons by the com and hitting some graphics, the legend PRIVATE QUARTERS LOCKED coming up and a little red light appearing over each door. Except Kaylee's. He comes to Kaylee's room and the door is open. He listens a moment — nothing — then looks down the length of the ship.

INT. ENGINE ROOM - LATER

Kaylee is lying on her back, working under the engine. She yawns, goes back to work — hears something.

She sits up, looks out into the dark of the hall. Maybe a little unnerved. It's dark in here, most of the light comes from the lamp she's working by, and the hall itself is pitch.

KAYLEE
River...?

She stands, looks. Nothing.

She turns back to the toolbox, squats down to toss in a part, comes back up and Early is RIGHT behind her. She spins to see his face staring impassively, inches from hers.

She gasps, stumbles back. She's up against the wall here.

EARLY
I like this ship.

She says nothing. Looks frantically around.

EARLY (cont'd)
Serenity. She's good-looking. I mean she looks good.

KAYLEE
How did you get on...?

EARLY
It strains the mind a bit, don't it? You think you're all alone... Maybe I come down the chimney, Kaylee, bring presents to the good girls and boys. Maybe not, though.

He comes closer to her. She shrinks closer to the wall.

EARLY (cont'd)
Maybe I've always been here.

KAYLEE
What do you want?

He looks at the turning engine, mesmerized.

EARLY
That's her beating heart, isn't it? You pull off any one of a thousand parts, she'll just die. Such a slender thread...
(still looking at the engine)
Have you ever been raped?

A small beat —

KAYLEE
The Captain's right by —

J E W E L   S T A I T E

The scene where Early corners me in the engine room and basically threatens to rape me was probably one of the most emotional scenes in the whole series for me.

EARLY
The Captain's locked in his quarters. They all are. There's nobody can help you. Say it.

KAYLEE
There's... There's nobody can help me.

EARLY
I'm gonna tie you up now. And you know what I'm gonna do then?
(she can't answer)
I'm gonna give you a present. Get rid of a problem you've got. And I won't touch you in any wrong fashion, nor hurt you at all, unless you make some kind of ruckus. You throw a monkey wrench into my dealings in any way, your body is forfeit. Ain't nothing but a body to me, and I can find all unseemly manner of use for it. Do you understand?

KAYLEE
(tiny voice)
Yes.

EARLY
Turn around and put your hands behind your back.

She slowly does, terror on her face, as he pulls out a thin roll of tape. Pulls a strip out, says:

EARLY (cont'd)
Now tell me, Kaylee... Where does River sleep?

INT. PASSENGER DORM/SIMON AND RIVER'S ROOMS - NIGHT

Book exits the bathroom, in his sleepwear, towel over his shoulder, kit in hand. It's dark here as well, though there are safety lights enough to keep one from bumping into shit.

Book heads for his room, hears something at the top of the stairs. Turns back that way, looks up.

ANGLE: up the stairs — is complete blackness.

BOOK
Hello?

Nothing. He turns to go, hears another sound. Starts up the stairs, merely curious.

Early SLIDES down the handrails on both hands, shooting down at Book with both feet out, catching the Shepherd in the face at two steps up, sends him flying back as Early lands gracefully by him.

ANGLE: SIMON

wakes, hearing the thumps. There is silence after, but he's not satisfied. He climbs out of bed (he's just wearing drawstring pants) and opens his door, looking out at:

ANGLE: the hall where Book got slammed — is now empty. Simon looks around for a sec — then crosses to River's room to check on her. He slides the door open —

ANGLE: RIVER'S ROOM is empty.

SIMON
River...

He comes back into the hall, stands between the two bedrooms, not sure what to do... and the camera finds Early PERCHED on both ladders above him, almost spider-like.

Simon almost has time to look up as Early drops, lands straddling Simon's head, holding the ladders and swinging the Doctor up and SLAMMING him to the ground.

Simon's in pain, but Early comes over him and Simon GRABS him, throws him as he himself gets up, ready for a fight — but Early comes up with his weapon pointed at Simon.

EARLY
Doctor Tam, why don't you sit yourself down?

SIMON
Rather die standing.

EARLY
The intention is not for you to die. The warrant doesn't specify any particular need for you to be alive, but...

Early waves the gun. Backed into the curved corner of the hall, Simon sits on the steps. Early peers into the rooms.

EARLY (cont'd)
Where's your sister?

SIMON
Are you Alliance?

EARLY
(not understanding)
Am I a lion?

SIMON
What?

EARLY
I don't think of myself as a lion.
(smiles)
You may as well, though: I have a mighty roar.

SIMON
I said "Alliance".

EARLY
Oh. I thought —

SIMON
No, I was...

EARLY
That's weird.
(beat)
Where's your sister?

SIMON
I don't know. Who do you work for?

EARLY
This is her room.

SIMON
Yes.

EARLY
It's empty.

SIMON
I know.

EARLY
So is it still her room when it's empty? Does the room, the thing have purpose? Or are we... What's the word...

SIMON
I really can't help you.

EARLY
The plan is to take your sister, get the reward, which is substantial. "Imbue." That's the word.

SIMON
So you're a bounty hunter.

EARLY
That ain't it at all.

SIMON
Then what are you?

EARLY
I'm a bounty hunter.

SIMON
That's what I said.

EARLY
Yeah, but you didn't say it well. I'm named Early. I'm known to some — probably not your set, though. She sleep with anybody?

SIMON
River?

EARLY
Yeah, she grapple with any of the crew? Might be in their quarters?

SIMON
No!

EARLY
Maybe she does that you don't know about.

SIMON
This is insane. I'm not gonna help you find her in any case.

Early holds up his gun — not pointed at Simon, just observing it.

EARLY
I think this is very pretty. I like the weight of it.

SIMON
I thought the intention was not to kill me.

EARLY
You're missing the point. The design. Of the thing. It's functional. The plan is not to shoot you, the plan is to get the girl. If there's no girl, then the plan... well, it's like the room. You are gonna help me look for her.

SIMON
I don't think my last act in this 'verse is gonna be betraying my sister.

EARLY
You're gonna help me because every second you're with me is a chance to turn the tables, get the better of me, and it's the only chance your sister has. Maybe you'll find your moment. Maybe I'll slip. Or you'll refuse to help me, I'll shoot your brain out, and then I'll go upstairs and spend some time violating the little mechanic I got

trussed up in the engine room. I take no pleasure in the thought but she will die weeping if you cross me.

SIMON
(quietly)
You're out of your mind.

EARLY
That's between me and my mind. Let's start with these rooms.

ANGLE ON: BOOK, whose unconscious form is slumped in the other hallway. Simon (having grabbed a shirt) comes upon him quickly, checking to see he's not dead.

EARLY (cont'd)
He's not killed. Be a while before he comes to, but he'll mend.

SIMON
And which part of your plan dictated the necessity of beating up a Shepherd?

EARLY
That ain't a Shepherd.

Simon looks at Early, unsure if this is just more of his off-centerness. Early is looking down the hall.

EARLY (cont'd)
Open the rooms.

INT. INFIRMARY/PASSENGER DORM - A BIT LATER

The infirmary doors open. Simon steps in, Early behind, gun still held on the Doctor.

SIMON
She wouldn't come in here anyway. She hates this room. You see, Early, the people you're planning to sell her to cut up her brain in a lab like this. Tortured her. Teenage girl. Not some bandit on a murder run, just an innocent girl —

EARLY
You ever been shot?

A small beat.

SIMON
No.

EARLY
You oughta be shot, or stabbed, lose a leg... to be a surgeon. You know? Know the kind of pain you're dealing with.

What seemed like a threat becomes more like a distant observation — not that Simon is particularly comforted by this.

EARLY (cont'd)
They make psychiatrists get psychoanalyzed before they can get certified, but they don't make surgeons get cut on. That seem right to you?

Simon has no answer.

INT. CARGO BAY - MOMENTS LATER

The two of them enter the big, darkened bay. Early pulls out a small, powerful flashlight, shines it about. The locker with the spacesuits is near him, and the door is ajar. He moves to it — swings it open, gun at the ready. It's empty (except for a couple of spacesuits).

Early steps into the middle of the room, looks about at it.

SIMON
Come on out, River, the nice man wants to kidnap you...

EARLY
Shhh.

He looks at the walls, holds his arms out, moving them up parallel to the slanted walls.

EARLY (cont'd)
I like the way the walls go out. Gives you an open feeling. Firefly's a good design.

He motions with his gun for Simon to go upstairs. Heads up after.

EARLY (cont'd)
People don't appreciate the substance of things. Objects in space. People miss out on what's solid.

They reach the landing as he speaks, and he looks out over the room. Simon stands by him, unnoticed. He could just give a little shove —

And Early's gun is in his face, Early not even looking at him.

Richard Brooks
=EARLY=

♥ MAMA

helmet from FX base

Back

ShawnaTrpcic
=Firefly= ep II

Back

front

Nov 1?
Nov

zip from

silver

Chin guards
New rock
MOD:
OLANA
MICHAEL
COLOR:
ITALI NEGRO
N AUTIC
ACERO

Lycra

Boot
New rock
MOD: 373C #.174
SOLE: planing ung ro #8
ACERO PAINT Zone 6
COLOR: ITALI negro
Y AUTIC
ACER

SHOULD LOOK AND
FIT LIKE DARE DEVIL
or X-MEN

310·822·6518
© 310 962 1813,
Richard Brooks
6'3" 195 lbs
44L
35/35
14 shoe
7⅜

ACCESS FILE:

EARLY'S SPACESUIT

Chris Gilham of Global Effects: "The bounty hunter leather suit was something that the wardrobe department already had made. The helmet was a variant of the *Firefly* helmet but with parts re-sculpted and different details. We wanted to give the impression that they might have been made at the same factory. This one was painted with a silver undercoat which had areas peeling off to make it look like it's an aluminum helmet underneath. We bought a bunch of cast resin parts from another FX company which had closed down, and there are two details on the helmet we can't identify, one on the forehead and one on the chin. They could be part of Johnny Five from *Short Circuit* or even from *Aliens*. The two discs on the neck are from *Armageddon*."

Costume designer Shawna Trpcic: "One of my favorite guest characters was the bounty hunter, Early. I took his costume from everywhere from the *X-Men* to *Daredevil* to spacesuits — I did a lot of research on spacesuits to make sure that it looked like it could be airtight and he could actually survive. The helmet has the shape of the Alien's head in the *Aliens* movie, it's pointed in the back. Then there's the side-slung gun, which is Han Solo — I wanted to echo Mal, because if Mal just took one step further, he could end up doing something like that."

EARLY (cont'd)
It's not your moment, Doctor.

Simon takes a step back. Early points his light at Inara's shuttle.

EARLY (cont'd)
Companion lives there?

SIMON
Yes.

EARLY
Let's visit.

INT. INARA'S SHUTTLE - LATER

Inara is sitting up in bed. Simon stands near the entrance of the room, looking tense.

Inara, vulnerable and more than a little confused, looks from him to Early, who is peeking in the back room, gun trained steadily on Inara.

INARA
This is pointless, you know that.

EARLY
Two-hundred thousand seems fairly pointed to me. Money like that, I could retire, not that I would. What's life without work?

INARA
This is a smuggling ship. I've been here a year, I couldn't name all the places she might hide.

EARLY
I don't have a year.
(to Simon)
Your sister's becoming a real annoyance.

SIMON
I feel for you.

He heads to the exit, herding Simon ahead of him, talking to Inara.

EARLY
I'm not gonna waste my time threatening you, because I think you believe that I will kill people if someone upsets my plan. I'm gonna seal you in,

though. You just sit.

INARA
You can still walk away from this. I know you're tired.

He violently pistol-whips her, pointing the gun back at Simon as she feels the blood on her lip.

EARLY
Don't go visiting in my intentions. Don't ever.

He moves to the entrance. Before he shuts the door:

EARLY (cont'd)
(to Inara)
Man is stronger by far than woman. But only woman can create a child. That seem right to you?

He shuts the door on her.

INT. BRIDGE - LATER

Simon comes up the stairs from the front of the bridge while Early stands at the very front, looking down into the space, gun trained on Simon. He steps over to the middle with Simon, his manner tenser and the gun held with both hands at arm's length.

EARLY
(calls out)
All right! That's all the hide and seek I got time for!

INT. MAL'S ROOM - CONTINUING

Mal stirs, the voice barely reaching him.

INT. WASH AND ZOE'S ROOM - CONTINUING

She does the same.

INT. JAYNE'S ROOM - CONTINUING

He's sleeping right through it.

INT. BRIDGE - CONTINUING

EARLY
Now I know you're on this ship, little girl, so here's how this goes!

He points the gun at Simon's temple.

EARLY (cont'd)
You show yourself, and we finish this exchange, or your brother's brains'll be flying every which way.
(to Simon)
You understand, I'm sort of on a clock here, it's frustrating —

RIVER (O.S.)
You're wrong, Early.

He looks around, what the fuck — but realizes she's just coming over the com.

He speaks in a more normal voice, knowing she can hear him.

EARLY
I'm not wrong, dumpling. I will shoot your brother dead if you don't —

RIVER (V.O.)
Wrong about River. River's not on the ship. They didn't want her here, but she couldn't make herself leave, so she melted. Melted away.

INT. MAL'S ROOM - CONTINUING

He is hearing this also, and is more than a mite confused.

RIVER (V.O.)
They didn't know she could do that... but she did.

INT. WASH AND ZOE'S ROOM - CONTINUING

Even Wash is waking up... as Early's voice also sounds on the general com.

EARLY (V.O.)
Not sure I take your meaning there...

The two of them look at each other.

INT. BRIDGE - CONTINUING

RIVER (V.O.)
I'm not on the ship. I'm in the ship.

Simon looks almost as perturbed as Early.

RIVER (cont'd; V.O.)
I am the ship.

SIMON
River...

RIVER (V.O.)
River's gone.

EARLY
Then who exactly are we talking to?

RIVER (V.O.)
You're talking to Serenity. And Early... Serenity is very unhappy.

Early looks over at Simon, a bit freaked. Simon just shrugs. What are you gonna do?

END OF ACT TWO

ACT THREE

INT. ENGINE ROOM - MOMENTS LATER

Kaylee is sitting in the corner, hands tied behind her back, legs tied together. She hasn't moved since Early left her, she's so scared. After a moment...

JOSE MOLINA

One of our more veteran actors, who has been in everything under the sun, said that it was the rare time in his career that he would walk onto a set and he would talk to people and he could tell, at the time that they were doing the work, that people realized they were working on something special. Usually, you do a job, you go in, the product comes in and you go, 'Wow, that was pretty cool, I was a part of something great.' But in the middle of doing it, people were aware that this was something special.

Another moment I remember: I'm sure you'll hear this from every other person you talk to, but this cast was such a rarity and so fantastic to work with. I remember one time, about two-and-a-half months into production, Nathan called Gareth Davies, the producer, to book some time with him. And Gareth called Joss to go, 'Uh-huh, here we go. So it begins. This guy is going to talk to me because he has some problems.' And the entire reason Nathan was calling Gareth was because he wanted to sit down with him to tell him what a great time everybody was having and how happy they all were to show up to work every day, and what a joy it was to work on the show. Believe me, [an actor setting up a meeting to thank a producer] has never happened in my, or anybody else's experience, before or since. These guys were fantastic.

RIVER (V.O.)
Kaylee?

The voice is quieter, more intimate — this is not being broadcast for the public.

RIVER (cont'd; V.O.)
Kaylee, can you hear me?

KAYLEE
River...?

RIVER (V.O.)
You're afraid.

KAYLEE
(near tears)
He tied me up... I don't know where he came from, he just...

RIVER (V.O.)
It's okay. Gonna be okay.

KAYLEE
Is he gone?

There is a small beat.

KAYLEE (cont'd)
(panicked)
Is he coming back?

RIVER (V.O.)
He's not gonna hurt you, Kaylee; he's only visiting.

KAYLEE
I told him where you were, I'm sorry, I didn't know what —

RIVER
Shhhh... I'm fine. Only I need you to do something for me. Gotta be brave.

KAYLEE
I'm tied up, I can't —

RIVER
Got tools. Something sharp. Don't be scared. I'm right here.

INT. BRIDGE - CONTINUING

Early and Simon are very still. After a beat:

EARLY
Where'd she go?

SIMON
I can't keep track of her when she's NOT incorporeally possessing a spaceship, don't look at me —

EARLY
That's some nonsensical crap! Ain't nobody can do that.
(to the air)
You're somewhere on this boat! Somewhere with a com, playing games!

Her LAUGHTER filters over the com. It's somewhat unsettling.

EARLY (cont'd)
That's somewhat unsettling.

RIVER (V.O.)
Early, Mr. Jubel Early, bounty hunter... Can I call you Jubel?

Okay, freak time. How'd she know that?

EARLY
Ain't nobody calls me that.

RIVER (V.O.)
Your mother does. I'm sorry. Did. She's gone now.

EARLY
That supposed to scare me? Bringing up my mother?

RIVER (V.O.)
You're a liar.

A beat.

RIVER (cont'd; V.O.)
I don't think your intentions are honorable.

EARLY
Well, no, I'm a bounty hunter, it's not generally considered "honorable" so much as... I live by a code, though, which I think is worth —

BOOK

"You can't fix the bible, River."

Despite the fact that *Firefly* only lasted for an abbreviated season, one thing that has become legend was the amazing chemistry and rapport amongst the cast — a fact that is rare indeed in Hollywood. Having worked on more than fifty television series during his long career, Ron Glass admits that connection to the cast, among many other things, made *Firefly* a truly unique experience. Talking about the group dynamic, he offers, "When you sit around the table for a family dinner, you connect with all the people in your family, but you don't want to spend the same amount of time around each individual, all the time," he chuckles. "It was kind of like that. There were some people that you immediately feel more simpatico with than others, but the most significant thing for me was that I was really impressed with the commitment and the potential and the excitement that everybody seemed to feel toward the project and their individual characters. I think that kind of thing happens from the top down and that's really to Joss's credit that he was able to generate that kind of commitment and enthusiasm from people. I also think that because Nathan was the Captain, that his particular personality was just ideal for the character he was playing. His own commitment and willingness to do anything and for however long, helping to keep everyone's spirits up, was contagious. It made it easy to fall in line, whether it was in the script or just on the set. The tendency was to support wherever he was leading and that is pretty unusual. It wasn't a drag to do it," he laughs. "It was a pretty seamless experience as far as the chemistry and the devotion to the material. That is part of the reason it was so hard to let go. You

want to hold onto that type of experience because it feels good."

Of all the characters on the series, Shepherd Book was arguably the least revealed. His history was left largely unexplored, save for the occasional cryptic hints or comments the character would dangle from episode to episode. Alternately frustrating and engaging for fans, Glass admits he felt the same way. "Whenever I had a conversation with Joss about Book's background, he was generally as mysterious and evasive as what you saw played," he chuckles. "At times that felt a little aggravating, but ultimately it made it really, really interesting for me every time I saw a new script. It was intriguing! I still maintain and harbor great curiosity about how this character would have unfolded had the series continued. It was an uncertain thing for me and was at times unsettling, but it always remained exciting and adventurous. It was like two sides of a sharp sword, which ultimately I came to really enjoy and appreciate."

The legacy of the show has been the life it still maintains, even years after cancellation. The cast has traveled the world meeting fans who adore the show, and the actors that brought it to life. For Glass, that outpouring of support has truly been the least expected but most welcome aspect of the show. "It's a unique experience out of the many years of experience that I have had. It will always be singular and special and really close to my heart. I still have the opportunity to do conventions and meet people one-on-one and hear what they have to say. I get to have a human exchange between myself and the other person. It's very fulfilling and at the same time, it's an unusual honor to be able to thank people in person for their tremendous support. I like to let them know how much I really appreciate the response they have had for the whole work and towards me individually. One of the things I have really felt is how there is so much gentleness amongst these *Firefly* fans. There is a gentleness and respectfulness that is really humbling to be in the presence of. I've never had this kind of experience before and I might never again. In the moment, it's very special and I am really very honored to be a part of the whole thing." ◑

RIVER (V.O.)
You hurt people.

EARLY
Only when the job requires it.

RIVER (V.O.)
WRONG. You're a bad liar. You crawl inside me uninvited and you hurt my crew. I see everything that passes —

EARLY
I only hurt people 'cause they keep getting in the way of finding you!
(to Simon)
Tell her!

SIMON
What am I, your advocate?

EARLY
(thrusts out gun)
You are starting now.

SIMON
(to River)
He's really very gentle and fuzzy. We're becoming fast friends.

She giggles again.

EARLY
You folk are all insane!

SIMON
Well, my sister's a ship, I just have issues going way back.

EARLY
Does anybody care that I have a finely crafted gun pointed at this boy's head?

RIVER (V.O.)
I care.

EARLY
Then are you gonna come out, stop me from doing what I don't want to? You gonna be smart here, River?

There is no answer.

EARLY (cont'd)
River?
(beat)
Serenity?

INT. MAL'S ROOM - CONTINUING

He's shaking off the beating he took, pulling himself up.

MAL
(groggy)
What in the hell is going on here?

RIVER (V.O.)
I need you to do me a favor, Captain.

MAL
There was a guy, he was very blurry. You gotta be careful... How come there's a guy on board and

how come you're all of a sudden the ship?

RIVER (V.O.)
I know you have questions...

MAL
Yeah, that would be why I just asked them —

RIVER (V.O.)
But there isn't a lot of time. Captain, I need you to trust me.

MAL
Am I dreaming?

RIVER (V.O.)
We all are.

The Captain rolls his eyes.

RIVER (cont'd; V.O.)
Don't make faces.

He looks around. That was creepy.

INT. AFT HALL - CONTINUING

The door opens slowly and Kaylee peers out, still very afraid. A moment, then she starts down the hall, hugging the wall.

INT. BRIDGE - A BIT LATER

Early is getting a little more hyper.

EARLY
Just gotta think here...
(turns to Simon)
You know, with the exception of one deadly and unpredictable midget, this girl is the smallest cargo I have ever had to transport and by far the most troublesome. Does that seem right to you?

SIMON
What'd he do?

EARLY
Who?

SIMON
The midget.

EARLY
Arson.
(beat)
Little man loooved fire.

INT. FOREDECK HALL - CONTINUING

Kaylee peeks out around the corner. She can just see a piece of Early. She ducks her head back, then braves it, comes around and works the console.

GINA TORRES

On whether she misses *Firefly*: "You know, not so much, because I get to see the people that I worked with. That was the biggest joy for me, to meet and get to work with Nathan and Morena and Jewel and Alan and Adam and we're in touch and we love each other a great deal, so that's great. So I don't miss it so much, because I still have them in my life."

The red lights over the rooms go out.

Kaylee bolts down toward the cargo bay.

INT. WASH AND ZOE'S ROOM - CONTINUING

They are talking with River's voice.

ZOE
I can take this guy out.

RIVER (V.O.)
He's faster than you. All of you. And he's wearing armor.

WASH
What about his face? Is his face wearing armor?

RIVER (V.O.)
No touching guns. You just have to sit and be good. He'll leave soon.

Wash looks at Zoe.

WASH
This is all very surreal. I hate surreal.

INT. MAL'S ROOM - CONTINUING

He is standing right under his ladder, waiting.

RIVER (V.O.)
It's soon now. Are you ready?

MAL
How do you know what this guy's gonna do?

RIVER (V.O.)
I'm very close to him. He doesn't even see it.

MAL
Okay, but —

RIVER (V.O.)
Go now.

INT. BRIDGE - CONTINUING

The lights go completely out in the bridge and the hall. We may or may not see Mal scrambling up his ladder and disappearing around the corner in the far background as Early looks around, NOT seeing him.

Now Early's very freaked.

RIVER (V.O.)
You're not welcome here anymore, Early.

EARLY
And you think I'm gonna leave here empty handed?

RIVER (V.O.)
I know it.

EARLY
Yeah, you know me real well.

RIVER (V.O.)
Wish I didn't. You like to hurt folk.

EARLY
It's part of the job.

RIVER (V.O.)
It's why you TOOK the job. Not the chase, not the money... Power. Control. Pain. Your mother knew. Sadness in her when she waved goodbye, but she's relieved. Saw darkness in you. You're not well.

EARLY
You'll be wanting to shut up now.

RIVER (V.O.)
Big golden retriever, sitting on the lawn. Never took to you. Smell on you, the neighbors' pets, you did things to 'em... Cleaned up after. Shined and polished. Everything in here gleams.

Realization dawns on Early.

EARLY
Well, I'll be a son of a whore. You're not in my gorramn mind. You're on my gorramn SHIP!

EXT./INT. - EARLY'S SHIP - CONTINUING

We push in on River, who is in fact sitting in the pilot's seat of Early's ship, spacesuit on and helmet off. She is giggling again.

BEN EDLUND

Firefly really came at the right time in my life, helped restore my faith in television and just having the opportunity to work with a Joss, a Tim, a Jose and everybody was really, really valuable and important for me.

RIVER
It's very interesting. All these buttons...

INTERCUT THE TWO LOCATIONS:

EARLY
Okay, we're not touching those, okay?
(to Simon)
How the hell did she get on my ship?

SIMON
At this point, I'm as lost as you.

RIVER
Can see everyone from here. Wave to mommy. Put the gun away.

EARLY
(not putting it away)
Okay, I'm putting it away...

SIMON
No he's not.

He glares at Simon. Puts it away.

EARLY
I'm putting it away 'cause we're all reasonable people, don't want to be doing anything rash, fiddling with any dials.

RIVER
You're not right, Early. You're not righteous. Got issues.

EARLY
No! Or, yes, I could have that, you might have me figured out, that... Good job, I'm not a hundred percent — Are we gonna be reasonable?

RIVER
Talk too much.

EARLY
I'm flawed in that way, I sometimes go on, it's been said —

RIVER
It's okay, Early. I'm going with you.

Now it's Simon's turn to be unhappy.

SIMON
River, what are you —

RIVER
Don't belong. Dangerous. Like you.

INT. WASH AND ZOE'S ROOM - CONTINUING

They listen in, somber.

RIVER (V.O.)
Can't be controlled. Can't be trusted. Every-

---

body could just go on without me, not have to worry.

INT. PASSENGER DORM - CONTINUING

Where Kaylee is tending a groggy Book, also hearing this.

RIVER (V.O.)
People could be who they wanted to be, could be with the people they wanted... Could live simple. No secrets.

We move in on Kaylee, the words clearly affecting her.

INT. BRIDGE INTERCUT WITH EARLY'S SHIP - CONTINUING

The realization of what she's saying truly hits him.

SIMON
(quietly)
No...

RIVER
And I'll be fine. I'll be your bounty, Jubel Early. And then I'll just fade away.

Early smiles. Heads for the door.

EARLY
Well, finally something goes according to —

Simon throws himself at him, they clatter to the ground, tussling —

RIVER
Simon?

Early throws him off, pulls out his gun — and fires. Simon's eyes go wide.

River starts screaming.

END OF ACT THREE

ACT FOUR

INT. BRIDGE - CONTINUING

Early stands, looking at Simon, who's shot in the upper thigh. He holds his hand over the spilling wound, face blanching.

EARLY
See? That's what it feels like.

He takes off —

INT. FOREDECK HALL - CONTINUING

Takes a moment to make sure no one is waiting in the hall —

EARLY
You just hang tight, darlin'... Early's on the move.

Comes down the steps just as Simon launches himself at him, flying, knocking them both down, getting a couple of blows in before Early recovers enough to ninja his face.

Early takes off, rounding the corner —

EARLY (cont'd)
Spirited boy...

SPACE EFFECTS

Visual effects supervisor Loni Peristere: "I really liked working on 'Objects in Space'. We played with the quiet of space and how alone our crew could feel when they're being invaded. The only way to get rid of the nemesis was to go outside and kick him into space. I loved playing that sequence between the two vessels tied together, with the threat and jeopardy of the vastness of space. I loved that sequence on the top of Serenity. Making that feel real was a challenge and fun.

"We had a wonderful shot at the beginning where we approach Serenity from the back and enter in through the engine ducts and the vent shafts and the next thing you know we are in River's room. I loved that CGI helped tell that story. We were creating effects to create tension — it was great storytelling."

ANGLE ON SIMON trying to shake it off.

RIVER (V.O.)
Simon...

SIMON
River don't let him.... Don't let him do this...

RIVER (V.O.)
Have to.
(quieter)
Have to.

EXT. TOP OF SERENITY - CONTINUING

Early comes out the hatch, helmet on. He looks up to see his ship following perfectly, smiles.

EARLY
You made the right move, darlin'. Best for you to go with old Early.

MAL
You think so?

Early turns awkwardly (magnetic boots) to see

Mal, suited up and cabled to the ship, right behind him.

MAL (cont'd)
Some of us feel differently.

Mal double palms him in the chest, an inelegant move, but the force of it sends Early flying off the ship, gone, just like that, long gone.

Mal watches him go a moment, then looks up. After a long beat, River floats down to him. He steadies her as she lands. Looks at her affectionately.

RIVER
Permission to come aboard?

MAL
You know, you ain't quite right.

RIVER
It's the popular theory.

MAL
Get on in there. Give your brother a thrashing for messing up your plan.

RIVER
(going down)
He takes so much looking after...

INT. INFIRMARY/PASSENGER DORM/CARGO BAY - LATER

(This is possibly a one-er.)

Simon is on the table, talking Zoe through pulling

out his bullet. He watches her progress on the screen...

SIMON
To the left — your left. Now, very gently, pull that aside.

ZOE
This is really not my area of expertise, Doctor. I tend to be putting these into people more than the other thing.

WASH
(to Zoe)
Can I mop your brow? I'm at the ready with the fearsome brow mopping.

SIMON
You got the bullet. Okay, I'm gonna pass out for a minute, but you're doing great.

We find Mal and Inara at the entrance, watching.

MAL
So we live to fight another day.

INARA
Any chance that <SHIONG-mung duh kuang-ren> [violent lunatic] might survive?

MAL
Air he had left... chance'd be one in about... a very big number. Ain't odds I'd play. How's your lip?

He touches her face to look and she pulls away. They look at each other a moment, and she goes off into the cargo bay, where we find Book and Jayne coming downstairs to do some weights. (Jayne going first, Book spotting.)

BOOK
I just feel such a fool.

JAYNE
Yeah, all those years of priest training and you get taken out by one bounty hunter.

BOOK
Don't get me wrong — I gave him a hell of a fight.

JAYNE
Epic, I'm guessing.

BOOK
There'll be poems and songs, you just wait.

JAYNE
Hey, at least you got some play. I missed every damn thing.

We are moving off them to find the girls, Kaylee and River, sitting in the corner. They are playing, of all things, jacks. It's Kaylee's turn, and she's tellin' a tale, the ease between them returned...

KAYLEE
And then his folks come by to fetch him, and it turns out he's fourteen years old!
(they both laugh)
I mean, he must have been some kind of genetic experiment, 'cause I swear he was... My daddy whupped me so hard...

SUMMER GLAU

My favorite episode is 'Objects in Space'. It's a special, special memory for me working with Joss. It's the one episode when I got to work every day. I just felt like an important part of that episode. It was one Joss wrote and directed and there are so many images from it that I think about all the time and mean a lot to me. I loved working with Richard [Brooks], who played Jubal Early. He was fantastic, but that suit was really loud and smelled really bad. I felt so bad that he had to wear that. It was this huge, purple, leather suit!

There were some moments of River's physicality that I really worked hard on in that episode. River communicates a lot with her face and body. She's not good at talking to people: what she says never makes sense. So with 'Objects in Space', I really felt like her physicality was important to her expression. Joss said that there were things that he noticed after shooting it that he didn't even realize I was doing: ways that I was moving and touching the ship. He said that it really added to the episode.

The one mistake I wish I had never made started the 'Summer Blame Game'. It was the end of 'Objects in Space', and Jewel and I are sitting on the floor of the cargo bay, playing jacks. It was this long shot that everybody was in and it was a oner — where they move the camera through the entire ship and it's very complicated and delicate. I was the very last shot of the scene and they went through the whole scene perfectly and they come to me at the very end and I have one line! I'm looking at the ball and I don't remember to say my line. Nathan was all the way in the other end of the ship and I could just hear him say, '*Summmmer!* You ruined the whole shot!' So now it's a game — when anything wrong happens to anybody, it's my fault. It was so funny, when Nathan was working on *Buffy*, playing Caleb, and somebody messed up something, he yelled my name and I'm not even on that show!

She misses —

KAYLEE (cont'd)
Dyah! I'm at fours. Let's see you match that.

RIVER
(seriously)
I can win this.

KAYLEE
I'm hearing a lot of talk, genius. Come on. Show me what you got.

River looks at the ball in her hand.

CLOSE ON the ball, as she contemplates it. The solidity of the thing. We might notice it has a similar coloring to the moon we saw at the beginning of the show.

CLOSER STILL as she throws it down, camera goes slowly with it. It hits ground but the camera keeps going down, through the ship one last time, and out the bottom to:

EXT. SPACE - CONTINUING

Looking up at Serenity and panning left as she rockets away into the distance.

EXT. SPACE - ELSEWHERE - LATER

We see him, floating, turning slowly in space.

His helmet comes into view, his face amusedly resigned.

EARLY
Well... Here I am...

Tiny, alone, he floats.

END OF SHOW

STILL FLYING

A Celebration of Joss Whedon's Acclaimed Television Series

CONTRIBUTIONS FROM
BEN EDLUND
JANE ESPENSON
BRETT MATTHEWS
JOSE MOLINA

FEATURES AND INTERVIEWS BY
TARA BENNETT
ABBIE BERNSTEIN
KARL DERRICK

THE LEGACY OF FIREFLY

By Way of an Introduction...

Simon: Are you always this sentimental?

Mal: Had a good day.

Simon: You had the Alliance on you, criminals and savages... half the people on the ship have been shot or wounded including yourself, and you're harboring known fugitives.

Mal: We're still flying.

Simon: That's not much.

Mal: It's enough.

FROM THE FIREFLY EPISODE 'SERENITY', BY JOSS WHEDON

"*Firefly* was a family like I've never known. *Firefly* spoiled me rotten. You hope and dream that you will get a job where you get to go to work every day and say, "Oh my god – look what I get to do today! I kicked him in the engine!" You want to work with people that you really enjoy, and people whose work you can respect. You want to work with people, a crew, that every day not only wants to go to work and do their jobs well, and that are creative and capable, but also want to have a good time doing it. And are willing to sacrifice just to make it better and make it fun. I had that."

NATHAN FILLION, SPEAKING ON STAGE
AT THE 'STARFURY' CONVENTION, 2004

"The *Firefly* fans – the Browncoats – the charity work they've done remains extremely important to me and sort of stunning, and they themselves have become enough of an industry myth – a legend, I should say – that they make people think that my fanbase is much bigger than it actually is. I think they've helped other projects of mine, because people see that the revenue stream is about the long haul and not the opening weekend. These people have also proved that fans are not just people who chase actors around, but they're also people who form communities and help people for the joy of doing it. They have done as much as any group I know to change the face of fandom. I'm not entirely sure I deserve them, but I ain't giving them up."

JOSS WHEDON, INTERVIEW WITH ABBIE BERNSTEIN, 2009

❖ This page: On set during filming of the original pilot episode, 'Serenity'.

// BY JANE ESPENSON

Kaylee's hands were shaking. They had blood on them, too, not so much under the nails, but around the edges. A' course, she didn't need steady right yet. She needed strong. Later, if there was a later, the blood would wash clean. There was wordplay in there somewhere. Wash's blood.

Plan had been to break into this floating junkyard and steal replacement parts for her girl Serenity. Money was tight and supplies were thin and the place was run by Bad Guys anyway, guys who stole ships off humble smugglers. Only it turned out that the Bad Guys were smarter than they'd made provision for and now Wash was dying and Kaylee was hurt and Serenity had flown away without them. And now she and Wash were on this scrapped Series One Firefly they'd found in the yard. The ship felt a little like home but not at all *really* like home.

The deck plate was awful heavy. She wiped her hands on her coveralls, the teddy-bear patch taking the worst of it, and she reached for the incised handhold again. But the plates were gummed into place, held fast by their own weight and the grime of years — coagulated oil and, in places, the droppings of the scrapyard rats. She'd

seen some dead rats in the corners of the hold already, a few inside the radiation shielding, too — a bad place to nest, even in a dead ship. Rats are none too bright on the best of days.

She tried to ignore the pained noises that Wash was making as she got the edge of a plate lifted up and jammed a wedge under it. It felt not quite right to listen to someone's pain like that. He wasn't properly awake, neither, which made it even more private.

She made a lever, *Simple machines for simple people*, she recited in her mind, only slightly hysterically.

The Bad Guys had to be searching for them.

Her plan was going to require time and she was pretty sure time was something they had none of. Then she was sliding the plate aside. She had to go slow, since the metal on metal of it made a *skreel* noise that had her aching head beating like a drum and would surely bring the Bad Guys arunning if they heard it.

Wash woke up from the noise and his eyes were wide and scared. They made Kaylee's heart hurt. They both waited, holding their breath, listening for running footsteps and shouts that would mean they'd been discovered. They didn't hear anything, but that didn't mean too much. They might be Crepe-Soled Bad Guys. She hadn't really noticed.

She pulled Wash down into the opening between decks, carefully gripping him, neck-and-side, then ass-and-legs as she eased his lower half down, trying to be unaware of his body under her hands, trying to pretend there wasn't something awful in the intimacy. He hissed from the pain. More blood got on her hands, mixing with the oil and grime from the deck.

They were under the deck, now. It was dark and hot and full of massive grav dampeners. If she hadn't already known this ship was dead, she'd've known because down was still down here. If the grav dampeners were working, then the gravity underdeck would've been opposite and they'd've been pulled up toward the underside of the deck plating. Instead, down remained down, meaning that the gravity of the floating junkyard was still king here. She knelt on the subfloor. The rats down here weren't quite as dead and she heard them skittering. Kaylee had to figure rat-dancing as the least of their problems.

She hauled Wash as far astern in the ship as she could get him, bumping him over and under obstacles 'tween decks, her hands under his sweaty pits, his heels kicking at the subfloor as he tried to help push himself along. When she was exhausted and he was more or less unconscious again from the pain, she left him and made her way back to the treasure chests — to the dampeners.

The damps were big, a' course, taller than she was. She lifted open the metal shielding at the bottom of the first damp, exposing the control assembly. There, held in a big clamp like a fig in a baby's hand was a short, fat rod with copper rings around it. That was a honey, and that was what she needed. They were Honnecourt Capacitors, but everyone just called them honeys. It took a little muscle work to pull 'em, but she worked her way down the line, trying to be quiet and fast. She fashioned a leather strap into something like a bandolier and tucked them into that, crossways to her body. But even then, five was as many as she could carry. She crawled her way back to Wash, listening for people outside the ship, even though she wasn't sure she'd hear 'em until it was too late.

Series One Fireflies were rare as hen's lips and it wasn't often you'd get to play in one. A' course, it would be better if Wash wasn't wheezing now, making a very slight bubbling noise that she hated with her whole being. She sat down next to him and started working on the rods. These were set to work in the damps, making it so the contents of the ship didn't float around. She needed 'em to work in the rotor, so they'd make

the ship able to resist the pull of the junkyard's own gravity system. It required some math and some guesswork, but she figured she was as apt to get it right as anyone was, which wasn't very, but worth a shot. It would make for a hell of a bothersome ride, but escapers can't be choosers.

"Hey, Wash? You're not sleeping there, are you?"

"Me? No way. I'm dying. No time to sleep."

"You're not dying."

"No? I'll show you."

"Shut up." Then, after a moment's thought, she added, "Keep talking."

She heard definite footsteps then, from outside the ship. From right below, sounded like. And voices. Men, saying things like "Back half a' the yard's clear." and "Look over there." She locked eyes with Wash until the voices faded.

"They might come back for us," she said. She didn't mean the searching men.

He knew what she meant.

"That would be stupid. Mal isn't stupid."

"Well..."

"He's not stupid about stuff like this."

"Zoe might make him come get you."

He made a face, rejecting that.

"Not her style. She's a soldier."

"But she loves you."

"Like air."

She was pretty sure the bullet that had gone through his shoulder was higher than his lungs. She was also pret' sure it was that same bullet that had knocked her on the head. Went through him on its way to her. All its velocity spent, it was like a thrown rock. A sharp hard heavy tiny rock thrown by a machine. Her injury made it hard for her to concentrate. Also, *his* injury made it impossible for her to concentrate, since she was thinking he might've developed a tendency to stop talking and die all of a sudden.

She heard a sound and she froze. Maybe a footstep inside the ship. Maybe not.

She had to leave him to carry the honeys out to the grav rotor. It was an interior scramble through the ship, through hot tight passages. The rotor was another string of damps, only these were arranged in a ring 'round the ass of the ship, not in a line underdeck. She popped 'em open, one by one, pulled out their spent and charred honeys and put in the new ones. Like changing light bulbs, only maybe with the chance to save their lives. She traded out the five she had and went back for more.

Every time she passed Wash, he'd wake up and look at her like he was surprised. He was a little less there every time. She sat down next to him with another bunch of honeys and set about adjusting them.

She thought about Simon and how she would feel if he was gone. Like she couldn't breathe. Like air. She didn't want to think about that.

"Hey, Wash. I can fix this ship, but I can't fly it."

He opened his eyes, which surprised her a little. For a minute he'd been more landscape than person. He grinned, then looked like he regretted it.

"You make this pile of *gou shi* fly and I'll pilot it."

"It's not a pile of *gou shi.*"

He moved a hand and pointed at something.

Kaylee looked and then smiled.

"It has piles of *gou shi in it*. Not the same thing."

He closed his eyes and she felt colder.

She heard the footsteps and the voices more often now outside the ship. That meant they were working a search grid. Sooner or later, this ship, this hulk among the other hulks, would be searched.

"What are you doing?" He coughed after he asked the question, but she ignored it.

"Fixing it."

"How?"

"Moving the gravity around."

"Well, of course."

She crawled to the grav rotor again. A five-minute trip there. Then ten minutes to get the honeys into place. Then five minutes back, her bandolier empty. Sometimes she'd hear Wash coughing before she got to him. That made her worry because sound carried. The times when she didn't hear him made her worry more. She pulled the last batch of honeys and sat next to him again.

"Does it bother you? About Mal and Zoe?"

"What?"

The way he said "What?" was all drifty and unsure, as if what he meant was "What are you and why are you standing between me and the vivid blue peace that is death?" So she set a honey on the sub-deck *hard*, so it made noise, and she asked again, more loudly:

"Does it bother you that her first loyalty is to him?"

He went "Huh," at that. A little irked, which struck her as shiny. Seemed to her a man couldn't die with irk in him.

"Does it?"

"She loves me helplessly."

"Mal's a hero. Coat and hair and tight pants and big ol' shoulders with no holes in them."

"You're provoking me."

"Ain't I though?"

"This hurts." It was the first time he'd talked about pain. She didn't like it.

"Why in the whole 'verse does Zoe love you, Wash?"

"I'm funny."

"Really? I'd love to hear that some time."

"I'm good in bed."

"Not what she told me." This was a lie. Zoe had said he was good. She'd used gestures.

"I'm cute."

"Not at the moment. Gotta say, I'm finding this to be an enduring mystery."

After a while, he said, "She loves me because I love her for the right reasons."

"Clearly nonsense."

"Well, yes."

The work with the honeys had become

automatic. Kaylee carried the last ones out through the hot cramped obstacle course of the ship and returned. She crouched and touched his non-holey shoulder and asked him, "Got an answer yet?"

He didn't answer for a while, but finally he said, "I'm a carrier."

"What? Like for a disease?"

"Yeah. I don't suffer from heroism, but everyone around me does, so I figure I'm a carrier."

"Zoe was a big damn war hero before you even knew her..."

"'S retroactive." His voice sort of sank over the horizon and she hoped he was just asleep.

All the honeys had been moved, so she went back and faced the grav rotor. Looking at the big exterior spinning ring from the inside, while it wasn't spinning, made it hard to figure out if this was going to work. She couldn't turn anything on, run any power through the system without calling the attention of the still-circling Bad Guys to them. So she sat and stared and played a game she liked to call "Kaylee is an electron" in which she traced the interior mechanism in her head. She found a half-dozen places to be concerned. Parts to check, connections to verify. But a voice rang out, way too close – "Did anyone check the Firefly?"

She raced back through the internal jungle of the ship and found Wash looking around with wild eyes. He smelled like sweaty metal and she

realized it was the blood. It had soaked near half his less-than-tasteful shirt now. She dropped down next to him and whispered, "Be quiet."

"Kaylee —" he whispered back, "they're getting in. Go start the engine."

"It's not done."

"Will it start?"

"No."

"Are you sure?"

"I'm almost certain."

"Go and start the damn engine."

She shook her head. Then he started talking louder. And louder:

"Go. START IT. *GO.*"

Now from outside there was a shout and there were running feet. So she had no choice. She swore at Wash over her shoulder as she ran.

She approached the main body of the engine. She was out of breath, shaking. She started the reactor. It made a sound not unlike Wash's wet cough. Then it died.

She reached past the shielding, thinking of Wash, feeling the awful hot-ants feeling on her skin. This was the deadly life's-blood of the ship. A definite no-touch-'em, but... she forced open a tiny stuck valve... The reactor coughed again and then her feet left the floor. So did a dozen dead rats and a few live ones, twisting and exclaiming.

She whipped her hand out of the engine. She had done it. They were floating. The grav rotor was negating the junkyard's gravity as it buoyed the ship.

The lack of gravity made her feel much worse. She'd already felt light-headed and making that literal was too much for her. The only thing that really helped was seeing Wash swimming toward her. If the lack of gravity had been bad for her, it had been very good for him. He was holding his left arm braced across his chest, but he was swimming with the right, brushing floating rats out of the way as he pushed off in the direction of the bridge.

A live rat did a fancy little swan dive into her line of sight. Kaylee shoved it away and watched Wash go.

———

Six hours later, Simon was assessing the amount of radiation she'd been exposed to. Across the room, Zoe was bent over Wash's cot, doing her best to embrace him without causing him pain. Kaylee tried to watch them, but Simon was being distracting on account of his existing.

"You'll be okay," he told her. She knew that's what he liked to say when he didn't have instruments good enough to tell him the truth.

"And Wash?"

"He'll be fine. I have everything I need to fix him."

Kaylee thought Zoe was probably everything he needed. Which brought the opposite question back to her mind again. Why was he what Zoe needed?

"I know why Zoe loves him," she told Simon, speaking softly, which made him lean in. Bonus.

He glanced over at them.

"Why?"

"He's a carrier."

"What? Like with a disease?"

"Yeah. Just like that."

"I don't understand."

Kaylee remembered their conversations between the decks of the Series One and she knew one of them had kept the other alive.

"He's a man what makes heroes." ◑

THE WRITING PROCESS

By Jane Espenson

I've been asked to describe the writing process on a Joss Whedon show. I am primarily a *Buffy* writer, and I'm not in the *Firefly* writing room that often, but the general procedure is similar.

Okay, first there is the idea. This is usually something that Joss brings in, and it always begins with the main character – in my case, almost always with Buffy. We spend a lot of time discussing her emotional state, and how we want her to change over the course of the season. Frequently this in itself will suggest a story area – we will find a story in which we explore her mental state metaphorically. The episode 'Same Time, Same Place', was centered around Willow... we wanted to explore her emotional distance from the other characters. This turned into a story in which no one could see or touch Willow and vice versa. The episode 'Conversations with Dead People' dealt in part with Buffy's ambivalent feelings about her calling. She explored the feelings during a mock therapy session with a vampire she was destined to kill. Notice that the episode ideas *begin* with "what is she going through?" and never with "what would be a cool Slaying challenge?"

Once we have the central theme of the episode, and we understand how the main character will change during it, we begin "breaking" the story. This is done as a group, with the entire staff participating, except for anyone who is currently out writing the script for the previous week's episode. Breaking the story means organizing it into acts and scenes. When the break is complete, the white board in the writers' room is covered in blue marker, with a brief ordered description of each scene.

The first step in breaking an episode, once we know what the story is about, is deciding on the act breaks. These are the moments before each commercial that introduce danger or unexpected revelations into the story... the moments that make you come back after the commercials. Finding these moments in the story help give it shape: think of them as tentpoles that support the structure.

Selecting the moments that will be the act breaks is crucial. Writers who are just starting out, writing sample scripts that they will use to find that first job, often fail to realize this – I remember changing what the act break would be in a script because I wanted it to fall on the correct page. This is a bad sign. The act break moments

should be clear and large. In my *Firefly* episode, 'Shindig', the third act ends with Mal stabbed, badly injured, in danger of losing the duel. It does not end when Mal turns the fight around, when he stands victorious over his opponent. They're both big moments, but one of them leaves you curious and the other doesn't.

After the act breaks are set, the writers work together to fill in the surrounding scenes. When this is done, there is one white board full of material. At this point the work-dynamic changes completely, and it stops being a group project. At this point, the single author of the episode takes over. She takes the broken story and turns it into an outline. (Or possibly a "beat sheet", a less detailed version of an outline.) An outline is usually between nine and fourteen pages of typed material that fleshes out the broken story. It clarifies the attitudes of the characters, the order in which events happen within scenes, and often includes sample dialogue and jokes. A writer usually writes an outline in a single day.

The complete outline is turned in to the showrunners – Joss Whedon and Marti Noxon on *Buffy* or Joss and Tim Minear on *Firefly*. The writer is given notes on the outline very quickly, usually within the day. These notes are often quite brief and almost always have to do with the *tone* of the scenes – "make sure this doesn't get too silly," or "I see this as more genuinely scary."

At that point, the writer starts work, writing the script itself. Many of the writers go home to do this. They are excused from story breaking until their first draft is done. (The rest of the staff, of course, moves on to breaking the next episode.) The writing of a first draft takes anywhere from three days to two weeks, depending on the demands of production. Sometimes

the production schedule requires that more than one writer work on a given episode, splitting it into halves or even thirds – interestingly, this often results in very nice episodes and isn't as jarring as you might expect, because we've all learned to write in the same style.

The first draft turns a dozen-page outline into approximately 52 pages of action and dialogue. People outside the writing process are sometimes disappointed to learn that we are following a detailed outline. They feel that there can be little creative work left to do in the actual writing, but this is not the case. This is, in fact, the most exciting and freeing part of the process... every word spoken, every punch thrown, is spelled out by the writer at this stage. For me, this, more than during filming, is when the episode actually becomes *real*.

After the first draft is turned in, the writer gets another set of notes. These may be light or extensive, but on a Joss Whedon show, these rarely result in a rethinking of the episode. The broken story remains the same, although the words expressing it may change. Even an extensive note session rarely lasts more than an hour, and usually is much shorter than that. The writer takes these notes and in the next few days, produces a second draft. *Buffy* scripts usually go to a third draft and sometimes a fourth, but by the end of the process the changes become very small indeed – "change this word" or "cut this joke."

At the end of the process, Joss or Marti or Tim usually take the script and make a quick rewriting pass of their own. This produces the SHOOTING DRAFT.

Then it is filmed!

Congratulations – that's an episode! ◀

ORIGINALLY PUBLISHED ON FOX.COM, 2002

NATHAN FILLION

Captain Malcolm Reynolds

NATHAN ON THE LONGEVITY OF THE FANBASE:
When I was doing *Firefly*, I thought the show would last a long time. That it didn't was a surprise to me, and then likewise, for such a short life, that it's had such incredible legs, that has been a surprise. I knew it would live in my heart, because I really enjoyed it, I had a great time, and I can't deny that I learned so much from that project, I learned so much from Joss, but no, I had no idea [the fandom would last so long]. Pleasantly surprised!

INTERVIEW WITH ABBIE BERNSTEIN, 2009

ON WHY HE LOVES THE FANS:
There's nothing like going to Edinburgh, a place where I've never been – it's a whole other country – and you come in and there's a theatre full of 800 people who are right there, hanging on your every word, and laughing at all my crappy jokes.

INTERVIEW WITH CHUCK THE MOVIE GUY, 2005

ON STARTING OUT HIS CAREER IN THE SOAP
ONE LIFE TO LIVE:
Bob Woods, he played my uncle, he played Bo Buchanan. I was Joey Buchanan, and two years into my three-year contract he pulled me aside and said, "Look,

I'm here to tell you that they are going to come and renegotiate your contract. I'm telling you, say no. The harder you say no, the harder they are going to make it to leave. They offer you more money, but daytime drama is the golden handcuffs; they're gold, but they're handcuffs. If you leave and go to LA and try it out, if it doesn't work out they'll take you back, so go out there and try your luck." So every time I go to New York, I buy Bob a bottle of something nice.

INTERVIEW WITH ZETAMINOR.COM, 2005

ON A SOURCE OF INSPIRATION FOR HIS PERFORMANCE AS MAL:
A friend of mine grew up in Texas and he worked on a farm with his grandfather. He would tell me these amazing stories of his grandfather, who can't be flustered. This one story that particularly struck me was, they were castrating bulls. The process is that you throw them into this stall, close the gate behind them, do your business and get the next one in there. While they're getting this one bull in, they're shutting the gate, the bull kicked and hit the gate between his thumb and a post. And it severed his thumb, which remained inside his glove, but it was hanging. He was, "Oh well, we have six more to do, so let's keep this going." He didn't show the pain in any way. And there's my friend Cory, nine, ten years old going, "Grandpa, you have to go to the hospital!" crying. Because of him he decided to go, but I think he was a tough man. He's had some hard living. That's the kind of man I imagined Malcolm to be, he grew up on a ranch. He's a hard worker, not somebody who cries from a little pain.

INTERVIEW WITH ZETAMINOR.COM, 2005

ON HIS 'FIGHT CLUB' TRAINING REGIME FOR THE MOVIE, COMPARED TO SUMMER GLAU'S:
I was there barely three weeks. And I would complain about my time there, and every time I'd come in, I'd see

NATHAN FILLION

Summer doing her thing, kicking something above her head about sixty times. I'd be warming up and doing my stuff, cool down and leave, and she's in the corner fighting nine guys. And she had to start months before us. She worked really hard.

INTERVIEW WITH ZETAMINOR.COM, 2005

from each other and the work, and I attribute a lot of that to Nathan. I felt like we were a family and I would be taken care of – there were several incidences during the shoot in which I came to Nathan for help with certain things and he was right there. I feel like that's 100 percent the case.

SPEAKING ON STAGE AT THE 'SERENITY' CONVENTION, 2005

JEWEL STAITE AND MORENA BACCARIN ON NATHAN BEING THE 'LEADER' OF THE CAST, BOTH ONSCREEN AND OFF:

Jewel: I think we all naturally follow Nathan without realizing that we are following Nathan. We were all on set one day and sitting in our chairs on a break and somebody walked by with a platter of sandwiches to take to the craft services table. Nathan said, "Oh hey they've got sandwiches, let's go check it out." And everybody went [mimes standing up and following after Nathan], and then we kind of looked at each other and said, "Why are we following him? We just ate. I'm not even hungry!" I just do as he tells me.

Morena: It's true, we all kind of just follow the Captain. It's written in there, we may as well do it! But no joke, I'm going to take a serious note here – I'm not kidding. When I first came to the set everybody was already there, and I found the tone had been set for what we were to expect

ON 'OUT OF GAS':

I really enjoy that moment of seeing Malcolm Reynolds looking across that ship yard and seeing Serenity lying up there in the blowing sand. I think that's the moment where he fell in love. Joss Whedon said it was like seeing a girl across a dance floor and falling for them – love at first sight.

SPEAKING ON STAGE AT 'THE WHITE ROOM' CONVENTION, 2004

ON WHY *FIREFLY* IS PARTICULARLY SPECIAL TO HIM:

I've had jobs that I've preferred more than others simply because I've gotten to meet and make friends with great people. I've pulled at least one very close friend from every project I've done with the exception of *Firefly*, where I pulled all of them – they're *all* my friends. ◐

INTERVIEW WITH FIRSTSHOWING.NET, 2007

BATTLE PLANS

Storyboarding the Battle of Serenity Valley

"I got involved with *Firefly* in the very beginning stages," remembers Charles Ratteray, a Los Angeles-based storyboard artist, concept designer and illustrator, who started out as a special effects intern at Stan Winston Studio thirteen years ago, and has since worked as a freelancer on such memorable TV shows as *Battlestar Galactica*, *Buffy the Vampire Slayer* and *CSI*.

It was Ratteray's job to help turn the Battle of Serenity Valley from the 'EXT. SERENITY VALLEY – NIGHT: Battle rages' of Joss Whedon's script into the tense, attention-grabbing sequence that was originally planned to launch the entire series.

"Loni Peristere of Zoic Studios came to me and asked me to board out the first battle sequence in episode one," Ratteray continues. "He was my main window into the production part of the *Firefly* experience. When necessary I accompanied him into meetings with Joss and the rest of the creative crew over there. For the most part I completed the boards at Zoic and at my private studio."

Though the artist also contributed some ship designs, and storyboarded other sequences for the series (some of which are featured in the 'Ships of the 'Verse' section

❖ This spread and overleaf: Ratteray's storyboards for the sequence contain some shots that were ultimately not filmed.

of this book), that opening scene remains his favorite: "It really set the mood, and had loads of action and emotion driving the visuals. And of course it was a kick-ass way to set the tone of the episode."

All these years later, as he dug deep into his archive to supply the art that is published here for the first time, he still has fond memories of his time on the series. "*Firefly* was an awesome show. Masterfully thought out and thoroughly entertaining. It's not surprising it has generated such a loyal following. As far as the Browncoats go, they're really, really cool. 'Keep the torch burning, never give up' – I can definitely identify with that line of thinking." ◐

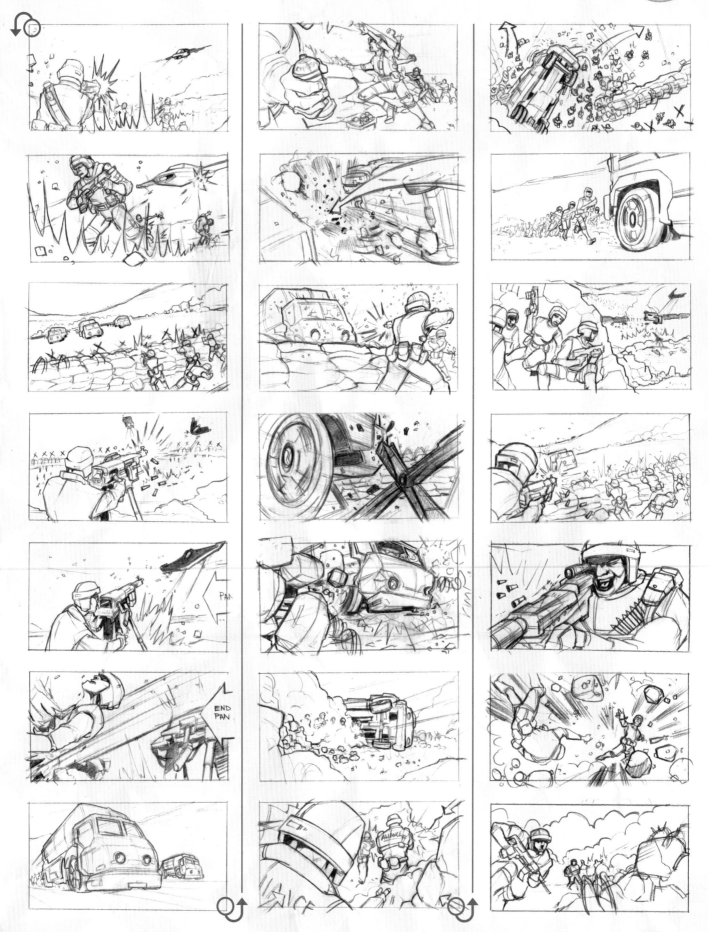

GINA TORRES

Zoe Washburne

GINA ON WHY JOSS CAST HER AS ZOE:
I think he hired me because he saw a great deal of what he had written and so there was never really a whole lot of discussion. He felt confident and comfortable with what I was bringing to the table, which is a quiet authority. Zoe's presence is more often more important than anything that she can say. When she speaks, it's always for a reason; for a particular reason. She's not talking just to be talking. I think that if Zoe is displeased or if she's happy, we want to feel like the temperature is literally changing in the room, and that was my job.

INTERVIEW WITH BLACKFILM.COM, 2005

ON THE PROMINENT ROLES FOR WOMEN IN THE 'VERSE:
I was happy about it. Clearly when you are looking into the future... as far as we've come now, you have women in the trenches now, they are in Iraq and in the work place. If you project that 500 years into the future, of course we are going to be in positions of power and be even more capable, because we are part of the workforce. As human beings we have to use each other and what we're best at. And my character Zoe is clearly a fabulous, kick-ass, capable soldier. Why wouldn't you want that person to be your right hand?

INTERVIEW WITH ZETAMINOR.COM, 2005

GINA TORRES

ON THE SHOW'S DISTINCTIVE DIALOGUE:
What is so interesting about the writing, is that [Joss] has taken this futuristic world that he has created and all the circumstances that have sort of fed into this world that you see in front of you, and an element of that is what we refer to as 'Joss speak'. It's the English language ever so tweaked enough to make you a little crazy [laughs] as an actor, but it sort of informs everything else surrounding it, so maybe a line that you may have heard before doesn't sound the same. Because it doesn't sound the same it holds a different weight, or it resonates differently in the ears, and I think that just makes it more interesting.

INTERVIEW WITH ZETAMINOR.COM, 2005

ON THE FANS' REACTION TO THE CANCELLATION:

Some were angry [laughs], most of them were sad. They found us early, they were sort of shocked that we disappeared because we were on the air for eleven episodes and we were pre-empted as often as we aired. We might be on one week and then we wouldn't be on for two weeks because of the baseball playoffs or whatever it was. They felt like they were teased with the promise of a show that they could be dedicated to and be interested in and see how it played out. And then we were gone as quickly as we appeared. I think that's what helped with the sales of the DVD, suddenly there was enough talk about it, maybe enough people had seen it, but they were just completely dissatisfied and wanted to know what happened. Because it is good storytelling, they are intriguing characters, and, you know, how do you feel when your favorite show is cancelled? You feel lost a little bit. *Cheers* was on the air for years and people still miss that show! I think we just sort of filled a niche that wasn't available on television at the time.

But it is incredibly gratifying to be a part of something that you knew was special from the very beginning, that was not understood. There was really no effort, that we could see, to make that happen and then it [was] released to the world and the world responded in the way that it has... yes, absolutely it's incredibly vindicating.

INTERVIEW WITH ZETAMINOR.COM, 2005

ON HER REACTION TO WASH'S DEATH IN THE MOVIE:

There was definitely a collective gasp heard across the nation when we all got the script and read it. I adored Alan, and I adored him as Wash, as my pretend husband. I thought we were an amazing couple. In a way, it might hurt you to hear this, but since there is no sequel to *Serenity* it is a relief, because I can't imagine Zoe without him. I really can't.

INTERVIEW WITH IFMAGAZINE.COM, 2006

OBJECTS IN SPACE

A selection of Firefly props

Some of the props in this section have become iconic amongst the Browncoats, while others were only glimpsed onscreen. All of them, however, played their part in adding to the rich texture of the 'verse...

ALLIANCE SONIC RIFLE

EPISODES: 'TRASH' AND 'ARIEL'

This is an unusual prop. It's a rare example of a non-lethal weapon in science fiction. It's in good company: the phaser from the original *Star Trek* had a stun setting.

The design is a deliberate choice by Joss Whedon and the producers to allow the possibility of an essentially harmless weapon in the 'verse. The theory is simple: compressed and focused sound waves in a narrow frequency band.

Originally one of eight made by Applied Effects in Los Angeles, this prop appeared twice in *Firefly*, both times in the hands of purplebellies. At the time of printing of the first *Official Companion* books, the whereabouts of the screen-used props was unknown. One has since come to light.

This prop is also unusual in that there was not time to make rubber stunt copies of it, so the Sonics used in the fight and action sequences are fully detailed 'hero' versions. The four surviving Sonics do show evidence of a tough life.

It is a heavy, solid piece, made in five resin sections

cemented together. The emitter tip is of machined aluminum with red painted details. The models for the emitter focus dishes were modified *Flintstones* jello dishes. The color scheme is a dark metallic blue with gunmetal and silver details.

There's an interesting 'technical' section on each side, apparently made from bashed model kit parts.

The base prop for the original model was a 'Foosh' rifle from the Arnold Schwarzenegger film *The Sixth Day*, also made by Applied Effects.

Not bad for "high-tech Alliance crap".

BOOK'S BIBLE
MULTIPLE EPISODES

At a mere 6 inches by 4.25 inches by 1.25 inches, this King James compact reference version of the Holy Bible, from Thomas Nelson publishers, doesn't look like anything special, other than being the 'Good Book' of course.

This leather-clad tome, now bearing the signature of one Ron Glass, appears in the opening sequence of *Firefly* and is the badge of office of Shepherd Derrial Book.

The script for the episode 'Jaynestown' required River

to mutilate Book's Bible in an attempt to 'fix' it. Summer Glau insisted on undertaking the task herself. The prop is annotated throughout with blue, red, green and orange marker; some of the pages are folded and some torn out altogether.

On page 108, "Jesus loves me this I know" is written in blue pen.

The Bible was sourced by the on-set propmaster Skip Crank, and was one of several shown to Joss Whedon as likely candidates for the Shepherd's constant companion. Gifted to Ron Glass when the show was cancelled, the Bible remained in Ron's care until it was auctioned for charity at the Flanvention in December 2005. Ron signed the book for the lucky winner.

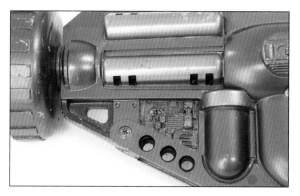

JUBAL EARLY'S PISTOL
EPISODE: 'OBJECTS IN SPACE'

Jubal Early is dangerous. So's his shiny pistol.

It doesn't obey any of the rules of practical, real-world weapons. It has no ammunition storage, no means of loading ammo or removing it, no power source, no apparent safety device, no front sight, no rear sight. It's a nonsensical sci-fi collection of mercurial silver blobs and brass bits on a set of slick black rubber grips.

It's very cool though.

The prop is constructed largely from pieces of machined and polished alloy. It seems to have been machined from solid metal. The barrel is a single piece of thick walled brass tubing, with a matching brass rod underneath. The rod is still bent from use on set.

The grips are a set of commercial black Pachmayr rubbers. The trigger is a simple pivoted lever on a return spring. There seems to be no internal mechanism of any kind.

But "I like the weight of it."

BURGESS' LASER
EPISODE: 'HEART OF GOLD'

Few bad guys are as bad as Rance Burgess, the archetypal evil-local-landowner-who's-brought-a-town-to-its-knees. Burgess is self-appointed judge, jury and executioner who makes his own "distinction between legality and morality".

'Heart of Gold' is a very traditional story of good versus evil. Folks in distress (usually some kind of dress, anyway), rescued by hired guns from out of town — its theme is repeated throughout the history of film and television. Clint Eastwood's *Unforgiven* is a good modern example.

So — Burgess is a bad man. It's only fitting that such a villain has an appropriately evil weapon: a Silk-Trigger, Active Return-Bolt Laser, with the Auto Target-Adjust "crafted special".

This is quite an unexpected sight. Weirdly for *Firefly*, it's actually a bona fide Sci-Fi Raygun. The best, and flashiest, that money can buy. Does he have a horse, like his men?

No, he has a silver hovercraft...

Joss Whedon leads us once again down the garden

path of blindly trusting technology. Burgess puts his misplaced trust in the Laser and is, naturally, let down at the crucial moment by a flat battery.

The prop itself is extremely well made. It seems to have been machined from solid alloy billets — a tremendous amount of work. It has a lot of very cool light functions, including two rows of red running lights on the top, red firing 'lasers' in the twin barrels and a circular chase circuit in the side window that changes colors when you open the side panel.

And then there's the oversized 'Check Battery' warning. Hilarious.

Yep, "She is a beauty."

EMERGENCY BREATHING MASKS
MULTIPLE EPISODES

The 'verse can be a dangerous place. It pays to have certain safeguards to hand should the worst-case scenario materialize.

Serenity's interior sets were designed to reflect the difficulties faced by her crew in an imperfect world. Every part of the ship's design shows an awareness of the potential issues of the environment. Nowhere is this more clearly seen than at the hatchways in the ship's bulkheads.

In sea-going vessels on Earth, watertight doors were placed in bulkheads strategically positioned to enable areas of the ship to be sealed off, should they become damaged. This would prevent the flooding of additional compartments if the vessel became holed.

Designers of ships intended for use in space would face a similar issue should a meteorite strike or weapons fire breach the hull of their ship. The air in the damaged compartment would be vented to space. Sure, you wouldn't drown, but the upshot is the same; bloated and blue, curled in the fetal position. Far from ideal, you'll agree.

Serenity has airtight bulkheads between each major section of the ship, and at either side of each door is an emergency breathing mask. Thoughtfully located for your safety and convenience, should you end up on the wrong side of a door.

The sixteen masks used on the set are obsolete high-altitude emergency masks, used to deliver oxygen to military aircrews.

The masks are primarily rubber and retro white and grey plastic, but have exciting anodized aluminum parts and hoses and a push-to-talk microphone button. The little audio connectors on the end of the cable were added by the Art Department, so they could plug into the bulkhead on the set.

Though if you were to be trapped in a compartment with no air, it might be better to have a little air cylinder with your mask. That way, you could move more than five feet away from the door...

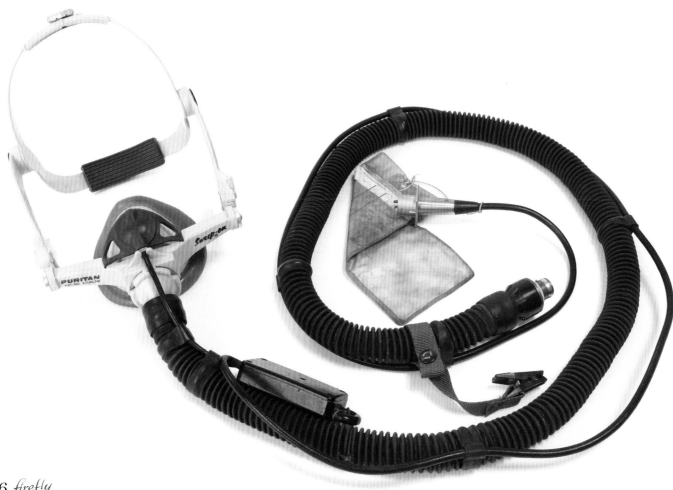

GALLEY WARE
MULTIPLE EPISODES

The galley is the heart of the ship. Bad things as well as good can happen to a heart, and Serenity's galley has seen the best of times and the worst of times for our intrepid crew. Birthdays, arguments, conflict, love and war.

The set was designed to be a little part of home in space. It's a warm, inviting space and the huge table brings Thanksgiving and Christmas family gatherings to mind. You can almost see Kaylee stenciling the flowers on the bulkheads.

Essential dressing for any galley set are the tools of the trade: pots, pans, knives and spoons.

The set was dressed by the *Firefly* Art Department, using items from prop rental houses in the Los Angeles area. Many of these rental houses have 'themed' sections, such as Medical or Police equipment. These props would be from the Restaurant section.

The chopsticks used in the mess are typical *Firefly*: a motley crew of mix-and-match items from many different cultures. Some are expensive Core Planet lacquer-ware, others the basic wooden sticks of a farmer out on the Rim.

The orange/brown, oriental serving containers appear in virtually every episode, as do the big pans and spoons hanging on the rack.

The two aluminum dredgers are standard kitchen equipment, used in *Firefly* as salt shakers. One has a bent handle, damaged when Zoe was blown up in 'Out of Gas'.

In many ways the galley is the most important set in the show. For many of the cast and crew, the happiest times on *Firefly* were in the mess hall, gathered around the table laughing.

JAYNE'S FLYING GEAR
EPISODES: 'THE TRAIN JOB', 'JAYNESTOWN'

Never averse to taking a risk, Jayne is seen hanging out the bottom of a spaceship more than once.

Back in the real world, the prospect of one of your lead actors dangling in space above a stage floor is a pretty daunting one for any producer. This kind of activity is usually reserved for stunt performers. Adam Baldwin is an intrepid type though, and you can clearly see it's Adam himself in many of the fight sequences and stunts throughout the series.

This is actually a custom-made flying harness, used by stunt performers in film and television. It's constructed of very sturdy nylon strapping and has a safe 'lifting point' on the back of the shoulders. There are leg loops, like a parachute harness, to help keep the wearer's body in a stable attitude and to help spread the load of their bodyweight around.

The goggles are standard issue US Military eyewear, now obsolete. They have a soft foam face seal, which on the pair used in 'Jaynestown' was cut away to show Adam's face more clearly.

JAYNE'S KNIFE
EPISODE: 'JAYNESTOWN'

In 'Jaynestown', we get a little glimpse into the past of our enigmatic mercenary. Here's a look at a key prop from the episode: Jayne's 'other' knife.

The knife is actually a whole set of props, comprising four versions for different purposes.

The first is the detailed 'hero' version. This is a heavy, solid metal knife, used in close up shots. The antler hilt is a resin casting of a real deer antler, and the brass ferrule is exactly what it appears to be. Although made from steel, the blade is 'safe', with no live, sharpened edge.

There is also a rubber, 'stunt' version of the knife, less detailed than the hero. This is a prop used in medium or long shots, whenever the actor is moving in an action sequence, and could possibly hurt himself with it. You can spot the stunt version in Adam Baldwin's hand when he pushes the statue over.

The third version seen here is a 'plate' knife. It is made of steel, but is only half a knife. The flat, steel end of the blade is drilled and tapped and can be screwed to a flat metal plate worn under the actor's

clothing. This same trick was used for Mal, when stabbed by Crow in 'The Train Job'.

There is a fourth version, not pictured — a retractable knife. This has one section of the blade which telescopes into another, to give the illusion of the knife stabbing someone. Such props tend to work better when being 'pulled out' of the stab victim.

We can only guess at why the producers decided to give Jayne a different knife for this episode. One suspects there was no plate or retractable version of Jayne's regular knife, and no time or budget to have them made.

A memorable prop, from "the man they call Jayne".

DOBSON'S CORTEX ACCESS DEVICE
EPISODE: 'SERENITY'

Shot in the face? Well, he had it coming...

Laurence Dobson, Alliance agent, hot on the trail of Simon and River Tam is hiding out aboard the independent freighter, Serenity.

An essential piece of equipment for the Alliance-mole-in-hiding is the Personal Cortex Access Device.

The concept is similar to that of an Earth-That-Was PDA or notebook computer. A compact, hand-held device capable of connecting the user to the 'verse's equivalent of the Internet, The Cortex.

Although perfect for purpose as a sci-fi device, the actual prop comprises two found items, real-world personal organizers, both now obsolete.

The two items were made by two separate companies and are in no way related, but the propmaster has managed to fuse them into a utilitarian-looking single unit.

The prop is constructed entirely from injection-molded plastics, the outer shell painted silver. The screen is not functional and never was — the active Cortex screen seen in the show was added in post-production.

The original operating stylus is missing, but other than that, it's in pretty good condition. Especially since it was thrown across the cabin by the frustrated Dobson!

The diligence of *Firefly* fans from all over the world, all wanting their own Cortex Device for costuming, has now made these two objects — the Franklin RF 8110 Rolodex and the Fellowes Type 'N' Go PDA/Organiser — very hard to find!

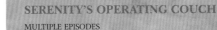

SERENITY'S OPERATING COUCH
MULTIPLE EPISODES

This chair is quite unusual.

It's an examination table, dentist's chair, operating table, psychiatrist's couch, pathologist's bench, field hospital, restraint device, morgue slab ... it even has stirrups for birthing, should the need arise.

This is, of course, the operating table from Serenity's infirmary set.

Somewhat unusually for a permanent dressing prop on a major television show, the chair was a rental from a large Hollywood prop house.

It was made by a company called Ritter, who still make medical examination tables. It is quite old, possibly 1940s or 50s, and weighs an incredible 300 pounds.

To the eye, it's a great deal less red than it appeared in *Firefly*, more russet or brown. Its silky smooth, precision engineered, positional locking system still operates perfectly, and its padded sections can be locked in any position. A substantial, solid piece of equipment.

Kaylee lay here shot and bleeding, Zoe was carried here injured, Jayne's 'Pine' was pronounced OK, Simon himself had Early's bullet extracted on it, River was sedated, a Reaver restrained, Book almost died here.

Mal injected himself in the heart with adrenalin here when he was Serenity's last hope.

It's seen a lot of action.

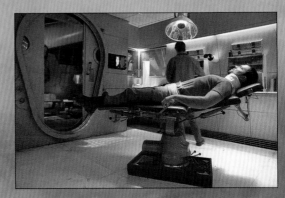

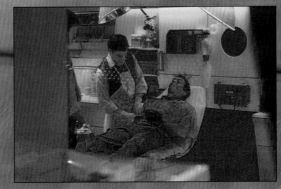

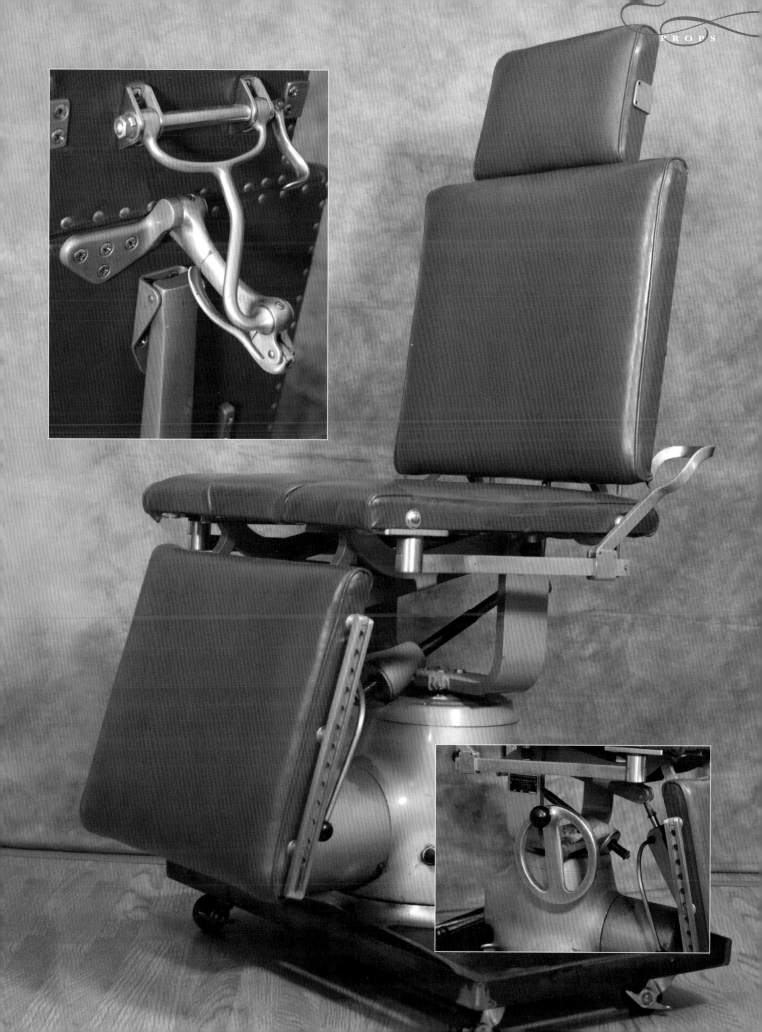

THE LASSITER

EPISODE: 'TRASH'

In *Firefly* the Lassiter is an historic relic, the first practical Laser weapon from Earth-That-Was. It's also a priceless antique, worthy of a traditional heist caper. This is not a new prop created for the show, but rather one that has served in Hollywood productions for many decades. It is known to have been in the inventory of a prominent prop rental house in Los Angeles as far back as 1992.

Firefly simply didn't have the budget to have every special prop custom made. Instead, the propmaster would go to rental houses and bring back samples of different styled weapons for the director to choose from. This is how the Lassiter was selected for *Firefly*. Though the spelling in the script is slightly different, the prop is named for John Lasseter, a friend and collaborator of Joss Whedon, and Oscar-winning animator and director.

The Lassiter is never seen working in 'Trash', but the prop has several functions. The large display screen on the rear has several working lights and there is a functional red LED under each of the buttons at the side. There is also a descending numerical countdown on the top right of the screen. There is a red 'laser' light in the machined sight/probe on the top, and two transparent probes on the front end also light up.

Made largely from cast and machined metal, the prop has some weight to it — Morena Baccarin did very well to hold it at arm's length for any time in 'Trash'. It was smeared with some of the mud make-up from 'Jaynestown' to give it a weathered look for the episode, then wiped clean after use.

The main body of the prop is an old, converted rechargeable flashlight: the First Alert ReadyLite (below left). This would suggest the prop was made some time in the Eighties. The silver handle seems to be a solid aluminum foundry casting of a Sixties plastic toy ray gun called a 'Galactronic Gun' (below).

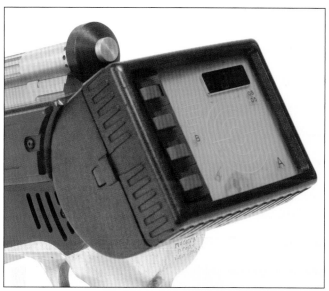

WASH'S DINOSAURS
MULTIPLE EPISODES

Wash never looks more at home than when in Serenity's cockpit, surrounded by his plastic pals.

Like the rest of the ship's crew, Wash's Dinos are an eclectic bunch. Their number includes models of all different colors, sizes and scales and seems to obey no collective rules whatsoever. They are all commercially made, mass produced figures bought by the Art Department from dime stores in Los Angeles.

Several of the most memorable are, regrettably, still missing in action. But some have been saved for posterity.

All have been seen around the cockpit at one time or another, sometimes not so obviously, but they are there. As to which is where and when? Skip Crank, the on-set propmaster: "I used to have a big box of them and Joss and Alan Tudyk would reach in and choose their favorites for that day."

INARA'S PISTOL

EPISODE: 'TRASH'

'Trash' showed us Inara uncharacteristically brandishing not one, but two guns in a single episode, the Lassiter and this elegant, silver pistol.

It's based on a real-world firearm: the Ruger Mark 2 target pistol. This is a small caliber sporting piece, produced in both blued and nickel finishes. The black plastic grips are original. Although now legally deactivated, the action still functions and the pressed-steel magazine is removable.

There are two additions to the base gun which mark this prop as unique. The first is the machined aluminum suppressor/brake at the end of the muzzle. The brake is machined from a solid billet and has no

aperture through which the gun could fire when live. It's screwed into place in a thread purpose-cut in the barrel.

The second addition is the outrigger/nacelle on the receiver. This piece is machined steel and features a working red light. It's secured in place with an Allen bolt, the thread tapped into a block mounted on the receiver.

In the hand the pistol is solid and weighty, but balanced and elegant. The machined add-ons do make the Ruger very sexy and sci-fi, but without taking us into the flamboyant, Golden Age of laser guns.

The pistol is contemporary and believable.

Elegant and beautiful, but still dangerous and business-like, this pistol is pure Inara.

JAYNE'S HOLD-OUT PIECE

EPSIODE: 'JAYNESTOWN'

This interesting prop is glimpsed briefly in 'Jaynestown', being taped to Jayne's belly in the infirmary, before they touch down in Mudder central. Joss Whedon had spoken to propmaster Randy Eriksen about the need for Jayne to own an all-plastic gun, to avoid detection by sensors on Core planets. The prop was originally made as part of Jayne's bunk arsenal.

The design is interesting and the sharp-eyed will notice a more than passing similarity to Jubal Early's pistol. Perhaps both were made by the same prop maker.

The all-plastic pistol sports a set of black rubber Pachmayr grips, smaller than on the Early piece, and has graphite-colored holo-tape wrapping the barrel. The detailing is crisp and interesting, with at least a

nod to functionality, whereas the Early pistol has no obvious controls at all.

The gun feels good in the hand. It's understandably light, but seems to point instinctively at the target, like the best real-world guns do.

Watching Jayne tape the gun industriously to his belly in 'Jaynestown' did raise a question though: how did he plan to draw it in a hurry?

SERENITY CONTROL KEYBOARD

MULTIPLE EPISODES

Part of the charm of the design of Serenity's interior sets is the attention to detail in the spit-and-bailing wire set dressing.

The Motorola KDT480 keyboard is an integral part of the look of the bridge. There are six in evidence there, ready to have their buttons frantically punched by a stressed out Wash.

Originally rented from a Hollywood prop house, and designed as part of a mobile computer terminal for police cruisers and fire trucks, the keyboards fit nicely into the jury-rigged design ethic of the Old Girl's bridge.

The KDT480 keyboard is also found on each and every one of the ship's interior com-panels. They also make a guest appearance in the Parcel office in 'The Message'.

The units feature an integral light bar at the top of the keyboard so the operator can use it in subdued lighting or even total darkness. As with most military/police equipment, the lighting is red. This is the only color of light which won't ruin your night vision. Often ship or aircraft controls are red lit for this purpose.

Many regional police and fire departments still use the system to this day. ◉

ALAN TUDYK

Hoban 'Wash' Washburne

ALAN ON MEETING THE FANS:

After *Firefly* was canceled, Nathan started going to conventions. I didn't. I didn't know what it [the fan experience] was about. Nathan talked me into it – I went to a convention in England. I could see there is a lot of passion there. But it's grown since then. I think *Firefly* fans are responsible for doing a lot of good.

INTERVIEW WITH ABBIE BERNSTEIN, 2009

NATHAN FILLION AND ALAN REMEMBER THE FIRST SCRIPT READ-THROUGH FOR THE SHOW:

Nathan: We did a table reading and I was sitting across from Alan Tudyk and he was being hilarious and self-deprecating and I'm a fan, and I'm like, "What is *he* doing here? He's a movie star, he's slumming!"

Alan: When I first got there and I was sitting around the table, I looked around and I thought, "I'm slumming, what am I doing here?" So [Nathan and I] we had that connection!"

SPEAKING ON STAGE AT THE 'SERENITY' CONVENTION, 2005.

ON MEETING GINA TORRES FOR THE FIRST TIME:

When I met Gina I was like [incredulous] "You're *my* wife? Wow, I really gotta step up here, how do I pull this off?"

SPEAKING ON STAGE AT THE 'SERENITY' CONVENTION, 2005.

ON HIS OPINION OF THE BIG DAMN MOVIE:

I loved the movie. I really liked the look of it, I liked the style of it, I thought Joss did a great job with it. There was one part of that movie where I was like, "Really?", which is where I *died*, but other than that, it was pretty awesome.

INTERVIEWED AT THE SUNDANCE FILM FESTIVAL, 2010

JEWEL STAITE ON ALAN'S MASTERY OF LANGUAGE:

Alan always screwed up his Chinese. He always came up with the most hilarious things to say just because he couldn't remember his lines and he thought he'd go with it. It was total gibberish in the end.

SPEAKING ON STAGE AT THE 'FUSION' CONVENTION, 2004.

NATHAN REMEMBERS HIS FAVORITE 'SLOW-COOKED' PRANK ON ALAN:

When we first did the pilot I made friends with everybody and Alan Tudyk was one of those people. I had to go to Vancouver for four weeks and do an independent film, and he was in Los Angeles looking for a place to live. I said, "You can live at my house, help feed my cat, for four weeks while you find your apartment," and it worked out great. And while he was at my house he left [behind] a calendar – it's one of those calendars where you go to the shopping mall and you get a bunch of family photos and you create a calendar putting one for each month. So it was family photos of him since he was a child. There were lots of really goofy photos of Alan Tudyk as a kid. So I saved it. I took all the goofiest pictures and I saved them for *three years*, and when we were doing the bar scene [in

ALAN TUDYK

NATHAN ON ALAN BEING PROTECTIVE OF THE BRIDGE SET:

If you changed the tilt on Alan's chair – look out! [As Alan] "Who was sitting in this... who did... If this isn't in the right... I'm not going to... If you guys don't... I'll be in my trailer!"

SPEAKING ON STAGE AT THE 'SERENITY' CONVENTION, 2005.

the movie] I posted them all over the set – all these really, really goofy pictures of Alan. That made me happy!

SPEAKING ON STAGE AT 'THE WHITE ROOM' CONVENTION, 2004.

ALAN'S EPISODE IDEAS:

Ever since I started on *Firefly*, I've been pitching Joss Whedon ideas. One involves us capturing a bunch of wolves, to sell for like dog fights on a planet, but then River teaches the dogs peace, so they're no good...

[Another idea] Inara has us as her servants, and somebody says "I need two strippers, can we use your servants?", and she's in a position where she has to say yes, and then we get sort of thrust into it. And Wash is really good – so you understand a bit more why Zoe and Wash are together, 'cause he's got *moves*.

INTERVIEWED ON SET, 2002

ON HIS HARDEST SCENE:

Any action scenes were easy for me, because I was on the ship [mimes sitting there, flicking a few switches]. The hardest one would have been when [Nathan and I] did 'War Stories'... our electrocution thing? My God... You tense your muscles and jiggle around... You try doing that for eight hours in a day, and see if you don't wake up the next day feeling like you were *actually* electrocuted.

SPEAKING ON STAGE AT DRAGON CON, 2008

HE'S STILL AT IT...

I'm pitching to Joss Whedon a new TV show, it's not so much a series as a cycle, and I'm going to call it *The Wash Cycle...*

INTERVIEWED AT THE SUNDANCE FILM FESTIVAL, 2010

BEHIND THE SCENES

Danny Nero's Photo Album

When he first heard that *Firefly* was in pre-production, Danny Nero had spent three years on *Angel* as David Boreanaz's stand-in — the person who stands where the actor will be during a scene, so that lighting and camera moves can be planned without the actor having to be there in person during the often lengthy set up.

Nero explains, "As much as I enjoyed the people on *Angel*, the working conditions of so many nights in so many unsavory back alley locations in downtown LA... I thought, '*Firefly* is science fiction, which I love, and it's going to be a lot on a spaceship, which means being on a soundstage a lot, that's great.' I hadn't considered that we would have to go on location on *Firefly* occasionally, either to some of the local ranches or out into the desert, which would mean sometimes getting up at three in the morning to be there by six a.m. — but we enjoyed every minute on that show. It was such a fun place to work that we didn't mind going out to the desert every once in a while."

Nero's job was to stand in primarily for Nathan Fillion

❖ Right: Danny Nero with Nathan Fillion.

❖ Below: with Adam Baldwin, on the set of 'The Message'.

and occasionally for Adam Baldwin. "[Baldwin] is about six-six, and I'm about six-three, so three inches just about makes all the difference," Nero notes. "I was very lucky in that [original *Firefly* pilot costume designer] Jill Ohanneson found in Fox wardrobe a pair of Converse high-top tennis shoes that had six-inch platforms on them. I tried those on and people were in hysterics. I can't imagine why they were there, who would have used them on what show. I was in fear of falling and breaking something, so [Ohanneson] chopped off three inches, and I still have them to this day."

When Fillion and Baldwin shared a scene, another stand-in would be brought in to work with Nero. "There might be a day where Nathan worked in the morning and Adam worked later on, so I could do both, but if they're both in the same scene, then you would have to have someone for each guy, and there was someone to cover each of the regular cast members. We had pretty much the same group of people the whole time. It was a great group all around, cast and crew, and it's always sad when that gets broken up."

Asked about particularly memorable days on set, Nero recalls, "Being out in the desert for a scene where Mal is completely naked. That required being at that desert location at least a full hour before the sun came up and it was quite cold. It was *very* cold." Fortunately, Nero was not called upon to be likewise bare. "No, I wore my closest

flesh-colored clothes and I sat on that rock for a good bit of time before Nathan had to come out and do it. He was wearing something, but not very much, and he joked about it, but everyone was like, 'Oh, boy, there but for the grace of whoever ...'

"Because of Joss, people would do just about anything," Nero continues. "One day, I couldn't tell you what episode it was, but we were in one of the narrow corridors between the engine room and the dining room. And I don't know how it happened, but Joss started singing the song 'Oklahoma'. There were at least six or seven of us in there that all sang along and knew all the lyrics – including Nathan Fillion of course. We sang the entire theme song of *Oklahoma* and then just went around and continued working as if it had never happened," he laughs.

As for *Firefly* fandom, Nero says, "I would love to meet some of the fans. I never considered while I was working on it how popular the show would become. Of course, we never thought we would only do those few episodes, but we had no control over that. No one anticipated the fact that the DVD would help spawn a feature and that we would be doing that [Nero again stood in for Fillion and

Baldwin]. But once we were doing the feature, we were convinced, 'This will now spawn even more, there will be more features.' So it just goes to show you how you can never really be sure of anything in this business. Any time they're ready to get it back together and start the series up, I'd like to be involved somehow."

In the meantime, Nero still has his memories, and some great photos from his time on set... ◁

❖ Top: Filming 'The Message'.

❖ Above: Nero with Jewel Staite, during filming for 'Shindig'.

❖ Left: Tracey's family assemble in 'The Message'.

❖ Below: In the 'Ariel' ambulance; filming 'Safe'.

❖ Bottom: Capturing a moment of history: this moment from 'Heart of Gold' was the last ever shot to be filmed on *Firefly*.

❖ Top: Ron Glass says hello during filming for 'The Message'.

❖ Above: Shooting the opening scene of 'Ariel'.

❖ Far left center: Haymer's parlor from 'Trash'. The Lassiter is on the left.

❖ Far left bottom: Nero in front of the painted flat of Serenity, on location for 'Safe'.

❖ Left: Nero in costume as an extra for the ball scene in 'Shindig'.

❖ Top: Filming on the Serenity exterior set.

❖ Far right center: "No power in the 'verse can stop me." Filming 'War Stories'.

❖ Far right bottom: Nero in costume for 'The Message'.

❖ Right: Set detail. The sign warns of loud noise.

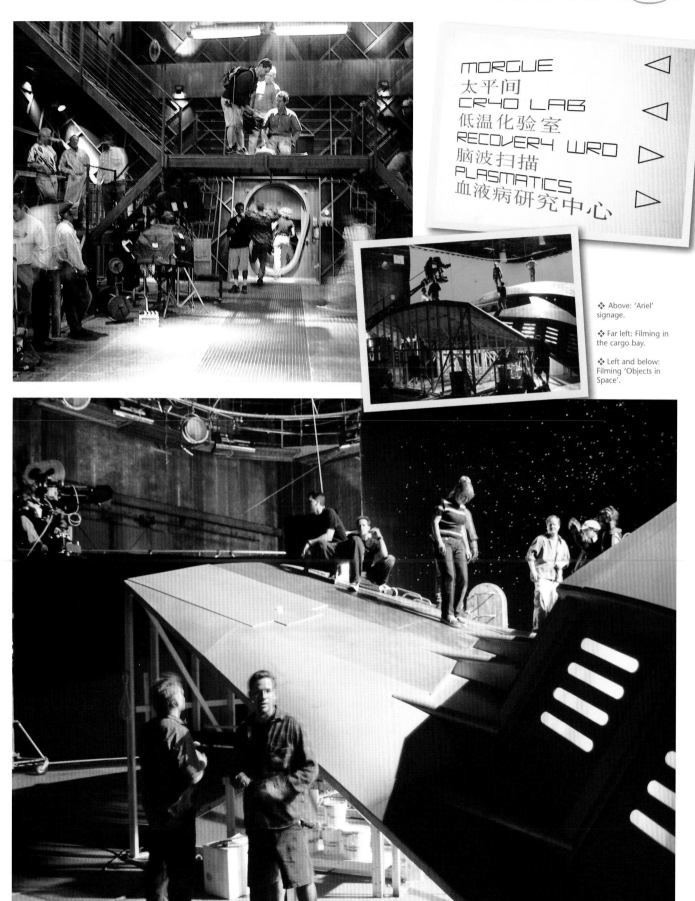

MORGUE
太平间
CRYO LAB
低温化验室
RECOVERY WRD
脑波扫描
PLASMATICS
血液病研究中心

❖ Above: 'Ariel' signage.

❖ Far left: Filming in the cargo bay.

❖ Left and below: Filming 'Objects in Space'.

THE STORY OF MONKEY SHINES

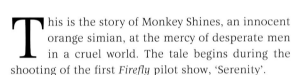

The on-set practical joke that has passed into legend...

This is the story of Monkey Shines, an innocent orange simian, at the mercy of desperate men in a cruel world. The tale begins during the shooting of the first *Firefly* pilot show, 'Serenity'.

Propmasters standing-by on set often have a hand-wagon containing key props and set dressing for use in that day's scenes. Being a legendary practical joker, *Firefly* propmaster Skip Crank would tend to keep more esoteric items to hand as well: a small model of Han Solo in Carbonite for example, or realistic severed limbs, heads and body parts to surprise the cast with.

Skip had acquired a stuffed orange monkey toy with the most annoying screech known to man. The screech was so irritating in fact that eventually Joss Whedon banned the toy from the soundstage.

On this particular day, Skip was busy dressing the set for the upcoming scene and had left his wagon unattended. Not usually an issue, but a certain cast member was tired, a little cranky, and saw his chance...

This actor was between shooting some of the salvage scenes from the start of the episode and, rather than his usual tight pants, was dressed in one of Serenity's familiar khaki-colored space suits. He spotted Monkey Shines languishing on Skip's wagon and grabbed him, stuffing him down inside the suit and sauntering casually away.

Skip returned and was naturally distraught at the theft of his little buddy. He vowed to get him back.

What ensued is a very good example of what can happen when two imaginative, articulate and intelligent men have too much time on their hands...

MISSING
THIS <u>WAS</u> A KIDNAPPING
NOT A BOATING ACCIDENT

I only hope he isn't suffering from *Mal* nutrition!

POSSIBLY THE WORK
OF REAVERS

ANY LEADS OR CLUE
CONTACT- 310

This page, anti-clockwise from left:

❖ The poster that Skip made upon Monkey Shines' disappearance. Copies were posted all over the Fox Studio, soundstages and back-lot. The reference to *Mal*-nutrition shows he had his suspicions as to who the culprit may be, even at this stage.

❖ Several days after Monkey Shines' kidnapping, this envelope arrived on Skip's desk at the studio. The actor involved had taken to riding a small motor scooter around the lot. The tread on the tires is identical to that which made the muddy track across the envelope. More clues…

❖ This is the first of the ransom notes. It's clear the kidnapper is a desperate man. The pictures of the hapless Monkey Shines lashed to a chair are very moving. It is somewhat ironic that the word 'smart' is misspelled in the note.

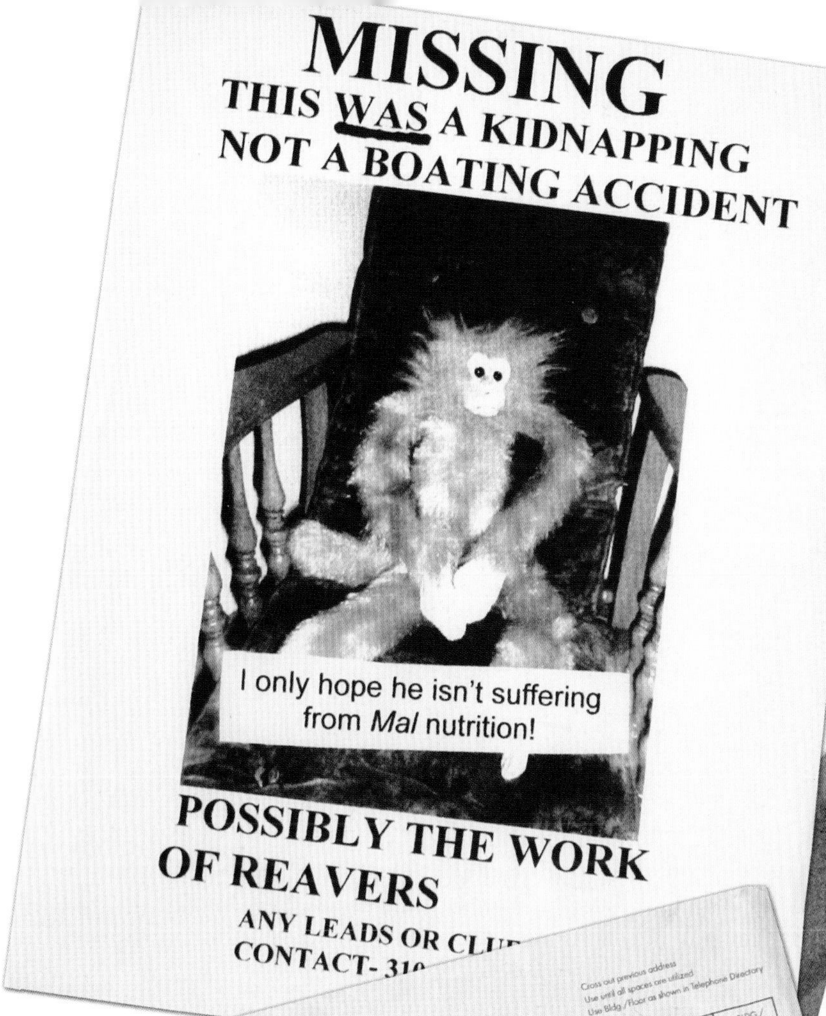

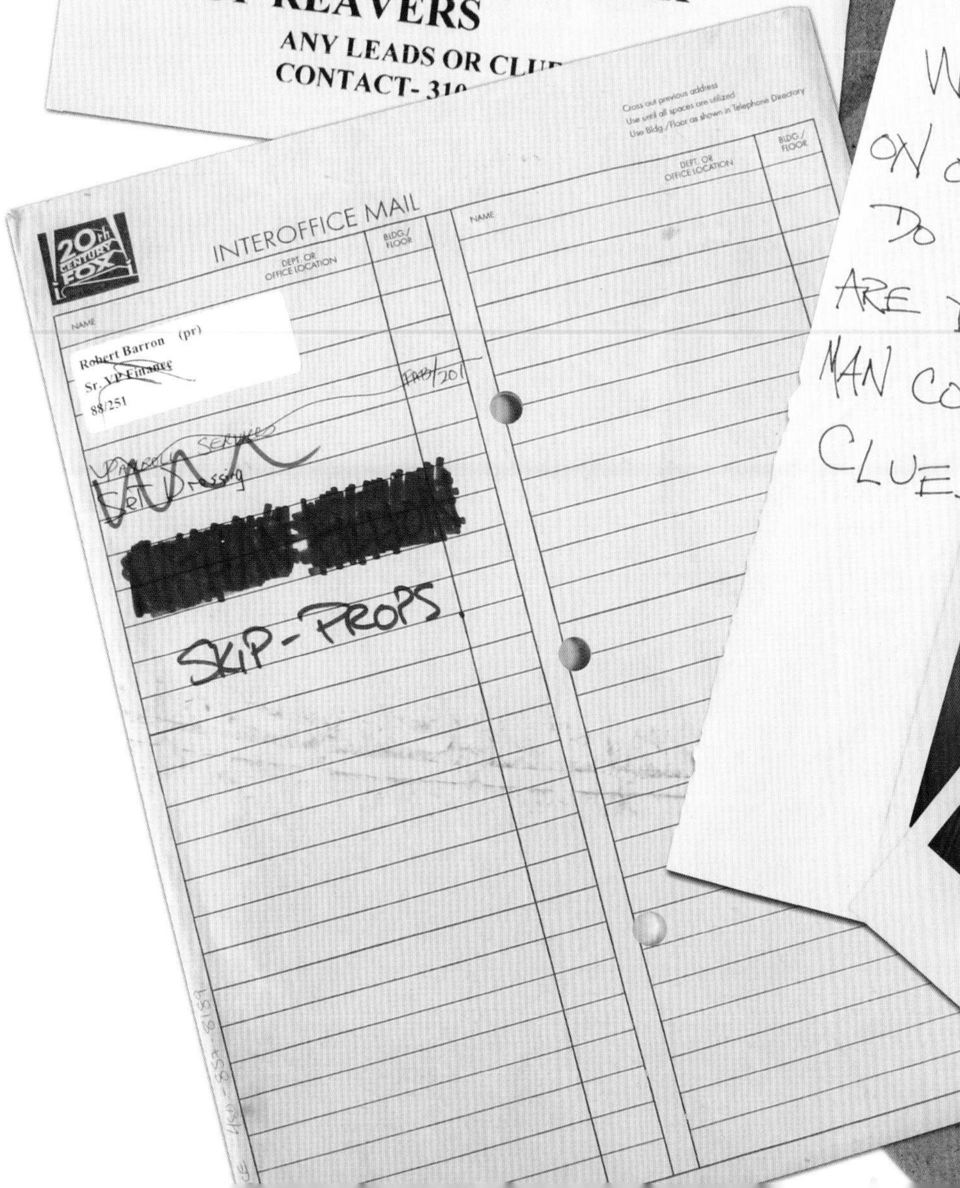

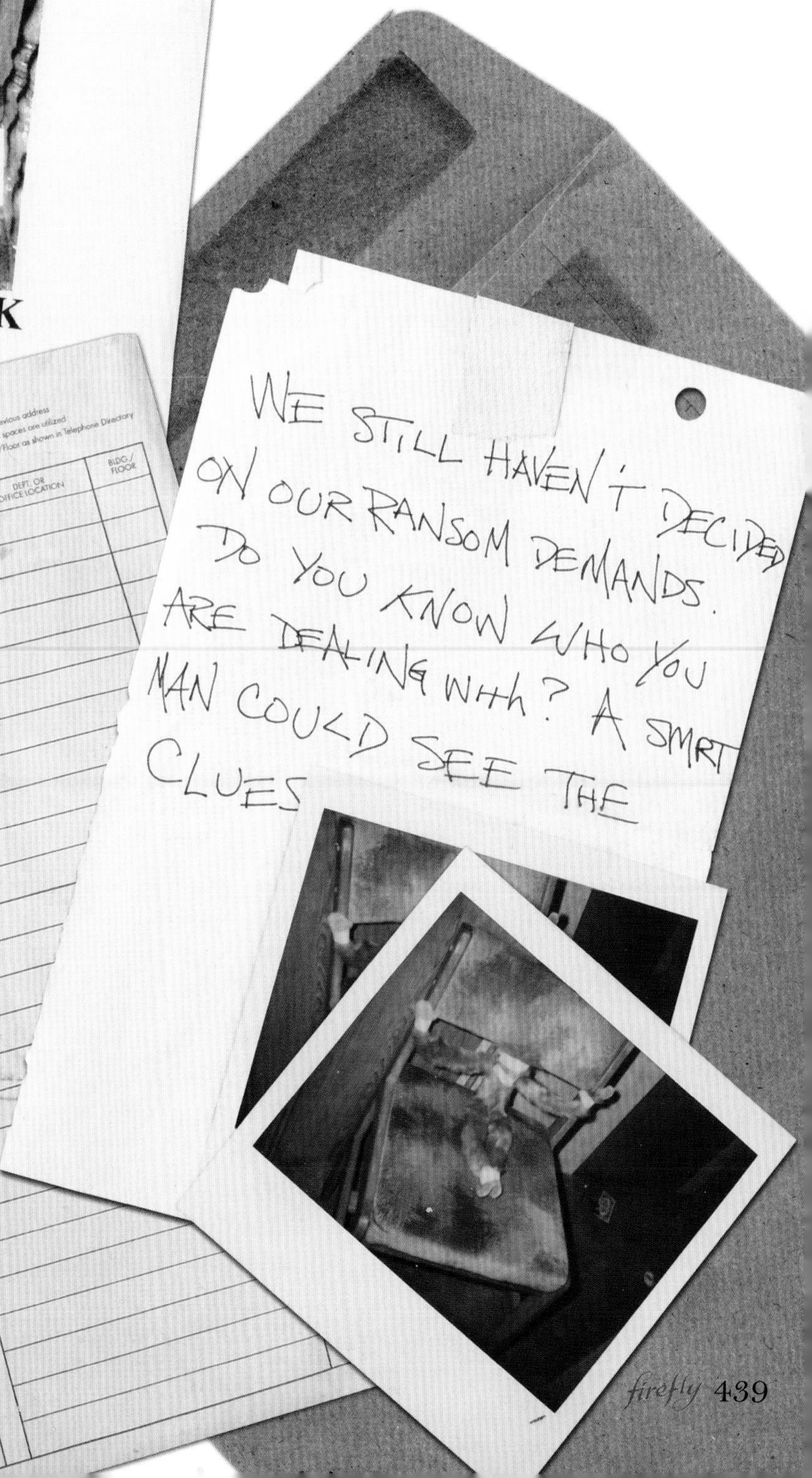

INTEROFFICE MAIL

Robert Barron (pr)
Sr. VP Features

SKIP-PROPS

WE STILL HAVEN'T DECIDED ON OUR RANSOM DEMANDS. DO YOU KNOW WHO YOU ARE DEALING WITH? A SMRT MAN COULD SEE THE CLUES

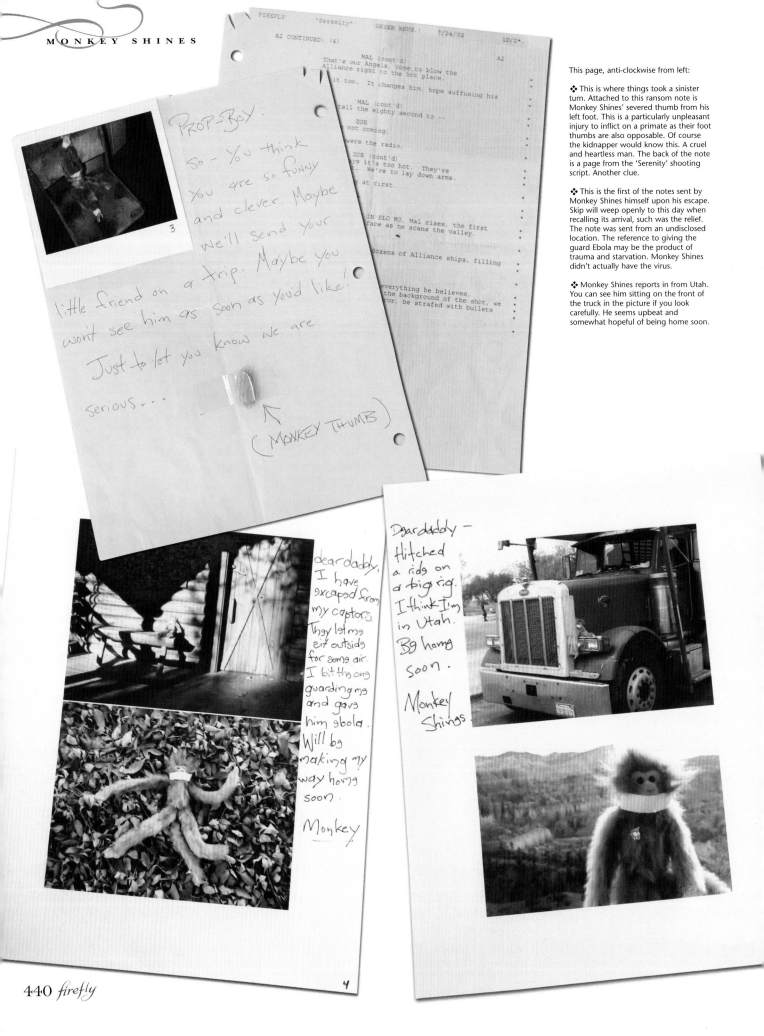

FIREFLY   "Serenity"   (GREEN REVS.)   7/24/02   1D/2*.

A2 CONTINUED: (4)   A2

                          MAL (cont'd)
              That's our Angels, come to blow the
              Alliance right to the hot place.

              it too. It changes him, hope suffusing his

                          MAL (cont'd)
              tell the eighty second to --

                          ZOE
              not coming.

              lowers the radio.

                          ZOE (cont'd)
              says it's too hot. They're
              . We're to lay down arms.

              at first.

              IN SLO MO, Mal rises, the first
              face as he scans the valley.

              dozens of Alliance ships, filling

              everything he believes,
              the background of the shot, we
              or, be strafed with bullets

PROP-BOY.

So - You think
you are so funny
and clever. Maybe
we'll send your
little friend on a trip. Maybe you
won't see him as soon as you'd like!
Just to let you know we are
serious....

↑
(MONKEY THUMB)

dear daddy,
I have
excaped from
my captors.
They let me
sit outside
for some air.
I bit the one
guarding me
and gave
him ebola.
Will be
making my
way home
soon.

Monkey

Dear daddy -
Hitched
a ride on
a big rig.
I think I'm
in Utah.
Be home
soon.

Monkey
Shines.

This page, anti-clockwise from left:

❖ This is where things took a sinister turn. Attached to this ransom note is Monkey Shines' severed thumb from his left foot. This is a particularly unpleasant injury to inflict on a primate as their foot thumbs are also opposable. Of course the kidnapper would know this. A cruel and heartless man. The back of the note is a page from the 'Serenity' shooting script. Another clue.

❖ This is the first of the notes sent by Monkey Shines himself upon his escape. Skip will weep openly to this day when recalling its arrival, such was the relief. The note was sent from an undisclosed location. The reference to giving the guard Ebola may be the product of trauma and starvation. Monkey Shines didn't actually have the virus.

❖ Monkey Shines reports in from Utah. You can see him sitting on the front of the truck in the picture if you look carefully. He seems upbeat and somewhat hopeful of being home soon.

dear daddy –
don't know exactly
where I
am. Got
turned
around
in Kentucky.
Be home
soon.

Monkey
Shines.

dear daddy. Shoot. Definitely took wrong turn. Back
in Utah. Will get back on track. Be home soon.
Monkey
Shines.

STATE PROPERTY
NO DUMPING
NO PARKING
NO TRESPASSING
VIOLATORS WILL BE PROSECUTED

DANGEROUS CLIFFS
WATCH YOUR CHILDREN
STAY IN YOUR CAR DURING
LIGHTNING STORMS
NO PETS OR BICYCLES
ON TRAILS
DO NOT LEAVE
VALUABLES IN YOUR CAR

❖ Top left: Another update from the brave little
fellow. Why he's lashed to the post is a bit of a
mystery. The psychological effects of malnutrition
may be a factor.

❖ Left: It seems he was a little addled and ended up
back in Utah again. Definitely something amiss here.
On the upside, he seems positive. Almost chipper.

7

dear daddy - Getting closer. finding food where i can. Raided campground. Slowed down in Washington, long story.
Monkey Shines.

dear daddy - This nice lady (who wishes to remain almost namless) helped me get home by mailing me from Canada. I'm home!
Monkey Shines.

WELCOME TO
ALBERTA
WILD ROSE COUNTRY

This page, clockwise from above:

❖ Monkey Shines seems to be back on track. He's managed to find a banana in a Washington campground. Although now properly nourished, he still seems somewhat confused. The self-imposed gag may be a silent cry for help.

❖ Rescued and posted home by a nice lady from Alberta, Canada.

❖ Skip was overjoyed to see Monkey Shines alive and well, and alerted the media. Monkey Shines himself, psychologically and emotionally bruised by the ordeal, was operating on his own agenda.

❖ This candid and somewhat unsettling shot was taken by Skip while visiting his friend during his recovery. It seems Monkey Shines was not willing to let bygones be bygones and seemed intent on revenge. The need for retribution reached obsessive levels and Monkey Shines was eventually taken into care for his own protection. He now resides in a peaceful rest home for damaged toys in West London, England.

DAILY VARIETY

LOS ANGELES • NEW YORK

$3.25
NEWSPAPER

WEDNESDAY
November 19, 2003

VARIETY.COM

AMC, Loews eyeing major screen team

MONKEY SURFACES !
Simian Vows Vengeance for Kidnappings

442

THE KIDNAPPER... REVEALED!

NATHAN FILLION CONFESSES ALL

There was a monkey on set and if you squeezed it, it made this monkey noise. It was fine enough, but once you've heard it more than once, it got a little annoying. I had to wear a space suit all day and that's the worst.

You're claustrophobic, you're sweating and Sean Maher had to wear it before me because we didn't have enough space suits to go around. The space suit was sweaty and hot and it's awful. Sean's worked all day and he takes it and hands it to me and he says, "Sorry." And there's nothing you can do, and I say, "No problem man." So I'm getting into an already hot and sweaty space suit and it's claustrophobic and you can't really hear anybody, and everybody is tugging on it to get you in it and everyone is smacking you around... It had to weigh about 120, 130 pounds. I hated it. I loved that job, but if you wanted to see me with a sour face and all cranky, put me in a space suit.

And that damn monkey would not shut up.

So when I left I pulled up my helmet, grabbed the monkey and shoved him in my spacesuit, walked back to my trailer and hid him in a drawer. Then I took a Polaroid camera and I taped up the monkey's eyes and his mouth, taped him to a chair and started taking Polaroids of him, with little items in the back as clues as to who it would be that stole him. Of course they recognized my trailer in the photos! Not too bright. One too many knocks with the helmet. So they put out an ad saying that they hoped the monkey wasn't Mal-nourished. Then I wrote a letter back to them – a ransom note with the monkey's thumb taped to it saying, "Quit messing around." Then I mailed the monkey to my parents, who took it on a cross-country trip across Canada and into the States, and took pictures of this monkey all over [yes, that's Nathan's mother in the picture opposite]. Then I finally returned the monkey... 🌀

SPEAKING ON STAGE AT THE 'WHITE ROOM' CONVENTION, 2004

MORENA BACCARIN

Inara Serra

MORENA ON THE FEEDBACK SHE GETS FROM FANS:

They have a very mutual understanding of the work, I think. They really enjoy the same things that we enjoy in it. They have such an in-depth understanding of the world, the universe that was created. They really do their research, and they read things about it. They're very intelligent. And they're really passionate about it. They get really into the world, and they dress up as us sometimes. They have these really intelligent questions about the Alliance vs. the Browncoats, it's really cool.

INTERVIEW WITH ZETAMINOR.COM, 2005

ON THE FANS:

I still can't believe that people were as into that show as they were, and are. It's great and I loved the series, because I was in it and working and loved the people that I worked with. I am always amazed and humbled by the amount of fans out there for *Firefly* and it's so touching to me that people feel as passionately about it as I did.

Just the other day I went to eat in a restaurant here in Los Angeles, and the owners were huge *Firefly* fans wearing *Serenity* shirts. I had no idea and told the owner that I liked her shirt and she said, "Oh my God, I was

hoping one of you would come in eventually!" It's so great. It's so sweet.

INTERVIEW WITH IFMAGAZINE.COM, 2007

ON INARA'S SHUTTLE SET:

Morena: My room was kind of great because nobody ever came in it except Nathan, and then we just bickered and he would storm out. I had it all to myself.
Nathan: Actually when we weren't filming, I twice went in there for a nap.

SPEAKING ON STAGE AT THE 'SERENITY' CONVENTION, 2005

ON JOINING THE SHOW AFTER EVERYONE ELSE HAD BEEN CAST:

I felt that everybody was leagues ahead of me and I was just playing catch up the whole time, but my first

MORENA BACCARIN

impression of Joss was kind of funny. I read for the casting director first and she said, "OK Joss is downstairs on set we'll get him up," because they were rushing to get this going. And he comes in and he's got a hat on and a ragged T-shirt and a beard and he's like, "Hi" and I was like, "Who is this guy? How is he directing this and what is this person in front of me?" And he started talking, and I hadn't even read the script at that point, I hadn't had any time, and I thought, "Oh my god I will do anything this man does. It doesn't matter what my part is. I know I can trust him and I know that I'm in good hands." That kicked it off really well.

SPEAKING ON STAGE AT THE 'SERENITY' CONVENTION, 2005

MORENA AND NATHAN ON INARA'S RELATIONSHIP WITH MAL:

Morena: You can see in 'Out of Gas' they met when she was looking for shuttles to rent, and right away you can tell that they're attracted to each other. Not necessarily in a sexual way, but there is something which brings them together, and the minute he calls her a whore – it's all downhill.

Nathan: I think that Malcolm Reynolds pegged her right off the bat seeing that she's running away from something.

Morena: Takes one to know one!

SPEAKING ON STAGE AT 'THE WHITE ROOM' CONVENTION, 2005

JEWEL STAITE ON MORENA:

Morena and I got really, really close very quickly. We have like the same birthday on the same day. We were just like two peas in a pod. She was the maid of honor at my wedding and we just became really, really close. But we would say mean, horrible things to each other in front of people, just to get a reaction. We were in this room full of extras on 'Shindig' and there was just this lull, this silent moment and she turned around and she looked at me and she said, "I am so sick of looking at your face." Everyone was like [mimes shock] and I just burst out laughing.

SPEAKING ON STAGE AT THE 'SERENITY' CONVENTION, 2005

ON HER FAVORITE EPISODE:

Maybe it was 'Shindig'. One of the most satisfying things for me, apart from watching Nathan get the crap kicked out of him [laughs] – well, it doesn't suck to be a girl and wear pretty dresses and have two guys fight over you.

SPEAKING ON STAGE AT 'THE WHITE ROOM' CONVENTION, 2005

ON GIFTS FROM FANS:

I didn't get this as a gift, but Christina Hendricks did. She received coasters with all of our faces on them, so she gets a really big kick whenever I go to her house giving me the coaster with my face on it, so I can put a glass on top of it.

INTERVIEW WITH IFMAGAZINE.COM, 2007

COSTUMES

Selections from the wardrobes of Inara and Jayne

FIREFLY COSTUME DESIGNER SHAWNA TRPCIC

I went and spoke at Comic-Con this year, at the Browncoat panel, and as I was answering questions about the *Firefly* costumes, we also did a flashpoint [presentation] of the Jayne hats and sang 'A Man Called Jayne'. Also, Nathan Fillion came in right in the middle of the interview – big hugs and kisses and it was awesome. I saw many replicas at Comic-Con, after almost six years, of the Browncoat Mal outfit.

INTERVIEW WITH ABBIE BERNSTEIN, 2009

❖ Opposite: The design for Inara's costume from 'Ariel'.

❖ This page top right: Inara's dress for 'Shindig' was adapted from Shawna Trpcic's own wedding dress.

❖ This page right: The design for a costume seen in 'War Stories'.

❖ Below: Shawna Trpcic at San Diego Comic-Con 2009.

❖ Overleaf: Jayne's iconic T-shirts and hat. Kept by Adam Baldwin after filming ended, he later auctioned them off, raising thousands of dollars for charity.

INARA going to core hospital ep 8

sleeve

larger to ba g

COSTUME DESIGNERS GUILD
IATSE 892
494

= INARA'S sweatsuit =

ADAM BALDWIN ON THAT CUNNING-LOOKING GIFT FROM JAYNE'S MOM:

It was very much of sentimental value for Jayne. We haven't met his mom yet, but I always pictured her as someone short and feisty, like Ruth Gordon, that Jayne could carry around in his arms... [The hat has] a lot of sentimental value for me. I love it, I think it's great [seeing fans wear it at conventions]. It stands out. It really pops!

INTERVIEW WITH HYPA SPACE, 2006

ADAM BALDWIN

Jayne Cobb

ADAM ON THE CHARACTER'S APPEAL:

Jayne is this guy who says what everybody wishes they could say. He's that big elephant in the room that will just spew the truth and I think people relate to that... Joss gave me some really fun words to say and I just got to drop my voice [in Jayne's gruff tones] *like this*.

INTERVIEW WITH ZETAMINOR.COM, 2005

ON HIS INSPIRATION:

I had just been trying to do Warren Oates from *The Wild Bunch* meets Eli Wallach from *The Good, the Bad and the Ugly*. Guys like that. Those are guys I was trying to impersonate, mixed in with some Strother Martin. Those are great Western guys. I just always approached it as a Western, with that sensibility. You can shoot someone in the back and rationalize it, because you're out on the frontier, and survival of the fittest. It was up to Joss to infuse him with a little bit of a heart of gold and honor for Mal. The rest of them, he could take or leave them. And later I saw *Alien* again, and it turns out I was just doing Yaphet Kotto.

INTERVIEW WITH THE ONION A.V. CLUB, 2009

ON COMING BACK FOR THE MOVIE:

It fit like a glove. I still had the boots from the series. I slipped right back into those, and a couple of the T-shirts. We upgraded them a little bit, and put on some cooler beltwork and weaponry. The gun sling that the prop guy made for the movie used a quick-release parachute capo. That was pretty cool. It was great to have that group back again, because at that point, we all appreciated what it was. It was probably the most fun job I've ever worked on. It was so sweet. Such redemption. I'm sorry the movie didn't make more money at the theaters. If we'd had three more million viewers for the show, we'd still be on the air, and if we'd had three million more butts in the seats, we'd probably have made a sequel or two.

INTERVIEW WITH THE ONION A.V. CLUB, 2009

ON WHETHER JAYNE HAD A CRUSH ON INARA:

It wasn't that tough [to play that]! I've been to a couple of panel discussions with Morena, and I've mentioned that, and she said, "Do you have a crush on me?" And I'm like... "Nah... my character does though." But Joss

ADAM BALDWIN

would say, "No, you don't have a crush on Inara!" "Yes I do. I don't care what you say, I'm going to play it!"

I love those guys. It was really a family affair. It's so rare to have a cast like that.

SPEAKING ON STAGE AT A CONVENTION, 2005

ON JAYNE IN 'ARIEL', AND THE QUALITY OF THE WRITING:

Even though he's a bit of a ne'er do well, that's the realm into which he's painted, but he has that sort of honor among thieves. Even in the episode in the series where I quote unquote 'betrayed' the Captain by trying to dump off the loony fugitives ['Ariel'] – in my own mind, I wasn't betraying the Captain, I was trying to do better and just make a buck along the way. When he clocked me in the head with a wrench – "Hello, now I'm awake. OK, I get it now."

I think what that shows is Joss's brilliance. I think that shows his ability to connect with an audience in writing profound stories, with action and quite a bit of sense of humor, that are universal in nature. That touch people across a wide spectrum of age ranges. I'm not saying that he has the most gigantic audience in the world, but the audience that he has is very varied. You can't put them in a box you know — young and old, men and women, freaks and geeks — you got 'em all. I'm just happy to be part of that world. I'm so proud to have been given... I think it's a role of a lifetime.

INTERVIEW WITH SMRT-TV.COM, 2005

ON WHAT JAYNE COBB AND JOHN CASEY (HIS CHARACTER IN *CHUCK*) WOULD TALK ABOUT IF THEY MET:

"Weaponry first, hot girls second."

INTERVIEW WITH JOHN PATRICK BARRY, 2010

"Port Control is paying four credits for every stray we kill!"

"Stop it, Dick," says Jayne. "Stop it."

"Now we have enough money to back
our own hobo in the Meat Raffle!"

"Sic'em, Speshal!" shouts Jayne. "Yay!"

THE HEAD THEY CALL JAYNE

Whatever happened to the Jaynestown statue?

One of the more memorable pieces of *Firefly* set dressing was the statue of Jayne created for 'Jaynestown'. Mike Schotte of Dallas, Texas, wound up in possession of the statue's head.

"Adam Baldwin brought it as a charity auction item for the Flanvention [held in Burbank, California in 2005]," Schotte relates. "It's in good shape. Basically, at the end of the day's shooting, he broke the head off the body of the statue and took it home! Then the production office called him and said they had to do some pick-up shots, so they had to put it back together, which is why it's got a pole in the head, so they could stick it back on. If you look in the episode, you can see the crack around the head in some of the shots. During opening ceremonies of the Flanvention, they mentioned the charity auction, which they hadn't said much about, but Adam just said, 'Oh, by the way, I brought the Jayne statue.' I immediately freaked out, went and found money. It is just an iconic prop. I mean, that's so obviously *Firefly*. There were a lot of great things there, but that was something that I just said, 'I'm going to go for it and do whatever I can to get it.'"

It's been challenging to place such a unique item within a household. "It's kind of a hard thing to display," Schotte acknowledges. "Right now, it's packed away safely. I've been trying for years and years to research if the rest of it was out there anywhere. But everybody I've talked to has basically said that they think that the body went into the trash at the end of shooting. I went to Mutant Enemy Strike Day [organized by Joss Whedon in support of the 2007/2008 Writers Guild of America strike], and Jane Espenson introduced me to Joss. Since I just ask everybody, I said, 'Somebody told me there was a rumor that you might have the Jayne statue in your garage.' He said, 'Nope, that's not true.' I said, 'Yeah, I figured it probably wasn't true. Who's going to keep a headless body in their garage for five years?' He said, 'Well, I didn't say I didn't have *any* headless bodies, just not that one,'" Schotte laughs.

"I know the special effects house, Almost Human, who made the statue, and I talked to Shawna Trpcic, who provided the clothing for when they made the statue, but I haven't been able to track down any more pieces of it."

Schotte does have at least one complementary piece of memorabilia. "When Adam sold his shooting scripts in charity auctions, I bought his 'Jaynestown' script to go with the head, and his notes that he's written in the margin crack me up. Next to Jayne's line, 'The magistrate of this company town ain't exactly a forgiving sort of fella,' he's written in the margin, 'We're all going to die a horrible muddy death.' That alone makes it worth the price." ◉

❖ Opposite top: The Jaynestown statue, as immortalized in a poster produced by QMx.

JAYNESTOWN

CANTON

A. Leverance

JEWEL STAITE

Kaywinnit Lee Frye

JEWEL ON GETTING READY TO PLAY KAYLEE:

When I first auditioned for *Firefly*, I read the breakdown of the characters and the one that caught my eye was River. I read it and I thought, "Oh that sounds meaty, I like that." There was a lot of crying and hysteria and every actor wants to do that. But then I read Kaylee, and they said, "Well actually Joss wants to see you for Kaylee," and I thought "Oh," because it said "chubby" on the breakdown, and I'm not chubby, and I didn't know if they meant 'Hollywood chubby' or what. So I put myself on tape and kind of forgot about it, and then a few weeks later I got the call and I flew down to meet Joss, and he told me flat out. He said, "You know I need this character to be full of life, and by full of life I mean she has to look like she enjoys life. She has to look like she eats a burger now and then, and drinks a few beers once in a while." He didn't want her to be a typical size zero actress, which I understand. I'm naturally this way. I was a little taken aback because I'm really into yoga, and I like to stay healthy. But I loved the role so much it wasn't like I was going to say no. So I just stuffed my face for about three weeks, and got to eat lots of mayonnaise. I got to eat doughnuts every morning and I felt so sick because I was so full all the time, but I had to keep eating like that to keep the weight on. It was interesting. My husband loved it – guys apparently like a little weight on women! It was awesome.

SPEAKING ON STAGE AT THE 'FUSION' CONVENTION, 2004

ON THE EVOLUTION OF THE CHARACTER:

Once I had the part and we started to shoot, it was a bit unclear how bubbly Kaylee was supposed to be. Is she just happy or is she more manic? Is she hiding something and that's why she puts on the happy facade, or is she just drunk? I figured the best route to go was to play up her innocence, her frankness, and her warmth more than anything. 'Out of Gas' put me straight on the whole innocence thing, so after that I added horny flirt to her repertoire.

INTERVIEW WITH RAYGUNREVIVAL.COM, 2007

ON KAYLEE'S LIFE BEFORE JOINING THE SERENITY CREW:

I did a bit of imagining, but I also trusted Joss with any kind of backstory questions I had. I knew she had a great family, maybe not such a well-off one, but a family that was supportive of her and her abilities, otherwise why would they have let her go with someone like Mal? That's one of the things that was most disappointing for me when the series got canceled so prematurely; I would have loved to learn more about her life off the ship... I would have loved to meet her family. I've always had this desire to see Kaylee become a mother. She's child-like in a lot of ways, but also loving and maternal. I think she would have been a really great mom.

INTERVIEW WITH RAYGUNREVIVAL.COM, 2007

JEWEL STAITE

ON 'JOSS SPEAK':
Once I got used to it, it became really easy. I can't help myself doing it off set, that broken English he sometimes writes for us.

INTERVIEW WITH ZETAMINOR.COM, 2005

ON HER HARDEST SCENE TO SHOOT:
The hardest for me was probably the one in 'Objects in Space', in the engine room with Early, even though he [Richard Brooks] was a very nice man. That was a tough day at work. The not-hardest was any time I had to make

out with Sean. Just being honest! He smells *beautiful*.

SPEAKING ON STAGE AT DRAGON CON, 2008

ON HER FEELINGS TOWARDS THE SHOW:
I had such a love affair with this show in a really crazy, mad way. I still watch the episodes when I'm feeling glum, and just the fact that we got to do the movie and that we got to work together again and that being canceled wasn't the end was so incredible.

SPEAKING ON STAGE AT THE 'SERENITY' CONVENTION, 2005

ON FOREVER BEING KNOWN AS THE 'SMUDGY, SMILEY MECHANIC'.
It's kind of funny: I've met some fans at certain events and conventions and things who say I look "sooooo much better" with grease on my face and overalls on. Like, thanks. But at least she's a likeable character! I never imagined when I signed on to *Firefly* that this would happen. I think we all knew from the very beginning that we were creating something quite special, so when I meet people that understand and appreciate it, it feels really nice. The whole experience holds a lot of wonderful memories for me. Like when Nathan put hand lotion under the door handles of my trailer and laughed at me when I fell down the stairs. Other than that, I love all those guys, and I miss them a lot. ◉

INTERVIEW WITH RAYGUNREVIVAL.COM, 2007

THRILLING HEROICS

An interview with Firefly Stunt Coordinator Nick Brandon

Australian-accented Nick Brandon was born in Singapore, where he studied martial arts as a youth. He refined his craft in the Hong Kong film industry, then moved to the US and began doing stunts in Hollywood. "I decided this is where it was happening," Brandon laughs. As he grew more experienced, he began dividing his time between doing stunts and stunt coordination. He worked for Mutant Enemy on both *Buffy the Vampire Slayer* and *Angel. Angel* stunt coordinator Mike Massa suggested Brandon for the *Firefly* gig after Eddie Braun had coordinated the pilot, 'Serenity'.

ON THE GENERAL STYLE OF *FIREFLY* STUNTS:

I didn't want to go too Hong Kong *Matrix*-y. I tried to blend more of a powerful, almost a realistic look with some of the Hong Kong stuff and also with the kind of lifelike fights that happen a lot in English film and television. The fighting styles developed based on the characters, how they moved and what would work out best for them, so basically it grew with them.

The *Firefly* regulars were all great, they were all very physical. The main two that I worked with were Nathan and Adam. They both have their own styles that developed, Adam being a lot more powerful-looking in his style of fighting; Nathan is very talented in most of the things he does. They were both awesome to work with, very easy.

ON 'THE TRAIN JOB':

We had a stunt where we had Adam's stunt double Tim Sitarz jump out of the spaceship and land on the roof of the train. He jumped out of the full-sized spaceship into a hole, basically. We put a green screen down below, so he jumped out onto pads, out of the full-sized ship.

For the second part of the stunt, we had one or two carriages of the train that we built on stage that I landed him down on. He was actually suspended in mid-air on a wire that just released and then decelerated him as he lands on top of the carriage.

When Mal kicks Crow into the engine, that was actually done CG. They scanned the actor [Andrew Bryniarski] and then used a completely computer-generated character that flew into the engine. I had ideas of how to do it practically; time was probably the reason that they went with purely CG. The kick was for real. We just cut out of him as soon as he started to go backwards. He hardly went backwards at all. As soon as the kick happened, they cut out of it.

ON 'SHINDIG':

In the story, Mal couldn't swordfight at all. Atherton Wing [played by Edward Atterton], who challenged him to the duel, was supposedly an expert sword-fighter. It was interesting to do a swordfight where one person's obviously not very skilled and the other person is an expert. In reality, the actors were both very good. Nathan was great. I brought in a sword guy, Tim Weske, to help choreograph the sword stuff and work with the actors on getting them up to scratch sword-wise. Pretty much, I'll give him the outline of the fight, the important beats and then see what he comes up with. The stunt doubles did quite a bit of the sword-fighting stuff. Usually, you film over the shoulder of one guy looking at the other guy, and the guy you're looking at is going to be the actor and you're over the shoulder of the stunt double. The stunt double is really accurate, so they can get really close to the actor with their moves, and they can make it look great.

ON 'SAFE':

There was a gun battle with a few stunt people in that. Generally speaking, if they're not actors, i.e., if they're just nondescript people in the scenes who come in and have a gun battle, they'll be stunt people. We'll talk about it and it'll be, "You come around the corner and this guy shoots you, you take a hit here," and the director will require a squib hit, a blood pack, so special effects will work that out and then we'll do our part of it. All the stunt people I hire would know how to take any of those kinds of hits and go to the ground, no problem. Where the hits are on the body will be up to the director. A lot of times, that'll be decided in a pre-production meeting, so it will be known by everybody way beforehand.

ON 'JAYNESTOWN':

There was a bit where a guy jumped in front of a shotgun blast. That was in fact a stunt double, although you do see his face. I put him on a wire to change his direction in mid-air, so he actually dove in front heading one way, and as he got hit, spun around and landed. When wire stunts are done outdoors, you can go with anything to hold the wire, from cranes to great forklift pieces of machinery of adjustable height, that weigh a lot. Basically, you're looking for anything solid!

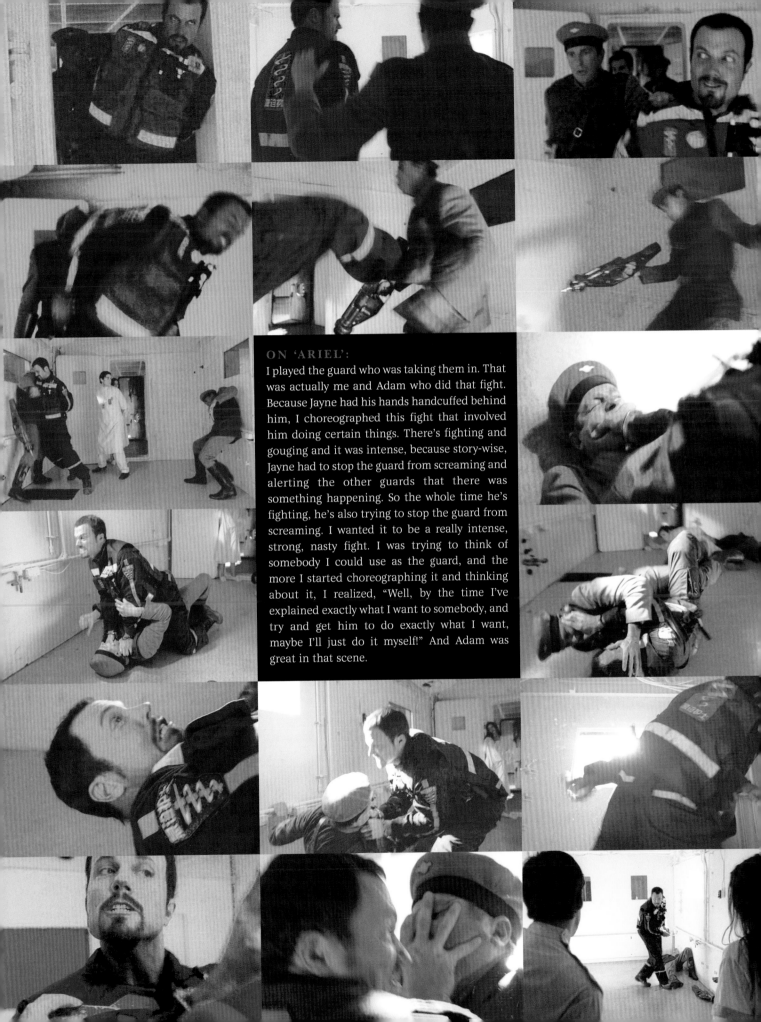

ON 'ARIEL':

I played the guard who was taking them in. That was actually me and Adam who did that fight. Because Jayne had his hands handcuffed behind him, I choreographed this fight that involved him doing certain things. There's fighting and gouging and it was intense, because story-wise, Jayne had to stop the guard from screaming and alerting the other guards that there was something happening. So the whole time he's fighting, he's also trying to stop the guard from screaming. I wanted it to be a really intense, strong, nasty fight. I was trying to think of somebody I could use as the guard, and the more I started choreographing it and thinking about it, I realized, "Well, by the time I've explained exactly what I want to somebody, and try and get him to do exactly what I want, maybe I'll just do it myself!" And Adam was great in that scene.

ON 'TRASH':

I think the biggest mishap we had was [Jayne double] Tim Sitarz, who hit his head doing the stunt on 'Trash'. We did a wire thing as one of the containers explodes and throws him back. He landed on the outside of the ship. He went backwards about ten, twelve feet, something like that. In that instance, a cable went up to the perms [permanent cable-bearing fixtures] on the stage and then down to a ratchet, the piece of machinery that pulled him backwards. The wire was attached to a harness that he's wearing underneath his wardrobe. In that case, it was attached to his back. When we pulled him backwards, he basically whipped back and hit the back of his head. He went and got it checked out though, and he was fine.

ON 'HEART OF GOLD':

The horse stuff in that one was pretty cool, because we had saddle falls and horse falls. Saddle falls are where the rider will fall off the horse, and the horse fall is where the actual horse will go down as well. We had two or three of both of those in there, and then there was a hovercraft deal that had a big machine gun on on the back that was quite fun. There were a couple of different rigs. There was one where the hovercraft was actually towed behind another vehicle on a trailer [as seen on page 99], and the trailer was painted out to make it look like it was floating. Then there were pieces of it – there was another one that was on the soundstage that just kind of moved as if it was going over bumps and stuff with green screen in the back. There were a lot of people taking bullet hits, the one guy in the back of the hover vehicle took a nice hit coming off of that.

ON 'OBJECTS IN SPACE':

We had a sequence in that where Jubal Early [played by Richard Brooks] fights Mal in the confines of the ship itself. Obviously, for the moves in that, you're restricted to a lot of close combat kind of stuff, rather than nice big flashy jumping kicks, because there's no room. It can work in two ways. It can make the fight look more intense or it can limit you so much that it looks pretty boring, so you've got to try to use the space that you have in the best way you can.

IN CONCLUSION:

I think the whole concept was unique. I love the way that Joss developed it. I haven't talked to anybody who saw it that didn't like it. In terms of stunts, I think we were a very safe show. I had a great time filming it and we all got along very well. It was just a great series. ◀

SEAN MAHER

Dr Simon Tam

SEAN ON THE WORLD OF THE SHOW, AND THE MOVIE:

What I love about the world of *Firefly* is it's 500 years in the future but there's this big 'what if?', like, what if we used up the resources of Earth and here we are, people are trying to survive, trying to get by, trying to just eat and get a job... For me it instilled this faith in humanity that, yes, 500 years in the future we have this Alliance trying to do this horrible thing to this girl and trying to change people, [but] at the end of the day it's like, "OK, let's just have faith." There is innate goodness, and people will prevail as human beings... there's just a wonderful sense of humanity to it. No matter how far in the future you go, hopefully people are people in how they work and function together. We are trying to rebuild and figure things out.

INTERVIEW WITH ZETAMINOR.COM, 2005

ON JOSS WHEDON:

He's just this incredible man, he's really a wonderful guy, a friend and a mentor. The instant I met him... I was so intrigued. I really wanted to work with him. And it just continually grew, like every time on set, watching him work, everything he said was so smart. I felt that I was being steered into the right direction.

He's this incredible ring leader.

INTERVIEW WITH ZETAMINOR.COM, 2005

ON THE FRUSTRATION OF BEING IN TV SHOWS THAT GOT CANCELED:

It got easier. I think the first time it happened, it was like a death. When *Ryan Caulfield* got canceled... Y'know, it was my first job, and you do kind of live in this bubble before you air. You think this show is the most amazing thing, and you're doing six, seven episodes before you go to air, so you've created bonds with people and you feel like a family. So *Ryan Caulfield* felt a bit like a death. And then, by the time I got to *Firefly*... The irony of the *Firefly* journey, for me, was that when it was canceled, I was like, "Oh well, chalk it up to another canceled show." And that was when Joss was like, "No way. We're not done. We're gonna make a movie." And I was like, "Yeah, right. I've heard this before." Because I felt like I had been jaded, because I think that was my... fourth canceled show. So,

SEAN MAHER

yeah, by the time *Firefly* got canceled, I think I was a little used to it, and just felt like, "All right, well, let's move on to something else." So that's why I'm always so shocked at the *Firefly* phenomenon. It was the exact opposite of what I had been used to. Because when *Ryan Caulfield* was canceled, all those discussions were going on. "It's not done. We're going to a different network. We're doing this. We're doing that..." Like I even related that to my agent, "Oh no, this isn't finished. Don't you worry. We're going to find a home for this. That's what they're telling me on set. It's fine." And you know, it never happens, or rarely happens, I guess. *Firefly* is the little engine that could. It's a phenomenon of its own.

INTERVIEW WITH SEANMAHER.INFO, 2009

ON GETTING THE PHONE CALL ABOUT THE MOVIE:

I remember exactly where I was. I was on Orlando, it's a street in LA just north of Melrose, and I pulled off to the side of the road because I was just like, "Wait, what? We're really doing this?" And my agent was like, "We have the offer." And I was, "All right, I gotta go!" And then we [the cast] all called each other: "Did you get an offer?" [Laughs.] ... I honestly didn't believe that it was going to happen. Even at the read-through... We kept laughing because we couldn't believe we were doing this. I'd look over at Jewel and she'd be like, "Heeheehee!"

INTERVIEW WITH SEANMAHER.INFO, 2009

ON THE FANS:

It's just wonderful, it just brings you home. I mean, all the time, people... like the Immigrations Officer tonight [Sean had just flown into Vancouver when this interview took place] was all, this is business business, talk talk talk, and then as I'm walking away, he said, "*Firefly* rules." And I was like, "Thanks, buddy." They're everywhere, the fans... It's extraordinary to be part of something that reached so many people. And I feel like people continue [to find it]... People who have recently seen the show, new fans who are like, "Oh my gosh, my girlfriend made me watch it this weekend and I was so happy and what an amazing show!" I just feel like everybody who gets a taste of it, loves it. I'm always amazed at that. I feel like I've rarely met – or maybe people don't tell me – people who've seen the show, who didn't like it."

INTERVIEW WITH SEANMAHER.INFO, 2009

HIS FAVORITE MEMORY OF JOSS:

My favorite moment – and he wasn't on the set – but we were shooting the series and I remember the time when his first child was born. That sort of epitomizes to me how much of a family I feel with these people. To be on set and get word that Joss had his first child, and how moving that was."

INTERVIEW WITH ABOUT.COM, 2005

While most of the interiors for *Firefly*, including the sets for the ship Serenity, existed on the soundstages of Twentieth Century Fox Studios in Los Angeles, when it came time to visit a planet, the cast and crew often headed off for a location shoot.

This is where *Firefly* location manager Peter M. Robarts came in. So what exactly does the job entail? Robarts explains: "A location manager reads the script, and all the different locations that are written in the storyline – whether it's a gas station, the beach, a building, a rooftop, a bar or whatever it is – a location manager needs to go out and find different options for each of them. Then he'll present them all to the director for him to choose which one he thinks is best for the show. And then a location manager has to arrange for all the city and county permits for filming in those locations, as well as arrange for all the physical choreography of getting a group of people into a location – parking lots for crew, places to park all the trucks – all that kind of stuff."

Robarts had been working for Mutant Enemy for over a year as location manager on *Buffy the Vampire Slayer* when *Firefly* came along. "A lot of the people went from *Buffy* to *Firefly* – I was one of those – to do the pilot and the series," Robarts notes. "The premise was a pretty interesting one. I love sci-fi, and it was also combined with a frontier setting, in which you went to these different planets and people rode horses and used guns — not ray guns. We weren't looking for a whole lot of hi-tech buildings and hi-tech exteriors. We kept it much more open, out in the frontier regions, where the Serenity crew were shipping their trade. A lot of the stuff that we in the location department were looking for were old abandoned towns, vacant valleys, a lot of mines and just interesting terrain that you'd probably shoot more in a Western than you would normally think of in sci-fi. We were looking for really interesting, otherworldly geography that could be on some other remote planet somewhere."

ON LOCATION

An interview with Location Manager Peter Robarts

How does one find such locations? "If you've been in the business long enough," Robarts points out, "you know all these different places, because over the years, you've shot them from time to time on different shows. So most of the stuff that we shot, I knew all about from before."

Many of the desert 'Western' locations were several hours' drive out of Los Angeles. Why were such distant sites chosen? "Well, it just depends on what you're looking for," Robarts says. "If you want real desert, you've got to go out to Palmdale or Lancaster. Those are your closest ones. Also, you want to get away from a lot of houses. Every time you go out, every couple of months, there are more houses on your horizon, which is sort of what's happening to Los Angeles in a lot of ways. But the best deserts, you have to go out to that area, out toward Mojave. Not *to* Mojave, but on the way out to Mojave, which is where Lancaster and Palmdale are."

'SERENITY':

"In the pilot, they had a huge battle scene in Serenity Valley. That was a really interesting look that we needed to find, and we found it in a valley out toward the Mojave Desert, in the Palmdale/Lancaster area. There is this really terrific desert valley full of huge boulders and lots of sand, really nice and wide with a sort of desert bowl area off to one side of it. And it was quite large: hundreds of yards long and hundreds of yards wide, so it fit what we needed very well. There's another place that we shot the big scene with Patience and her gang, down in a big dry wash. That was a ranch out by Acton, by the 14 freeway."

❖ Opposite: Meeting Patience and her gang, out by Acton, CA.

❖ Above and top: Filming the battle of Serenity Valley.

'THE TRAIN JOB':

"There was a high-speed train that came into an old desert town and a mine. That was out at Rosamond, just north of Lancaster, about two hours north of Los Angeles, and it's an old gold mine that sits on a hill. I think they went back there on the feature [*Serenity*]. That was an interesting location — the Tropico Gold Mine it's called."

❖ Above and right: The Tropico Gold Mine became Paradiso.

❖ Right: A callsheet for one of the days spent filming 'Jaynestown' at Sable Ranch, along with a map given to cast and crew to help orient them.

❖ Opposite left center and bottom: Sable Ranch as it is today.

'JAYNESTOWN':

"That was a neat set. We shot that at a place called Sable Ranch, which is out in the Santa Clarita area north of Los Angeles. It's a film ranch — it's about four hundred acres and easily a thousand shows have been shot out there. It's a great location. They have lots of different buildings and they have this remarkably large area with a pond — well, they have several, actually. We used one of those for where they were digging the mud out and doing the bricks, and we used one of the other ponds that was a little higher up for the prison where people were in cages over water."

'ARIEL':
"We were on the Fox lot, because it was a Fox show, so for a lot of the exteriors we needed we shot some of the nice modern buildings that they have there, in Century City."

❖ Above and opposite: Filming 'War Stories'. That's a painted flat of the shuttle.

❖ Below: The Japanese Garden in Van Nuys, onscreen in 'Trash' and as it is today.

'WAR STORIES':
The scenes of Wash and Mal delivering their cargo, and then Zoe, Jayne and Book discovering the aftermath, were filmed on a desert location out beyond Lancaster. It's on private property, up behind a standing set of a run-down gas station and motel.

'TRASH':
Robarts did not work on the last two *Firefly* episodes to be filmed, 'Trash' and 'The Message'. "At that time," he says, "they weren't sure if they had been picked up to do a couple more episodes and I went off to do another show." The exteriors for Durran Haymer's estate on Bellerophon in 'Trash' were shot at the Japanese Garden in Van Nuys, California. The garden's Japanese name, Suiho-en, means "garden of water and fragrance", which is somewhat ironic given that it is right next to the Tillman Water Reclamation Plant, which treats sewage. However, the garden itself is a beautiful location, with migratory waterfowl, tilapia and carp inhabiting its ponds and a variety of traditional Japanese tea garden architecture and landscaping. The garden is open to the general public.

'HEART OF GOLD':
"That was a private compound that's way, way out past Lancaster. I'd heard about it, so I went out there and it was this two-story or two-and-a-half-story old mansion that some desert person had half-built. He'd built it on the inside, but a lot of the outside was left unfinished – actually, some of the inside, too – and there was all kinds of trash and everything all over the place. It was a bizarre but really unique location, and that's what we used for the ladies of ill repute. There was some kind of an airfield there, too, that he had outlined with tires. It was a very eclectic property, and it really fit what we were looking for on that particular show."

❖ Above: Prepping a shot for 'Heart of Gold'.

❖ Right: Filming the attack. The gunmen on the right are firing pellets to simulate bullet hits on the house.

❖ Far right: Adding some prop blood.

WHAT MIGHT HAVE BEEN:

Having used several places within striking distance of LA, Robarts looked further afield at Death Valley for possible future locations, though ultimately *Firefly* never filmed there. "I went for a big scout out there, thinking that we would be using a lot of that stuff. I'm sure that had we gone another season, if it had been picked up, we probably would have gone to a lot of really interesting areas out towards Death Valley, because there's some *really* otherworldly places out there, which would have been great to shoot." He's sorry it didn't last longer. "*Firefly* had a very interesting group of people, very talented. It was a fun shoot, and it was a great crew." ◁

❖ Top right: The house encased in foil during filming, and (top left) as it is today.

❖ Above left: The hovercraft trailer rig.

❖ Left: Actor Fredric Lehne takes a test drive.

SUMMER GLAU

River Tam

SUMMER ON DEVELOPING HER ACTING SKILLS:

The thing about River that I like is that she doesn't have a lot of lines. Especially in the series she had to show what she was thinking just by the way she moved, or by how her face was moving. I think that has helped me a lot as an actor. I still have a hard time sometimes, expressing my anger with words, I'm better at moving and being in a room and showing how I feel that way. It's a thing that I had to work on because I was very shy as a kid. I think that's why I love dancing, because I felt that people were watching me but I didn't have to connect with them. They were out there and I could feel that they were watching me, but I didn't have to look at them. Now with acting it's very therapeutic for me, having to actually say and communicate.

INTERVIEW WITH ZETAMINOR.COM, 2005

ON JOSS WHEDON:

If you stand by him on set for ten minutes you realize every detail that runs by him, you realize how special, creative and patient he is. He is kind, and he speaks well to everybody. He gave me what I have now in my career, he cast me in my very first TV show, he believed in me when nobody believed in me. He saw something that other people were not seeing. He's my hero in a way. I'll never forget what he's done for me.

INTERVIEW WITH ZETAMINOR.COM, 2005

ON FILMING THE 'SESSION 416' VIRAL MARKETING CAMPAIGN FOR THE MOVIE:

It was very exciting for me to be involved in that. I was in Texas... Joss called me and said, "Where are you? Can you come back for the weekend? I have this idea but I need to write it!" I was thrilled and I felt it was really important for people to see River before anything happened to her, when she was happy and full of hope.

I loved doing it. It was just Joss and me and it's a really special memory for me. I thought the script was very haunting. I remember when I was trying to memorize it, I hadn't been in my LA apartment for a month. I was lying in bed trying to memorize the dialogue that I was going to shoot the next morning. I couldn't sleep that night going in and out of bad dreams and talking to myself. I got scared from trying to prepare for those emotional scenes. It was a hard night to get through, the words were powerful.

INTERVIEW WITH SUMMERGLAU.CO.UK, 2005

JEWEL STAITE ON MEETING SUMMER FOR THE FIRST TIME:

Jewel: [Summer was] very quiet and shy and beautiful and fairy-like. Very elegant in her posture – you could tell she was a dancer. We were all at the read-through and you opened your mouth and you gave this crazy-ass performance out of nowhere. At read-throughs you sort of give it fifty percent, and Summer gave it like 100 percent and I was like, "Oh my god!" She just floored me; I just couldn't believe how good she was, and how perfect she was for the role.

Summer: I get really sappy when I talk about everyone. I was the new kid and I'd never done anything before and

SUMMER GLAU

when Jewel said that we were at the table read and I was reading full out — I didn't *know* that we were supposed to read through the script, I thought that we had to perform at the table. I finally grew into learning how to be an actor... I love everybody, I really do. I admire everyone.

SPEAKING ON STAGE AT THE 'SERENITY' CONVENTION, 2005

ON WHERE RIVER, WHO ARRIVED ON THE SHIP NAKED, GOT HER CLOTHES FROM:

I think River collected clothes from Kaylee and Inara, and also there were a few dresses that we made up a little backstory for ourselves that Simon would pick them up from stops along the way. Like the pink dress that I wore in 'The Message', which was my favorite actually. It was an old vintage dress from the forties. We just figured that one day Simon was out shopping and he saw it and picked it up because he thought River would like it. I loved my wardrobe. I thought it was the most comfortable out of anybody's. So I think she just picked up little scraps and wore strange little things, whatever might fit on her, and I think she raided Inara's closet and Kaylee's too.

SPEAKING ON STAGE AT THE 'FUSION' CONVENTION, 2004

ON HER CHARACTER'S 'DEFINING MOMENT':

I think that one of the favorite scenes I ever did was in 'Objects in Space' after I had been up in Jubal Early's ship. The crew had been trying to get rid of me for so many episodes and when Mal comes up onto the ship to bring me back, that's one of my favorite moments. I felt like they were really my family and that they were going to take care of me, and that I was accepted. I think that was an important moment for my character, and a scene that I really love.

SPEAKING ON STAGE AT THE 'FUSION' CONVENTION, 2004

CRYSTAL

// BY BRETT MATTHEWS

Simon looked...

It was hard to find the word. He wasn't helping, not offering anything beyond the gentle smile he had not worn sincerely in too long. He looked at her directly, but it wasn't a stare. Didn't make her uncomfortable in the smallest way.

The word came suddenly, as obvious and clear to her as it had been elusive only moments before.

Simon Tam was happy. They were finally safe.

"River."

Simon's face resolved slowly, lines drawing out of thin air to form it. His brow was furrowed. He was no longer happy. He stared at River, more as a clinician than her brother, which *always* made her uncomfortable.

"How do you feel?"

She could see the hypo he had used to inject her sitting on a surface in the infirmary. River had come to hate the place and its cold, even light. She didn't say anything for a while. She wasn't sure of the answer. She watched as Simon continued to sharpen, to the point she felt she could count all the pores of his face.

"*River.*" More urgently this time. It had been

about a minute.

It made River lose count, somewhere in the hundreds. She brought her eyes to Simon, slow and steady and sure. He flinched as if he didn't recognize her... or as though he *did*. Like when you see someone you haven't for a very long time.

"*Crystal.*" That was the word. And with it River Tam was off, wandering Serenity's twisting corridors. She hoped as she had so many times before...

Simon let her go. As always, he would not be far behind.

———————

I t's hard to describe what River saw next. Bodies. Limbs. Tongues. Writhing like oiled snakes. She could all but feel their slickness on the surface of her skin...

And the *sounds*. Pleasure or pain. Maybe even both.

———————

"W hy you lookin' at me like that, Moon Pie?"

Jayne was in the kitchen area. He brought a steaming pot of soy-something over to the large, wooden surface where River sat. The table had enough room for all of them, but it occurred to her that soon, they'd start removing chairs. In this moment, River felt she could divine exactly how and when the seats would turn up empty.

No. She *knew* it...

"What's the matter? You gone deaf on top of *dinlo*?"

He had used the masculine form — as Jayne often did, overcompensating — but the translation

was one of River's very favorites. *Dinlo*. Crazy. But it was the literal that she loved. *Electric man.*

"I reckon this stuff would taste just as good coming out the other end..." Jayne mumbled as he took a seat across from her, at the spot he'd carved his name, long ago. He'd etched other expressions into the table, too. None for polite company. Marking his territory from the moment he had decided to stay aboard the ship. When he grudgingly realized, though he would never admit it, that the lot of everyone aboard and Jayne Cobb's were one and the same.

His knife speared a block of purple tofu, worked it around the stump of tobacco clenched in his teeth and into his mouth. Jayne's face twisted, not much different from the times he'd been shot.

"I were runnin' this boat, it'd be strawberries and salmon. *Guaranteed.*"

The sound of his eating jogged her to what she'd just seen and heard so clearly, no matter that it was the future. River's stomach turned despite being empty. Maybe that was why the mixture of drugs Simon had injected her with was having such a profound effect. He had told her to eat before her treatment. She should have listened.

"You'll never captain your own ship, but it's going to be fine. You'll be happy as you define it. Even heroic, from time to time."

River swept out of the dining room before Jayne could get the mouthful down. He had no idea what any of it meant. Maybe time would tell. He was not blind to the fact that it often did, where River was concerned.

"*Dinlo.*" Jayne said it again. That was a hell of a lot easier to deal with than the alternative...

———————

"**Y**ou die, Shepherd."

Book didn't so much as blink.

"We all die, child. It's merely a question of when. And more importantly, for what." His answer reassured River. His answers often did.

"Yes. But you die first."

He blinked, that time. But Book was immediately at peace.

"Seems to me the normal way of things. I am the eldest aboard this ship —"

"It's *painful.*" River continued. "And it's not aboard the ship." She felt that she could talk to him, at once more easily and directly than anyone else. "Do you want to know how it happens? Do you want to know where?"

Book fingered the braided locks of his hair, didn't notice it made her fear they might pop loose. Of the questions that occurred to him since River had broken the silence of his morning prayers, neither of the two she had asked.

"No. What I would want to know is this. Am I alone? Is it for something I believe is *right...?*"

River relaxed profoundly. Those were so much easier to answer than her own. She knew them innately, as an infant knows to draw its first breath. Took air herself, preparing to share what she had seen — was it *experienced?* — with the Shepherd. She would have told him anything he asked. Anything in her power, which on this day, this hour, seemed limitless...

"On second thought," Book spoke before River had the chance. "I'd prefer not knowing." He smiled, broad and brilliant and white.

"I've chased mysteries my whole life, divine and otherwise. I see no point in stopping now."

———————

"**A**in't interrupting, River. Doing the count's easy, you can count all that we got on one hand."

She had found Zoe in the cargo bay, taking inventory of their supplies. But River didn't come any further down the suspended catwalk than she already was.

"You're going to be okay," she said from the

shadows above.

It didn't come as any surprise to Zoe, not even enough to warrant looking up from the work. For her, there simply was no other option.

"'Course we are. We've been without before, will be again." She scratched four lines with lead into a piece of brown paper as she spoke. There wasn't enough stock to warrant a fifth, the slash that should have gone through them. "Not that I'd mind having to carry a one, from time to time."

"It will seem impossible. It's almost going to break you. In the small hours, when no one is around..."

Now Zoe's head snapped up. River met her gaze and held it, not something that happened to Zoe often.

"But you're going to be okay."

Zoe nodded almost imperceptibly and River took a step back, disappearing into the darkness. She'd said what she came to and she'd been heard. That was about as much as anyone could ever ask of words.

Zoe started the count over.

"It looks like a pig."

Of this River was certain.

Kaylee squirmed in her hammock to clock where she stood, at the threshold of the engine room. River spun a finger in a circle, pantomiming the action of Serenity's cabled heart, revolving around its spit of a piston.

Kaylee took it as a compliment of the highest order. Impossibly, her face brightened even more.

"Pigs is yummy!"

She motioned that River should join her in the hammock, an image Jayne would have deemed *bunk-worthy*. River shook her head.

"I can't stay. It's running out. But I wanted to thank you..." Her voice was serene. If Kaylee wasn't looking at River as she spoke, she might not have recognized it at all.

"Thank me? Whatever for?"

"Long story." River smiled. "*Beautiful* story." Then she was simply gone.

"You're welcome!" Kaylee's voice echoed down the hall, bouncing around its slanted shape. She sighed and swung herself out of the rope's embrace, yellowed picture novels and technical manuals spilling out along with her, equal in her eyes as pleasure reading. In the former, the boy and girl often ended up together. Or failing that, died wonderfully in the pursuit. But the latter had *schematics*. Annotations on hydraulics and fluid mechanics. And gobs of other things, even if they were wrong sometimes or Kaylee knew from experience the method they advised could be done twenty-five to fifty percent better.

She sighed again, plucking her favorite socket wrench off a loop of her coveralls and approaching the engine, which had begun to emit a funny sound.

Kaywinnit Lee Frye had a pig to attend to.

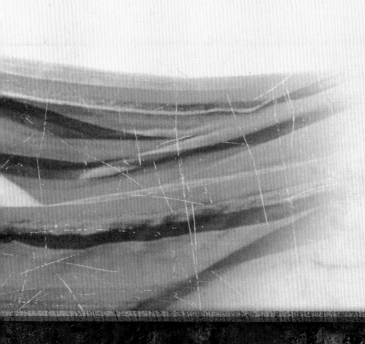

Wash looked over the flight yoke, into the familiar black of space. The dash was void of dinosaurs, making it easy. You put dinosaurs up there — *one time* — and it was all anyone wanted to talk about. It was much the same with flowered shirts...

He felt River's presence and spun the jump seat around to greet her. Wash got used to people coming up behind him, working in a cockpit. And though he couldn't always tell who was there so instantly, apart from his wife, there was never any mistaking River. She radiated something no one else aboard the ship — that Wash had ever known, for that matter — put out. She *crackled*.

"Howdy, Sunshine. Come to keep a pilot company while we limp to the cheapest fuel deck?"

River stepped into the light of the instrument panels. Her appearance concerned him. It looked to Wash like she was going to cry.

"River. What's the matter? Has Jayne been telling you where babies come from again...?"

She continued forward, throwing her arms around Wash and embracing him. *Urgently.* So tight the air was squeezed from his lungs and his question trailed off, unanswered. River was stronger than she looked. Stronger than anyone knew...

She released him just as suddenly. Her hand was last to break contact, fingertips describing an erratic shape around the whole of his chest, like a heart but larger and lopsided. Finally withdrew reluctantly. River spun on her bare heel and left the cockpit without crying, or even saying a word.

"*Right.* Because that happens every day. Is there some obscure holiday I don't know about —"

"You know what would happen, I found you huggin' on some sweet young thing, wasn't

certifiable?" River and Zoe had crossed paths, again in the hall.

"You'd murder me?" Wash opened his arms the familiar, perfect amount.

"No." Zoe said. "Most places, murder requires them finding the body."

She kicked the door shut and lowered herself into his lap.

"We got anything in our path?"

Wash shook his head.

"No ma'am. Nothing but empty space the next eight or so hours."

They kissed. It was exactly the right answer.

"Ask me."

River had entered the shuttle un-announced. Inara ended the conversation she was having over the Cortex immediately, somehow gracefully. Her potential client was not offended when the wave was cut short, instead even more intrigued.

"River —"

"*Ask me.*" It was more demand than question,

this time.

Inara took River's hand and led her to the bed, piled high with fabrics from a dozen different worlds. She was cold to the touch, sweating hail.

"Ask you what?"

"What you *want*." Her teeth were chattering, now. "Ask me and I'll tell you."

The way River said it made Inara believe her. She was more open-minded than most, given her profession as a Companion. Was not one to hold a grudge against things that were not easily explained.

"Running out of time…"

Two questions formed in Inara's mind at once, so distinctly they had faces. One was her own. The other familiar and handsome, if very stubborn. It occurred to her if she could only ask one, she didn't know which she would choose…

And then the faces were gone, replaced by River's. River was Inara's concern, not matters she had been too afraid to address with anyone — herself included — in far too long.

"Stay here. I'm going to find Simon."

"Yes and no." Inara was at the door when she heard them. The answers to her questions, but in which order? One would happen. The other would not. The revelation brought relief, maybe even joy…

But only for a moment. The other possibility soon seeped in, became every bit as palpable. Regret and despair.

Inara turned back to say something, just in time to see River hit the floor.

Malcolm Reynolds was dead.

He forced himself out of his bunk just the

People might say that. But they'd be wrong.

He'd been up all night — it was *always* night in space — reaching out. Sending out feelers to various contacts, trying to find where the next tank of fuel or table of food might come from. Nothing so far, but it didn't worry Mal. His employers weren't the type to keep regular business hours.

Six of them, he figured, between now and when they'd be refueling. Plenty of time to suss how he was to pay for it. Something would come up. It always did. And if not, then Mal would have to make it...

Mal started up the ladder that led out of his quarters. The hatch atop popped open and he was in the hallway, which ran from stem to stern. And right on time, apparently. He stepped aside, letting the crush of crew and passengers pass.

"We didn't get paid, as you well know. So's I don't see the need for a parade —"

The sentence died on his lips the moment he saw they were carrying River.

same, pulled a coarse woolen shirt over too many scars and hitched up his suspenders. No shower today. Not out of preference, but because they hadn't been able to fill the reservoir before pushing off the latest rock that had offered them a job. Mal didn't even remember the planet's name at the moment, only that it was overly self-important in retrospect. He supposed people might say the same about the one he had chosen for his ship...

"*Serenity.*" Mal whispered it to himself as she sailed as silently as she ever did through the black. He touched her rusted hull, could feel her pulse as surely as his own.

Black. Stretching out indefinitely, without beginning or end...

It took River a moment to realize that it was space. The understanding allowed her to resolve the pinpricks of light that were very distant stars. So far away that were she to set course for them, she would not reach them in her lifetime. Not in ten.

The ship thrummed beneath her feet. Up the flight yoke and into the tips of her fingers, reverberating down the length of her arms and into her core. Her heart. Serenity's vibration was a promise between lovers, yearning to be fulfilled.

Of power just waiting to be unleashed...

River knew exactly how she — *the ship* — felt.

She reached up, flipping switches on and cutting others off, knowing where each was and what it did without looking. She increased the engine's gain and allowed Serenity to accumulate speed... not as much as either of them wanted, but River knew firsthand that a little bit of what you desired was often better than the whole.

River looked left to the co-pilot's seat, found Mal. Did he seem older? *Was* he older? It was hard to say. Malcolm Reynolds had a timeless quality about him she had always found comforting, that was constant and never went out of style. His expression asked the question for him, as it often did. *"We in a hurry or something?"* She smiled and answered aloud, though he had never spoke:

"No, Captain. We're just getting where we're going."

———

Mal was the first thing River saw when she awoke. He *had* looked older, just before.

It was the final moment of clarity before the fog set in, so fast and so thick it was soon raining in her head, making a mess of all that had come previously. River Tam began to... *wonder* about things. Large and small, consequential and not, all at once. Wonder wasn't the right word, but it was now as close as she could come.

More faces beyond Mal, all of them staring holes into her. River could feel the sear on her skin. All but smell her own flesh, going up...

River screamed and Mal smiled.

"There's our girl."

Jayne turned on the thick sole of his boot, stalking out of the infirmary.

"Seems fine to me, Doc. When do we eat?" Simon watched River, considering...

———

River found Mal in the sunken area beneath the cockpit. It didn't have a name, really. There was never much reason to be there, beyond the occasional electrical issue and that it afforded perhaps the best view on the ship. This was as far

forward as one could get, just a sliver of transparent canopy between you and the cold crush of space...

Mal sometimes took his coffee there, as he did now. He looked up from the rim of his battered tin cup as River descended the ladder with a dancer's grace to join him.

"Sorry. Wanted to find you before. Ran out of time." She reached the deck. Mal kicked a stool over and River joined him, the two of them sitting before the quiet glory of the 'verse in mismatched chairs.

"Well, you found me now," Mal replied. "What was it you need?"

River craned her neck, listening to a song that only she could hear. Tried to filter its noise, to settle on the one frequency amidst thousands that would provide the answer... couldn't. The best she could do was:

"*This*. I don't know, but I think it was this."

Mal raised his cup. It was enough for him.

"Don't worry, sailor. It'll come to you. We've got all the time in the world..."

River looked out through the viewport as he did, hoping it were true. Even if she'd known, just hours before and with crystal clarity, that it wasn't.

"Sad, simple Simon..."

He looked down at River where she laid tucked in bed. Her eyes were heavy. Her cadence once again her own, more accurately that which had been imposed upon her. Scored into her brain with electrode-laced needles.

"I'm not sad, River. I'd like to think simple." Simon meant the words. He smiled as proof.

"Thought you fixed broken me." She yawned it out, was fading fast.

River was right. Neurologically, she was never closer to what she'd been before her abduction than today. And yet she was wrong, too.

"You're fine." Simon meant it every bit as much. "You're happier now than you were this morning. That means more to me than any readout from a machine."

Jayne's diagnosis — the irony of those two words paired was not lost on Simon — had been correct. River was undeniably different, now. And yet, in her own particular way, she was also right as rain. While Simon Tam would never abandon the search for the sister he knew, that he had helped raise and loved more than anything on any world he would ever visit, the events of the day had made him come to realize that he loved River — as she was now, falling asleep in front of him — every bit as much.

"You're fine." He said it again as he leaned low, kissing her forehead. Then Simon shut off the lights and slipped out of the berth.

And for one night, River slept without the interruption of dreams. ◐

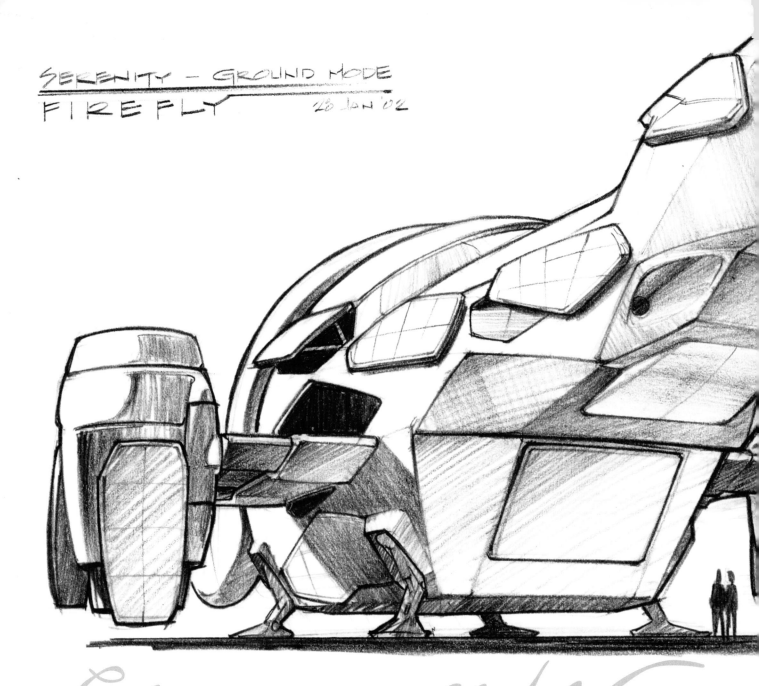

SERENITY — GROUND MODE
FIREFLY   28 JAN '02

SHIPS OF THE 'VERSE

Designing the ships of Firefly

I f Whedon was the master of the mythology and stories behind *Firefly*, then it was production designer Carey Meyer and visual effects supervisor/co-creator of Zoic Studios Loni Peristere who were the visual magicians, overseeing the design of all of the brilliant ships, vehicles and space stations that are now synonymous with the series. The two sat down together to reminisce about how they came to create the myriad of vehicles that were such an integral part of the show.

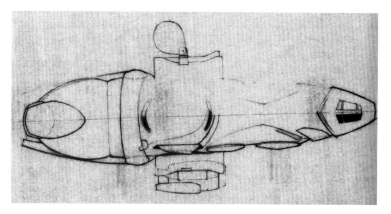

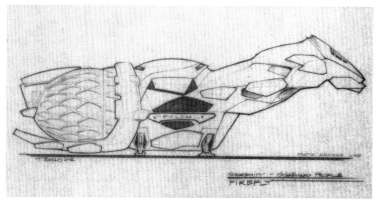

J. EARLES '02

SERENITY

First and foremost let's make it clear – there really is no *Firefly* series without the Firefly class transport Serenity. In fact the ship was so important to Whedon, he told Meyer and Peristere that it was to be considered a character equal in standing to the cast. That mandate set the tone for how they approached its creation.

Meyer remembers, "When we were first starting the project, Joss was just getting the green light from Fox and we were all working on *Buffy* at the time. After a couple of weeks Joss came up to me and said he really wanted me to work on it and to pitch some ideas for what the ship would look like, because that was the starting point for him. Once he got an idea of what the world was like inside the ship, he could start formulating the stories. Joss said his one key was for it to have an ironic flair to it. It had to

be cool, but there had to be some reality to it. So I started playing around with paper airplanes. There was this cool design I had always played around with as a child, and always loved. It's this conical-shaped airplane all made out of paper and I shoved a balloon into it.

"I still have the original model that I built," he chuckles. "I was up for 24 hours building this thing. We came in the next morning at nine o'clock and I think I nailed it. I brought the plane with the balloon shoved into it and a little sketch of what I was thinking. We all sit down and Joss says, 'Well, it's cool, but I think it's too far. We need to bring it back a little bit.' The shape was very asymmetrical, and he wanted a sleeker line to it. I took that original model and spread clay all over it, smoothing out the original into something resembling

❖ Opposite and above: Designs by illustrator Tim Earls helped refine Carey Meyer's original concept for Serenity.

what we have today. Then he really fell in love with what we now know as the ring that wraps around the rear."

Meyer continues, "From that point it was a series of sketches for how the rest of it all would look. He wanted a lot of it to look like an insect — a firefly obviously. One of the main designers I was looking at was Lebbeus Woods, who is a futurist architect. Joss liked that look as well, so we started sketching in that style, which got us an overall shape that we were able to cross-section and start developing the interior. From that Joss was able to ask for a bridge and a hallway that leads to the corridors, a galley, a corridor to the engine room and the main cargo bay. Once he nailed down the different spaces that were inside, we were able to lay it all out as set designs and work it back into the exterior shape."

Meanwhile Peristere says he was working in concert with Meyer in the digital realm. "I was keying off of what Carey was doing," he explains. "I began to build a

temporary version of that ship in 3-D, so once we had a physical model we could immediately bring it into 3-D space. A lot of what we were doing was coming up with how the rooms fit, and fitting that into the 3-D model, adjusting so all the rooms would fit in a logical manner. And Carey had this cool idea that the ship was put together and then reconstructed a little bit, because it had been in a junkyard for a long time. So the idea was that the external panels weren't all original. We spent some time going in the direction of having a lot of variety of textures, with a lot of colors and patinas from other ships. We went too far at first because it was like a quilt of a spaceship, but we pulled back and streamlined it. We also took a look at the logistics of the neck of the ship, and played with how steep it was, and how close to the ground based on how you would drive stuff into the cargo bay when the landing gear was down. Then we had to come up with the right kind of landing gear, and the door/ramp into the cargo bay."

❖ Right and far right: More designs by Tim Earls.

❖ Below: Carey Meyer's early concept design for the ship.

❖ Opposite: Serenity, seen both as Zoic's CG model (above) and the sets, including the exterior of the shuttle cockpit set (center row, left).

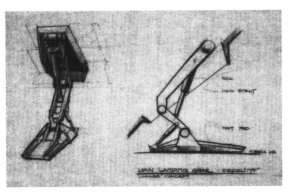

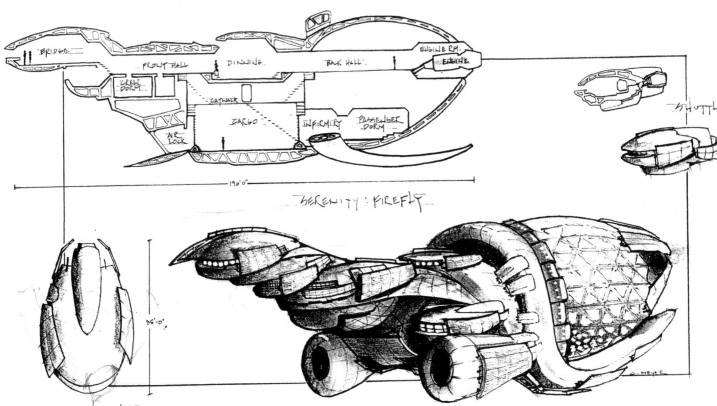

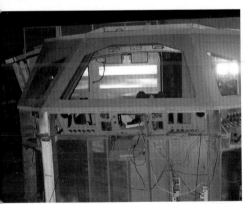

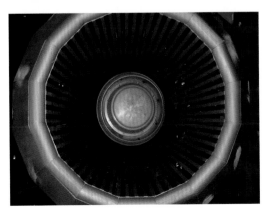

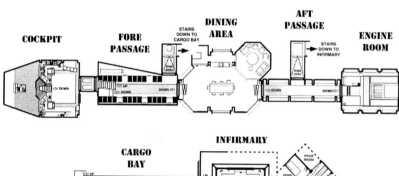

COCKPIT   **FORE PASSAGE**   STAIRS DOWN TO CARGO BAY   **DINING AREA**   **AFT PASSAGE**   STAIRS DOWN TO INFIRMARY   **ENGINE ROOM**

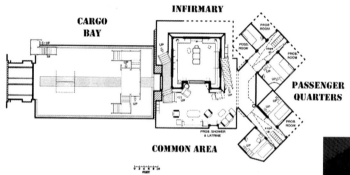

CARGO BAY   **INFIRMARY**   PROB. ROOM   **PASSENGER QUARTERS**   **COMMON AREA**

He continues, "In addition, we came up with where the gravity on the ship came from – we used the ring that Carey created. We called it the 'gravity ring' and put a widget in there that spun around. We built lighting effects for it with our DP on set, so they were built into the set lighting so you could see the changing flicker. We also had to come up with the trans-warp drive, the 'firefly engine'. Carey built these honeycomb shapes on the inside set, so we mirrored that on the outside. We came up with the logic of a cooling process, so we created these panels on the butt of the ship that opened up to reveal the same honeycomb pattern you saw on the inside, on the outside. There were insect-like panels that would show this glowing butt on Serenity, which was kinda cool."

SHUTTLE

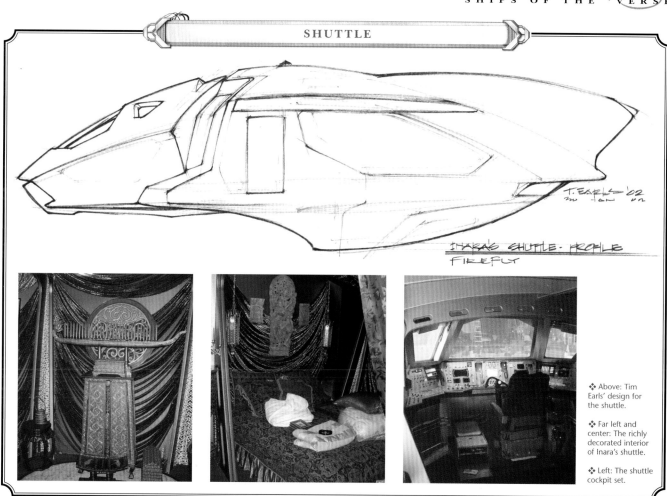

INARA'S SHUTTLE · PROFILE
FIREFLY

❖ Above: Tim Earls' design for the shuttle.

❖ Far left and center: The richly decorated interior of Inara's shuttle.

❖ Left: The shuttle cockpit set.

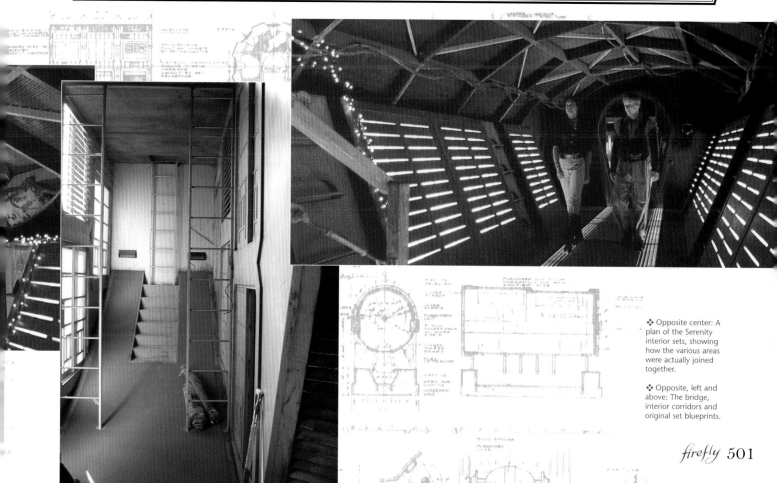

❖ Opposite center: A plan of the Serenity interior sets, showing how the various areas were actually joined together.

❖ Opposite, left and above: The bridge, interior corridors and original set blueprints.

Peristere laughs as he reveals an insiders' joke: "I always wanted Serenity's cargo bay to be detachable. Carey thought it was cool, but Joss was worried it was too similar to something that happened in *Star Trek*. I always thought a cargo ship's hold should be like a shipping container, where you can drop one off and pick one up. Believe it or not, I actually built it into the design of the CG model so that it does do that, because I figured at some time I would win that argument. I never won that fight, but it's still there."

Of their final product, Meyer muses, "Joss didn't just want a ship, he wanted a tenth character. I think we pulled it off and to this day he's very emotionally tied to that vehicle."

❖ Above: A bulkhead doorway, from blueprint to final set piece.

❖ Right: The infirmary.

❖ Below: The galley.

CONTROL PANEL SCREENS

❖ Top: A selection of control panel displays, which were printed onto transparencies and backlit.

❖ Above: The engine room.

❖ Above left and left: The cargo bay.

ALLIANCE CRUISER

These massive ships serve as functional cities that house military, police and civilians, patrolling the space between Alliance planets. After designing Serenity, Meyer says these were the next ships they tackled.

"We immediately knew we needed the Alliance ship and that it was a big craft – a sort of cityscape concept on a wing," Meyer details. "Joss was pretty clear right away that he didn't want to make something super long like the *Star Wars* Destroyer. He wanted it to be vertical... since it can go through space it doesn't have to worry about atmosphere. It can move whatever shape it is, so we started playing with it being tall. We did rough concept illustrations then sat down with illustrator Tim Earls and started creating."

Peristere continues, "The whole concept of a city in space was interesting to me. I love the notion of revealing a ship in an entirely new way, and one which embraced the fact that in space there is no up, down, right or left. There are no hard and fast rules of what you are looking at. I love how we introduce I.A.V. Dortmunder seeing two towers, thinking they are just great shapes, but then we reveal they are essentially Empire State buildings – these massive things! I love the idea that the tiny fighter craft show just how big this thing is. There's no need for scale in space – you can build ships as big as you like – so the idea of having this giant thing moving through the black was really cool. I was actually disappointed we didn't use the ship more, because we spent a lot of time working out the design of all of it, like the interesting bays on the underside where the fighter craft were stationed."

Carey adds, "The other concept we were playing with was that the textures and colors were completely divergent. The Alliance ship was stark grey with blacks and whites, while Serenity was very warm and had texture and felt real."

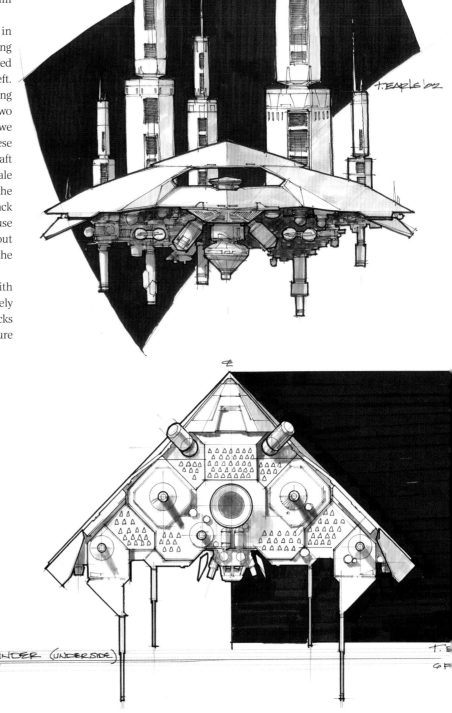

DORTMUNDER (UNDERSIDE)
FIREFLY

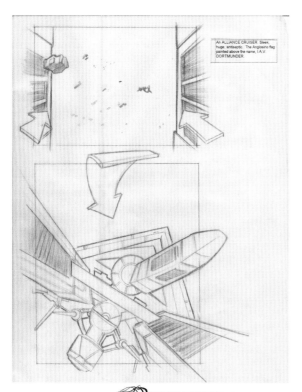

An ALLIANCE CRUISER. Sleek, huge, antiseptic. The Anglosino flag painted above the name, I.A.V. DORTMUNDER

ROCCO PASSIONINO

As the digital visual effects supervisor on the Emmy-winning Zoic team that created the *Firefly* pilot 'Serenity', Rocco Passionino was in charge of guiding the team of artists that translated Carey Meyer and Loni Peristere's designs and concept sketches into the finished CG ships and vehicles featured in the episode.

As the visual effects supervisor on *Angel*, Passionino says it was exciting to follow Whedon to his next creative endeavor. "I had such a strong feeling for Joss's work to begin with, so it was nice to jump onto a pilot he was doing, and for it to be sci-fi which was fantastic because... who doesn't like sci-fi?"

He continues, "*Firefly* gave us the opportunity to do something that had never been done before. It was this fun sci-fi show that we could geek out over back at the office creating wacky space ships we would then deliver back to Joss."

Detailing his responsibilities, Passionino explains, "Because this was such a CG-heavy show, my role as the digital visual effects supervisor was paying attention to the 3-D and the 2-D sides of things, so that Loni could focus on creating. He was doing a lot of the artistic stuff, so my role was after everything was created, was, 'How do we execute it?' As far as the design of the space ships, a lot of that was taking what the art department had done and fleshing it out and giving it a little bit more life. With it being the large show that it was, it was tricky for us to do a lot of that stuff. My job was focusing the vision that both Joss and

Loni had for the show into a physical constraint. A lot of what I was doing was making sure the CG could be created and that the composites could be completed the way they were."

From day one, Passionino says the visual effects required for the series were ambitious. "At the time, it was very difficult, but the team was so brilliant about everything. I know a lot of people say that," he laughs, "but I have worked with bad teams before. But the guys on *Firefly* loved the show, and they had a lot of freedom. I think having that freedom to allow their creativity to happen and not have the supervisors jamming things down their throats allowed them to offer ideas and we'd pitch them."

Passionino says another aspect of *Firefly*'s visual effects was that they were always in service of the story, a rarity in sci-fi film and TV, where the initial impulse is often to dazzle. "When you are in the thick of a show, you don't think of the grander scheme of things, or the impact some of these shows will have. But it was great for us to do a sci-fi show on a network channel. We really loved that it was well-written drama. A lot of the visual effects we were doing helped that along, but they weren't the focus of the show. They weren't in your face. It wasn't about the space ships; rather it was about the drama between the actors, which was great. That's what visual effects are supposed to be about. Effects should be about augmenting, not shove-it-in-your-face graphics."

❖ Opposite: Designs for the Dortmunder by Tim Earls.

❖ Above left: Frames from Charles Ratteray's storyboard for the introduction of the Dortmunder.

PERSEPHONE

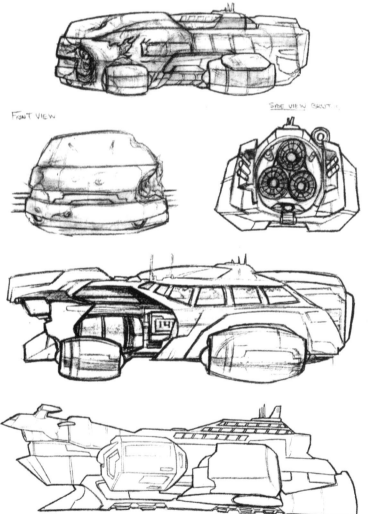

FRONT VIEW

SIDE VIEW (CUT)

PERSEPHONE'S EAVESDOWN DOCKS

In the episode 'Serenity', Mal's crew lands at a quasi-Skid Row-type docking station filled with a motley assortment of ships. Peristere says all of those vehicles were designed and created for the scene. "Between our department and Carey's department we threw around different sketches for that particular place. We asked what other kinds of ships would you find there? We came up with transportation vessels for people and other kinds of cargo ships. We pulled a bunch of real-world reference and then started deconstructing that material. It became a first set of library rules [vehicles] that inform the series."

MEDSHIP

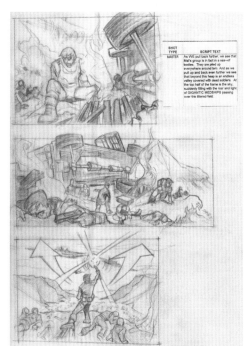

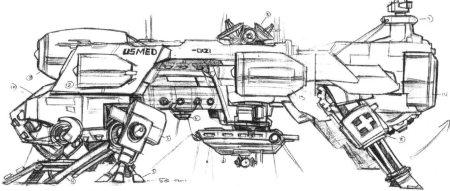

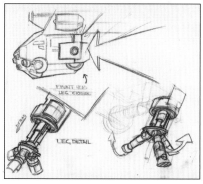

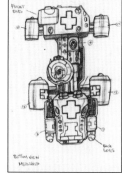

❖ Opposite: Eavesdown docks: A storyboard frame and ship designs (including the Brutus and at the bottom, the Paragon) by Charles Ratteray.

❖ Above and left: Ratteray's storyboard and designs for the Medships glimpsed at the end of the Battle of Serenity.

❖ Below: An early Tim Earls design, adapted to become the Hands of Blue's ship in 'Ariel'.

HANDS OF BLUE SHIP

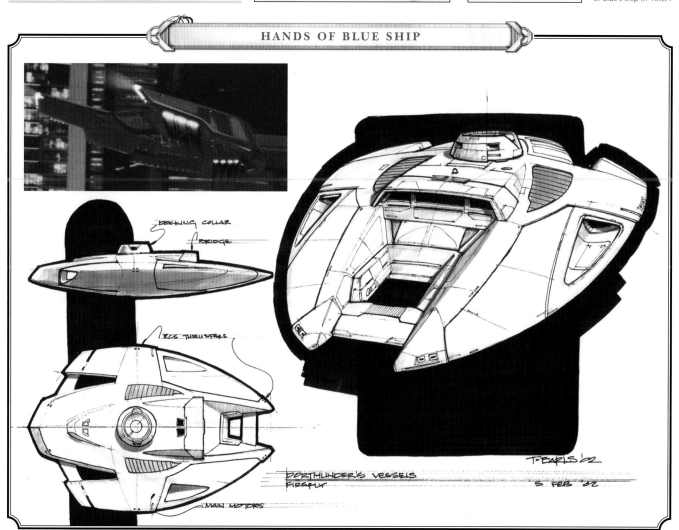

DOCKING COLLAR

BRIDGE

RCS THRUSTERS

DORTHUNDER'S VESSELS
FIREFLY

5. FEB. 02

MAIN MOTORS

T. EARLS '02

"Loni Peristere is a mad genius, which, apart from his endless attempts to destroy Metropolis, is useful. He and Zoic have provided the best digital effects I've ever seen on TV, which is *very* useful. They've been integral in creating a look, a style – in point of fact, a world. I couldn't imagine having done it without them."

JOSS WHEDON
INTERVIEW WITH AWN.COM, 2002

MK. V

REAVER SHIPS

❖ Top: Design for the Reaver ship by Tim Earls.

❖ Above: A storyboard frame by Charles Ratteray from the Reaver chase, and the onscreen result.

To represent the nightmarish savages that terrorize the outer planets, it was essential for Meyer and Zoic to come up with a visual concept for the Reavers' ships that was just as terrifying as the monsters that lurk within.

"We said that Serenity is this rough-and-tumble ship patched together with pieces of another ship; but it was all from another Firefly class ship," Meyer says about their design rationale. "With the Reaver ship, we decided they would make a ship out of ten ships. The original idea was that the main body was made from a really old super liner cruise ship. They took it and ripped

it apart and put engines front, so it was a complete fabrication of ripped-up other ships."

He continues, "Around that time in-house we were building the Serenity interiors on stage and I worked out a short-hand with illustrator Tim Earls, who had finalized some designs for Serenity and the Alliance. He had a good feel for the world we were creating, so when Joss started talking about the Reaver ship, it was literally as quick as saying to Tim, 'Let's go even further than what Serenity was.' We talked about a wide-body 747 and started deconstructing that, along with the idea of a wild boar."

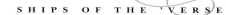

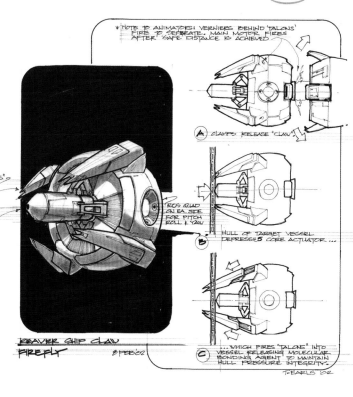

Note to animators: verniers behind 'talons' fire to seperate. Main motor fires after 'safe' distance is achieved.

ARTICULATED "TALONS" (4)

CORE ACTUATOR

FIRES QUAD ON EA. SIDE FOR PITCH ROLL & YAW

(A) CLAMPS RELEASE "CLAW"

HULL OF TARGET VESSEL DEPRESSES CORE ACTUATOR...

(B)

REAVER SHIP CLAW
FIREFLY   8 FEB '02

... WHICH FIRES "TALONS" INTO VESSEL RELEASING MOLECULAR BONDING AGENT TO MAINTAIN HULL PRESSURE INTEGRITY.

(C)

T. EARLS '02

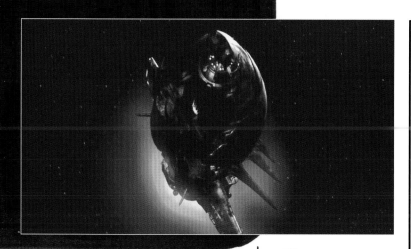

T. EARLS '02

"Then we added the idea they wanted to paint their ships with war paint," Peristere details. "And that they would *purposefully* rip open their containment engine so it would leak. They didn't *care* that they would get radiation poisoning, so the idea was to be as menacing as possible by design. They haphazardly construct the meanest-looking things they can. They create a mask of intimidation so you get scared."

Carey smiles as he remembers, "When I saw the first pre-viz of the Reaver ship chasing Serenity I just about fell out of my chair. It was the coolest thing I had seen in sci-fi."

❖ Top right: The Reavers' grapple claw, as envsioned by Tim Earls.

JUBAL EARLY'S SHIP

The bounty hunter's ship only appeared in 'Objects in Space', but it was an important extension of the charismatic character. Meyer shares, "Ron Cobb [the legendary illustrator who also worked on the likes of *Alien* and *Back to the Future*] worked on that design. Colin De Rouin, my art director said to me, 'I have worked with this guy before and he would *love* to design one of these ships.' What I remember about Early's ship was that Joss and Loni kept remarking about Boba Fett's ship Slave One. If you go back and look at the design process for that ship, they took an old sodium vapor light hood and started playing around with it. They flipped it vertically and it looked really cool, so we played around with a similar idea."

THE 'SPACE BAZAAR'

In 'The Message', the Serenity crew visits a space station, described in the script as a Space Bazaar. Inside it's a colorful, bustling marketplace full of people, shops and stalls. The exterior design is similarly striking, and had a very definite inspiration, as Meyer reveals: "It was a whole other idea of how a city in space would work, with bits added on and added on, like the modern day International Space Station works today, as opposed to a thought-out Alliance ship. It wasn't like a Reaver ship, meant to look mean," he clarifies, "but a conglomeration of thousands of people's ideas. We referenced the book *City of Darkness – Life In Kowloon Walled City* [by Ian Lambot and Greg Girard], which is based on a housing development in Hong Kong that had its own police force and its own laws. It was literally this block of humanity that sat in the middle of a city, with its own boundaries. We really went at the bazaar with that book in mind."

THE 'TRASH' FREIGHTER

❖ For 'Trash', Tim Earls designed a full exterior for Monty's freighter, though ultimately only the underside and landing struts were seen.

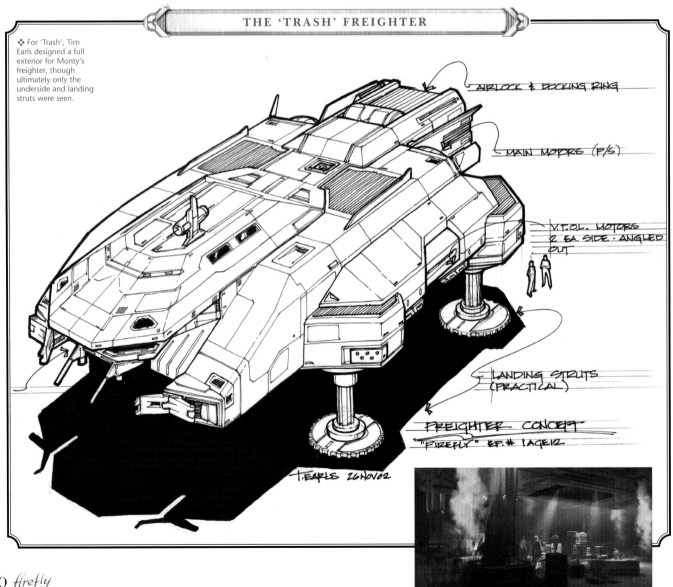

NISKA'S SKYPLEX

For the episodes 'The Train Job' and 'War Stories', the design team needed to create a space station that was a contrast to the Alliance ships, but with a menace all its own. Meyer explains, "It was another design that was both an exterior CG model and interior sets – especially for 'War Stories'. But Loni just took it to the nth degree on the outside."

Peristere continues, "For this space station we imagined that an independent contractor had taken it over, and it had been retrofitted many times. It's almost like a house you rebuild five or six times, and then Serenity has to squeeze and slide in. We created these tubes that were like a claw that would grab Serenity and take it into its folds; inside a deep, dark place."

Meyer says his favorite design aspect was featured inside the station. "The whole station had a central core of a long, long tube that everything glommed onto. Loni knocked it out of the park in Niska's office when they throw the guy over the balcony and you look down and it's basically that core. Amazing."

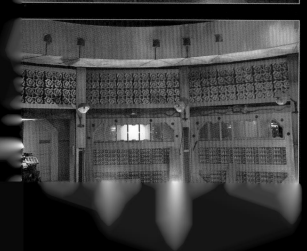

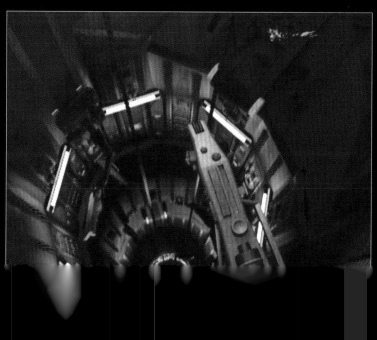

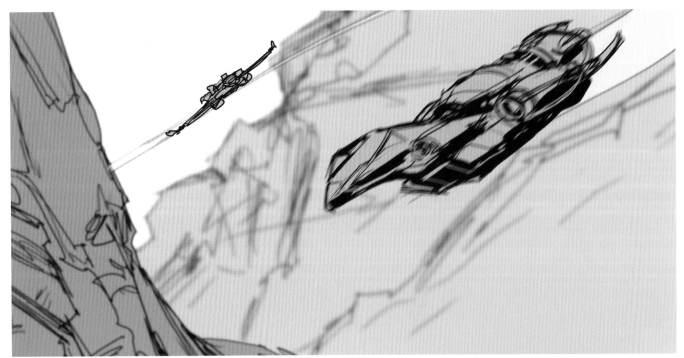

ALLIANCE SHORT RANGE ENFORCEMENT VESSEL (ASREV)

These small gun ships were housed within the larger Alliance vessels, and were originally glimpsed in 'Trash' before one had a starring role in the memorable chase sequence in 'The Message'. Meyer explains that these ships represented the point where he handed off the intricate design work to the Zoic team.

"We were so deep into production of the show that Loni completely took over in terms of getting the design process finished on these kinds of vehicles," Meyer explains.

"So we brought in some superstar freelance designers [like Ron Cobb] to help us out," Peristere continues. "With this ship, the idea was to take technology of today and advance it several hundred years and imagine what would be functional both in space and in atmosphere. I wanted to think about what would work in both spaces. Again we employed a joint strike fighter VTOL system where a panel opened up in the wing so it could lift off vertically instead of needing a runway. At the same time we wanted a sleek, bad-ass look that was intimidating and looked like a creature. We wanted it to be familiar, yet fresh and functional." ◐

❖ Opposite and below: Charles Ratteray's storyboards for the chase sequence in 'The Message'.

RON GLASS

Shepherd Derrial Book

RON ON THE CAST:
From the very beginning it was like... people were perfectly cast. Everybody was slightly different but were versatile and had a good work ethic. It was a very harmonious atmosphere to work in.

INTERVIEW WITH FRACTALMATTER.COM, 2006

ON EMBRACING FANDOM:
I'm surprised that the popularity lingers. It was very fulfilling but I've never been associated with a show that did conventions. Yeah, they're quite wonderful. The people have a reputation for being... let's just say the reputation is not totally sane, but there's the other side that I think is very warm and really gentle. So I feel privileged to be able to partake in it. In a certain kind of way, the *Firefly* fans are much more informed and aware about the *Firefly* universe than I am. In a way they are more interested. Most of the sci-fi genre can be a large part of their lives. For me, I just slipped into it, I was just fascinated by the characterisation, but again, I'm grateful for it and it's opened my perspective in ways that I couldn't have anticipated.

INTERVIEW WITH FRACTALMATTER.COM, 2006

NATHAN FILLION ON RON:
"I could listen to Ron Glass read the phone book. When you ask Ron Glass a question he does this [impersonates Ron deep in thought] and then he answers you. He's always connected, he's always connecting and I just admire him. He's a smart guy and he picks his moments and he's always shiny."

SPEAKING ON STAGE AT THE 'SERENITY' CONVENTION, 2005

GINA TORRES ON RON:
I adore Ron. I was watching Ron as most people of our generation were on *Barney Miller* – my earliest memories of television. When he walked on stage for the first time when we did the series, I was like, "I love you!"

INTERVIEW WITH BLACKFILM.COM, 2005

THE CAST DISCUSS MEETING RON FOR THE FIRST TIME, AND DISCOVERING HIS UNIQUE SENSE OF HUMOR:
Jewel: [Ron] just appeared to be very zen and calm and kind and genuine. It's true he is. And then we got to know him and this twisted, sick sense of humor came out. It came out of nowhere.
Nathan: And you'll never see it coming...
Jewel: You won't see it coming. He'll say the sickest, funniest, most insulting thing and we'll just be on the floor laughing.
Morena: I just have to tell my Ron story. We're standing doing a shoot for 'Heart of Gold', in what's supposed to be the tinfoil whore house and I'm standing there in my normal Inara outfit which was always more extravagant than everybody else's, who are all in canvas pants or overalls or whatever. And I see Ron looking at me from across the room kind of like [shakes head] and I walk up to him and I'm like, "Hi Ron!" and he says [about Inara's costume], "What is this? A f***ing carnival act?"

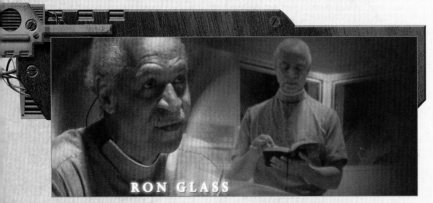

RON GLASS

Jewel: And yesterday when we were all sort of reunited here in the UK [for the convention], Ron came up to Morena and looked her up and down and gave her a hug and said, "Hi honey, so where are the elephants?"

SPEAKING ON STAGE AT THE 'SERENITY' CONVENTION, 2005

actually I think that Book, before he became a Shepherd, was a choreographer." So I'm going to stick with that! [Laughs].

SPEAKING ON STAGE AT THE DALLAS COMIC CON, 2006

RON'S ANSWER WHEN ASKED AT A CONVENTION WHAT HE KNOWS OF BOOK'S BACKSTORY:

This whole experience of dealing with fans in a convention environment was totally new for me. The very first convention that I went to was in England, and somebody asked me that question, and I said, "Well

A STORY HE WAS TOLD BY A FAN:

This guy was telling me he'd been to a place where you could get used DVDs, and he was standing there in line waiting to check out, and some woman is going through a box, and she picks up a used DVD. It turns out that it was a copy of *Serenity*, and she yelled really loud in the store, "Whoever brought this here is going to *hell*!"

SPEAKING ON STAGE AT THE DALLAS COMIC CON, 2006

THE BROWNCOATS

An overview of Firefly fandom

WRITER AND EXECUTIVE PRODUCER TIM MINEAR

❖ Below: *Firefly* in space! In June 2007, Astronaut and Browncoat Steven Swanson, pictured here with Sunita Williams, took a set of DVDs to the International Space Station on NASA Shuttle mission STS-117.

What is there to say about the fandom? *Firefly* has got its own vibe. It's a little bit different than the other stuff. I mean, I have been involved in stuff that has been very fan-friendly. Everything from *Lois & Clark*, *The X-Files* to *Angel*, but for some reason, the *Firefly* fans are their own special thing. And it could be because it was killed so early – there's a sort of tragedy to the whole thing [laughs]. If only the network had the tiniest bit of farsightedness that the fans of *Firefly* have shown over the last five years, then we'd probably be in our sixth or seventh season by now. But we love the fans and we love the show, too. We are fans as well.

INTERVIEW WITH ABBIE BERNSTEIN, 2009.

*F*irefly fans, universally known as the Browncoats, have a special place in sci-fi fandom. This brief overview can only hope to scratch the surface of the story of how they have kept the show alive in the years since cancellation, but one thing's for sure: you can't stop the signal!

CONVENTIONS

While the Internet is certainly integral to *Firefly* fandom, if one wants to encounter a cross-section of ardent Browncoats in the same place at the same time, there's nothing like a convention. Creation Entertainment's Salute to *Firefly* and *Serenity* at the LAX Marriott in November 2009 had an impressive guest list, including Morena Baccarin, Adam Baldwin, Jewel Staite, Mark Sheppard and Alan Tudyk (who ran an impromptu trivia quiz and gave out *Firefly*-related prizes for the right answers), and writers Jane Espenson and Tim Minear. The convention was abuzz with fans who had come from not only all over the country, but all over the world, both to see the guests and to visit with one another.

Wendy Scott has come from England, where she runs a *Firefly/Serenity* podcast called Sending the Wave. Describing the appeal of *Firefly* fandom, Scott says, "For a start, it's so much fan-led. The great thing is certainly everybody here, seriously, within thirty seconds, you know them. They're so friendly, they're so open. It's kind of like we've bonded in the trenches of Serenity Valley," she laughs. "We all share this very, very precious thing, and it's great when we get feedback from the podcast and we know that there are so many people listening to it across the world. We feel that we're doing our part to keep the fandom going. I've loved Westerns since I was a child and when I first saw the pilot, I genuinely wasn't sure if I was going to like it, but when we got to Eavesdown Docks, it was, 'Oh, my God, I know this place,' because I was a huge *Star Wars* fan. To me, that was Mos Eisley. I see *Firefly* as *Star Wars*'

first cousin. And I thought, 'Oh, I'm home.' And then it just kept going. I think we had something very precious in the episodes that we had. It was very rich, and you can keep going back."

Nicole Hoye is an Australian currently living in Toronto. She says her UK friends also attending the convention persuaded her to come to Los Angeles for the event. "I had been to a couple of the Starfury [*Firefly* conventions] in the UK, so that's how I met all of those friends. So I came along to this one to see them, and the guests, and to see what a US convention is like. It's been great. Really good panels and the dealer room is *amazing*." Hoye says she is attracted to *Firefly* because of "the characters. It's a really character-driven story. Sometimes I find with a lot of sci-fi that it tends to roll around the setting and idea of, 'Oh, it's sci-fi' so much that *Firefly* really stands on its own."

A woman who goes by the *Nom de Web* Raven

❖ Above: Nathan Fillion meets the fans at San Deigo Comic-Con 2009.

❖ Left: Tim Minear (center) with the California Browncoats (CABC) team at Comic-Con 2007.

❖ Top: "Check this out, I rock at these," Nathan Fillion told fan Sean Koo as he took this photo for him.

❖ Right: The CABC in action at Wondercon 2009.

❖ Below: Would you buy a T-shirt from this man? Adam Baldwin helps out on the CABC stand at Wondercon 2009.

Underwood has come to the convention from Chicago, Illinois. She's been involved in all the Joss Whedon-related fandoms and, in her opinion, "The difference between *Firefly* and a lot of the other ones is, it's sci-fi. It hit a chord with sci-fi people. And there are a lot more costumes involved," she notes with a laugh. "I think because it was canceled so quickly, this is something special. Like *Star Trek* was in the sixties, *Firefly* is in the 2000s, they're similar in that respect, fighting to keep it alive. These convention events do that, as well as everything the fans are doing, and it brings a lot of people together."

Tony Arlen has traveled from Northern California. This is his first convention. "This is the first time I've ever done anything like this. And it's kind of scary – I came by myself, I couldn't talk my wife into coming. I'm just kind of star-struck and very shy but trying to do my best to really enjoy everything. *Firefly* – I can't stop watching it. I love it. It's very real and very honest – even though it's set in space and it's 500 years from now. I feel a lot of chemistry, a family atmosphere, among the characters, among the actors. And I read something in [one of the previous *Firefly* volumes] that Christina Hendricks said, that she felt so warm and welcomed when she came and did her guest shots on the show, which was not the case for a lot of her guest-starring work. So that's the feeling I get – it's family." ◗

CHARITY

Browncoats are very active in fundraising for good causes. Many of these are favorites of Whedon and the cast. Whedon is a proponent of Equality Now, an organization that promotes women's rights worldwide, which has been the beneficiary of Browncoat-raised funds. Ron Glass has brought attention to the Al Wooten Jr Heritage Center in South Central Los Angeles, which helps underprivileged children; Adam Baldwin has spoken up for the Marine Corps and Law Enforcement Foundation, which raises money to help the children of fallen US military and law enforcement personnel; Jewel Staite is a proponent of the Dyslexia Foundation. All of these and more have received monies raised at Browncoat-sponsored events.

James Riley, president of the California Browncoats, explains this is both fun and a serious business. "As a non-profit corporation, we have existed since June 2007. Our main purpose is to raise funds for the charities selected by the cast and crew of *Firefly* and *Serenity*, and we do that by running fan tables at conventions like Creation's and Wonder-Con and Comic-Con. I'd have to go look at the spreadsheet again, but I'm pretty sure since

2007, the California Browncoats alone have raised close to $100,000 for charity, and Browncoats as a whole I think have raised somewhere close to half a million dollars for charity."

Riley continues, "I think the best thing about *Firefly* and *Serenity* is not the fact that the fandom for the show has lasted so long, but that the community that was built around the show has lasted too. I think that's why it's lasted so long, because the Browncoats themselves have kept it alive. Don't get me wrong, the performers and writers are definitely all a very large part of it, but not since some other key fandoms like *Star Wars* and *Star Trek* has there been a fandom built around the fandom itself and the community that it has developed. The need to do good seems to have developed inside the community itself. The Backup Bash [a convention set up literally at the last minute, when a major *Firefly* convention fell apart the day it was supposed to begin] was definitely something that brought a lot of the fans closer together, it kind of made us huddle around ourselves instead of relying on others, and I think it showed that we could do things if we had to."

Beth Nelson, a New Yorker who has relocated to Austin, Texas, is one of the Austin Browncoats. She's involved with both the charitable "Can't Stop the Serenity" screenings and licensed *Firefly/Serenity* collectibles. "I've been a fan since the very beginning. I'm a huge space Western fan, so I had to get involved. Charity-wise, I started getting really active in 2007. There is one global organizer who usually has a team that helps them run the events, and then each city has their own organizer. And so we try to keep it very central. Everybody has similar rules, but we get to put a lot of individual thought into each event, so that they're unique."

Kids Need to Read is a charity started in 2007 by author P.J. Haarsma and Nathan Filllion, with assistance from Alan Tudyk and many Browncoats. Denise Gary, the organization's executive director, explains how Kids began and what it does. "P.J. Haarsma has a children's sci-fi book. He's gone around to schools presenting his book and found out that a lot of them didn't have any funding for new books. It was a large problem. Haarsma is very good friends with Nathan Fillion and actually Alan Tudyk as well. He went to Nathan and asked if he would be interested in helping solve this problem. Nathan said, 'You bet, I want to help.' P.J. came to me, because I had a group of Browncoats that had worked with him before on another project, and asked if we would like to also help and make his vision come about. We are based out of Phoenix, Arizona, but we are a national program. Our core program is to buy new books for under-funded schools and libraries and clinics and shelters, any place that has a good literacy program for children, especially disadvantaged children. It is also about giving the right kind of books. Most of our kids are very underprivileged, very poverty-stricken, they're not surrounded with a culture of reading. So we give books that have valuable substance and a lot of uplifting messages. That's a very big part of our mission as well. The core people running the charity are Browncoats, and most of the volunteers that we have coming in are Browncoats, who hear about Kids Need to Read and want to help."

Why is Gary a Browncoat? "Oh, because *Firefly* to me is simply unforgettable. I cannot get it out of my system. It's just a part of me." ◔

❖ Above: Nathan and Kids Need to Read founder P. J. Haarsma sign for fans at the 2008 Comic-Con.

❦ MERCHANDISE ❦

Whether it's a fan-made costume or prop replica, or a professional licensed product, *Firefly* has inspired an outpouring of creativity, including artwork, models, podcasts, audio plays, a role-playing game, 'Filk' music, even *Serenity*-shaped cakes. On the pro side, a highlight came in 2005 when Dark Horse Comics teamed with Joss Whedon to bring forth *Those Left Behind*, a three-issue chronicle of the adventures of our Big Damn Heroes between the events of *Firefly* and *Serenity*. Written by Whedon and Brett Matthews, with art from Will Conrad, it was a great success, leading to follow-up *Better Days* in 2008, with *Float Out* and *A Shepherd's Tale* announced for 2010.

Quantum Mechanix, or QMx for short, is a licensed collectibles/props replica company that came into being in 2005 out of love for *Firefly*. CEO Andy Gore relates, "*Firefly* was the sole reason why I got into it. I had actually not been in the collectibles business previously, but I have a fairly extensive background in web development. The founders of the company wanted me to build the interactive strategy for the company and I basically said, 'Well, you can pay me,' and what I normally get paid was way more than they could afford, 'or you can pick up the *Serenity* license.' And they said, 'Okay, we'll pick up the *Serenity* license.' So I basically traded a website for the opportunity to do the things that I'm doing now. We only just picked up the *Firefly* license, but we've been interested in it for a long time. We have a lot of stuff in development. Our categories include prop replicas, ship replicas, T-shirts, posters, maquettes [small statue likenesses of the characters],

key chains and bumper stickers and so forth."

Fans are very involved in QMx product development, Gore adds. "As a matter of fact, we developed a secure confidential collaboration space online where we invite particularly dedicated fans to come in and look at early versions of the products we're developing and let us know what they think and give us advice, catch mistakes. A number of the products we do are very, very detailed and they take years to create, and so there are lots of opportunities for fans to give input and also, frankly, to find errors when they happen. These cutaways," Gore indicates a series of detailed plans of Serenity and other 'verse craft, "are only four pages, but there are thousands of pieces of information in them, and while we have a wonderful research team and we're lucky to be working with the production designers from both the movie and the series [Geoffrey Mandel and Timothy Earls], even they will tell you that the fans find things that they've missed. So we're very engaged with the fan community. In terms of what they're like, fans aren't shy about letting you know what they're interested in. Fans oftentimes have some of the best ideas. But in a sense, we're fans as well, and so I almost view it as a collaboration with the community."

In at least one case, QMx has afforded the opportunity for a fan artist to turn pro. Gore explains, "Adam Levermore started as a fan designer, but – I will quote a Hollywood designer who works with us on a regular basis – 'There are fan designers who are incredibly skilled and the only real difference between them and a quote-unquote professional is knowledge of the franchise.' Oftentimes, the fan designer is every bit as good as the

professional, but the fan knows more about the material. So we love fan designers. Not all of them are working at that level of skill, but the ones who are ultimately end up being the best designers to work with."

Levermore connected with Gore at the Backup Bash, where QMx needed dealer space at the last minute and Levermore had a table for his fan art company, Black Market Beagles. Levermore recalls, "Andy came and we talked and really got along well. He asked if I was interested in doing some work for them and it grew from there." He believes his artwork, largely of 'verse ships, props and locations, has improved since joining the company. "It ramped up very quickly. I've always doodled and sketched, but I'd never really worked professionally, certainly never selling any of my art before Black Market Beagles, and when I got together with QMx, it took a big jump from there as well, getting to work on officially licensed stuff for *Firefly* and *Serenity*, and also *Battlestar Galactica* and *Star Trek* and *Stargate: SG-1*, so it's been really exciting and fast-paced and I've really enjoyed working with them."

Like James Riley, Levermore says he feels the fan-run, totally not-for-profit Backup Bash was a major event for the Browncoats. "There's no question. It's something that I think changed a lot of people's lives and set a lot of things in motion in terms of what people were doing with the fandom and how they felt about it. For me personally, I made a lot of contacts through it, a lot of new friends, a lot of memories, but I think everybody who was involved in it, whether they were involved in arranging it or just participating in it, had an experience of a lifetime."

As for what drew QMx's CEO to *Firefly*, Gore says, "Everything, honestly. *Firefly* will be remembered decades from now as being one of the most innovative pieces of entertainment that was ever done – for its characterization, production design, gritty realism, even the way that the show was shot. I mean, *Battlestar Galactica* is one of the most successful sci-fi series ever, and even they will tell you how much they owe to *Firefly* – Steadicam, ships that don't make noise in space, gritty, realistic, lived-in ship design, sci-fi plots that are character-driven as opposed to technology-driven or scenario-driven, all these things. *Firefly* is literally the Rosetta Stone of what I would consider the modern wave of sci-fi on TV." ◐

❖ Top and above left: QMx's double-sided Map of the 'verse was two years in the making.

❖ Far left: The Map of Serenity Valley comes complete with handwritten annotations and blood stains!

❖ Left: This limited edition Kaylee maquette is now sold out.

FAN FILMS

In written form, fan fiction – taking the universe and characters created by professionals and coming up with new stories that are distributed not for profit, but simply for the love of doing it – has been around almost as long as fiction. However, filmed fan fiction is relatively new. Fan-made feature-length documentaries aren't quite so rare, but they are still fairly uncommon. However, Browncoat enthusiasm has brought forth a number of cinematic endeavors.

On the documentary side, the best-known Browncoat-made film is *Done The Impossible: The Fans' Tale of Firefly & Serenity*, a chronicle of fan efforts to help *Firefly* continue, culminating with the release of *Serenity*. *Done The Impossible* was produced and directed by the team of Brian Wiser, Jeremy Neish, Jared Nelson, Jason Heppler and Tony Hadlock. Wiser explains their impetus. "We couldn't let the *Firefly* fan community and their major efforts be forgotten. What the fans accomplished and the way they did it was unparalleled and unexpected. We wanted to share the unique journey from *Firefly* to *Serenity* and contribute something to the 'verse that people could enjoy and connect with. Additionally, we wanted to create something for existing Browncoats, as well as people who were new to the 'verse, to keep the Browncoat momentum moving forward."

Done The Impossible began production in 2005. "During that time," Wiser says, "I arranged interviews with fans, cast, crew and executives. We were filming, editing and developing unique special features. We felt it was very important to

have someone from the series help convey the story and Adam Baldwin was a perfect fit. When I asked Adam at Dragon Con if he would be willing to host the documentary, he was genuinely interested in a way that demonstrated he not only believed in our film, but in the importance of the message of *Firefly* and the fans. Jewel Staite took her vacation time to record the timeline and trivia voiceover as Kaylee. The fans and cast were incredibly cooperative. People were very eager to share their feelings about why *Firefly* has such a following and how it affected their lives. *Firefly* composer Greg Edmonson invited us into his home and Tim Minear took time away from a very important engagement. I was surprised at how many people had stories and experiences we can all relate to, and how willing and excited people were to be involved. I also contacted Joss and several executives – they were all very supportive of our project."

First screened at Comic-Con in 2006, now available on DVD and with a Blu-ray released in 2010, *Done The Impossible* has played at a number of film festivals around the world and raised money for charity. "Donating to charity is an important part of who the Browncoats are. That's why we initially donated $5,000 to Equality Now. Each year we donate and support charitable events like Can't Stop the Serenity." Wiser says the film has in some instances helped fans find one another. "Fans have found connections to the Browncoat community that they may not have known about if they had only watched *Firefly*." However, most gratifying for Wiser is that "I have enjoyed deep

friendships with fans and cast that have continued to this day. I find many of the relationships I hold most dear have originated through *Firefly*."

Wiser was also one of the organizers of the 2007 Browncoat Cruise, a weeklong floating convention with Ron Glass as a headlining guest, and is one of the producers on *Browncoats: Redemption*, a feature-length narrative film about what happens in the 'verse once it's discovered that the Alliance created the dreaded Reavers through a backfired effort at mind control.

"We took the premise that was already there from the content that's been established so far," reveals *Browncoats: Redemption* writer/director/producer/co-creator Michael C. Dougherty. "It's a new ship and a new crew, on a total opposite end of the 'verse [than Mal Reynolds and the Serenity crew], having to deal with the Alliance and trying to make sense of everything that's going on. For the Core planets, the Alliance is pretending that the information about the Reavers is anti-propaganda, but the Rim planets are all up in arms because they know it's true. You have a crew who normally do the right things, completely unlike Mal, but are now forced to start taking the jobs that Mal would normally take to be able to survive. The story flows from there."

Steven Fisher, the other *Browncoats: Redemption* co-creator/producer, explains the project's origins. "In July 2008, I was talking to a friend who had done a lot of *Star Trek* fan films and we were talking about *Firefly* fan films. At the time, I didn't know there were any, so I thought we should try something like this. I'd known Mike for about six months at the time, and I said, 'I want to do a *Firefly* film.' Mike is a great writer, and we started to work on this together. We obviously didn't want to impinge on anything that Joss was going to create with his crew, so what we did was to create a new crew and tell a different perspective."

Whedon gave his blessing, Dougherty relates. We [Dougherty and Fisher] agreed that we couldn't go forward without letting Joss know. I finally got Joss's assistant on the phone and did our pitch in about fifteen seconds flat without breathing, and when she stopped laughing, she said, 'Slow down, say it again.' I told her what we were trying to do. She said, 'Send a detailed email. I'll get you a response one way or the other.' After a month and a half of pins and needles waiting, we finally got an email that said, 'Joss gives his blessing, but he cannot speak for Fox or Universal.'"

Fisher adds, "Fox and Universal seemed to be fine with it, because we're non-profit and we're not making any

❖ Opposite top: A new ship, a new crew. The cast of the non-profit fan-film *Browncoats: Redemption*.

❖ Opposite center, top to bottom: Adam Baldwin, Mark A. Sheppard (aka Badger), Ron Glass and Michael Fairman (Niska) show their support for *Browncoats: Redemption*'s charity fund-raising aims.

❖ Opposite bottom: The feature length fan-documentary *Done the Impossible*.

❖ Above: Filming a ship's galley scene for *Browncoats: Redemption*.

money from it. All of it goes to charity [and] it gives awareness and continued support for their original properties."

Browncoats have been intensely supportive of *Redemption*, Fisher says. "As of this date, we've had a 153 people donate their time for 200 different jobs on the film. So in terms of the crew, a lot of professionals who've been in the industry were involved in this and have brought their talents to it, and all the actors have waived any fee to do the film. It's been quite a humbling experience."

Where did all those Browncoats come from? "Besides the love of the fans," Dougherty replies, "social media – Twitter, Facebook and YouTube –

❖ Top: Filming an ship's interior scene.

❖ Above: Shootig a fight scene at Frontier Town.

have been our lifeblood."

"People came from all over the country on their own dime to be extras," Fisher relates. "It was like the biggest shindig you've ever seen."

Heather Fagan, who stars as Captain Laura Matthews, is one of the people who pulled multiple duties. "I was a Browncoat before," she says. "I've actually known Mike for years and he sent me the script, just kind of, 'Hey, I'm writing this, what do you think?' 'I really like that. I want to audition for this!' He made me go through the audition process. I told him, 'I will be involved in this in any way, shape or form.' So I was a jack-of-all-trades on the set occasionally, everything from supplying food to being in front of the camera, for fifteen hours a day."

The film was shot with the digital Red One camera. "That gave us a level of production quality that's a cinema level of film," Fisher relates.

Fisher reckons that the out-of-pocket cost of *Browncoats: Redemption* is just under $30,000, with approximately another $100,000 in in-kind donations. "We've had donations from Neo Effects, who donated about $70,000 worth of CGI. Jones Soda is sponsoring the film."

Browncoats: Redemption was shot in Maryland. "Frontier Town in Ocean City donated a Western theme park for three weekends," Dougherty says.

Redemption

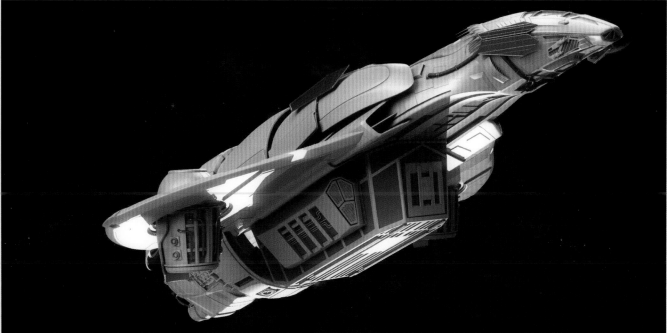

"Saint John's Properties donated their warehouse space for four months where we could build our ship. The city of Bowie donated a state park where we could film our Alliance scenes. Everything was donated because of the non-profit aspect."

With the film scheduled to premiere at Dragon Con in Atlanta in Fall 2010, there are five charities that are intended beneficiaries of any funds raised from DVD sales of *Browncoats: Redemption*: Equality Now, Kids Need to Read, the Dyslexia Foundation, the Al Wooten Jr Heritage Center and the Marine Corps and Law Enforcement Foundation. "These are charities that are actually on the ground doing stuff and affecting people," Fisher says. "If we could accomplish our goal of 32,000 units over the course of a year, then we'll definitely move forward on any sequels. I'm just humbled by everybody who's come to the table to be a part of this."

[2012 Update: After a successful launch at Dragon Con 2010, and DVDs shipped to fans on seven continents, the makers of *Browncoats: Redemption* announced at the project's 'Wrap Party' at Dragon Con 2011 that the film had raised over $113,000 for its charities.] ◐

❖ Above: Two views of Neo f/x's CG model of the new ship, Redemption. CG model by Dustin Elmore, original design by Alex Bradley.

ON 'ARIEL'

By Jose Molina

Hello, everyone –
I've been asked by our cyberfriends at Fox to pitch in with an article detailing how 'Ariel' came to life. So here I am. About to detail.

Cairo, 1843. Wait, that's wrong.

Santa Monica, September of 2002. Yeah, that's better. To quote a famous dead guy, I was nervous. Very, very dreadfully nervous. I'd been a fan of *Buffy* and *Angel* and the whole Mutant Enemy camp for years, and this was my first shot at showing the best writers in television that I didn't suck. Still waiting for confirmation on that one. Um... guys?

So, it started with an idea from Joss: he wanted to do a story where Simon hired the crew for a heist. The rest was up for grabs. But since the folks around the office didn't take kindly to my random grabbing, I decided it was best for everyone if I worked at home.

After approaching the story from a few different angles, the staff and I finally landed on a take we liked. I

pitched it to executive producer Tim Minear, who in typical Tim fashion said, "That's great! What else ya got?" He was kidding. (I think.) We spent the next couple of days hammering out the details, then rolled on over to the Paramount lot to pitch our ideas to Joss, who was in the middle of playing spin the bottle with David Boreanaz. Or he was directing 'Spin the Bottle' for *Angel*, I get confused. He said something along the lines of "me like" and producer Ben Edlund and I trucked back to our Santa Monica offices to put the finishing touches on the outline. At around 1:30 that morning, we finished the outline and cracked a celebratory beverage. I think Ben enjoyed it more than I did because he was laughing on his way out the door; it might have had something to do with the four days I had to write the script. He'd recently written 'Jaynestown' in about that amount of time and he was anticipating how much fun I was about to have. That must have been it, right?

So I spent four crazy days writing constantly, cursing

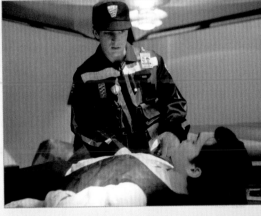

in Chinese, sleeping very little and having dreams about playing bocci ball with Adam Baldwin. I love Adam dearly, but in my dreams he cheats. When I emerged from my cocoon on Monday, I had a script... and an epiphany. Despite all my anxiety, I actually had tons of fun writing the script. I loved writing these characters, I loved living in this world, I loved everything. YOU GUYS! (sniff)

I also loved being done! And watching as the best cast and crew in town turned the pretty pictures in my head into reality was a blast. I'm extremely grateful and indebted to everyone who worked their gluteal regions off to make this episode as cool as it is. It's a bit of a departure – we have a Core planet, sonic rifles, and some big bad villains swooping in to complicate things. It's sort of *Ocean's Eleven* meets *The X-Files* in space. Or *Curse of the Mummy* meets *The A-Team*. Also heavily influenced by *Chico and the Man*. All right, I don't know. Just watch it and you can tell me.

I hope you enjoy the show as much as we enjoyed making it. I think you will! ◉

ORIGINALLY PUBLISHED ON FOX.COM, 2002

TAKE THE SKY

// BY JOSE MOLINA

The handwritten scrawl on the post-box read "Reynolds". A few steps past, the sign before the porch read "Trespassers Will Be Shot." Beyond, inked in red, a final warning was scratched out on the waterlogged wood of the front door.

"NO, SERIOUSLY."

Fist-sized shotgun blasts in the wood confirmed the truth of the message.

The small, wooden house sat on a remote mesa, and a gangly kid with a dust-streaked face stood by the post-box, contemplating the end of his journey. He was no more than twenty steps from the front door. He'd been paid handsomely to deliver his parcel, but not handsomely enough to get shot.

Who was he fooling? This wasn't about the delivery, or the parcel, or the pay. It was about getting a first-hand look at Malcolm Reynolds.

The kid girded himself, approached the door and raised his hand to knock. The door swung open before his knuckles landed.

"Ni dao di yao shen me?"

The kid looked up at Reynolds. He was taller than expected. Broader. His eyes bore into the young man like a fishhook, and immediately he understood why some men followed Reynolds to their grave while others strove to dig him one.

The kid was staring, and he knew it. Seventy-odd years had carved Reynolds' face with countless stories, and he wanted to hear every one of them. Especially the ones about the countless slingers who'd thought they could take out the one and only Malco—

"Spit it out." The voice snapped the kid back to reality, and he extended his hands for the old man to see the parcel he'd brought.

"P-post for you, sir."

Reynolds eyed the box — a long, thin object — then took it and swiped his thumb across the kid's ident scanner before stepping back and reaching for his door.

"S-scuse me, sir —" the kid interrupted before the door shut. "I was curious about some—"

"Make up your own story," said Reynolds.

He slammed the door shut.

<hr>

Mal ripped into the package as he walked into what passed for his living room: a chair, a vidscreen, a collection of mostly empty bottles, a rack of mostly loaded weapons. He didn't receive much mail out here on the rim; few people knew where to find him, and those few knew to leave him be unless there was trouble. So what kind of trouble did this small box spell?

He pulled the contents out one at a time: a note, a vidstrip, and an oblong velvet box. A jewelry box. Curiosity scratched at the back of Mal's brain, but he didn't believe in opening presents on Christmas Eve. He'd leave the box for last, and start with the note.

It was from Zoe.

"Jayne stole this. Thought you'd want it back."

Eight words. Sounded like Zoe. She didn't talk much these days. She spent too much time out in the black with no one to talk to. The last time she and Mal had spoken was two years back, when she'd brought Serenity home for a visit.

A pang of jealousy had shot through him when he saw his old boat, but it was Zoe's home now, not his. She needed it more than Mal did. It no longer afforded Mal the anonymity he craved anyway. The ship was synonymous with "The Signal." With galaxy-shattering heroics no one man could or should have to embody. Once upon a time, Serenity had been a place of refuge for Mal. It was no longer that for him. It could still be that for Zoe.

Let her have the sky. They'd taken it from him.

<hr>

Mal passed his finger across the vidstrip, sparking it to life. Why Zoe would think him interested in a news vid was beyond his comprehension, but he'd give her the benefit of the doubt. If he found a single story about himself, however, he'd have to wave her with some words.

But the story she wanted Mal to see wasn't about him. It was about Jayne.

"BILLIONAIRE COBB FOUND DEAD IN BED," was the headline. Exactly as Jayne would've wanted, thought Mal. Then he played the rest of the story, and laughed for the first time in weeks.

After the events at Mr. Universe's complex, Jayne had been the only one to embrace celebrity. For Mal, fame brought questions he didn't want to answer, scrutiny that he would not abide. For Jayne, being a hero meant money.

It meant women. It meant respect. Yes, it also caused a lifetime of rats to skitter from the proverbial woodwork, but whatever bygones he couldn't buy he could mostly achieve via shooting, stabbing or garroting.

"BILLIONAIRE COBB FOUND DEAD IN BED." Mal expected a story of debauchery to follow — four women, a weeklong binge, several broken laws of both man and nature. Instead, a sober-faced journalist reported the reality.

Apparently, after being booted from a half-dozen watering holes the night before he was found, Jayne returned home alone and collapsed in bed from a combination of exhaustion and drink. As usual, he took his beloved Vera to bed with him.

The reporter proceeded to explain — with a solemnity that plainly masked her embarrassment — how Jayne appeared to

mistake his semi-automatic rifle for a woman... whether in his sleep or inebriation... and accidentally shot himself in the neck. Twice.

Mal set aside the vidstrip and picked up the jewelry box. Jayne stole this from him? Mal couldn't recall ever owning jewelry, especially not the kind that came in a fancy velvet box. That was Inara's stock in trade. He shook the name from his mind and opened the box. Inside was a silver crucifix; he hadn't worn it since the Independents' defeat at Serenity Valley.

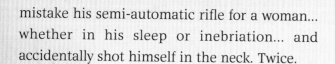

It all made sense now. Mal could never bring himself to dispose of the crucifix. Jayne could never bring himself to sell it. Neither would've been able to explain why, nor would they have accepted another's explanation. Jayne's simple truth was that he feared "gettin' smote." Mal's less-simple truth was that the cross was a token — an emblem. Not of Salvation or whatever other nonsense got peddled in the Fat Book or any assortment of lesser-known fat books. It was a token of hope. It had nothing to do with religion, or faith, or God, but simple symbolism. Mal could live without a lot, but not without hope... or, at the very least, the hope of hope.

It was that same hope that had always kept him going back to Inara. Hope that she'd one day turn her back on her vocation and ask him to lay down his guns and his burdens. A normal life with the most extraordinary woman he'd ever met — that was worth holding out hope.

The problem with hope was that the rug-pull was always all the more painful when it came. And it always came. Mal should've known better; if he expected nothing, then something was a pleasant surprise. If he hoped for something...

...he put it out of his mind. He'd gone over this enough to know where it led. Both he and

Inara would've endured far less if they'd gone on their merry. And now there was no going back.

Mal forced himself to think happy thoughts. Kittens and bunnies, gorramit. Big fat babies. That was better. Big fat babies. Violet and Caleb Tam. They were far from babies anymore, but that was still how Mal chose to remember them — the way they looked when Mal last visited Kaylee and Simon on Ariel.

Violet took after her mother. She was a sweet, kind little soul who exhibited heaps of confusion during the inevitable occasions when she made little Caleb cry. No matter how many times Kaylee asked her not to take apart his toys to see how they worked, little Violet couldn't help herself. The three year-old spent most of Mal's last visit trying to increase the nav-thrust on Caleb's tri-mobile by replacing its battery-powered motor with an internal combustion engine. Caleb spent most of the visit on his mother's lap.

The boy definitely took after his father. He was far tougher than he looked. Smart as a whip and stubborn as the day was long. He'd go to bed only when he was tired, not because Kaylee "said so." He couldn't be convinced that it was beneficial to sleep at any time other than when one was, in fact, sleepy. Only Simon could get little Caleb to bed with the promise of reading him some doorstop of a book.

Ultimately, though, both kids had as much of River in them as they did their own parents. After all, it was River who spent the most time with them, sitting for the twins any time of day or night to accommodate for Simon and Kaylee's busy Cityfolk schedules.

And the twins loved their Auntie River. She'd hold cockroach races for them and tell them which one was going to win before they even started. She'd tell hour-long stories that would literally hypnotize them and make them believe they were part of the tale. She'd clean up scrapes with such vivid descriptions of the gruesome wars being waged by microscopic organisms inside their tiny bodies that the twins would forget the pain in lieu of being nauseous.

If Simon was brain and Kaylee was heart, then River was spirit. The Tam family was a confluence of all good things, and it eased Mal's weary mind to think of them on some distant place far, far away from his desolate rock.

At his age, Mal often found himself lost in musings. He didn't know how much longer he'd have to wait for a grave to call his own, but he knew he'd done a lot of living in his years. He would die alone. Here, in this box of sticks he called a house. None of his remaining friends would attend his funeral, simply because weeks would go by before they heard of his passing.

It was how it had to be.

He'd come to terms with all that. Mal had lost a lot. Sacrificed a lot. Happiness had visited him rarely in his waning years, the quiet and the stillness of age replacing the chaotic commotion of his youth.

But Mal was lonely. Very lonely out here on the rim.

It was how it had to be.

It had been his decision. He'd come to terms with that, too.

But this — the here and now — is no time for musings. This is time to act.

Mal stands before The Operative. He's mere steps from the console that will allow him to broadcast the Parliament's sins to the entire 'verse. The people will know the truth...

"...'cause they need to," Mal tells The Operative.

"Do you really believe that?" asks The Operative.

"I do."

"You willing to die for that belief?"

Mal stops to think. He is willing to die for that belief. Dying is easy. Living is hard.

But is Mal willing to *live* with the decision he's about to make? To forever alter the course of his life, for better or — most like — for worse. To become, in the eyes of the 'verse, something he's not: a savior.

But no man can know the future. Mal can only *hope*.

He lets the same principles that have always guided him dictate his choice. It's not about what's best for him. It's about what's best, period.

"I am," says Mal, unwavering.

The Operative nods his understanding. He and Captain Reynolds may have different worldviews, but The Operative can't help respecting the man's convictions. That is, until he starts shooting.

"'course, that ain't exactly Plan A." ◑

MUTANT ENEMIES?

Some closing words...

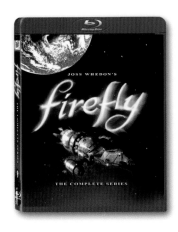

In 2008, Joss Whedon, Nathan Fillion, Alan Tudyk and Ron Glass reunited to record a roundtable discussion for inclusion as a bonus extra on the *Firefly* Blu-ray set. There was a lot of laughter. Here's an excerpt, where Whedon discusses a script idea he had back in 2002:

Joss: I wanted to do – was dead serious about doing – monster cattle... And the way I was going to justify monster cattle was the idea that they didn't send animals to the distant planets, they'd send DNA scrip, you know, "Here's the test tube, you grow your own." And it went *badly*... so we were going to have monsters. We had a telepathic girl... so I felt we could get away with a little mutation stuff.

Alan: But Cows?

Joss: But cows are my favorite. Probably I would have been talked into something else.

Nathan: Monkeys!

Joss: Well, horses, because then, you know, the executives who said, "Why are there horses?" and it would be [makes mutant horse noises] ripping people apart and stuff, "That's why there's horses! 'Cause they're *awesome*!"
[Pause.]
Or they could be *bad* horses. Nah, we would never do that...

BEN EDLUND was a producer on Firefly, wrote the episode 'Jaynestown', and co-wrote 'Trash' with Jose Molina. His other TV credits include Angel, Point Pleasant, Supernatural and The Tick, which he also created.

JANE ESPENSON wrote the episode 'Shindig' for Firefly. Her other TV writing and producing credits include Buffy the Vampire Slayer, Angel, Battlestar Galactica, Dollhouse, and Caprica.

BRETT MATTHEWS wrote the episode 'Heart of Gold' for Firefly, and co-wrote the Serenity graphic novels Those Left Behind and Better Days with Joss Whedon. His other writing credits include Chronicles of Riddick: Dark Fury.

JOSE MOLINA was executive story editor on Firefly, wrote the episode 'Ariel', and co-wrote 'Trash' with Ben Edlund. His other TV writing and producing credits include Law and Order: Special Victims Unit, Without a Trace, and Castle, starring Nathan Fillion.

ACKNOWLEDGMENTS:

The publishers are indebted to many people for their help in putting this book together. Firstly, huge thanks to Ben Edlund, Jane Espenson, Brett Matthews and Jose Molina for taking time out of their busy schedules to write (and draw!) their contributions.

Thanks to the writers who conducted interviews and wrote features: Tara Bennett (Ships of the 'Verse, Rocco Passionino) Abbie Bernstein (Behind the Scenes, A Head Called Jayne, On Location, Thrilling Heroics, The Browncoats and interview quotes where credited) and Karl Derrick (Monkey Shines, Objects in Space).

Our gratitude to Firefly veterans Nick Brandon, Skip Crank, Tim Earls, Carey Meyer, Danny Nero, Rocco Passionino, Loni Peristere, Charles Ratteray, and Peter Robarts for sharing their memories, photos and artwork.

Thanks to James Riley of the California Browncoats, and the makers of Browncoats: Redemption, especially Steve Fisher, Mike Dougherty and Brian Wiser, for photographs and assistance.

Thanks too to Beth Nelson, Andy Gore and the crew at QMx for some shiny visuals, and assisting Jane Espenson with the Firefly class tech queries she had when writing her story! Visit them at www.quantummechanix.com

Thanks to Julian Knott at Zeta Minor, Paul Christian Glenn at Ray Gun Revival and Joey at seanmaher.info for their help, and to those notable Browncoats Christopher Frankonis, Craig Latimore, Sean Koo, Michael B. McGuirk, Mike Schotte and especially Steven R. Swanson, NASA Astronaut, for supplying visuals. Credit is also due to Naomi Roper, who originally posted the 2004/2005 convention transcripts this book excerpts from on summerglau.co.uk.

Thanks once again to Debbie Olshan at Fox for her help and support.

Finally, thanks must of course go to Joss Whedon, without whom...

Mike Schotte: p458

Steven R. Swanson/NASA: p518 (while the publishers would like to make it clear that NASA does not formally endorse/promote Firefly, it's fair to say that more than a few Browncoats work there!)

Shawna Trpcic: pp448-449

Props courtesy of Karl Derrick, with photos by Elena Kanouris and Karl Derrick, except Book's Bible (special thanks to its owner Sean Crowley for his photos and assistance). Thanks to Charles Kline for the photo p422 bottom left.

SOME USEFUL WEB ADDRESSES:

Please note: this is not intended to be a comprehensive list!

Fan Sites and Fan Films:
California Browncoats – www.californiabrowncoats.org
Austin Browncoats – www.austinbrowncoats.com
Can't Stop the Serenity – www.cantstoptheserenity.com
Done the Impossible: The Fans' Tale of Firefly & Serenity –
    www.donetheimpossible.com
Browncoats: Redemption – www.browncoatsmovie.com
Bellflower – www.thebellflower.com/
Serenity Stuff – www.serenitystuff.com
Still Flying – www.stillflying.net
Can't Take the Sky – http://still-flying.net/images/
The Signal Podcast – http://signal.serenityfirefly.com/
Badger Books – http://badger.serenityfirefly.com/
Whedonesque – www.whedonesque.com
Charities:
Equality Now – www.equalitynow.org
Al Wooten Jr Heritage Center – www.wootencenter.org
Marine Corps and Law Enforcement Foundation – www.mc-lef.org
Dyslexia Foundation – www.dyslexiafoundation.org
Kids Need to Read – www.kidsneedtoread.org

IMAGE CREDITS:

Images in this book are courtesy of 20th Century Fox, with the exception of:

The makers of Browncoats: Redemption: pp526-529
Tim Earls: pp496-497; p498 (top left and right), p499 (center middle; bottom left and right), p501 (top; center right); p504; p507 (bottom); 508 (top); p509 (top right)
Christopher Frankonis: p519 (top)
Julie Hamburg: pp478-479 (Japanese Garden photos)
Sean Koo: p520 (top)
Carey Meyer: p498 (bottom)
Danny Nero: pp432-437; p476 bottom left; p477 left center and bottom; p478 top left; p479 top right; p480-481
Rocco Passionino: p499 (center left and right; bottom middle); p500 (top); p501 (center left and middle; bottom left); p502 (top and center); p503 (center left; bottom left)
QMx: p8; p459; p523; pp524-525
Charles Ratteray: pp404-407; p505, p506; p507 (top); p508 (center left); pp512-513
James Riley: p448 (bottom left); pp450-451 (T-shirt photos and p451 bottom right); p519 (bottom); p520 (middle and bottom); p521; p522

❖ Above: A couple of the promotional items sent out by Twentieth Century Fox when they launched the series in 2002.

"I WOULD NEVER RULE IT OUT,
I LOVE THOSE PEOPLE."

Joss Whedon on a possible return to *Firefly*